The essential
JOHN
STOTT

THE Cross of Christ

THE Contemporary Christian

Inter-Varsity Press

INTER-VARSITY PRESS
38 De Montfort Street, Leicester LE1 7GP, England

The Cross of Christ first published 1986; reprinted 1986, 1987, 1989, 1990,
1991, 1992, 1994, 1995, 1996, 1998, 1999.

The Contemporary Christian first published 1992; reprinted 1992, 1993 (twice),
1995, 1996, 1999.

Combined volume (*The Essential John Stott*) first published 1999.
Reprinted 1999

British Library Cataloguing in Publication Data
A catalogue record for this book is available from the British Library.

ISBN 0–85111–758–9

Set in Garamond
Typeset in Great Britain by Avocet Typeset, Brill, Aylesbury, Bucks.
Printed in Great Britain by Creative Print and Design Group (Wales), Ebbw Vale.

*Inter-Varsity Press is the book-publishing division of the Universities and Colleges
Christian Fellowship (formerly the Inter-Varsity Fellowship), a student movement
linking Christian Unions in universities and colleges throughout the United
Kingdom and the Republic of Ireland, and a member movement of the
International Fellowship of Evangelical Students. For information about local and
national activities write to UCCF, 38 De Montfort Street, Leicester LE1 7GP.*

All royalties from this book have been irrevocably assigned to the Evangelical
Literature Trust (UK), which distributes evangelical books to pastors, theological
teachers and students and seminary libraries in the developing world. Further
information may be obtained from, and donations sent to, The Director,
Evangelical Literature Trust, St Peter's Church Office, Stoke Park Drive,
Ipswich, IP2 9TH, UK.

Preface to the
Combined Edition

I am glad and grateful that IVP have decided to publish in one volume this new edition of *The Cross of Christ* (1986) and *The Contemporary Christian* (1992). There is a certain appropriateness in their decision, since the topics of the two books dovetail with one another.

Although *The Cross of Christ* is concerned with the meaning of an event which took place nearly two millennia ago, and although *The Contemporary Christian* focuses on what it means to follow Jesus Christ today, both are reflections on the relations between the past and the present, the 'then' and the 'now'. Indeed, one of the distinctive characteristics of the gospel, whether declared in word or dramatized in sacrament, is that it brings the past out of the past and makes it present; that is, it confronts us with past events as present realities. Paul could claim, for example, that he had clearly portrayed Jesus Christ as crucified before the Galatians' very eyes (Gal. 3:1). So vivid had his proclamation been that in their imagination they could see their Saviour dying for them and could kneel before his cross in penitence and faith.

I have written elsewhere, I think, that more of my heart and mind went into the writing of *The Cross of Christ* than into any other book I have written. This is understandable, because the cross remains the very centre of our Christian faith, life and mission. 'You do not understand Christ', wrote

P. T. Forsyth, 'till you understand his cross.' He was right. I would go so far as to say that I could not be a Christian at all if it were not for the cross. What I believe about God himself, about his character and purpose, about time and eternity, about evil, suffering, salvation, reality, faith, love – and everything else besides – is largely determined by the cross.

At the same time, the writing of *The Contemporary Christian* was also very important to me because of its subtitle: *An urgent plea for double listening*. Over the years I have come to an increasingly firm conviction that, as followers of the Lord Jesus, we must listen attentively to both the Word and the world. We listen to God as he continues to speak his word to us particularly through Scripture. But we must also listen to the often strident voices of the modern world, its cries and sighs of pain, its questioning, alienation and bewilderment, even its shouts of anger. Not of course that we listen to the Word and the world with an equal degree of respect. We listen to God in order to believe and obey him. We listen to the world rather in order to understand and feel its predicament.

Double listening is vital if we are ever to communicate the gospel, to speak God's Word to God's world with a necessary combination of faithfulness and sensitivity.

JOHN STOTT
Christmas 1998

THE Cross of Christ

Dedicated to Frances Whitehead
in gratitude for 30 years of outstanding
loyal and efficient service
1956–1986

Contents

Preface

I count it an enormous privilege to have been invited by Inter-Varsity Press to write a book on that greatest and most glorious of all subjects, the cross of Christ. I have emerged from the several years of work involved spiritually enriched, with my convictions clarified and strengthened, and with a firm resolve to spend the rest of my days on earth (as I know the whole redeemed company will spend eternity in heaven) in the liberating service of Christ crucified.

It is appropriate that a book on the cross should form part of the Golden Jubilee celebrations of Inter-Varsity Press, to which (under its dedicated leaders Ronald Inchley and Frank Entwistle) the whole Christian reading public is greatly indebted. For the cross is at the centre of the evangelical faith. Indeed, as I argue in this book, it lies at the centre of the historic, biblical faith, and the fact that this is not always everywhere acknowledged is in itself a sufficient justification for preserving a distinctive evangelical testimony. Evangelical Christians believe that in and through Christ crucified God substituted himself for us and bore our sins, dying in our place the death we deserved to die, in order that we might be restored to his favour and adopted into his family. Dr J. I. Packer has rightly written that this belief 'is a distinguishing mark of the world-wide evangelical fraternity' (even though it 'often gets misunderstood and caricatured by its critics'); it 'takes us to the very heart of the Christian gospel'.[1]

The centrality of the cross has certainly been a vital factor in the history of what is now the Universities and Colleges Christian Fellowship, together with the world body to which it is affiliated, namely the International Fellowship of Evangelical Students. Two events, which took place earlier in this century, were particularly important.

The first was the disafffiliation in 1910 of the Cambridge Inter-Collegiate Christian Union (founded in 1877) from the Student Christian Movement (founded in 1895). CICCU members were conscious of standing in the tradition of Bilney, Tyndale, Latimer, Ridley and Cranmer, the great names of the Cambridge Reformation. They also looked back with pride and affection to Charles Simeon, who for fifty-four years (1782–1836) as Vicar of Holy Trinity Church had faithfully expounded the Scriptures and, as his memorial plaque testifies, 'whether as the ground of his own hopes or as the subject of all his ministrations, determined to know nothing but Jesus Christ and him crucified'. It is not surprising, therefore, that they were becoming increasingly disenchanted with the liberal tendencies of the SCM, and specially with its weak doctrines of the Bible, the cross and even the deity of Jesus. So when Tissington Tatlow, General Secretary of the SCM, met CICCU members in March 1910, the vote to disafffiliate the Union was taken. The following year Howard Mowll (later to be Archbishop of Sydney and Primate of Australia) became President of CICCU and helped to establish it on firm evangelical foundations from which it has never been moved.[2]

After the First World War ended in 1918, many ex-servicemen went up to Cambridge as students. CICCU by now was much smaller than the SCM. Yet the SCM leaders (notably Charles Raven, the Dean of Emmanuel) made overtures to the CICCU, hoping that they would re-join and supply the missing devotional warmth and evangelistic thrust. To resolve the issue, Daniel Dick and Norman Grubb (President and Secretary of CICCU) met the SCM committee in the rooms in Trinity Great Court of their secretary, Rollo Pelly. Here is Norman Grubb's own account of the crucial issue:

> After an hour's talk, I asked Rollo point-blank, 'Does the SCM put the atoning blood of Jesus Christ central?' He hesitated, and then said, 'Well, we acknowledge it, but not necessarily central.' Dan Dick and I then said that this settled the matter for us in the CICCU. We could never join something that did not maintain the atoning blood of Jesus Christ as its centre; and we parted company.[3]

This decision not only confirmed the pre-war vote to disaffiliate, but 'was also the real foundation of the I.V.F., for it was only a few months later that the realization dawned on us that if a C.I.C.C.U. was a necessity in

Cambridge, a union of the same kind was also a necessity in every University of the world'.[4] The first Inter-Varsity Conference was held in London in December 1919.

During this period Norman Grubb quoted 1 Corinthians 15:3–4 as a key text in their thinking: 'For I delivered to you as of first importance what I also received, that Christ died for our sins in accordance with the scriptures, that he was buried, that he was raised on the third day in accordance with the scriptures' (RSV). It would be hard to square with this the SCM's 1919 Aim and Basis, which included the following statement about the cross: 'it is only as we see on Calvary the price of suffering paid day by day by God himself for all human sin, that we can enter into the experience of true penitence and forgiveness, which sets us free to embark upon a wholly new way of life ... This is the meaning of the Atonement.'[5] But we have respectfully to respond that the meaning of the atonement is not to be found in *our* penitence evoked by the sight of Calvary, but rather in what *God* did when in Christ on the cross he took our place and bore our sin.

This distinction between an 'objective' and 'subjective' understanding of the atonement needs to be made clear in every generation. According to Dr Douglas Johnson, the first General Secretary of the IVF, this discovery was the turning-point in the ministry of Dr Martyn Lloyd-Jones, who occupied an unrivalled position of evangelical leadership in the decades following the Second World War. He confided in several friends that 'a fundamental change took place in his outlook and preaching in the year 1929'. He had, of course, emphasized from the beginning of his ministry the indispensable necessity of the new birth. But, after preaching one night in Bridgend, South Wales, the minister challenged him that 'the cross and the work of Christ' appeared to have little place in his preaching. He went 'at once to his favourite secondhand book shop and asked the proprietor for the two standard books on the Atonement. The bookseller ... produced R. W. Dale's *The Atonement* (1875) and James Denney's *The Death of Christ* (1903). On his return home he gave himself to study, declining both lunch and tea, and causing his wife such anxiety that she telephoned her brother to see whether a doctor should be called. But when he later emerged, he claimed to have found 'the real heart of the gospel and the key to the inner meaning of the Christian faith'. So the content of his preaching changed, and with this its impact. As he himself put it, the basic question was not Anselm's 'Why did God become man?' but 'Why did Christ die?'[6]

Because of the vital importance of the atonement, and of an understanding of it which reclaims from misrepresentation the great biblical concepts of 'substitution', 'satisfaction' and 'propitiation', two things have greatly surprised me. The first is how unpopular the doctrine remains. Some theologians evince a strange reluctance to subscribe to it, even when its biblical basis becomes clear to them. I think, for example, of that noted Methodist New

Testament scholar, Vincent Taylor. His careful and comprehensive scholarship is exemplified in his three books on the cross, *Jesus and His Sacrifice* (1937), *The Atonement in New Testament Teaching* (1940) and *Forgiveness and Reconciliation* (1946). He employs many adjectives to describe the death of Christ, such as 'vicarious', 'redemptive', 'reconciling', 'expiatory', 'sacrificial' and especially 'representative'. But he cannot bring himself to call it 'substitutionary'. After a close examination of primitive Christian preaching and belief, of Paul, Hebrews and John, he writes of the work of Christ: 'In none of the passages we have examined is it described as that of a substitute ... Nowhere have we found any support for such views' (*Atonement*, p. 258). No, Christ's work was 'a ministry accomplished on our behalf, but not in our stead' (p. 270). Yet even as Vincent Taylor made these astonishing statements, he was clearly uneasy in making them. Their vehemence leaves us unprepared for the concessions which he later feels obliged to make. 'Perhaps the most striking feature of New Testament teaching concerning the representative work of Christ', he writes, 'is the fact that it comes so near, without actually crossing, the bounds of substitutionary doctrine. Paulinism, in particular, is within a hair's breadth of substitution' (p. 288). He even confesses of New Testament theologians that 'too often we are content to deny substitution without replacing it' (p. 289), and that it is a notion 'we have perhaps been more anxious to reject than to assess' (p. 301). What, however, I shall try to show in this book, is that the biblical doctrine of atonement is substitutionary from beginning to end. What Vincent Taylor shrank from was not the doctrine itself, but the crudities of thought and expression of which the advocates of substitution have not infrequently been guilty.

My second surprise, in view of the centrality of the cross of Christ, is that no book on this topic has been written by an evangelical author for thoughtful readers (until two or three years ago) for nearly half a century. True, there have been several small paperbacks, and there have been some scholarly works. I would like to pay special tribute to the outstanding labours in this field of Dr Leon Morris of Melbourne, Australia. His *The Apostolic Preaching of the Cross* (1955) has put all of us in his debt, and I am glad that he has brought its contents within reach of lay people in *The Atonement* (1983). He has made himself master of the extensive literature of the ages on this theme, and his *The Cross in the New Testament* (1965) remains probably the most comprehensive survey available. From it I quote with warm endorsement his statement that 'the cross dominates the New Testament' (p. 365).

Until the recent publication, however, of Ronald Wallace's *The Atoning Death of Christ* (1981) and Michael Green's *The Empty Cross of Jesus* (1984), I do not know of an evangelical book for the readership I have in mind since H. E. Guillebaud's *Why the Cross?* (1937), which was one of the very first books published by IVF. It was a courageous work, meeting the critics of a substitutionary atonement head on, and asking the three questions: (1) 'is it Christian?' (*i.e.* compatible with the teaching of Jesus and his apostles); (2) 'is it immoral?' (*i.e.* compatible or incompatible with justice); and (3) 'is it incredible?' (*i.e.* compatible or incompatible with such problems as time and the transfer of guilt).

My concern is to range more widely, for this is not a book on the atonement only, but on the cross. After the three introductory chapters which form Part One, I come in Part Two to what I have called 'the heart of the cross', in which I argue for a truly biblical understanding of the notions of 'satisfaction' and 'substitution'. In Part Three, I move on to the three great achievements of the cross, namely saving sinners, revealing God and conquering evil. But Part Four grapples with areas which are often omitted from books on the cross, namely what it means for the Christian community to 'live under the cross'. I try to show that the cross transforms everything. It gives us a new, worshipping relationship to God, a new and balanced understanding of ourselves, a new incentive to give ourselves in mission, a new love for our enemies, and a new courage to face the perplexities of suffering.

In developing my theme, I have had in mind the triangle of Scripture, tradition and the modern world. My first anxiety has been to be true to the Word of God, allowing it to say what it has to say and not asking it to say what I might want it to say. There is no alternative to careful exegesis of the text. Secondly, I have endeavoured to share some of the fruits of my reading. In seeking to understand the cross, one cannot ignore the great works of the past. To be disrespectful of tradition and of historical theology is to be disrespectful of the Holy Spirit who has been actively enlightening the church in every century. Then, thirdly, I have tried to understand Scripture, not only in its own light and in the light of tradition, but also in relation to the contemporary world. I have asked what the cross of Christ says to us at the end of the twentieth century.

In daring to write (and read) a book about the cross, there is of course a great danger of presumption. This is partly because what actually happened when 'God was reconciling the world to himself in Christ' is a mystery whose depths we shall spend eternity plumbing; and partly because it would be most unseemly to feign a cool detachment as we contemplate Christ's cross. For willy-nilly we are involved. Our sins put him there. So, far from offering us flattery, the cross undermines our self-righteousness. We can stand before it only with a bowed head and a broken spirit. And there we remain until the Lord Jesus speaks to our hearts his word of pardon and acceptance, and we, gripped by his love and brimful of thanksgiving, go out into the world to live our lives in his service.

I am grateful to Roger Beckwith and David Turner for reading portions of the manuscript and for their helpful comments. I thank my four most recent study assistants – Mark Labberton, Steve Ingraham, Bob Wismer and Steve Andrews. Steve Andrews has been characteristically meticulous in reading the MS, compiling the bibliography and indexes, checking references and correcting the proofs.

But I reserve until last my heartfelt thanks to Frances Whitehead who in 1986 completes thirty years as my secretary. This book is the umpteenth she has typed. I cannot speak too highly of her efficiency, helpfulness, loyalty, and undiminished enthusiasm for the work of the Lord. With much gratitude I dedicate this book to her.

JOHN STOTT
Christmas, 1985

Notes

[1] J. 1. Packer, 'What Did the Cross Achieve?', p. 3.
[2] See *Archbishop Mowll* by Marcus L Loane, especially pp. 43–61. See also *Whatever Happened to the Jesus Lane Lot?* by O. R Barclay, especially pp. 65–70.
[3] Norman P. Grubb, *Once Caught, No Escape*, p. 56.
[4] F. Donald Coggan (ed.), *Christ and the Colleges*, p. 17.
[5] Tissington Tatlow, *Story of the SCM*, p. 630.
[6] I am grateful to Dr Douglas Johnson for supplying me with this information, which supplements the account given by Iain H. Murray in *David Martyn Lloyd-Jones*, pp. 190–191.

Abbreviations

The English text of biblical quotations is that of the New International Version, unless stated to the contrary.

AG   A *Greek-English Lexicon of the New Testament and Other Early Christian Literature* by William F. Arndt and F. Wilbur Gingrich (University of Chicago Press and Cambridge University Press, 1957).

AV   The Authorized (King James) Version of the Bible, 1611.

JB   The Jerusalem Bible (Darton, Longman and Todd, 1966).

LXX   The Old Testament in Greek according to the Septuagint, 3rd century BC.

NEB   The New English Bible (NT 1961, 2nd edition 1970; OT 1970).

NIV   The New International Version of the Bible (NT 1973; OT 1979).

RSV   The Revised Standard Version of the Bible (NT 1946, 2nd edition 1971; OT 1952).

PART ONE

Approaching the cross

ONE

The centrality of the cross

Do you know the painting by Holman Hunt, the leader of the Pre-Raphaelite Brotherhood, entitled 'The Shadow of Death'? It depicts the inside of the carpenter's shop in Nazareth. Stripped to the waist, Jesus stands by a wooden trestle on which he has put down his saw. He lifts his eyes towards heaven, and the look on his face is one of either pain or ecstasy or both. He also stretches, raising both arms above his head. As he does so, the evening sunlight streaming through the open door casts a dark shadow in the form of a cross on the wall behind him, where his tool-rack looks like a horizontal bar on which his hands have been crucified. The tools themselves remind us of the fateful hammer and nails.

In the left foreground a woman kneels among the wood chippings, her hands resting on the chest in which the rich gifts of the Magi are kept. We cannot see her face because she has averted it. But we know that she is Mary. She looks startled (or so it seems) at her son's cross-like shadow on the wall.

The Pre-Raphaelites have a reputation for sentimentality. Yet they were serious and sincere artists, and Holman Hunt himself was determined, as he put it, to 'do battle with the frivolous art of the day', its superficial treatment of trite themes. So he spent 1870–73 in the Holy Land, and painted 'The Shadow of Death' in Jerusalem, as he sat on the roof of his house.[1] Though the idea is historically fictitious, it is also theologically true. From Jesus' youth, indeed even from his birth, the cross cast its shadow ahead of him. His death was central to his mission. Moreover, the church has always recognized this.

Imagine a stranger visiting St Paul's Cathedral in London. Having been brought up in a non-Christian culture, he knows next to nothing about Christianity. Yet he is more than a tourist; he is personally interested and keen to learn.

Walking along Fleet Street, he is impressed by the grandeur of the building's proportions, and marvels that Sir Christopher Wren could have conceived such an edifice after the Great Fire of London in 1666. As his eyes attempt to take it in, he cannot help noticing the huge golden cross which dominates the dome.

He enters the cathedral and stands at its central point, under the dome. Trying to grasp the size and shape of the building, he becomes aware that its ground plan, consisting of nave and transepts, is cruciform. He walks round and observes that each side chapel contains what looks to him like a table, on which, prominently displayed, there stands a cross. He goes downstairs into the crypt to see the tombs of famous men such as Sir Christopher Wren himself, Lord Nelson and the Duke of Wellington: a cross is engraved or embossed on each.

Returning upstairs, he decides to remain for the service which is about to begin. The man beside him is wearing a little cross on his lapel, while the lady on his other side has one on her necklace. His eye now rests on the colourful, stained-glass east window. Though he cannot make out the details from where he is sitting, he cannot fail to notice that it contains a cross.

Suddenly, the congregation stands up. The choir and clergy enter, preceded by somebody carrying a processional cross. They are singing a hymn. The visitor looks down at the service paper to read its opening words:

> We sing the praise of him who died,
>   Of him who died upon the cross;
> The sinner's hope let men deride,
>   For this we count the world but loss.

From what follows he comes to realize that he is witnessing a Holy Communion service, and that this focuses upon the death of Jesus. For when the people around him go forward to the communion rail to receive bread and wine, the minister speaks to them of the body and blood of Christ. The service ends with another hymn:

> When I survey the wondrous cross
>   On which the Prince of glory died,
> My richest gain I count but loss,
>   And pour contempt on all my pride.

> Forbid it, Lord, that I should boast
> Save in the cross of Christ my God;
> All the vain things that charm me most,
> I sacrifice them to his blood.

Although the congregation now disperses, a family stays behind. They have brought their child to be baptized. Joining them at the font, the visitor sees the minister first pour water over the child and then trace a cross on its forehead, saying, 'I sign you with the cross, to show that you must not be ashamed to confess the faith of Christ crucified ...'.

The stranger leaves the cathedral impressed, but puzzled. The repeated insistence by word and symbol on the centrality of the cross has been striking. Yet questions have arisen in his mind. Some of the language used has seemed exaggerated. Do Christians really for the sake of the cross 'count the world but loss', and 'boast' in it alone, and 'sacrifice' everything for it? Can the Christian faith be accurately summed up as 'the faith of Christ crucified'? What are the grounds, he asks himself, for this concentration on the cross of Christ?

The sign and symbol of the cross

Every religion and ideology has its visual symbol, which illustrates a significant feature of its history or beliefs. The lotus flower, for example, although it was used by the ancient Chinese, Egyptians and Indians, is now particularly associated with Buddhism. Because of its wheel shape it is thought to depict either the cycle of birth and death or the emergence of beauty and harmony out of the muddy waters of chaos. Sometimes the Buddha is portrayed as enthroned in a fully open lotus flower.

Ancient Judaism avoided visual signs and symbols, for fear of infringing the second commandment which prohibits the manufacture of images. But modern Judaism now employs the so-called Shield or Star of David, a hexagram formed by combining two equilateral triangles. It speaks of God's covenant with David that his throne would be established for ever and that the Messiah would be descended from him. Islam, the other monotheistic faith which arose in the Middle East, is symbolized by a crescent, at least in West Asia. Originally depicting a phase of the moon, it was already the symbol of sovereignty in Byzantium before the Muslim conquest.

The secular ideologies of this century also have their universally recognizable signs. The Marxist hammer and sickle, adopted in 1917 by the Soviet government from a nineteenth-century Belgian painting, represent industry and agriculture; and they are crossed to signify the union of workers and peasants, of factory and field. The swastika, on the other hand, has been traced back some 6,000 years. The arms of its cross are bent clockwise to symbolize either the movement of the sun across the sky, or the cycle of the four seasons, or the process of creativity and prosperity ('svasti' being a Sanskrit word for 'well-being'). At the beginning of this century, however, it was taken up by some German groups as a symbol of the Aryan race. Then Hitler took it over, and it became the sinister sign of Nazi racial bigotry.

Christianity, then, is no exception in having a visual symbol. The cross was not its earliest, however. Because of the wild accusations which were levelled against Christians, and the persecution to which they were exposed, they 'had to be very circumspect and to avoid flaunting their religion. Thus the cross, now the universal symbol of Christianity, was at first avoided, not only for its direct association with Christ, but for its shameful association with the execution of a common criminal also'.[2] So on the walls and ceilings of the catacombs (underground burial-places outside Rome, where the persecuted Christians probably hid), the earliest Christian motifs seem to have been either non-committal paintings of a peacock (supposed to symbolize immortality), a dove, the athlete's victory palm or, in particular, a fish. Only the initiated would know, and nobody else could guess, that *ichthys* ('fish') was an acronym for *Iēsous Christos Theou Huios Sōtēr* ('Jesus Christ, Son of God, Saviour'). But it did not remain the Christian sign, doubtless because the association between Jesus and a fish was purely acronymic (a fortuitous arrangement of letters) and had no visual significance.

Somewhat later, probably during the second century, the persecuted Christians seem to have preferred to paint biblical themes like Noah's ark, Abraham killing the ram instead of Isaac, Daniel in the lions' den, his three friends in the fiery furnace, Jonah being disgorged by the fish, some baptisms, a shepherd carrying a lamb, the healing of the paralytic and the raising of Lazarus. All these were symbolic of Christ's redemption, while not being in themselves incriminating, since only the instructed would have been able to interpret their meaning. In addition, the Chi-Rho monogram (the first two letters of the Greek word *Christos)* was a popular cryptogram, often in the form of a cross, and sometimes with a lamb standing before it, or with a dove.

A universally acceptable Christian emblem would obviously need to speak of Jesus Christ, but there was a wide range of possibilities. Christians might have chosen the crib or manger in which the baby Jesus was laid, or the carpenter's bench at which he worked as a young man in Nazareth, dignifying manual labour, or the boat from which he taught the crowds in Galilee, or the apron he wore when washing the apostles' feet, which would have spoken of his spirit of humble service. Then there was the stone which, having been rolled from the mouth of Joseph's tomb, would have proclaimed his resurrection. Other possibilities were the throne, symbol of divine sovereignty, which John in his vision of heaven saw that Jesus was sharing, or the dove, symbol of the Holy Spirit sent from heaven on the Day of Pentecost. Any of these seven symbols would have been suitable as a pointer to some aspect of the ministry of the Lord. But instead the chosen symbol came to be a simple cross. Its two bars were already a cosmic symbol from remote antiquity of the axis between heaven and earth. But its choice by Christians had a more specific explanation. They wished to commemorate as central to their understanding of Jesus neither his birth nor his youth, neither his teaching nor his service, neither his resurrection nor his reign, nor his gift of the Spirit, but his death, his crucifixion. The crucifix (that is, a cross to which a figure of Christ is attached) does not appear to have been used before the sixth century.

It seems certain that, at least from the second century onwards, Christians not only drew, painted and engraved the cross as a pictorial symbol of their faith, but also made the sign of the cross on themselves or others. One of the first witnesses to this practice was Tertullian, the North African lawyer-theologian who flourished about AD 200. He wrote:

> At every forward step and movement, at every going in and out, when we put on our clothes and shoes, when we bathe, when we sit at table, when we light the lamps, on couch, on seat, in all the ordinary actions of daily life, we trace upon the forehead the sign [the cross].[3]

Hippolytus, the scholar-presbyter of Rome, is a particularly interesting witness, because he is known to have been 'an avowed reactionary who in his own generation stood for the past rather than the future'. His famous treatise *The Apostolic Tradition* (c. AD 215) 'claims explicitly to be recording only the forms and models of rites *already* traditional and customs *already* long established, and to be written in deliberate protest against innovations'.[4] When he describes certain 'church observances', therefore, we may be sure that they were already being practised a generation or more previously. He mentions that the sign of the cross was used by the bishop when anointing the candidate's forehead at Confirmation, and he recommends it in private prayer: 'imitate him [Christ] always, by signing thy forehead sincerely: for this is the sign of his passion.' It is also, he adds, a protection against evil: 'When tempted, always reverently seal thy forehead with the sign of the cross. For this sign of the passion is displayed and made manifest against the devil if thou makest it in faith, not in order that thou mayest be seen of men, but by thy knowledge putting it forth as a shield.'[5]

There is no need for us to dismiss this habit as superstitious. In origin at least, the sign of the cross was intended to identify and indeed sanctify each act as belonging to Christ.

In the middle of the third century, when another North African,

Cyprian, was Bishop of Carthage, a terrible persecution was unleashed by the Emperor Decius (AD 250–251) during which thousands of Christians died rather than offer sacrifice to his name. Anxious to strengthen the morale of his people, and to encourage them to accept martyrdom rather than compromise their Christian faith, Cyprian reminded them of the ceremony of the cross: 'let us take also for protection of our head the helmet of salvation ... that our brow may be fortified, so as to keep safe the sign of God.'[6] As for the faithful who endured prison and risked death, Cyprian praised them in these terms: 'your brows, hallowed by God's seal ... reserved themselves for the crown which the Lord would give.'[7]

Richard Hooker, the sixteenth-century Anglican theologian and Master of the Temple in London, applauded the fact that the early church Fathers, in spite of heathen scorn at the sufferings of Christ, 'chose rather the sign of the cross [*sc.* in baptism] than any other outward mark, whereby the world might most easily discern always what they were'.[8] He was aware of the forthright objections of the Puritans. 'Crossing and such like pieces of Popery,' they were saying, 'which the church of God in the Apostles' time never knew', ought not to be used, for human inventions ought not to be added to divine institutions, and there was always the danger of superstitious misuse. As King Hezekiah destroyed the brazen serpent, so crossing should be abandoned. But Hooker stood his ground. In 'matters indifferent', which were not incompatible with Scripture, Christians were free. Besides, the sign of the cross had a positive usefulness: it is 'for us an admonition ... to glory in the service of Jesus Christ, and not to hang down our heads as men ashamed thereof, although it procure us reproach and obloquy at the hands of this wretched world'.[9]

It was Constantine, the first emperor to profess to be a Christian, who gave added impetus to the use of the cross symbol. For (according to Eusebius), on the eve of the Battle of the Milvian Bridge which brought him supremacy in the West (AD 312–313), he saw a cross of light in the sky, along with the words *in hoc signo vinces* ('conquer by this sign'). He immediately adopted it as his emblem, and had it emblazoned on the standards of his army.

Whatever we may think of Constantine and of the development of post-Constantinian 'Christendom', at least the church has faithfully preserved the cross as its central symbol. In some ecclesiastical traditions the candidate for baptism is still marked with this sign, and the relatives of a Christian who after death is buried rather than cremated are likely to have a cross erected over his grave. Thus from Christian birth to Christian death, as we might put it, the church seeks to identify and protect us with a cross.

The Christians' choice of a cross as the symbol of their faith is the more surprising when we remember the horror with which crucifixion was regarded in the ancient world. We can understand why Paul's 'message of the cross' was to many of his listeners 'foolishness', even 'madness' (1 Cor. 1:18, 23). How could any sane person worship as a god a dead man who had been justly condemned as a criminal and subjected to the most humiliating form of execution? This combination of death, crime and shame put him beyond the pale of respect, let alone of worship.[10]

Crucifixion seems to have been invented by 'barbarians' on the edge of the known world, and taken over from them by both Greeks and Romans. It is probably the most cruel method of execution ever practised, for it deliberately delayed death until maximum torture had been inflicted. The victim could suffer for days before dying. When the Romans adopted it, they reserved it for criminals convicted of murder, rebellion or armed robbery, provided that they were also slaves, foreigners or other non-persons. The Jews were therefore outraged when the Roman general Varus crucified 2,000 of their compatriots in 4 BC, and when during the siege of Jerusalem the general Titus crucified so many fugitives from the city that neither 'space ... for the crosses, nor crosses for the bodies' could be found.[11]

Roman citizens were exempt from crucifixion, except in extreme cases of treason. Cicero in one of his speeches condemned it as *crudelissimum taeterrimumque supplicium,* 'a most cruel and disgusting punishment'.[12] A little later he declared: 'To bind a Roman citizen is a crime, to flog him is an abomination, to kill him is almost an act of murder: to crucify him is – What? There is no fitting word that can possibly describe so horrible a deed.'[13] Cicero was even more explicit in his successful defence in 63 BC of the elderly senator Gaius Rabirius who had been charged with murder: 'the very word "cross" should be far removed not only from the person of a Roman citizen, but from his thoughts, his eyes and his ears. For it is not only the actual occurrence of these things [*sc.* the procedures of crucifixion] or the endurance of them, but liability to them, the expectation, indeed the mere mention of them, that is unworthy of a Roman citizen and a free man.'[14]

If the Romans regarded crucifixion with horror, so did the Jews, though for a different reason. They made no distinction between a 'tree' and a 'cross', and so between a hanging and a crucifixion. They therefore automatically applied to crucified criminals the terrible statement of the law that 'anyone who is hung on a tree is under God's curse' (Dt. 21:23). They could not bring themselves to believe that God's Messiah would die under his curse, strung up on a tree. As Trypho the Jew put it to Justin the Christian apologist, who engaged him in dialogue: 'I am exceedingly incredulous on this point.'[15]

So then, whether their background was Roman or Jewish or both, the early enemies of Christianity lost no opportunity to ridicule the claim that God's anointed and man's Saviour ended his life on a cross. The idea was crazy. This is well illustrated by a graffito from the second century, discovered on the

Palatine Hill in Rome, on the wall of a house considered by some scholars to have been used as a school for imperial pages. It is the first surviving picture of the crucifixion, and is a caricature. A crude drawing depicts, stretched on a cross, a man with the head of a donkey. To the left stands another man, with one arm raised in worship. Unevenly scribbled underneath are the words ALEXAMENOS CEBETE [*sc. sebete*] THEON, 'Alexamenos worships God'. The cartoon is now in the Kircherian Museum in Rome. Whatever the origin of the accusation of donkey-worship (which was attributed to both Jews and Christians), it was the concept of worshipping a crucified man which was being held up to derision.

One detects the same note of scorn in Lucian of Samosata, the second-century pagan satirist. In *The Passing of Peregrinus* (a fictitious Christian convert whom he portrays as a charlatan) he lampoons Christians as 'worshipping that crucified sophist himself and living under his laws' (p. 15).

The perspective of Jesus

The fact that a cross became the Christian symbol, and that Christians stubbornly refused, in spite of the ridicule, to discard it in favour of something less offensive, can have only one explanation. It means that the centrality of the cross originated in the mind of Jesus himself. It was out of loyalty to him that his followers clung so doggedly to this sign. What evidence is there, then, that the cross stood at the centre of Jesus' own perspective?

Our only glimpse into the developing mind of the boy Jesus has been given us in the story of how at the age of twelve he was taken to Jerusalem at Passover and then left behind by mistake. When his parents found him in the temple, 'sitting among the teachers, listening to them and asking them questions', they scolded him. They had been anxiously searching for him, they said. 'Why were you searching for me?' he responded with innocent astonishment. 'Didn't you know I had to be in my Father's house?' (Lk. 2:41–50). Luke tells the story with a tantalizing economy of detail. We must therefore be careful not to read into it more than the narrative itself warrants. This much we may affirm, however, that already at the age of twelve Jesus was both speaking of God as 'my Father' and also feeling an inward compulsion to occupy himself with his Father's affairs. He knew he had a mission. His Father had sent him into the world for a purpose. This mission he must perform; this purpose he must fulfil. What these were emerges gradually in the narrative of the Gospels.

The evangelists hint that Jesus' baptism and temptation were both occasions on which he committed himself to go God's way rather than the devil's, the way of suffering and death rather than of popularity and acclaim. Yet Mark (who is followed in this by Matthew and Luke) pinpoints a later event when Jesus began to teach this clearly. It was the watershed in his public ministry. Having withdrawn with his apostles to the northern district round Caesarea Philippi in the foothills of Mount Hermon, he put to them the direct question who they thought he was. When Peter blurted out that he was God's Messiah, immediately Jesus 'warned them not to tell anyone about him' (Mk. 8:29–30). This injunction was consistent with his previous instructions about keeping the so-called 'Messianic secret'. Yet now something new took place: Jesus

> then began to teach them that the Son of Man must suffer many things and be rejected by the elders, chief priests and teachers of the law, and that he must be killed and after three days rise again. He spoke plainly about this (Mk. 8:31–32).

'Plainly' translates *parrēsia*, meaning 'with freedom of speech' or 'openly'. There was to be no secret about this. The fact of his Messiahship had been secret, because its character had been misunderstood. The popular Messianic expectation was of a revolutionary political leader. John tells us that at the peak of Jesus' Galilean popularity, after feeding the five thousand, the crowds had 'intended to come and make him king by force' (Jn. 6:15). Now that the apostles had clearly recognized and confessed his identity, however, he could explain the nature of his Messiahship and do so openly. Peter rebuked him, horrified by the fate he had predicted for himself. But Jesus rebuked Peter in strong language. The same apostle who in confessing Jesus' divine Messiahship had received a revelation from the Father (Mt. 16:17) had been deceived by the devil to deny the necessity of the cross. 'Out of my sight, Satan!' Jesus said, with a vehemence which must have astonished his hearers. 'You do not have in mind the things of God, but the things of men.'[16]

This incident is usually referred to as the first 'prediction of the passion'. There had been passing allusions before (*e.g.* Mk. 2:19–20); but this was quite unambiguous. The second was made a little later, as Jesus was passing through Galilee incognito. He said to the Twelve:

> 'The Son of Man is going to be betrayed into the hands of men. They will kill him, and after three days he will rise' (Mk. 9:31).

Mark says that the disciples did not understand what he meant, and were afraid to ask him. Matthew adds that they were 'filled with grief' (Mk. 9:30–32; *cf.* Mt. 17:22–23). This was probably the time when, according to Luke, Jesus 'resolutely set out for Jerusalem' (9:51). He was determined to fulfil what had been written of him.

Jesus made his third 'prediction of the passion' when they were heading for the Holy City. Mark introduces it with a graphic description of the awe which the Lord's resolution inspired in them:

> They were on their way up to Jerusalem, with Jesus leading the way, and the disciples were astonished, while those who followed were afraid. Again he took the Twelve aside and told them what was going to happen to him. 'We are going up to Jerusalem,' he said, 'and the Son of Man will be betrayed to the chief priests and teachers of the law. They will condemn him to death and will hand him over to the Gentiles, who will mock him and spit on him, flog him and kill him. Three days later he will rise.'

Luke adds his comment that 'everything that is written by the prophets about the Son of Man will be fulfilled'.[17]

This threefold repetition of the passion prediction adds a note of solemnity to Mark's narrative. It is in this way that he deliberately prepares his readers, as Jesus deliberately prepared the Twelve, for the terrible events which were to take place. Putting the three predictions together, the most impressive emphasis is neither that Jesus would be betrayed, rejected and condemned by his own people and their leaders, nor that they would hand him over to the Gentiles who would first mock and then kill him, nor that after three days he would rise from death. It is not even that each time Jesus designates himself 'Son of Man' (the heavenly figure whom Daniel saw in his vision, coming in the clouds of heaven, being given authority, glory and sovereign power, and receiving the worship of the nations) and yet paradoxically states that as Son of Man he will suffer and die, thus with daring originality combining the two Old Testament Messianic figures, the Suffering Servant of Isaiah 53 and the reigning Son of Man of Daniel 7. More impressive still is the determination he both expressed and exemplified. He *must* suffer and be rejected and die, he said. Everything written of him in Scripture *must* be fulfilled. So he set his face towards Jerusalem, and went ahead of the Twelve in the road. Peter's negative comment he instantly recognized as Satanic and therefore instantly repudiated.

Although these three predictions form an obvious trio because of their similar structure and wording, the Gospels record at least eight more occasions on which Jesus alluded to his death. Coming down from the mountain where he had been transfigured, he warned that he would suffer at the hands of his enemies just as John the Baptist had done,[18] and in response to the outrageously selfish request of James and John for the best seats in the kingdom, he said that he himself had come to serve, not to be served, and 'to give his life as a ransom for many'.[19] The remaining six allusions were all made during the last week of his life, as the crisis drew near. He saw his death as the culmination of centuries of Jewish rejection of God's message, and foretold that God's judgment would bring Jewish national privilege to an end.[20] Then on the Tuesday, mentioning the Passover, he said he was going to be 'handed over to be crucified'; in the Bethany home he described the pouring of perfume over his head as preparing him for burial; in the upper room he insisted that the Son of Man would go just as it was written about him, and gave them bread and wine as emblems of his body and blood, thus foreshadowing his death and requesting its commemoration. Finally, in the Garden of Gethsemane he refused to be defended by men or angels, since 'how then would the Scriptures be fulfilled that say it must happen in this way?'[21] Thus the Synoptic evangelists bear a common witness to the fact that Jesus both clearly foresaw and repeatedly foretold his coming death.

John omits these precise predictions. Yet he bears witness to the same phenomenon by his seven references to Jesus' 'hour' (usually *hōra* but once *kairos*, 'time'). It was the hour of his destiny, when he would leave the world and return to the Father. Moreover, his hour was in the Father's control, so that at first it was 'not yet', though in the end he could confidently say that 'the hour has come'.

When Jesus said to his mother at the Cana wedding after the wine had run out, and to his brothers when they wanted him to go to Jerusalem and advertise himself publicly, 'My time has not yet come', the surface meaning was plain. But John intended his readers to detect the deeper meaning, even though Jesus' mother and brothers did not.[22] John continues to share this secret with his readers, and uses it to explain why Jesus' apparently blasphemous statements did not lead to his arrest. 'They tried to seize him,' he comments, 'but no-one laid a hand on him, because his time had not yet come.'[23] Only when Jesus reaches Jerusalem for the last time does John make the reference explicit. When some Greeks asked to see him, he first said, 'The hour has come for the Son of Man to be glorified' and then, after speaking plainly of his death, he went on: 'Now my heart is troubled, and what shall I say? "Father, save me from this hour"? No, it was for this very reason I came to this hour. Father, glorify your name!'[24] Then twice in the upper room he made final references to the time having come for him to leave the world and to be glorified.[25]

However uncertain we may feel about the earlier allusions to his 'hour' or 'time', we can be in no doubt about the last three. For Jesus specifically called his 'hour' the time of his 'glorification', which (as we shall see later) began with his death, and added that he could not ask to be delivered from it because this was the reason he had come into the world. Indeed, the paradox John records can hardly have been accidental, that the hour for which he had come into the world was the hour in which he left it. Mark makes matters yet more explicit by identifying his 'hour' with his 'cup'.[26]

From this evidence supplied by the Gospel writers, what are we justified in saying about Jesus' perspective on his own death? Beyond question he knew that it was going to happen – not in the sense that all of us know we will have to die one day, but in the sense that he would meet a violent, premature, yet purposive death. More than that, he gives three intertwining reasons for its inevitability.

First, he knew he would die because of the hostility of the Jewish national leaders. It appears that this was aroused quite early during the public ministry. His attitude to the law in general, and to the sabbath in particular, incensed them. When he insisted on healing a man with a shrivelled hand in a synagogue on a sabbath day, Mark tells us that 'the Pharisees went out and began to plot with the Herodians how they might kill Jesus' (3:6). Jesus must have been aware of this. He was also very familiar with the Old Testament record of the persecution of the faithful prophets.[27] Although he knew himself to be more than a prophet, he also knew he was not less, and that therefore he could expect similar treatment. He was a threat to the leaders' position and prejudices. According to Luke, after his reading and exposition of Isaiah 61 in the Nazareth synagogue, in which he seemed to be teaching a divine preference for the Gentiles, 'all the people in the synagogue were furious .... They got up, drove him out of the town, and took him to the brow of the hill on which the town was built, in order to throw him down the cliff'. Luke adds that 'he walked right through the crowd and went on his way' (4:16–30). But it was a narrow escape. Jesus knew that sooner or later they would get him.

Secondly, he knew he would die because that is what stood written of the Messiah in the Scriptures. 'The Son of Man will go just as it is written about him' (Mk. 14:21). Indeed, when referring to the Old Testament prophetic witness, he tended to couple the death and resurrection, the sufferings and glory, of the Messiah. For the Scriptures taught both. And the Lord was still insisting on this after he had risen. He said to the disciples on the road to Emmaus: '"Did not the Christ have to suffer these things and then enter his glory?" And beginning with Moses and all the Prophets, he explained to them what was said in all the Scriptures concerning himself' (Lk. 24:25–27; *cf.* verses 44–47).

One would dearly love to have been present at this exposition of 'Christ in all the Scriptures'. For the actual number of his recognizable quotations from the Old Testament, in relation to the cross and resurrection, is not large. He predicted the falling away of the apostles by quoting from Zechariah that when the shepherd was struck the sheep would be scattered.[28] He concluded his Parable of the Tenants with a telling reference to the stone which, though rejected by the builders, subsequently became the building's capstone or cornerstone.[29] And while hanging on the cross, three of his so-called 'seven words' were direct quotations from Scripture: 'My God, my God, why have you forsaken me?' being Psalm 22:1, 'I thirst' coming from Psalm 69:21, and 'Father, into your hands I commit my spirit' from Psalm 31:5. These three psalms all describe the deep anguish of an innocent victim, who is suffering both physically and mentally at the hands of his enemies, but who at the same time maintains his trust in his God. Although of course they were written to express the distress of the psalmist himself, yet Jesus had evidently come to see himself and his own sufferings as their ultimate fulfilment.

It is, however, from Isaiah 53 that Jesus seems to have derived the clearest forecast not only of his sufferings, but also of his subsequent glory. For there the servant of Yahweh is first presented as 'despised and rejected by men, a man of sorrows, and familiar with suffering' (v. 3), on whom the Lord laid our sins, so that 'he was pierced for our transgressions' and 'crushed for our iniquities' (vv. 5–6), and then, at the end of both chapters 52 and 53, is 'raised and lifted up and highly exalted' (52:13) and receives 'a portion among the great' (53:12), as a result of which he will 'sprinkle many nations' (52:15) and 'justify many' (53:11). The only straight quotation which is recorded from Jesus' lips is from verse 12, 'he was numbered with the transgressors'. 'I tell you that this must be fulfilled in me,' he said (Lk. 22:37). Nevertheless, when he declared that he 'must suffer many things' and had 'not come to be served, but to serve, and to give his life as a ransom for many' (Mk. 8:31; 10:45), although these are not direct quotations from Isaiah 53, yet their combination of suffering, service and death for the salvation of others points straight in that direction. Moreover Paul, Peter, Matthew, Luke and John – the major contributors to the New Testament – together allude to at least eight of the chapter's twelve verses. What was the origin of their confident, detailed application of Isaiah 53 to Jesus? They must have derived it from his own lips. It was from this chapter more than from any other that he learnt that the vocation of the Messiah was to suffer and die for human sin, and so be glorified.

The opposition of the hierarchy and the predictions of Scripture, however, do not in themselves explain the inevitability of Jesus' death. The third and most important reason why he knew he would die was because of his own deliberate choice. He was determined to fulfil what was written of the Messiah, however painful it would be. This was neither fatalism nor a martyr complex. It was quite simply that he believed Old Testament Scripture to be his Father's revelation and that he was totally resolved to do his Father's will and finish his Father's work. Besides, his suffering and death would not be purposeless. He had come 'to seek and to save what was lost' (Lk. 19:10). It was for the salvation of sinners that he would die, giving his life as a ransom to set them free (Mk. 10:45). So he set his face steadfastly to go to Jerusalem. Nothing would deter or deflect him. Hence the reiterated 'must' when he spoke of his death. The Son of Man *must* suffer many things and be rejected. Everything that was written about him *must* be fulfilled. He refused to appeal for angels to rescue him, because then the Scriptures would not be fulfilled which said that it *must* happen in this way. Was it not *necessary* for the Christ to suffer before entering his glory?[30] He felt under constraint, even under compulsion: 'I have a baptism to undergo, and how distressed I am [RSV 'constrained', literally 'hemmed in'] until it is completed!' (Lk. 12:50).

So then, although he knew he must die, it was not because he was the helpless victim either of evil forces arrayed against him, or of any inflexible fate decreed for him, but because he freely embraced the purpose of his Father for the salvation of sinners, as it had been revealed in Scripture.

This was the perspective of Jesus on his death. Despite the great importance of his teaching, his example, and his works of compassion and power, none of these was central to his mission. What dominated his mind was not the living but the giving of his life. This final self-sacrifice was his 'hour', for which he had come into the world. And the four evangelists, who bear witness to him in the Gospels, show that they understand this by the disproportionate amount of space which they give to the story of his last few days on earth, his death and resurrection. It occupies between a third and a quarter of the three Synoptic Gospels, while John's Gospel has justly been described as having two parts, 'the Book of the Signs' and 'the Book of the Passion', since John spends an almost equal amount of time on each.

The apostles' emphasis

It is often asserted that in the book of Acts the apostles' emphasis was on the resurrection rather than the death of Jesus, and that in any case they gave no doctrinal explanation of his death. Neither of these arguments is sustained by the evidence. I am not of course wanting to claim that the apostles' sermons express a full doctrine of the atonement as it is later found in their letters. Luke's historical sense enables him to record what they said at the time, not what they might have said if they had been preaching several years later. Yet the seeds of the developed doctrine are there. Luke weaves his story round the two apostles Peter and Paul, and supplies five sample evangelistic sermons from each, in shorter or longer summaries. Thus we have Peter's sermons on the Day of Pentecost and in the Temple precincts, brief abstracts of what he said during his two trials by the Sanhedrin, and a fairly full account of his message to the Gentile centurion Cornelius and his household.[31] Then, when Luke is recounting the missionary exploits of his hero Paul, he contrasts his address to Jews in the synagogue at Pisidian Antioch with that to pagans in the open air at Lystra, contrasts two more in the second missionary journey, namely to Thessalonian Jews and Athenian philosophers, and summarizes his teaching to the Jewish leaders in Rome.[32] In each sermon the approach is different. To Jews

Paul spoke of the God of the covenant, the God of Abraham, Isaac and Jacob, but to Gentiles of the God of creation, who made the heavens, the earth and the sea and everything in them. Nevertheless, there was a core to the proclamation of both apostles, which might be reconstructed as follows:

> 'Jesus was a man who was accredited by God through miracles and anointed by the Spirit to do good and to heal. Despite this, he was crucified through the agency of wicked men, though also by God's purpose according to the Scriptures that the Messiah must suffer. Then God reversed the human verdict on Jesus by raising him from the dead, also according to the Scriptures, and as attested by the apostolic eyewitnesses. Next God exalted him to the place of supreme honour as Lord and Saviour. He now possesses full authority both to save those who repent, believe and are baptized in his name, bestowing on them the forgiveness of sins and the gift of the Spirit, and to judge those who reject him.'

Several important points emerge from this gospel core.

First, although the apostles attributed the death of Jesus to human wickedness, they declared that it was also due to a divine purpose.[33] Moreover, what God had foreknown, he had foretold. So the apostles repeatedly emphasized that the death and resurrection of Jesus happened 'according to the Scriptures'. Paul's own later summary of the gospel also stressed this: 'that Christ died for our sins according to the Scriptures ... that he was raised on the third day according to the Scriptures ...' (1 Cor. 15:3–4). Only sometimes are actual biblical quotations recorded. Many more unrecorded ones must have been used, as when in the Thessalonian synagogue Paul 'reasoned with them from the Scriptures, explaining and proving that the Christ had to suffer and rise from the dead' (Acts 17:2–3). It seems likely that these were – or at least included – the Scriptures which Jesus used, and therefore the doctrine which they expressed.

Secondly, although a full-scale atonement doctrine is missing, the apostolic preaching of the cross was not undoctrinal. Not only did they proclaim that Christ died according to the Scriptures, and so according to God's saving purpose, but they called the cross on which he died a 'tree'. Luke is careful to record this fact of both the leading apostles, Peter and Paul. Peter twice used the expression that the people 'killed him by hanging him on a tree', to the Jewish Sanhedrin and to the Gentile Cornelius. Similarly, Paul told the synagogue congregation in Pisidian Antioch that when the people and their rulers in Jerusalem 'had carried out all that was written about him, they took him down from the tree'.[34]

Now they were under no necessity to use this language. Peter also spoke of Jesus' 'crucifixion', and Paul of his 'sufferings' and 'execution'.[35] So why their references to the 'tree' and to his having been 'hanged' on it? The only possible explanation is to be found in Deuteronomy 21:22–23, where instructions were given for the body of a man, who had been executed for a capital offence by hanging, to be buried before nightfall, 'because anyone who is hung on a tree is under God's curse'. The apostles were quite familiar with this legislation, and with its implication that Jesus died under the divine curse. Yet, instead of hushing it up, they deliberately drew people's attention to it. So evidently they were not embarrassed by it. They did not think of Jesus as in any sense deserving to be accursed by God. They must, therefore, have at least begun to understand that it was our curse which he was bearing. Certainly both apostles stated this plainly in their later letters. Paul in Galatians, probably written very soon after his visit to Pisidian Antioch, wrote that 'Christ redeemed us from the curse of the law by becoming a curse for us, for it is written: "Cursed is everyone who is hanged on a tree"' (3:13). And Peter wrote: 'He himself bore our sins in his body on the tree' (1 Pet. 2:24). If then Peter and Paul in their letters plainly saw the cross of Jesus in sin-bearing or curse-bearing terms, and both linked this fact with the verses in Deuteronomy about being hanged on a tree, is it not reasonable to suppose that already in their Acts speeches, in which they called the cross a tree, they had glimpsed the same truth? In this case there is more doctrinal teaching about the cross in the early sermons of the apostles than they are often credited with.

Thirdly, we need to consider how the apostles presented the resurrection. Although they emphasized it, it would be an exaggeration to call their message an exclusively resurrection gospel. For in the nature of the case the resurrection cannot stand by itself. Since it is a resurrection from death, its significance is determined by the nature of this death. Indeed, the reason for emphasizing the resurrection may be rather to emphasize something about the death which it cancels and conquers. This proves to be the case. At its simplest their message was: 'You killed him, God raised him, and we are witnesses.'[36] In other words, the resurrection was the divine reversal of the human verdict. But it was more than this. By the resurrection God 'glorified' and 'exalted' the Jesus who had died.[37] Promoting him to the place of supreme honour at his right hand, in fulfilment of Psalm 110:1 and on account of the achievement of his death, God made the crucified and risen Jesus 'both Lord and Christ', both 'Prince and Saviour', with authority to save sinners by bestowing upon them repentance, forgiveness and the gift of the Spirit.[38] Moreover, this comprehensive salvation is specifically said to be due to his powerful 'Name' (the sum total of his person, death and resurrection), in which people must believe and into which they must be baptized, since there is 'no other name under heaven given to men' by which they must be saved.[39]

When we turn from the apostles' early sermons recorded in the Acts to the maturer utterances of their letters, the prominent place they give to the cross is even more marked. True, some of the shortest letters do not mention it (such as Paul's to Philemon, Jude's, and John's second and third), and it is not altogether surprising that James's largely ethical homily does not refer to it. Yet the three major letter-writers of the New Testament – Paul, Peter and John – are unanimous in witnessing to its centrality, as are also the letter to the Hebrews and the Revelation.

We begin with Paul. He found no anomaly in defining his gospel as 'the message of the cross', his ministry as 'we preach Christ crucified', baptism as initiation 'into his death' and the Lord's Supper as a proclamation of the Lord's death. He boldly declared that, though the cross seemed either foolishness or a 'stumbling block' to the self-confident, it was in fact the very essence of God's wisdom and power.[40] So convinced was he of this that he had deliberately resolved, he told the Corinthians, to renounce worldly wisdom and instead to know nothing among them 'except Jesus Christ and him crucified' (1 Cor. 2:1–2). When later in the same letter he wished to remind them of his gospel, which he had himself received and had handed on to them, which had become the foundation on which they were standing and the good news by which they were being saved, what was 'of first importance' (he said) was 'that Christ died for our sins according to the Scriptures, that he was buried, that he was raised on the third day according to the Scriptures, and that he appeared ...' (1 Cor. 15:1–5). And when a few years later he developed this outline into the full gospel manifesto which his letter to the Romans is, his emphasis is even more strongly on the cross. For having proved all humankind sinful and guilty before God, he explains that God's righteous way of putting the unrighteous right with himself operates 'through the redemption that came by Christ Jesus', whom 'God presented as a sacrifice of atonement, through faith in his blood' (Rom. 3:21–25). Consequently, we are 'justified by his blood' and 'reconciled to God through the death of his Son' (Rom. 5:9–10). Without Christ's sacrificial death for us salvation would have been impossible. No wonder Paul boasted in nothing except the cross (Gal. 6:14).

The apostle Peter's testimony is equally clear. He begins his first letter with the startling statement that his readers have been sprinkled with the blood of Jesus Christ. And a few verses later, he reminds them that the price of their redemption from their former empty way of life has not been 'perishable things such as silver or gold', but rather 'the precious blood of Christ, a lamb without blemish or defect' (1 Pet. 1:18–19). Although the remaining references in his letter to the death of Jesus relate it to the unjust sufferings of Christians ('glory through suffering' being the principle for them as for him), Peter nevertheless takes the opportunity to give some profound instruction about the Saviour's death. 'He himself bore our sins in his body on the tree' and 'Christ died for sins once for all, the righteous for the unrighteous, to bring you to God' (2:24; 3:18), in fulfilment of the prophecy of Isaiah 53. Because in the context Peter is emphasizing the cross as our example, it is all the more striking that he should at the same time write of Christ our sinbearer and substitute.

John's emphasis in his letters was on the incarnation. Because he was combating an early heresy which tried to sever Christ from Jesus, the divine Son from the human being, he insisted that Jesus was 'the Christ come in the flesh' and that anyone who denied this was Antichrist.[41] Nevertheless, he saw the incarnation as being with a view to the atonement. For God's unique love was seen not so much in the coming as in the dying of his Son, whom he 'sent ... as an atoning sacrifice for our sins' and whose 'blood ... purifies us from every sin'.[42]

The letter to the Hebrews, which is more a theological tract than a letter, was written to Jewish Christians who, under the pressure of persecution, were being tempted to renounce Christ and relapse into Judaism. The author's tactic was to demonstrate the supremacy of Jesus Christ, not only as Son over the angels and as Prophet over Moses, but in particular as Priest over the now obsolete Levitical priesthood. For the sacrificial ministry of Jesus, our 'great high priest' (4:14), is incomparably superior to theirs. He had no sins of his own for which to make sacrifice; the blood he shed was not of goats and calves, but his own; he had no need to offer the same sacrifices repeatedly, which could never take away sins, because he made 'one sacrifice for sins for ever'; and he has thus obtained an 'eternal redemption' and established an 'eternal covenant' which contains the promise, 'I will forgive their wickedness and will remember their sins no more.'[43]

Still more striking than all this, however, is the portraiture of Jesus in the last book of the Bible, the Revelation. He is introduced to us in its first chapter as 'the firstborn from the dead' (v. 5) and 'the Living One', who was dead but now is alive for ever, and who holds the keys of death and Hades (v. 18). An appropriate doxology is added: 'To him who loves us and has freed us from our sins by his blood ... to him be glory and power for ever and ever!' (vv. 5–6).

John's commonest designation of Jesus, consonant with the symbolic imagery of the Revelation, is simply 'the Lamb'. The reason for this title, which is applied to him twenty-eight times throughout the book, has little to do with the meekness of his character (although once his qualities as both 'Lion' and 'Lamb' are deliberately contrasted (5:5–6)); it is rather because he has been slain as a sacrificial victim and by his blood has set his people free. In order to grasp the broad perspective from which John views the influence of the Lamb, it may be helpful to divide it into four spheres – salvation, history, worship and eternity.

The redeemed people of God (that 'great multitude that no-one could count'), who are drawn from every nation and language, and stand before God's throne, specifically attribute their salvation to God and the Lamb. They cry with a loud voice:

> 'Salvation belongs to our God,
> who sits on the throne,
> and to the Lamb.'

By a very dramatic figure of speech the robes they are wearing are said to have been 'washed … and made white in the blood of the Lamb'. In other words, they owe their righteous standing before God entirely to the cross of Christ, through which their sins have been forgiven and their defilement cleansed. Their salvation through Christ is also secure, for not only are their names written in the Lamb's book of life, but the Lamb's name is written on their foreheads.[44]

In John's vision, however, the Lamb is more than the Saviour of a countless multitude; he is depicted also as the lord of all history. To begin with, he is seen 'standing in the centre of the throne', that is, sharing in the sovereign rule of Almighty God. More than that, the occupant of the throne is holding in his right hand a seven-sealed scroll, which is generally identified as the book of history. At first John 'wept and wept' because no-one in the universe could open the scroll, or even look inside it. But then at last the Lamb is said to be worthy. He takes the scroll, breaks the seals one by one, and thus (it seems) unfolds history chapter by chapter. It is significant that what has qualified him to assume this role is his cross; for this is the key to history and the redemptive process it inaugurated. Despite their sufferings from war, famine, plague, persecution and other catastrophes, God's people can yet overcome the devil 'by the blood of the Lamb', and are assured that the final victory will be his and theirs, since the Lamb proves to be 'Lord of lords and King of kings'.[45]

It is not surprising to learn that the author of salvation and the lord of history is also the object of heaven's worship. In chapter 5 we listen as one choir after another is brought in to swell the praise of the Lamb. First, when he had taken the scroll, 'the four living creatures and the twenty-four elders' (probably representing the whole creation on the one hand and the whole church of both Testaments on the other) 'fell down before the Lamb … and sang a new song':

> 'You are worthy to take the scroll
>   and to open the seals,
> because you were slain,
> and with your blood you purchased men for God
> from every tribe and language and people and nation …'

Next, John heard the voice of a hundred million angels, or more, who constituted the outer circle of those surrounding the throne. They too sang with a loud voice:

> 'Worthy is the Lamb, who was slain,
> to receive power and wealth and wisdom and strength
> and honour and glory and praise!'

Then finally he 'heard every creature in heaven and on earth and under the earth and on the sea, and all that is in them' – universal creation – singing:

> 'To him who sits on the throne and to the Lamb
> be praise and honour and glory and power,
>   for ever and ever!'

To this the four living creatures responded with their 'Amen', and the elders fell down and worshipped.[46]

Jesus the Lamb does more than occupy the centre of the stage today, in salvation, history and worship; in addition, he will have a central place when history ends and the curtain rises on eternity. On the day of judgment those who have rejected him will try to escape from him. They will call to the mountains and rocks to engulf them: 'Fall on us and hide us from the face of him who sits on the throne and from the wrath of the Lamb! For the great day of their wrath has come, and who can stand?' For those who have trusted and followed him, however, that day will be like a wedding day and a wedding feast. For the final union of Christ with his people is depicted in terms of the Lamb's marriage to his bride. Changing the metaphor, the new Jerusalem will descend from heaven. It will have no temple in it, 'because the Lord God Almighty and the Lamb are its temple'; nor will it need either sun or moon, 'for the glory of God gives it light, and the Lamb is its lamp'.[47]

One cannot fail to notice, or to be impressed by, the seer's repeated and uninhibited coupling of 'God and the Lamb'. The person he places on an equality with God is the Saviour who died for sinners. He depicts him as mediating God's salvation, sharing God's throne, receiving God's worship (the worship due to him) and diffusing God's light. And his worthiness, which qualifies him for these unique privileges, is due to the fact that he was slain, and by his death procured our salvation. If (as may be) the book of life is said in 13:8 to belong to 'the Lamb that was slain from the creation of the world', then John is telling us nothing less than that from an eternity of the past to an eternity of the future the centre of the stage is occupied by the Lamb of God who was slain.

Persistence despite opposition

This survey leaves us in no doubt that the principal contributors to the New Testament believed in the centrality of the cross of Christ, and believed that their conviction was derived from the mind of the Master himself. The early post-apostolic church, therefore, had a firm double base – in the teaching of Christ and his apostles – for making a cross the sign and symbol of Christianity. Church tradition proved in this to be a faithful reflection of Scripture.

Moreover, we must not overlook their remarkable tenacity. They knew that those who had crucified the Son of God had subjected him to 'public disgrace' and that in order to endure the cross Jesus had had to humble himself to it and to 'scorn its shame'.[48] Nevertheless, what was shameful, even odious, to the critics of Christ, was in the eyes of his followers most glorious. They had learnt that the servant was not greater than the master, and that for them as for him suffering was the means to glory. More than that, suffering was glory, and whenever they were 'insulted because of the name of Christ', then 'the Spirit of glory' rested upon them.[49]

Yet the enemies of the gospel neither did nor do share this perspective. There is no greater cleavage between faith and unbelief than in their respective attitudes to the cross. Where faith sees glory, unbelief sees only disgrace. What was foolishness to Greeks, and continues to be to modern intellectuals who trust in their own wisdom, is nevertheless the wisdom of God. And what remains a stumbling-block to those who trust in their own righteousness, like the Jews of the first century, proves to be the saving power of God (1 Cor. 1:18–25).

One of the saddest features of Islam is that it rejects the cross, declaring it inappropriate that a major prophet of God should come to such an ignominious end. The Koran sees no need for the sin-bearing death of a Saviour. At least five times it declares categorically that 'no soul shall bear another's burden'. Indeed, 'if a laden soul cries out for help, not even a near relation shall share its burden'. Why is this? It is because 'each man shall reap the fruits of his own deeds', even though Allah is merciful and forgives those who repent and do good. Denying the need for the cross, the Koran goes on to deny the fact. The Jews 'uttered a monstrous falsehood' when they declared 'We have put to death the Messiah Jesus the son of Mary, the apostle of Allah', for 'they did not kill him, nor did they crucify him, but they thought they did'.[50] Although Muslim theologians have interpreted this statement in different ways, the commonly held belief is that God cast a spell over the enemies of Jesus in order to rescue him, and that either Judas Iscariot[51] or Simon of Cyrene was substituted for him at the last moment. In the nineteenth century the Ahmadiya sect of Islam borrowed from different liberal Christian writers the notion that Jesus only swooned on the cross, and revived in the tomb, adding that he subsequently travelled to India to teach, and died there; they claim to be the guardians of his tomb in Kashmir.

But Christian messengers of the good news cannot be silent about the cross. Here is the testimony of the American missionary Samuel M. Zwemer (1867–1952), who laboured in Arabia, edited *The Muslim World* for forty years, and is sometimes called 'The Apostle to Islam':

> The missionary among Moslems (to whom the Cross of Christ is a stumbling-block and the atonement foolishness) is driven daily to deeper meditation on this mystery of redemption, and to a stronger conviction that here is the very heart of our message and our mission ...
>
> If the Cross of Christ is anything to the mind, it is surely everything – the most profound reality and the sublimest mystery. One comes to realize that literally all the wealth and glory of the gospel centres here. The Cross is the pivot as well as the centre of New Testament thought. It is the exclusive mark of the Christian faith, the symbol of Christianity and its cynosure.
>
> The more unbelievers deny its crucial character, the more do believers find in it the key to the mysteries of sin and suffering. We rediscover the apostolic emphasis on the Cross when we read the gospel with Moslems. We find that, although the offence of the Cross remains, its magnetic power is irresistible.[52]

'Irresistible' is the very word an Iranian student used when telling me of his conversion to Christ. Brought up to read the Koran, say his prayers and lead a good life, he nevertheless knew that he was separated from God by his sins. When Christian friends brought him to church and encouraged him to read the Bible, he learnt that Jesus Christ had died for his forgiveness. 'For me the offer was irresistible and heaven-sent,' he said, and he cried to God to have mercy on him through Christ. Almost immediately 'the burden of my past life was lifted. I felt as if a huge weight ... had gone. With the relief and sense of lightness came incredible joy. At last it had happened. I was free of my past. I *knew* that God had forgiven me, and I felt clean. I wanted to shout, and tell everybody.' It was through the cross that the character of God came clearly into focus for him, and that he found Islam's missing dimension, 'the intimate fatherhood of God and the deep assurance of sins forgiven'.

Muslims are not by any means the only people, however, who repudiate the gospel of the cross. Hindus also, though they can accept its historicity, reject its saving significance. Gandhi, for example, the founder of modern India, who while working in South Africa as a young lawyer was attracted to Christianity, yet wrote of himself while there in 1894:

I could accept Jesus as a martyr, an embodiment of sacrifice, and a divine teacher, but not as the most perfect man ever born. His death on the cross was a great example to the world, but that there was anything like a mysterious or miraculous virtue in it, my heart could not accept.[53]

Turning to the West, perhaps the most scornful rejection of the cross has come from the pen of the German philosopher and philologist, Friedrich Nietzsche (died 1900). Near the beginning of *The Anti-Christ* (1895) he defined the good as 'the will to power', the bad as 'all that proceeds from weakness', and happiness as 'the feeling that power *increases* ...' while 'what is more harmful than any vice' is 'active sympathy for the ill-constituted and weak – Christianity'. Admiring Darwin's emphasis on the survival of the fittest, he despised all forms of weakness, and in their place dreamt of the emergence of a 'superman' and a 'daring ruler race'. To him 'depravity' meant 'decadence', and nothing was more decadent than Christianity which 'has taken the side of everything weak, base, ill-constituted'. Being 'the religion of *pity*', it 'preserves what is ripe for destruction' and so 'thwarts the law of evolution' (pp. 115-118). Nietzsche reserved his bitterest invective for 'the Christian conception of God' as 'God of the sick, God as spider, God as spirit', and for the Christian Messiah whom he dismissed contemptuously as 'God on the Cross' (pp. 128, 168).

If Nietzsche rejected Christianity for its 'weakness', others have done so for its supposedly 'barbaric' teachings. Professor Sir Alfred Ayer, for example, the Oxford philosopher who is well known for his antipathy to Christianity, wrote in a recent newspaper article that, among religions of historical importance, there was quite a strong case for considering Christianity the worst. Why so? Because it rests 'on the allied doctrines of original sin and vicarious atonement, which are intellectually contemptible and morally outrageous'.[54]

How is it that Christians can face such ridicule without shifting their ground? Why do we 'cling to the old rugged cross' (in the words of a rather sentimental popular hymn), and insist on its centrality, refusing to let it be pushed to the circumference of our message? Why must we proclaim the scandalous, and glory in the shameful? The answer lies in the single word 'integrity'. Christian integrity consists partly in a resolve to unmask the caricatures, but mostly in personal loyalty to Jesus, in whose mind the saving cross was central. Indeed, readers who have come without bias to the Scriptures all seem to have come to the same conclusion. Here is a sample from this century.

P. T. Forsyth, the English Congregationalist, wrote in *The Cruciality* of *the* Cross (1909):

Christ is to us just what his cross is. All that Christ was in heaven or on earth was put into what he did there ... Christ, I repeat, is to us just what his cross is. You do not understand Christ till you understand his cross (pp. 44–45).

And the following year (1910) in *The Work of Christ* he wrote:

On this interpretation of the work of Christ [*sc.* the Pauline doctrine of reconciliation] the whole Church rests. If you move faith from that centre, you have driven *the* nail into the Church's coffin. The Church is then doomed to death, and it is only a matter of time when she shall expire (p. 53).

Next, Emil Brunner, the Swiss theologian, whose book *The Mediator* was first published in German in 1927, sub-titled *A Study of the Central Doctrine of the Christian Faith*, defended his conviction with these words:

In Christianity faith in the Mediator is not something optional, not something about which, in the last resort, it is possible to hold different opinions, if we are only united on the 'main point'. For faith in the Mediator – in the event which took place once for all, a revealed atonement – is the Christian religion itself; it is the 'main point'; it is not something alongside of the centre; it is the substance and kernel, not the husk. This is so true that we may even say: in distinction from all other forms of religion, the Christian religion is faith in the one Mediator ... And there is no other possibility of being a Christian than through faith in that which took place once for all, revelation and atonement through the Mediator (p. 40).

Later Brunner applauds Luther's description of Christian theology as a *theologia crucis*, and goes on:

The Cross is the sign of the Christian faith, of the Christian Church, of the revelation of God in Jesus Christ ... The whole struggle of the Reformation for the *sola fide*, the *soli deo gloria*, was simply the struggle for the right interpretation of the Cross. He who understands the Cross aright – this is the opinion of the Reformers – understands the Bible, he understands Jesus Christ (p. 435).

Again,

the believing recognition of this uniqueness, faith in the Mediator, is the sign of the Christian faith. Whoever considers this statement to be a sign of exaggeration, intolerance, harshness, non-historical thought, and the like, has not yet heard the message of Christianity (p. 507).

My final quotation comes from the Anglican scholar, Bishop Stephen Neill:

> In the Christian theology of history, the death of Christ is the central point of history; here all the roads of the past converge; hence all the roads of the future diverge.[55]

The verdict of scholars has understandably percolated through into popular Christian devotion. Allowances should be made for Christians who at Christ's cross have found their pride broken, their guilt expunged, their love kindled, their hope restored and their character transformed, if they go on to indulge in a little harmless hyperbole. Perceiving the cross to be the centre of history and theology, they naturally perceive it also to be the centre of all reality. So they see it everywhere, and have always done so. I give two examples, one ancient and the other modern.

Justin Martyr, the second-century Christian apologist, confessed that wherever he looked, he saw the cross. Neither the sea is crossed nor the earth is ploughed without it, he writes, referring to a ship's mast and yard, and to a plough's blade and yoke. Diggers and mechanics do not work without cross-shaped tools, alluding presumably to a spade and its handle. Moreover, 'the human form differs from that of the irrational animals in nothing else than in its being erect and having the arms extended'. And if the torso and arms of the human form proclaim the cross, so do the nose and eyebrows of the human face.[56] Fanciful? Yes, entirely, and yet I find myself willing to forgive any such fancies which glorify the cross.

My modern example is the most eloquent description I know of the universality of the cross. It is Malcolm Muggeridge unconsciously updating Justin Martyr. Brought up in a Socialist home, and familiar with Socialist Sunday Schools and their 'sort of agnosticism sweetened by hymns', he became uneasy about 'this whole concept of a Jesus of good causes'. Then:

> I would catch a glimpse of a cross – not necessarily a crucifix; maybe two pieces of wood accidentally nailed together, on a telegraph pole, for instance – and suddenly my heart would stand still. In an instinctive, intuitive way I understood that something more important, more tumultuous, more passionate, was at issue than our good causes, however admirable they might be ...
>
>   It was, I know, an obsessive interest ... I might fasten bits of wood together myself, or doodle it. This symbol, which was considered to be

derisory in my home, was yet also the focus of inconceivable hopes and desires ...

As I remember this, a sense of my own failure lies leadenly upon me. I should have worn it over my heart; carried it, a precious standard, never to be wrested out of my hands; even though I fell, still borne aloft. It should have been my cult, my uniform, my language, my life. I shall have no excuse; I can't say I didn't know. I knew from the beginning, and turned away.[57]

Later, however, he turned back, as each of us must who has ever glimpsed the reality of Christ crucified. For the only authentic Jesus is the Jesus who died on the cross.

But why did he die? Who was responsible for his death? That is the question to which we turn in the next chapter.

Notes

[1] See *Pre-Raphaelite Paintings* from the Manchester City Art Gallery, where 'The Shadow of Death' hangs, by Julian Treuherz.

[2] Michael Gough, *Origins of Christian Art*, p. 18. See also J. H. Miller, 'Cross' and Crucifix'; *Christian World*, ed. Geoffrey Barraclough; and *Cross and Crucifix* by Cyril E. Pocknee.

[3] Tertullian, *De Corona*, Ch. III, p. 94.

[4] Gregory Dix (ed.), *Apostolic Tradition of St Hippotyus*, p. xi.

[5] *Ibid.*, pp. 68–69.

[6] Cyprian, *Ad Thibaritanos* IX.

[7] Cyprian, *De Lapsis* 2.

[8] Richard Hooker, *Ecclesiastical Polity*, Book V, Ch. lxv.20, 'Of the Cross in Baptism'.

[9] *Ibid.*, Book V, Ch. lxv.6.

[10] See especially pp. 1–10 of *Crucifixion* by Martin Hengel, whose original title was *Mors turpissima crucis*, 'the utterly vile death of the cross', an expression first used by Origen.

[11] See the accounts given by Josephus in *Antiquities* xvii.10.10 and *Jewish War* V.xi.1.

[12] Cicero, *Against Verres* II.v.64, para. 165.

[13] *Ibid.*, II.v.66, para. 170.

[14] Cicero, *In Defence of Rabirius* V.16, p. 467.

[15] Justin Martyr, *Dialogue with Trypho a Jew*, Ch. lxxxix.

[16] Mk. 8:31ff.; *cf.* Mt. 16:21ff.; Lk. 9:22ff.

[17] Mk. 10:32–34; *cf.* Mt. 20:17–19; Lk. 18:31–34.

[18] Mt. 17:9–13; Mk. 9:9–13; *cf.* Lk. 9:44.

[19] Mk. 10:35–45; Mt. 20:20–28.

[20] Mk. 12:1–12; *cf.* Mt. 21:33–46; Lk. 20:9–19.

[21] For the Passover saying see Mt. 26:2; for the 'burial' references Mk. 14:3–9 and *cf.* Mt. 26:6–13; for the woe on Judas Mk. 14:10ff. and *cf.* Mt. 26:14ff. and Lk. 22:22; for the institution of the supper Mk. 14:22–25 and *cf.* Mt. 26:26–29, Lk. 22:14–20 and 1 Cor. 11:23–26; and for the arrest Mt. 26:47–56 and *cf.* Mk. 14:43–50, Lk. 22:47–53 and Jn. 18:1–11.

[22] Jn. 2:4; 7:8.

[23] Jn. 7:25ff. especially v. 30, and 8:12ff. especially v. 20.

[24] Jn. 12:20–28.

[25] Jn.13:1; 17:1.

[26] Jn. 12:27; 13:1; Mk.14:35, 41. *Cf.* Mt.26:18.

[27] Joachim Jeremias develops this argument in *Central Message*. See especially p. 41.

[28] Zc. 13:7; Mt. 26:31; Mk. 14:27.

[29] Ps. 118:22; Mt. 21:42; Mk. 12:10–11; Lk. 20:17. *Cf.* Acts 4:11; 1 Pet. 2:7.

[30] Mk. 8:31; Lk. 24:44; Mt. 26:54; Lk. 24:26.

[31] Acts 2:14–39; 3:12–26; 4:8–12; 5 29–32 and 10:34–43.

[32] Acts 13:16–41; 14:15–17; 17:2–3 and 22–31; 28:23–31.

[33] *E.g.* Acts 2:23; 3:18; 4:28.

[34] Acts 5:30; 10:39; 13:29.

[35] Acts 2:23, 36; 4:10; 17:3 and 13:28.

[36] *Cf.* Acts 2:23–24; 3:15; 4:10; 5:30; 10:39–40; 13:28–30.

[37] Acts 3:13 and 2:33.

[38] *Cf.* Acts 2:33–36; 3:26; 5:31–32; 10:43 and 13:38–39.

[39] Acts 2:38; 3:16; 4:10, 12; *cf.* Lk. 24:46–47.

[40] 1 Cor. 1:18–25; Rom. 6:3; 1 Cor. 11:26.

[41] *E.g.* 1 Jn. 2:22; 4:1–3; 2 Jn. 7.

[42] 1 Jn. 3:16; 4:9, 14; 4:10 and *cf.* 2:1–2; 17.

[43] See especially Hebrews 8 – 10.

[44] Rev. 7:9–14, 16–17; 13:8; 21:27; 14:1ff.

[45] Rev. 5:1–6; 22:1, 3; 12:11; 17:14.

[46] Rev. 5:8–9, 11–14.

[47] Rev. 6:15–17; 19:6–7; 21:9–10, 22–23.

[48] Heb. 6:6; Phil. 2:8; Heb. 12:2.

[49] Lk. 24:26; Jn. 12:23–24; 1 Pet. 1:11; 4:13; 5:1, 10; 4:14.

[50] Quotations are from *The Koran*. The five rejections of the possibility of 'substitutions' are on pages 114 (liii.38), 176 (xxv.18), 230 (xvii.15), 274 (xxxix.7) and 429 (vi.164).

[51] The spurious 'Gospel of Barnabas', written in Italian in the fourteenth or fifteenth century by a Christian convert to Islam, contains parts of the Koran as well as of the four canonical Gospels. It tells the fantastic tale that, when Judas came with the soldiers to arrest Jesus, he withdrew into a house. There angels rescued him through a window, while Judas 'was so changed in speech and in face to be like Jesus' that everybody was deceived, and Judas was crucified in Jesus' place.

[52] Samuel M. Zwemer, *Glory of the Cross*, p. 6.

[53] Gandhi, *An Autobiography*, p. 113.

[54] *The Guardian,* 30 August 1979.

[55] From the chapter entitled 'Jesus and History' in *Truth of God Incarnate*, ed. E. M. B. Green, p. 80.

[56] Justin Martyr's *First Apology*, Ch. lv, 'Symbols of the Cross'.

[57] Malcolm Muggeridge, *Jesus Rediscovered*, pp. 24–25.

Two

Why did Christ die?

Why did Christ die? Who was responsible for his death?

Many people see no problem in these questions and therefore have no difficulty in answering them. The facts seem to them as plain as day. Jesus did not 'die', they say; he was killed, publicly executed as a felon. The doctrines he taught were felt to be dangerous, even subversive. The Jewish leaders were incensed by his disrespectful attitude to the law and by his provocative claims, while the Romans heard that he was proclaiming himself King of the Jews, and so challenging the authority of Caesar. To both groups Jesus appeared to be a revolutionary thinker and preacher, and some considered him a revolutionary activist as well. So profoundly did he disturb the *status quo* that they determined to do away with him. In fact, they entered into an unholy alliance with one another in order to do so. In the Jewish court a theological charge was brought against him, blasphemy. In the Roman court the charge was political, sedition. But whether his offence was seen to be primarily against God or against Caesar, the outcome was the same. He was perceived as a threat to law and order, which could not be tolerated. So he was liquidated. Why did he die? Ostensibly he died as a law-breaker, but in reality as the victim of small minds, and as a martyr to his own greatness.

One of the fascinating features of the Gospel writers' accounts of the trial of Jesus is this blending of the legal and moral factors.[1] They all indicate that in both Jewish and Roman courts a certain legal procedure was followed. The prisoner was arrested, charged and cross-examined, and witnesses were called. The judge then reached his verdict and pronounced the sentence. Yet the evangelists also make it clear that the prisoner was not guilty of the charges laid, that the witnesses were false, and that the sentence of death was a gross miscarriage of justice. Further, the reason for this was the presence of personal, moral factors which influenced the course of the law. Caiaphas the Jewish high priest and Pilate the Roman procurator were not just officers of church and state, fulfilling their official roles; they were fallen and fallible human beings, swayed by the dark passions which rule us all. For our motives are always mixed. We may succeed in preserving a modicum of rectitude in the performance of our public duty, but behind this façade lurk violent and sinful emotions, which are always threatening to erupt. These secret sins the evangelists expose, as they tell their story of the arrest, custody, trial, sentence and execution of Jesus. It is one of the purposes of their narrative, for the material of the Gospels was used in the moral instruction of converts.

The Roman soldiers and Pilate

Those immediately responsible for the death of Jesus were of course the Roman soldiers who carried out the sentence. The actual process of crucifying him is not, however, described by any of the four evangelists.

If we had to rely exclusively on the Gospels, we would not have known what happened. But other contemporary documents tell us what a crucifixion was like.[2] The prisoner would first be publicly humiliated by being stripped naked. He was then laid on his back on the ground, while his hands were either nailed or roped to the horizontal wooden beam (the *patibulum*), and his feet to the vertical pole. The cross was then hoisted to an upright position and dropped into a socket which had been dug for it in the ground. Usually a peg or rudimentary seat was provided to take some of the weight of the victim's body and prevent it from being torn loose. But there he would hang, helplessly exposed to intense physical pain, public ridicule, daytime heat and night-time cold. The torture would last several days.

None of this is described by the Gospel writers. Piecing together what they do tell us, it seems that, according to known Roman custom, Jesus began by carrying his own cross to the place of execution. Presumably, however, he stumbled under its weight. For a man named Simon, from Cyrene in North Africa, who was at that moment coming into the city from the country, was stopped and forced to carry the cross for Jesus. When they arrived at 'the place called Golgotha (which means The Place of the Skull)', Jesus was offered some wine mixed with myrrh, which was a merciful gesture intended to dull the worst pain. But, although according to Matthew he tasted it, he refused to drink it. Next, all four evangelists write simply: 'and they crucified him'.[3] That is all. They have previously described in some detail how the soldiers mocked him in the Praetorium (the governor's residence): they dressed him in a purple robe, placed a crown of thorns on his head and a sceptre of reed in his right hand, blindfolded him, spat on him, slapped him in the face and struck him on the head, at the same time challenging him to identify who was hitting him. They also knelt down before him in mock homage. But the evangelists give no details of the crucifixion; they make no reference at all to hammer or nails or pain, or even blood.

All we are told that is 'they crucified him'. That is, the soldiers carried out their gruesome task. There is no evidence that they enjoyed it, no suggestion that they were cruel or sadistical. They were just obeying orders. It was their job. They did what they had to do. And all the while, Luke tells us, Jesus kept praying out loud, 'Father, forgive them, for they do not know what they are doing' (23:34).

Although the Gospel writers seem to be implying that no particular blame attached to the Roman soldiers for crucifying Jesus (and they add that later the centurion in charge of them believed, or at least semi-believed), the case is quite different with the Roman procurator who ordered the crucifixion. 'Finally Pilate handed him over to them to be crucified. So the soldiers took charge of Jesus ... they crucified him' (Jn. 19:16–18). Pilate was culpable. In fact, his guilt is written into our Christian creed, which declares that Jesus was 'crucified under Pontius Pilate'.

Pilate is known to have been appointed procurator (*i.e.* Roman governor) of the border province of Judea by the Emperor Tiberius, and to have served for ten years from about AD 26 to 36. He acquired a reputation as an able administrator, with a typically Roman sense of fair play. But he was hated by the Jews because he was contemptuous of them. They did not forget his provocative act, at the beginning of his period of office, of exhibiting the Roman standards in Jerusalem itself. Josephus describes another of his follies, namely that he misappropriated some Temple money to build an aqueduct.[4] Many think that it was in the ensuing riot that he had mixed the blood of certain Galileans with their sacrifices (Lk. 13:1). These are only samples of his hot temper, violence and cruelty. According to Philo, King Agrippa I described him in a letter to the Emperor Caligula as 'a man of a very inflexible disposition, and very merciless as well as very obstinate'.[5] His overriding aim was to maintain law and order, to keep those troublesome Jews firmly under control, and, if necessary for these ends, to be ruthless in the suppression of any riot or threat of one.

The portrait of Pontius Pilate in the Gospels tallies well with this external evidence. When the Jewish leaders brought Jesus to him with the words 'We have found this man subverting our nation', and added that 'he opposes the payment of taxes to Caesar and claims to be Christ, a king' (Lk. 23:2), Pilate could not fail to take notice. As his investigation proceeded, the evangelists emphasize two important points.

First, Pilate was convinced of Jesus' innocence. He was obviously impressed by the prisoner's noble bearing, self-control and political harmlessness. So three times he declared publicly that he could find no ground for charging him. The first was soon after daybreak on the Friday morning when the Sanhedrin referred the case to him. Pilate listened to them, asked Jesus a few questions, and after this preliminary hearing announced, 'I find no basis for a charge against this man.'[6]

The second occasion was when Jesus came back from being examined by Herod. Pilate said to the priests and people: 'You brought me this man as one who was inciting the people to rebellion. I have examined him in your presence and have found no basis for your charges against him. Neither has Herod, for he sent him back to us: as you can see, he has done nothing to deserve death.'[7] At this the crowd shouted, 'Crucify him! Crucify him!' But Pilate responded for the third time: 'Why? What crime has this man committed? I have found in him no grounds for the death penalty.'[8] Moreover, the procurator's personal conviction about the innocence of Jesus was confirmed by the message his wife sent him: 'Don't have anything to do with that innocent man, for I have suffered a great deal today in a dream because of him' (Mt. 27:19).

Pilate's repeated insistence on the innocence of Jesus is the essential background to the second point about him which the evangelists emphasize, namely his ingenious attempts to avoid having to come down clearly on one side or the other. He wanted to avoid sentencing Jesus (since he believed he was innocent) and at the same time avoid exonerating him (since the Jewish leaders believed he was guilty). How could he contrive to reconcile these irreconcilables? We watch him wriggling, as he attempts to release Jesus and pacify the Jews, *i.e.* to be just and unjust simultaneously. He tried four evasions.

First, on hearing that Jesus was a Galilean, and therefore under Herod's jurisdiction, he sent him to Herod for trial, hoping to transfer to him the responsibility of decision. But Herod sent Jesus back unsentenced (Lk. 23:5–12).

Secondly, he tried half-measures: 'I will have him punished [*i.e.* scourged] and then release him' (Lk. 23:16, 22). He hoped the crowd might be satisfied by something less than the supreme penalty, and their blood-lust sated by the sight of his lacerated back. It was despicable. For if Jesus was innocent, he should have been immediately released, not flogged first.

Thirdly, he tried to do the right thing (release Jesus) for the wrong reason (because the crowd chose him for release). Remembering the procurator's established custom to grant a Passover amnesty to some prisoner, he hoped the people would select Jesus for this favour. Then he could release him as an act of clemency instead of as an act of justice. It was an astute idea, but inherently shameful, and the people thwarted it by demanding instead that the procurator's pardon be granted to a notorious criminal and murderer, Barabbas.

Fourthly, he tried to protest his innocence. He took water and washed his hands before the crowd, saying, 'I am innocent of this man's blood' (Mt. 27:24). And then, before his hands were dry, he handed Jesus over to be crucified. How could he bring himself to incur this great guilt immediately after proclaiming his innocence?

It is easy to condemn Pilate and overlook our own equally devious behaviour. Anxious to avoid the pain of a whole-hearted commitment to Christ, we too search for convenient subterfuges. We either leave the decision to somebody else, or opt for a half-hearted compromise, or seek to honour Jesus for the wrong reason (*e.g.* as teacher instead of as Lord), or even make a public affirmation of loyalty while at the same time denying him in our hearts.

Three tell-tale expressions in Luke's narrative illumine what in the end Pilate did: 'their shouts prevailed', 'Pilate decided to grant their demand', and he 'surrendered Jesus to their will' (Lk. 23:23–25). *Their* shouts, *their* demand, *their* will: to these Pilate weakly capitulated. He was 'wanting to release Jesus' (Lk. 23:20), but he was also 'wanting to satisfy the crowd' (Mk. 15:15). The crowd won. Why? Because they said to him: 'If you let this man go, you are no friend of Caesar. Anyone who claims to be a king opposes Caesar' (Jn. 19:12). This clinched it. The choice was between honour and ambition, between principle and expediency. He had already been in trouble with Tiberius Caesar on two or three previous occasions. He could not afford another.

Sure, Jesus was innocent. Sure, justice demanded his release. But how could he champion innocence and justice if thereby he denied the will of the people, flouted the nation's leaders, and above all provoked an uprising, thereby forfeiting the imperial favour? His conscience was drowned by the loud voices of rationalization. He compromised because he was a coward.

The Jewish people and their priests

Although we cannot exonerate Pilate, we can certainly acknowledge that he was on the horns of a difficult dilemma, and that it was the Jewish leaders who impaled him there. For it was they who committed Jesus to him for trial, who accused him of subversive claims and teaching, and who stirred up the crowd to demand his crucifixion. Therefore, as Jesus himself said to

Pilate, 'the one who handed me over to you is guilty of a greater sin' (Jn. 19:11). Perhaps, since he used the singular, he was referring to the high priest Caiaphas, but the whole Sanhedrin was implicated. Indeed, so were the people, as Peter boldly said to them soon after Pentecost: 'Men of Israel, … you handed him [Jesus] over to be killed, and you disowned him before Pilate, though he had decided to let him go. You disowned the Holy and Righteous One and asked that a murderer be released to you. You killed the author of life … ' (Acts 3:12–15). The very same crowds, it seems, who had given Jesus a tumultuous welcome into Jerusalem on Palm Sunday, were within five days screaming for his blood. Yet their leaders were even more to blame for inciting them.

Jesus had upset the Jewish establishment from the outset of his public ministry. To begin with, he was an irregular. Though he posed as a Rabbi, he had not entered by the correct door or climbed up by the right ladder. He had no credentials, no proper authorization. Next, he had courted controversy by his provocative behaviour, fraternizing with disreputable people, feasting instead of fasting, and profaning the sabbath by healing people on it. Not content with disregarding the traditions of the elders, he had actually rejected them wholesale, and criticized the Pharisees for exalting tradition above Scripture. They cared more for regulations than for persons, he had said, more for ceremonial cleansing than for moral purity, more for laws than for love. He had even denounced them as 'hypocrites', called them 'blind leaders of the blind', and likened them to 'whitewashed tombs, which look beautiful on the outside but on the inside are full of dead men's bones and everything unclean' (Mt. 23:27). These were intolerable accusations. Worse still, he was undermining their authority. And at the same time he was making outrageous claims to be lord of the sabbath, to know God uniquely as his Father, even to be equal with God. It was blasphemy. Yes, that's what it was, blasphemy.

So they were full of self-righteous indignation over Jesus. His doctrine was heretical. His behaviour was an affront to the sacred law. He was leading the people astray. And there were rumours that he was encouraging disloyalty to Caesar. So his ministry must be stopped before he did any further damage. They had good political, theological and ethical reasons for demanding that he be arrested, put on trial and silenced. Moreover, when they had him in court, and put him on oath to testify, even then he made blasphemous claims for himself. They heard him with their own ears. No more witnesses were necessary. He was a self-confessed blasphemer. He deserved to die. It was absolutely clear. He was guilty. Their hands were clean.

And yet, and yet, there were flaws in the Jewish leaders' case. Leaving aside the fundamental question whether Jesus' claims were true or false, there was the matter of motivation. What was the fundamental reason for the priests' hostility to Jesus? Was it entirely that they were concerned for political stability, doctrinal truth and moral purity? Pilate did not think so. He was not taken in by their rationalizations, especially their pretence of loyalty to the Emperor. As H. B. Swete put it, 'he detected under their disguise the vulgar vice of envy'.[9] In Matthew's words, 'he knew it was out of envy that they had handed Jesus over to him'.[10] There is no reason to question Pilate's assessment. He was a shrewd judge of human character. Besides, the evangelists appear, by recording his judgment, to endorse it.

Envy! Envy is the reverse side of a coin called vanity. Nobody is ever envious of others who is not first proud of himself. And the Jewish leaders were proud, racially, nationally, religiously and morally proud. They were proud of their nation's long history of a special relationship with God, proud of their own leadership role in this nation, and above all proud of their authority. Their contest with Jesus was essentially an authority struggle. For he challenged their authority, while at the same time possessing himself an authority which they manifestly lacked. When they came to him with their probing questions, 'By what authority are you doing these things? And who gave you authority to do this?' (Mk. 11:28), they thought they had nailed him. But instead they found themselves nailed by his counter-question: 'John's baptism – was it from heaven, or from men? Tell me!' (v. 30). They were trapped. They could not answer 'From heaven' or he would want to know why they did not believe him. Nor could they answer 'From men', because they feared the people who were convinced that John was a true prophet. So they gave no reply. Their prevarication was a symptom of their insincerity. If they could not face the challenge of John's authority, they certainly could not face the challenge of Christ's. He claimed authority to teach about God, to drive out demons, to forgive sins, to judge the world. In all this he was utterly unlike them, for the only authority they knew was an appeal to other authorities. Besides, there was a self-evident genuineness about his authority. It was real, effortless, transparent, from God.

So they felt threatened by Jesus. He undermined their prestige, their hold over the people, their own self-confidence and self-respect, while leaving his intact. They were 'envious' of him, and therefore determined to get rid of him. It is significant that Matthew recounts two jealous plots to eliminate Jesus, the first by Herod the Great at the beginning of his life, and the other by the priests at its end. Both felt their authority under threat. So both sought to 'destroy' Jesus.[11] However outwardly respectable the priests' political and theological arguments may have appeared, it was envy which led them to 'hand over' Jesus to Pilate to be destroyed (Mk. 15:1, 10).

The same evil passion influences our own contemporary attitudes to Jesus. He is still, as C. S. Lewis called him, 'a transcendental interferer'.[12] We resent his intrusions into our privacy, his demand for our homage, his expectation of our obedience. Why can't he mind his own business, we ask petulantly, and leave us alone? To which he instantly replies that we are his business and that he will never leave us alone. So we too perceive him as a threatening rival, who disturbs our peace, upsets our *status quo*, undermines our authority and diminishes our self-respect. We too want to get rid of him.

Judas Iscariot the traitor

Having seen how Jesus was handed over by the priests to Pilate, and by Pilate to the soldiers, we now have to consider how in the first place he was handed over to the priests by Judas. This 'handing over' is specifically termed a 'betrayal'. Indeed, Maundy Thursday will always be remembered as 'the night on which he was betrayed' (1 Cor. 11:23), and Judas as 'he who betrayed him'. This accusing epitaph is already attached to his name when it is first mentioned in the Gospels among the Twelve. All three Synoptic evangelists put him at the bottom of their list of the apostles.[13]

It is not unusual to hear people expressing sympathy for Judas. They feel he was given an unfair deal in his lifetime and has had an unfair press ever since. 'After all,' they say, 'if Jesus had to die, somebody had to betray him. So why blame Judas? He was but the tool of providence, the victim of pre-destination.' Well, the biblical narrative certainly indicates that Jesus foreknew the identity of his betrayer[14] and referred to him as 'doomed to destruction so that Scripture would be fulfilled'.[15] It is also true that Judas did what he did only after Satan first 'prompted' him and then actually 'entered into him'.[16]

Nevertheless, none of this exonerates Judas. He must be held responsible for what he did, having no doubt plotted it for some time previously. The fact that his betrayal was foretold in the Scriptures does not mean that he was not a free agent, any more than the Old Testament predictions of the death of Jesus mean that he did not die voluntarily. So Luke referred later to his 'wickedness' (Acts 1:18). However strong the Satanic influences upon him were, there must have been a time when he opened himself to them. Jesus seems clearly to have regarded him as responsible for his actions, for even at the last minute in the upper room he made a final appeal to him by dipping a piece of bread in the dish and giving it to him (Jn. 13:25–30). But Judas rejected Jesus' appeal, and his betrayal has always seemed the more odious because it was a flagrant breach of hospitality. In this it fulfilled another Scripture which said: 'Even my close friend, whom I trusted, he who shared my bread, has lifted up his heel against me' (Ps. 41:9). Judas' ultimate cynicism was to choose to betray his Master with a kiss, using this sign of friendship as a means to destroy it. So Jesus affirmed his guilt, saying, 'Woe to that man who betrays the Son of Man! It would be better for him if he had not been born' (Mk. 14:21). Not only did Jesus thus condemn him, but he came in the end to condemn himself. He acknowledged his crime in betraying innocent blood, returned the money for which he had sold Jesus, and committed suicide. Doubtless he was seized more with remorse than repentance, but at least he confessed his guilt.

The motive for Judas' crime has long occupied the curiosity and ingenuity of students. Some have been convinced that he was a Jewish zealot,[17] had joined Jesus and his followers in the belief that theirs was a national liberation movement, and finally betrayed him either out of political disillusion or as a ploy to force Jesus' hand and compel him to fight. Those who attempt a reconstruction of this kind think they find confirmatory evidence in his name 'Iscariot', although everybody admits that it is obscure. It is generally taken to indicate his origin as a 'man of Kerioth', a town in the southern territory of Judah which is mentioned in Joshua 15:25. But those who think Judas was a zealot suggest that 'Iscariot' is linked to the word *sikarios,* an assassin (from the Latin *sica* and Greek *sikarion,* a 'dagger'). Josephus refers to the *sikarioi*.[18]

Fired with a fanatical Jewish nationalism, they were determined to recover their country's independence from the colonial domination of Rome, and to this end did not shrink from assassinating their political enemies, whom they despised as collaborators. They are referred to once in the New Testament, namely when the Roman commander who had rescued Paul from being lynched in Jerusalem told him he had thought he was 'the Egyptian who started a revolt and led four thousand terrorists [*sikarioi*] out into the desert some time ago' (Acts 21:38).

Other commentators consider the basis for this reconstruction too flimsy, and attribute the defection of Judas to a moral fault rather than a political motivation, namely the greed which the fourth evangelist mentions. He tells us that Judas was the 'treasurer' (as we would say) of the apostolic band, having been entrusted with the common purse. The occasion of John's comment was the anointing of Jesus by Mary of Bethany. She brought an alabaster jar containing very expensive perfume ('pure nard' according to Mark and John), which she proceeded to pour over him as he was reclining at table, until the house was filled with the fragrant scent. It was a gesture of lavish, almost reckless devotion, which Jesus himself later called a 'beautiful thing'. But some present (of whom Judas was the spokesman) reacted in a totally different way. Watching her with incredulity, they 'snorted' (literally) with self-righteous indignation. 'What a waste!' they said. 'What wicked extravagance! The perfume could have been sold for more than a year's wages, and the money given to the poor.' But their comment was sick and insincere, as John goes on to say. Judas 'did not say this because he cared about the poor but because he was a thief; as keeper of the money bag, he used to help himself to what was put into it'. Indeed, having witnessed and denounced what he saw as Mary's irresponsible wastefulness, he seems to have gone straight to the priests to recoup some of the loss. 'What are you willing to give me if I hand him over to you?' he asked them. No doubt they then began to bargain, and in the end agreed on thirty silver coins, the ransom price of a common slave. The evangelists with their sense of high drama deliberately contrast Mary and Judas, her uncalculating generosity and his coldly calculated bargain. What other dark passions were seething in his heart we can only guess, but John insists that it was monetary greed which finally overwhelmed him. Incensed by the waste of a year's wages, he went and sold Jesus for barely a third of that amount.[19]

It is not for nothing that Jesus tells us to 'beware of all covetousness', or that Paul declares the love of money to be 'a root of all kinds of evil'.[20] For in pursuit of material gain human beings have descended to deep depravity. Magistrates have perverted justice for bribes, like the judges of Israel of whom Amos said: 'They sell the righteous for silver, and the needy for a pair of sandals' (2:6). Politicians have used their power to give contracts to the highest bidder, and spies have sunk low enough to sell their country's secrets to the enemy. Businessmen have entered into shady transactions, jeopardizing the prosperity of others in order to get a better deal. Even supposedly spiritual teachers have been known to turn religion into a commercial enterprise, and some are still doing it today, so that a candidate for the pastorate is warned not to be 'a lover of money'.[21] The language of all such people is the same as that of Judas: 'what are you willing to give me, and I will hand him over to you?' For 'everybody has his price', the cynic asserts, from the hired assassin, who is prepared to bargain over somebody's life, to the petty official who delays the issue of a permit or passport until his bribe has been paid. Judas was not exceptional. Jesus had said that it is impossible to serve God and money. Judas chose money. Many others have done the same.

Their sins and ours

We have looked at the three individuals – Pilate, Caiaphas and Judas – on whom the evangelists fasten the major blame for the crucifixion of Jesus, and at those associated with them, whether priests or people or soldiers. Of each person or group the same verb is used, *paradidōmi*, to 'hand over' or 'betray'. Jesus had predicted that he would be 'betrayed into the hands of men' or 'handed over to be crucified'.[22] And the evangelists tell their story in such a way as to show how his prediction came true. First, Judas 'handed him over' to the priests (out of greed). Next, the priests 'handed him over' to Pilate (out of envy). Then Pilate 'handed him over' to the soldiers (out of cowardice), and they crucified him.[23]

Our instinctive reaction to this accumulated evil is to echo Pilate's astonished question, when the crowd howled for his blood: 'Why? What crime has he committed?' (Mt. 27:23). But Pilate received no rational answer. The hysterical crowd only shouted all the louder, 'Crucify him!' But why?

> Why? What has my Lord done?
>   What makes this rage and spite?
> He made the lame to run
> And gave the blind their sight.
>   Sweet injuries!
>   Yet they at these
>   Themselves displease,
> And 'gainst him rise.

It is natural to make excuses for them, for we see ourselves in them and we would like to be able to excuse ourselves. Indeed, there were some mitigating circumstances. As Jesus himself said, in praying for the forgiveness of the soldiers who were crucifying him, 'they do not know what they are doing'. Similarly, Peter said to a Jewish crowd in Jerusalem, 'I know that you acted in ignorance, as did your leaders.' Paul added that, if 'the rulers of this age' had understood, 'they would not have crucified the Lord of glory'.[24] Yet they knew enough to be culpable, to accept the fact of their guilt and to be condemned for their actions. Were they not claiming full responsibility when they cried out, 'Let his blood be on us and on our children!'?[25] Peter was quite outspoken on the Day of Pentecost: 'Let all Israel be assured of this: God has made this Jesus, *whom you crucified*, both Lord and Christ.' Moreover, far from disagreeing with his verdict, his hearers were 'cut to the heart' and asked what they should do to make amends (Acts 2:36–37). Stephen was even more direct in his speech to the Sanhedrin which led to his martyrdom. Calling the Council 'stiffnecked people, with uncircumcised hearts and ears', he accused them of resisting the Holy Spirit just like their ancestors. For their ancestors had persecuted the prophets and killed those who predicted the Messiah's coming, and now they had betrayed and murdered the Messiah himself (Acts 7:51–52). Paul was later to use similar language in writing to the Thessalonians about contemporary Jewish opposition to the gospel: they 'killed the Lord Jesus and the prophets and also drove us out'. Because they were trying to keep the Gentiles from salvation, God's judgment would fall upon them (1 Thes. 2:14–16).

This blaming of the Jewish people for the crucifixion of Jesus is extremely unfashionable today. Indeed, if it is used as a justification for slandering and persecuting the Jews (as it has been in the past), or for anti-Semitism, it is absolutely indefensible. The way to avoid anti-Semitic prejudice, however, is not to pretend that the Jews were innocent, but, having admitted their guilt, to add that others shared in it. This was how the apostles saw it.

Herod and Pilate, Gentiles and Jews, they said, had together 'conspired' against Jesus (Acts 4:27). More important still, we ourselves are also guilty. If we were in their place, we would have done what they did. Indeed, we *have* done it. For whenever we turn away from Christ, we 'are crucifying the Son of God all over again and subjecting him to public disgrace' (Heb. 6:6). We too sacrifice Jesus to our greed like Judas, to our envy like the priests, to our ambition like Pilate. 'Were you there when they crucified my Lord?' the old negro spiritual asks. And we must answer, 'Yes, we were there.' Not as spectators only but as participants, guilty participants, plotting, scheming, betraying, bargaining, and handing him over to be crucified. We may try to wash our hands of responsibility like Pilate. But our attempt will be as futile as his. For there is blood on our hands. Before we can begin to see the cross as something done *for* us (leading us to faith and worship), we have to see it as something done *by* us (leading us to repentance). Indeed, 'only the man who is prepared to own his share in the guilt of the cross', wrote Canon Peter Green, 'may claim his share in its grace'.[26]

Horatius Bonar (1808–89), who has been called 'the prince of Scottish hymn-writers', expressed it well:

> 'Twas I that shed the sacred blood;
>   I nailed him to the tree;
> I crucified the Christ of God;
>   I joined the mockery.
>
> Of all that shouting multitude
>   I feel that I am one;
> And in that din of voices rude
>   I recognize my own.
>
> Around the cross the throng I see,
>   Mocking the Sufferer's groan;
> Yet still my voice it seems to be,
>   As if I mocked alone.

The answer which we have so far given to the question 'Why did Christ die?' has sought to reflect the way in which the Gospel writers tell their story. They point to the chain of responsibility (from Judas to the priests, from the priests to Pilate, from Pilate to the soldiers), and they at least hint that the greed, envy and fear which prompted their behaviour also prompt ours. Yet this is not the complete account which the evangelists give. I have omitted one further and vital piece of evidence which they supply. It is this: that although Jesus was brought to his death by human sins, he did not die as a martyr. On the contrary, he went to the cross voluntarily, even deliberately. From the beginning of his public ministry he consecrated himself to this destiny.

In his baptism he identified himself with sinners (as he was to do fully on the cross), and in his temptation he refused to be deflected from the way of the cross. He repeatedly predicted his sufferings and death, as we saw in the last chapter, and steadfastly set himself to go to Jerusalem to die there. His constant use of the word 'must' in relation to his death expressed not some external compulsion, but his own internal resolve to fulfil what had been written of him. 'The good shepherd lays down his life for the sheep,' he said. Then, dropping the metaphor, 'I lay down my life ... No-one takes it from me, but I lay it down of my own accord' (Jn. 10:11, 17–18).

Moreover, when the apostles took up in their letters the voluntary nature of the dying of Jesus, they several times used the very verb (*paradidōmi*) which the evangelists used of his being 'handed over' to death by others. Thus Paul could write that 'the Son of God ... loved me and gave [*paradontos*] himself for me'.[27] It was perhaps a conscious echo of Isaiah 53:12, which says that 'he poured out [LXX, *paredothē*] his life unto death'. Paul also used the same verb when he looked behind the voluntary self-surrender of the Son to the Father's surrender of him. For example, 'he who did not spare his own Son, but gave him up [*paredōken*] for us all – how will he not also, along with him, graciously give us all things?'[28] Octavius Winslow summed it up in a neat statement: 'Who delivered up Jesus to die? Not Judas, for money; not Pilate, for fear; not the Jews, for envy; – but the Father, for love!'[29]

It is essential to keep together these two complementary ways of looking at the cross. On the human level, Judas gave him up to the priests, who gave him up to Pilate, who gave him up to the soldiers, who crucified him. But on the divine level, the Father gave him up, and he gave himself up, to die for us. As we face the cross, then, we can say to ourselves both '*I* did it, my sins sent him there', and '*He* did it, his love took him there.' The apostle Peter brought the two truths together in his remarkable statement on the Day of Pentecost, both that 'this man was handed over to you by God's set purpose and foreknowledge' and that 'you, with the help of wicked men, put him to death by nailing him to the cross'.[30] Peter thus attributed Jesus' death simultaneously to the plan of God and to the wickedness of men. For the cross which, as we have particularly considered in this chapter, is an exposure of human evil, is at the same time a revelation of the divine purpose to overcome the human evil thus exposed.

I come back at the end of this chapter to the question with which I began it: why did Jesus Christ die? My first answer was that he did not die; he was killed. Now, however, I have to balance this answer with its opposite. He was not killed; he died, giving himself up voluntarily to do his Father's will.

In order to discern what the Father's will was, we have to go over the same events again, this time looking below the surface.

Notes

[1] For a recent scholarly defence by a lawyer of the historical accuracy of the trials, as described in the Gospels, see *Le Procès de Jésus* by Prof. Jean Imbert.

[2] For a summary of available information about crucifixion see Martin Hengel's *Crucifixion*.

[3] Mt. 27:32–35; Mk. 15:21–25; Lk. 23:26–33; Jn. 19:17–18.

[4] *Antiquities* xviii.3.2.

[5] *Ad Gaium* 38, p. 165.

[6] Lk. 23:4; Jn. 18:38.

[7] Lk. 23:13–15; *cf.* Jn. 19:4–5.

[8] Lk. 23:22; Jn. 19:6.

[9] H. B. Swete, *The Gospel According to St Mark*, p. 350.

[10] Mt. 27:18; *cf.* Mk. 15:10.

[11] Mt. 2:13 and 27:20, AV.

[12] C. S. Lewis, *Surprised by Joy*, p. 163.

[13] Mt. 10:4; Mk. 3:19; Lk. 6:16.

[14] Jn. 6:64, 71; 13:11.

[15] Jn. 17:12. *Cf.* Acts 1:15–17, 25.

[16] Jn. 13:2, 27. *Cf.* Lk. 22:3.

[17] The founder of the zealot party was Judas' namesake, namely 'Judas the Galilean', who in AD 6 led an armed revolt against Rome (mentioned in Acts 5:37). The rebellion was crushed and Judas was killed, but his sons continued the struggle. Masada was the final stronghold of zealot resistance to Rome; it fell in AD 74. William Barday is one of those who considered it 'more than likely' that Judas was a zealot, and that the kiss in the Garden of Gethsemane was 'no intended treachery', but rather a signal meant to provoke Jesus to abandon his wavering and launch his long-awaited campaign (*Crucified and Crowned*, pp. 36–38).

[18] See Josephus' *Antiquities* xx.163–165, 186–188 and *Jewish War* ii.254–257.

[19] Mt. 26:6–16; Mk. 14.3–11, Jn. 12:3–8 and 13:29.

[20] Lk. 12:15, RSV; 1 Tim. 6:10.

[21] 1 Tim. 3:3, 8; Tit. 1:7. *Cf.* Acts 8:18–23 and 20:33–34.

[22] Mt. 17:22; 26:2.

[23] Mt. 26:14–16 (Judas); 27:18 (the priests); 27:26 (Pilate).

[24] Lk. 23:34; Acts 3:17; 1 Cor. 2:8.

[25] Mt. 27:25. *Cf.* Acts 5:28.

[26] Peter Green, *Watchers by the Cross*, p. 17.

[27] Gal. 2:20. *Cf.* Eph. 5:2, 25 and also Lk. 23:46.

[28] Rom. 8:32; *cf.* 4:25.

[29] I am grateful to David Kingdon for drawing my attention to this quotation, which John Murray indudes in his *Romans*, Vol. 1, p. 324, having taken it from Winslow's *No Condemnation in Christ Jesus* (1857).

[30] Acts 2:23; *cf.* 4:28. Later, in his first letter, Peter was to describe Jesus the Lamb as having been 'chosen before the creation of the world' (1 Pet. 1:1–20).

THREE

Looking below the surface

In the previous chapters I have sought to establish two facts about the cross. First, its central importance (to Christ, to his apostles and to his world-wide church ever since), and secondly its deliberate character (for, though due to human wickedness, it was also due to the set purpose of God, voluntarily accepted by Christ who gave himself up to death).

But why? We return to this basic puzzle. What was there about the crucifixion of Jesus which, in spite of its horror, shame and pain, makes it so important that God planned it in advance and Christ came to endure it?

An initial construction

It may be helpful to answer this question in four stages, beginning with the straightforward and the non-controversial, and gradually penetrating more deeply into the mystery.

First, Christ *died* for us. In addition to being necessary and voluntary, his death was altruistic and beneficial. He undertook it for our sake, not for his own, and he believed that through it he would secure for us a good which could be secured in no other way. The Good Shepherd, he said, was going to lay down his life 'for the sheep', for their benefit. Similarly, the words he spoke in the upper room when giving them the bread were, 'This is my body given for you.' The apostles picked up this simple concept and repeated it, sometimes making it more personal by changing it from the second person to the first: 'Christ died for us.'[1] There is no explanation yet, and no identification of the blessing he died to procure for us, but at least we are agreed over the 'for you' and 'for us'.

Secondly, *Christ died for us that he might bring us to God* (1 Pet. 3:18). The beneficial purpose of his death focuses down on our reconciliation. As the Nicene Creed expresses it, 'for us [general] and for our salvation [particular] he came down from heaven ...'. The salvation he died to win for us is variously portrayed. At times it is conceived negatively as redemption, forgiveness or deliverance. At other times it is positive – new or eternal life, or peace with God in the enjoyment of his favour and fellowship.[2] The precise vocabulary does not matter at present. The important point is that it is in consequence of his death that he is able to confer upon us the great blessing of salvation.

Thirdly, *Christ died for our sins.* Our sins were the obstacle preventing us from receiving the gift he wanted to give us. So they had to be removed before it could be bestowed. And he dealt with our sins, or took them away, by his death. This expression 'for our sins' (or very similar phrases) is used by most of the major New Testament authors; they seem to have been quite clear that – in some way still to be determined – Christ's death and our sins were related to each other. Here is a sample of quotations: 'Christ died for our sins according to the Scriptures' (Paul); 'Christ died for sins once for all' (Peter); 'he has appeared once for all ... to do away with sin by the sacrifice of himself', and he 'offered for all time one sacrifice for sins' (Hebrews); 'the blood of Jesus, [God's] Son, purifies us from all sin' (John); 'to him who loves us and has freed us from our sins by his blood ... be glory' (Revelation).[3] All these verses (and many more) link his death with our sins. What, then, is the link?

Fourthly, *Christ died our death,* when he died for our sins. That is to say, granted that his death and our sins are linked, the link is not merely that of consequence (he was the victim of our human brutality) but of penalty (he endured in his innocent person the penalty our sins had deserved). For, according to Scripture, death is related to sin as its just reward: 'the wages of sin is death' (Rom. 6:23). The Bible everywhere views human death not as a *natural* but as a *penal* event. It is an alien intrusion into God's good world, and not part of his original intention for humankind. To be sure, the fossil record indicates that predation and death existed in the animal kingdom before the creation of man. But God seems to have intended for his human image-bearers a more noble end, akin perhaps to the 'translation' which Enoch and Elijah experienced, and to the 'transformation' which will take place in those who are alive when Jesus comes.[4] Throughout Scripture, then, death (both physical and spiritual) is seen as a divine judgment on human disobedience.[5] Hence the expressions of horror in relation to death, the sense of anomaly that man should have become 'like the beasts that perish', since 'the same fate awaits them both'.[6] Hence too the violent 'snorting' of indignation which Jesus experienced in his confrontation with death at the graveside of Lazarus.[7] Death was a foreign body. Jesus resisted it; he could not come to terms with it.

If, then, death is the penalty of sin, and if Jesus had no sin of his own in his nature, character or conduct, must we not say that he need not have died? Could he not instead have been translated? When his body became translucent on the occasion of his mountain-top transfiguration, were the apostles not given a preview of his resurrection body (hence his instruction to tell nobody about it until he had risen from the dead, Mk. 9:9)? Could he not at that point have stepped straight into heaven and escaped death? But he came back into our world in order to go *voluntarily* to the cross. No-one would take his life from him, he insisted; he was going to lay it down of his own accord. So when the moment of death came, Luke represented it as his own self-determined act. 'Father,' he said, 'into your hands I commit my spirit.'[8] All this means that the simple New Testament statement that 'he died for our sins' implies much more than appears on the surface. It affirms that Jesus Christ, who being sinless had no need to die, died our death, the death our sins had deserved.

We shall need in subsequent chapters to penetrate further into the rationale, the morality and the efficacy of these statements. For the time being we must be content with this preliminary fourfold construction, that Christ died for us, for our good; that the 'good' he died to procure for us was our salvation; that in order to procure it he had to deal with our sins; and that in dying for them it was our death that he died.

The question I want to ask now, and seek to answer during the rest of this chapter, is whether this preliminary theological construction fits the facts. Is it a rather complex theory imposed on the story of the cross, or does the evangelists' narrative itself supply evidence for it and even remain unintelligible without it? I shall argue the latter. Further, I shall seek to show that what the evangelists portray, although it is their witness, is not their invention. What they are doing is to allow us to enter a little way into the mind of Christ himself.

So we shall look at three of the main scenes of Jesus' last twenty-four hours on earth – the upper room, the Garden of Gethsemane and the place called Golgotha. As we do so, we shall be unable to limit ourselves to the mere telling of a poignant story, since each scene contains sayings of Jesus which demand explanation and cannot be swept under the carpet. Something deeper was happening than mere words and deeds, something below the surface. Theological truth keeps breaking through, even when we wish it would leave us alone. In particular, we feel obliged to ask questions about the institution of the Lord's Supper in the upper room, the 'agony' in the Garden of Gethsemane, and the 'cry of dereliction' on the cross.

Before we do so, however, there is a noteworthy fact which needs to delay us. It concerns Jesus' perspective throughout. Our story begins on the evening of Maundy Thursday. Jesus had already seen the sun set for the last time. Within about fifteen hours his limbs would be stretched out on the cross. Within twenty-four hours he would be both dead and buried. And he knew it. Yet the extraordinary thing is that he was thinking of his mission as still future, not past. He was a comparatively young man, almost certainly between thirty and thirty-five years of age. He had lived barely half the allotted span of human life. He was still at the height of his powers. At his age most people have their best years ahead of them. Mohammed lived until he was sixty, Socrates until he was seventy, and Plato and the Buddha were over eighty when they died. If death threatens to cut a person's life short, a sense of frustration plunges him or her into gloom. But not Jesus, for this simple reason: he did not regard the death he was about to die as bringing his mission to an untimely end, but as actually necessary to accomplish it. It was only seconds before he died (and not till that moment) that he would be able to shout, 'Finished!' So then, although it was his last evening, and although he had but a few more hours to live, Jesus was not looking *back* at a mission he had completed, still less that had failed; he was still looking *forward* to a mission which he was about to fulfil. The mission of a lifetime of thirty to thirty-five years was to be accomplished in its last twenty-four hours, indeed, its last six.

The Last Supper in the upper room

Jesus was spending his last evening on earth in quiet seclusion with his apostles. It was the first day of the Feast of Unleavened Bread, and they had met to eat the Passover meal together in a friend's house. The place is described as 'a large upper room, furnished and ready', and we can picture them round a low meal-table, reclining on cushions on the floor. Evidently no servant was in attendance, so that there had been no-one to wash their feet before the meal began. Nor was any of the apostles humble enough to undertake this menial task. It was to their intense embarrassment, therefore, that during supper Jesus put on a slave's apron, poured water into a basin, and went round washing their feet, thus doing what none of them had been willing to do. He then proceeded to tell them how authentic love always expresses itself in humble service and how the world would identify them as his disciples only if they loved one another. In contrast to the priority of sacrificial and serving love, he warned them that one of them was going to betray him. He also spoke much of his impending departure, of the coming of the Comforter to take his place, and of this Spirit of truth's varied ministry of teaching and witnessing.

Then, at some point while the meal was still in progress, they watched enthralled as he took a loaf of bread, blessed it (that is, gave thanks for it), broke it into pieces and handed it round to them with the words, 'This is my body, which is given for you; do this in remembrance of me.' In the same way, after supper had ended, he took a cup of wine, gave thanks for it, passed it round to them, and said either, 'This cup is the new covenant in my blood', or 'This is my blood of the new covenant, which is poured out for many for the forgiveness of sins; do this, whenever you drink it, in remembrance of me.'[9]

These are tremendously significant deeds and words. It is a pity that we are so familiar with them that they tend to lose their impact. For they throw floods of light on Jesus' own view of his death. By what he did with the bread and wine, and by what he said about them, he was visibly dramatizing his death before it took place and giving his own authoritative explanation of its meaning and purpose. He was teaching at least three lessons.

The first lesson concerned *the centrality of his death*. Solemnly and deliberately, during his last evening with them, he was giving instructions for his own memorial service. It was not to be a single occasion, however, like our modern memorial services, the final tribute paid by friends and relatives. Instead, it was to be a regular meal or service or both. He specifically told them to repeat it: 'do this in remembrance of me'. What were they to do? They were to copy what he had done, both his acts and his words, namely to take, break, bless, identify and share bread and wine. What did the bread and wine signify? The words he had spoken explained. Of the bread he had said, 'This is my body given for you', and of the wine, 'This is my blood shed for you.' So his death spoke to them from both the elements. The bread did not stand for his living body, as he reclined with them at table, but his body as it was shortly to be 'given' for them in death. Similarly, the wine did not stand for his blood as it flowed in his veins while he spoke to them, but his blood which was shortly to be 'poured out' for them in death. The evidence is plain and irrefutable. The Lord's Supper, which was instituted by Jesus, and which is the only regular commemorative act authorized by him, dramatizes neither his birth nor his life, neither his words nor his works, but only his death. Nothing could indicate more clearly the central significance which Jesus attached to his death. It was by his death that he wished above all else to be remembered. There is then, it is safe to say, no Christianity without the cross. If the cross is not central to our religion, ours is not the religion of Jesus.

Secondly, Jesus was teaching about *the purpose of his death*. According to Paul and Matthew, Jesus' words about the cup referred not only to his 'blood' but to the 'new covenant' associated with his blood, and Matthew adds further that his blood was to be shed 'for the forgiveness of sins'. Here is the truly fantastic assertion that through the shedding of Jesus' blood in death God was taking the initiative to establish a new pact or 'covenant' with his people, one of the greatest promises of which would be the forgiveness of sinners. What did he mean?

Many centuries previously God had entered into a covenant with Abraham, promising to bless him with a good land and an abundant posterity. God renewed this covenant at Mount Sinai, after rescuing Israel (Abraham's descendants) from Egypt. He pledged himself to be their God and to make them his people. Moreover, this covenant was ratified with the blood of sacrifice: 'Moses ... took the blood, sprinkled it on the people and said, "This is the blood of the covenant that the LORD has made with you in accordance with all these words." '[10] Hundreds of years passed, in which the people forsook God, broke his covenant and provoked his judgment, until one day in the seventh century BC the word of the Lord came to Jeremiah, saying:

> 'The time is coming,' declares the LORD,
> 'when I will make a new covenant
> with the house of Israel
> and with the house of Judah.
> It will not be like the covenant
> I made with their forefathers
> when I took them by the hand
> to lead them out of Egypt,
> because they broke my covenant,
> though I was a husband to them,'
>   declares the LORD.
> 'This is the covenant that I will make
>   with the house of Israel
>   after that time,' declares the LORD.
> 'I will put my law in their minds
> and write it on their hearts.
> I will be their God,
> and they will be my people.
> No longer will a man teach his neighbour,
> or a man his brother, saying, "Know the LORD,"
> because they will all know me,
> from the least of them to the greatest,'
>   declares the LORD.
> 'For I will forgive their wickedness
> and will remember their sins no more.'
>   (Je. 31:3–34)

More than six more centuries passed, years of patient waiting and growing expectancy, until one evening in an upper room in Jerusalem a Galilean peasant, carpenter by trade and preacher by vocation, dared to say in effect: 'this new covenant, prophesied in Jeremiah, is about to be established; the forgiveness of sins promised as one of its distinctive blessings is about to become available; and the sacrifice to seal this covenant and procure this forgiveness will be the shedding of my blood in death.' Is it possible to exaggerate the staggering nature of this claim? Here is Jesus' view of his death. It is the divinely appointed sacrifice by which the new covenant with its promise of forgiveness will be ratified. He is going to die in order to bring his people into a new covenant relationship with God.

The third lesson Jesus was teaching concerned *the need to appropriate his death personally*. If we are right in saying that in the upper room Jesus was giving an advance dramatization of his death, it is important to observe what form the drama took. It did not consist of one actor on the stage, with a dozen in the audience. No, it involved them as well as him, so that they took part in it as well as he. True, he took, blessed and broke the bread, but then he explained its significance as he gave it to them to eat. Again he took and blessed the cup, but then he explained its meaning as he gave it to them to drink. Thus they were not just spectators of this drama of the cross; they were participants in it. They can hardly have failed to get the message. Just as it was not enough for the bread to be broken and the wine to be poured out, but they had to eat and drink, so it was not enough for him to die, but they had to appropriate the benefits of his death personally. The eating and drinking were, and still are, a vivid acted parable of receiving Christ as our crucified Saviour and of feeding on him in our hearts by faith. Jesus had already taught this in his great discourse on the Living Bread which followed his feeding of the five thousand:

> 'I tell you the truth, unless you eat the flesh of the Son of Man and drink his blood, you have no life in you. Whoever eats my flesh and drinks my blood has eternal life, and I will raise him up at the last day. For my flesh is real food and my blood is real drink' (Jn. 6:53–55).

His words on that occasion and his actions in the upper room both bear witness to the same reality. For him to give his body and blood in death was one thing; for us to make the blessings of his death our own is another. Yet many have not learnt this distinction. I can still remember what a revelation it was to me as a young man to be told that any action on my part was necessary. I used to imagine that because Christ had died, the world had been automatically put right. When someone explained to me that Christ had died for *me,* I responded rather haughtily, 'Everybody knows that,' as if the fact itself or my knowledge of the fact had brought me salvation. But God does not impose his gifts on us willy-nilly; we have to receive them by faith. Of both the divine gift and the human reception the Lord's Supper remains the perpetual outward sign. It is intended to be 'a participation in the body and blood of Christ' (1 Cor. 10:16).

Here then are the lessons of the upper room about the death of Christ. First, it was central to his own thinking about himself and his mission, and he desired it to be central to ours. Secondly, it took place in order to establish the new covenant and procure its promised forgiveness. Thirdly, it needs to be appropriated individually if its benefits (the covenant and the forgiveness) are to be enjoyed. The Lord's Supper which Jesus instituted was not meant to be a slightly sentimental 'forget-me-not', but rather a service rich in spiritual significance.

What makes the events of the upper room and the significance of the Lord's Supper yet more impressive is that they belong to the context of the Passover. That Jesus thought of his death in terms of an Old Testament sacrifice we have already seen. But which sacrifice did he have in mind? Not only, it seems, the Mount Sinai sacrifice of Exodus 24, by which the covenant was decisively renewed, but also the Passover sacrifice of Exodus 12, which became an annual commemoration of God's liberation of Israel and covenant with them.

According to the Synoptic evangelists, the last supper was the Passover meal which followed the sacrificing of the Passover lambs. This is clear because the disciples asked Jesus where they should make preparations to 'eat the Passover', and Jesus himself referred to the meal as 'this Passover'.[11] According to John, however, the Passover meal would not be eaten until the Friday evening, which meant that Jesus was dying on the cross at the very time that the Passover lambs were being killed.[12] In his important book *The Eucharistic Words of Jesus,* Joachim Jeremias elaborated the three main attempts which have been made to harmonize these two chronologies (pp. 20–62). The best seems to be to declare both correct, each having been followed by a different group. Either the Pharisees and Sadducees were using alternative calendars, which differed from each other by a day, or there were so many pilgrims in Jerusalem for the festival (perhaps as many as 100,000) that the Galileans killed their lambs on the Thursday and ate them that evening, while the Judeans observed the celebration one day later.

However the two chronologies are to be reconciled, the Passover context further enforces the three lessons that we have already considered. The central importance which Jesus attached to his death is underlined by the fact that he was actually giving instructions for the annual celebration of the Passover to be replaced by his own supper. For he spoke words of explanation over the bread and wine ('This is my body ... this is my blood ...'), just as the head of an Aramaic Jewish household did over the Passover food ('This is the bread of affliction which our fathers had to eat as they came out of Egypt', pp. 54–57).[13] Thus 'Jesus modelled his sayings upon the ritual of interpreting the Passover' (p. 61).

This further clarifies Jesus' understanding of the purpose of his death. He 'presupposes', wrote Jeremias, 'a slaying that has separated flesh and blood. In other words, *Jesus spoke of himself as a sacrifice*'. Indeed, he was 'most probably speaking of himself as the paschal lamb', so that the meaning of his last parable was: 'I go to death as the true Passover sacrifice' (pp. 222–224). The implications of this are far-reaching. For in the original Passover in Egypt each paschal lamb died instead of the family's first-born son, and the first-born was spared only if a lamb was slain in his place. Not only had the lamb to be slain, but also its blood had to be sprinkled on the front door and its flesh eaten in a fellowship meal. Thus the Passover ritual taught the third lesson too, that it was necessary for the benefits of Christ's sacrificial death to be personally appropriated.

The agony in the Garden of Gethsemane

Supper is now over, and Jesus has finished his instruction of the apostles. He has urged them to abide in him, as the branches abide in the vine. He has warned them of the opposition of the world, yet encouraged them to bear witness to him none the less, remembering that the Spirit of truth will be the chief witness. He has also prayed – first for himself that he may glorify his Father in the coming ordeal, then for them that they may be kept in truth, holiness, mission and unity, and lastly for all those of subsequent generations who would believe in him through their message. Probably now they sing a hymn, and then together they leave the upper room. They walk through the streets of the city in the stillness of the night, and in the soft light of the paschal moon, cross the Kidron Valley, begin to climb the Mount of Olives, and turn off into an olive orchard, as its name 'Gethsemane' ('oil press') suggests. It is evidently a favourite retreat for Jesus, for John comments that he 'had often met there with his disciples' (18:2). Here something takes place which, despite the sober way the evangelists describe it, simply cries out for an explanation, and begins to disclose the enormous costliness of the cross to Jesus. We rightly call it 'the agony in the garden'.

Leaving most of the apostles behind, and urging them to watch and pray, he takes Peter, James and John – the intimate three – a stone's throw farther into the olive grove with him, shares with them that he feels 'overwhelmed with sorrow to the point of death', and asks them to keep watch with him. He then goes on a little farther alone, falls prostrate with his face to the ground and prays: 'My Father, if it is possible, may this cup be taken from me. Yet not as I will, but as you will.' Returning to the apostles, he finds them sleeping and remonstrates with them. Going away a second time, he prays: 'My Father, if it is not possible for this cup to be taken away unless I drink it, may your will be done.' Again he finds the disciples sleeping. So he leaves them once more and prays the third time, saying the same thing. After this third season of prayer he returns to find them asleep again, for they cannot enter into the fathomless mystery of his suffering. This is a path he has to walk alone. At some point, Luke says, he was 'in anguish' (or 'agony'), and prayed yet more earnestly, so that 'his sweat was like drops of blood falling to the ground'.[14]

As we approach this sacred scene, we should first consider the forceful words which Jesus and the evangelists used to express his strong emotions. We have been prepared for these a little by two of his earlier statements. The first, which Luke records, was that he had 'a baptism to undergo' and felt 'distressed' (or 'pressed', even 'tormented', *synechō*) until it was completed. The second was a saying which John records that his heart was 'troubled' (or 'agitated', *tarassō*), so that he even wondered if he should ask his Father to save him from 'this hour'. It was an anticipation of Gethsemane.[15]

B. B. Warfield wrote a careful study entitled 'On the Emotional Life of Our Lord', in the course of which he referred to the terms employed by the Synoptic evangelists in relation to Gethsemane. Luke's word *agōnia* he defines as 'consternation, appalled reluctance'. Matthew and Mark share two expressions. The primary idea of 'troubled' (*adēmoneō*), he suggests, is 'loathing aversion, perhaps not unmixed with despondency', while Jesus' self-description as 'overwhelmed with sorrow' (*perilypos*) 'expresses a sorrow, or perhaps we would better say, a mental pain, a distress, which hems him in on every side, from which there is therefore no escape'. Mark uses another word of his own, 'deeply distressed' (*ekthambeomai*), which has been rendered 'horror-struck'; it is 'a term', Warfield adds, 'which more narrowly defines the distress as consternation – if not exactly dread, yet alarmed dismay'.[16] Put together, these expressive words indicate that Jesus was feeling an acute emotional pain, causing profuse sweat, as he looked with apprehension and almost terror at his future ordeal.

This ordeal he refers to as a bitter 'cup' which he ardently prays may, if possible, be taken from him, so that he does not have to drink it. What is this cup? Is it physical suffering from which he shrinks, the torture of the scourge and the cross, together perhaps with the mental anguish of betrayal, denial and desertion by his friends, and the mockery and abuse of his enemies? Nothing could ever make me believe that the cup Jesus dreaded was any of these things (grievous as they were) or all of them together. His physical and moral courage throughout his public ministry had been indomitable. To me it is ludicrous to suppose that he was now afraid of pain, insult and death. Socrates in the prison cell in Athens, according to Plato's account, took his cup of hemlock 'without trembling or changing colour or expression'. He then 'raised the cup to his lips, and very cheerfully and quietly drained it'. When his friends burst into tears, he rebuked them for their 'absurd' behaviour and urged them to 'keep quiet and be brave'.[17] He died without fear, sorrow or protest. So was Socrates braver than Jesus? Or were their cups filled with different poisons?

Then there have been the Christian martyrs. Jesus had himself told his followers that when insulted, persecuted and slandered, they were to 'rejoice and be glad'. Did Jesus not practise what he preached? His apostles did. Leaving the Sanhedrin with backs bleeding from a merciless flogging, they were actually 'rejoicing because they had been counted worthy of suffering disgrace for the Name'. Pain and rejection were to them a joy and a privilege, not an ordeal to be shrunk from in dismay.[18]

In the post-apostolic period there was even a longing to be united with Christ in martyrdom. Ignatius, Bishop of Antioch in Syria at the beginning of the second century, on his way to Rome, begged the church there not to attempt to secure his release lest they should deprive him of this honour! 'Let fire and the cross,' he wrote, 'let the companies of wild beasts, let breaking of bones and tearing of limbs, let the grinding of the whole body, and all the malice of the devil, come upon me; be it so, if only I may gain Christ Jesus!'[19] A few years later, in the middle of the second century, Polycarp, the eighty-six-year-old Bishop of Smyrna, having refused to escape death either by fleeing or by denying Christ, was burnt at the stake. Just before the fire was lit, he prayed, 'O Father, I bless thee that thou hast counted me worthy to receive my portion among the number of martyrs.'[20] As for Alban, the first known British Christian martyr during one of the severe persecutions of the third century, he was first 'cruelly beaten, yet suffered he the same patiently, nay rather joyfully, for the Lord's sake', and was then beheaded.[21] And so it has continued in every generation. 'O the joy that the martyrs of Christ have felt', cried Richard Baxter, 'in the midst of the scorching flames!' Although made of flesh and blood like us, he continued, their souls could rejoice even 'while their bodies were burning'.[22]

Of many examples which could be given from the present century I choose only those mentioned by Sadhu Sundar Singh, the Indian Christian mystic and evangelist. He told, for instance, of a Tibetan evangelist, flogged by tormentors who then rubbed salt into his wounds, whose 'face shone with peace and joy', and of another who, sewn into a damp yak skin and left in the sun for three days, 'was joyful all the time' and thanked God for the privilege of suffering for him. It is true that the Sadhu sometimes embellished or romanticized his stories, yet there seems no reason to doubt his testimony, from his own experience and others', that even in the midst of torture God gives his people a supernatural joy and peace.[23]

We turn back to that lonely figure in the Gethsemane olive orchard –

prostrate, sweating, overwhelmed with grief and dread, begging if possible to be spared the drinking of the cup. The martyrs were joyful, but he was sorrowful; they were eager, but he was reluctant. How can we compare them? How could they have gained their inspiration from him if he had faltered when they did not? Besides, up till now he had been clear-sighted about the necessity of his sufferings and death, determined to fulfil his destiny, and vehement in opposing any who sought to deflect him. Had all that suddenly changed? Was he now after all, when the moment of testing came, a coward? No, no! All the evidence of his former teaching, character and behaviour is against such a conclusion.

In that case the cup from which he shrank was something different. It symbolized neither the physical pain of being flogged and crucified, nor the mental distress of being despised and rejected even by his own people, but rather the spiritual agony of bearing the sins of the world; in other words, of enduring the divine judgment which those sins deserved. That this is the correct understanding is strongly confirmed by Old Testament usage, for in both the Wisdom literature and the prophets the Lord's 'cup' was a regular symbol of his wrath. A wicked person was said to 'drink of the wrath of the Almighty' (Jb. 21:20). Through Ezekiel, Yahweh warned Jerusalem that she would shortly suffer the same fate as Samaria, which had been destroyed:

> 'You will drink your sister's cup,
>   a cup large and deep;
> it will bring scorn and derision,
>   for it holds so much.
> You will be filled with drunkenness and sorrow,
>   the cup of ruin and desolation,
>   the cup of your sister Samaria.
> You will drink it and drain it dry ...'
>   (Ezk. 23:32–34)

Not long afterwards this prophecy of judgment came true, and then the prophets began to encourage the people with promises of restoration. Describing Jerusalem as 'you who have drunk from the hand of the Lord the cup of his wrath, you who have drained to its dregs the goblet that makes men stagger', Isaiah summoned her to wake up and to get up, for Yahweh had now taken the cup out of her hand and she would never have to drink it again. Nor was the cup of the Lord's wrath given only to his disobedient people. Psalm 75 is a meditation on the universal judgment of God: 'In the hand of the Lord is a cup full of foaming wine mixed with spices; he pours it out, and all the wicked of the earth drink it down to its very dregs.' Similarly, Jeremiah was told to take from God's hand a cup filled with the wine of his wrath and to make all the nations drink it to whom he was sent. The same figure of speech recurs in the book of Revelation, where the wicked 'will drink of the wine of God's fury, which has been poured full strength into the cup of his wrath', and the final judgment is depicted as the pouring out of 'the seven bowls of God's wrath on the earth'.[24]

This Old Testament imagery will have been well known to Jesus. He must have recognized the cup he was being offered as containing the wine of God's wrath, given to the wicked, and causing a complete disorientation of body (staggering) and mind (confusion) like drunkenness. Was he to become so identified with sinners as to bear their judgment? From this contact with human sin his sinless soul recoiled. From the experience of alienation from his Father which the judgment on sin would involve, he hung back in horror. Not that for even a single instant he rebelled. His vision had evidently become blurred, as a dreadful darkness engulfed his spirit, but his will remained surrendered. Each prayer began, 'My Father, if it is possible, may this cup be taken from me', and each prayer ended, 'yet not as I will, but as you will'. Although in theory 'everything is possible' to God, as Jesus himself affirmed in Gethsemane (Mk. 14:36), yet this was not possible. God's purpose of love was to save sinners, and to save them righteously; but this would be impossible without the sin-bearing death of the Saviour. So how could he pray to be saved from 'this hour' of death? 'No,' he had said, he would not, since 'it was for this very reason I came to this hour' (Jn. 12:27).

From his agony of dread, as he contemplated the implications of his coming death, Jesus emerged with serene and resolute confidence. So when Peter drew his sword in a frantic attempt to avert the arrest, Jesus was able to say: 'Shall I not drink the cup the Father has given me?' (Jn. 18:11). Since John has not recorded Jesus' agonized prayers for the cup to be removed, this reference to it is all the more important. Jesus knows now that the cup will not be taken away from him. The Father has given it to him. He will drink it. Moreover, bitter and painful though the draining of the cup will be, he will yet find that to do the will of the Father who sent him and to finish his work will be his 'meat and drink' (as we might say), deeply and completely satisfying to his thirst (Jn. 4:34).

The agony in the garden opens a window on to the greater agony of the cross. If to bear man's sin and God's wrath was so terrible in anticipation, what must the reality have been like?

> We may not know, we cannot tell,
>   What pains he had to bear;
> But we believe it was for us
>   He hung and suffered there.

The cry of dereliction on the cross

We must now pass by the details of the betrayal and arrest of Jesus, his trials before Annas and Caiaphas, Herod and Pilate, Peter's denials, the cruel mockery by priests and soldiers, the spitting and the scourging, and the hysteria of the mob who demanded his death. We move on to the end of the story. Condemned to death by crucifixion, 'he was led like a lamb to the slaughter, and as a sheep before her shearers is silent, so he did not open his mouth' (Is. 53:7). Carrying his own cross, until Simon of Cyrene was compelled to carry it for him, he will have walked along the Via Dolorosa, out of the city, to Golgotha, 'the place of the skull'. 'Here they crucified him', the evangelists write, declining to dwell on the stripping, the clumsy hammering home of the nails, or the wrenching of his limbs as the cross was hoisted and dropped into its place. Even the excruciating pain could not silence his repeated entreaties: 'Father, forgive them, for they do not know what they are doing.' The soldiers gambled for his clothes. Some women stood afar off. The crowd remained a while to watch. Jesus commended his mother to John's care and John to hers. He spoke words of kingly assurance to the penitent criminal crucified at his side. Meanwhile, the rulers sneered at him, shouting: 'He saved others, but he can't save himself!' Their words, spoken as an insult, were the literal truth. He could not save himself and others simultaneously. He chose to sacrifice himself in order to save the world.

Gradually the crowd thinned out, their curiosity glutted. At last silence fell and darkness came – darkness perhaps because no eye should see, and silence because no tongue could tell, the anguish of soul which the sinless Saviour now endured. 'At the birth of the Son of God', Douglas Webster has written, 'there was brightness at midnight; at the death of the Son of God there was darkness at noon.'[25] What happened in the darkness is expressed by biblical writers in a variety of ways:

> ... he was pierced for our transgressions,
>   he was crushed for our iniquities;
> the punishment that brought us peace was upon him,
>   and by his wounds we are healed.
> We all, like sheep, have gone astray,
>   each of us has turned to his own way;
> and the LORD has laid on him
>   the iniquity of us all.

Look, the Lamb of God, who takes away the sin of the world!

The Son of Man came ... to give his life as a ransom for many.

Christ was sacrificed once to take away the sins of many people.

He himself bore our sins in his body on the tree.

Christ died for sins once for all, the righteous for the unrighteous, to bring you to God.

God made him who had no sin to be sin for us, so that in him we might become the righteousness of God.

Christ redeemed us from the curse of the law by becoming a curse for us.[26]

The fearful concept of Jesus 'bearing', even actually 'becoming', our sin and curse, how it could be and what it could mean, we will leave until the next chapters. Meanwhile, it seems that the darkness of the sky was an outward symbol of the spiritual darkness which enveloped him. For what is darkness in biblical symbolism but separation from God who is light and in whom 'there is no darkness at all' (1 Jn. 1:5)? 'Outer darkness' was one of the expressions Jesus used for hell, since it is an absolute exclusion from the light of God's presence. Into that outer darkness the Son of God plunged for us. Our sins blotted out the sunshine of his Father's face. We may even dare to say that our sins sent Christ to hell – not to the 'hell' (*hadēs*, the abode of the dead) to which the Creed says he 'descended' after death, but to the 'hell' (*gehenna*, the place of punishment) to which our sins condemned him before his body died.

The darkness seems to have lasted for three hours. For it was at the third hour (9 a.m.) that he was crucified, at the sixth hour (12 noon) that the darkness came over the whole land, and at the ninth hour (3 p.m.) that, emerging out of the darkness, Jesus cried out in a loud voice in Aramaic: '*Eloi, Eloi, lama sabachthani?*' meaning, 'My God, my God, why have you forsaken me?'[27] The Greek speakers present misunderstood his words and thought he was calling for Elijah. What he said is still misunderstood by many today. Four main explanations of his terrible cry of 'dereliction' (desertion, abandonment) have been offered. All commentators agree that he was quoting Psalm 22:1. But they are not agreed as to why he did so. What was the significance of this quotation on his lips?

First, some suggest that it was *a cry of anger, unbelief or despair*. Perhaps he had clung to the hope that even at the last moment the Father would send angels to rescue him, or at least that in the midst of his utter obedience to the Father's will he would continue to experience the comfort of the Father's presence. But no, it was now clear to him that he had been abandoned, and he cried out with a heart-rending 'why?' of dismay or defiance.

His faith failed him. But of course, these interpreters add, he was mistaken. He imagined he was forsaken, when he was not. Those who thus explain the cry of dereliction can scarcely realize what they are doing. They are denying the moral perfection of the character of Jesus. They are saying that he was guilty of unbelief on the cross, as of cowardice in the garden. They are accusing him of failure, and failure at the moment of his greatest and supremest self-sacrifice. Christian faith protests against this explanation.

A second interpretation, which is a modification of the first, is to understand the shout of dereliction as *a cry of loneliness*. Jesus, it is now maintained, knew God's promises never to fail or forsake his people.[28] He knew the steadfastness of God's covenant love. So his 'why?' was not a complaint that God had actually forsaken him, but rather that he had allowed him to *feel* forsaken. 'I have sometimes thought', wrote T. R. Glover, 'there never was an utterance that reveals more amazingly the distance between feeling and fact.'[29] Instead of addressing God as 'Father', he could now call him only 'my God', which is indeed an affirmation of faith in his covenant faithfulness, but falls short of declaring his fatherly loving-kindness. In this case Jesus was neither mistaken, nor unbelieving, but experiencing what the saints have called 'the dark night of the soul', and indeed doing so deliberately out of solidarity with us. In this condition, as Thomas J. Crawford puts it, the people of God 'derive no conscious satisfaction from the joys of his favour and the comforts of his fellowship'. They are granted 'no approving smile, no commending voice, no inward manifestation of the divine favour'.[30] This explanation is possible. It does not cast a slur on the character of Jesus like the first. Yet there seems to be an insuperable difficulty in the way of adopting it, namely that the words of Psalm 22:1 express an experience of *being*, and not just *feeling*, God-forsaken.

A third quite popular interpretation is to say that Jesus was uttering *a cry of victory*, the exact opposite of the first explanation, the cry of despair. The argument now is that, although Jesus quoted only the first verse of Psalm 22, he did so to represent the whole Psalm which begins and continues with an account of appalling sufferings, but ends with great confidence, and even triumph: 'I will declare your name to my brothers; in the congregation I will praise you. You who fear the LORD, praise him! ... For he has not despised or disdained the suffering of the afflicted one; he has not hidden his face from him but has listened to his cry for help' (vv. 22). This is ingenious but (it seems to me) far-fetched. Why should Jesus have quoted from the Psalm's beginning if in reality he was alluding to its end? It would seem rather perverse. Would anybody have understood his purpose?

The fourth explanation is simple and straightforward. It is to take the words at their face value and to understand them as *a cry of real dereliction*. I agree with Dale who wrote: 'I decline to accept any explanation of these words which implies that they do not represent the actual truth of our

Lord's position.'[31] Jesus had no need to repent of uttering a false cry. Up to this moment, though forsaken by men, he could add, 'Yet I am not alone, for my Father is with me' (Jn. 16:32). In the darkness, however, he was absolutely alone, being now also God-forsaken. As Calvin put it, 'If Christ had died only a bodily death, it would have been ineffectual ... Unless his soul shared in the punishment, he would have been the Redeemer of bodies alone.' In consequence, 'he paid a greater and more excellent price in suffering in his soul the terrible torments of a condemned and forsaken man'.[32] So then an actual and dreadful separation took place between the Father and the Son; it was voluntarily accepted by both the Father and the Son; it was due to our sins and their just reward; and Jesus expressed this horror of great darkness, this God-forsakenness, by quoting the only verse of Scripture which accurately described it, and which he had perfectly fulfilled, namely, 'My God, my God, why have you forsaken me?' The theological objections and problems we shall come to later, although we already insist that the God-forsakenness of Jesus on the cross must be balanced with such an equally biblical assertion as 'God was reconciling the world to himself in Christ'. C. E. B. Cranfield is right to emphasize both the truth that Jesus experienced 'not merely a felt, but a real, abandonment by his Father' and 'the paradox that, while this God-forsakenness was utterly real, the unity of the Blessed Trinity was even then unbroken'.[33] At this point, however, it is enough to suggest that Jesus had been meditating on Psalm 22, which describes the cruel persecution of an innocent and godly man, as he was meditating on other Psalms which he quoted from the cross;[34] that he quoted verse 1 for the same reason that he quoted every other Scripture, namely that he believed he was fulfilling it; and that his cry was in the form of a question ('Why ... ?'), not because he did not know its answer, but only because the Old Testament text itself (which he was quoting) was in that form.

Almost immediately after the cry of dereliction, Jesus uttered three more words or sentences in quick succession. First, 'I am thirsty', his great spiritual sufferings having taken their toll of him physically. Secondly, he called out, again (according to Matthew and Mark) in a loud voice, 'It is finished.' And thirdly the tranquil, voluntary, confident self-commendation, 'Father, into your hands I commit my spirit,' as he breathed his last breath.[35] The middle cry, the loud shout of victory, is in the Gospel text the single word *tetelestai*. Being in the perfect tense, it means, 'It has been and will for ever remain finished.' We note the achievement Jesus claimed just before he died. It is not men who have finished their brutal deed; it is he who has accomplished what he came into the world to do. He has borne the sins of the world. Deliberately, freely and in perfect love he has endured the judgment in our place. He has procured salvation for us, established a new covenant between God and humankind, and made available the chief covenant blessing, the forgiveness of sins. At once the curtain of the Temple, which for centuries had symbolized the alienation of sinners from God, was torn in two from top to bottom, in order to demonstrate that the sin-barrier had been thrown down by God, and the way into his presence opened.

Thirty-six hours later God raised Jesus from the dead. He who had been condemned for us in his death was publicly vindicated in his resurrection. It was God's decisive demonstration that he had not died in vain.

All this presents a coherent and logical picture. It gives an explanation of the death of Jesus which takes into proper scientific account all the available data, without avoiding any. It explains the central importance which Jesus attached to his death, why he instituted his supper to commemorate it, and how by his death the new covenant has been ratified, with its promise of forgiveness. It explains his agony of anticipation in the garden, his anguish of dereliction on the cross, and his claim to have decisively accomplished our salvation. All these phenomena become intelligible if we accept the explanation given by Jesus and his apostles that 'he himself bore our sins in his body on the tree'.

In conclusion, the cross enforces three truths – about ourselves, about God and about Jesus Christ.

First, our sin must be extremely horrible. Nothing reveals the gravity of sin like the cross. For ultimately what sent Christ there was neither the greed of Judas, nor the envy of the priests, nor the vacillating cowardice of Pilate, but our own greed, envy, cowardice and other sins, and Christ's resolve in love and mercy to bear their judgment and so put them away. It is impossible for us to face Christ's cross with integrity and not to feel ashamed of ourselves. Apathy, selfishness and complacency blossom everywhere in the world except at the cross. There these noxious weeds shrivel and die. They are seen for the tatty, poisonous things they are. For if there was no way by which the righteous God could righteously forgive our unrighteousness, except that he should bear it himself in Christ, it must be serious indeed. It is only when we see this that, stripped of our self-righteousness and self-satisfaction, we are ready to put our trust in Jesus Christ as the Saviour we urgently need.

Secondly, God's love must be wonderful beyond comprehension. God could quite justly have abandoned us to our fate. He could have left us alone to reap the fruit of our wrongdoing and to perish in our sins. It is what we deserved. But he did not. Because he loved us, he came after us in Christ. He pursued us even to the desolate anguish of the cross, where he bore our sin, guilt, judgment and death. It takes a hard and stony heart to remain unmoved by love like that. It is more than love. Its proper name is 'grace', which is love to the undeserving.

Thirdly, Christ's salvation must be a free gift. He 'purchased' it for us at the high price of his own life-blood. So what is there left for us to pay? Nothing! Since he claimed that all was now 'finished', there is nothing for us to contribute. Not of course that we now have a licence to sin and can always count on God's forgiveness. On the contrary, the same cross of Christ, which is the ground of a free salvation, is also the most powerful incentive to a holy life. But this new life follows. First, we have to humble ourselves at the foot of the cross, confess that we have sinned and deserve nothing at his hand but judgment, thank him that he loved us and died for us, and receive from him a full and free forgiveness. Against this self-humbling our ingrained pride rebels. We resent the idea that we cannot earn – or even contribute to – our own salvation. So we stumble, as Paul put it, over the stumbling-block of the cross.[36]

Notes

[1] Jn. 10:11, 15; Lk. 22:19; Rom. 5:8; Eph. 5:2; 1 Thes. 5:10; Tit. 2:14. Professor Martin Hengel has shown with great erudition that the concept of a person voluntarily dying for his city, family and friends, truth, or to pacify the gods, was widespread in the Graeco-Roman world. A special composite word, *hyperapothnēskein* ('to die for'), had been formed to express it. The gospel that 'Christ died for us' would, therefore, have been readily intelligible to first-century pagan audiences. (Martin Hengel, *Atonement*, pp.1–32.)

[2] For the negative see, *e.g.*, Gal. 1:4; Eph. 1:7; Heb. 9:28. For the positive see, *e.g.*, Jn. 3 14–16; Eph. 2:16; Col. 1:20; 1 Thes. 5:10; 1 Pet. 3:18.

[3] 1 Cor. 15:3; 1 Pet. 3:18; Heb. 9:26; 10:12; 1 Jn. 1:7; Rev. 1:5–6.

[4] See Gn. 5:24; 2 Ki. 2:1–11, 1 Cor. 15:50–54.

[5] *E.g.* Gn. 2:17; 3:3, 19, 23; Rom. 5:12–14; Rev. 20:14; 21:8.

[6] Ps. 49:12, 20; Ec. 3:19–21.

[7] See the occurrence of the verb *embrimaomai* in John 11:33, 38. Used of the snorting of horses, it was transferred to the strong human emotions of displeasure and indignation.

[8] Jn. 10:18; Lk. 23:46.

[9] The words of administration are recorded somewhat differently by Paul and the Synoptic evangelists. See 1 Cor. 11:23–25; Mt. 26:26–28; Mk. 14:22–24; Lk. 22:17–19.

[10] Ex. 24:8. See also the covenant references in Is. 42:6; 49:8; Zc. 9:11 and Heb. 9:18–20.

[11] Mk. 14:12–16; Lk. 22:15.

[12] Jn. 18:28. *Cf.* Jn. 19:36 and Ex. 12:46.

[13] Cf. Ex. 12:26–27; 13:8; Dt. 16:3.

[14] Jesus' agony in the Garden of Gethsemane is described by Matthew (26:36–46), Mark (14:32–42) and Luke (22:39–46). John does not refer to it, although he does tell of the walk to the olive orchard at the foot of the Mount of Olives where Jesus was betrayed and arrested (18:1–11).

[15] Lk. 12:50; Jn. 12:27.

[16] These particular Greek words occur in Mt. 26:37; Mk. 14:33 and Lk. 22:44. B. B. Warfield's essay is published in his *Person and Work*, pp. 93–145. His translations of these words occur on pp. 130–131.

[17] *Phaedo*, 117–118.

[18] Mt. 5:1–12; Acts 5:41; Phil. 1:29–30.

[19] Quoted in Foxe's *Book of Martyrs*, p. 19.

[20] *Ibid.*, pp. 20–25.

[21] *Ibid.*, pp. 31–33.

[22] From *Saints' Everlasting Rest*, p. 393.

[23] Friedrich Heiler, *Gospel of Sadhu Sundar Singh*, pp. 173–178.

[24] Is. 51:17–22; Ps. 75:8; Je. 25:15–29 (*cf.* Hab. 2:16); 49:12; Rev. 14:10; 16:1ff. and 18:6.

[25] Douglas Webster, *In Debt to Christ*, p. 46.

[26] Is. 53:5–6; Jn. 1:29; Mk. 10:45; Heb. 9:28; 1 Pet. 2:24; 3:18; 2 Cor. 5:21; Gal. 3:13.

[27] Mk. 15:25, 33–34.

[28] *E.g.* Jos. 1:5, 9 and Is. 41:10.

[29] T. R. Glover, *Jesus of History*, p. 192.

[30] Thomas J. Crawford, *Doctrine of Holy Scripture*, pp. 137–138.

[31] R. W. Dale, *Atonement*, p. 61.

[32] Calvin's *Institutes*, II.xvi.10 and 12. It is true, and somewhat strange, that Calvin (following Luther) believed this to be the explanation of Jesus' 'descent into hell' after his death. What matters most is the fact that he experienced God-forsakenness for us, however, and not precisely *when* he did so.

[33] C E. B. Cranfield, *Mark*, pp. 458–459.

[34] *E.g.* 'I am thirsty' (Jn. 19:28) is an allusion to Ps. 69:21 (*cf.* Ps. 22:15), and 'Into your hands I commit my spirit' (Lk. 23:46), a quotation of Ps. 31:5.

[35] Jn. 19:28, 30; Lk. 23:46.

[36] 1 Cor. 1:23; Gal. 5:11; *cf.* Mt. 11:6; Rom. 9:32; 1 Pet. 2:8.

PART TWO

The heart of the cross

FOUR

The problem of forgiveness

The last chapter's 'look below the surface' may well have provoked in some readers an impatient response. 'That simple supper in the upper room,' you may be saying, 'and even the confessedly agonized prayer in the garden and cry from the cross, all admit of much more straightforward explanations. Why must you complicate everything with your tortuous theologizing?' It is an understandable reaction.

In particular, our insistence that according to the gospel the cross of Christ is the only ground on which God forgives sins bewilders many people. 'Why should our forgiveness depend on Christ's death?' they ask. 'Why does God not simply forgive us, without the necessity of the cross?' As the French cynic put it, 'Le bon Dieu me pardonnera; c'est son metier.'[1] 'After all,' the objector may continue, 'if we sin against one another, we are required to forgive one another. We are even warned of dire consequences if we refuse. Why can't God practise what he preaches and be equally generous? Nobody's death is necessary before we forgive each other. Why then does God make so much fuss about forgiving us and even declare it impossible without his Son's "sacrifice for sin"? It sounds like a primitive superstition which modern people should long since have discarded.'

It is essential to ask and to face these questions. Two answers may be given to them immediately, although we shall need the rest of the chapter in which to elaborate them. The first was supplied by Archbishop Anselm in his great book *Cur Deus Homo?* at the end of the eleventh century. If anybody imagines, he wrote, that God can simply forgive us as we forgive others, that person has 'not yet considered the seriousness of sin', or literally 'what a heavy weight sin is' (i.xxi). The second answer might be expressed similarly: 'You have not yet considered the majesty of God.' It is when our perception of God and man, or of holiness and sin, are askew that our understanding of the atonement is bound to be askew also.

The fact is that the analogy between our forgiveness and God's is far from being exact. True, Jesus taught us to pray: 'Forgive us our sins, as we forgive those who sin against us.' But he was teaching the impossibility of the unforgiving being forgiven, and so the obligation of the forgiven to forgive, as is clear from the Parable of the Unmerciful Servant; he was not drawing any parallel between God and us in relation to the *basis* of forgiveness.[2] For us to argue, 'We forgive each other unconditionally, let God do the same to us', betrays not sophistication but shallowness, since it overlooks the elementary fact that we are not God. We are private individuals, and other people's misdemeanours are personal injuries. God is not a private individual, however, nor is sin just a personal injury. On the contrary, God is himself the maker of the laws we break, and sin is rebellion against him.

The crucial question we should ask, therefore, is a different one. It is not why God finds it *difficult* to forgive, but how he finds it *possible* to do so at all. As Emil Brunner put it, 'Forgiveness is the very opposite of anything which can be taken for granted. Nothing is less obvious than forgiveness.'[3] Or, in the words of Carnegie Simpson, 'forgiveness is to man the plainest of duties; to God it is the profoundest of problems'.[4]

The problem of forgiveness is constituted by the inevitable collision between divine perfection and human rebellion, between God as he is and us as we are. The obstacle to forgiveness is neither our sin alone, nor our guilt alone, but also the divine reaction in love and wrath towards guilty sinners. For, although indeed 'God is love', yet we have to remember that his love is 'holy love',[5] love which yearns over sinners while at the same time refusing to condone their sin. How, then, could God express his holy love – his love in forgiving sinners without compromising his holiness, and his holiness in judging sinners without frustrating his love? Confronted by human evil, how could God be true to himself as holy love? In Isaiah's words, how could he be simultaneously 'a righteous God and a Saviour' (45:21)? For, despite the truth that God demonstrated his righteousness by taking action to save his people, the words 'righteousness' and 'salvation' cannot be regarded as simple synonyms. Rather his saving initiative was compatible with, and expressive of, his righteousness. At the cross in holy love God through Christ paid the full penalty of our disobedience himself. He bore the judgment we deserve in order to bring us the forgiveness we do not deserve. On the cross divine mercy and justice were equally expressed and eternally reconciled. God's holy love was 'satisfied'.

I am running on too fast, however. The reason why many people give the wrong answers to questions about the cross, and even ask the wrong questions, is that they have carefully considered neither the seriousness of sin nor the majesty of God. In order to do so now, we shall review four basic biblical concepts, namely the gravity of sin, human moral responsibility, true and false guilt, and the wrath of God. We shall thus see ourselves successively as sinful, responsible, guilty and lost. It will not be a pleasant exercise, and our integrity will be tested in the course of it.

The gravity of sin

The very word 'sin' has in recent years dropped from most people's vocabulary. It belongs to traditional religious phraseology which, at least in the increasingly secularized West, is now declared by many to be meaningless. Moreover, if and when 'sin' is mentioned, it is most likely to be misunderstood. What is it, then?

The New Testament uses five main Greek words for sin, which together portray its various aspects, both passive and active. The commonest is *hamartia*, which depicts sin as a missing of the target, the failure to attain a goal. *Adikia is* 'unrighteousness' or 'iniquity', and *poneria* is evil of a vicious or degenerate kind. Both these terms seem to speak of an inward corruption or perversion of character. The more active words are *parabasis* (with which we may associate the similar *paraptōma*), a 'trespass' or 'transgression', the stepping over a known boundary, and *anomia*, 'lawlessness', the disregard or violation of a known law. In each case an objective criterion is implied, either a standard we fail to reach or a line we deliberately cross.

It is assumed throughout Scripture that this criterion or ideal has been established by God. It is, in fact, his moral law, which expresses his righteous character. It is not the law of his own being only, however; it is also the law of ours, since he has made us in his image and in so doing has written the requirements of his law in our hearts (Rom. 2:15). There is, thus, a vital correspondence between God's law and ourselves, and to commit sin is to commit 'lawlessness' (1 Jn. 3:4), offending against our own highest welfare as well as against the authority and love of God.

The emphasis of Scripture, however, is on the godless self-centredness of sin. Every sin is a breach of what Jesus called 'the first and great commandment', not just by failing to love God with all our being, but by actively refusing to acknowledge and obey him as our Creator and Lord. We have rejected the position of dependence which our createdness inevitably involves, and made a bid for independence. Worse still, we have dared to proclaim our self-dependence, our autonomy, which is to claim the position occupied by God alone. Sin is not a regrettable lapse from conventional standards; its essence is hostility to God (Rom. 8:7), issuing in active rebellion against him. It has been described in terms of 'getting rid of the Lord God' in order to put ourselves in his place in a haughty spirit of 'God-almightiness'. Emil Brunner sums it up well: 'Sin is defiance, arrogance, the desire to be equal with God ... the assertion of human independence over against God ... the constitution of the autonomous reason, morality and culture.' It is appropriate that he entitled the book from which this quotation is taken *Man in Revolt* (p. 129).

Once we have seen that every sin we commit is an expression (in differing degrees of self-consciousness) of this spirit of revolt against God, we shall be able to accept David's confession: 'Against you, you only, have I sinned and done what is evil in your sight' (Ps. 51:4). In committing adultery with Bathsheba, and in arranging to have her husband Uriah killed in battle, David had committed extremely serious offences against them and against the nation. Yet it was God's laws which he had broken and thereby ultimately against God that he had chiefly offended.

Perhaps it is a deep-seated reluctance to face up to the gravity of sin which has led to its omission from the vocabulary of many of our contemporaries. One acute observer of the human condition, who has noticed the disappearance of the word, is the American psychiatrist Karl Menninger. He has written about it in his book, *Whatever Became of Sin?* Describing the malaise of western society, its general mood of gloom and doom, he adds that 'one misses any mention of "sin"'. 'It was a word once in everyone's mind, but is now rarely if ever heard. Does that mean', he asks, 'that no sin is involved in all our troubles ...? Has no-one committed any sins? Where, indeed, did sin go? What became of it?' (p. 13). Enquiring into the causes of sin's disappearance, Dr Menninger notes first that 'many former sins have become crimes', so that responsibility for dealing with them has passed from church to state, from priest to policeman (p. 50), while others have dissipated into sicknesses, or at least into symptoms of sickness, so that in their case punishment has been replaced by treatment (pp. 74ff.). A third convenient device called 'collective irresponsibility' has enabled us to transfer the blame for some of our deviant behaviour from ourselves as individuals to society as a whole or to one of its many groupings (pp. 94ff.).

Dr Menninger goes on to plead not only for the reinstatement of the word 'sin' in our vocabulary, but also for a recognition of the reality which the word expresses. Sin cannot be dismissed as merely a cultural taboo or social blunder. It must be taken seriously. He takes preachers to task for soft-pedalling it, and adds: 'The clergyman cannot minimize sin and maintain his proper role in our culture' (p. 198). For sin is 'an implicitly aggressive quality – a ruthlessness, a hurting, a breaking away from God and from the rest of humanity, a partial alienation, or act of rebellion ... Sin has a willful, defiant or disloyal quality: *someone* is defied or offended or hurt' (p. 19). To ignore this would be dishonest. To confess it would enable us to do something about it. Moreover, the reinstatement of sin would lead inevitably to 'the revival or reassertion of personal responsibility'. In fact the 'usefulness' of reviving sin is that responsibility would be revived with it (pp. 178f.).

Human moral responsibility

But is it fair to blame human beings for their misconduct? Are we really responsible for our actions? Are we not more often victims of other agencies than free agencies ourselves, and so more sinned against than sinning? A whole gamut of scapegoats is ready at hand – our genes, our chemistry (a temporary hormonal imbalance), our inherited temper and temperament, our parents' failures during our early childhood, our upbringing, our educational and social environment. Together these seem to constitute an infallible alibi.

Perhaps no more comprehensive attempt has been made to undermine the traditional concept of personal responsibility than Professor B. F. Skinner's book *Beyond Freedom and Dignity.* His thesis is that 'the terrifying problems that face us in the world today' (especially the threats of population overgrowth, nuclear war, famine, disease and pollution) could all be solved by 'a technology of human behaviour'. That is, 'vast changes in human behaviour' could be secured by changes in the human environment. Man could be programmed to behave properly. What stands in the way, then? Answer: the concept of 'autonomous man', his supposed 'freedom' (in that he is held responsible for his actions) and his supposed 'dignity' (in that he is given credit for his achievements). But these things are an illusion, for 'a scientific analysis shifts both the responsibility and the achievement to the environment' (pp. 9–30). Man must have the courage to create a social environment or culture which adequately 'shapes and maintains the behaviour of those who live in it' (p. 141). This is essential for the survival of humankind, which is more important than the traditional, 'flattering' concept of our 'freedom and dignity' (p. 208). To be sure, C. S. Lewis called this 'the abolition of man'. What would be abolished, however, is only 'autonomous man ... the man defended by the literature of freedom and dignity'. Indeed, 'his abolition has been long overdue' (p. 196). Peering into the future, in which man creates an environment which controls him, and so performs 'a gigantic exercise in self-control', B. F. Skinner ends his book with the words: 'We have not yet seen what man can make of man' (p. 210). It is a chilling prospect of self-determined determinism.

The human spirit rebels against it, however. The concept of 'diminished responsibility' we certainly accept, but not the total dissolution of all responsibility, except in the most extreme circumstances. The parallel between moral responsibility and legal liability is instructive at this point. Generally speaking, the criminal law assumes that people have it in their power to choose whether they will obey or break the law, and it treats them accordingly. Nevertheless, responsibility for crime can be diminished, and even excluded, by certain 'excusing' conditions. In his essays in the philosophy of law entitled *Punishment and Responsibility*, H. L. A. Hart defines the principle as follows: 'In all advanced legal systems liability to conviction for serious crimes is made dependent, not only on the offender having done those outward acts which the law forbids, but on his having done them in a certain frame of mind or with a certain will' (p. 187).[6] This state of mind and will is known technically as *mens rea*, which, though a literal translation would be 'a guilty mind', really refers to the person's 'intention'. For example, the distinction between intentional and unintentional homicide, that is, between murder and manslaughter, goes right back to the Mosaic law. The principle also has a wider bearing. If a person commits an offence while insane, under duress or as an automaton, criminal liability cannot be established. Provocation may reduce murder to manslaughter. The plea of insanity has been accepted for centuries, and has been interpreted since the MacNaghten Rules of 1843 as 'disease of the mind', leading to such 'a defect of reason' that the offender either did not know 'the nature and quality of the act he was doing' or, if he did know it, 'did not know he was doing what was wrong'.

The Rules were criticized, however, for concentrating on the ignorance of the offender, rather than on his lack of capacity for self-control. So the Infanticide Act of 1938 made provision for acts done by a woman when 'the balance of her mind was disturbed by reason of her not having fully recovered from the effect of giving birth ...', and the Homicide Act of 1957 provided that a person 'shall not be convicted of murder if he was suffering from such abnormality of mind ... as substantially impaired his mental responsibility for his acts ...' So, too, the British Parliament has decided that no child under ten years can be held guilty of an offence, while between the ages of ten and fourteen it has to be proved specifically that an offending child knew that what he or she was doing was seriously wrong.

Thus, legal liability depends on mental and moral responsibility, that is, on *mens rea*, the intention of mind and will. But pleas based on lack of consciousness or control will always need to be precisely defined, and exceptional. An accused person certainly cannot plead his genetic inheritance or social upbringing as an excuse for criminal behaviour, let alone personal negligence ('I simply wasn't thinking what I was doing'). No, generally speaking, the whole procedure of trying, convicting and sentencing in the courts rests on the assumption that human beings are free to make choices and are responsible for the choices they make.

It is the same in everyday situations. Admittedly we are conditioned by our genes and upbringing, but the human spirit (not to mention the Christian mind) protests against the reductionism which declares a human being to be nothing but a computer (programmed to perform and respond) or an animal (at the mercy of his instincts). Over against these concepts we appeal to the ineradicable sense which men and women have that within reasonable limits we are free agents, able to make up our own minds and decide our own actions. Faced with an alternative, we know we are able to choose. And when we make a wrong choice, we reproach ourselves, because we know we could have behaved differently. We also act on the assumption that other people are free and responsible, for we try to persuade them to our point of view, and 'we all praise or blame people from time to time'.[7]

Sir Norman Anderson is, I think, right to draw attention to this human sense of responsibility. On the one hand, he writes, we can speculate about the extent to which people are 'preconditioned by the constitution and condition of their brains, by the psychological make-up they have inherited or acquired, by the blind and inevitable course of "nature" or by the sovereignty of a Creator God, to behave in the way they do'. But on the other hand it is possible 'unequivocally to affirm that there is no reason whatever to suppose that ordinary men and women are mistaken in their firm conviction that they have, within limits, a genuine freedom of choice and action, and that this necessarily entails a corresponding measure of moral responsibility'.[8]

The three contributors to the 1982 London Lectures in Contemporary Christianity, entitled *Free to Be Different,* came to the same conclusion. Professor Malcolm Jeeves spoke and wrote as a psychologist, Professor Sam Berry as a geneticist, and Dr David Atkinson as a theologian. Together they investigated the respective influences on human behaviour of 'nature' (our genetic inheritance), 'nurture' (our social conditioning) and 'grace' (God's loving and transforming initiative). They agreed that these things evidently both shape and constrain our behaviour. Nevertheless, their lectures were a vigorous, interdisciplinary rejection of determinism and assertion of human responsibility. Although the whole subject is admittedly complex and it is not possible neatly to disentangle all the threads, yet the three contributors were able to express this common conclusion:

We are not automata, able to do nothing but react mechanically to our genes, our environment or even God's grace. We are personal beings created by God for himself ... Moreover, what God has given us is not to be regarded as a static endowment. Our character can be refined. Our behaviour can change. Our convictions can mature. Our gifts can be cultivated ... We are indeed free to be different ...[9]

When we turn to the Bible, we find the same tension, of which we are aware in our personal experience, between the pressures which condition and even control us, and our abiding moral responsibility nonetheless. There is a strong biblical emphasis on the influence of our inheritance, of what we are 'in Adam'. The doctrine of original sin means that the very nature we have inherited is tainted and twisted with self-centredness. It is, therefore, 'from within, out of men's hearts', Jesus taught, that evil thoughts and actions come (Mk. 7:21–23). It is not surprising that he also described the sinner as 'a slave to sin' an. 8:34). We are, in fact, enslaved to the world (public fashion and opinion), the flesh (our fallen nature) and the devil (demonic forces). Even after Christ has liberated us and made us his slaves instead, we are not yet entirely rid of the insidious power of our fallenness, so that Paul can conclude his argument in Romans 7 with the summary: 'So then, I myself in my mind am a slave to God's law, but in the sinful nature a slave to the law of sin' (v. 25b).

Scripture recognizes the subtlety and strength of these forces, which indeed diminish our responsibility. It is because God 'knows how we are formed' and 'remembers that we are dust' that he is patient towards us, slow to anger, and 'does not treat us as our sins deserve' (Ps. 103:10, 14). Similarly, God's Messiah is gentle with the weak, refusing to break bruised reeds or to snuff out smouldering wicks.[10]

At the same time, the biblical recognition that our responsibility is diminished does not mean that it is destroyed. On the contrary, Scripture invariably treats us as morally responsible agents. It lays upon us the necessity of choice between 'life and good, death and evil', between the living God and idols.[11] It exhorts us to obedience and remonstrates with us when we disobey. Jesus himself pleaded with recalcitrant Jerusalem to acknowledge and welcome him. Often, he said, addressing the city in direct speech, 'I have longed to gather your children together, as a hen gathers her chicks under her wings, but you were not willing' (Mt. 23:37). He thus attributed Jerusalem's spiritual blindness, apostasy and coming judgment to her obstinacy. It is true that he also said, 'No-one can come to me unless the Father … draws him', but only after he had said, 'You refuse to come to me.'[12] Why is it that people do not come to Christ? Is it that they cannot, or is it that they will not? Jesus taught both. And in this 'cannot' and 'will not' lies the ultimate antinomy between divine sovereignty and human responsibility. But however we state it, we must not eliminate either part. Our responsibility before God is an inalienable aspect of our human dignity. Its final expression will be on the day of judgment. Nobody will be sentenced without trial. All people, great and small, irrespective of their social class, will stand before God's throne, not crushed or browbeaten, but given this final token of respect for human responsibility, as each gives an account of what he or she has done.

Emil Brunner is surely right to emphasize our responsibility as an indispensable aspect of our humanness. 'Today our slogan must be: no determinism, on any account! For it makes all understanding of man as man impossible.'[13] Man has to be seen as 'a thinking-willing being', responsive and responsible to his Creator, 'the creaturely counterpart of his divine self-existence'. Further, this human responsibility is in the first instance 'not ... a task but a gift ... not law but grace'. It expresses itself in 'believing, responsive love' (p. 98). So then, 'one who has understood the nature of responsibility has understood the nature of man. Responsibility is not an attribute, it is the "substance" of human existence. It contains everything ... [it is] that which distinguishes man from all other creatures ...' (p. 50). Therefore 'if responsibility be eliminated, the whole meaning of human existence disappears' (p. 258).

But has not the Fall seriously weakened man's responsibility? Is he responsible for his actions any longer? Yes, he is. 'Man never sins purely out of weakness, but always also in the fact that he "lets himself go" in weakness. Even in the dullest sinner there is still a spark of decision', indeed of defiant rebellion against God. So man cannot shuffle off his responsibility for his own wickedness. 'No Fate, no metaphysical constitution, no weakness of his nature, but himself, man, in the centre of his personality is made responsible for his sin' (pp. 130–131).

True and false guilt

If human beings have sinned (which they have), and if they are responsible for their sins (which they are), then they are guilty before God. Guilt is the logical deduction from the premises of sin and responsibility. We have done wrong, by our own fault, and are therefore liable to bear the just penalty of our wrongdoing.

This is the argument of the early chapters of the letter to the Romans. Paul divides the human race into three major sections, and shows how each knows something of its moral duty, but has deliberately suppressed its knowledge in order to pursue its own sinful course. As John put it, 'This is the verdict: Light has come into the world, but men loved darkness instead of light because their deeds were evil' (Jn. 3:19). Nothing is more serious than this deliberate rejection of the light of truth and goodness. Paul begins with decadent Roman society. Its people have known God's power and glory from the creation, and his holiness from their conscience, but they have refused to live up to their knowledge. Instead, they have turned from worship to idolatry. So God has given them over to immorality and other forms of anti-social behaviour (Rom. 1:18–32).

The second section of humanity that Paul addresses is the self-righteous world, whose knowledge of God's law may be either in the Scriptures (Jews) or in their hearts (Gentiles). In either case they do not live up to their knowledge (2:1–16). The third section is the specifically Jewish world, whose members pride themselves on the knowledge they have and on the moral instruction they give to others. Yet the very law they teach they also disobey. This being so, their privileged status as God's covenant people will not render them immune to his judgment (2:17 – 3:8).

What, then, is the conclusion? Paul answers his own question. 'We have already made the charge that Jews and Gentiles alike are all under sin' (3:9). Old Testament Scripture confirms this verdict. We are all without excuse, since we have all known our duty, and none of us has done it. Every protest is silenced, and the whole world is guilty and accountable to God (3:19–20).

Is this a rather morbid viewpoint? Christians have often been criticized (not least evangelical Christians) for continuously harping on sin, for becoming obsessed with it in our own lives and, particularly in our evangelism, for trying to induce in others a sense of their guilt. Nietzsche, for example, bitterly complained that 'Christianity *needs* sickness ... *Making* sick is the true hidden objective of the Church's whole system of salvation procedures ... One is not "converted" to Christianity – one must be sufficiently sick for it'.[14] Nietzsche was partly correct, namely that Christianity is medicine for the sin-sick. After all, Jesus himself defended his concentration on 'tax collectors and sinners' by saying, 'It is not the healthy who need a doctor, but the sick.' 'I have not come to call the righteous,' he added, 'but sinners' (Mk. 2:17). We vigorously deny, however, that it is the church's role to 'make' people sick in order to convert them. Instead, we have to make them aware of their sickness, so that they will turn to the Great Physician.

Yet the criticism persists that Christians are unhealthily preoccupied with sin. An eloquent contemporary spokesman of this viewpoint is the BBC's former Religious Affairs Correspondent, Gerald Priestland. One of his talks in the radio series *Priestland's Progress* was entitled 'Guilt-edged Religion'. He told us how at the age of ten he thought Christianity was about sin and that by the time he was fifteen he was having 'glimpses into the abyss of depression', accompanied by fears of divine vengeance for his 'unnameable secret crimes', fears which kept growing for the next thirty years. His Christianity gave him no help. 'When I looked at the Cross, with its suffering victim, its only message to me was: "You did this – and there is no health in you!"' His equivalent of a Damascus Road conversion came to him at last 'on the psychiatrist's couch', for that was where he learnt 'the missing element of forgiveness'. Since then he confesses to 'a fairly low level of personal guilt and relatively little interest in the matter of sin' (pp. 59–60).

That is not the whole of Gerald Priestland's story, but it is enough to illustrate the grievous damage done by half-truths. How could anyone imagine that Christianity is about sin rather than about the forgiveness of sin? How could anyone look at the cross and see only the shame of what we did to Christ, rather than the glory of what he did for us? The prodigal son had to 'come to himself' (acknowledge his self-centredness) before he could 'come to his father'. The humiliation of penitence was necessary before the joy of reconciliation. There would have been no ring, no robe, no kiss, no feast if he had remained in the far country or returned impenitent. A guilty conscience is a great blessing, but only if it drives us to come home.

This does not mean that our conscience is always a reliable guide. There is such a thing as a morbid, overscrupulous conscience, and it would be mischievous to seek deliberately to create one. Not all guilt feelings are pathological, however. On the contrary, those who declare themselves sinless and guiltless are suffering from an even worse sickness. For to manipulate, smother and even 'cauterize' (1 Tim. 4:2) the conscience, in order to escape the pain of its accusations, renders us impervious to our need for salvation.

Is it, then, healthy or unhealthy to insist on the gravity of sin and the necessity of atonement, to hold people responsible for their actions, to warn them of the peril of divine judgment, and to urge them to confess, repent and turn to Christ? It is healthy. For if there is 'false guilt' (feeling bad about evil we have not done), there is also 'false innocence' (feeling good about the evil we *have* done). If false contrition is unhealthy (an ungrounded weeping over guilt), so is false assurance (an ungrounded rejoicing over forgiveness). It may be, therefore, that it is not we who exaggerate, when we stress the seriousness of sin, but our critics, who underestimate it. God said of the false prophets in Old Testament days: 'They dress the wound of my people as though it were not serious. "Peace, peace," they say, when there is no peace.'[15] Superficial remedies are always due to a faulty diagnosis. Those who prescribe them have fallen victim to the deceiving spirit of modernity which denies the gravity of sin. To make a true diagnosis of our condition, however, grave as it is, could never be unhealthy, provided that we go on immediately to the remedy. So the law which condemns us is nevertheless God's good gift, because it sends us to Christ to be justified. And the Holy Spirit came to 'convict the world of guilt', but only in order that he might more effectively bear witness to Christ as the Saviour from guilt (Jn. 16:8; 15:26–27). There is no joy comparable to the joy of the forgiven.

It is here that some recent American psychologists and psychiatrists go wrong, for they go only half-way. They start right, however, even some who make no Christian profession, for they insist that we must take sin, responsibility and guilt seriously. This is certainly great gain, but to diagnose well without being able to prescribe well is to embrace a dangerous and disillusioning half-measure.

Dr Hobart Mowrer, who was Research Professor of Psychology at the

University of Illinois when his critique of Freudian psychoanalysis *The Crisis in Psychiatry and Religion* was published (1961), rejected the notion that 'psychoneurosis implies no moral responsibility'. For 'just so long as we deny the reality of sin, we cut ourselves off ... from the possibility of radical redemption ("recovery")' (p. 40). Dr Mowrer created quite a stir within his profession by his use of the word 'sin'. But he persisted in teaching the fact of sin and the need for an acknowledgment of it.

> Just so long as a person lives under the shadow of real, unacknow-ledged, and unexpiated guilt, he *cannot* ... 'accept himself' ... He will continue to hate himself and to suffer the inevitable consequences of self-hatred. But the moment he ... begins to accept his guilt and his sinfulness, the possibility of radical reformation opens up, and with this ... a new freedom of self-respect and peace (p. 54).

A few years later, also rebelling against the Freudian insistence that guilt is pathological, Dr William Glasser began in Los Angeles to develop a dif-ferent approach in treating juvenile delinquents and others which he called 'Reality Therapy'. His thesis was that a person who is 'unable to fulfil his essential needs', especially love and self-worth, denies the reality of the world around him and acts irresponsibly. So the therapist seeks 'to make him face a truth he has spent his life trying to avoid: *he is responsible for his behaviour*'.[16] Dr Mowrer in his Foreword sums up the essence of Dr Glasser's therapeutic method as 'a psychiatric version of the three R's, namely reality, responsibility and right-and-wrong' (p. xii).

Similarly, 'sin must be dealt with in the private courts of the human heart', writes Karl Menninger.[17] Well and good. But how? Especially, he goes on, by 'repentance, reparation, restitution and atonement'. Karl Menninger here betrays his very partial grasp of the gospel. For those four words cannot be bracketed in this way. The first three do indeed belong together. Reparation (a general word for making amends) and restitution (the more particular restoration of what has been stolen) are both necessary to signify the genuineness of repentance. But 'atonement' is not something we can do; only God can atone for our sins, and indeed has done so through Christ.

It is true that Dr Menninger mentions the forgiveness of God once or twice in passing (though without any basis in Christ's cross). Dr Hobart Mowrer, however, studiously avoids both the word and the concept. Like Karl Menninger he concentrates on the acknowledging of faults and the making of restitution. He calls his therapy groups 'integrity groups' because their foundation is personal integrity in the acknowledgment of wrong-doing. Initiation into a group is by means of 'a complete unqualified self-disclosure' which he calls *exomologēsis*. When, during a personal conversation with Dr Mowrer at the University of Illinois in 1970,1 mentioned that *exomologēsis* is the Greek word for 'confession', and that in the Christian tradition the purpose of confession is to receive forgiveness from the injured party, he immediately responded, 'Oh, we never talk about forgiveness.' His concept of sin is that in each case it is the breach of a contractual obligation for which the guilty person must make restitution. Forgiveness is therefore unnecessary, either by the injured person or even by God.

Although, as has been pointed out, Dr Menninger does not share Dr Mowrer's inhibition about mentioning forgiveness, neither of them ever refers to the cross, let alone regards it as the only and sufficient ground on which God forgives sins. To recover the concepts of human sin, responsibility, guilt and restitution, without simultaneously recovering confidence in the divine work of atonement, is tragically lopsided. It is diagnosis without prescription, the futility of self-salvation in place of the salvation of God, and the rousing of hope only to dash it to the ground again.

A full acknowledgment of human responsibility and therefore guilt, far from diminishing the dignity of human beings, actually enhances it. It presupposes that men and women, unlike the animals, are morally responsible beings, who know what they are, could be and should be, and do not make excuses for their poor performance. This is the thesis of Harvey Cox in his book *On Not Leaving it to the Snake*. Eve's sin in the Garden of Eden, he urges, was not so much her disobedience in eating the forbidden fruit as her feeble surrender of responsibility which preceded it, not her pride but her sloth. Although Dr Cox is surely mistaken in his refusal to accept the biblical view of sin as essentially pride, and is tainted with the 'man come of age' misconception, he nevertheless makes an important point when he says that 'apathy is the key form of sin in today's world ... For Adam and Eve apathy meant letting a snake tell them what to do. It meant abdicating ... the exercise of dominion and control of the world' (p. xvii). But decision-making belongs to the essence of our humanness. Sin is not only the attempt to be God; it is also the refusal to be man, by shuffling off responsibility for our actions. 'Let's not let any snake tell us what to do' (p. xviii). The commonest defence of the Nazi war criminals was that they were merely following orders. But the court held them responsible all the same.

The Bible takes *sin* seriously because it takes *man* (male and female) seriously. As we have seen, Christians do not deny the fact – in some circumstances – of diminished responsibility, but we affirm that diminished responsibility always entails diminished humanity. To say that somebody 'is not responsible for his actions' is to demean him or her as a human being. It is part of the glory of being human that we are held responsible for our actions. Then, when we also acknowledge our sin and guilt, we receive God's forgiveness, enter into the joy of his salvation, and so become yet more completely human and healthy. What is unhealthy is every wallowing in guilt which does not lead to confession, repentance, faith in Jesus Christ and so forgiveness.

In his justly famous essay 'The Humanitarian Theory of Punishment', C. S. Lewis bemoans the modern tendency to abandon the notion of just retribution and replace it with humanitarian concerns both for the criminal (reform) and for society as a whole (deterrence). For this means, he argues, that every lawbreaker 'is deprived of the rights of a human being. The reason is this. The Humanitarian theory removes from punishment the concept of desert. But the concept of desert is the only connecting link between punishment and justice. It is only as deserved or undeserved that a sentence can be just or unjust.' Again, 'when we cease to consider what the criminal deserves and consider only what will cure him or deter others, we have tacitly removed him from the sphere of justice altogether; instead of a person, a subject of rights, we now have a mere object, a patient, a "case".' By what right may we use force to impose treatment on a criminal, either to cure him or to protect society, unless he *deserves* it?

> To be 'cured' against one's will, and cured of states which we may not regard as disease, is to be put on a level with those who have not yet reached the age of reason or those who never will; to be classed with infants, imbeciles, and domestic animals. But to be punished, however severely, because we have deserved it, because we 'ought to have known better', is to be treated as a human person made in God's image.[18]

God's holiness and wrath

We have considered the seriousness of sin as rebellion against God, the continuing responsibility of men and women for their actions, and their consequent guilt in God's sight and liability to punishment. But can we think of God as 'punishing' or 'judging' evil? Yes, we can and must. Indeed the essential background to the cross is not only the sin, responsibility and guilt of human beings but the just reaction of God to these things, in other words his holiness and wrath.

That God is holy is foundational to biblical religion. So is the corollary that sin is incompatible with his holiness. His eyes are 'too pure to look on evil' and he 'cannot tolerate wrong'. Therefore our sins effectively separate us from him, so that his face is hidden from us and he refuses to listen to our prayers.[19] In consequence, it was clearly understood by the biblical authors that no human being could ever set eyes on God and survive the experience. They might perhaps be permitted to see his 'back' but not his 'face', the sunshine but not the sun.[20] And all those who were granted even a glimpse of his glory were unable to endure the sight. Moses 'hid his face, because he was afraid to look at God'. When Isaiah had his vision of

Yahweh enthroned and exalted, he was overwhelmed by the sense of his uncleanness. When God revealed himself personally to Job, Job's reaction was to 'despise' himself and to 'repent in dust and ashes'. Ezekiel saw only 'the appearance of the likeness of the glory of the LORD', in burning fire and brilliant light, but it was enough to make him fall prostrate to the ground. At a similar vision David also collapsed and fainted, with his face to the ground. As for those who were confronted by the Lord Jesus Christ, even during his earthly life when his glory was veiled, they felt a profound discomfort. For example, he provoked in Peter a sense of his sinfulness and of his unfitness to be in his presence. And when John saw his ascended magnificence, he 'fell at his feet as though dead'.[21]

Closely related to God's holiness is his wrath, which is in fact his holy reaction to evil. We certainly cannot dismiss it by saying that the God of wrath belongs to the Old Testament, while the God of the New Testament is love. For God's love is clearly seen in the Old Testament, as is also his wrath in the New. R. V. G. Tasker correctly wrote: 'It is an axiom of the Bible that there is no incompatibility between these two attributes of the divine nature; and for the most part the great Christian theologians and preachers of the past have endeavoured to be loyal to both sides of the divine self-disclosure.'[22] Yet the concept of an angry God continues to raise problems in Christian minds. How can an emotion, they ask, which Jesus equated with murder, and which Paul declared to be one of the 'acts of the sinful nature' of which we must rid ourselves, possibly be attributed to the all-holy God?[23]

One attempted explanation is associated particularly with the name of C. H. Dodd, and with his commentary on *The Epistle of Paul to the Romans*. He pointed out that, although alongside references to God's love Paul also writes that he 'loved' us, yet alongside references to God's anger he never writes that he 'is angry' with us. In addition to this absence of the verb to 'be angry', the noun *orgē* (anger or wrath) is constantly used by Paul 'in a curiously impersonal way' (p. 21). He refers to 'wrath' or 'the wrath' without specifying whose wrath it is, and thus almost absolutizes it. For example, he writes of 'the day of God's wrath', of how 'law brings wrath', and of how wrath 'has come upon' disbelieving Jews, while believers will be rescued from 'the coming wrath' through Jesus Christ.[24] Dodd's deduction from this evidence was that Paul retained the concept of wrath 'not to describe the attitude of God to man, but to describe an inevitable process of cause and effect in a moral universe' (p. 23).

Professor A. T. Hanson has elaborated C. H. Dodd's thesis in his comprehensive biblical survey *The Wrath of the Lamb*. Drawing attention to 'a marked tendency' among post-exilic biblical authors 'to speak of the divine wrath in a very impersonal manner', he defines it as 'the inevitable process of sin working itself out in history' (pp. 21 and 37). Coming to the New

Testament, he writes: 'there can be little doubt that for Paul the impersonal character of the wrath was important; it relieved him of the necessity of attributing wrath directly to God, it transformed the wrath from an attribute of God into the name for a process, which sinners bring upon themselves.' For wrath is 'wholly impersonal' and 'does not describe an attitude of God but a condition of men' (pp. 69 and 110).

That expression 'relieved him of the necessity' is revealing. It suggests that Paul was uncomfortable with the notion of God's personal wrath, looked round for an escape from having to believe and teach it, and was 'relieved' of his burden by discovering that wrath was not a divine emotion, attribute or attitude, but an impersonal historical process affecting sinners. In this Professor Hanson seems to be projecting on to Paul his own dilemma, for he is candid enough to confess that he has just such an *a priori* problem himself. Towards the end of his discussion he writes: 'If we once allow ourselves to be led into thinking that a reference to the wrath of God in the New Testament means that God is conceived of as angry ... we cannot avoid maintaining that in some sense the Son endured the wrath of the Father, we cannot help thinking in forensic terms, with all the strain and violence to our God-given sense of moral justice that such a theory involves' (pp. 193–194). He seems to be saying that it is in order to overcome these 'appalling difficulties' that he has reinterpreted the wrath of God. To say that Christ bore 'wrath' on the cross, he maintains, means that he 'endured the consequences of men's sins', not their penalty (p. 194).

We must watch our presuppositions, therefore. It is perilous to begin with any *a priori*, even with a 'God-given sense of moral justice' which then shapes our understanding of the cross. It is wiser and safer to begin inductively with a God-given doctrine of the cross, which then shapes our understanding of moral justice. I hope later to demonstrate that it is possible to hold a biblical and Christian concept of 'wrath' and 'propitiation' which, far from contradicting moral justice, both expresses and safeguards it.

The attempts by C. H. Dodd, A. T. Hanson and others to reconstruct 'wrath' as an impersonal process must be declared at least 'not proven'. To be sure, sometimes the word is used without explicit reference to God, and with or without the definite article, but the full phrase 'the wrath of God' is used as well, apparently without embarrassment, by both Paul and John. Without doubt also, Paul taught that God's wrath is being revealed in the present both through the moral deterioration of pagan society and through the state's administration of justice.[25] These processes are not identified with God's wrath, however, but declared to be manifestations of it. The truth that God's wrath (*i.e.* his antagonism to evil) is active through social and legal processes does not necessitate the conclusion that it is itself a purely impersonal continuum of cause and effect. Perhaps the reason for

Paul's adoption of impersonal expressions is not to affirm that God is never angry, but to emphasize that his anger is void of any tinge of personal malice. After all, Paul sometimes refers to *charis* (grace) without referring to God. He can write, for example, of grace 'increasing' and of grace 'reigning' (Rom. 5:20–21). Yet we do not on that account depersonalize grace and convert it into an influence or process. On the contrary, grace is the most personal of all words; grace is God himself acting graciously towards us. And just as *charis* stands for the gracious personal activity of God himself, so *orgē* stands for his equally personal hostility to evil.

How, then, shall we define anger? Writing particularly of righteous human anger, James Denney called it 'the instinctive resentment or reaction of the soul against anything which it regards as wrong or injurious' and 'the vehement repulsion of that which hurts'.[26] Similarly, God's wrath in the words of Leon Morris is his 'personal divine revulsion to evil' and his 'personal vigorous opposition' to it.[27] To speak thus of God's anger is a legitimate anthropomorphism, provided that we recognize it as no more than a rough and ready parallel, since God's anger is absolutely pure, and uncontaminated by those elements which render human anger sinful. Human anger is usually arbitrary and uninhibited; divine anger is always principled and controlled. Our anger tends to be a spasmodic outburst, aroused by pique and seeking revenge; God's is a continuous, settled antagonism, aroused only by evil, and expressed in its condemnation. God is entirely free from personal animosity or vindictiveness; indeed, he is sustained simultaneously with undiminished love for the offender. Charles Cranfield's summary is that God's *orgē* is 'no nightmare of an indiscriminate, uncontrolled, irrational fury, but the wrath of the holy and merciful God called forth by, and directed against, men's *asebeia* (ungodliness) and *adikia* (unrighteousness)'.[28]

What is common to the biblical concepts of the holiness and the wrath of God is the truth that they cannot coexist with sin. God's holiness exposes sin; his wrath opposes it. So sin cannot approach God, and God cannot tolerate sin. Several vivid metaphors are used in Scripture to illustrate this stubborn fact.

The first is *height*. Frequently in the Bible the God of creation and covenant is called 'the Most High God', and is personally addressed in several Psalms as 'Yahweh Most High'.[29] His lofty exaltation expresses both his sovereignty over the nations, the earth and 'all gods',[30] and also his inaccessibility to sinners. True, his throne is called 'the throne of grace' and is encircled by the rainbow of his covenant promise. Nevertheless, it is 'high and exalted' and he himself is 'the high and lofty One', who does not live in man-made temples, since heaven is his throne and the earth his footstool; so sinners should not presume.[31] True again, he condescends to the contrite and lowly, who find security in his shadow. But proud sinners he knows only 'from afar', and he cannot stand the high and haughty looks of the arrogant.[32]

The 'high' exaltation of God is not literal, of course, and was never meant to be taken literally. The recent hue and cry about abandoning a God 'up there' was largely superfluous. The biblical writers used height as a symbol of transcendence, just as we do. It is more expressive than depth. 'The Ground of Being' may speak of ultimate reality to some people, but 'the high and lofty One' conveys God's otherness more explicitly. When thinking of the great and living God, it is better to look up than down, and outside than inside ourselves.

The second picture is that of *distance*. God is not only 'high above' us, but 'far away' from us also. We dare not approach too close. Indeed, many are the biblical injunctions to keep our distance. 'Do not come any closer,' God said to Moses out of the burning bush. So it was that the arrangements for Israel's worship expressed the complementary truths of his nearness to them because of his covenant and his separation from them because of his holiness. Even as he came down to them at Mount Sinai to reveal himself to them, he told Moses to put limits for the people around the base of the mountain and to urge them not to come near. Similarly, when God gave instructions for the building of the Tabernacle (and later the Temple), he both promised to live among his people and yet warned them to erect a curtain before the inner sanctuary as a permanent sign that he was out of reach to sinners. Nobody was permitted to penetrate the veil, on pain of death, except the high priest, and then only once a year on the Day of Atonement, and then only if he took with him the blood of sacrifice.[33] And when the Israelites were about to cross the Jordan into the promised land, they were given this precise command: 'Keep a distance of about a thousand yards between you and the ark; do not go near it' Jos. 3:4). It is against the background of this plain teaching about God's holiness and about the perils of presumption that the story of Uzzah's death must be understood. When the oxen carrying the ark stumbled, he reached out and took hold of it. But 'the LORD's anger burned against Uzzah because of his irreverent act',[34] and he died. Commentators tend to protest at this 'primitive' Old Testament understanding of God's wrath as 'fundamentally an irrational and in the last resort inexplicable thing which broke out with enigmatic, mysterious and primal force' and which bordered closely on 'caprice'.[35] But no, there is nothing inexplicable about God's wrath: its explanation is always the presence of evil in some form or other. Sinners cannot approach the all-holy God with impunity. On the last day, those who have not found refuge and cleansing in Christ will hear those most terrible of all words: 'Depart from me.'[36]

The third and fourth pictures of the holy God's unapproachability to sinners are those of *light* and *fire*: 'God is light', and 'our God is a consuming fire'. Both discourage, indeed inhibit, too close an approach. Bright light is blinding; our eyes cannot endure its brilliance, and in the heat of the fire everything shrivels up and is destroyed. So God 'lives in unapproach-able light'; 'no-one has seen or can see' him. And those who deliberately reject the truth have 'only a fearful expectation of judgment and of raging fire that will consume the enemies of God ... It is a dreadful thing to fall into the hands of the living God.'[37]

The fifth metaphor is the most dramatic of all. It indicates that the holy God's rejection of evil is as decisive as the human body's rejection of poison by *vomiting*. Vomiting is probably the body's most violent of all reactions. The immoral and idolatrous practices of the Canaanites were so disgusting, it is written, that 'the land vomited out its inhabitants', and the Israelites were warned that if they committed the same offences, the land would vomit them out as well. Moreover, what is said to be the land's repudiation of evil was in reality the Lord's. For in the same context he is represented as declaring that he 'abhorred' the Canaanites because of their evil doings. The identical Hebrew word is used of him in relation to the stubborn disobedi-ence of Israel in the wilderness: 'For forty years I was angry with [literally 'loathed'] that generation.' Here too the verb probably alludes to nauseat-ing food, as it does in the statement, 'We detest this miserable food!' Our delicate upbringing may find this earthy metaphor distinctly embarrassing. Yet it continues in the New Testament. When Jesus threatens to 'spit' the lukewarm Laodicean church people out of his mouth, the Greek verb liter-ally means to 'vomit' (*emeō*). The picture may be shocking, but its meaning is clear. God cannot tolerate or 'digest' sin and hypocrisy. They cause him not distaste merely, but disgust. They are so repulsive to him that he must rid himself of them. He must spit or vomit them out.[38]

All five metaphors illustrate the utter incompatibility of divine holiness and human sin. Height and distance, light, fire and vomiting all say that God cannot be in the presence of sin, and that if it approaches him too closely it is repudiated or consumed.

Yet these notions are foreign to modern man. The kind of God who appeals to most people today would be easygoing in his tolerance of our offences. He would be gentle, kind, accommodating, and would have no violent reactions. Unhappily, even in the church we seem to have lost the vision of the majesty of God. There is much shallowness and levity among us. Prophets and psalmists would probably say of us that 'there is no fear of God before their eyes'. In public worship our habit is to slouch or squat; we do not kneel nowadays, let alone prostrate ourselves in humility before God. It is more characteristic of us to clap our hands with joy than to blush with shame or tears. We saunter up to God to claim his patronage and friendship; it does not occur to us that he might send us away. We need to hear again the apostle Peter's sobering words: 'Since you call on a Father who judges each man's work impartially, live your lives ... in reverent fear.'[39] In other words, if we dare to call our Judge our Father, we must beware of presuming on him. It must even be said that our evangelical emphasis on the atonement is dangerous if we come to it too quickly. We learn to appreciate the access to God which Christ has won for us only after we have first seen God's inaccessibility to sinners. We can cry 'Hallelujah' with authenticity only after we have first cried, 'Woe is me, for I am lost.' In Dale's words, 'it is partly because sin does not provoke our own wrath, that we do not believe that sin provokes the wrath of God'.[40]

We must, therefore, hold fast to the biblical revelation of the living God who hates evil, is disgusted and angered by it, and refuses ever to come to terms with it. In consequence, we may be sure that, when he searched in his mercy for some way to forgive, cleanse and accept evil-doers, it was not along the road of moral compromise. It had to be a way which was expressive equally of his love and of his wrath. As Brunner put it, 'where the idea of the wrath of God is ignored, there also will there be no understanding of the central conception of the Gospel: the uniqueness of the revelation in the Mediator'.[41] Similarly, 'only he who knows the greatness of wrath will be mastered by the greatness of mercy'.[42]

All inadequate doctrines of the atonement are due to inadequate doctrines of God and man. If we bring God down to our level and raise ourselves to his, then of course we see no need for a radical salvation, let alone for a radical atonement to secure it. When, on the other hand, we have glimpsed the blinding glory of the holiness of God, and have been so convicted of our sin by the Holy Spirit that we tremble before God and acknowledge what we are, namely 'hell-deserving sinners', then and only then does the necessity of the cross appear so obvious that we are astonished we never saw it before.

The essential background to the cross, therefore, is a balanced understanding of the gravity of sin and the majesty of God. If we diminish either, we thereby diminish the cross. If we reinterpret sin as a lapse instead of a rebellion, and God as indulgent instead of indignant, then naturally the cross appears superfluous. But to dethrone God and enthrone ourselves not only dispenses with the cross; it also degrades both God and man. A biblical view of God and ourselves, however, that is, of our sin and of God's wrath, honours both. It honours human beings by affirming them as responsible for their own actions. It honours God by affirming him as having moral character.

So we come back to where we began this chapter, namely that forgiveness is for God the profoundest of problems. As Bishop B. F. Westcott expressed it, 'nothing superficially seems simpler than forgiveness', whereas 'nothing if we look deeply is more mysterious or more difficult'.[43] Sin and wrath stand in the way. God must not only respect us as the responsible beings we are, but he must also respect himself as the holy God he is. Before the holy God can forgive us, some kind of 'satisfaction' is necessary. That is the subject of our next chapter.

Notes

[1] 'The good God will forgive me; that's his job [or his speciality].' Quoted by S. C. Neill in *Christian Faith Today*, p. 145. James Denney attributed the quotation to Heine in his *Death of Christ*, p. 186.

[2] Mt. 6:12–15; 18:21–35.

[3] Emil Brunner, *Mediator*, p. 448.

[4] P. Carnegie Simpson, *Fact of Christ*, p. 109.

[5] For the emphasis on 'holy love' see P. T. Forsryth in both *Cruciality of the Cross* and *Work of Christ*, William Temple in *Christus Veritas*, e.g. pp. 257, 269, and Emil Brunner in *Mediator*.

[6] Similar statements appear on pp. 28 and 114.

[7] Alec R. Vidler, *Essays in Liberality*, p. 45.

[8] J. N. D. Anderson, *Morality, Law and Grace*, p. 38.

[9] Malcolm Jeeves, R. J. Berry and David Atkinson, *Free to Be Different*, p. 155.

[10] Is. 42:1–3; Mt. 12:15–21. God also distinguishes between sins committed in ignorance and those committed knowingly and deliberately. See, *e.g.*, Lk. 23:34; Acts 3:17; 1 Tim. 1:13.

[11] Dt. 30:15–20; Jos. 24:15.

[12] Jn. 6:44; 5:40.

[13] Emil Brnnner, *Man in Revolt*, p. 257.

[14] Friedrich Nietzsche, *The Anti-Christ*, pp. 167–168.

[15] Je. 6:14; 8:11.

[16] William Glasser, *Reality Therapy*, pp. 5–41.

[17] Karl Menninger, *Whatever Became of Sin?*, p. 180.

[18] C. S. Lewis's essay 'The Humanitarian Theory of Punishment' has been published in several collections of his writings. I have used the text as it appears *in Churchmen Speak*, ed. Philip E. Hughes, pp. 39–44. See also C. S. Lewis's letter to T. S. Eliot on 25 May 1962 in *Letters of C. S. Lewis*, ed. W. H. Lewis, p. 304. He writes: 'It is vile tyranny to submit a man to compulsory "cure" ... unless he *deserves* it.'

[19] Hab. 1:13; Is. 59:1ff.

[20] *E.g.* Ex. 33:20–23; Jdg. 13:22.

[21] Ex. 3:6; Is. 6:1–5; Jb. 42:5–6; Ezk. 1:28; Dn. 10:9; Lk. 5:8; Rev. 1:17.

[22] R. V. G. Tasker, *Biblical Doctrine of the Wrath of God*, p. vii. 'Wrath' is attributed to Jesus in Mk. 3:5 and (perhaps, following some manuscripts) Mk. 1:41.

[23] Mt. 5:21–26; Gal. 5:20; Eph. 4:31; Col. 3:8.

[24] Rom. 2:5; 4:15; 1 Thes. 2:16; 1:10; Rom. 5:9.

[25] Rom. 1:18–32 and 13:1–7. C. H. Dodd refers to these on pp. 26 and 204 of his commentary.

[26] James Denney, article 'Anger', pp. 60–62.

[27] Leon Morris, *Cross in the New Testament*, pp. 190–191. See also his *Apostolic Preaching*, pp. 161–166.

[28] C. E. B. Cranfield, *Romans*, Vol. I, p. 111.

[29] *E.g.* Gn. 14:18–22; Pss. 7:17; 9:2; 21:7; 46:4; 47:2; 57:2; 83:18; 92:8; 93:4; 113:4;

Dn.3:26; 4:2,17, 24–25, 32, 34; 5:18–21; 7:18–27; Ho. 7:16; 11:7; Mi. 6:6.

[30] *E.g.* Pss. 97:9 and 99:2.

[31] Heb. 4:16: Rev. 4:3; Is. 6:1; 57:15; Acts 7:48–49.

[32] Is. 57:15; Pss. 91:1, 9; 138:6; Pr. 21:4; Is. 10:12.

[33] Ex. 3:5; 19:3–25 *(cf.* Heb. 12:18–21); 20:24; 25 – 40, especially 29:45–46; Lv. 16 (*cf.* Heb. 9:7–8).

[34] 2 Sa. 6:6–7. *Cf.* 1 Sa. 6:19. Plain warnings had been given to the Levites, whose responsibility it was to dismantle, carry and reassemble the Tabernacle. See Nu. 1:51, 53.

[35] Johannes Fichtner in his article on *orgē,* pp. 401–402.

[36] *E.g.* Mt. 7:23; 25:41.

[37] 1 Jn. 1:5; Heb.12:29 (*cf.* Dt. 4:24); 1 Tim. 6:16; Heb. 10:27, 31.

[38] Lv. 18:25–28; 20:22–23; Ps. 95:10; Nu. 21:5; Rev.3:16.

[39] 1 Pet. 1:17.

[40] R. W. Dale, *Atonement,* pp. 338–339.

[41] Emil Brunner, *Mediator,* p. 152.

[42] Gustav Stählin in his article on *orgē,* p. 425.

[43] B. F. Westcott, *Historic Faith,* p. 130.

FIVE

Satisfaction for sin

No two words in the theological vocabulary of the cross arouse more criticism than 'satisfaction' and 'substitution'. Yet it is in defence of these words that this chapter and the next are written. In combination ('satisfaction through substitution') they may even seem intolerable. How, people ask, can we possibly believe that God needed some kind of 'satisfaction' before he was prepared to forgive, and that Jesus Christ provided it by enduring as our 'substitute' the punishment we sinners deserved? Are not such notions unworthy of the God of the biblical revelation, a hangover from primitive superstitions, indeed frankly immoral?

Sir Alister Hardy, for example, formerly Linacre Professor of Zoology at Oxford, who was friendly to all kinds of religious experience because he spent a lifetime investigating it, nevertheless expressed his inability to come to terms with the 'crude' beliefs he thought 'so many orthodox churchmen' entertain. In his 1965 Gifford Lectures, published under the title *The Divine Flame,* he asked whether Jesus himself would be a Christian if he were to live today. 'I very much doubt it,' Sir Alister replied. 'I feel certain that he would not have preached to us of a God who would be appeased by the cruel sacrifice of a tortured body ... I cannot accept either the hypothesis that the appalling death of Jesus was a sacrifice in the eyes of God for the sins of the world, or that God, in the shape of his son, tortured himself for our redemption. I can only confess that, in my heart of hearts, I find such religious ideas to be amongst the least attractive in the whole of anthropology. To me they belong to quite a different philosophy – different psychology – from that of the religion that Jesus taught' (p. 218).

Sir Alister Hardy was right to say that Jesus would not (because he did not) explain his death in those crude terms, but wrong to suppose that 'many orthodox churchmen' do so. He caricatured the Christian understanding of the cross in order the more readily to condemn it. The real question is whether we can hold fast to the saving effficacy of the death of Jesus, and to its traditional vocabulary (including 'satisfaction' and 'substitution'), without denigrating God. I believe we can and must. To be sure, neither 'satisfaction' nor 'substitution' is a biblical word, and therefore we need to proceed with great caution. But each is a biblical concept. There is, in fact, a biblical revelation of 'satisfaction through substitution', which is uniquely honouring to God, and which should therefore lie at the very heart of the church's worship and witness. That is why Cranmer included a clear statement of it at the beginning of his Prayer of Consecration (1549). In consequence, for 400 years Anglicans have described Jesus Christ as having made on the cross, by his 'one oblation of himself once offered', 'a full, perfect, and sufficient sacrifice, oblation, and satisfaction for the sins of the whole world'.

But the way in which different theologians have developed the concept of satisfaction depends on their understanding of the obstacles to forgiveness which need first to be removed. What demands are being made which stand in the way until they are satisfied? And who is making them? Is it the devil? Or is it the law, or God's honour or justice, or 'the moral order'? All these have been proposed. I shall argue, however, that the primary 'obstacle' is to be found within God himself. He must 'satisfy himself' in the way of salvation he devises; he cannot save us by contradicting himself.

Satisfying the devil

The notion that it was the devil who made the cross necessary was widespread in the early church.[1] To be sure, Jesus and his apostles did speak of the cross as the means of the devil's overthrow (as we shall consider in a later chapter). But some of the early Fathers were extremely injudicious in the ways in which they represented both the devil's power and how the cross deprived him of it. They all recognized that since the Fall, and on account of it, mankind has been in captivity not only to sin and guilt but to the devil. They thought of him as the lord of sin and death, and as the major tyrant from whom Jesus came to liberate us.

But with the benefit of hindsight we may say that they made three mistakes. First, they credited the devil with more power than he has. Even though they portrayed him as a rebel, a robber and a usurper, they tended to speak as if he had acquired certain 'rights' over man which even God himself was under obligation to satisfy honourably. Gregory of Nazianzus in the fourth century was one of the few early theologians who vigorously repudiated this idea. He called it an 'outrage'.[2]

Secondly, they therefore tended to think of the cross as a divine transaction with the devil; it was the ransom-price demanded by him for the release of his captives, and paid to him in settlement of his rights. This was a very popular belief in the early centuries of the church.

Thirdly, some went further and represented the transaction in terms of a deception. Theologically, they pictured the devil as having over-reached himself. Although in the case of us sinners he 'holds the power of death' (Heb. 2:14), he had no such authority over the sinless Jesus, and in hounding him to death he shed innocent blood. Therefore, having thus abused his power, he was deprived of it. Some Fathers added at this point that he did not altogether realize what he was doing, either because he did not recognize who Jesus was, or because, seeing Godhead in human form, he thought he now had a unique opportunity to overpower him. But he was deceived. Origen was the first to teach unequivocally that the death of Jesus was both the ransom-price paid to the devil and the means of his deception and overthrow. Gregory of Nyssa, a shy Cappadocian scholar of the fourth century, further developed these ideas in his *Great Catechism* or *Catechetical Oration*, using vivid imagery:

> God ... in order to secure that the ransom in our behalf might be easily accepted by him [*sc.* the devil] who required it ... was hidden under the veil of our nature, that so, as with ravenous fish, the hook of the Deity might be gulped down along with the bait of flesh, and thus, life being introduced into the house of death ... (the devil) might vanish.[3]

To us the analogy of the fish-hook is grotesque, as is also Augustine's sermonic use of mousetrap imagery. Peter Lombard was to use it centuries later, affirming that 'the cross was a mousetrap (*muscipula*) baited with the blood of Christ'.[4] To be sure, these theologians may well have developed such pictures as a concession to the popular mind, and the early Fathers saw a certain justice in the idea that he who had deceived the human race into disobedience should himself be deceived into defeat. But to attribute fraudulent action to God is unworthy of him.

What is of permanent value in these theories is first that they took seriously the reality, malevolence and power of the devil (the 'strong man, fully armed' of Lk. 11:21), and secondly that they proclaimed his decisive, objective defeat at the cross for our liberation (by the 'someone stronger' who attacked and overpowered him, Lk. 11:22).[5] Nevertheless, R. W. Dale was not exaggerating when he dubbed them 'intolerable, monstrous and profane'.[6] We deny that the devil has any rights over us which God is obliged to satisfy. Consequently, any notion of Christ's death as a necessary transaction with, let alone deception of, the devil is ruled out.

Satisfying the law

Another way of explaining the moral necessity of the divine 'satisfaction' at the cross has been to exalt the law. Sin is 'lawlessness' (1 Jn. 3:4), a disregard for God's law and a disobedience of it. But the law cannot be broken with impunity. Sinners therefore incur the penalty of their law-breaking. They cannot simply be let off. The law must be upheld, its dignity defended, and its just penalties paid. The law is thereby 'satisfied'.

A popular illustration of this truth is the story of King Darius in the book of Daniel (chapter 6). He appointed 120 satraps to rule Babylonia, and set three administrators over them, of whom Daniel was one. Further, such were Daniel's exceptional qualities and distinguished service that the king planned to promote him over all his colleagues. This aroused their jealousy, and they immediately began to plot his downfall. Watching him like hawks, they tried to find some inconsistency or ineffficiency in his conduct of public affairs, so that they could lodge charges against him. But they failed, 'because he was trustworthy and neither corrupt nor negligent' (v. 4). So they turned their scrutiny upon his private life; their only hope, they reckoned, was to find him guilty of some technical fault in connection with his regular religious devotion. They managed to persuade the king to 'issue an edict and enforce the decree that anyone who prays to any god or man during the next thirty days', except to the king himself, would be thrown into the lions' den (v. 7). With incredible naivety the king fell into their trap. By putting the decree into writing he even made it unalterable, 'in accordance with the laws of the Medes and Persians, which cannot be repealed' (vv. 8–9).

The publication of the decree reached Daniel's ears, but did not lead him to change his routine. On the contrary, he continued three times a day to pray to his God. His practice was to do so kneeling in his upstairs room, whose windows opened towards Jerusalem. There he was visible to passers-by, and there his enemies duly saw him. They went back to the king immediately, and reported David's flagrant breach of the royal decree. 'When the king heard this, he was greatly distressed; he was determined to rescue Daniel and made every effort until sundown to save him' (v. 14). But he could find no solution to the legal problem he had created for himself. His administrators and satraps reminded him that 'according to the law of the Medes and Persians no decree or edict that the king issues can be changed' (v. 15). So Darius reluctantly bowed to the inevitable and gave the order for Daniel to be thrown into the lions' den. The law had triumphed.

Many are the preachers (myself among them) who have used this story to highlight the divine dilemma. Darius respected Daniel and laboured long to find some way of saving him, but the law must take its course and not be tampered with. So God loves us sinners and longs to save us, but cannot do so by violating the law which has justly condemned us. Hence the cross, in which the penalty of the law was paid and its sanctity vindicated. As one recent exponent of this view, I cite Henry Wace, Dean of Canterbury from 1903 to 1924:

> A law which has no sanction, in the technical sense of that expression
> – in other words, a law which can be broken without an adequate
> penalty, is no law at all; and it is inconceivable that God's moral law
> can be violated without entailing consequences of the most terrible
> kind. The mere violation of one of his physical laws may entail,
> whether men intend the violation or not, the most lasting and wide-
> spread misery; and can it reasonably be supposed that the most fla-
> grant and wilful violation of the highest of all laws – those of truth and
> righteousness – should entail no such results?[7]

Again, 'God cannot abolish that moral constitution of things which he has established'. It is true that Dean Wace went on to qualify these state-ments, by reminding us that the moral world is not 'a kind of moral machine in which laws operate as they do in physical nature', and that 'we have to do not simply with an established order but with a living personal-ity, with a living God'. Nevertheless, he refers again to 'the penalty neces-sarily involved in the violation of the Divine law'.[8]

I am not wanting to disagree with this language, and indeed I continue to use it myself. It has, in fact, good scriptural warrant. For Paul quotes Deuteronomy with approval to the effect that every law-breaker is 'cursed', and then goes on to affirm that 'Christ redeemed us from the curse of the law by becoming a curse for us' (Gal. 3:10, 13). If therefore Paul was not afraid to use an impersonal expression like 'the curse of the law', we should not be either.

The fourth-century Latin Fathers such as Ambrose and Hilary regularly expounded the cross in these terms. Going further than Tertullian, who was the first to use the legal terms 'merit' and 'satisfaction' of the Christian's rela-tion to God, they interpreted texts such as Galatians 3:13 in the light of 'the *satisfactio* of the Roman public law, which means the endurance of the law's sentence'.[9] The sixteenth-century Reformers developed this further. They rightly emphasized that Jesus Christ's personal submission to the law was indispensable to our rescue from its condemnation. They also taught that his submission took two forms, his perfect obedience to it in his life and his bearing of its penalty in his death. They called the first his 'active' and the second his 'passive' obedience. These adjectives are inexact, however, since Jesus' obedience unto death on the cross was just as 'active' (*i.e.* voluntary and determined) as his obedient submission to the moral law. His obedience to the Father's will is one and the same, whether in his conduct or mission, his life or death. The value of continuing to speak of Christ's 'double' obedience is that we then distinguish between his fulfilling the demands of the law and his enduring the condemnation of the law. Both kinds of submission to the law were essential to the effficacy of the cross.

Nevertheless, we need to be alert to the dangers of law-language and to the inadequacy of likening God's moral law either to the civil laws of the country or to the physical laws of the universe. True, a part of the glory of a constitutional monarchy is that even the monarch is not above the law but under it, being required to obey its provisions and (if in breach of them) to bear its penalties. Darius provides a good example of this. Yet the decree he made was rash and foolish, since it contained no religious conscience clause, and so led to the punishment of a righteous man for a righteous deed which the king had never intended his decree to make a punishable offence. We cannot think of God as caught in a technical legal muddle of this kind. Nor is it wise to liken God's moral laws to his physical laws and then declare them equally inflexible. For example, 'if you put your hand in the fire it will be burnt, and if you break the ten commandments you will be punished'. There is truth in the analogy, but the concept of mechanical penalties is misleading. It may be true of the laws of nature, even though strictly they are not 'laws' which bind God's action but a description of the normal uniformity of his action which human beings have observed. The real reason why disobedience of God's moral laws brings condemnation is not that God is their prisoner, but that he is their creator.

As R. W. Dale put it, God's connection with the law is 'not a relation of subjection but of identity ... In God the law is *alive;* it reigns on his throne, sways his sceptre, is crowned with his glory'.[10] For the law is the expression of his own moral being, and his moral being is always self-consistent. Nathaniel Dimock captures this truth well in the following words:

> There can be nothing ... in the demands of the law, and the severity of the law, and the condemnation of the law, and the death of the law, and the curse of the law, which is not a reflection (in part) of the perfections of God. Whatever is due to the law is due to the law because it is the law of God, and is due therefore to God himself.[11]

Satisfying God's honour and justice

If the early Greek Fathers represented the cross primarily as a 'satisfaction' of the devil, in the sense of being the ransom-price demanded by him and paid to him, and the early Latin Fathers saw it as a satisfaction of God's law, a fresh approach was made by Anselm of Canterbury in the eleventh century, who in his *Cur Deus Homo?* made a systematic exposition of the cross as a satisfaction of God's offended honour. His book was 'epoch-making in the whole history of our doctrine', wrote R. S. Franks, 'in that it for the first time in a thoroughgoing and consistent way applies to the elucidation of the subject the conceptions of satisfaction and merit'.[12] James Denney went further and called it 'the truest and greatest book on the atonement that has ever been written'.[13]

Anselm was a godly Italian, who first settled in Normandy, and then in 1093, following the Norman Conquest, was appointed Archbishop of Canterbury. He has been described as the first representative of medieval 'scholasticism', which was an attempt to reconcile philosophy and theology, Aristotelian logic and biblical revelation. Although he included in his writings a number of biblical quotations, however, and referred to Holy Scripture as 'a firm foundation', his overriding concern was to be 'agreeable to reason' (ii.xi). As his imaginary interlocutor Boso put it, 'the way by which you lead me is so walled in by reasoning on each side that I do not seem able to turn out of it either to the right hand or the left' (ii.ix).

In *Cur Deus Homo?*, Anselm's great treatise on the relationship between the incarnation and the atonement, he agrees that the devil needed to be overcome, but rejects the patristic ransom-theories on the ground that 'God owed nothing to the devil but punishment' (ii.xix). Instead, man owed something to God, and this is the debt which needed to be repaid. For Anselm defines sin as 'not rendering to God what is his due' (i.xi), namely the submission of our entire will to his. To sin is, therefore, to 'take away from God what is his own', which means to steal from him and so to dishonour him. If anybody imagines that God can simply forgive us in the same way that we are to forgive others, he has not yet considered the seriousness of sin (i.xxi). Being an inexcusable disobedience of God's known will, sin dishonours and insults him, and 'nothing is less tolerable ... than that the creature should take away from the Creator the honour due to him, and not repay what he takes away' (i.xiii). God cannot overlook this. 'It is not proper for God to pass by sin thus unpunished' (i.xii). It is more than improper; it is impossible. 'If it is not becoming to God to do anything unjustly or irregularly, it is not within the scope of his liberty or kindness or will to let go unpunished the sinner who does not repay to God what he has taken away' (i.xii). 'God upholds nothing more justly than he doth the honour of his own dignity' (i.xiii).

So what can be done? If we are ever to be forgiven, we must repay what we owe. Yet we are incapable of doing this, either for ourselves or for other people. Our present obedience and good works cannot make satisfaction for our sins, since these are required of us anyway. So we cannot save ourselves. Nor can any other human being save us, since 'one who is a sinner cannot justify another sinner' (i.xxiii). Hence the dilemma with which Book i ends: 'man the sinner owes to God, on account of sin, what he cannot repay, and unless he repays it he cannot be saved' (i.xxv).

Near the beginning of Book ii, the only possible way out of the human dilemma is unfolded: 'there is no-one ... who *can* make this satisfaction except God himself ... But no-one ought to make it except man; otherwise man does not make satisfaction.' Therefore, 'it is necessary that one who is God-man should make it' (ii.vi). A being who is God and not man, or man and not God, or a mixture of both and therefore neither man nor God, would not qualify. 'It is needful that the very same Person who is to make this satisfaction be perfect God and perfect man, since no-one *can* do it except one who is truly God, and no-one *ought* to do it except one who is truly man' (ii.vii). This leads Anselm to introduce Christ. He was (and is) a unique Person, since in him 'God the Word and man meet' (ii.ix). He also performed a unique work, for he gave himself up to death – not as a debt (since he was sinless and therefore under no obligation to die) but freely for the honour of God. It was also reasonable that man, 'who by sinning stole himself away from God as completely as he possibly could do so, should, in making satisfaction, surrender himself to God as completely as he can do so', namely by his voluntary self-offering unto death. Serious as human sin is, yet the life of the God-man was so good, so exalted and so precious that its offering in death 'outweighs the number and greatness of all sins' (ii.xiv), and due reparation has been made to the offended honour of God.

The greatest merits of Anselm's exposition are that he perceived clearly the extreme gravity of sin (as a wilful rebellion against God in which the creature affronts the majesty of his Creator), the unchanging holiness of God (as unable to condone any violation of his honour), and the unique perfections of Christ (as the God-man who voluntarily gave himself up to death for us). In some places, however, his scholastic reasoning took him beyond the boundaries of the biblical revelation, as when he speculated whether Christ's payment was exactly what sinners owed or more, and whether the number of redeemed humans would exceed the number of fallen angels. Moreover, his whole presentation reflects the feudal culture of his age, in which society was rigidly stratified, each person stood on the dignity which had been accorded him, the 'proper' or 'becoming' conduct of inferiors to superiors (and especially to the king) was laid down, breaches of this code were punished, and all debts must be honourably discharged.

When God is portrayed, however, in terms reminiscent of a feudal over-lord who demands honour and punishes dishonour, it is questionable whether this picture adequately expresses the 'honour' which is indeed due to God alone. We must certainly remain dissatisfied whenever the atone-ment is presented as a necessary satisfaction either of God 'law' or of God's 'honour' in so far as these are objectified as existing in some way apart from him.

It was during the twelfth century that three distinct interpretations of the death of Christ were clarified. Anselm (died 1109) as we have seen, emphasized the objective satisfaction to the honour of God which had been paid by the God-man Jesus, while his younger contemporary Peter Abelard of Paris (died 1142) (Abelard's teaching is considered in greater detail on pp. 200ff.) emphasized the subjective moral influence which the cross has on believers. Meanwhile, Bernard of Clairvaux (died 1153), the mystic theologian, continued to teach that a ransom-price had been paid to the devil. It was the Anselmian view, however, which prevailed, for careful students of Scripture were unable to eliminate from it the notion of satisfaction. So the 'scholastics' or 'schoolmen' (so-called because they taught in the recently founded medieval Eurpean 'schools', *i.e.* universities) further developed Anselm's position – both the 'Thomists' who were Dominicans looking to Thomas Aquinas (died 1274) and the 'Scotists' who were Franciscans looking to Duns Scotus (died 1308). Although these two groups of 'schoolmen' differed in details, they both taught that the demands of divine justice were satisfied by Christ's cross.

With the Reformation, and the Reformers' emphasis on justification, it is understandable that they stressed the justice of God and the impossibility of a way of salvation which did not satisfy his justice. For, as Calvin wrote in the *Institutes,* 'there is a perpetual and irreconcilable disagreement between righteousness and unrighteousness' (II.xvi.3). It was necessary therefore for Christ 'to undergo the severity of God's vengeance, to appease his wrath and satisfy his just judgment'.[14] Thomas Cranmer in his 'Homily of Salvation' explained that three things had to go together in our justification: on God's part 'his great mercy and grace', on Christ's part 'the satisfaction of God's justice', and on our part 'true and lively faith'. He concluded the first part of the homily: 'It pleased our heavenly Father, of his infinite mercy, without any our desert or deserving, to prepare for us the most precious jewels of Christ's body and blood, whereby our ransom might be fully paid, the law fulfilled, and his justice fully satisfied.'[15]

This same teaching can be found in Luther's works. After his death, however, the Protestant 'scholastics' systematized the doctrine of the death of Christ into a double satisfaction, namely of God's law and of God's justice. God's law was satisfied by Christ's perfect obedience in his life, and God's justice by his perfect sacrifice for sin, bearing its penalty in his death. This is rather too neat a formulation, however. Since God's law is an expression of his justice, the two cannot be precisely separated.

Then was God's concern to satisfy the 'moral order'? This concept, like that of 'law', is an expression of the justice or moral character of God. It is perhaps at once more general and more broad than 'law', since it embraces not only moral standards but a built-in system of sanctions. It rests on the belief that the holy God who rules the world rules it morally. He has established an order in which the good is to be approved and rewarded, while the evil is to be condemned and punished. To approve the evil or to condemn the good would subvert this moral order. In such a world the unprincipled forgiveness of sins would be equally subversive.

The beginnings of this concept in relation to the death of Christ may be seen in Hugo Grotius (died 1645), the Dutch lawyer and statesman, who deplored Christian controversies and divisions, and dreamt of a reunited, reformed Christendom. His understanding of the atonement was something of a compromise between Anselm and Abelard. Sometimes he taught an almost Abelardian view of the subjective influence of the cross, which leads sinners to repentance and so enables God to forgive them. Usually, however, he preserved the objectivity of the cross, and saw it as a satisfaction of God's justice. In addition, he had a jurist's concern for public morality, both the preventing of crime and the upholding of law. He saw God neither as the offended party, nor as creditor, nor even as judge, but as the Supreme Moral Governor of the world. So public justice was more important to him than retributive justice, and it was this in particular which he believed was satisfied at the cross. To be sure, Christ died for our sins in our place. But what part or office did God occupy in this? he asked. 'The right of inflicting punishment does not belong to the injured party as injured' but rather 'to the ruler as ruler'.[16] Again, 'to inflict punishment ... is only the prerogative of the ruler as such ... for example, of a father in a family, of a king in a state, of God in the universe' (p. 51). So Grotius developed his 'rectoral' or 'governmental' interpretation of the cross. He taught that God ordained it 'for the order of things and for the authority of his own law' (p. 137). He was preoccupied with the public vindication of God's justice. 'God was unwilling to pass over so many sins, and so great sins, without a distinguished example', that is, of his serious displeasure with sin (p. 106). 'God has ... most weighty reasons for punishing', but chief among them in Grotius' mind was the resolve to uphold the established order of law, so that we might 'estimate the magnitude and multitude of sins' (p. 107).

Several twentieth-century theologians have taken up Grotius' vision of God as 'the moral governor of the world' and developed it further in relation to the atonement. P. T. Forsyth, for example, wrote of 'this cosmic order of holiness', and added: 'God's moral order demands atonement wherever moral ideas are taken with final seriousness, and man's conscience re-echoes the demand.'[17]

Another example is B. B. Warfield, who drew attention to the universal sense of guilt among human beings. It is a 'deep moral self-condemnation which is present as a primary factor in all truly religious experience. It cries out for satisfaction. No moral deduction can persuade it that forgiveness of sins is a necessary element in the moral order of the world. It knows on the contrary that indiscriminate forgiveness of sin would be precisely the subversion of the moral order of the world .... It cries out for expiation.'[18]

But the most striking statement of the inviolability of the moral order has been made by Emil Brunner in his famous book *The Mediator*. Sin is more than 'an attack on God's honour', he wrote (p. 444); it is an assault on the moral world order which is an expression of God's moral will.

> The law of his divine Being, on which all the law and order in the world is based ... the logical and reliable character of all that happens, the validity of all standards, of all intellectual, legal and moral order, the Law itself, in its most profound meaning, demands the divine reaction, the divine concern about sin, the divine resistance to this rebellion and this breach of order ... If this were not true, then there would be no seriousness in the world at all; there would be no meaning in anything, no order, no stability; the world order would fall into ruins; chaos and desolation would be supreme. All order in the world depends upon the inviolability of his [*sc.* God's] honour, upon the certitude that those who rebel against him will be punished (pp. 444–445).

Later Brunner drew an analogy between natural law and moral law, asserting that neither can be infringed with impunity. Forgiveness without atonement would be a contravention of logic, law and order more serious and vast 'than the suspension of the laws of nature' (p. 447). How is forgiveness possible, then, if 'punishment is the expression of the divine law and order, of the inviolability of the divine order of the world' (p. 449)? Since law is 'the expression of the will of the Lawgiver, of the personal God' (p. 459), then, if it is broken, it cannot and does not heal by itself. Sin has caused a 'break in the world order', a disorder so deep-seated that reparation or restitution is necessary, that is, 'Atonement' (p. 485).

God satisfying himself

Here, then, are five ways in which theologians have expressed their sense of what is necessary before God is able to forgive sinners. One speaks of the overthrow of the devil by 'satisfying' his demands, others of 'satisfying' God's law, honour or justice, and the last of 'satisfying the moral order of the world'. In differing degrees all these formulations are true. The limitation they share is that, unless they are very carefully stated, they represent God as being subordinate to something outside and above himself which controls his actions, to which he is accountable, and from which he cannot free himself. 'Satisfaction' is an appropriate word, providing we realize that it is he himself in his inner being who needs to be satisfied, and not something external to himself. Talk of law, honour, justice and the moral order is true only in so far as these are seen as expressions of God's own character. Atonement is a 'necessity' because it 'arises from within God himself'.[19]

To be sure, 'self-satisfaction' in fallen human beings is a particularly unpleasant phenomenon, whether it refers to the satisfying of our instincts and passions or to our complacency. Since we are tainted and twisted with selfishness, to say 'I must satisfy myself' lacks self-control, while to say 'I am satisfied with myself' lacks humility. But there is no lack of self-control or humility in God, since he is perfect in all his thoughts and desires. To say that he must 'satisfy himself' means that he must be himself and act according to the perfection of his nature or 'name'. The necessity of 'satisfaction' for God, therefore, is not found in anything outside himself but within himself, in his own immutable character. It is an inherent or intrinsic necessity. The law to which he must conform, which he must satisfy, is the law of his own being. Negatively, he 'cannot disown himself' (2 Tim. 2:13); he cannot contradict himself; he 'never lies' (Tit. 1:2, RSV: *apseudēs*, 'free from all deceit'), for the simple reason that 'it is impossible for God to lie' (Heb. 6:18); he is never arbitrary, unpredictable or capricious; he says, 'I will not ... be false to my faithfulness' (Ps. 89:33, RSV). Positively, he is 'a faithful God who does no wrong' (Dt. 32:4). That is, he is true to himself; he is always invariably himself.

Scripture has several ways of drawing attention to God's self-consistency, and in particular of emphasizing that when he is obliged to judge sinners, he does it because he must, if he is to remain true to himself.

The first example is *the language of provocation*. Yahweh is described (and indeed describes himself) as 'provoked' by Israel's idolatry to anger or jealousy or both. For example, 'they made him jealous with their foreign gods and angered him with their detestable idols'.[20] The exilic prophets, such as Jeremiah and Ezekiel, were constantly employing this vocabulary.[21] They did not mean that Yahweh was irritated or exasperated, or that Israel's behaviour had been so 'provocative' that his patience had run out. No, the language of provocation expresses the inevitable reaction of God's perfect nature to evil. It indicates that there is within God a holy intolerance of idolatry, immorality and injustice. Wherever these occur, they act as stimuli to trigger his response of anger or indignation. He is never provoked without reason. It is evil alone which provokes him, and necessarily so since God must be (and behave like) God. If evil did *not* provoke him to anger he would forfeit our respect, for he would no longer be God.

Secondly, there is *the language of burning*. Under this heading may be mentioned the verbs which depict God's anger as a fire and speak of its 'kindling', 'burning', 'quenching' and 'consuming'. It is true that human beings are also said to 'burn with anger'.[22] But this vocabulary is much more frequently applied in the Old Testament to Yahweh, who 'burns with anger' whenever he sees his people disobeying his law and breaking his covenant.[23] In fact, it is precisely when he is 'provoked' to anger that he is said to 'burn' with it,[24] or his anger is said to 'break out and burn like fire'.[25] In consequence, we read of 'the fire of his anger' or 'the fire of his jealousy'; indeed God himself unites them by referring to 'the fire of my jealous anger'.[26] As with the provocation of Yahweh to anger, so with the fire of his anger, a certain inevitability is implied. In the dry heat of a Palestinian summer fires were easily kindled. It was the same with Yahweh's anger. Never from caprice, however; always only in response to evil. Nor was his anger ever uncontrolled. On the contrary, in the early years of Israel's national life 'time after time he restrained his anger and did not stir up his full wrath'.[27] But when he 'could no longer endure' his people's stubborn rebellion against him, he said: 'The time has come for me to act. I will not hold back; I will not have pity, nor will I relent. You will be judged according to your conduct and your actions, declares the Sovereign Lord.'[28]

If a fire was easy to kindle during the Palestinian dry season, it was equally difficult to put out. So with God's anger. Once righteously aroused, he 'did not turn away from the heat of his fierce anger, which burned against Judah'. Once kindled, it was not readily 'quenched'.[29] Instead, when Yahweh's anger 'burned' against people, it 'consumed' them. That is to say, as fire leads to destruction, so Yahweh's anger leads to judgment. For Yahweh is 'a consuming fire'.[30] The fire of his anger was 'quenched', and so 'subsided' or 'ceased', only when the judgment was complete,[31] or when a radical regeneration had taken place, issuing in social justice.[32]

The imagery of fire endorses what is taught by the vocabulary of provocation. There is something in God's essential moral being which is 'provoked' by evil, and which is 'ignited' by it, proceeding to 'burn' until the evil is 'consumed'.

Thirdly, there is *the language of satisfaction itself*. A cluster of words seems to affirm the truth that God must be himself, that what is inside him must come out, and that the demands of his own nature and character must be met by appropriate action on his part. The chief word is *kālah*, which is used particularly by Ezekiel in relation to God's anger. It means 'to be complete, at an end, finished, accomplished, spent'. It occurs in a variety of contexts in the Old Testament, nearly always to indicate the 'end' of something, either because it has been destroyed, or because it has been finished in some other way. Time, work and life all have an end. Tears are exhausted by weeping, water used up and grass dried up in drought, and our physical strength is spent. So through Ezekiel Yahweh warns Judah that he is about to 'accomplish' (AV), 'satisfy' (RSV) or 'spend' (NIV) his anger 'upon' or 'against' them.[33] They have refused to listen to him and have persisted in their idolatry. So now at last 'the time has come, the day is near … I am about to pour out my wrath on you and spend my anger against you' (Ezk. 7:7–8). It is significant that the 'pouring out' and the 'spending' go together, for what is poured out cannot be gathered again, and what is spent is finished. The same two images are coupled in Lamentations 4:11, 'The LORD has given full vent [*kālah*] to his wrath; he has poured out his fierce anger.' Indeed, only when Yahweh's wrath is 'spent' does it 'cease'. The same concept of inner necessity is implied by these verbs. What exists within Yahweh must be expressed; and what is expressed must be completely 'spent' or 'satisfied'.

To sum up, God is 'provoked' to jealous anger over his people by their sins. Once kindled, his anger 'burns' and is not easily quenched. He 'unleashes' it, 'pours' it out, 'spends' it. This threefold vocabulary vividly portrays God's judgment as arising from within him, out of his holy character, as wholly consonant with it, and therefore as inevitable.

So far the picture has been one-sided, however. Because of the history of Israel's apostasy, the prophets concentrated on Yahweh's anger and consequent judgment. But the reason why this threat of national destruction is so poignant is that it was uttered against the background of God's love for Israel, his choice of them and his covenant with them. This special relationship with Israel, which God had initiated and sustained, and which he promised to renew, had also arisen out of his character. He had acted 'for the sake of his name'. He had not set his love upon Israel and chosen them because they were more numerous than other peoples, for they were the fewest. No, he had set his love upon them only because he loved them (Dt. 7:7–8). No explanation of his love for them could be given, except his love for them.

So there is a fourth way in which Scripture emphasizes the self-consistency of God, namely by using *the language of the Name*. God always acts 'according to his name'. To be sure, this is not the only criterion of his activity. He also deals with us 'according to our works'. By no means invariably, however. Indeed, if he did, we would be destroyed. So 'he does not treat us as our sins deserve or repay us according to our iniquities'.[34] For he is 'the compassionate and gracious God, slow to anger, abounding in love and faithfulness' (Ex. 34:6). Although he does not always treat us 'according to our works', however, he always does 'according to his name', that is, in a manner consistent with his revealed nature.[35] The contrast is deliberately drawn in Ezekiel 20:44: 'You will know that I am the LORD, when I deal with you for my name's sake and not according to your evil ways and your corrupt practices, O house of Israel, declares the Sovereign LORD.'

Jeremiah 14 expresses with emphatic thoroughness the recognition that Yahweh is and always will be true to his name, that is to himself. The situation was one of devastating drought: the cisterns were empty, the ground cracked, the farmers dismayed and the animals disorientated (vv. 1–6). In their extremity Israel cried to God: 'Although our sins testify against us, O LORD, do something for the sake of your name' (v. 7). In other words, 'although we cannot appeal to you to act on the ground of who *we* are, we can and do on the ground of who *you* are'. Israel remembered that they were God's chosen people, and begged him to act in a way which would be consistent with his gracious covenant and steadfast character, for, they added, 'we bear your name' (vv. 8–9). In contrast to the pseudo-prophets, who were preaching a lopsided message of peace without judgment (vv. 13–16), Jeremiah prophesied 'sword, famine and plague' (v. 12). But he also looked beyond judgment to restoration, convinced that Yahweh would act, he said to him, 'for the sake of your name' (v. 21).

The same theme was further developed in Ezekiel 36. There Yahweh promised his people restoration after judgment, but was disconcertingly candid about his reasons. 'It is not for your sake, O house of Israel, that I am going to do these things, but for the sake of my holy name' (v. 22). They had profaned it, caused it to be despised and even blasphemed by the nations. But Yahweh would take pity on his great name and once more demonstrate its holiness, its uniqueness, before the world. For then the nations would know that he was the Lord, the Living One (vv. 21, 23). When God thus acts 'for the sake of his name', he is not just protecting it from misrepresentation; he is determining to be true to it. His concern is less for his reputation than for his consistency.

In the light of all this biblical material about the divine self-consistency, we can understand why it is impossible for *God* to do what Christ commanded *us* to do. He told us to 'deny ourselves', but 'God cannot deny himself'.[36] Why is that? Why is it that God will not do, indeed cannot do, what he tells us to do? It is because God is God and not man, let alone fallen man. We have to deny or disown everything within us which is false to our true humanity. But there is nothing in God which is incompatible with his true deity, and therefore nothing to deny. It is in order to be our true selves that we have to deny ourselves; it is because God is never other than his true self that he cannot and will not deny himself. He can empty himself of his rightful glory and humble himself to serve. Indeed, it is precisely this that he has done in Christ (Phil. 2:7–8). But he cannot repudiate any part of himself, because he is perfect. He cannot contradict himself. This is his integrity. As for us, we are constantly aware of our human inconsistencies; they usually arouse a comment. 'It's so uncharacteristic of him', we say, or 'You are not yourself today', or 'I've come to expect something better from you.' But can you imagine saying such things to or about God? He is always himself and never inconsistent. If he were ever to behave 'uncharacteristically', in a way that is out of character with himself, he would cease to be God, and the world would be thrown into moral confusion. No, God is

God; he never deviates one iota, even one tiny hair's breadth, from being entirely himself.

The holy love of God

What has this to do with the atonement? Just that the way God chooses to forgive sinners and reconcile them to himself must, first and foremost, be fully consistent with his own character. It is not only that he must overthrow and disarm the devil in order to rescue his captives. It is not even only that he must satisfy his law, his honour, his justice or the moral order: it is that he must satisfy himself. Those other formulations rightly insist that at least one expression of himself must be satisfied, either his law or honour or justice or moral order; the merit of this further formulation is that it insists on the satisfaction of God himself in *every* aspect of his being, including both his justice and his love.

But when we thus distinguish between the attributes of God, and set one over against another, and even refer to a divine 'problem' or 'dilemma' on account of this conflict, are we not in danger of going beyond Scripture? Was P. T. Forsyth correct in writing that 'there is nothing in the Bible about the strife of attributes'?[37] I do not think he was. To be sure, talk about 'strife' or 'conflict' in God is very anthropomorphic language. But then the Bible is not afraid of anthropomorphisms. All parents know the costliness of love, and what it means to be 'torn apart' by conflicting emotions, especially when there is a need to punish the children. Perhaps the boldest of all human models of God in Scripture is the pain of parenthood which is attributed to him in Hosea, chapter 11. He refers to Israel as his 'child', his 'son' (v. 1), whom he had taught to walk, taking him in his arms (v. 3) and bending down to feed him (v. 4). Yet his son proved wayward and did not recognize his Father's tender love. Israel was determined to turn from him in rebellion (vv. 5–7). He therefore deserved to be punished. But can his own father bring himself to punish him? So Yahweh soliloquizes:

> How can I give you up, Ephraim?
> How can I hand you over, Israel?
> How can I treat you like Admah?
> How can I make you like Zeboiim?
> My heart is changed within me;
> all my compassion is aroused.
> I will not carry out my fierce anger,
> nor devastate Ephraim again.
> For I am God, and not man
> the Holy One among you.
> I will not come in wrath (Ho. 11:8–9).

Here surely is a conflict of emotions, a strife of attributes, within God. The four questions beginning with the words 'How can 1 ...?' bear witness to a struggle between what Yahweh *ought* to do because of his righteousness and what he *cannot* do because of his love. And what is the 'change of heart' within him but an inner tension between his 'compassion' and his 'fierce anger'?

The Bible includes a number of other phrases which in different ways express this 'duality' within God. He is 'the compassionate and gracious God ... Yet he does not leave the guilty unpunished'; in him 'love and faithfulness meet together; righteousness and peace kiss each other'; he announces himself as 'a righteous God and a Saviour', besides whom there is no other; and in wrath he remembers mercy. John describes the Word made flesh, the Father's one and only Son, as 'full of grace and truth'; and Paul, contemplating God's dealings with both Jews and Gentiles, invites us to consider 'the kindness and sternness of God'. In relation to the cross and to salvation Paul also writes of God demonstrating his justice 'so as to be just and the one who justifies the man who has faith in Jesus', and he finds nothing anomalous about juxtaposing references to God's 'wrath' and God's 'love', while John assures us that, if we confess our sins, God will be 'faithful and just' to forgive us.[38] Here are nine couplets, in each of which two complementary truths about God are brought together, as if to remind us that we must beware of speaking of one aspect of God's character without remembering its counterpart.

Emil Brunner in *The Mediator* did not hesitate to write of God's 'dual nature' as 'the central mystery of the Christian revelation' (p. 519). For 'God is not simply Love. The nature of God cannot be exhaustively stated in one single word' (pp. 281–282). Indeed, modern opposition to forensic language in relation to the cross is mainly 'due to the fact that the idea of the Divine Holiness has been swallowed up in that of the Divine love; this means that the biblical idea of God, in which the decisive element is this twofold nature of holiness and love, is being replaced by the modern, unilateral, monistic idea of God' (p. 467). Yet 'the dualism of holiness and love, ... of mercy and wrath cannot be dissolved, changed into *one* synthetic conception, without at the same time destroying the seriousness of the biblical knowledge of God, the reality and the mystery of revelation and atonement ... Here arises the "dialectic" of all genuine Christian theology, which simply aims at expressing in terms of thought the indissoluble nature of this dualism' (p. 519, footnote). So then, the cross of Christ 'is the event in which God makes known his holiness and his love simultaneously, in one event, in an absolute manner' (p. 450). 'The cross is the only place where the loving, forgiving merciful God is revealed in such a way that we perceive that his holiness and his love are equally infinite' (p. 470). In fact, 'the objective aspect of the atonement ... may be summed up thus: it consists in the combination of inflexible righteousness, with its penalties, and transcendent love' (p. 520).

At the same time, we must never think of this duality within God's being as irreconcilable. For God is not at odds with himself, however much it may appear to us that he is. He is 'the God of peace', of inner tranquillity, not turmoil. True, we find it difficult to hold in our minds simultaneously the images of God as the Judge who must punish evil-doers and of the Lover who must find a way to forgive them. Yet he is both, and at the same time. In the words of G. C. Berkouwer, 'in the cross of Christ God's justice and love are *simultaneously* revealed',[39] while Calvin, echoing Augustine, was even bolder. He wrote of God that 'in a marvellous and divine way he loved us even when he hated us'.[40] Indeed, the two are more than simultaneous, they are identical, or at least alternative expressions of the same reality. For 'the wrath of God is the love of God', Brunner wrote in a daring sentence, 'in the form in which the man who has turned away from God and turned against God experiences it'.[41]

One theologian who has struggled with this tension is P. T. Forsyth, who coined – or at least popularized – the expression 'the holy love of God'.

> Christianity [he wrote] is concerned with God's holiness before all else, which issues to man as love ... This starting-point of the supreme holiness of God's love, rather than its pity, sympathy or affection, is the watershed between the Gospel and ... theological liberalism ... My point of departure is that Christ's first concern and revelation was not simply the forgiving love of God, but the holiness of such love.

Again,

> If we spoke less about God's love and more about his holiness, more about his judgment, we should say much more when we did speak of his love.[42]

Yet again,

> Without a holy God there would be no problem of atonement. It is the holiness of God's love that necessitates the atoning cross ...[43]

This vision of God's holy love will deliver us from caricatures of him. We must picture him neither as an indulgent God who compromises his holiness in order to spare and spoil us, nor as a harsh, vindictive God who suppresses his love in order to crush and destroy us. How then can God express his holiness without consuming us, and his love without condoning our sins? How can God satisfy his holy love? How can he save us and satisfy *himself* simultaneously? We reply at this point only that, in order to satisfy himself, he sacrificed – indeed substituted – himself for us. What that meant will be our concern in the next chapter to understand.

> Beneath the cross of Jesus
> I fain would take my stand
> The shadow of a mighty rock
> Within a weary land ....
>
> O safe and happy shelter!
> O refuge tried and sweet!
> O trysting-place, where heaven's love
> And heaven's justice meet!

Notes

[1] For historical surveys of the different theories of the atonement see H. E. W. Turner, *Patristic Doctrine*, J. K Mozley, *Doctrine of the Atonement*, Robert Mackintosh, *Historic Theories* and Robert S. Franks, *History of the Doctrine of the Work of Christ.*

[2] *Orat.* xlv. 22.

[3] *Catechetical Oration* 22 – 26. See A. S. Dunstone, *Atonement in Gregory of Nyssa*, p. 15, footnote 7.

[4] *Sentences*, Liber III, Distinctio xix.1.

[5] Nathaniel Dimock, while not accepting 'the unguarded language or misleading statements of *some* of the Fathers', since God does not trade with the devil, nevertheless believes that in over-reaction 'undue condemnation has been bestowed on the Patristic view of this subject'. He therefore salvages some biblical truths from it in his Additional Note B, 'on Christ's Redemption as viewed in relation to the dominion and works of the devil'. See his *Doctrine of the Death of Christ*, pp. 121–136.

[6] R. W. Dale, *Atonement*, p. 277.

[7] Henry Wace, *Sacrifice of Christ*, p. 16.

[8] *Ibid.*, pp. 22, 28–29, 36.

[9] Robert S. Franks, *Work of Christ*, p. 135.

[10] R. W. Dale, *Atonement*, p. 372.

[11] Nathaniel Dimock, *Doctrine of the Death of Christ*, p. 32, footnote 1.

[12] Robert S. Franks, *Work of Christ*, p. 126.

[13] James Denney, *Atonement*, p. 116.

[14] *Institutes*, II.xvi.10. *Cf.* II.xii.3.

[15] Thomas Cranmer, *First Book of Homilies*, p. 130. The Westminster Confession of Faith (1647) also declares that the Lord Jesus, by his perfect obedience and self-sacrifice, has 'fully satisfied the justice of his Father' (VIII.5). Indeed, it was 'a proper, real, and full satisfaction to his Father's justice' on behalf of the justified (XI.3).

[16] Hugo Grotius, *Defence of the Catholic Faith*, p. 57.

[17] P. T. Forsyth, *Cruciality of the Cross*, pp. 137–138. See also his *Work of Christ*, pp. 122—129.

[18] B. B. Warfield, *Person and Work*, p. 292.

[19] Ronald S. Wallace, *Atoning Death*, p. 113.

[20] Dt. 32:16, 21. *Cf.* Jdg. 2:12; 1 Ki. 15:30; 21:22; 2 Ki. 17:17; 22:17; Ps. 78:58.

[21] *E.g.* Je. 32:30–32; Ezk. 8:17; Ho. 12:14.

[22] *E.g.* Gn. 39:19; Ex. 32:19;1 Sa. 11:6; 2 Sa. 12:5; Est. 7:10.

[23] *E.g.* Jos. 7:1; 23:16; Jdg. 3:8; 2 Sa. 24:1; 2 Ki. 13:3; 22:13; Ho. 8:5.

[24] *E.g.* Dt. 29:27–28; 2 Ki. 22:17; Ps. 79:5.

[25] *E.g.* Je. 4:4; 21:12.

[26] *E.g.* Ezk. 36:5-6; 38:19; Zp. 1:18; 3:8.

[27] Ps. 78:38. *Cf.* Is. 48:9; La. 3:22; and in the New Testament Rom. 2:4 and 2 Pet. 3:9.

[28] Je. 44:22; Ezk. 24:13–14; *cf.* Ex. 32:10.

[29] 2 Ki. 23:26; 22:17; 2 Ch. 34:25; Je. 21:12.

[30] Dt. 4:24, quoted in Heb. 12:29. Some examples of the portrayal of God's judgment as a devouring fire are: Nu. 11:1; Dt. 6:15; Ps. 59:13; Is. 10:17; 30:27; La. 2:3; Ezk. 22:31; Zp. 1:18.

[31] *E.g.* Jos. 7:26; Ezk. 5:13; 16:42; 21:17.

[32] *E.g.* Je. 4:4; 21:12.

[33] Ezk. 5:13; 6:12; 7:8; 13:15; 20:8, 21.

[34] Ps. 103:10. For God's forbearance, the restraining of his anger and the delaying of his judgment, see also Ne. 9:31; La. 3:22; Rom. 2:4–16; 3:25; 2 Pet. 3:9. Contrast, for example, Ezk. 7:8–9, 27.

[35] *E.g.* Pss. 23:3; 143:11.

[36] Mk. 8:34; 2 Tim. 2:13, RSV.

[37] P. T. Forsyth, *The Work of Christ*, p. 118.

[38] Ex. 34:6–7; Ps. 85:10; Is. 45:21; Hab. 3:2; Mi. 7:18; Jn. 1:14; Rom. 11:22; 3:26; Eph. 2:3–4; 1 Jn. 1:9.

[39] G. C. Berkouwer, *Work of Christ*, p. 277.

[40] *Institutes*, II.xvi.4. *Cf.* II.xvii.2.

[41] Emil Brunner, *Man in Revolt*, p. 187.

[42] P. T. Forsyth, *Cruciality of the Cross*, pp. 5–6 and 73.

[43] P. T. Forsyth, *Work of Christ*, p. 80. He also uses the expression 'holy love' in *The Justification of God*, especially pp. 124–131 and 190–195. William Temple picked it up in *Christus Veritas*, especially pp. 257–260.

Six

The self-substitution of God

We have located the problem of forgiveness in the gravity of sin and the majesty of God, that is, in the realities of who we are and who he is. How can the holy love of God come to terms with the unholy lovelessness of man? What would happen if they were to come into collision with each other? The problem is not outside God; it is within his own being. Because God never contradicts himself, he must be himself and 'satisfy' himself, acting in absolute consistency with the perfection of his character. 'It is the recognition of this divine necessity, or the failure to recognise it,' wrote James Denney, 'which ultimately divides interpreters of Christianity into evangelical and non-evangelical, those who are true to the New Testament and those who cannot digest it.'[1]

Moreover, as we have seen, this inward necessity does not mean that God must be true to only a part of himself (whether his law or honour or justice), nor that he must express one of his attributes (whether love or holiness) at the expense of another, but rather that he must be completely and invariably himself in the fullness of his moral being. T. J. Crawford stressed this point: 'It is altogether an error ... to suppose that God acts at one time according to one of his attributes, and at another time according to another. He acts in conformity with all of them at all times ... As for the divine justice and the divine mercy in particular, the end of his [*sc.* Christ's] work was not to bring them into harmony, as if they had been at variance with one another, but jointly to manifest and glorify them in the redemption of sinners. It is a case of *combined action,* and not of *counteraction,* on the part of these attributes, that is exhibited on the cross.'[2]

How then could God express simultaneously his holiness in judgment and his love in pardon? Only by providing a divine substitute for the sinner, so that the substitute would receive the judgment and the sinner the pardon. We sinners still of course have to suffer some of the personal, psychological and social consequences of our sins, but the penal consequence, the deserved penalty of alienation from God, has been borne by Another in our place, so that we may be spared it. I have not come across a more careful statement of the substitutionary nature of the atonement than that made by Charles E. B. Cranfield in his commentary on *Romans.* Although it summarizes the conclusion towards which this chapter will argue, it may be helpful to quote it near the beginning, so that we know the direction in which we are heading. The quotation is part of Dr Cranfield's comment on Romans 3:25. He writes:

> God, because in his mercy he willed to forgive sinful men, and, being truly merciful, willed to forgive them righteously, that is, without in any way condoning their sin, purposed to direct against his own very self in the person of his Son the full weight of that righteous wrath which they deserved (p. 217).

The vital questions which must now occupy us are these: who is this 'Substitute'? And how are we to understand and justify the notion of his substituting himself for us? The best way to approach these questions is to consider the Old Testament sacrifices, since these were the God-intended preparation for the sacrifice of Christ.

Sacrifice in the Old Testament

'The interpretation of Christ's death as a sacrifice is imbedded in every important type of the New Testament teaching.'[3] Sacrificial vocabulary and idiom are widespread. Sometimes the reference is unambiguous, as when Paul says Christ 'gave himself up for us as a fragrant offering [*prosphora*] and sacrifice [*thysia*] to God' (Eph. 5:2). At other times the allusion is less direct, simply that Christ 'gave himself' (*e.g.* Gal. 1:4) or 'offered himself' (*e.g.* Heb. 9:14) for us, but the background of thought is still the Old Testament sacrificial system. In particular, the statement that he died 'for sin' or 'for sins' (*e.g.* Rom. 8:3, RSV, and 1 Pet. 3:18) self-consciously borrows the Greek translation of the 'sin offering' (*peri hamartias*). Indeed, the letter to the Hebrews portrays the sacrifice of Jesus Christ as having perfectly fulfilled the Old Testament 'shadows'. For he sacrificed himself (not animals), once and for all (not repeatedly), and thus secured for us not only ceremonial cleansing and restoration to favour in the covenant community but the purification of our consciences and restoration to fellowship with the living God.

What did the Old Testament sacrifices signify, however? And did they have a substitutionary meaning? In order to answer these questions, we must not make the mistake of turning first to anthropological studies. To be sure, priests, altars and sacrifices seem to have been a universal phenomenon in the ancient world, but we have no right to assume *a priori* that Hebrew and pagan sacrifices had an identical meaning. They may well have had a common origin in God's revelation to our earliest ancestors. But it would be more consonant with a recognition of the special status of Scripture to say that the Israelites (despite their backslidings) preserved the substance of God's original purpose, whereas pagan sacrifices were degenerate corruptions of it.

Sacrifices were offered in a wide variety of circumstances in the Old Testament. They were associated, for example, with penitence and with celebration, with national need, covenant renewal, family festivity and personal consecration. This diversity warns us against imposing on them a single or simple significance. Nevertheless, there do seem to have been two basic and complementary notions of sacrifice in God's Old Testament revelation, each being associated with particular offerings. The first expressed the sense human beings have of belonging to God by right, and the second their sense of alienation from God because of their sin and guilt. Characteristic of the first were the 'peace' or 'fellowship' offering which was often associated with thanksgiving (Lv. 7:12), the burnt offering (in which everything was consumed) and the ritual of the three annual harvest festivals (Ex. 23:14–17). Characteristic of the second were the sin offering and the guilt offering, in which the need for atonement was clearly acknowledged. It would be incorrect to distinguish these two kinds of sacrifice as representing respectively man's approach to God (offering gifts, let alone bribes to secure his favour) and God's approach to man (offering forgiveness and reconciliation). For both kinds of sacrifice were essentially recognitions of God's grace and expressions of dependence upon it. It would be better to distinguish them, as B. B. Warfield did, by seeing in the former 'man conceived merely as creature' and in the latter 'the needs of man as sinner'. Or, to elaborate the same distinction, in the first the human being is 'a creature claiming protection', and in the second 'a sinner craving pardon'.[4]

Then God is revealed in the sacrifices on the one hand as the Creator on whom man depends for his physical life, and on the other as simultaneously the Judge who demands and the Saviour who provides atonement for sin. Of these two kinds of sacrifice it was further recognized that the latter is the foundation of the former, in that reconciliation to our Judge is necessary even before worship of our Creator. It is therefore significant that in Hezekiah's purification of the Temple, the sin offering 'to atone for all Israel' was sacrificed before the burnt offering (2 Ch. 29:20–24). Further, it may be that we can discern the two kinds of offering in the sacrifices of Cain and Abel, although both are termed *minha,* a gift offering. The reason why Cain's was rejected, we are told, was that he did not respond in faith like Abel to God's revelation (Heb. 11:4). In contrast to God's revealed will, either he put worship before atonement or he distorted his presentation of the fruits of the soil from a recognition of the Creator's gifts into an offering of his own.

The notion of substitution is that one person takes the place of another, especially in order to bear his pain and so save him from it. Such an action is universally regarded as noble. It is good to spare people pain; it is doubly good to do so at the cost of bearing it oneself. We admire the altruism of Moses in being willing for his name to be blotted out of Yahweh's book if only thereby Israel might be forgiven (Ex. 32:32). We also respect an almost identical wish expressed by Paul (Rom. 9:1–4), and his promise to pay Philemon's debts (Phm. 18–19). Similarly in our own century we cannot fail to be moved by the heroism of Father Maximilian Kolbe, the Polish Franciscan, in the Auschwitz concentration camp. When a number of prisoners were selected for execution, and one of them shouted that he was a married man with children, 'Father Kolbe stepped forward and asked if he could take the condemned man's place. His offer was accepted by the authorities, and he was placed in an underground cell, where he was left to die of starvation'.[5]

So it is not surprising that this commonly understood principle of substitution should have been applied by God himself to the sacrifices. Abraham 'sacrificed … as a burnt offering instead of his son' the ram which God had provided (Gn. 22:13). Moses enacted that, in the case of an unsolved murder, the town's elders should first declare their own innocence and then sacrifice a heifer in place of the unknown murderer (Dt. 21:1–9). Micah evidently understood the substitutionary principle well, for he soliloquized about how he should come before Yahweh, and wondered if he should bring burnt offerings, animals, rivers of oil or even 'my firstborn for my transgression, the fruit of my body for the sin of my soul'. The fact that he gave himself a moral instead of a ritual answer, and especially that he rejected the horrific thought of sacrificing his own child in place of himself, does not mean that he rejected the substitutionary principle which was built into the Old Testament sacrificial system (Mi. 6:6–8).

This elaborate system provided for daily, weekly, monthly, annual and occasional offerings. It also included five main types of offering, which are detailed in the early chapters of Leviticus, namely the burnt, cereal, peace, sin and guilt offerings. Because the cereal offering consisted of grain and oil, rather than flesh and blood, it was atypical and was therefore made in association with one of the others. The remaining four were blood sacrifices and, although there were some differences between them (relating to their proper occasion, and the precise use to which the flesh and blood were put), they all shared the same basic ritual involving worshipper and priest. It was very vivid. The worshipper brought the offering, laid his hand or hands on it and killed it. The priest then applied the blood, burnt some of the flesh, and arranged for the consumption of what was left of it. This was significant symbolism, not meaningless magic. By laying his hand(s) on the animal, the offerer was certainly identifying himself with it and 'solemnly' designating 'the victim as standing for him'.[6] Some scholars go further and see the laying-on of hands as 'a symbolic transferral of the sins of the worshipper to the animal',[7] as was explicitly so in the case of the scapegoat, to be considered later. In either case, having taken his place, the substitute animal was killed in recognition that the penalty for sin was death, its blood (symbolizing that the death had been accomplished) was sprinkled, and the offerer's life was spared.

The clearest statement that the blood sacrifices of the Old Testament ritual had a substitutionary significance, however, and that this was why the shedding and sprinkling of blood was indispensable to atonement, is to be found in this statement by God explaining why the eating of blood was prohibited:

> For the life of a creature is in the blood, and I have given it to you to make atonement for yourselves on the altar; it is the blood that makes atonement for one's life (Lv. 17:11).

Three important affirmations about blood are made in this text. First, blood is the symbol of life. This understanding that 'blood is life' seems to be very ancient. It goes back at least to Noah, whom God forbade to eat meat which had its 'lifeblood' still in it (Gn. 9:4), and was later repeated in the formula 'the blood is the life' (Dt. 12:23). The emphasis, however, was not on blood flowing in the veins, the symbol of life being lived, but on blood shed, the symbol of life ended, usually by violent means.

Secondly, blood makes atonement, and the reason for its atoning significance is given in the repetition of the word 'life'. It is only because 'the life of a creature is in the blood' that 'it is the blood that makes atonement for one's life'. One life is forfeit; another life is sacrificed instead. What makes atonement 'on the altar' is the shedding of substitutionary lifeblood. T. J. Crawford expressed it with: 'The text, then, according to its plain and obvious import, teaches the *vicarious* nature of the rite of sacrifice. *Life was given for life,* the life of the victim for the life of the offerer', indeed 'the life of the innocent victim for the life of the sinful offerer'.[8]

Thirdly, blood was given by God for this atoning purpose. 'I have given it to you', he says, 'to make atonement for yourselves on the altar.' So we are to think of the sacrificial system as God-given, not man-made, and of the individual sacrifices not as a human device to placate God but as a means of atonement provided by God himself.

This Old Testament background helps us to understand two crucial texts in the letter to the Hebrews. The first is that 'without the shedding of blood there is no forgiveness' (9:22), and the second that 'it is impossible for the blood of bulls and goats to take away sins' (10:4). No forgiveness without blood meant no atonement without substitution. There had to be life for life or blood for blood. But the Old Testament blood sacrifices were only shadows; the substance was Christ. For a substitute to be effective, it must be an appropriate equivalent. Animal sacrifices could not atone for human beings, because a human being is 'much more valuable ... than a sheep', as Jesus himself said (Mt. 12:12). Only 'the precious blood of Christ' was valuable enough (1 Pet. 1:19).

The Passover and 'sin-bearing'

We turn now from the principle of substitution, as it is seen in what the Old Testament says about blood sacrifices in general, to two particular examples of it, namely the Passover and the concept of 'sin-bearing'.

It is right for two reasons to start with the Passover. The first is that the original Passover marked the beginning of Israel's national life. 'This month is to be for you the first month,' God had said to them, 'the first month of your year' (Ex. 12:2). It was to inaugurate their annual calendar because in it God redeemed them from their long and oppressive Egyptian bondage, and because the exodus led to the renewal of God's covenant with them at Mount Sinai. But before the exodus and the covenant came the Passover. That day they were to 'commemorate for the generations to come'; they were to 'celebrate it as a festival to the LORD – a lasting ordinance' (12:14, 17).

The second reason for beginning here is that the New Testament clearly identifies the death of Christ as the fulfilment of the Passover, and the emergence of his new and redeemed community as the new exodus. It is not only that John the Baptist hailed Jesus as 'the Lamb of God, who takes away the sin of the world' Jn. 1:29, 36),[9] nor only that according to John's chronology of the end Jesus was hanging on the cross at the precise time when the Passover lambs were being slaughtered,[10] nor even that in the book of Revelation he is worshipped as the slain Lamb who by his blood has purchased men for God.[11] It is specially that Paul categorically declares: 'Christ, our Passover lamb, has been sacrificed. Therefore let us keep the Festival ...' (1 Cor. 5:7–8).

What then happened at the first Passover? And what does this tell us about Christ, our Passover lamb?

The Passover story (Ex. 11 – 13) is a self-disclosure of the God of Israel in three roles. First, Yahweh revealed himself as the Judge. The background was the threat of the final plague. Moses was to warn Pharaoh in the most solemn terms that at midnight Yahweh himself was going to pass through Egypt and strike down every firstborn. There would be no discrimination either between human beings and animals, or between different social classes. Every firstborn male would die. There would be only one way of escape, by God's own devising and provision.

Secondly, Yahweh revealed himself as the Redeemer. On the tenth day of the month each Israelite household was to choose a lamb (a year-old male without defect), and on the fourteenth evening to kill it. They were then to take some of the lamb's blood, dip a branch of hyssop in it and sprinkle it on the lintel and side-posts of their front door. They were not to go out of their house at all that night. Having shed and sprinkled the blood, they must shelter under it. For Yahweh, who had already announced his intention to 'pass through' Egypt in judgment, now added his promise to 'pass over' every blood-marked house in order to shield it from his threatened destruction.

Thirdly, Yahweh revealed himself as Israel's covenant God. He had redeemed them to make them his own people. So when he had saved them from his own judgment, they were to commemorate and celebrate his goodness. On Passover night itself they were to feast on the roasted lamb, with bitter herbs and unleavened bread, and they were to do so with their cloak tucked into their belt, their sandals on their feet and their staff in their hand, ready at any moment for their rescue. Some features of the meal spoke to them of their former oppression (*e.g.* the bitter herbs), and others of their future liberation (*e.g.* their dress). Then on each anniversary the festival was to last seven days, and they were to explain to their children what the whole ceremony meant: 'It is the Passover sacrifice to the LORD, who passed over the houses of the Israelites in Egypt and spared our homes when he struck down the Egyptians.' In addition to the celebration in which the whole family would share, there was to be a special ritual for the firstborn males. It was they who had been personally rescued from death by the death of the Passover lambs. Thus redeemed, they belonged in a special way to Yahweh who had purchased them by blood, and they were therefore to be consecrated to his service.

The message must have been absolutely clear to the Israelites; it is equally clear to us who see the fulfilment of the Passover in the sacrifice of Christ. First, the Judge and the Saviour are the same person. It was the God who 'passed through' Egypt to judge the firstborn, who 'passed over' Israelite homes to protect them. We must never characterize the Father as Judge and the Son as Saviour. It is one and the same God who through Christ saves us from himself. Secondly, salvation was (and is) by substitution. The only firstborn males who were spared were those in whose families a firstborn lamb had died instead. Thirdly, the lamb's blood had to be sprinkled after it had been shed. There had to be an individual appropriation of the divine provision. God had to 'see the blood' before he would save the family. Fourthly, each family rescued by God was thereby purchased for God. Their whole life now belonged to him. So does ours. And consecration leads to celebration. The life of the redeemed is a feast, ritually expressed in the Eucharist, the Christian festival of thanksgiving, as we shall consider more fully in chapter 10.

The second major illustration of the principle of substitution is the notion of 'sin-bearing'. In the New Testament we read of Christ that 'he himself bore our sins in his body on the tree' (1 Pet. 2:24), and similarly that he 'was once offered to bear the sins of many' (Heb. 9:28, AV). But what does it mean to 'bear sin'? Must it be understood in terms of the bearing of sin's penalty, or can it be interpreted in other ways? And is 'substitution' necessarily involved in 'sin-bearing'? If so, what kind of substitution is in mind? Can it refer only to the innocent, God-provided substitute taking the place of the guilty party and enduring the penalty instead of him? Or are there alternative kinds of substitution?

During the last one hundred years a number of ingenious attempts have been made to retain the vocabulary of 'substitution', while rejecting 'penal substitution' ('penal' being derived from *poena,* a penalty or punishment). Their origin can be traced back to Abelard's protest against Anselm in the twelfth century, and even more to Socinus' scornful rejection of the Reformers' doctrine in the sixteenth. In his book *De Jesu Christo Servatore* (1578), Faustus Socinus denied not only the deity of Jesus but any idea of 'satisfaction' in his death. The notion that guilt can be transferred from one person to another,[12] he declaimed, was incompatible with both reason and justice. It was not only impossible, but unnecessary. For God is perfectly capable of forgiving sinners without it. He leads them to repentance, and so makes them forgivable.

John McLeod Campbell's *The Nature of the Atonement* (1856) stands in the same general tradition. Christ came to do God's will, he wrote, and in particular to bear men's sins. Not in the traditional sense, however, but in two others. First, in dealing with men on behalf of God, Christ's sufferings were not 'penal sufferings endured in meeting a demand of divine justice', but 'the sufferings of divine love suffering from our sins according to its own nature' (pp. 115–116). Secondly, in dealing with God on behalf of men, the 'satisfaction' due to divine justice took the form of 'a perfect confession of our sins'. In this way Christ acknowledged the justice of God's wrath against sin, 'and in that perfect response he absorbs it' (pp. 117–118). He was so much one with God as to be 'filled with the sense of the Father's righteous condemnation of our sin', and so much one with us as to 'respond with a perfect Amen to that condemnation' (p. 127). In this way 'sin-bearing' has dissolved into sympathy, 'satisfaction' into sorrow for sin, and 'substitution' into vicarious penitence, instead of vicarious punishment.

Ten years later *The Vicarious Sacrifice* was published, by Horace Bushnell, the American Congregationalist.[13] Like McLeod Campbell he rejected 'penal' substitution. Yet the death of Jesus was 'vicarious' or 'substitutionary' in the sense that he bore our pain rather than our penalty. For 'love is itself an essentially vicarious principle' (p. 11). Consequently, God's love entered through the incarnation and public ministry of Jesus (not only his death) into our sorrows and sufferings, and 'bore' them in the sense of identifying with them and feeling burdened by them. 'There is a cross in God before the wood is seen upon Calvary' (p. 35). This loving sacrifice of God in Christ – expressed in his birth, life and death – is 'the power of God unto salvation' because of its inspiring influence upon us. Christ is now able 'to bring us out of our sins ... and so out of their penalties' (p. 7). It is thus that the Lamb of God takes away our sins. 'Atonement ... is a change wrought in us, a change by which we are reconciled to God' (p. 450). But the 'subjective atoning' (*i.e.* the change in us) comes first, and only then 'God is objectively propitiated' (p. 448).

R. C. Moberly developed similar ideas in his *Atonement and Personality* (1901). He rejected all forensic categories in relation to the cross, and in particular any idea of retributive punishment. He taught that penitence (worked in us by the Spirit of the Crucified One) makes us first 'forgivable' and then holy. Christ may be said to take our place only in terms of vicarious penitence, not of vicarious penalty.

The attempt by these theologians to retain the language of substitution and sin-bearing, while changing its meaning, must be pronounced a failure. It creates more confusion than clarity. It conceals from the unwary that there is a fundamental difference between 'penitent substitution' (in which the substitute offers what we could not offer) and 'penal substitution' (in which he bears what we could not bear). Here is Dr J. I. Packer's definition of the latter. It is the notion

> that Jesus Christ our Lord, moved by a love that was determined to do everything necessary to save us, endured and exhausted the destructive divine judgment for which we were otherwise inescapably destined, and so won us forgiveness, adoption and glory. To affirm penal substitution is to say that believers are in debt to Christ specifically for this, and that this is the mainspring of all their joy, peace and praise both now and for eternity.'[14]

The essential question, however, concerns how the biblical authors themselves employ 'sin-bearing' language.

It is clear from Old Testament usage that to 'bear sin' means neither to sympathize with sinners, nor to identify with their pain, nor to express their penitence, nor to be persecuted on account of human sinfulness (as others have argued), nor even to suffer the consequences of sin in personal or social terms, but specifically to endure its penal consequences, to undergo its penalty. The expression comes most frequently in the books of Leviticus and Numbers. It is written of those who sin by breaking God's laws that they 'will bear their iniquity [or sin]' (AV and RSV). That is, they 'will be held responsible' or 'will suffer for their sins' (NIV). Sometimes the matter is put beyond question by the fact that the penalty is specified: the offender is to be 'cut off from his people' (*i.e.* excommunicated) and even, for example in the case of blasphemy, put to death.[15]

It is in this context of sin-bearing that the possibility is envisaged of somebody else bearing the penalty of the sinner's wrongdoing. For example, Moses told the Israelites that their children would have to wander in the desert, 'suffering for your unfaithfulness' (Nu. 14:34); if a married man failed to nullify a foolish vow or pledge made by his wife, then (it was written) 'he is responsible for her guilt' (Nu. 30:15, NIV) or more simply 'he shall bear her iniquity' (RSV); again, after the destruction of Jerusalem in 586 BC the remnant who stayed in the otherwise deserted ruins said: 'Our fathers sinned and are no more, and we bear their punishment' (La. 5:7).

These are examples of involuntary vicarious sin-bearing. In each case innocent people found themselves suffering the consequences of others' guilt. The same phraseology was used, however, when the vicarious sin-bearing was intended. Then the notion of deliberate substitution was introduced, and God himself was said to provide the substitute, as when he instructed Ezekiel to lie down, and in dramatic symbolism to 'bear the sin of the house of Israel' (Ezk. 4:4–5). The sin offering was also referred to in terms of sin-bearing. Moses said of it to the sons of Aaron: 'it was given to you to take away the guilt of the community by making atonement for them before the LORD' (Lv. 10:17). Clearer still was the ritual of the annual Day of Atonement. The high priest was to 'take two male goats for a sin offering' in order to atone for the sins of the Israelite community as a whole (Lv. 16:5). One goat was to be sacrificed and its blood sprinkled in the usual way, while on the living goat's head the high priest was to lay both his hands, 'and confess over it all the wickedness and rebellion of the Israelites all their sins – and put them on the goat's head' (v. 21). He was then to drive the goat away into the desert, and it would 'carry on itself all their sins to a solitary place' (v. 22). Some commentators make the mistake of driving a wedge between the two goats, the sacrificed goat and the scapegoat, overlooking the fact that the two together are described as 'a sin offering' in the singular (v. 5). Perhaps T. J. Crawford was right to suggest that each embodied a different aspect of the same sacrifice, 'the one exhibiting the means, and the other the results, of the atonement'.[16] In this case the public proclamation of the Day of Atonement was plain, namely that reconciliation was possible only through substitutionary sin-bearing. The author of the letter to the Hebrews has no inhibitions about seeing Jesus both as 'a merciful and faithful high priest' (2:17) and as the two victims, the sacrificed goat whose blood was taken into the inner sanctuary (9:7, 12) and the scapegoat which carried away the people's sins (9:28).

Although the sin offering and the scapegoat both in their different ways had a sin-bearing role, at least the more spiritually minded Israelites must have realized that an animal cannot be a satisfactory substitute for a human being. So, in the famous 'servant songs' in the second part of Isaiah, the prophet began to delineate one whose mission would embrace the nations, and who, in order to fulfil it, would need to suffer, to bear sin and to die. Matthew applies to Jesus the first song about the quietness and gentleness of the servant in his ministry,[17] and Peter in his early speeches is recorded four times as calling Jesus God's 'servant' or 'holy servant'.[18]

But it is particularly the fifty-third chapter of Isaiah, describing the servant's suffering and death, which is applied consistently to Jesus Christ. 'No other passage from the Old Testament', Joachim Jeremias has written, 'was as important to the Church as Isaiah 53.'[19] The New Testament writers quote eight specific verses as having been fulfilled in Jesus. Verse 1 ('who has believed our message?') is applied to Jesus by John (12:38). Matthew sees the statement of verse 4 ('he took up our infirmities and carried our diseases') as fulfilled in Jesus' healing ministry (8:17). That we have gone astray like sheep (v. 6), but that by his wounds we have been healed (v. 5) are both echoed by Peter (1 Pet. 2:22–25), and so in the same passage are verse 9 ('nor was any deceit in his mouth') and verse 11 ('he will bear their iniquities'). Then verses 7 and 8, about Jesus being led like a sheep to the slaughter and being deprived of justice and of life, were the verses the Ethiopian eunuch was reading in his chariot, which prompted Philip to share with him 'the good news about Jesus' (Acts 8:30–35). Thus verses 1, 4, 5, 6, 7, 8, 9 and 11– eight verses out of the chapter's twelve – are all quite specifically referred to Jesus.

Careful students of the Gospels have detected numerous references by Jesus himself, sometimes only in a single word, to Isaiah 53. For example, he said he would be 'rejected',[20] 'taken away'[21] and 'numbered with the transgressors'.[22] He would also be 'buried' like a criminal without any preparatory anointing, so that (he explained) Mary of Bethany gave him an advance anointing, 'to prepare for my burial'.[23] Other allusions may well be his description of the stronger man who 'divides up the spoils',[24] his deliberate silence before his judges,[25] his intercession for the transgressors[26] and his laying down his life for others.[27] If these be accepted, then every verse of the chapter except verse 2 ('he had no beauty or majesty to attract us to him') is applied to Jesus in the New Testament, some verses several times. Indeed, there is good evidence that his whole public career, from his baptism through his ministry, sufferings and death to his resurrection and ascension, is seen as a fulfilment of the pattern foretold in Isaiah 53. Oscar Cullmann has argued that at his baptism he deliberately made himself one with those whose sins he had come to bear, that his resolve to 'fulfil all right-eousness' (Mt. 3:15) was a determination to be God's 'righteous servant', who by his sin-bearing death would 'justify many' (Is. 53:11), and that the Father's voice from heaven, declaring himself 'well pleased' with his Son, also identified him as the servant (Is. 42:1).[28] Similarly, Vincent Taylor pointed out that already in the very first apostolic sermon in Acts 2 'the dominating conception is that of the Servant, humiliated in death and exalted ...'[29] More recently, Professor Martin Hengel of Tübingen has reached the same conclusion, arguing that this use of Isaiah 53 must go back to the mind of Jesus himself.[30]

So far my purpose in relation to Isaiah 53 has been to show how foun-dational the chapter is to the New Testament's understanding of Jesus. I have left to the last his two most important sayings, which focus on the sin-bearing nature of his death. The first is the 'ransom saying': 'for even the Son of Man did not come to be served, but to serve, and to give his life as a ransom for many' (Mk. 10:45). Here Jesus unites the divergent 'Son of man' and 'Servant' prophecies. The Son of Man would 'come with the clouds of heaven' and all peoples would 'serve him' (Dn. 7:13–14), whereas the Servant would not be served but serve, and complete his service by suf-fering, specially by laying down his life as a ransom instead of many. It was only by serving that he would be served, only by suffering that he would enter into his glory. The second text belongs to the institution of the Lord's Supper, when Jesus declared that his blood would be 'poured out for many',[31] an echo of Isaiah 53:12, 'he poured out his life unto death'.[32] Moreover, both texts say that he would either give his life or pour out his blood 'for many', which again echoes Isaiah 53:12, 'he bore the sin of many'. Some have been embarrassed by the apparently restrictive nature of this expression. But Jeremias has argued that, according to the pre-Christian Jewish interpretation of it, 'the many' were 'the godless among both the Jews and the Gentiles'. The expression therefore is 'not exclusive ("many, but not all") but, in the Semitic manner of speech, inclusive ("the totality, consisting of many")', which was 'a (Messianic) concept unheard of in con-temporary rabbinical thought'.[33]

It seems to be definite beyond doubt, then, that Jesus applied Isaiah 53 to himself and that he understood his death in the light of it as a sin-bearing death. As God's 'righteous servant' he would be able to 'justify many', because he was going to 'bear the sin of many'. This is the thrust of the whole chapter, not just that he would be despised and rejected, oppressed and afflicted, led like a lamb to the slaughter and cut off from the land of the living, but in particular that he would be pierced for our transgressions, that the Lord would lay on him the iniquity of us all, that he would thus be numbered with the transgressors, and that he would himself bear their iniquities. 'The song makes twelve distinct and explicit statements', wrote J. S. Whale, 'that the servant suffers the *penalty* of other men's sins: not only vicarious suffering but penal substitution is the plain meaning of its fourth, fifth and sixth verses.'[34]

In the light of this evidence about the sin-bearing nature of Jesus' death, we now know how to interpret the simple assertion that 'he died for us'. The preposition 'for' can translate either *hyper* ('on behalf of') or *anti* ('instead of'). Most of the references have *hyper*. For example, 'while we were still sinners, Christ died for us' (Rom. 5:8), and again 'one died for all' (2 Cor. 5:14). *Anti* comes only in the ransom verses, namely in Mark 10:45 (literally 'to give his life as a ransom instead of many') and in 1 Timothy 2:6 ('who gave himself as a ransom for all men', where 'for' is again *hyper*, but the preposition *anti* is in the noun, *antilytron*).

The two prepositions do not always adhere to their dictionary definitions, however. Even the broader word *hyper* ('on behalf of') is many times shown by its context to be used in the sense of *anti* ('instead of'), as, for example, when we are said to be 'ambassadors for Christ' (2 Cor. 5:20), or when Paul wanted to keep Onesimus in Rome to serve him 'on behalf of' his master Philemon, that is, in his place (Phm. 13). The same is clear in the two most outspoken statements of the meaning of Christ's death in Paul's letters. One is that 'God made him who had no sin to be sin for us' (2 Cor. 5:21), and the other that Christ has 'redeemed us from the curse of the law by becoming a curse for us' (Gal. 3:13). Some commentators have found these assertions difficult to accept. Karl Barth called the first 'almost unbearably severe'[35] and A. W. F. Blunt described the language of the second as 'almost shocking'.[36] It will be observed that in both cases what happened to Christ on the cross ('made sin', 'becoming a curse') is said by Paul to have been intended 'for us', on our behalf or for our benefit. But what exactly did happen? The sinless one was 'made sin for us', which must mean that he bore the penalty of our sin instead of us, and he redeemed us from the law's curse by 'becoming a curse for us', which must mean that the curse of the law lying upon us for our disobedience was transferred to him, so that he bore it instead of us.

Both verses go beyond these negative truths (that he bore our sin and curse to redeem us from them) to a positive counterpart. On the one hand he bore the curse in order that we might inherit the blessing promised to Abraham (Gal. 3:14), and on the other, God made the sinless Christ to be sin for us, in order that 'in him we might become the righteousness of God' (2 Cor. 5:21). Both verses thus indicate that when we are united to Christ a mysterious exchange takes place: he took our curse, so that we may receive his blessing; he became sin with our sin, so that we may become righteous with his righteousness. Elsewhere Paul writes of this transfer in terms of 'imputation'. On the one hand, God declined to 'impute' our sins to us, or 'count' them against us (2 Cor. 5:19), with the implication that he imputed them to Christ instead. On the other, God has imputed Christ's righteousness to us.[37] Many are offended by this concept, considering it both artificial and unjust on God's part to arrange such a transfer. Yet the objection is due to a misunderstanding, which Thomas Crawford clears up for us. Imputation, he writes, 'does not at all imply the transference of one person's moral qualities to another'. Such a thing would be impossible, and he goes on to quote John Owen to the effect that 'we ourselves have done nothing of what is imputed to us, nor Christ anything of what is imputed to him'. It would be absurd and unbelievable to imagine, Crawford continues, 'that the moral turpitude of our sins was transferred to Christ, so as to make him personally sinful and ill-deserving; and that the moral excellence of his righteousness is transferred to us, so as to make us personally upright and commendable'. No, what was transferred to Christ was not moral qualities but legal consequences: he voluntarily accepted liability for our sins. That is what the expressions 'made sin' and 'made a curse' mean. Similarly, 'the righteousness of God' which we become when we are 'in Christ' is not here righteousness of character and conduct (although that grows within us by the working of the Holy Spirit), but rather a righteous standing before God.[38]

When we review all this Old Testament material (the shedding and sprinkling of blood, the sin offering, the Passover, the meaning of 'sin-bearing', the scapegoat and Isaiah 53), and consider its New Testament application to the death of Christ, we are obliged to conclude that the cross was a substitutionary sacrifice. Christ died for us. Christ died instead of us. Indeed, as Jeremias put it, this use of sacrificial imagery 'has the intention of expressing the fact that Jesus died without sin in substitution for our sins'.[39]

Who is the substitute?

The key question we now have to address is this: exactly who was our substitute? Who took our place, bore our sin, became our curse, endured our penalty, died our death? To be sure, 'while we were still sinners, Christ died for us' (Rom. 5:8). That would be the simple, surface answer. But who was this Christ? How are we to think of him?

Was he just a man? If so, how could one human being possibly – or justly – stand in for other human beings? Was he then simply God, seeming to be a man, but not actually being the man he seemed? If so, how could he represent humankind? Besides this, how could he have died? In that case, are we to think of Christ neither as man alone, nor as God alone, but rather as the one and only God-man who because of his uniquely constituted person was uniquely qualified to mediate between God and man? Whether the concept of substitutionary atonement is rational, moral, plausible, acceptable, and above all biblical, depends on our answers to these questions. The possibility of substitution rests on the identity of the substitute. We need therefore to examine in greater depth the three explanations which I have sketched above.

The first proposal is that the substitute was *the man Christ Jesus,* viewed as a human being, and conceived as an individual separate from both God and us, an independent third party. Those who begin with this *a priori* lay themselves open to gravely distorted understandings of the atonement and so bring the truth of substitution into disrepute. They tend to present the cross in one or other of two ways, according to whether the initiative was Christ's or God's. In the one case Christ is pictured as intervening in order to pacify an angry God and wrest from him a grudging salvation. In the other, the intervention is ascribed to God, who proceeds to punish the innocent Jesus in place of us, the guilty sinners who had deserved the punishment. In both cases God and Christ are sundered from one another: either Christ persuades God or God punishes Christ. What is characteristic of both presentations is that they denigrate the Father. Reluctant to suffer himself, he victimizes Christ instead. Reluctant to forgive, he is prevailed upon by Christ to do so. He is seen as a pitiless ogre whose wrath has to be assuaged, whose disinclination to act has to be overcome, by the loving self-sacrifice of Jesus.

Such crude interpretations of the cross still emerge in some of our evangelical illustrations, as when we describe Christ as coming to rescue us from the judgment of God, or when we portray him as the whipping-boy who is punished instead of the real culprit, or as the lightning conductor to which the lethal electric charge is deflected. Even some of our time-honoured hymns express this view:

> Jehovah lifted up his rod;
>   O Christ, it fell on thee!
> Thou wast sore stricken of thy God;
>   There's not one stroke for me.

There is, of course, some justification in Scripture for both kinds of formulation, or they would never have been developed by Christians whose desire and claim are to be biblical.

Thus, Jesus Christ is said to be the 'propitiation' for our sins and our 'advocate' with the Father (1 Jn. 2:2, AV), which at first sight suggests that he died to placate God's anger and is now pleading with him in order to persuade him to forgive us. But other parts of Scripture forbid us to interpret the language of propitiation and advocacy in that way, as we shall see in the next chapter. The whole notion of a compassionate Christ inducing a reluctant God to take action on our behalf founders on the fact of God's love. There was no *Umstimmung* in God, no change of mind or heart secured by Christ. On the contrary, the saving initiative originated in him. It was 'because of the tender mercy of our God' (Lk. 1:78) that Christ came, 'because of his great love for us',[40] because of 'the grace of God that brings salvation' (Tit. 2:11).

As for the other formulation (that God punished Jesus for our sins), it is true that the sins of Israel were transferred to the scapegoat, that 'the LORD laid on him', his suffering servant, all our iniquity (Is. 53:6), that 'it was the LORD's will to crush him' (Is. 53:10), and that Jesus applied to himself Zechariah's prophecy that God would 'strike the shepherd'.[41] It is also true that in the New Testament God is said to have 'sent' his Son to atone for our sins (1 Jn. 4:9–10), 'delivered him up' for us,[42] 'presented him as a sacrifice of atonement' (Rom. 3:25), 'condemned sin' in his flesh (Rom. 8:3), and 'made him ... to be sin for us' (2 Cor. 5:21). These are striking statements. But we have no liberty to interpret them in such a way as to imply either that God compelled Jesus to do what he was unwilling to do himself, or that Jesus was an unwilling victim of God's harsh justice. Jesus Christ did indeed bear the penalty of our sins, but God was active in and through Christ doing it, and Christ was freely playing his part (*e.g.* Heb. 10:5–10).

We must not, then, speak of God punishing Jesus or of Jesus persuading God, for to do so is to set them over against each other as if they acted independently of each other or were even in conflict with each other. We must never make Christ the object of God's punishment or God the object of Christ's persuasion, for both God and Christ were subjects not objects, taking the initiative together to save sinners. Whatever happened on the cross in terms of 'God forsakenness' was voluntarily accepted by both in the same holy love which made atonement necessary. It was 'God in our nature forsaken of God'.[43] If the Father 'gave the Son', the Son 'gave himself'. If the Gethsemane 'cup' symbolized the wrath of God, it was nevertheless 'given' by the Father (Jn. 18:11) and voluntarily 'taken' by the Son. If the Father 'sent' the Son, the Son 'came' himself. The Father did not lay on the Son an ordeal he was reluctant to bear, nor did the Son extract from the Father a salvation he was reluctant to bestow. There is no suspicion anywhere in the New Testament of discord between the Father and the Son, 'whether by the Son wresting forgiveness from an unwilling Father or by the Father demanding a sacrifice from an unwilling Son'.[44] There was no unwillingness in either. On the contrary, their wills coincided in the perfect self-sacrifice of love.

If then our substitute was not Christ alone as a third party independent of God, is the truth that God *alone* took our place, bore our sin and died our death? If we may not so exalt the initiative of Christ as virtually to eliminate the contribution of the Father, may we reverse their roles, ascribing the whole initiative and achievement to the Father, thus virtually eliminating Christ? For if God has himself done everything necessary for our salvation, does that not make Christ redundant?

This proposed solution to the problem is at first sight attractive theologically, for it avoids all the distortions which arise when Jesus is conceived as a third party. As we saw in the last chapter, it is God who must satisfy himself as holy love. He was unwilling to act in love at the expense of his holiness or in holiness at the expense of his love. So we may say that he satisfied his holy love by himself dying the death and so bearing the judgment which sinners deserved. He both exacted and accepted the penalty of human sin. And he did it 'so as to be just and the one who justifies the man who has faith in Jesus' (Rom. 3:26). There is no question now either of the Father inflicting punishment on the Son or of the Son intervening on our behalf with the Father, for it is the Father himself who takes the initiative in his love, bears the penalty of sin himself, and so dies. Thus the priority is neither 'man's demand on God' nor 'God's demand on men', but supremely 'God's demand on God, God's meeting his own demand'.[45]

Many theologians ancient and modern, representing different traditions, have seen the necessity of emphasizing that God himself was there on the cross, and have therefore expressed their understanding of the atonement in these terms. In the Old English poem 'The Dream of the Rood', which may date from as early as the seventh or eighth century, the author tells how in 'the most treasured of dreams' he saw 'the strangest of trees':

> Lifted aloft in the air, with light all around it,
> Of all beams the brightest. It stood as a beacon,
> Drenched in gold; gleaming gems were set
> Fair around its foot ...

Then in the dream the cross spoke, telling its own story. Having been cut from the forest, it was carried up the hill. Then it saw what its destiny was to be:

> The King of all mankind coming in great haste,
> With courage keen, eager to climb me.

> Then the young hero – it was God Almighty –
> Strong and steadfast, stripped himself for battle;

He climbed up on the high gallows, constant in his purpose,
Mounted it in sight of many, mankind to ransom.

At the end of the poem, having seen God dying for him, the dreamer prays to 'that blessed beam' and, putting his trust in it, declares: 'My refuge is the Rood.'[46]

'God dying for man', wrote P. T. Forsyth. 'I am not afraid of that phrase; I cannot do without it. God dying for men; and for such men – hostile, malignantly hostile men.'[47] Again, because 'the holiness of God ... is meaningless without judgment', the one thing God could not do in the face of human rebellion was nothing. 'He must either inflict punishment or assume it. And he chose the latter course, as honouring the law while saving the guilty. He took his own judgment.'[48]

It was 'God himself' giving himself for us. Karl Barth did not shrink from using those words. 'God's own heart suffered on the cross', he added. 'No-one else but God's own Son, and hence the eternal God himself ...'[49] Similarly, Bishop Stephen Neill wrote: 'If the crucifixion of Jesus ... is in some way, as Christians have believed, the dying of God himself, then ... we can understand what God is like.'[50] And hymns of popular devotion have echoed it, like this phrase from Charles Wesley's 'And can it be':

Amazing love! How can it be
That thou, my God, should'st die for me?

The reason why both scholarly and simple Christians have felt able to use this kind of language is of course that Scripture permits it. When the apostles wrote of the cross, they often indicated by a tell-tale expression who it was who died there and gave it its efficacy. Thus, he who humbled himself even to death on a cross was none other than he who 'being in very nature God' made himself nothing in order to become human and to die (Phil. 2:6–8). It was 'the Lord of glory' whom the rulers of this age crucified (1 Cor. 2:8). And the blood by which the robes of the redeemed have been washed clean is that of the Lamb who shares the centre of God's throne (Rev. 5:6, 9; 7:9). Moreover, the logic of the letter to the Hebrews requires us to say that it is God who died. It plays on the similarity between a 'covenant' and a 'will'. The terms of a will come into force only after the death of the testator. So he who makes promises in his will has to die before the legacies can be received. Since, then, the promises in question are God's promises, the death must be God's death (Heb. 9:15–17).

There is one other verse which we must not overlook. It occurs in Paul's farewell speech at Miletus to the elders of the Ephesian church. The flock over which the Holy Spirit has made them overseers and shepherds, he says, is nothing less than 'the church of God, which he bought with his own blood' (Acts 20:28). It is true that the text is uncertain (some manuscripts read 'the church of the Lord', referring to Christ, instead of 'the church of God'), and so is the translation (it might mean 'the church of God which he bought with the blood of his own', referring again to Christ). Nevertheless, the context seems to demand the readings 'the church of God' and 'his own blood'. For Paul's purpose is to remind the elders of the precious value of the church they have been called to serve. It is God's church. God's Spirit has appointed them elders over it, and the price paid for its purchase is actually 'God's blood' – an almost shocking phrase which was used by some of the church Fathers such as Ignatius and Tertullian,[51] and which medieval churchmen continued to use, albeit often as an oath.

In spite of this biblical justification, however, no verse specifically declares that 'God himself' died on the cross. Scripture bears witness to the deity of the person who gave himself for us, but it stops short of the unequivocal affirmation that 'God died'. The reasons for this are not far to seek. First, immortality belongs to God's essential being ('God ... alone is immortal', 1 Tim. 6:16), and therefore he cannot die. So he became man, in order to be able to do so: 'Since the children have flesh and blood, he too shared in their humanity so that by his death he might destroy him who holds the power of death – that is, the devil' (Heb. 2:14). Similarly, he became man in order to be the 'one mediator between God and men' (1 Tim. 2:5).

The second reason why it is misleading to say that 'God died' is that 'God' in the New Testament frequently means 'the Father' (*e.g.* 'God sent his Son'), and the person who died on the cross was not the Father but the Son. At the beginning of the third century AD some denied this. They had difficulties with the doctrine of the Trinity and could not see how to believe in the Father, the Son and the Spirit without thereby becoming tritheists. So they began by emphasizing the unity of God, and then spoke of Father, Son and Spirit not as three eternally distinct 'persons' within the Godhead, but rather as three temporal 'modes' in which God successively revealed himself. Hence their name 'Modalists'. The Father became the Son, they taught, and then the Son became the Spirit. They were also referred to as 'Sabellians' because Sabellius was one of their leaders. Another was Praxeas, whose teaching is known to us through Tertullian's powerful refutation of it. Praxeas taught (or, according to Tertullian, the devil taught through him) 'that the Father himself came down into the virgin, was himself born of her, himself suffered, indeed was himself Jesus Christ'. Because Praxeas also opposed the Montanists, who have been loosely described as the charismatics of that era, Tertullian continued, 'Praxeas did a twofold service for the devil at Rome; he drove away prophecy and he brought in heresy; he put to flight the Paraclete, and he crucified the Father'.[52] The droll notion that the Father was crucified led the critics of Praxeas' followers to give them the nickname 'Patripassians' (those who taught that the Father suffered). Over against this Tertullian urged: 'Let us be content with saying that Christ died, the Son of the Father; and *let this suffice,* because the Scriptures have told us so much.'[53]

A somewhat similar deviation arose in the sixth century in Constantinople, which came to be known as 'theopaschitism' (the belief that God suffered). Its adherents rejected the definition of the Council of Chalcedon (AD 451) that Jesus, though one person, had two natures, being both truly God and truly man. Instead, they were 'Monophysites', teaching that Christ had only one composite nature (*physis,* 'nature'), which was essentially divine. Thus underplaying the humanity of Jesus, they naturally emphasized that God suffered in and through him.

Although these controversies seem very remote to us in the twentieth century, we need to take warning from them. An over-emphasis on the sufferings of God on the cross may mislead us either into confusing the persons of the Trinity and denying the eternal distinctness of the Son, like the Modalists or Patripassians, or into confusing the natures of Christ, and denying that he was one person in two natures, like the Monophysites or Theopaschites. It is true that, since Jesus was both God and man, the Council of Ephesus (AD 431) declared it correct to refer to the virgin Mary as *theotokos* ('mother of God', literally 'God-bearer'). Similarly, and for the same reason, it seems permissible to refer to God suffering on the cross. For if God could be born, why could he not also die? The value of these expressions is that they eliminate the possibility of thinking of Jesus as an independent third party. Nevertheless, the words *theotokos* and 'Theopaschite' are misleading, even if technically legitimate, because they emphasize the deity of the person who was born and died, without making any comparable reference to his humanity. It would be wiser instead to say what the New Testament authors said, faithfully echoed by the Apostles' Creed, namely that he who 'was conceived by the Holy Spirit, born of the Virgin Mary, suffered under Pontius Pilate, was crucified, died and was buried' was not 'God', still less the Father, but 'Jesus Christ, his only Son, our Lord'. The apostles further clarify this by stressing the Son's willing obedience to the Father.[54]

God in Christ

Our substitute, then, who took our place and died our death on the cross, was neither Christ alone (since that would make him a third party thrust in between God and us), nor God alone (since that would undermine the historical incarnation), but *God in Christ,* who was truly and fully both God and man, and who on that account was uniquely qualified to represent both God and man and to mediate between them. If we speak only of Christ suffering and dying, we overlook the initiative of the Father. If we speak only of God suffering and dying, we overlook the mediation of the Son. The New Testament authors never attribute the atonement either to Christ in such a way as to disassociate him from the Father, or to God in such a way as to dispense with Christ, but rather to God and Christ, or to God acting in and through Christ with his whole-hearted concurrence.

The New Testament evidence for this is plain. In surveying it, it seems logical to begin with the announcement of the Messiah's birth. The names he was given were Jesus ('divine Saviour' or 'God saves') and Emmanuel ('God with us'). For in and through his birth God himself had come to the rescue of his people, to save them from their sins (Mt. 1:21–23). Similarly, according to Luke, the Saviour who had been born was not just, in the familiar expression, the Christ of the Lord, the Lord's anointed, but actually 'Christ the Lord', himself both Messiah and Lord (Lk. 2:11).

When Jesus' public ministry began, his personal self-consciousness confirmed that God was at work in and through him. For though he did speak of 'pleasing' the Father (Jn. 8:29) and 'obeying' him (Jn. 15:10), of doing his will and finishing his work,[55] yet this surrender was entirely voluntary, so that his will and the Father's were always in perfect harmony.[56] More than that, according to John he spoke of a mutual 'indwelling', he in the Father and the Father in him, even of a 'union' between them.[57]

This conviction that Father and Son cannot be separated, especially when we are thinking about the atonement, since the Father was taking action through the Son, comes to its fullest expression in some of Paul's great statements about reconciliation. For example, 'all this is from God' (referring to the work of the new creation, 2 Cor. 5:17–18), who 'reconciled us to himself through Christ' and 'was reconciling the world to himself in Christ' (vv. 18–19). It does not seem to matter much where, in translating the Greek, we place the expressions 'through Christ' and 'in Christ'. What matters is that God and Christ were together active in the work of reconciliation, indeed that it was in and through Christ that God was effecting the reconciliation.

Two other important Pauline verses forge an indissoluble link between Christ's person and work, and so indicate that he was able to do what he did only because he was who he was. Both speak of God's 'fullness' dwelling in him and working through him (Col. 1:19–20 and 2:9). This work is variously portrayed, but it is all attributed to the fullness of God residing in Christ – reconciling all things to himself, making peace by the blood of the cross, resurrecting us with Christ, forgiving all our sins, cancelling the written code that was against us, taking it away, nailing it to the cross, and disarming the principalities and powers, triumphing over them either 'by it' (the cross) or 'in him' (Christ).

Anselm was right that only *man should* make reparation for his sins, since it is he who has defaulted. And he was equally right that only *God could* make the necessary reparation, since it is he who has demanded it. Jesus Christ is therefore the only Saviour, since he is the only person in whom the 'should' and the 'could' are united, being himself both God and man. The weakness of Anselm's formulation, due probably to his cultural background in medieval feudalism, is that he overemphasized the humanity of Christ, since man the sinner must pay the debt he has incurred and repair the damage he has done. But the New Testament emphasis is more on the initiative of God, who 'sent' or 'gave' or 'delivered up' his Son for us,[58] and who therefore suffered in his Son's sufferings.

George Buttrick wrote of a picture which hangs in an Italian church, although he did not identify it. At first glance it is like any other painting of the crucifixion. As you look more closely, however, you perceive the difference, because 'there's a vast and shadowy Figure behind the figure of Jesus. The nail that pierces the hand of Jesus goes through to the hand of God. The spear thrust into the side of Jesus goes through into God's.'[59]

We began by showing that God must 'satisfy himself', responding to the realities of human rebellion in a way that is perfectly consonant with his character. This internal necessity is our fixed starting-point. In consequence, it would be impossible for us sinners to remain eternally the sole objects of his holy love, since he cannot both punish and pardon us at the same time. Hence the second necessity, namely substitution. The only way for God's holy love to be satisfied is for his holiness to be directed in judgment upon his appointed substitute, in order that his love may be directed towards us in forgiveness. The substitute bears the penalty, that we sinners may receive the pardon. Who, then, is the substitute? Certainly not Christ, if he is seen as a third party. Any notion of penal substitution in which three independent actors play a role – the guilty party, the punitive judge and the innocent victim – is to be repudiated with the utmost vehemence. It would not only be unjust in itself but would also reflect a defective Christology. For Christ is not an independent third person, but the eternal Son of the Father, who is one with the Father in his essential being.

What we see, then, in the drama of the cross is not three actors but two, ourselves on the one hand and God on the other. Not God as he is in himself (the Father), but God nevertheless, God-made-man-in-Christ (the Son). Hence the importance of those New Testament passages which speak of the death of Christ as the death of God's Son: for example, 'God so loved the world that he gave his one and only Son', 'he ... did not spare his own Son', and 'we were reconciled to God through the death of his Son'.[60] For in giving his Son he was giving himself. This being so, it is the judge himself who in holy love assumed the role of the innocent victim, for in and through the person of his Son he himself bore the penalty which he himself inflicted. As Dale put it, 'the mysterious unity of the Father and the Son rendered it possible for God at once to endure and to inflict penal suffering'.[61] There is neither harsh injustice nor unprincipled love nor Christological heresy in that; there is only unfathomable mercy. For in order to save us in such a way as to satisfy himself, God through Christ substituted himself for us. Divine love triumphed over divine wrath by divine self-sacrifice. The cross was an act simultaneously of punishment and amnesty, severity and grace, justice and mercy.

Seen thus, the objections to a substitutionary atonement evaporate. There is nothing even remotely immoral here, since the substitute for the law-breakers is none other than the divine Lawmaker himself. There is no mechanical transaction either, since the self-sacrifice of love is the most personal of all actions. And what is achieved through the cross is no merely external change of legal status, since those who see God's love there, and are united to Christ by his Spirit, become radically transformed in outlook and character.

We strongly reject, therefore, every explanation of the death of Christ which does not have at its centre the principle of 'satisfaction through substitution', indeed divine self-satisfaction through divine self-substitution. The cross was not a commercial bargain with the devil, let alone one which tricked and trapped him; nor an exact equivalent, a *quid pro quo* to satisfy a code of honour or technical point of law; nor a compulsory submission by God to some moral authority above him from which he could not otherwise escape; nor a punishment of a meek Christ by a harsh and punitive Father; nor a procurement of salvation by a loving Christ from a mean and reluctant Father; nor an action of the Father which bypassed Christ as Mediator. Instead, the righteous, loving Father humbled himself to become in and through his only Son flesh, sin and a curse for us, in order to redeem us without compromising his own character. The theological words 'satisfaction' and 'substitution' need to be carefully defined and safeguarded, but they cannot in any circumstances be given up. The biblical gospel of atonement is of God satisfying himself by substituting himself for us.

The concept of substitution may be said, then, to lie at the heart of both sin and salvation. For the essence of sin is man substituting himself for God, while the essence of salvation is God substituting himself for man. Man asserts himself against God and puts himself where only God deserves to be; God sacrifices himself for man and puts himself where only man deserves to be. Man claims prerogatives which belong to God alone; God accepts penalties which belong to man alone.

If the essence of the atonement is substitution, at least two important inferences follow, the first theological and the second personal. The theological inference is that it is impossible to hold the historic doctrine of the cross without holding the historic doctrine of Jesus Christ as the one and only God-man and Mediator. As we have seen, neither Christ alone as man nor the Father alone as God could be our substitute. Only God in Christ, God the Father's own and only Son made man, could take our place. At the root of every caricature of the cross there lies a distorted Christology. The person and work of Christ belong together. If he was not who the apostles say he was, then he could not have done what they say he did. The incarnation is indispensable to the atonement. In particular, it is essential to affirm that the love, the holiness and the will of the Father are identical with the love, the holiness and the will of the Son. God was in Christ reconciling the world to himself.

Perhaps no twentieth-century theologian has seen this more clearly, or expressed it more vigorously, than Karl Barth.[62] Christology, he insisted, is the key to the doctrine of reconciliation. And Christology means confessing Jesus Christ the Mediator, he repeated several times, as 'very God, very man, and very God-man'. There are thus 'three Christological aspects' or 'three perspectives' for understanding the atonement. The first is that 'in Jesus Christ we have to do with very God. The reconciliation of man with God takes place as God himself actively intervenes' (p. 128). The second is that 'in Jesus Christ we have to do with a true man ... He is altogether man, just as he is altogether God ... That is how he is the reconciler between God and man' (p. 130). The third is that, although very God and very man, 'Jesus Christ himself is one. He is the God-man' (p. 135). Only when this biblical account of Jesus Christ is affirmed can the uniqueness of his atoning sacrifice be understood. The initiative lay with 'the eternal God himself, who has given himself in his Son to be man, and as man to take upon himself this human passion ... It is the Judge who in this passion takes the place of those who ought to be judged, who in this passion allows himself to be judged in their place' (p. 246). 'The passion of Jesus Christ is the judgment of God, in which the Judge himself was the judged' (p. 254).

The second inference is personal. The doctrine of substitution affirms not only a fact (God in Christ substituted himself for us) but its necessity (there was no other way by which God's holy love could be satisfied and rebellious human beings could be saved). Therefore, as we stand before the cross, we begin to gain a clear view both of God and of ourselves, especially in relation to each other. Instead of inflicting upon us the judgment we deserved, God in Christ endured it in our place. Hell is the only alternative. This is the 'scandal', the stumbling-block, of the cross. For our proud hearts rebel against it. We cannot bear to acknowledge either the seriousness of our sin and guilt or our utter indebtedness to the cross. Surely, we say, there must be something we can do, or at least contribute, in order to make amends? If not, we often give the impression that we would rather suffer our own punishment than the humiliation of seeing God through Christ bear it in our place.

George Bernard Shaw, who had considerable insight into the subtleties of human pride, dramatized this in his comedy about the Salvation Army entitled *Major Barbara* (1905). Bill Walker, 'a rough customer of about 25', arrives at the Army's West Ham shelter one cold January morning drunk and infuriated because his girlfriend Mog has not only been converted but 'got another bloke'. Bill's rival is Todger Fairmile, a champion music-hall wrestler in Canning Town, who has also been converted. Accusing Jenny Hill, a young Salvation Army lass, of having set his girlfriend against him, Bill first seizes her by the hair until she screams and then strikes her with his fist in the face, cutting her lip. The bystanders mock him for his cowardice. He attacks a girl, they say, but he would not have the courage to hit Todger Fairmile. Gradually Bill's conscience and pride nag him, until he can no longer bear the insult. He determines to do something to redeem his reputation and expiate his guilt. He says in broad Cockney:

'Aw'm gowin to Kennintahn, to spit in Todger Fairmawl's eye. Aw beshed Jenny Ill's fice; an nar Aw'll git me aown fice beshed ... Ee'll itt me ardem Aw itt er. Thatll mike us square ...'

But Todger refuses to co-operate, so Bill returns shamefaced:

'Aw did wot Aw said Aw'd do. Aw spit in is eye. E looks ap at the skoy and sez, "Ow that Aw should be fahnd worthy to be spit upon for the gospel's sike!" ... an Mog sez "Glaory Allelloolier!".'

Jenny Hill says she is sorry and that he did not really hurt her, which makes him angrier still:

'Aw downt want to be forgive be you, or be ennybody. Wot Aw did Aw'll py for. Aw trawd to gat me aown jawr browk to settisfaw you.' Because that way has failed, however, he tries another ruse. He offers to pay a fine which one of his mates has just incurred, and produces a sovereign.

'Eahs the manney. Tike it; and lets ev no more o your forgivin an pryin an your Mijor jawrin me. Let wot Aw dan be dan an pide for; ant let there be a end of it ... This bloomin forgivin an neggin an jawrin ... mikes a menn thet sore that iz lawf's a burdn to im. Aw wownt ev it, Aw tell yer ... Awve offered to py. Aw can do no more. Tike it or leave it. There it is.' And he throws the sovereign down.

The proud human heart is there revealed. We insist on paying for what we have done. We cannot stand the humiliation of acknowledging our bankruptcy and allowing somebody else to pay for us. The notion that this somebody else should be God himself is just too much to take. We would rather perish than repent, rather lose ourselves than humble ourselves.

Moreover, only the gospel demands such an abject self-humbling on our part, for it alone teaches divine substitution as the only way of salvation. Other religions teach different forms of self-salvation. Hinduism, for example, makes a virtue of refusing to admit to sinfulness. In a lecture before the Parliament of Religions in Chicago in 1893, Swami Vivekananda said: 'The Hindu refuses to call you sinners. Ye are the children of God; the sharers of immortal bliss, holy and perfect beings. Ye divinities on earth, sinners? It is a sin to call a man a sinner. It is a standing libel on human nature.' Besides, if it has to be conceded that human beings do sin, then Hinduism insists that they can save themselves.[63]

As Brunner put it, 'all other forms of religion – not to mention philosophy – deal with the problem of guilt apart from the intervention of God, and therefore they come to a "cheap" conclusion. In them man is spared the final humiliation of knowing that the Mediator must bear the punishment instead of him. To this yoke he need not submit. He is not stripped absolutely naked.'[64]

But we cannot escape the embarrassment of standing stark naked before God. It is no use our trying to cover up like Adam and Eve in the garden. Our attempts at self-justification are as ineffectual as their fig-leaves. We have to acknowledge our nakedness, see the divine substitute wearing our filthy rags instead of us, and allow him to clothe us with his own righteousness.[65] Nobody has ever put it better than Augustus Toplady in his immortal hymn 'Rock of Ages':

> Nothing in my hand I bring,
> Simply to your Cross I cling;
> Naked, come to you for dress;
> Helpless, look to you for grace;
> Foul, I to the fountain fly;
> Wash me, Saviour, or I die.

Notes

[1] James Denney, *Atonement*, p. 82.

[2] Thomas J. Crawford, *Doctrine of Holy Scripture*, pp. 453–454.

[3] From the article 'Sacrifice' by W. P. Paterson, p. 343.

[4] From the essay 'Christ our Sacrifice' by B. B. Warfield, published in *Biblical Doctrines*, pp. 401–435; especially p. 411.

The story is told by Trevor Beeson in *Discretion and Valour*, p. 139.

[6] F. D. Kidner, *Sacrifice in the Old Testament*, p. 14. See also the article 'Sacrifice and Offering' by R. J. Thompson and R. T. Beckwith, and the additional note on 'Old Testament sacrifice' by G. J. Wenham in his *Commentary on Numbers*, pp. 202–205.

[7] Leon Morris, *Atonement*, p. 47.

[8] T. J. Crawford, *Doctrine of Holy Scripture*, pp. 237, 241.

[9] Scholarly debate continues as to whether John the Baptist's 'Lamb of God' was a reference to the Passover lamb, the *tamid* (the lamb of the daily sacrifice), the binding of Isaac (Gn. 22), the horned lamb of Jewish apocalyptic, or the suffering servant of Isaiah 53. For a competent summary of the arguments, in the light of the Fourth Evangelist's use of the Old Testament, see George L. Carey's lecture 'Lamb of God', pp. 97–122.

[10] *E.g.* Jn. 13:1; 18:28; 19:14, 31.

[11] Rev. 5:6, 9, 12; 12:11. Jesus is identified as 'the Lamb' twenty-eight times in Revelation.

[12] Calvin had written: 'This is our acquittal: the guilt that held us liable for punishment has been transferred to the head of the Son of God (Is. 53:12). We must, above all, remember this substitution, lest we tremble and remain anxious throughout life', that is, in fear of God's judgment (*Institutes*, II.xvi.5).

[13] Horace Bushnell somewhat modified his views in his later publication, *Forgiveness and Law*. While still repudiating the traditional doctrine, he nevertheless affirmed that there was in the cross an objective propitiation of God, and that he was 'incarnated into the curse', in order to rescue us from it. He added, however, that Christ consciously suffered the curse or shame of our sin throughout his life.

[14] J. I. Packer, 'What Did the Cross Achieve?', p. 25.

[15] Some examples of 'sin-bearing' expressions are Ex. 28:43; Lv. 5:17; 19:8; 22:9; 24:15 and Nu. 9:13; 14:34 and 18:22.

[16] T. I. Crawford, *Doctrine of Holy Scripture*, p. 225. See also chapter 3, 'The Day of Atonement' in Leon Morris, *Atonement*, pp. 68–87.

[17] Is. 42:1–4; *cf.* Mt. 12:17–21.

[18] Acts 3:13, 26; 4:27, 30.

[19] J. Jeremias, *Eucharistic Words*, p. 228. See also his *Servant of God* and the article on *pais theou* ('servant of God') by Jeremias and Zimmerli, pp. 712ff. Compare chapter 3, 'Jesus the Suffering Servant of God', in Oscar Cullmann's *Christology of the New Testament*.

[20] Mk. 9:12; *cf.* Is. 53:3.

[21] Mk. 2:20; *cf.* Is. 53:8.

[22] Lk. 22:37; *cf.* Is. 53:12.

[23] Mk. 14:8; *cf.* Is. 53:9.

[24] Lk. 11:22; *cf.* Is. 53:12.

[25] Mk. 14:61; 15:5; Lk. 23:9 and Jn. 19:9; *cf.* Is. 53:7.

[26] Lk. 23:34; *cf.* Is. 53:12.

[27] Jn. 10:11, 15, 17; *cf.* Is. 53:10.

[28] Oscar Cullmann, *Baptism in the New Testament*, p. 18.

[29] Vincent Taylor, *Atonement*, p. 18.

[30] Martin Hengel, *Atonement*, pp. 33–75.

[31] Mk. 14:24; *cf.* Mt. 26:28.

[32] In his thorough study, *Atonement*, Professor Martin Hengel argues convincingly that behind Paul's statements that Christ 'died for our sins (1 Cor. 15:3) and 'was given up for our sins' (Rom. 4:25) there lie the 'ransom-saying' and 'supper-sayings' of Jesus, recorded by Mark (10:45; 14:22–25); and that behind these there lies Isaiah 53 and Jesus' own understanding of it (pp. 33–75).

[33] Joachim Jeremias, *Eucharistic Words*, pp. 228–229. Elsewhere Jeremias interprets Jesus' two sayings as referring to 'a vicarious dying for the countless multitude ... of those who lay under the judgment of God'. See also his *Central Message*, pp. 45–46.

[34] J. S. Whale, *Victor and Victim*, pp. 69–70.

[35] Karl Barth, *Church Dogmatics*, vol. IV, 'The Doctrine of Reconciliation', p. 165.

[36] A. W. F. Blunt, *Galatians*, p. 96. See the last chapter for a fuller quotation.

[37] Rom. 4:6; 1 Cor. 1:30; Phil. 3:9.

[38] See T. J. Crawford, *Doctrine of Holy Scripture*, pp. 444–45.

[39] Joachim Jeremias, *Central Message*, p. 36.

[40] Eph. 2:4; *cf.* Jn. 3:16; 1 Jn. 4:9–10.

[41] Zc. 13:7; Mk. 14:27.

[42] Acts 2:23; Rom. 8:32.

[43] John Murray, *Redemption Accomplished*, p. 77.

[44] I. H. Marshall, *Work of Christ*, p. 74.

[45] P. T. Forsyth, *Justification of God*, p. 35.

[46] The quotations are from Helen Gardner's translation. 'Rood', from the old English word *rōd*, was used for the gallows, and especially for Christ's cross.

[47] P. T. Forsyth, *Work of Christ*, p. 25.

[48] P. T. Forsyth *Cruciality of the Cross*, pp. 205–206.

[49] Karl Barth, *Church Dogmatics*, II.1, pp. 446ff. See also pp. 396–403.

[50] S. C. Neill, *Christian Faith Today*, p. 159.

[51] Ignatius refers to 'the blood of God' and to 'the suffering of my God' in the shorter versions of his Letters to the Ephesians (ch. I) and the Romans (ch. VI) respectively. In his *De Carne Christi* Tertullian is even more explicit. 'Was not God really crucified?' he asks. In fact it is he who first used the startling expression 'a crucified God' (ch. V). Another example is Gregory of Nazianzus, who wrote of 'the precious and lordly blood of our God ...' (*Orat.* xlv. 22).

[52] Tertullian, *Adversus Praxean*, ch. I.

[53] *Ibid.*, ch. XXIV.

[54] *E.g.* Rom. 5:12–19; Gal. 4:4; Phil. 2:7–8; Heb. 5:8.

[55] *E.g.* Jn. 4:34; 6:38–39; 17:4; 19:30.

[56] *E.g.* Jn. 10:18; Mk. 14:36; Heb. 10:7 (Ps. 40:7–8).

[57] *E.g.* Jn. 14:11; 17:21–23; 10:30.

[58] *E.g.* Gal. 4:4; 1 Jn. 4:14; Jn. 3:16; Rom. 8:32.

[59] George A. Buttrick, *Jesus Came Preaching*, p. 207.

[60] Jn. 3:16; Rom. 8:32 and 5:10.

[61] R. W. Dale, *Atonement*, p. 393.

[62] Karl Barth, *Church Dogmatics*, IV.1.

[63] From *Speeches and Writings* by Swami Vivekananda, pp. 38–39. *Cf.* p. 125. See also *Crises of Belief* by S. C. Neill, p. 100.

[64] Emil Brunner, *Mediator*, p. 474.

[65] *Cf.* Rev. 3:17–18.

PART THREE

The achievement of the cross

Seven

The salvation of sinners

Moved by the perfection of his holy love, God in Christ substituted himself for us sinners. That is the heart of the cross of Christ. It leads us to turn now from the event to its consequences, from what happened on the cross to what was achieved by it. Why did God take our place and bear our sin? What did he accomplish by his self-sacrifice, his self-substitution?

The New Testament gives three main answers to these questions, which may be summed up in the words 'salvation', 'revelation' and 'conquest'. What God in Christ has done through the cross is to rescue us, disclose himself and overcome evil. In this chapter we shall focus on salvation through the cross.

It would be hard to exaggerate the magnitude of the changes which have taken place as a result of the cross, both in God and in us, especially in God's dealings with us and in our relations with him. Truly, when Christ died and was raised from death, a new day dawned, a new age began.

This new day is 'the day of salvation' (2 Cor. 6:2), and the blessings of 'such a great salvation' (Heb. 2:3) are so richly diverse that they cannot be neatly defined. Several pictures are needed to portray them. Just as the church of Christ is presented in Scripture as his bride and his body, the sheep of God's flock and the branches of his vine, his new humanity, his household or family, the temple of the Holy Spirit and the pillar and but-tress of the truth, so the salvation of Christ is illustrated by the vivid imagery of terms like 'propitiation', 'redemption', 'justification' and 'reconciliation', which are to form the theme of this chapter. Moreover, as the images of the church are visually incompatible (one cannot envisage the body and the bride of Christ simultaneously), yet underlying them all is the truth that God is calling out a people for himself, so the images of salvation are incompatible (justification and redemption conjure up respectively the divergent worlds of law and commerce), yet underlying them all is the truth that God in Christ has borne our sin and died our death to set us free from sin and death. Such images are indispensable aids to human understanding of doctrine. And what they convey, being God-given, is true. Yet we must not deduce from this that to have understood the images is to have exhausted the meaning of the doctrine. For beyond the images of the atonement lies the mystery of the atonement, the deep wonders of which, I guess, we shall be exploring throughout eternity.

'Images' of salvation (or of the atonement) is a better term than 'theories'. For theories are usually abstract and speculative concepts, whereas the biblical images of the atoning achievement of Christ are concrete pictures and belong to the data of revelation. They are not alternative explanations of the cross, providing us with a range to choose from, but complementary to one another, each contributing a vital part to the whole. As for the imagery, 'propitiation' introduces us to rituals at a shrine, 'redemption' to transactions in a market-place, 'justification' to proceedings in a lawcourt, and 'reconciliation' to experiences in a home or family. My contention is that 'substitution' is not a further 'theory' or 'image' to be set alongside the others, but rather the foundation of them all, without which each lacks cogency. If God in Christ did not die in our place, there could be neither propitiation, nor redemption, nor justification, nor reconciliation. In addition, all the images begin their life in the Old Testament, but are elaborated and enriched in the New, particularly by being directly related to Christ and his cross.

Propitiation

Western Christians of earlier generations were quite familiar with the language of 'propitiation' in relation to the death of Christ. For the Authorized (King James) Version of the Bible, on which they were brought up, contained three explicit affirmations of it by Paul and John:

Paul: '... Christ Jesus, whom God hath set forth to be a propitiation through faith in his blood' (Rom. 3:24–25).
John: 'We have an advocate with the Father, Jesus Christ the righteous: and he is the propitiation for our sins.' Again, 'Herein is love, not that we loved God, but that he loved us, and sent his Son to be the propitiation for our sins' (1 Jn. 2:1–2; 4:10).

Although this language was well known to our forebears, they were not necessarily comfortable in using it. To 'propitiate' somebody means to appease or pacify his anger. Does God then get angry? If so, can offerings or rituals assuage his anger? Does he accept bribes? Such concepts sound more pagan than Christian. It is understandable that primitive animists should consider it essential to placate the wrath of gods, spirits or ancestors, but are notions like these worthy of the Christian God? Should we not have grown out of them? In particular, are we really to believe that Jesus by his death propitiated the Father's anger, inducing him to turn from it and to look upon us with favour instead?

Crude concepts of anger, sacrifice and propitiation are indeed to be rejected. They do not belong to the religion of the Old Testament, let alone of the New. This does not mean, however, that there is no biblical concept of these things at all. What is revealed to us in Scripture is a pure doctrine (from which all pagan vulgarities have been expunged) of God's holy wrath, his loving self-sacrifice in Christ and his initiative to avert his own anger. It is obvious that 'wrath' and 'propitiation' (the placating of wrath) go together. It is when the wrath is purged of unworthy ideas that the propitiation is thereby purged. The opposite is also true. It is those who cannot come to terms with any concept of the wrath of God who repudiate any concept of propitiation. Here, for example, is Professor A. T. Hanson: 'If you think of the wrath as an attitude of God, you cannot avoid some theory of propitiation. But the wrath in the New Testament is never spoken of as being propitiated, because it is not conceived of as being an attitude of God.'[1]

It is this discomfort with the doctrines of wrath and propitiation which has led some theologians to re-examine the biblical vocabulary. They have concentrated on a particular word-group which the Authorized Version translated in 'propitiatory' terms, namely the noun *hilasmos* (1 Jn. 2:2; 4:10), the adjective *hilastērios* (Rom. 3:25, where it may be used as a noun) and the verb *hilaskomai* (Heb. 2:17; also Lk. 18:13 in the passive, which should perhaps be rendered 'be propitiated – or propitious – to me, a sinner'). The crucial question is whether the object of the atoning action is God or man. If the former, then the right word is 'propitiation' (appeasing God); if the latter, the right word is 'expiation' (dealing with sin and guilt).

The British theologian who led the way in this attempted reinterpretation was C. H. Dodd.[2] Here is his comment on Romans 3:25: 'the meaning conveyed ... is that of expiation, not that of propitiation. Most translators and commentators are wrong.'[3] He expresses a similar opinion in relation to 1 John 2:2, namely that the translation 'propitiation for our sins' is 'illegitimate here as elsewhere'.[4] Since C. H. Dodd was director of the panels which produced the New English Bible (New Testament 1961), it is not surprising that his view was reflected in its rendering of the verses just referred to. Romans 3:25 is translated 'God designed him to be the means of expiating sin by his sacrificial death', while in 1 John 2:2 and 4:10 the key phrase is rendered 'he is himself the remedy for the defilement of our sins'. The RSV, whose New Testament was published a few years earlier (1946), has 'expiation' in all three verses.

C. H. Dodd's argument, developed with his customary erudition, was linguistic. He acknowledged that in pagan Greek (both classical and popular) the regular meaning of the verb *hilaskomai* was to 'propitiate' or 'placate' an offended person, especially a deity. But he denied that this was its meaning either in Hellenistic Judaism, as evidenced in the Septuagint (LXX), or, on that account, in the New Testament. He argued that in the LXX *kipper* (the Hebrew verb for 'atone') was sometimes translated by Greek words other than *hilaskomai*, which mean to 'purify' or 'cancel'; that *hilaskomai* in the LXX sometimes translates other Hebrew words than *kipper*, which mean to 'cleanse' or 'forgive'; and that when *hilaskomai* does translate *kipper* the meaning is expiation or the removal of defilement. This is how he sums up: 'Hellenistic Judaism, as represented by the LXX, does not regard the cultus as a means of pacifying the displeasure of the Deity, but as a means of delivering man from sin.'[5] Indeed, it was generally believed in antiquity that 'the performance of prescribed rituals ... had the value, so to speak, of a powerful disinfectant'.[6] Therefore, he concludes, the New Testament occurrences of the *hilaskomai* word group should be interpreted in the same way. By his cross Jesus Christ expiated sin; he did not propitiate God.

Professor Dodd's reconstruction, although accepted by many of his contemporaries and successors, was subjected to a rigorous critique by others, in particular by Dr Leon Morris[7] and Dr Roger Nicole.[8] Both showed that his conclusions rested on either incomplete evidence or questionable deductions. For example, his assessment of the meaning of the *hilaskomai* group in Hellenistic Judaism makes no reference either (1) to the books of the Maccabees, although they belong to the LXX and contain several passages which speak of 'the wrath of the Almighty' being averted, or (2) to the writings of Josephus and Philo, although in them, as Friedrich Büchsel shows, the meaning to 'placate' prevails.[9] As for the New Testament understanding of these words, F. Büchsel points out what C. H. Dodd overlooks, that in both Clement's First Letter (end of the first century) and the *Shepherd* of Hermas (beginning of the second) *hilaskomai* is plainly used of propitiating God. So then, for C. H. Dodd's theory about the LXX and New Testament usage to be correct, he would have to maintain that they 'form a sort of linguistic island with little precedent in former times, little confirmation from the contemporaries, and no following in after years!'[10]

But we have to declare his thesis incorrect. Even in the Old Testament canon itself there are numerous instances in which *kipper* and *hilaskomai* are used of propitiating the anger either of men (like Jacob pacifying Esau with gifts and a wise man appeasing a king's wrath)[11] or of God (like Aaron and Phinehas who turned God's anger away from the Israelites).[12] Even in passages where the natural translation is to 'make atonement for sin', the context often contains explicit mention of God's wrath, which implies that the human sin can be atoned for only by the divine anger being turned away.[13] These instances, Roger Nicole points out, are consistent with 'the predominant use in classical and *koinē* Greek, in Josephus and Philo, in patristic writers and in the Maccabees'.[14] Leon Morris's conclusion in regard to the Old Testament is that, although *hilaskomai* is 'a complex word', yet 'the averting of anger seems to represent a stubborn substratum of meaning from which all the usages can be naturally explained'.[15]

The same is true of the New Testament occurrences. The description of Jesus as the *hilasmos* in relation to our sins (1 Jn. 2:2; 4:10) could be understood as meaning simply that he took them away or cancelled them. But he is also named our 'advocate with the Father' (2:1), which implies the displeasure of the One before whom he pleads our cause. As for the passage in Romans 3, the context is determinative. Whether we translate *hilastērion* in verse 25 'the place of propitiation' (*i.e.* the mercy-seat, as in Heb. 9:5) or 'the means of propitiation' (*i.e.* a propitiatory sacrifice), the Jesus who is so described is set forth by God as the remedy for universal human guilt under his wrath, which Paul has taken two and a half chapters to demonstrate. As Leon Morris justly comments, 'wrath has occupied such an important place in the argument leading up to this section that we are justified in looking for some expression indicative of its cancellation in the process which brings about salvation'.[16] It is true that in Hebrews 2:17 *hilaskomai is* a transitive verb, with 'the sins of the people' as its object. It could therefore be translated 'expiate' (NEB) or 'make atonement for' (NIV). This meaning is not indubitable, however. The NIV margin renders it 'that he might turn aside God's wrath, taking away' the people's sins.

If we grant that C. H. Dodd's linguistic argument has been lost, or at the very least that his case is 'not proven', and that the *hilaskomai* word-group means 'propitiation' not 'expiation', we still have to decide how to portray God's anger and its averting. It would be easy to caricature them in such a way as to dismiss them with ridicule. This William Neil has done in the following passage:

It is worth noting that the 'fire and brimstone' school of theology who revel in ideas such as that Christ was made a sacrifice to appease an angry God, or that the cross was a legal transaction in which an innocent victim was made to pay the penalty for the crimes of others, a propitiation of a stern God, find no support in Paul. These notions came into Christian theology by way of the legalistic minds of the medieval churchmen; they are not biblical Christianity.[17]

But of course this is the Christianity neither of the Bible in general, nor of Paul in particular. It is doubtful if anybody has ever believed such a crude construction. For these are pagan notions of propitiation with but a very thin Christian veneer. If we are to develop a truly biblical doctrine of propitiation, it will be necessary to distinguish it from pagan idols at three crucial points, relating to why a propitiation is necessary, who made it and what it was.

First, the reason why a propitiation is necessary is that sin arouses the wrath of God. This does not mean (as animists fear) that he is likely to fly off the handle at the most trivial provocation, still less that he loses his temper for no apparent reason at all. For there is nothing capricious or arbitrary about the holy God. Nor is he ever irascible, malicious, spiteful or vindictive. His anger is neither mysterious nor irrational. It is never unpredictable, but always predictable, because it is provoked by evil and by evil alone. The wrath of God, as we considered more fully in chapter 4, is his steady, unrelenting, unremitting, uncompromising antagonism to evil in all its forms and manifestations. In short, God's anger is poles apart from ours. What provokes our anger (injured vanity) never provokes his; what provokes his anger (evil) seldom provokes ours.

Secondly, who makes the propitiation? In a pagan context it is always human beings who seek to avert the divine anger either by the meticulous performance of rituals, or by the recitation of magic formulae, or by the offering of sacrifices (vegetable, animal or even human). Such practices are thought to placate the offended deity. But the gospel begins with the outspoken assertion that nothing we can do, say, offer or even contribute can compensate for our sins or turn away God's anger. There is no possibility of persuading, cajoling or bribing God to forgive us, for we deserve nothing at his hands but judgment. Nor, as we have seen, has Christ by his sacrifice prevailed upon God to pardon us. No, the initiative has been taken by God himself in his sheer mercy and grace.

This was already clear in the Old Testament, in which the sacrifices were recognized not as human works but as divine gifts. They did not make God gracious; they were provided by a gracious God in order that he might act graciously towards his sinful people. 'I have given it to you', God said of the sacrificial blood, 'to make atonement for yourselves on the altar' (Lv. 17:11). And this truth is yet more plainly recognized in the New Testament, not least in the main texts about propitiation. God himself 'presented' (NIV) or 'put forward' (RSV) Jesus Christ as a propitiatory sacrifice (Rom. 3:25). It is not that we loved God, but that he loved us and sent his Son as a propitiation for our sins (1 Jn. 4:10). It cannot be emphasized too strongly that God's love is the source, not the consequence, of the atonement. As P. T. Forsyth expressed it, 'the atonement did not procure grace, it flowed from grace'.[18] God does not love us because Christ died for us; Christ died for us because God loved us. If it is God's wrath which needed to be propitiated, it is God's love which did the propitiating. If it may be said that the propitiation 'changed' God, or that by it he changed himself, let us be clear he did not change from wrath to love, or from enmity to grace, since his character is unchanging. What the propitiation changed was his dealings with us. 'The distinction I ask you to observe', wrote P. T. Forsyth, 'is between a change of feeling and a change of treatment ... God's feeling toward us never needed to be changed. But God's treatment of us, God's practical relation to us – that had to change.'[19] He forgave us and welcomed us home.

Thirdly, what was the propitiatory sacrifice? It was neither an animal, nor a vegetable, nor a mineral. It was not a thing at all, but a person. And the person God offered was not somebody else, whether a human person or an angel or even his Son considered as somebody distinct from or external to himself. No, he offered himself. In giving his Son, he was giving himself. As Karl Barth wrote repeatedly, 'it was the Son of God, *i.e.* God himself'. For example, 'the fact that it was God's Son, that it was God himself, who took our place on Golgotha and thereby freed us from the divine anger and judgment, reveals first the full implication of the wrath of God, of his condemning and punishing justice'. Again, 'because it was the Son of God, *i.e.* God himself, who took our place on Good Friday, the substitution could be effectual and procure our reconciliation with the righteous God ... Only God, our Lord and Creator, could stand surety for us, could take our place, could suffer eternal death in our stead as the consequence of our sin in such a way that it was finally suffered and overcome'.[20] And all this, Barth makes clear, was an expression not only of God's holiness and justice, but of 'the perfections of the divine loving', indeed of God's 'holy love'.

So then, God himself is at the heart of our answer to all three questions about the divine propitiation. It is God himself who in holy wrath needs to be propitiated, God himself who in holy love undertook to do the propitiating, and God himself who in the person of his Son died for the propitiation of our sins. Thus God took his own loving initiative to appease his own righteous anger by bearing it his own self in his own Son when he took our place and died for us. There is no crudity here to evoke our ridicule, only the profundity of holy love to evoke our worship.

In seeking thus to defend and reinstate the biblical doctrine of propitiation, we have no intention of denying the biblical doctrine of expiation. Although we must resist every attempt to replace propitiation by expiation, we welcome every attempt to see them as belonging together in salvation. Thus F. Büchsel wrote that '*hilasmos* ... is the action in which God is propitiated and sin expiated'.[21] Dr David Wells has elaborated this succinctly:

In Pauline thought, man is alienated from God by sin and God is alienated from man by wrath. It is in the substitutionary death of

Christ that sin is overcome and wrath averted, so that God can look on man without displeasure and man can look on God without fear. Sin is expiated and God is propitiated.[22]

Redemption

We now move on from 'propitiation' to 'redemption'. In seeking to understand the achievement of the cross, the imagery changes from Temple court to market-place, from the ceremonial realm to the commercial, from religious rituals to business transactions. For at its most basic to 'redeem' is to buy or buy back, whether as a purchase or a ransom. Inevitably, then, the emphasis of the redemption image is on our sorry state – indeed our captivity – in sin which made an act of divine rescue necessary. 'Propitiation' focuses on the wrath of God which was placated by the cross; 'redemption' on the plight of sinners from which they were ransomed by the cross.

And 'ransom' is the correct word to use. The Greek words *lytroō* (usually translated 'redeem') and *apolytrōsis* ('redemption') are derived from *lytron* ('a ransom' or 'price of release'), which was almost a technical term in the ancient world for the purchase or manumission of a slave. In view of 'the unwavering usage of profane authors', namely that this word-group refers to 'a process involving release by payment of a ransom price',[23] often very costly, wrote Leon Morris, we have no liberty to dilute its meaning into a vague and even cheap deliverance. We have been 'ransomed' by Christ, not merely 'redeemed' or 'delivered' by him. B. B. Warfield was right to point out that we are 'assisting at the death bed of a word. It is sad to witness the death of any worthy thing – even of a worthy word. And worthy words do die, like any other worthy thing – if we do not take good care of them'. Sadder still is 'the dying out of the hearts of men of the things for which the words stand'.[24] He was referring to his generation's loss of a sense of gratitude to him who paid our ransom.

In the Old Testament property, animals, persons and the nation were all 'redeemed' by the payment of a price. The right (even the duty) to play the role of 'kinsman redeemer' and buy back a property which had been alienated, in order to keep it in the family or tribe, was illustrated in the case of both Boaz and Jeremiah.[25] As for animals, the firstborn males of all livestock belonged by right to Yahweh; donkeys and unclean animals, however, could be redeemed (*i.e.* bought back) by the owner.[26] In the case of individual Israelites, each had to pay 'a ransom for his life' at the time of the national census; firstborn sons (who since the first Passover belonged to God), and especially those in excess of the number of Levites who replaced them, had to be redeemed; the owner of a notoriously dangerous bull, which gored a man to death, was himself to be put to death, unless he redeemed his life by the payment of an adequate fine; and an impoverished

Israelite compelled to sell himself into slavery could later either redeem himself or be redeemed by a relative.[27] In all these cases of 'redemption' there was a decisive and costly intervention. Somebody paid the price necessary to free property from mortgage, animals from slaughter, and persons from slavery, even death.

What about the nation? Certainly the vocabulary of redemption was used to describe Yahweh's deliverance of Israel both from slavery in Egypt[28] and from exile in Babylon.[29] But in this case, since the redeemer was not a human being but God himself, can we still maintain that to 'redeem' is to 'ransom'? What price did Yahweh pay to redeem his people? Bishop B. F. Westcott seems to have been the first to suggest an answer: 'the idea of the exertion of a mighty force, the idea that the "redemption" costs much, is everywhere present.'[30] Warfield enlarged on this: 'the idea that the redemption from Egypt was the effect of a great expenditure of the divine power and in that sense cost much, is prominent in the allusions to it, and seems to constitute the central idea sought to be conveyed.'[31] For God redeemed Israel 'with an outstretched arm' and 'with a mighty hand'.[32] We conclude that redemption *always* involved the payment of a price, and that Yahweh's redemption of Israel was not an exception. Even here, Warfield sums up, 'the conception of price-paying intrinsic in *lutrousthai* is preserved ... A redemption without a price paid is as anomalous a transaction as a sale without money passing.'[33]

When we enter the New Testament and consider its teaching about redemption, two changes immediately strike us. Although it is still inherent in the concept both that those needing redemption are in a bad plight and that they can be redeemed only by the payment of a price, yet now the plight is moral rather than material, and the price is the atoning death of God's Son. This much is already evident in Jesus' famous 'ransom-saying', which is foundational to the New Testament doctrine of redemption: 'The Son of Man did not come to be served, but to serve, and to give his life as a ransom for many' (Mk. 10:45). The imagery implies that we are held in a captivity from which only the payment of a ransom can set us free, and that the ransom is nothing less than the Messiah's own life. Our lives are forfeit; his life will be sacrificed instead. F. Buchsel is surely correct that the saying 'undoubtedly implies substitution'. This is made plain by the combination of the two adjectives in the Greek expression *antilytron hyper pollōn* (literally, 'a ransom in place of and for the sake of many'). 'The death of Jesus means that there happens to him what would have had to happen to the many. Hence he takes their place.'[34] A parallel expression (perhaps an echo of it) occurs in 1 Timothy 2:5–6, 'Christ Jesus ... gave himself as a ransom for all men.'

It is instructive that the Jewish historian Josephus used similar language when he described the Roman general Crassus' visit to the Temple in

Jerusalem in 54–53 BC, intent on plundering the sanctuary. A priest named Eleazar, who was guardian of the sacred treasures, gave him a large bar of gold (worth 10,000 shekels) as *lytron anti pantōn*, 'a ransom instead of all'. That is, the gold bar was offered as a substitute for the Temple treasures.[35]

What then, first, is the human plight, from which we cannot extricate ourselves and which makes it necessary for us to be redeemed? We have seen that in the Old Testament people were redeemed from a variety of grave social situations such as debt, captivity, slavery, exile and liability to execution. But it is a moral bondage from which Christ has ransomed us. This is described now as our 'transgressions' or 'sins' (since in two key verses 'redemption' is a synonym for 'the forgiveness of sins'),[36] now as 'the curse of the law' (namely the divine judgment which it pronounces on law-breakers),[37] and now as 'the empty way of life handed down to you from your forefathers'.[38] Yet even our release from these captivities does not complete our redemption. There is more to come. For Christ 'gave himself for us to redeem us from all wickedness',[39] to liberate us from *all* the ravages of the Fall. This we have not yet experienced. Just as the Old Testament people of God, though already redeemed from their Egyptian and Babylonian exiles, were yet waiting for the promise of a fuller redemption, 'looking forward to the redemption of Jerusalem',[40] so the New Testament people of God, though already redeemed from guilt and judgment, are yet waiting for 'the day of redemption' when we shall be made perfect. This will include 'the redemption of our bodies'. At that point the whole groaning creation will be liberated from its bondage to decay and be brought to share in the freedom of the glory of God's children. Meanwhile, the indwelling Holy Spirit is himself the seal, the guarantee and the first-fruits of our final redemption.[41] Only then will Christ have redeemed us (and the universe) from all sin, pain, futility and decay.

Secondly, having considered the plight *from* which, we need to consider the price *with* which, we have been redeemed. The New Testament never presses the imagery to the point of indicating to whom the ransom was paid, but it leaves us in no doubt about the price: it was Christ himself. To begin with, there was the cost of the incarnation, of entering into our condition in order to reach us. Certainly we are told that when God sent his Son, he was 'born under law, to redeem those under law' (Gal. 4:4–5). Jeremias wonders if Paul was alluding to 'the dramatic act of entering into slavery in order to redeem a slave', just as the giving of the body to be burnt (1 Cor. 13:3) may refer to being 'branded with the slave-mark'.[42] Beyond the incarnation, however, lay the atonement. To accomplish this he gave 'himself' (1 Tim. 2:6; Tit. 2:14) or his 'life' (his *psychē*, Mk.10:45), dying under the law's curse to redeem us from it (Gal. 3:13).

When indicating the costly price paid by Christ to ransom us, however, the commonest word used by the New Testament authors was neither 'himself' nor his 'life' but his 'blood'. It was 'not with perishable things such as silver or gold', wrote Peter, 'that you were redeemed ..., but with the precious blood of Christ, a lamb without blemish or defect' (1 Pet. 1:18–19). The writer to the Hebrews, steeped as he was in sacrificial imagery, emphasized that Christ was victim as well as priest, since 'he entered the Most Holy Place once for all by his own blood'.[43]

But what is meant by Christ's 'blood'? Everybody agrees that it alludes to his death, but in what sense? Picking on the threefold assertion in Leviticus 17:11–14 that 'the life of a creature is in the blood' or 'the life of every creature is its blood', and the even more straightforward statement of Deuteronomy 12:23 that 'the blood is the life', a strangely popular theory was developed by British theologians at the end of the last century that Christ's blood stands not for his death but for his life, which is released through death and so made available for us. Vincent Taylor, C. H. Dodd and even P. T. Forsyth were among those who developed this idea. Its origin is usually traced back, however, to Bishop B. F. Westcott's *Commentary on the Epistles of John* (1883), in which he wrote:

> By the outpouring of the Blood the life which was in it was not destroyed, though it was separated from the organism which it had before quickened ... Thus two distinct ideas were included in the sacrifice of a victim, the death of the victim by the shedding of its blood, and the liberation, so to speak, of the principle of life by which it had been animated, so that this life became available for another end.[44]

Just so, Christ's blood was his life first given *for us* and then given *to us.*

In his later commentary on the Epistle to the Hebrews Westcott was still teaching the same concept. Blood is life 'regarded as still living', and 'the blood poured out is the energy ... made available for others'.[45]

James Denney was outspoken in his rejection of this thesis. In his book *The Death of Christ* (1902) he urged his readers not to adopt 'the strange caprice which fascinated Westcott', who distinguished in the blood of Christ between his death and his life, his blood shed and offered, his life laid down and liberated for men. 'I venture to say', he continued, 'that a more groundless fancy never haunted and troubled the interpretation of any part of Scripture' (p. 149).

Then in 1948 Alan Stibbs' excellent Tyndale Monograph was published, *The Meaning of the Word 'Blood' in Scripture*, which should have laid this ghost to rest for ever. He makes a thorough examination of the occurrences of 'blood' in both Old and New Testaments, and has no difficulty in demonstrating that it is 'a word-symbol for death'. True, 'the blood is the life of the flesh'. But 'this means that if the blood is separated from the flesh, whether in man or beast, the present physical life in the flesh will come to an end. Blood shed stands, therefore, not for the release of life from the burden of the flesh, but for the bringing to an end of life in the flesh. It is a witness to physical death, not an evidence of spiritual survival.' To 'drink Christ's blood', therefore, describes 'not participation in his life but appropriation of the benefits of his life laid down'.[46] We cannot do better than conclude as he does with a quotation from Johannes Behm's article on 'blood' in Kittel's Dictionary: '"Blood of Christ" is (like "Cross") only another, clearer expression for the death of Christ in its salvation meaning' or 'redemptive significance'.[47]

The 'redemption' image has a third emphasis. In addition to the plight from which, and the price with which, we are ransomed, it draws attention to the person of the redeemer who has proprietary rights over his purchase. Thus Jesus' lordship over both church and Christian is attributed to his having bought us with his own blood. Presbyters, for example, are summoned to conscientious oversight of the church on the ground that God in Christ has bought it with his own blood (Acts 20:28). If the church was worth his blood, is it not worth our labour? The privilege of serving it is established by the preciousness of the price paid for its purchase. That seems to be the argument. Again, the redeemed community in heaven is singing a new song which celebrates the worthiness of the Lamb:

> You are worthy to take the scroll
>   and to open its seals,
> because you were slain,
>   and with your blood you purchased men for God
>   from every tribe and language and people and nation.[48]

A remembrance that Jesus Christ has bought us with his blood, and that in consequence we belong to him, should motivate us as individual Christians to holiness, just as it motivates presbyters to faithful ministry and the heavenly host to worship. We detect a note of outrage in Peter's voice when he speaks of false teachers who by their shameful behaviour are 'denying the sovereign Lord who bought them' (2 Pet. 2:1). Since he bought them, they are his. They should therefore acknowledge and not deny him. Paul's urgent summons to us to 'flee from sexual immorality' is based on the doctrine of the human body and who owns it. On the one hand, 'Don't you know', he asks incredulously, 'that your body is a temple of the Holy Spirit, who is in you, whom you have received from God?' On the other, 'You are not your own; you were bought at a price. Therefore honour God with your body.'[49] Our body has not only been created by God and will one day be resurrected by him, but it has been bought by Christ's blood and is indwelt by his Spirit. Thus it belongs to God three times over, by creation, redemption and indwelling. How then, since it does not belong to us, can we misuse it? Instead, we are to honour God with it, by obedience and self-control. Bought by Christ, we have no business to become the slaves of anybody or anything else. Once we were the slaves of sin; now we are the slaves of Christ, and his service is the true freedom.

Justification

The two pictures we have so far considered have led us into the temple precincts (propitiation) and the market-place (redemption). The third image (justification) will take us into the lawcourt. For justification is the opposite of condemnation (*e.g.* Rom. 5:18; 8:34), and both are verdicts of a judge who pronounces the accused either guilty or not guilty. There is logic in the order in which we are reviewing these great words which describe the achievement of the cross. Propitiation inevitably comes first, because until the wrath of God is appeased (that is, until his love has found a way to avert his anger), there can be no salvation for human beings at all. Next, when we are ready to understand the meaning of salvation, we begin negatively with redemption, meaning our rescue at the high price of Christ's blood from the grim captivity of sin and guilt. Justification is its positive counterpart. True, some scholars have denied this. Sanday and Headlam wrote that justification 'is simply forgiveness, free forgiveness',[50] and more recently Jeremias has asserted that 'justification is forgiveness, nothing but forgiveness'.[51] The two concepts are surely complementary, however, not identical. Forgiveness remits our debts and cancels our liability to punishment; justification bestows on us a righteous standing before God.

The sixteenth-century Reformers, whom God enlightened to rediscover the biblical gospel of 'justification by faith', were convinced of its central importance. Luther called it 'the principal article of all Christian doctrine, which maketh true Christians indeed'.[52] And Cranmer wrote:

> This faith the holy Scripture teacheth: this is the strong rock and foundation of Christian religion: this doctrine all old and ancient authors of Christ's church do approve: this doctrine advanceth and setteth forth the true glory of Christ, and beateth down the vain glory of man: this whosoever denieth is not to be counted for a true Christian man … but for an adversary of Christ …[53]

Let me add a statement by some contemporary Anglican Evangelicals:

> Justification by Faith appears to us, as it does to all evangelicals, to be the heart and hub, the paradigm and essence of the whole economy of God's saving grace. Like Atlas, it bears a world on its shoulders, the

entire evangelical knowledge of God's love in Christ towards sinners.[54]

Despite the paramount importance of this truth, there have been many objections to it. First, there are those who have a strong antipathy to legal categories in all talk about salvation, on the ground that they represent God as Judge and King, not as Father, and therefore cannot adequately portray either his personal dealings with us or our personal relationship with him. This objection would be sustained if justification were the only image of salvation. But its juridical flavour is balanced by the more personal imagery of 'reconciliation' and 'adoption' (in which God is Father, not Judge), which we shall consider next. Other critics, secondly, attempt to dismiss the doctrine as a Pauline idiosyncrasy, originating in his peculiarly forensic mind. We should not hesitate to dismiss this dismissal, however, since what is Pauline is apostolic and therefore authoritative. In any case the statement is false. The concept of justification was not invented by Paul. It goes back to Jesus, who said that the tax collector in his parable 'went home justified before God', rather than the Pharisee (Lk. 18:14). Indeed, it goes further back still to the Old Testament, in which God's righteous and suffering servant 'will justify many', because 'he will bear their iniquities' (Is. 53:11).

Thirdly, we need to look at the reasons for the Roman Catholic rejection of the Reformers' teaching on justification by faith. We might not unfairly sum up the Council of Trent's doctrine under three headings which concern the nature of justification, what precedes and occasions it, and what follows it. First, the Council taught that justification takes place at baptism and includes both forgiveness and renewal. The baptized person is cleansed from all original and actual sins, and is simultaneously infused with a new and supernatural righteousness. Secondly, before baptism God's prevenient grace predisposes people 'to convert themselves to their own justification by freely assenting to and co-operating with that grace'. Thirdly, post-baptismal sins (if 'mortal', causing the loss of grace) are not included within the scope of justification. They have to be purged by contrition, confession and penance (also, if any remain at death, by purgatory), so that these and other post-baptismal good works may be said to 'merit' eternal life.[55]

The Protestant churches had good reason to be deeply disturbed by this teaching. At the same time, neither side was listening carefully to the other, and both were marked by the acrimonious and polemical spirit of their age. Today the basic issue, which is the way of salvation, remains crucial. Very much is at stake. Yet the atmosphere has changed. Also Hans Küng's astonishing monograph on Karl Barth's doctrine of justification[56] has opened up fresh possibilities for dialogue. So has the Second Vatican Council of the early 1960s.[57]

Hans Küng's book is in two parts. Concerning the first, which expounds

'Karl Barth's Theology of Justification', Barth himself wrote to Hans Küng: 'You have fully and accurately reproduced my views as I myself understand them ... You have me say what I actually do say and ... I mean it in the way you have me say it' (p. xvii). Concerning the second part, which offers 'An Attempt at a Catholic Response', and in its conclusion claims 'a fundamental agreement between Catholic and Protestant theology, precisely in the theology of justification' (p. 271), Barth wrote: 'If this is the teaching of the Roman Catholic Church, then I must certainly admit that my view of justification agrees with the Roman Catholic view, if only for the reason that the Roman Catholic teaching would then be most strikingly in accord with mine!' He then asks how this agreement 'could remain hidden so long and from so many', and mischievously enquires whether Hans Küng discovered it before, during or after his reading of the *Church Dogmatics* (pp. xvii-xviii)!

Hans Küng certainly makes some remarkable statements, although perhaps it is a pity that his thesis seeks to demonstrate Trent's accord with Barth, rather than with Luther for whom he appears to have less sympathy. In chapter 27 he defines grace according to Scripture as 'graciousness', God's 'favour' or 'generous kindness'. 'The issue is not *my having* grace, but *his being* gracious' (pp. 189–190). In chapter 28 he writes that justification 'must be defined as a *declaring just by court order,* and that in the New Testament 'the association with a juridical situation is never absent' (p. 200). Again, it is 'a judicial event', 'a wonderfully gracious saving justice' (pp. 205–206). Then in chapter 31 Hans Küng strongly affirms the truth of *sola fide* (by faith alone), and says that Luther was entirely correct and orthodox to add the word 'alone' to the text of Romans 3:28, since it was 'not Luther's invention', it had already appeared in several other translations, and Trent had not intended to contradict it (p. 237). So 'we have to acknowledge a fundamental agreement', he writes, 'in regard to the *sola fides* formula ... Man is justified by God on the basis of faith alone' (p. 246). Moreover, 'justification through "faith alone" bespeaks the complete incapacity and incompetence of man for any sort of self-justification' (p. 301). 'Thus man is justified through God's grace alone; man achieves nothing; there is no human activity. Rather man simply submits to the justification of God; he does not do works; he believes' (p. 240).

Professor Küng does not stop there, however. Despite his emphasis on the judicial nature of justification as a divine declaration, he insists that God's Word is always efficacious, so that whatever God pronounces comes into being. Therefore, when God says, 'You are just', 'the sinner is just, really and truly, outwardly and inwardly, wholly and completely. His sins *are* forgiven, and man is just in his heart ... In brief, God's *declaration* of justice is ... at the same time and in the same act a *making just*' (p. 204). Justification is 'the single act which simultaneously declares just and makes just' (p. 210).

But there is a dangerous ambiguity here, especially in the rhetorical sentence about the justified sinner being 'wholly and completely' just. What does this imply?

If 'just' here means 'forgiven, accepted, right with God', then indeed we become immediately, wholly and completely what God declares us to be; we enjoy the righteous status which he has conferred upon us. This is the true meaning of 'justification'.

If 'just' is used to signify 'made new, made alive', then again God's creative word immediately makes us what he declares. This would be a misuse of the word 'just', however, for what is being described now is not justification, but regeneration.

If 'just' means 'having a righteous character' or 'being conformed to the image of Christ', then God's declaration does not immediately secure it, but only initiates it. For this is not justification but sanctification, and is a continuous, lifelong process.

Even Hans Küng's explanatory Excursus II, 'Justification and Sanctification in the New Testament', does not disclose unambiguously what he means by God 'making' the sinner 'just'. He recognizes the problem that the language of 'sanctification' is used in the New Testament in two distinct senses. Sometimes it is almost a synonym for justification, because it denotes the holiness of our *status,* not our character. In this sense, at the very moment of our justification we become 'saints', for we have been 'sanctified in Christ Jesus', set apart to belong to the holy people of God.[58] At other times 'sanctification' describes the process of growing in holiness and becoming Christlike.[59]

The confusion seems to arise because Hans Küng does not maintain this distinction consistently. He refers to justification and sanctification now as happening together instantaneously ('God simultaneously justifies and sanctifies', p. 308) and now as being together capable of growth (Trent spoke of 'the necessity of ... growth in justification', p. 228). This is very misleading, however. In the debate about justification it would be wise to reserve the word 'sanctification' for its distinctive meaning of 'growing in holiness'. For then we can affirm that justification (God declaring us righteous through his Son's death) is instantaneous and complete, admitting no degrees, while sanctification (God making us righteous through his Spirit's indwelling), though begun the moment we are justified, is gradual and throughout this life incomplete, as we are being transformed into the likeness of Christ 'from one degree of glory to another' (2 Cor. 3:18, RSV).

In desiring a greater clarification at this point, I am not wishing to belittle Hans Küng's *tour de force.* At the same time, more than a quarter of a century has passed since the publication of his book, and one is not conscious of any widespread proclamation in the Roman Catholic Church of the gospel of justification by grace alone through faith alone.

Risking the danger of oversimplification, one may say that evangelicals and Roman Catholics together teach that God by his grace is the only Saviour of sinners, that self-salvation is impossible, and that the death of Jesus Christ as a propitiatory sacrifice is the ultimate ground of justification. But precisely what justification is, how it relates to other aspects of salvation, and how it takes place – these are areas of continuing and anxious debate.

Evangelicals feel the need to press Roman Catholics about sin, grace, faith and works. Roman Catholics are uncomfortable when we talk about 'total depravity' (that every part of our humanness has been twisted by the Fall), which lies behind our insistence on the need both for a radical salvation and for non-contributory grace. They find this a pessimistic view of the human condition, involving an inadequate doctrine of creation. They add that human beings have not lost their free will, and are therefore able to co-operate with grace and contribute to salvation. We, however, see the need to underline the New Testament antitheses regarding salvation. 'It is by grace you have been saved, through faith – and this not from yourselves, it is the gift of God – not of works, so that no-one can boast.' 'We ... know that a man is not justified by observing the law, but by faith in Jesus Christ.' Again, 'he saved us, not because of righteous things we had done, but because of his mercy'.[60] We cannot avoid the stark alternative which such texts put before us. Not works, but grace. Not law, but faith. Not our righteous deeds, but his mercy. There is no co-operation here between God and us, only a choice between two mutually exclusive ways, his and ours. Moreover, the faith which justifies is emphatic ally not another work. No, to say 'justification by faith' is merely another way of saying 'justification by Christ'. Faith has absolutely no value in itself; its value lies solely in its object. Faith is the eye that looks to Christ, the hand that lays hold of him, the mouth that drinks the water of life. And the more clearly we see the absolute adequacy of Jesus Christ's divine-human person and sin-bearing death, the more incongruous does it appear that anybody could suppose that we have anything to offer. That is why justification by faith alone, to quote Cranmer again, 'advances the true glory of Christ and beats down the vain glory of man'.

If we desire to press Roman Catholics on these points, however, we need also to respond to their pressures upon us. The chief might be a series of questions like the following. 'Do you still insist that when God justifies sinners he "pronounces" but does not "make" them righteous? That justification is a legal declaration, not a moral transformation? That righteousness is "imputed" to us, but neither "infused" in us nor even "imparted" to us? That we put on Christ's righteousness like a cloak, which conceals our continuing sinfulness? That justification, while changing our status, leaves our character and conduct unchanged? That every justified Christian, as the

Reformers taught, is *simul justus et peccator* (at one and the same time a righteous person and a sinner) ? If so, is not justification a legal action, even a giant hoax, a phoney transaction external to yourself, which leaves you inwardly unrenewed? Are you not claiming to be changed when in fact you are not changed? Is not your doctrine of "justification by faith alone" a thinly disguised free licence to go on sinning?'

These are searching questions. In one way or another, I have heard all of them asked. And there is no doubt that we evangelicals, in our zeal to emphasize the utter freeness of salvation, have sometimes been incautious in our phraseology, and have given the impression that good works are of no importance. But then the apostle Paul could evidently be incautious too, since his critics flung exactly the same charge at him, which led him to cry: 'What shall we say, then? Shall we go on sinning, so that grace may increase?' (Rom. 6:1). His indignant riposte to his own rhetorical question was to remind his readers of their baptism. Did they not know that, when they were baptized into Christ Jesus, they were baptized into his death? Having thus died with him to sin, how could they possibly live in it any longer (vv. 2–3)?

What Paul was doing by this response was to show that justification is not the only image of salvation. It would be entirely mistaken to make the equation 'salvation equals justification'. 'Salvation' is the comprehensive word, but it has many facets which are illustrated by different pictures, of which justification is only one. Redemption, as we have seen, is another, and bears witness to our radical deliverance from sin as well as guilt. Another is re-creation, so that 'if anyone is in Christ, he is a new creation' (2 Cor. 5:17). Yet another is regeneration or new birth, which is the inward work of the Holy Spirit, who then remains as a gracious indwelling presence, transforming the believer into the image of Christ, which is the process of sanctification. All these belong together. Regeneration is not an aspect of justification, but both are aspects of salvation, and neither can take place without the other. Indeed, the great affirmation that 'he saved us' is broken down into its component parts, which are 'the washing of rebirth and renewal by the Holy Spirit' on the one hand and being 'justified by his grace' on the other (Tit. 3:5–7). The justifying work of the Son and the regenerating work of the Spirit cannot be separated. It is for this reason that good works of love follow justification and new birth as their necessary evidence. For salvation, which is never 'by works', is always 'unto works'. Luther used to illustrate the correct order of events by reference to the tree and its fruit: 'The tree must be first, and then the fruit. For the apples make not the tree, but the tree makes the apples. So faith first makes the person, who afterwards brings forth works.'[61]

Once we hold fast that the work of the Son for us and the work of the Spirit in us, that is to say, justification and regeneration, are inseparable twins, it is quite safe to go on insisting that justification is an external, legal declaration that the sinner has been put right with God, forgiven and re-instated. This is plain from the popular use of the word. As Leon Morris has pointed out, 'when we speak of justifying an opinion or an action, we do not mean that we change or improve it. Rather we mean that we secure a verdict for it, we vindicate it.'[62] Similarly, when Luke says that everybody, on hearing Jesus' teaching, 'justified God', what he means is that they 'acknowledged that God's way was right' (Lk. 7:29).

The vocabulary of justification and condemnation occurs regularly in the Old Testament. Moses gave instructions to the Israelite judges that they were to decide cases referred to them, 'acquitting (*i.e.* justifying) the inno-cent and condemning the guilty' (Dt. 25:1). Everybody knew that Yahweh would never 'acquit [justify] the guilty' (Ex. 23:7), and that 'acquitting the guilty and condemning the innocent – the LORD detests them both' (Pr. 17:15). The prophet Isaiah pronounced a fierce woe against magistrates who 'acquit the guilty for a bribe, but deny justice to the innocent' (5:23). To condemn the righteous and justify the unrighteous would be to turn the administration of justice on its head. It is against this background of accepted judicial practice that Paul must have shocked his Roman readers when he wrote that 'God … justifies the wicked' (Rom. 4:5). How could God conceivably do such a thing? It was outrageous that the Divine Judge should practise what – in the very same Greek words – he had forbidden human judges to do. Besides, how could the Righteous One declare the unrighteous righteous? The very thought was preposterous.

In order to summarize Paul's defence of the divine justification of sinners, I will select four of his key phrases, which relate successively to justification's source, ground, means and effects. First, the *source* of our justification is indicated in the expression *justified by his grace* (Rom. 3:24), that is, by his utterly undeserved favour. Since it is certain that 'there is no-one righteous, not even one' (Rom. 3:10), it is equally certain that no-one can declare himself to be righteous in God's sight.[63] Self-justification is a sheer impos-sibility (Rom. 3:20). Therefore, 'it is God who justifies' (Rom. 8:33); only he can. And he does it 'freely' (Rom. 3:24, *dōrean,* 'as a free gift, gratis'), not because of any works of ours, but because of his own grace. In Tom Wright's neat epigram, 'no sin, no need for justification: no grace, no possibility of it'.[64]

Grace is one thing, however; justice is another. And justification has to do with justice. To say that we are 'justified by his grace' tells us the source of our justification, but says nothing about a righteous basis of it, without which God would contradict his own justice. So another key expression of Paul's, which introduces us to the *ground* of our justification, is *justified by his blood* (Rom. 5:9). Justification is not a synonym for amnesty, which strictly is pardon without principle, a forgiveness which overlooks – even forgets (*amnēstia* is 'forgetfulness') – wrongdoing and declines to bring it to justice. No, justification is an act of justice, of gracious justice. Its synonym is 'the righteousness of God' (Rom. 1:17; 3:21), which might for the moment be explained as his 'righteous way of righteoussing the unrighteous'. Dr J. I. Packer defines it as 'God's gracious work of bestowing upon guilty sinners a justified justification, acquitting them in the court of heaven without prejudice to his justice as their Judge'.[65] When God justifies sinners, he is not declaring bad people to be good, or saying that they are not sinners after all; he is pronouncing them legally righteous, free from any liability to the broken law, because he himself in his Son has borne the penalty of their law-breaking. That is why Paul is able to bring together in a single sentence the concepts of justification, redemption and propitiation (Rom. 3:24–25). The reasons why we are 'justified freely by God's grace' are that Christ Jesus paid the ransom-price and that God presented him as a propitiatory sacrifice. In other words, we are 'justified by his blood'. There could be no justification without atonement.

Thirdly, the *means* of our justification is indicated in Paul's favourite expression *justified by faith*.[66] Grace and faith belong indissolubly to one another, since faith's only function is to receive what grace freely offers. We are not, therefore, justified 'by' our faith, as we are justified 'by' God's grace and 'by' Christ's blood. God's grace is the source and Christ's blood the ground of our justification; faith is only the means by which we are united to Christ. As Richard Hooker put it with his usual precision: 'God doth justify the believing man, yet not for the worthiness of his belief, but for his worthiness who is believed.'[67]

Further, if faith is only the means, it is also the only means. Although the word 'only' does not occur in the Greek of Romans 3:28, it was a right instinct of Luther's, as we have seen, and indeed a correct translation, to render Paul's expression 'we maintain that a man is justified by faith only, apart from observing the law'. The point of his writing 'by faith apart from works of law' was to exclude law-works altogether, leaving faith as the sole means of justification. And Paul has already given his reason in the previous verse, namely to exclude boasting. For unless all human works, merits, co-operation and contributions are ruthlessly excluded, and Christ's sin-bearing death is seen in its solitary glory as the only ground of our justification, boasting cannot be excluded. Cranmer saw this clearly: 'This saying, that we be justified by faith only, freely, and without works, is spoken for to take away clearly all merit of our works, as being unable to deserve our justification at God's hands … and thereby wholly for to ascribe the merit and deserving of our justification unto Christ only and his most precious bloodshedding … And this form of speaking we use in the humbling of ourselves to God, and to give all the glory to our Saviour Christ, who is best worthy to have it.'[68]

Fourthly, what are the *effects* of our justification? I think we can deduce them from another, and sometimes neglected, Pauline expression, namely that we are *justified in Christ*.[69] To say that we are justified 'through Christ' points to his historical death; to say that we are justified 'in Christ' points to the personal relationship with him which by faith we now enjoy. This simple fact makes it impossible for us to think of justification as a purely external transaction; it cannot be isolated from our union with Christ and all the benefits which this brings. The first is membership of the Messianic community of Jesus. If we are in Christ and therefore justified, we are also the children of God and the true (spiritual) descendants of Abraham. Further, no racial, social or sexual barrier can come between us. This is the theme of Galatians 3:26–29. Tom Wright is surely correct in his emphasis that 'justification is not an individualist's charter, but God's declaration that we belong to the covenant community'.[70] Secondly, this new community, to create which Christ gave himself on the cross, is to be 'eager to do what is good', and its members are to devote themselves to good works.[71] So there is no ultimate conflict between Paul and James. They may have been using the verb 'justify' in different senses. They were certainly writing against different heresies, Paul against the self-righteous legalism of the Judaizers and James against the dead orthodoxy of the intellectualizers. Yet both teach that an authentic faith works, Paul stressing the faith that issues in works, and James the works that issue from faith.[72]

The new community of Jesus is an eschatological community which lives already in the new age he inaugurated. For justification is an eschatological event. It brings forward into the present the verdict which belongs to the last judgment. That is why the church is a community of hope, which looks with humble confidence into the future. To be sure, we can say with Paul that the law condemned us. But 'there is now no condemnation for those who are in Christ Jesus'. Why not? Because God has done for us what the law could not do. By sending his own Son in the likeness of our sinful nature to be a sin offering, he actually condemned our sin in the human Jesus. It is only because he was condemned that we could be justified. What then have we to fear? 'Who will bring any charge against those whom God has chosen? It is God who justifies. Who is he that condemns? Christ Jesus, who died – more than that, who was raised to life – is at the right hand of God and is also interceding for us.' That is why, once we have been justified, nothing can separate us from the love of God that is in Christ Jesus our Lord.[73]

Reconciliation

The fourth image of salvation, which illustrates the achievement of the cross, is 'reconciliation'. It is probably the most popular of the four because it is the most personal. We have left behind us the Temple precincts, the slave-market and the lawcourts; we are now in our own home with our family and friends. True, there is a quarrel, even 'enmity', but to reconcile means to restore a relationship, to renew a friendship. So an original relationship is presupposed which, having been broken, has been recovered by Christ.

A second reason why people feel at ease with this imagery is that reconciliation is the opposite of alienation, and many people nowadays refer to themselves as 'alienated'. Marxists continue to speak of the economic alienation of workers from the product of their labour. Others talk of political alienation, a sense of powerlessness to change society. But, for many more, 'alienation' encapsulates the modern mood. They do not feel at home in the materialism, emptiness and superficiality of the western world. On the contrary, they feel unfulfilled and disorientated, unable to find themselves, their identity or their freedom. To them talk of reconciliation sounds like the good news it is.

The first thing that has to be said about the biblical gospel of reconciliation, however, is that it begins with reconciliation to God, and continues with a reconciled community in Christ. Reconciliation is not a term the Bible uses to describe 'coming to terms with oneself', although it does insist that it is only through losing ourselves in love for God and neighbour that we truly find ourselves.

Reconciliation with God, then, is the beginning. This is the meaning of 'atonement'. It alludes to the event through which God and human beings, previously alienated from one another, are made 'at one' again. The word occurs only once in the New Testament's Authorized (King James) Version, namely in the statement that through Christ 'we have now received the atonement' (Rom. 5:11), that is to say, 'the reconciliation'. It is significant that in Romans 5:9–11, which is one of the four great passages on reconciliation in the New Testament, to be reconciled and to be justified are parallels. 'Since we have now been justified by his blood' is balanced by 'if, when we were God's enemies, we were reconciled to him through the death of his Son'. The two states, though both effected by the cross, are not identical, however. Justification is our legal standing before our Judge in the court; reconciliation is our personal relationship with our Father in the home. Indeed, the latter is the sequel and fruit of the former. It is only when we have been justified by faith that we have peace with God (Rom. 5:1), which is reconciliation.

Two other New Testament terms confirm this emphasis that reconciliation means peace with God, namely 'adoption' and 'access'. With regard to the former, it was Jesus himself, who always addressed God intimately as 'Abba, Father', who gave us permission to do the same, approaching him as 'our Father in heaven'. The apostles enlarged on it. John, who attributes our being children of God to our being born of God, expresses his sense of wonder that the Father should have loved us enough to call us, and indeed make us, his children.[74] Paul, on the other hand, traces our status as God's children rather to our adoption than to our new birth, and emphasizes the privileges we have in being sons instead of slaves, and therefore God's heirs as well.[75]

'Access' (*prosagōgē*) to God is another blessing of reconciliation. It seems to denote the active communion with God, especially in prayer, which his reconciled children enjoy. Twice Paul brackets 'access to God' and 'peace with God', the first time attributing them to our justification rather than our reconciliation (Rom. 5:1–2), and the second time explaining 'access' as a Trinitarian experience, in that we have access to the Father through the Son by the Spirit (Eph. 2:17–18), and 'we may approach God with freedom and confidence' (3:12). Peter uses the cognate verb, declaring that it was in order to 'bring' us to God (*prosagō*) that Christ died for us once for all, the righteous instead of the unrighteous (1 Pet. 3:18). And the writer to the Hebrews borrows from the Day of Atonement ritual, in order to convey the nearness to God which Christ by his sacrifice and priesthood has made possible. 'Since we have confidence to enter the Most Holy Place by the blood of Jesus,' he writes, 'let us draw near to God with a sincere heart in full assurance of faith ...' (10:19–22).

Thus, reconciliation, peace with God, adoption into his family and access into his presence all bear witness to the same new relationship into which God has brought us.

But reconciliation has a horizontal as well as a vertical plane. For God has reconciled us to one another in his new community, as well as to himself. A second great New Testament passage (Eph. 2:11–22) focuses on this, and in particular on the healing of the breach between Jews and Gentiles, so that sometimes it is not clear which reconciliation Paul is referring to. He reminds his Gentile Christian readers that formerly they were on the one hand 'excluded from citizenship in Israel and foreigners to the covenants of promise' and on the other 'separate from Christ ... and without God in the world' (v. 12). So they were 'far away' from both God and Israel, doubly alienated; 'but now in Christ Jesus', he goes on, 'you who once were far away have been brought near through the blood of Christ' – near to God and near to Israel (v. 13). In fact Christ, who 'himself is our peace', has broken down the barrier between these two halves of the human race, and 'made the two one' (v. 14). He has both 'abolished' the law's regulations which kept them apart and 'created' in himself 'one new man out of the two, thus making peace' (v. 15). Knowing the mutual bitterness and contempt which Jews and Gentiles felt for each other, this reconciliation was a miracle of God's grace and power. It has resulted in the emergence of a single, new, unified humanity, whose members through the cross have been reconciled both to God and to one another. Formerly enemies, they have had their reciprocal hostility put to death. They are now fellow citizens in God's kingdom, brothers and sisters in God's family (v. 19), fellow members of Christ's body and sharers together in the Messianic promise (3:6). This complete equality of Jew and Gentile in the new community is the 'mystery' which for centuries had been kept secret, but which now God had revealed to the apostles, especially to Paul, the apostle to the Gentiles (3:4–6).

Even this does not complete the reconciliation which God has achieved through Christ. In Colossians, which is a sister epistle to Ephesians because the two contain many parallels, Paul adds a cosmic dimension to the work of Christ. Whether the great Christological passage (Col. 1:15–20) is an early Christian hymn, as many scholars believe, or an original composition of Paul's, it is a sublime statement of the absolute supremacy of Jesus Christ in creation and redemption, in the universe and the church. At the same time, it is aptly addressed to the Colossian heretics who seem to have taught the existence of angelic intermediaries ('thrones, powers, rulers, authorities') between the Creator and the material creation, and may have suggested that Jesus was one of them. Paul will not have it. His emphasis is on 'all things', an expression he uses five times, which usually means the cosmos, but here evidently includes the principalities and powers. All things were created by God 'in', 'through' and 'for' Christ (v. 16). He is 'before' all things in time and rank, and 'in' him all things are sustained and integrated (v. 17). Since all things exist in, through, for and under Christ, he is the supreme lord by right. In addition, he is the head of the body, the church, being the first-born from among the dead, so that he might be pre-eminent in everything (v. 18). And this second sphere of his supremacy is due to the fact that God was pleased for his fullness both to dwell in him (v. 19) and to do his work of reconciliation through him, making peace through his blood shed on the cross. This time what is reconciled is again called 'all things', which are further described as 'things on earth or things in heaven' (v. 20).

We cannot be sure to what Paul was alluding. The presumption is that the 'all things' reconciled (v. 20) have the same identity as the 'all things' created (vv. 16–17). But if what was created through Christ needed later to be reconciled through Christ, something must have gone wrong in between. As Peter O'Brien puts it, 'the presupposition is that the unity and harmony of the cosmos have suffered a considerable dislocation, even a rupture, thus requiring reconciliation'.[76] If this is a reference to the natural order, then perhaps its 'reconciliation' is the same as the 'liberation from its bondage to decay' (Rom. 8:21), although this is a future event. If, on the other hand, the reference is to evil cosmic intelligences or fallen angels, there is no New Testament warrant for expecting that they have been (or will be) savingly reconciled to God. It seems more probable, therefore, that the principalities and powers have been 'reconciled' in the sense of the next chapter, namely that they have been 'disarmed' by Christ, who 'made a public spectacle of them, triumphing over them by the cross' (Col. 2:15). It is admittedly a strange use of the word 'reconciled', but, since Paul also describes this as 'making peace' (1:20), perhaps F. F. Bruce is right that he is thinking of a 'pacification' of cosmic beings 'submitting against their wills to a power which they cannot resist'.[77] In this case the same situation may be in mind which is elsewhere described as every knee bowing to Jesus and every tongue confessing his lordship (Phil. 2:9–11), and all things being placed by God under his feet until the day when they are brought together 'under one head, even Christ' (Eph. 1:10, 22).

So far we have been investigating the objects of God's reconciling work through Christ. He has reconciled sinners to himself, Jews and Gentiles to one another, and even the cosmic powers in the sense of disarming and pacifying them. We need now to consider how the reconciliation has taken place, and what in the great drama of reconciliation are the respective roles played by God, Christ and ourselves. For light on these questions we turn to the fourth reconciliation passage, 2 Corinthians 5:18–21.

> All this is from God, who reconciled us to himself through Christ and gave us the ministry of reconciliation: that God was reconciling the world to himself in Christ, not counting men's sins against them. And he has committed to us the message of reconciliation. We are therefore Christ's ambassadors, as though God were making his appeal through us – we implore you on Christ's behalf: Be reconciled to God. God made him who had no sin to be sin for us, so that in him we might become the righteousness of God.

The first truth this passage makes clear is that God *is the author of the reconciliation*. In fact, this is the principal emphasis throughout. 'All (*ta panta*, 'all things') is from God.' Perhaps the all things' look back to the 'new things' of the new creation with which the previous verse ended. God is the Creator; the new creation comes from him. Eight verbs follow in this paragraph which have God as their subject. They describe God's gracious initiative – God reconciling, God giving, God appealing, God making Christ to be sin for us. As the New English Bible translates the first sentence in verse 18: 'From first to last this has been the work of God.'

Therefore no explanation of the atonement is biblical which takes the initiative from God, and gives it instead either to us or to Christ. The initiative is certainly not ours. We have nothing to offer, to contribute, to plead. In William Temple's memorable phrase, 'all is of God; the only thing of my very own which I contribute to my redemption is the sin from which I need to be redeemed'. Nor has the primary initiative been Christ's. No interpretation of the atonement will do which attributes the initiative to

Christ in *such a way as to take it from the Father.* Christ did indeed take the initiative to come, but only in the sense that he could say, 'Here I am ... I have come to do your will, O God' (Heb. 10:7). The initiative of the Son was in submission to the initiative of the Father. There was no reluctance on the part of the Father. There was no intervention on the part of Christ as a third party. No, the reconciliation was conceived and born in the love of God. 'God so loved the world that he gave his one and only Son.'

We note here that wherever the verb 'to reconcile' occurs in the New Testament, either God is the subject (he reconciled us to himself) or, if the verb is passive, we are (we were reconciled to him). God is never the object. It is never said that 'Christ reconciled the Father to us'. Formally, linguistically, this is a fact. But we must be careful not to build too much on it theologically. For if we were right to say that God propitiated his own wrath through Christ, we could certainly say that he reconciled himself to us through Christ. If he needed to be propitiated, he equally needed to be reconciled. In other words, it is a mistake to think that the barrier between God and us, which necessitated the work of reconciliation, was entirely on our side, so that we needed to be reconciled and God did not. True, we were 'God's enemies', hostile to him in our hearts.[78] But the 'enmity' was on both sides. The wall or barrier between God and us was constituted both by our rebellion against him and by his wrath upon us on account of our rebellion. Three arguments support this contention.

First, the *language.* The very words 'enemy', 'enmity' and 'hostility' imply reciprocity. For example, in Romans 11:28 the word 'enemies' must be passive, since it is contrasted with the passive word 'loved'. Also the 'hostility' between Jews and Gentiles in Ephesians 2:14 was reciprocal, suggesting that the other 'hostility' (between God and sinners) was reciprocal too. So F. Büchsel writes that we should not interpret enemies 'unilaterally', as meaning only 'hostile to God', but as including 'standing under the wrath of God'.[79] The second argument concerns the *context,* both of each passage and of the whole Bible. In or near each major reconciliation passage there is a reference to God's wrath. The most striking is Romans 5, where 'saved from God's wrath' (v. 9) is immediately followed by 'we were God's enemies' (v. 10). Then there is the wider biblical context. Leon Morris particularly underlines this: 'there is, on the scriptural view, a definite hostility on the part of God to everything that is evil ... Thus, quite apart from details of interpretation of particular passages, there is strong and consistent teaching to the effect that God is active in his opposition to all that is evil.'[80] Thirdly, there is the *theology.* Paul's logic was that God had acted objectively in reconciliation *before* the message of reconciliation was proclaimed. So the 'peace' which evangelists preach (Eph. 2:17) cannot be that *our* enmity has been overcome (they are rather preaching in order that it may be), but that God has turned aside from *his* enmity because of Christ's cross. He has reconciled himself to us; we must now be reconciled to him.

Emil Brunner expressed himself forthrightly on this matter:

> Reconciliation presupposes enmity between two parties. To put it still more exactly: reconciliation, real reconciliation, an objective act of reconciliation, presupposes enmity on both sides; that is, that man is the enemy of God and that God is the enemy of man.[81]

Brunner goes on to explain that our enmity towards God is seen in our restlessness, ranging from frivolity to open renunciation and hatred of God, while his enmity to us is his wrath. Moreover, 'God is present in this anger, it is actually *his* anger' (p. 517).

Secondly, if God is the author, *Christ is the agent of the reconciliation*. This is crystal clear in 2 Corinthians 5:18–19: 'God ... reconciled us to himself through Christ' and 'God was reconciling the world to himself in Christ'. Both statements tell us that God took the initiative to reconcile, and that he did it in and through Christ. In this respect the sentences are identical. But the beneficiaries change from 'us' to 'the world', to show the universal scope of the reconciliation, and the preposition changes from 'through' to 'in', to show that God was not working through Christ as his agent at a distance but was actually present in him as he did the work.

We have now to notice the past tenses, especially the aorist ('reconciled', v. 18). Both verbs indicate that God was doing, indeed did, something in Christ. Let James Denney draw out the implication of this:

> The work of reconciliation, in the sense of the New Testament, is a work which is *finished*, and which we must conceive to be finished, *before the gospel is preached* ... Reconciliation ... is not something which is being done; it is something which is done. No doubt there is a work of Christ which is in process, but it has as its basis a finished work of Christ. It is in virtue of something already consummated on his cross that Christ is able to make the appeal to us which he does, and to win the response in which we *receive* the reconciliation.[82]

A few years later P. T. Forsyth pungently expressed the same truth:

> 'God was in Christ reconciling', actually reconciling, finishing the work. It was not a tentative, preliminary affair ... Reconciliation was finished in Christ's death. Paul did not preach a gradual reconciliation. He preached what the old divines used to call the finished work ... He preached something done once for all – a reconciliation which is the base of every soul's reconcilement, not an invitation only.[83]

What, then, was it which God did or accomplished in and through Christ? Paul answers this question in two complementary ways, negative and positive. Negatively, God declined to reckon our transgressions against us (v. 19b). Of course we deserved to have them counted against us. But if he were to bring us into judgment, we would die. 'If you, O LORD, kept a record of sins, O Lord, who could stand?' (Ps. 130:3). So God in his mercy refused to reckon our sins against us or require us to bear their penalty. What then has he done with them? For he cannot condone them. No, the positive counterpart is given in verse 21: 'God made him who had no sin to be sin for us, so that in him we might become the righteousness of God.' It is surely one of the most startling statements in the Bible, yet we must not on that account evade it. James Denney was not exaggerating when he wrote of it: 'Mysterious and awful as this thought is, it is the key to the whole of the New Testament.'[84] For our sake God actually made the sinless Christ to be sin with our sins. The God who refused to reckon our sins to us reckoned them to Christ instead. Indeed, his personal sinlessness uniquely qualified him to bear our sins in our place.

Moreover, Christ became sin for us, in order that 'in him we might become the righteousness of God'. In other words, our sins were imputed to the sinless Christ, in order that we sinners, by being united to him, might receive as a free gift a standing of righteousness before God. Christian disciples down the centuries have meditated on this exchange between the sinless Christ and sinners, and have marvelled at it. The first example is probably in the second-century *Epistle to Diognetus*, chapter 9: 'O sweet exchange! O unsearchable operation! O benefits surpassing all expectation! that the wickedness of many should be hid in a single Righteous One, and that the righteousness of One should justify many transgressors.' Then here is Luther writing to a monk in distress about his sins: 'Learn to know Christ and him crucified. Learn to sing to him and say "Lord Jesus, you are my righteousness, I am your sin. You took on you what was mine; yet set on me what was yours. You became what you were not, that I might become what I was not".'[85]

Half a century or so later (in 1585) Richard Hooker said in a sermon on Habakkuk 1:4:

> Such we are in the sight of God the Father, as is the very Son of God himself. Let it be counted folly or frenzy or fury or whatsoever. It is our wisdom and our comfort; we care for no knowledge in the world but this, that man hath sinned and God has suffered; that God hath made himself the sin of men, and that men are made the righteousness of God.[86]

As an example from this century let me choose Emil Brunner's epigram:

'Justification means this miracle: that Christ takes our place and we take his.'[87]

Looking back over the paragraph we are studying, it is important to note the paradox constituted by the first and last statements. On the one hand, God was in Christ reconciling. On the other, God made Christ to be sin for us. How God can have been in Christ when he made him to be sin is the ultimate mystery of the atonement. But we must hold both affirmations tenaciously, and never expound either in such a way as to contradict the other.

Thirdly, if God is the author and Christ is the agent, *we are the ambassadors of the reconciliation.* In considering verses 18 and 19 we have so far looked only at the first part of each sentence. But each is in two parts, the first stating the achievement of the reconciliation (God was in Christ reconciling the world to himself) and the second its announcement (he has committed to us the ministry and the message of reconciliation). Moreover, this ministry of reconciliation is itself in two stages. It begins as a proclamation that God was in Christ reconciling and that he made Christ to be sin for us. It continues with an appeal to people to 'be reconciled to God', that is, 'avail yourselves of the offered terms of reconciliation with God' (*cf.* Mt. 5:24), or simply 'receive it' (*cf.* Rom. 5:11).[88] We must keep these things distinct. God finished the work of reconciliation at the cross, yet it is still necessary for sinners to repent and believe and so 'be reconciled to God'. Again, sinners need to 'be reconciled to God', yet we must not forget that on God's side the work of reconciliation has already been done. If these two things are to be kept distinct, they will also in all authentic gospel preaching be kept together. It is not enough to expound a thoroughly orthodox doctrine of reconciliation if we never beg people to come to Christ. Nor is it right for a sermon to consist of an interminable appeal, which has not been preceded by an exposition of the gospel. The rule should be 'no appeal without a proclamation, and no proclamation without an appeal'.

In issuing this appeal, 'we are ... Christ's ambassadors' (v. 20). This was particularly true of Paul and his fellow apostles. They were the personal envoys and representatives of Jesus Christ. Yet in a secondary sense it is true of all Christian witnesses and preachers, who are heralds of the gospel: we speak in Christ's name and on his behalf. Then, as we issue our appeal, another voice is often heard, for it is 'as though God were making his appeal through us'. It is a remarkable truth that the same God who worked 'through Christ' to achieve the reconciliation now works 'through us' to announce it.

We have examined four of the principal New Testament images of salvation, taken from the shrine, the market, the lawcourt and the home. Their pictorial nature makes it impossible to integrate them neatly with one another. Temple sacrifices and legal verdicts, the slave in the market and the child in the home all clearly belong to different worlds. Nevertheless, certain themes emerge from all four images.

First, each highlights a different aspect of our human need. Propitiation underscores the wrath of God upon us, redemption our captivity to sin, justification our guilt, and reconciliation our enmity against God and alienation from him. These metaphors do not flatter us. They expose the magnitude of our need.

Secondly, all four images emphasize that the saving initiative was taken by God in his love. It is he who has propitiated his own wrath, redeemed us from our miserable bondage, declared us righteous in his sight, and reconciled us to himself. Relevant texts leave us in no doubt about this: 'God ... loved us, and sent his Son to be the propitiation for our sins.' 'God ... has come and has redeemed his people.' 'It is God who justifies.' 'God ... reconciled us to himself through Christ.'[89]

Thirdly, all four images plainly teach that God's saving work was achieved through the bloodshedding, that is, the substitutionary sacrifice, of Christ. With regard to the blood of Christ the texts are again unequivocal. 'God presented him as a propitiatory sacrifice, through faith in his blood.' 'In him we have redemption through his blood.' 'We have now been justified by his blood.' 'You who once were far away have been brought near [*i.e.* reconciled] through the blood of Christ.'[90] Since Christ's blood is a symbol of his life laid down in violent death, it is also plain in each of the four images that he died in our place as our substitute. The death of Jesus was the atoning sacrifice because of which God averted his wrath from us, the ransom-price by which we have been redeemed, the condemnation of the innocent that the guilty might be justified, and the sinless One being made sin for us.[91] So substitution is not a 'theory of the atonement'. Nor is it even an additional image to take its place as an option alongside the others. It is rather the essence of each image and the heart of the atonement itself. None of the four images could stand without it. I am not of course saying that it is necessary to understand, let alone articulate, a substitutionary atonement before one can be saved. Yet the responsibility of Christian teachers, preachers and other witnesses is to seek grace to expound it with clarity and conviction. For the better people understand the glory of the divine substitution, the easier it will be for them to trust in the Substitute.

Notes

[1] A. T. Hanson, *Wrath of the Lamb*, p. 192.

[2] C. H. Dodd contributed an article on *hilaskesthai* to the *Journal of Theological Studies*, which was subsequently re-published in his *Bible and the Greeks*. The same attempt to re-interpret 'propitiation' as 'expiation' is also expressed in his two Moffatt New Testament

Commentaries on *Romans* and the *Johannine Epistles*.

[3] C H. Dodd, *Bible and the Greeks*, p. 94. See also his *Romans*, pp. 54–55.

[4] C H. Dodd, *Johannine Epistles*, p. 25.

[5] C. H. Dodd, *Bible and the Greeks*, p. 93.

[6] C H. Dodd, *Johannine Epistles*, pp. 25–26.

[7] Leon Morris wrote an article on *hilaskesthai* in *The Expository Times*, and then expanded his thesis in his *Apostolic Preaching*. He has also produced a further development and simplification of this book in *Atonement*.

[8] Dr Roger R. Nicole's article entitled 'C. H. Dodd and the Doctrine of Propitiation' appeared in the *Westminster Theological Journal*, xvii.2 (1955), pp. 117–157. He acknowledges some indebtedness to Leon Morris, although it is an independent study.

[9] See the article on the *hikaskomai* word-group by F. Büchsel and J. Hermann in Kittel's *Theological Dictionary of the New Testament*, vol. I , pp. 300–323.

[10] Roger Nicole, 'C. H. Dodd', p. 132.

[11] Gn. 32:20; Pr. 16:14.

[12] Nu. 16:41–50 and 25:11–13. *Cf.* also Zc. 7:2; 8:22; Mal. 1:9.

[13] *E.g.* Ex. 32:30 (*cf.* v. 10); Dt. 21:1–9; 1 Sa. 3:14; 26:19.

[14] R. Nicole, 'C. H. Dodd', p. 134.

[15] L. Morris, *Apostolic Preaching*, p. 155.

[16] *Ibid.*, p. 169. In his large survey, *Cross in the New Testament*, Leon Morris writes: 'Throughout Greek literature, biblical and non-biblical alike *hilasmos* means "propitiation". We cannot now decide that we like another meaning better' (p. 349).

[17] William Neil, *Apostle Extraordinary*, pp. 89–90.

[18] P. T. Forsyth, *Cruciality of the Cross*, p. 78. Compare Calvin's statement: 'The work of atonement derives from God's love; therefore it did not establish it' (*Institutes*, II.xvi.4).

[19] P. T. Forsyth, *The Work of Christ*, p. 105.

[20] Karl Barth, *Church Dogmatics*, Vol. II, Part 1, pp. 398 and 403.

[21] F. Büchsel, '*hilaskomai*', p. 317.

[22] David F. Wells, *Search for Salvation*, p. 29.

[23] Leon Morris, *Apostolic Preaching*, p. 10. See also chapter 5, '*Redemption*', in his *Atonement*, pp. 106–131.

[24] From an article on '*Redemption*' by B. B. Warfield, first published in *The Princeton Theological Review* (Vol. xiv, 1916), and reprinted in his *Person and Work*, pp. 345 and 347.

[25] Lv. 25:25–28; Ru. 3 and 4; Je. 32:6–8. *Cf.* Lv. 27 for redeeming land which had been dedicated to the Lord by a special vow.

[26] Ex.13:13; 34:20; Nu. 18:14–17.

[27] Ex. 30:12–16; 13:13; 34:20 and Nu. 3:40–51; Ex. 21:28–32; Lv. 25:47–55.

[28] *E.g.* Ex. 6:6; Dt. 7:8; 15:15; 2 Sa. 7:23.

[29] *E.g.* Is. 43:1–4; 48:20; 51:11; Je. 31:11.

[30] B. F. Westcott, *Epistle to the Hebrews*, p. 298.

[31] B. B. Warfield, *Person and Work*, p. 448. Leon Morris makes the same point in his *Apostolic Preaching*, pp.14–17 and 19–20.

[32] *E.g.* Ex. 6:6; Dt. 9:26; Ne. 1:10; Ps. 77:15.

[33] B. B. Warfield, *Person and Work*, pp. 453–454.

[34] F. Büchsel, '*hilaskomai*', p. 343.

[35] Josephus, *Antiquities* xiv. 107.

[36] Eph. 1:7 and Col. 1:14. *Cf.* Heb. 9:15.

[37] Gal. 3:13; 4:5.

[38] 1 Pet. 1:18.

[39] Tit. 2:14. The noun is *anomia*, 'lawlessness'.

[40] Lk. 2:38. *Cf.* 1:68; 24:21.

[41] Lk. 21:28; Eph. 1:14; 4:30; Rom. 8:18–23.

[42] Jeremias, *Central Message*, pp. 37–38. *Cf.* l Clem. lv.

[41] Heb. 9:12. See also the references to Christ's blood in relation to our redemption in both Rom. 3:24–25 and Eph. 1:7.

[44] B. F. Westcott, *Epistles of John*, Additional Note on 1 John 1:7, 'The Idea of Christ's Blood in the New Testament', pp. 34ff.

[45] B. F. Westcott, *Epistle to the Hebrews*, Additional Note on Hebrews 9:9, pp. 283ff.

[46] Alan M. Stibbs, *Meaning of the Word 'Blood' in Scripture*, pp. 10, 12, 16 and 30. Leon Morris has a chapter entitled 'The Blood' in his *Apostolic Preaching* (pp. 108–124), and in his *Cross in the New Testament* writes: 'the Hebrews understood "blood" habitually in the sense of "violent death" ' (p. 219). F. D. Kidner also criticizes Westcott's thesis in his *Sacrifice in the Old Testament,* and points out that the prohibition of the use of blood in food 'is consistent with the idea of its preciousness, but hardly with that of its potency' (p. 24).

[47] Johannes Behm, '*haima*', p. 173.

[48] Rev. 5:9; *cf.* 1:5–6 and 14:3–4.

[49] 1 Cor. 6:18–20; *cf.* 7:23.

[50] Sanday and Headlam, *Romans*, p. 36.

[51] Jeremias, *Central Message*, p. 66.

[52] Martin Luther, *Galatians*, p. 143 (on Gal. 2:16). *Cf.* p. 101 (on Gal. 2:4–5).

[53] From Cranmer's 'Sermon on Salvation' in the *First Book of Homilies*, pp. 25–26.

[54] R. T. Beckwith, G. E. Duffield and J. I. Packer, *Across the Divide*, p. 58.

[55] See Council of Trent, Session VI, and its Decrees on Original Sin, on Justification and on Penance.

[56] Hans Küng, *Justification* (1957).

[57] For sympathetic but critical Protestant assessments of recent Roman Catholic thinking see *Revolution in Rome* by David F. Wells; *Across the Divide* by R. T. Beckwith, G. E. Duffield and J. I. Packer; *Justification Today: The Roman Catholic and Anglican Debate* by R. G. England; George Carey's contribution entitled 'Justification by Faith in Recent Roman Catholic Theology' to *Great Acquittal*; and James Atkinson's *Rome and Reformation Today*.

[58] *E.g.* Acts 20:32; 1 Cor. 1:2; 6:11; Heb. 10:29; 13:12.

[59] *E.g.* Rom. 6:19; 2 Cor. 7:1; 1 Thes. 4:3, 7; 5:23; Heb. 12:14.

[60] Eph. 2:8–9; Gal. 2:16; Tit. 3:5.

[61] Martin Luther, *Epistle to the Galatians*, p. 247, on Gal. 3:10.

[62] L. Morris, *Cross in the New Testament*, p. 242.

[63] Ps. 143:2. *Cf.* Pss. 51:4; 130:3; Jb. 25:4.

[64] From his essay 'Justification: The Biblical Basis and its Relevance for Contemporary Evangelicalism', in *Great Acquittal*, p. 16.

[65] From his article 'Justification' in *New Bible Dictionary*, p. 647.

[66] *E.g.* Rom. 3:28; 5:1; Gal. 2:16; Phil. 3:9.

[67] From Hooker's 'Definition of Justification' being Chapter xxxiii of his *Ecclesiastical Polity,* which began to be published in 1593.

[68] From Cranmer's 'Sermon on Salvation' in the *First Book of Homilies*, pp. 25 and 29.

[69] Gal. 2:17. *Cf.* Rom. 8:1; 2 cor. 5:21; Eph. 1:6.

[70] Tom Wright, 'Justification: The Biblical Basis' from *Great Acquittal*, p. 36.

[71] Tit. 2:14; 3:8.

[72] *E.g.* Gal. 5:6; 1 Thes. 1:3; Jas. 2:14–26.

[73] Rom. 7:7–25; 8:1, 3, 33–34, 39.

[74] Jn. 1:12–13; 1 Jn. 3:1–10.

[75] *E.g.* Rom. 8:14–17; Gal. 3:26–29; 4:1–7.

[76] Peter T. O'Brien, *Colossians*, p. 53.

[77] E. K Simpson and F. F. Bruce, *Ephesians and Colossians*, p. 210. Peter O'Brien follows F. F. Bruce in this interpretation (*Colossians*, p. 56).

[78] For references to human hostility to God see Rom. 5:10; 8:7; Eph. 2:14, 16; Col. 1:21; Jas. 4:4.

[79] From the article on *allassō* and *katallassō* by F. Büchsel, p. 257.

[80] L. Morris, *Apostolic Preaching*, p. 196. See Dr Morris's chapters on 'Reconciliation' in both *Apostolic Preaching*, pp. 186–223 and *Atonement*, pp. 132–150.

[81] E. Brunner, *Mediator*, p. 516.

[82] James Denney, *Death of Christ*, pp. 85–86. *Cf.* also p. 128.

[83] P. T. Forsyth, *Work of Christ*, p. 86.

[84] James Denney, *Death of Christ*, p. 88.

[85] Luther, *Letters of Spiritual Counsel*, p. 110.

[86] Hooker's 'Sermon on Habakkuk i.4', pp. 490f.

[87] E. Brunner *Mediator*. p. 524.

[88] T. J. Crawford, *Doctrine of Holy Scripture*, p. 75.

[89] Jn. 4:10, AV; Lk. 1:68; Rom. 8:33; 2 Cor. 5:18.

[90] Rom. 3:25; Eph. 1:7; Rom. 5:9; Eph. 2:13 (*cf.* Col. 1:20).

[91] Rom. 3:25; 1 Pet. 1:18–19; Rom. 8:3, 33; 2 Cor. 5:21.

EIGHT

The revelation of God

The achievement of Christ's cross must be seen in terms of revelation as well as salvation. To borrow some current jargon, it was a 'revelatory' as well as a 'salvific' event. For through what God did there for the world he was also speaking to the world. Just as human beings disclose their character in their actions, so God has showed himself to us in the death of his Son. The purpose of this chapter is to investigate in what way the cross was a word as well as a work, and to listen attentively to it.

The glory of God

According to John's Gospel Jesus referred to his death as a 'glorification', the event through which he and his Father would be supremely 'glorified' or manifested. This comes to many people as a surprise. In the Old Testament God's glory or splendour was revealed in nature and history, that is, in the created universe and in the redeemed nation. On the one hand, heaven and earth were filled with his glory, including (Jesus added) the flowers of a Galilean spring, whose glory exceeded even Solomon's.[1] On the other hand, God showed his glory in delivering Israel from their Egyptian and Babylonian captivities, and in revealing to them his character of mercy and justice.[2] Thus God displayed his majesty in his world and in his people.

It is not in the least surprising that, when the New Testament opens, glory should be associated with Jesus Christ. As Lord Ramsey of Canterbury has written, 'in so far as *doxa* is the divine splendour, Jesus Christ is that splendour'.[3] According to the Synoptic Gospels, however, although Jesus' glory was glimpsed at his transfiguration, its full manifestation would not take place until his parousia and the kingdom which would then be consummated.[4] It would be a revelation of 'power and glory'. What is striking about John's presentation is that, although his glory was manifested powerfully in his miracles or 'signs',[5] it was above all to be seen in his present weakness, in the self-humiliation of his incarnation. 'The Word became flesh and lived for a while among us. We have seen his glory, the glory of the one and only Son, who came from the Father, full of grace and truth' Jn. 1:14). One must not miss the Old Testament allusions. God's glory which overshadowed and filled the tabernacle in the wilderness was now displayed in him who 'lived for a while' (*eskēnōsen*, 'tabernacled') among us. And as Yahweh showed Moses his glory by declaring his name to be both merciful and righteous, so the glory we have seen in Jesus Christ was 'full of grace and truth'. More important still is the deliberate antithesis between 'flesh' and 'glory', and so 'the fundamental *paradox* of the glory of the divine humiliation'.[6]

The self-humiliation of the Son of God, which began in the incarnation, culminated in his death. Yet in that very abasement of himself he was 'lifted up', not just physically raised on to the cross, but spiritually exalted before the eyes of the world.[7] Indeed, he was 'glorified'. The cross which appeared to be 'shame' was in fact 'glory'. Whereas in the Synoptic Gospels suffering is the path to future glory,[8] to John it is also the arena in which the glorification actually takes place.[9] On three separate occasions Jesus referred to his coming death as the hour of his glorification. First, in response to the request of some Greeks to see him, Jesus said that 'the hour has come for the Son of Man to be glorified', and went on immediately to speak of his death in terms both of a kernel of wheat falling to the ground and of the Father's glorifying his own name. Secondly, as soon as Judas had left the upper room and gone out into the night, Jesus said, 'Now is the Son of Man glorified and God is glorified in him.' Thirdly, he began his great prayer, which terminated their evening in the upper room, with the words: 'Father, the time has come. Glorify your Son, that your Son may glorify you.'[10] What is notable about all three passages is first that each is introduced by either 'now' or 'the time has come', making the reference to the cross indisputable, and secondly that the glorification will be of the Father and the Son together.

So Father and Son are revealed by the cross. But what is it which they reveal of themselves? Certainly the self-humbling and self-giving of love are implicit there. But what about the holiness of that love, which made it necessary for the Lamb of God to take away the world's sin and for the

Good Shepherd to lay down his life for his sheep, and which made it more expedient (as Caiaphas correctly prophesied) 'that one man die for the people than that the whole nation perish'?[11] These statements were integral to John's understanding of the death by which the Father and Son would be glorified. The glory which radiates from the cross is that same combination of divine qualities which God revealed to Moses as mercy and justice, and which we have seen in the Word made flesh as 'grace and truth'.[12] This is God's 'goodness', which Calvin saw displayed in the 'theatre' of the cross:

> For in the cross of Christ, as in a splendid theatre, the incomparable goodness of God is set before the whole world. The glory of God shines, indeed, in all creatures on high and below, but never more brightly than in the cross ...

> If it be objected that nothing could be less glorious than Christ's death ... I reply that in that death we see a boundless glory which is concealed from the ungodly.[13]

When we turn from John to Paul the concept that God has revealed himself in and through the cross is yet more explicit. What in John is the manifestation of God's glory in Paul is the demonstration, indeed the vindication, of his character of justice and love. It may be helpful, before we study the two key texts separately, to look at them side by side. They both occur in the letter to the Romans:

> God ... did this [sc. presented Christ as an atoning sacrifice] to demonstrate his justice, because in his forbearance he had left the sins committed beforehand unpunished – he did it to demonstrate his justice at the present time, so as to be just and the one who justifies the man who has faith in Jesus (3:25–26).

> But God demonstrates his own love for us in this: While we were still sinners, Christ died for us (5:8).

The Greek verbs rendered 'demonstrate' in chapters 3 and 5 respectively are different. But it was a true instinct of the NIV translators to use the same English verb. For they mean the same thing, and Paul is declaring that in the death of Christ God has given us a clear, public demonstration of both his justice and his love. We have already seen how God 'satisfied' his wrath and love, justice and mercy, by giving himself in Christ to bear our sin and condemnation. Now we are to see how, in satisfying these divine attributes in the cross, he displayed and demonstrated them.

The justice of God

Men and women of moral sensitivity have always been perplexed by the seeming injustice of God's providence. This is far from being a modern problem. Ever since Abraham, indignant that God intended in the destruction of Sodom and Gomorrah to kill the righteous with the wicked, uttered his anguished cry, 'Will not the Judge of all the earth do right?' (Gn. 18:25), the characters and authors of the Bible have struggled with this question. It is one of the recurring themes of the Wisdom literature and dominates the book of Job. Why do the wicked flourish and the innocent suffer? 'Sin and death', human transgression and divine judgment, are said to be bracketed, even riveted together, so why do we not more frequently see sinners overwhelmed? Instead, more often than not, they seem to escape with impunity. The righteous, on the other hand, are frequently overtaken by disaster. Not only does God not protect them, he does not answer their prayers or even seem to care about their fate. So there is evidently a need for a 'theodicy', a vindication of the justice of God, a justification to humankind of the apparently unjust ways of God.

The Bible responds to this need in two complementary ways, first by looking on to the final judgment and secondly (from the perspective of New Testament believers) by looking back to the decisive judgment which took place at the cross. As to the first, this was the standard Old Testament answer to the problem, for example in Psalm 73. Evil people prosper. They are healthy and wealthy. In spite of their violence, their arrogance and their impudent defiance of God, they get away with it. No thunderbolt from heaven strikes them down. The psalmist admits that by envying their freedom to sin and their immunity to suffering, he had almost turned away from God, for his thoughts were more those of a 'brute beast' than of a godly Israelite. He failed to come to any satisfactory understanding until he 'entered the sanctuary of God'. But then he 'understood their final destiny'. The place on which they stand so self-confidently is more slippery than they realize, and one day they will fall, ruined by the righteous judgment of God.

This same certainty of ultimate judgment, when the imbalances of justice will be redressed, is several times repeated in the New Testament. Paul tells the Athenian philosophers that God has overlooked idolatry in the past only because 'he has set a day when he will judge the world with justice by the man he has appointed', and he warns his readers in Rome not to presume on the riches of God's 'kindness, tolerance and patience', which are giving them space in which to repent. Peter addresses the same message to 'scoffers' who ridicule the notion of a future day of judgment; the reason for its non-arrival is that God in his patience is holding the door of opportunity open a while longer, 'not wanting anyone to perish, but everyone to come to repentance'.[14]

If the first part of the biblical theodicy is to warn of future and final judgment, the second is to declare that the judgment of God has already taken place at the cross. That is why sins were allowed, as it were, to accumulate in Old Testament days without being either punished (as they deserved) or pardoned (since 'it is impossible for the blood of bulls and goats to take away sins'). But now, says the writer to the Hebrews, Christ 'has died as a ransom to set them free from the sins committed under the first covenant'.[15] In other words, the reason for God's previous inaction in the face of sin was not moral indifference but personal forbearance until Christ should come and deal with it on the cross. The classical passage on this theme is Romans 3:21–26, to which we now turn.

> But now a righteousness from God, apart from law, has been made known, to which the Law and the Prophets testify. This righteousness from God comes through faith in Jesus Christ to all who believe. There is no difference, for all have sinned and fall short of the glory of God, and are justified freely by his grace through the redemption that came by Christ Jesus. God presented him as a sacrifice of atonement, through faith in his blood. He did this to demonstrate his justice, because in his forbearance he had left the sins committed beforehand unpunished – he did it to demonstrate his justice at the present time, so as to be just and the one who justifies the man who has faith in Jesus.

Charles Cranfield has described these six verses as 'the centre and heart' of the whole letter to the Romans. In order to understand them, we shall have to begin with at least a brief discussion of that enigmatic phrase in verse 21, 'But now a righteousness from God ... has been made known'. The wording is almost identical with 1:17 ('for ... a righteousness from God is revealed'), except that the verbs are in the past and present tenses respectively. Whatever the 'righteousness from God' may be, it is clear that the revelation of it is in the gospel. It was revealed there when the gospel first came to be formulated, and it continues to be revealed there whenever the gospel is preached. To be sure, this is not the only revelation Paul mentions. He has already affirmed that God's power and deity are revealed in the creation (1:19–20), and that to the ungodly who suppress the truth God's wrath is revealed from heaven (1:18), particularly in the moral disintegration of society. But the same God who has revealed his power in creation and his wrath in society has also revealed his righteousness in the gospel.

The meaning of 'the (or 'a') righteousness of God' has been endlessly debated. Three main explanations have been given. First, according to the medieval tradition, it was said to be the divine attribute of righteousness or

justice, as in verses 25 and 26 where God is said to 'demonstrate' it. The
trouble with this interpretation is that God's justice normally issues in
judgment (*e.g.* Rev. 19:11), which is hardly the 'good news' revealed in the
gospel. Luther held this view at first, and it almost drove him to despair. Of
course, if God's justice could be shown in certain circumstances to issue in
justification rather than in judgment, that would be a different matter. But
I am anticipating.

Secondly, according to the Reformers the phrase meant a righteous status
which is 'of God' (genitive) in the sense that it is 'from God' (as the NIV
renders it), *i.e.* bestowed by him. It is 'apart from law' (v. 21), because the
function of the law is to condemn not to justify, although 'the Law and the
Prophets testify' to it, because it is an Old Testament doctrine. Since we are
all ourselves unrighteous (3:10) and cannot establish our own righteousness
(3:20; 10:3), God's righteousness is a free gift (5:17), which we 'submit to'
(10:3), 'receive' (9:30), 'have' (Phil. 3:9) and so even 'become' (2 Cor.
5:21). 'God's righteousness', being a gift to the unrighteous received by
faith in Christ alone (v. 22), is in fact nothing other than justification.

Thirdly, a number of scholars in recent years have drawn attention to the
Old Testament passages, especially in the Psalms and Isaiah, in which 'God's
righteousness' and 'God's salvation' are synonyms, and refer to God's initiative in coming to the rescue of his people and vindicating them when
oppressed.[16] In this case the 'righteousness of God' is neither his attribute
of justice, nor his gift of the justified status, but his dynamic, saving activity. The main objection to this interpretation is that Paul, although declaring that the law and the prophets testify to God's righteousness, does not
quote any of the appropriate verses.

The second of the three interpretations best fits each context in which
the expression occurs, and seems almost certainly correct. On the other
hand, it may not be necessary altogether to reject the other two. For if the
righteousness of God is the righteous standing he gives to those who believe
in Jesus, it is by his dynamic saving activity that such a gift is available and
bestowed, and the whole operation is fully consonant with his justice. The
'righteousness of God', then, might be defined as 'God's righteous way of
righteoussing the unrighteous'; it is the righteous status which he bestows
on sinners whom he justifies. Moreover, as we saw in the last chapter, his
free and gracious act of justifying is 'through the redemption that came by
Christ Jesus' (v. 24), whom 'God presented [some think 'purposed'] as a
propitiatory sacrifice' (v. 25). If God in Christ on the cross had not paid the
price of our ransom and propitiated his own wrath against sin, he could not
have justified us.

Now the reason why 'he did this', namely presented Christ as a sacrifice
of atonement, was 'to demonstrate his justice'. So important is this divine
objective that the apostle states it twice in virtually identical words,

although each time he adds a different explanation. The first time he looks back to the past, and says that God demonstrated his justice at the cross 'because in his forbearance he had left the sins committed beforehand unpunished' (v. 25). The second time he looks on from the cross to the present and future, and says that God demonstrated (indeed goes on demonstrating) his justice 'at the present time, so as to be just and the one who justifies the man who has faith in Jesus' (v. 26).

By his past forbearance towards sinners God had created a problem for himself. Sin, guilt and judgment are supposed to be inexorably linked in his moral world. Why, then, had he not judged sinners according to their works? A theodicy was needed to vindicate his justice. Although in self-restraint he might postpone his judgment, he could not allow the backlog of human sins to mount up indefinitely, let alone cancel the judgment altogether. If God does not justly punish sin, he would be 'unjust to himself', as Anselm put it, or, in James Denney's words, he would 'not do justice to himself' but rather 'do himself an injustice'.[17] In fact he would destroy both himself and us. He would cease to be God and we would cease to be fully human. He would destroy himself by contradicting his divine character as righteous Lawgiver and Judge, and he would destroy us by contradicting our human dignity as morally responsible persons created in his image. It is inconceivable that he should do either. So, although in his forbearance he temporarily left sins unpunished, now in justice he has punished them, by condemning them in Christ. He has thus demonstrated his justice by executing it. And he has done it publicly (which some think is the emphasis of the verb 'presented'), in order not only to be just but also to be seen to be just. Because of his past appearance of injustice in not punishing sins, he has given a present and visible proof of justice in bearing the punishment himself in Christ

No-one can now accuse God of condoning evil, and so of moral indifference or injustice. The cross demonstrates with equal vividness both his justice in judging sin and his mercy in justifying the sinner. For now, as a result of the propitiatory death of his Son, God can be 'just and the justifier' of those who believe in him. He is able to bestow a righteous status on the unrighteous, without compromising his own righteousness.

We should see more clearly now the relation between the achievement of the cross (illustrated in the four images examined in the last chapter) and the revelation of God. By bearing himself in Christ the fearful penalty of our sins, God not only propitiated his wrath, ransomed us from slavery, justified us in his sight, and reconciled us to himself, but thereby also defended and demonstrated his own justice. By the way he justified us, he also justified himself. This is the theme of P. T. Forsyth's book *The Justification of God*, which, being published in 1916, he subtitled *Lectures for Wartime on a Christian Theodicy*. 'There is no theodicy for the world', he wrote, 'except in a theology of the Cross. The only final theodicy is that self-justification of God which was fundamental to his justification of men. No reason of man can justify God in a world like this. He must justify himself, and he did so in the cross of his Son.[18]

The love of God

It is not only the justice of God which seems to be incompatible with the prevailing injustices of the world, but also his love. Personal tragedies, floods and earthquakes, accidents which cost hundreds of lives, hunger and poverty on a global scale, the cold vastness of the universe, the ferocities of nature, tyranny and torture, disease and death, and the sum total of the misery of the centuries – how can these horrors be reconciled with a God of love? Why does God allow them?

Christianity offers no glib answers to these agonized questions. But it does offer evidence of God's love, just as historical and objective as the evidence which seems to deny it, in the light of which the world's calamities need to be viewed. This evidence is the cross. Let me begin with two verses from John's first letter.

First, 'this is how we know what love is: Jesus Christ laid down his life for us' (3:16). Most people would have no difficulty in telling us what they think love is. They may know that whole books have been written with the purpose of distinguishing between different kinds of love, like Anders Nygren's *Agape and Eros* (1930) and C. S. Lewis's *The Four Loves* (1960). Nevertheless, they would claim that the meaning of love is self-evident. John would disagree with them, however. He dares to say that, apart from Christ and his cross, the world would never have known what true love is. Of course all human beings have experienced some degree and quality of love. But John is saying that only one act of pure love, unsullied by any taint of ulterior motive, has ever been performed in the history of the world, namely the self-giving of God in Christ on the cross for undeserving sinners. That is why, if we are looking for a definition of love, we should look not in a dictionary, but at Calvary.

John's second verse is more precise still. 'This is love: not that we loved God, but that he loved us and sent his Son as an atoning sacrifice [*hilasmos*] for our sins' (4:10). In the Romans 3 passage we have just been studying, Paul takes the propitiatory nature of the cross (*hilastērion*) as the demonstration of God's justice; here John takes it as the manifestation of God's love. It is both equally. True love is God's love, not ours, and he showed it among us (v. 9) by sending his one and only Son into the world that he might die for us and we might live through him. The two words 'live' (v. 9) and 'propitiation' (v. 10) both betray the extremity of our need. Because we were sinners, we deserved to die under the righteous anger of God. But God sent his only Son, and in sending him came himself, to die that death and bear that wrath instead of us. It was an act of sheer, pure, unmerited love.

We learn from John, then, that although in this world our attention is constantly arrested by the problems of evil and pain, which seem to contradict God's love, we will be wise not to allow it to be deflected from the cross, where God's love has been publicly and visibly made manifest. If the cross may be called a 'tragedy', it was a tragedy which illumines all other tragedies.

Paul also writes about the love of God in the first half of Romans 5. He refers to it twice, and thereby supplies us with two complementary ways of becoming assured of its reality. The first is that 'God has poured out his love into our hearts by the Holy Spirit, whom he has given us' (v. 5). The second is that 'God demonstrates his own love for us in this: While we were still sinners, Christ died for us' (v. 8). One of the most satisfying aspects of the gospel is the way in which it combines the objective and the subjective, the historical and the experimental, the work of God's Son and the work of God's Spirit. We may know that God loves us, Paul says, both because he has proved his love in history through the death of his Son, and because he continuously pours it into our hearts through the indwelling of his Spirit. And although we shall concentrate, as Paul does, on the objective demonstration of God's love at the cross, we shall not forget that the Holy Spirit confirms that historical witness by his own inward and personal witness, as he floods our hearts with the knowledge that we are loved. It is similar to our experience of the Holy Spirit testifying with our spirit that we are God's children – a witness he bears when, as we pray, he enables us to cry 'Abba, Father', because we then know ourselves to be God's justified, reconciled, redeemed and beloved children (Rom. 8:15–16).

Because of the cross, however, 'God demonstrates his own love for us' (Rom. 5:8). It is his very own, *sui generis*, for there is no other love like it. In what does the demonstration consist? It has three parts, which together build a convincing case.

First, God gave *his Son* for us. True, in verse 8 Paul affirms simply that 'Christ' died for us. But the context tells us who this Anointed One, this Messiah, was. For according to verse 10 the death of Christ was 'the death of his Son'. If God had sent a man to us, as he had sent the prophets to Israel, we would have been grateful. If he had sent an angel, as he did to Mary at the annunciation, we would have counted it a great privilege. Yet in either case he would have sent us a third party, since men and angels are creatures of his making. But in sending his own Son, eternally begotten from his own Being, he was not sending a creature, a third party, but giving himself. The logic of this is inescapable. How could the Father's love have been demonstrated if he had sent somebody else to us? No: since love is in its essence self-giving, then if God's love was seen in giving his Son, he must thereby have been giving himself. 'God so loved the world that he gave his one and only Son' (Jn. 3:16). Again, God 'did not spare his own Son, but gave him up for us all' (Rom. 8:32). P. T. Forsyth quite correctly added the gloss, 'he spared not his own Son, *i.e.* his own Self'.[19] It is because of the ultimacy of that self-giving love that Paul added his conviction that along with Christ God will 'graciously give us all things'. All lesser gifts are comprehended within 'his indescribable gift' of his Son (2 Cor. 9:15).

Secondly, God gave his Son *to die* for us. It would still have been wonderful if God had given his Son, and so himself, only to become flesh for us, to live and give and serve for us on earth. But the incarnation was but the begining of his self-giving. Having 'emptied himself' of his glory and taken the nature of a servant, he then 'humbled himself' and became 'obedient to death – even death on a cross!' (Phil. 2:7–8). This was to give himself to the uttermost, to the torture of crucifixion and to the horror of sin-bearing and God-forsakenness. 'Christ died for us.' His body died and, as we have seen, his soul died, died the death of separation from God. Sin and death are inseparable, but, whereas usually the one who sins and the one who dies are the same person, on this occasion they were not, since it was we who sinned, but *he* who died for our sins. This is love, holy love, inflicting the penalty for sin by bearing it. For the Sinless One to be made sin, for the Immortal One to die – we have no means of imagining the terror or the pain involved in such experiences.

Thirdly, God gave his Son to die *for us*, that is to say, for undeserving sinners like us. 'Sinners' is the first word Paul uses to describe us, failures who have missed the target and who invariably 'fall short of the glory of God' (3:23). Next, we were 'ungodly' (v. 6), for we had not given God the glory due to his name, and there was no fear of God before our eyes (3:18). Paul's third descriptive epithet is 'enemies' (v. 10). That is, we were 'God's enemies', as the NIV explains, for we had rebelled against his authority, rebuffed his love and been defiant of his law (8:7). The fourth and last word is 'powerless' (v. 6): it was 'when we were still powerless' that Christ died for us. For we had no power to save ourselves; we were helpless. These four words make an ugly cluster of adjectives. Very rarely, Paul argues in verse 7, somebody may be willing to die for a 'righteous' man (whose righteousness is cold, austere, forbidding), though for a 'good' man (whose goodness is warm, friendly and attractive) someone might possibly dare to die. 'But God demonstrates his own love for us' – his unique love – in this, that he died for sinful, godless, rebellious and helpless people like us.

The value of a love-gift is assessed both by what it costs the giver and by the degree to which the recipient may be held to deserve it. A young man who is in love, for example, will give his beloved expensive presents, often beyond what he can afford, as symbols of his self-giving love, because he considers she deserves them, and more. Jacob served seven years for Rachel because of his love for her. But God in giving his Son gave himself to die for his enemies. He gave everything for those who deserved nothing from him. 'And that is God's own proof of his love towards us' (Rom. 5:8, NEB).

Canon William Vanstone has a chapter in his book *Love's Endeavour, Love's Expense* which is entitled 'The Phenomenology of Love' (pp. 39–54). His thesis is that all human beings, even those who have been deprived of love from childhood, are able to discern authentic love instinctively. He then suggests that 'if we can describe the form of authentic love, we can hardly look elsewhere for a description of the love of God' (p. 42). Although this conflicts with what I wrote earlier about God's love defining ours, rather than *vice versa*, I know what he means and do not want to quarrel with it. He lists three marks of false love, by which its falsity is exposed. They are the mark of limitation (something is withheld), the mark of control (manipulating people), and the mark of detachment (we remain self-sufficient, unimpaired, unhurt). By contrast, authentic love is characterized by limitless self-giving, risk-taking with no certainty of success, and a vulnerability which is easily hurt. I happened to be reading Canon Vanstone's book while I was writing this chapter, and could hardly fail to observe the parallel (even though it is not exact) between his three marks of authentic love and the three marks of God's love unfolded by Paul in Romans 5:8. Here is Canon Vanstone's final summary (p. 115). God's love is 'expended in self-giving, wholly expended, without residue or reserve, drained, exhausted, spent'. That is, in giving his Son, he gave himself. Next, God's love is 'expended in precarious endeavour, ever poised upon the brink of failure ...' For he gave his Son to die, taking the risk of yielding up control over himself. Thirdly, God's love is seen 'waiting in the end, helpless before that which it loves, for the response which shall be its tragedy or its triumph'. For in giving his Son to die for sinners, God made himself vulnerable to the possibility that they would snub him and turn away.

Professor Jürgen Moltmann goes even further than this in his attempt to explain how God disclosed his love in the cross. He picks up Luther's striking expression 'the crucified God' (which Luther had himself borrowed from late medieval theology), and like Luther affirms both that God defines himself, and that we come to know him, at the cross. Luther's *theologia crucis*, therefore, 'is not a single chapter in theology, but the key signature for all Christian theology'.[20] No theology is genuinely Christian which does not arise from and focus on the cross. In particular, by 'the cross' Professor Moltmann means more than anything else the cry of dereliction. It shows, he writes, that Jesus was not only rejected by the Jews as a blasphemer and executed by the Romans as a rebel, but actually condemned and abandoned by his Father (pp. 149–152). It therefore prompts the question: 'Who is God in the cross of the Christ who is abandoned by God?' 'All Christian theology and all Christian life is basically an answer to the question which

Jesus asked as he died' (p. 4). That is why theology has to be developed 'within earshot of the dying cry of Jesus' (p. 201). What, then, do we understand of God when we see the crucified Jesus and hear his derelict cry? We certainly see his willingness in love to identify with human rejects. For 'the symbol of the cross in the church points to the God who was crucified not between two candles on an altar, but between two thieves in the place of the skull, where the outcast belong, outside the gates of the city' (p. 40). And in that awful experience which 'divides God from God to the utmost degree of enmity and distinction' (p. 152) we have to recognize that both Father and Son suffer the cost of their surrender, though differently. 'The Son suffers dying, the Father suffers the death of the Son. The grief of the Father here is just as important as the death of the Son. The Fatherlessness of the Son is matched by the Sonlessness of the Father' (p. 243). It is an arresting phrase. My own wish, I confess, is that Professor Moltmann had emphasized more strongly that it was with the *spiritually* outcast, not just the *socially* outcast, that is to say, with sinners not just criminals, that Jesus identified on the cross. He could then have clarified both the nature and the cause of the terrible God-forsakenness. Nevertheless, his outspoken acceptance that the dereliction was real, and is the greatest evidence of God's love, is moving.

The 'moral influence' theory

The cross remains such an evident display and demonstration of God's love that several theologians, in different eras of church history, have tried to find its atoning value there. To them the power of the cross lies not in any objective, sin-bearing transaction but in its subjective inspiration, not in its legal efficacy (changing our status before God) but in its moral influence changing our attitudes and actions).

The most famous exponent of this view, it is usually claimed, was the French philosopher-theologian Peter Abelard (1079–1142). He is best known for his passionate attachment to Heloïse (whom he secretly married after the birth of their son), which had such tragic consequences for them both. In his public academic life, however, his scintillating lectures and debates attracted large audiences. A younger contemporary of Anselm, he agreed with him in repudiating the notion that Christ's death was a ransom paid to the devil. But he violently disagreed with his teaching that it was a satisfaction for sin. 'How cruel and wicked it seems', he wrote, 'that anyone should demand the blood of an innocent person as the price for anything, or that it should in any way please him that an innocent man should be slain – still less that God should consider the death of his Son so agreeable that by it he should be reconciled to the whole world!'[21]

Instead, Abelard depicted Jesus as having been primarily our Teacher and

Example. Although he continued to use traditional phrases like 'redeemed by Christ', 'justified in his blood', and 'reconciled to God', he interpreted the efficacy of Christ's death in exclusively subjective terms. The voluntary self-sacrifice of the Son of God moves us to grateful love in response, and so to contrition and repentance.

> Redemption is that greatest love kindled in us by Christ's passion, a love which not only delivers us from the bondage of sin, but also acquires for us the true freedom of children, where love instead of fear becomes the ruling affection.[22]

In support of his thesis Abelard quoted Jesus' words: 'her sins are forgiven because she loved much' (Lk. 7:47). But he misunderstood the text, making love the ground of forgiveness instead of its result. Forgiveness to him was indeed the result of Christ's death, but indirectly, namely that the cross evokes our love for Christ, and when we love him, we are forgiven. 'Justification' has become for Abelard a divine infusion of love. As Robert Franks put it, 'he has reduced the whole process of redemption to one single clear principle, viz. the manifestation of God's love to us in Christ, which awakens an answering love in us'.[23]

Peter Lombard, who became Bishop of Paris in 1159 and could be described as a disciple of Abelard, wrote in his famous *Book of Sentences*:

> So great a pledge of love having been given us, we are both moved and kindled to love God who did such great things for us; and by this we are justified, that is, being loosed from our sins we are made just. The death of Christ therefore justifies us, inasmuch as through it charity is stirred up in our hearts.[24]

By the beginning of the twelfth century, then, a theological debate of immense importance had clarified, whose chief protagonists were Anselm and Abelard. Anselm taught that the death of Jesus Christ was an objective satisfaction for sin, Abelard that its efficacy was largely subjective in the moral influence it exerts on us. The ground on which God forgives our sins was to Anselm the propitiatory death of Christ; but to Abelard it was our own love, penitence and obedience which are aroused in us as we contemplate the death of Christ.

The most outspoken champion in this century of the 'moral influence' theory has probably been Dr Hastings Rashdall, whose 1915 Bampton Lectures were published under the title *The Idea of Atonement in Christian Theology*. He insisted that a choice had to be made between Anselm's objective and Abelard's subjective understandings of the atonement, and there was no question in his mind that Abelard was correct. For according to Jesus,

Rashdall maintained, the only condition of salvation was repentance: 'the truly penitent man who confesses his sins to God receives instant forgiveness' (p. 26). 'God is a loving Father who will pardon sin upon the sole condition of true repentance', and the death of Jesus Christ 'operates by actually helping to produce that repentance' (p. 48). More than that, 'God can only be supposed to forgive by making the sinner better, and thereby removing any demand for punishment' (p. 359). In other words, it is *our* repentance and *our* conversion, produced within us as we contemplate the cross, which enable God to forgive us. The significance of the cross is not that it expressed God's love in dealing with our sins, but that it has evoked our love and so made any divine dealing with sins unnecessary. Good works of love, instead of being the evidence of salvation, become the ground on which it is bestowed.

There are three reasons why the 'moral influence' or 'exemplarist' theory must be confidently declared to be untenable, at least by those who take Scripture seriously. The first is that those who hold this view tend not to take it seriously themselves. Rashdall rejected every text which was incompatible with his theory. Jesus' ransom-saying (Mk. 10:45) he declared to be a 'doctrinally coloured insertion', and his eucharistic words about the blood of the new covenant and the forgiveness of sins similarly secondary. On what ground? Simply that 'our Lord never taught that his death was necessary for the forgiveness of sins' (p. 45), which is a notable example of circular reasoning, assuming what he wishes to prove. He is more candid when he says that our belief in biblical inspiration must not prevent us from 'boldly rejecting any formulae which ... seem to say that sin cannot be forgiven without a vicarious sacrifice' (p. 207). In other words, first construct your atonement theory, then defend it against all objections, and do not allow a little matter like divine inspiration to stand in your way. Instead, simply maintain that the pure message of Jesus was corrupted by pre-Pauline Christianity, based on Isaiah 53, and that Paul completed the process.

Secondly, we need to quote against Abelard and Rashdall the words of Anselm, 'you have not yet considered the seriousness of sin'. The 'moral influence' theory offers a superficial remedy because it has made a superficial diagnosis. It appeals to Enlightenment man because it has boundless confidence in human reason and human ability. It entirely lacks the profound biblical understanding of man's radical rebellion against God, of God's wrath as his outraged antagonism to human sin, and of the indispensable necessity of a satisfaction for sin which satisfies God's own character of justice and love. James Orr was right that Abelard's 'view of atonement is defective precisely on the side on which Anselm's was strong',[25] namely in his analysis of sin, wrath and satisfaction.

Thirdly, the moral influence theory has a fatal flaw in its own central emphasis. Its focus is on the love of Christ, which both shines from the cross and elicits our responsive love. On these two truths we desire to lay an equal stress. We too know that it is because Christ loved us that he gave himself for us.[26] We too have found that his love awakens ours. In John's words, 'we love because he first loved us' (1 Jn. 4:19). We agree with Denney when he wrote: 'I do not hesitate to say that the sense of debt to Christ is the most profound and pervasive of all emotions in the New Testament.'[27] So far then we are agreed. The cross is the epitome of Christ's love and the inspiration of ours. But the question we desire to press is this: just how does the cross display and demonstrate Christ's love? What is there in the cross which reveals love? True love is purposive in its self-giving; it does not make random or reckless gestures. If you were to jump off the end of a pier and drown, or dash into a burning building and be burnt to death, and if your self-sacrifice had no saving purpose, you would convince me of your folly, not your love. But if I were myself drowning in the sea, or trapped in the burning building, and it was in attempting to rescue me that you lost your life, then I would indeed see love not folly in your action. Just so the death of Jesus on the cross cannot be seen as a demonstration of love in itself, but only if he gave his life in order to rescue ours. His death must be seen to have had an objective, before it can have an appeal. Paul and John saw love in the cross because they understood it respectively as a death for sinners (Rom. 5:8) and as a propitiation for sins (1 Jn. 4:10). That is to say, the cross can be seen as a proof of God's love only when it is at the same time seen as a proof of his justice. Hence the need to keep these two demonstrations together in our minds, as Berkouwer has insisted: 'In the cross of Christ God's justice and love are *simultaneously* revealed, so that we can speak of his love only in connection with the reality of the cross.'[28] Again, 'God's graciousness and justice are revealed only in the real substitution, in the radical sacrifice, in the reversing of roles' (p. 311). Similarly, Paul wrote in 2 Corinthians 5:14–15,

> Christ's love compels us [literally 'grips us' and so leaves us no choice], because we are convinced that one died for all, and therefore all died. And he died for all, that those who live should no longer live for themselves but for him who died for them and was raised again.

The constraint of Christ's love, Paul says, rests upon a conviction. It is because we are convinced of the purpose and costliness of the cross, namely that we owe our life to his death, that we feel his love tightening its grip upon us and leaving us no alternative but to live for him.

R. W. Dale's great book *The Atonement* was written in order to prove that Christ's death on the cross was objective before it could be subjective, and that 'unless the great Sacrifice is conceived under objective forms, the subjective power will be lost' (p. li). The cross is the supreme revelation in history of the love of God. But 'the revelation consists essentially in a redemption, rather than the redemption in a revelation'.[29]

We should not, therefore, allow Anselm and Abelard to occupy opposite poles. In general terms, Anselm was right to understand the cross as a satisfaction for sin, but he should have laid more emphasis on God's love. Abelard was right to see the cross as a manifestation of love, but wrong to deny what Anselm affirmed. Anselm and Abelard need each other's positive witness, the one to God's justice and the other to his love. For it was precisely in making a just satisfaction for sin that the manifestation of love took place.

Even after these arguments have been deployed, however, the advocates of the 'moral influence' theory consider that they have a trump card left. It is that Jesus himself, in at least three of his parables, taught forgiveness without atonement, on the basis of repentance alone. In the Parable of the Pharisee and the Tax Collector, the latter cried, 'God, have mercy on me, a sinner', and was immediately 'justified' (Lk. 18:9–14). In the Parable of the Unmerciful Servant, the king freely forgave him, cancelling his debt without insisting on its repayment (Mt. 18:23–35). And in the Parable of the Lost Son the father welcomed the young man home and reinstated him, when he returned in penitence; no punishment was exacted (Lk. 15:11–24). All three parables illustrate God's forgiving mercy, it is said, and contain no hint of the need for an atoning sacrifice. Three points may be made in reply, however.

First, the parables in question make no allusion to Christ either. Are we to deduce from this that not only his cross, but he himself, is unnecessary for our forgiveness? No. Parables are not allegories; we have no right to expect an exact correspondence, point by point, between the story and its message.

Secondly, each of the three parables contains two actors who are deliberately contrasted with each other – two worshippers in the temple (the self-righteous Pharisee and the self-humbling tax collector), two servants in the royal household (one freely forgiven by his king and the other refused forgiveness by his fellow servant), and two sons in the home (the one unrighteous but penitent, the other righteous but arrogant). The parables highlight, through this contrast, the condition of forgiveness, not its ground. They tell us what we must do, but say nothing directly about what God has done, for our forgiveness.

Nevertheless, thirdly, Christians see the cross in all three parables, because the forgiving mercy shown to the humble tax collector, the bankrupt servant and the prodigal son received its supreme historical demonstration in the self-giving love of God-in-Christ, who died that sinners might be forgiven.

Of these three parables it is that of the Prodigal Son which has seemed to many to teach most clearly a 'gospel' of forgiveness without atonement. This was the argument of Hastings Rashdall in his 1915 Bampton Lectures, mentioned above. Jesus taught, he said, that God is a loving Father who pardons all sinners who repent. This is the 'simple teaching about the forgiveness of God which is taught in the Parable of the Prodigal Son', and which the early church proceeded to corrupt (p. 27). A few years later Douglas White maintained the same thesis: 'Jesus taught ... that God loves us and longs for us to be reconciled to him. If he ever taught anything at all, it was the freedom of forgiveness ... There was no question of penance or punishment; only love and forgiveness. Its great illustration was the prodigal son ... According to this teaching, there is no pre-requisite to God's forgiveness, save the spirit of repentance.' It was Paul who perverted this simple message, making the cross necessary for salvation, using 'repugnant' phraseology, and thereby 'obscuring the doctrine of Jesus as to the unconditioned freedom of God's forgiveness'.[30]

Dr Kenneth Bailey has explained how this interpretation of the parable is common in the Muslim world:

> Islam claims that in this story the boy is saved without a saviour. The prodigal returns. The father forgives him. There is no cross, no suffering, and no saviour. If man seeks forgiveness, says Islam, God is merciful and will forgive. The incarnation, the cross, and the resurrection are all quite unnecessary. If God is truly great, he can forgive without these things. The story of the prodigal son is for them proof that Christians have sadly perverted Christ's own message.[31]

So in his book *The Cross and the Prodigal* Dr Bailey, who has for many years taught New Testament at the Near East School of Theology in Beirut, takes a fresh look at Luke 15 'through the eyes of Middle Eastern peasants'. He explains that the whole village would know that the returning prodigal was in disgrace, and that punishment of some kind was inevitable, if only to preserve the father's honour. But the father bears the suffering instead of inflicting it. Although 'a man of his age and position *always* walks in a slow, dignified fashion', and although 'he has not run *anywhere* for any purpose for 40 years', he yet 'races' down the road like a teenager to welcome his home-coming son. Thus risking the ridicule of the street urchins, 'he takes upon himself the shame and humiliation due to the prodigal'. 'In this parable', Kenneth Bailey continues, 'we have a father who leaves the comfort and security of his home and exposes himself in a humiliating fashion in the village street. The coming down and going out to his boy hints at the incarnation. The humiliating spectacle in the village street hints at the meaning of the cross' (pp. 54–55). Thus 'the cross and the incarnation are implicitly yet dramatically present in the story', for 'the suffering of the cross was not primarily the physical torture but rather the agony of rejected love'. What was essential for the prodigal's reconciliation was a 'physical demonstration of self-emptying love in suffering ... Is not this the story of the way of God with man on Golgotha?' (pp. 56–57).

We conclude, then, that the cross was an unparalleled manifestation of God's love; that he showed his love in bearing our penalty and therefore our pain, in order to be able to forgive and restore us, and that the Parable of the Prodigal Son, far from contradicting this, implicitly expresses it. I think T. J. Crawford was right to put it in this way, that before we can see in the sufferings of Christ any proof of the Father's love for us, 'some good must accrue to us from them, not otherwise to be obtained, or some evil must be averted from us by them, not otherwise to be removed or remedied'.[32] This 'otherwise unavoidable evil' is the fearful judgment of God, and this 'otherwise unattainable good' is his adoption of us into his family (p. 375). By securing such great blessings for us at the cost of such great sufferings, God has given us an unequalled demonstration of his love.

The wisdom and power of God

When Paul has finished his magisterial exposition of the gospel in the first eleven chapters of Romans, how God presented Christ as a propitiatory sacrifice, justifies sinners through faith in Christ, transforms them by the inward work of the Spirit and is creating his new community into which Gentiles are admitted on the same terms as Jews, he breaks off into a rapturous doxology: 'Oh, the depth of the riches of the wisdom and knowledge of God! How unsearchable his judgments, and his paths beyond tracing out! ... For from him and through him and to him are all things. To him be the glory for ever! Amen' (11:33–36). Earlier the apostle has seen the atoning death of Christ as a demonstration of God's justice and God's love; now he is overcome by a sense of God's wisdom – the wisdom to devise such a costly plan of salvation which both meets our needs and also satisfies his own character.

The cross as the wisdom and power of God is the main theme of 1 Corinthians 1:17 – 2:5, especially as contrasted with the wisdom and power of the world. It is Paul's mention of the 'gospel' which triggers his meditation, for he knows immediately that he is faced with a decision about its content. The choice is between 'words of human wisdom' and 'the cross of Christ'. If he were to choose human wisdom, the cross would be 'emptied', denuded, indeed destroyed (1:17). So he chooses 'the message of the cross', which he knows to be foolishness to those who are perishing, but at the same time is the power of God to those who are being saved (1:18). Powerless wisdom or foolish power: it was (and still is) a fateful choice. The one combination which is not an option is the wisdom of the world plus the power of God.

The reason Paul opts for power against wisdom, God's power against the world's wisdom, is that God in Old Testament Scripture has already declared his intention to destroy the wisdom of the wise and frustrate the cleverness of the clever (1:19). So, if God has set himself against them, where are the wise, the scholars and the philosophers of this age to be found? Has not God already decided against them by making their wisdom foolish (1:20)? This is how he has done so. In his wisdom God first decreed that the world through its own wisdom should not know him, and then was pleased through the foolishness of the revealed and preached gospel to save believers (1:21). So it is again clear that power (saving power) is not in the world's wisdom but in God's foolishness, namely the gospel of Christ crucified.

This principle can be seen operating in the evangelization of Jews and Greeks, for both groups lay down conditions on which the gospel would be acceptable to them. 'Jews demand miraculous signs and Greeks look for wisdom' (1:22). In other words, they insist that the message must authenticate itself to them by power and wisdom respectively. In total contrast to their demands, however, 'we preach Christ crucified' (1:23), who does not even begin to conform to their criteria. On the contrary, the Jews find the cross 'a stumbling block' and the Gentiles 'foolishness', for it offends instead of impressing them, whereas to those who are called by God, whether Jews or Greeks, it is the exact opposite. Though crucified in weakness Christ is God's power, and though apparently foolish he is God's wisdom (1:24). For what men regard as God's foolishness is wiser than their wisdom, and what they regard as God's weakness is stronger than their strength (1:25). In brief, divine and human values are completely at variance with one another. And the cross, which as a way of salvation seems the height of impotence and folly, is actually the greatest manifestation of God's wisdom and power.

Paul caps his argument with two illustrations, the first taken from the Corinthians' experience of their call and conversion (1:26–31), and the second from his own experience of evangelism (2:1–5). As for them, by human standards not many of them were wise or powerful. In fact God deliberately chose what the world regards as foolish and feeble people, in order to shame the wise and the strong; he chose even the lowly, the despised and the nonexistent to nullify what exists. His goal in this was to exclude human boasting. Boasting was entirely out of place, because it was God who had united them to Christ, and Christ who had become their wisdom (revealing God to them) and their power (bringing them justification, holiness and the promise of final redemption). Therefore, as Scripture says, if anybody boasts, he must boast neither in himself, nor in others, but in the Lord alone.

As for Paul the evangelist, when he came to Corinth, he had not come with a message of human wisdom. Nor had he come in his own strength.

Instead, he had brought the foolish, revealed message of the cross, and he had come in personal weakness, fear and trembling, relying on the Holy Spirit's power to confirm the word. His whole purpose in coming to them in such folly and feebleness was that their faith would rest firmly on God's power, not men's wisdom.

What we have been hearing throughout this passage is variations on the theme of the wisdom and power of God, his wisdom through human folly and his power through human weakness. The gospel of the cross will never be a popular message, because it humbles the pride of our intellect and character. Yet Christ crucified is both God's wisdom (1:24) and ours (1:30). For the cross is God's way to satisfy his love and justice in the salvation of sinners. It therefore manifests his power too, 'the power of God for the salvation of everyone who believes' (Rom. 1:16).

So when we look at the cross we see the justice, love, wisdom and power of God. It is not easy to decide which is the most luminously revealed, whether the justice of God in judging sin, or the love of God in bearing the judgment in our place, or the wisdom of God in perfectly combining the two, or the power of God in saving those who believe. For the cross is equally an act, and therefore a demonstration, of God's justice, love, wisdom and power. The cross assures us that this God is the reality within, behind and beyond the universe.

In one of his great hymns Isaac Watts brought together God's self-revelation in the creation and the cross. After speaking of his handiwork in nature, he continues:

> But in the grace that rescued man
>> His brightest form of glory shines.
> Here, on the cross, 'tis fairest drawn
>> In precious blood and crimson lines.

> Here his whole name appears complete:
>> Nor wit can guess, nor reason prove,
> Which of the letters best is writ,
>> The power, the wisdom or the love.

Notes

[1] Pss. 19:1; 29:9; Is. 6:3; Mt. 6:29.
[2] Nu. 14:22; Ps. 97:2–6; Is. 35:2; 40:5; Ex. 33:18 – 34:7.
[3] A. M. Ramsey, *Glory of God*, p. 28.
[4] For the transfiguration glory see Lk. 9:32 and 2 Pet.1:16; for the glory at the parousia see Mk. 13:26, and for the glory of the final kingdom see Mk. 10:37; Mt. 25:31.
[5] Jn. 2:11; 11:4, 40.
[6] F. Donald Coggan, *Glory of God*, p. 52.

7 John does not use the verb 'crucified' until chapter 19, where it occurs ten times. Before this he three times uses the term 'lifted up', with its deliberate *double entendre* (3:14; 8:28; 12:32).

8 Lk. 24:26. *Cf.* 1 Pet. 4:13; 5:1, 10 and Rom. 8:17–18.

9 I write 'also' because clearly John thinks of Christ being glorified in other ways too, *e.g.* by the work of the Spirit (16:14), in the church (17:10) and in heaven (17:5, 24).

10 Jn. 12:20–28; 13:30–32; 17:1.

11 Jn. 1:29; 10:11; 11:49–52 and 18:14.

12 Ex. 34:6; Jn. 1:14, 17.

13 Calvin's *St John*, p. 68 (on Jn. 13:31) and p. 135 (on Jn. 17:1).

14 Acts 17:30–31; Rom. 2:4; 2 Pet. 3:3–9.

15 Heb. 10:4 and 9:15.

16 *E.g.* Pss. 71:15; 98:2; Is. 45:21 ('a righteous God and a Saviour'); 46:13; 1:5–6; 56:1. See, for example, C. H. Dodd in *Romans*, pp. 10–13.

17 Anselm, *Cur Deus Homo?*, I. xiii, and James Denney, *Death of Christ*, p. 188.

18 P. T. Forsyth, *Justification of God*, pp. 124–125. Barth also wrote that the justification of man is the self-justification of God (*Church Dogmatics*, V1, pp. 559–564).

19 P. T. Forsyth, *Justification*, p. 154.

20 Jürgen Moltmann, *Crucified God*, p. 72.

21 Abelard's Commentary on Romans 3:19–26, in *A Scholastic Miscellany*, ed. Eugene Fairweather, p. 283.

22 *Ibid.*, p. 284. *Cf.* James Orr, *Progress of Dogma*, pp. 229–230. pp. 229—230.

23 Robert S. Franks, *Work of Christ*, p. 146. After writing these paragraphs my attention has been drawn to a penetrating article by Dr Alister McGrath, entitled 'The Moral Theory of the Atonement: An Historical and Theological Critique'. He maintains that to call the 'moral influence' theory 'Abelardian' is mistaken, that the mistake arose from regarding 'a single, small portion of Abelard's *Exposition in Epistolam ad Romanos* as representative of his teaching as a whole' (p. 208); and that the imitation of Christ he emphasized was not the means, but rather the result, of our redemption. Nevertheless, the passage in his commentary on the Letter to the Romans is quite explicit, so that I do not see how one can fairly eliminate this element from Abelard's view. At all events, the leaders of the German Enlightenment certainly taught the 'moral influence' theory as Dr McGrath shows. So did Hastings Rashdall, to whom I come soon.

24 Peter Lombard's *Book of Sentences*, iii, Dist. xix.1 (quoted by Rashdall, pp. 371, 438).

25 James Orr, *Progress of Dogma*, p. 229.

26 *E.g.* Gal. 2:20; Eph. 5:2 25; 1 Jn. 3:16.

27 James Denney, *Death of Christ*, p. 158.

28 G. C. Berkouwer, *Work of Christ*, pp. 277–278.

29 H. W. Robinson, *Suffering Human and Divine*.

30 Douglas White, 'Nature of Punishment', pp. 6–9.

31 Kenneth E. Bailey, *Cross and the Prodigal*, p. 56.

32 T. J. Crawford, *Doctrine of Holy Scripture*, p. 335.

NINE

The conquest of evil

It is impossible to read the New Testament without being impressed by the atmosphere of joyful confidence which pervades it, and which stands out in relief against the rather jejune religion that often passes for Christianity today. There was no defeatism about the early Christians; they spoke rather of victory. For example, 'thanks be to God! He gives us the victory ...' Again, 'in all these things [sc. adversities and dangers] we are more than conquerors ...' Once more, 'God ... always leads us in triumphal procession ...' And each of Christ's letters to the seven churches of Asia ends with a special promise 'to him who overcomes'.[1] Victory, conquest, triumph, overcoming – this was the vocabulary of those first followers of the risen Lord. For if they spoke of victory, they knew they owed it to the victorious Jesus. They said so in the texts which I have so far quoted only in truncated form. What Paul actually wrote was: 'he gives us the victory *through our Lord Jesus Christ*', 'we are more than conquerors *through him who loved us*', and 'God ... leads us in triumphal procession *in Christ*'. It is he who 'overcame', 'has triumphed', and moreover did it 'by the cross'.[2]

Of course any contemporary observer, who saw Christ die, would have listened with astonished incredulity to the claim that the Crucified was a Conqueror. Had he not been rejected by his own nation, betrayed, denied and deserted by his own disciples, and executed by authority from the Roman procurator? Look at him there, spread-eagled and skewered on his cross, robbed of all freedom of movement, strung up with nails or ropes or both, pinned there and powerless. It appears to be total defeat. If there is victory, it is the victory of pride, prejudice, jealousy, hatred, cowardice and brutality. Yet the Christian claim is that the reality is the opposite of the appearance. What looks like (and indeed was) the defeat of goodness by evil is also, and more certainly, the defeat of evil by goodness. Overcome there, he was himself overcoming. Crushed by the ruthless power of Rome, he was himself crushing the serpent's head (Gn. 3:15). The victim was the victor, and the cross is still the throne from which he rules the world.

> Fulfilled is now what David told
> In true prophetic song of old,
> How God the heathen's king should be,
> For God is reigning from the tree.

Here then is a further motif in the achievement of Christ's cross. In addition to the salvation of sinners (as indicated by the four images we considered in chapter 7) and the revelation of God (especially of his holy love, as considered in the last chapter), the cross secured the conquest of evil.

Gustav Aulén and *Christus Victor*

It is particularly Gustav Aulén, the Swedish theologian, who through his influential book *Christus Victor* (1930) reminded the church of this neglected truth. The book's original Swedish title means something like 'The Christian Concept of Atonement', but *Christus Victor* captures his emphasis better. His thesis, in a study which is more historical than apologetic, is that the traditional reconstruction of two main atonement theories is mistaken, namely the 'objective' or 'legal' view (Christ's death reconciling the Father), associated with Anselm, and the 'subjective' or 'moral' view (Christ's death inspiring and transforming us), associated with Abelard. For there is a third view which Aulén calls both 'dramatic' and 'classic'. It is 'dramatic' because it sees the atonement as a cosmic drama in which God in Christ does battle with the powers of evil and gains the victory over them. It is 'classic' because, he claims, it was 'the ruling idea of the Atonement for the first thousand years of Christian history' (pp. 22–23).

So Aulén was at pains to demonstrate that this concept of the atonement as a victory over sin, death and the devil was the dominant view of the New Testament; that it was held by all the Greek Fathers from Irenaeus at the end of the second century to John of Damascus at the beginning of the eighth, and is therefore held by Eastern Orthodox churches today; that the leading Western Fathers believed it too (though often side by side with the 'objective' view), including Ambrose and Augustine, and Popes Leo the

Great and Gregory the Great; that it was lost by medieval Catholic scholasticism; that Luther recovered it; but that subsequent Protestant scholasticism lost it again and reverted to the Anselmian notion of satisfaction.

Aulén is, therefore, very critical of Anselm's 'satisfaction' doctrine, which he calls 'Latin' and 'juridical'. He dismisses it a little contemptuously as 'really a sidetrack in the history of Christian dogma' (p. 31), in fact a deviation. His critique of Anselm is not altogether fair, however. He rightly underlines the truth that in the 'classic' view 'the work of atonement is regarded as carried through by God himself', that 'he himself is the effective agent in the redemptive work, from beginning to end' (p. 50), and that indeed 'the Atonement is, above all, a movement of God to man, not in the first place a movement of man to God' (p. 176). But he is unjust to represent Anselm's view of Christ's death as contradicting this, namely as 'an offering made to God by Christ as man' (p. 22), 'as it were from below' (p. 50), or 'a human work of satisfaction accomplished by Christ' (p. 104). For, as we saw in chapter 5, Anselm emphasized clearly that, although man *ought* to make satisfaction for sin, he *cannot,* for they are his sins for which satisfaction has to be made. Indeed, only God himself can, and therefore does, through Christ. In spite of what Aulén writes, Anselm's teaching is that, through the work of the unique God-man Christ Jesus, it is not only man who made satisfaction; it is God himself who was both the satisfier and the satisfied.

Nevertheless, Gustav Aulén was right to draw the church's attention to the cross as victory, and to show that by his death Jesus saved us not only from sin and guilt, but from death and the devil, in fact all evil powers, as well. His thesis was relevant too in a century torn apart by two World Wars and in a European culture aware of demonic forces. He was also correct in pointing out that 'the note of triumph', which 'sounds like a trumpet-call through the teaching of the early church' (p. 59), was largely absent from the cool logic of Anselm's *Cur Deus Homo?* Luther, on the other hand, struck this note again. His hymns and catechisms reverberate with joy that God has rescued us from that 'monster' or 'tyrant' the devil, who previously held us in the captivity of sin, law, curse and death.

Another just criticism of Aulén's thesis is that he made too sharp a contrast between the 'satisfaction' and the 'victory' motifs, as if they are mutually incompatible alternatives. But the New Testament does not oblige us to choose between them, for it includes them both. Thus, God took the initiative and won the victory through Christ, but one of the tyrants from whom he liberated us was the very guilt which, according to Anselm, he died to atone for. An admirable attempt to combine the two concepts was made by the nineteenth-century Scottish commentator John Eadie:

Our redemption is a work at once of price and of power – of expiation and of conquest. On the cross was the purchase made, and on the cross was the victory gained. The blood which wipes out the sentence against us was there shed, and the death which was the death-blow of Satan's kingdom was there endured.[3]

In fact all three of the major explanations of the death of Christ contain biblical truth and can to some extent be harmonized, especially if we observe that the chief difference between them is that in each God's work in Christ is directed towards a different person. In the 'objective' view God satisfies himself, in the 'subjective' he inspires us, and in the 'classic' he overcomes the devil. Thus Jesus Christ is successively the Saviour, the Teacher and the Victor, because we ourselves are guilty, apathetic and in bondage. P. T. Forsyth drew attention to this in the last chapter of his book *The Work of Christ* which he entitled 'The Threefold Cord'. He refers to the 'satisfactionary', 'regenerative' and 'triumphant' aspects of the work of Christ, and suggests that they are intertwined in 1 Corinthians 1:30, where Christ is made unto us 'justification, sanctification and redemption' (pp. 199–200). And although 'some souls … will gravitate to the great Deliverance, some to the great Atonement, and some to the great Regeneration' (p. 233), yet all are part of the Saviour's total accomplishment, 'the destruction of evil, the satisfaction of God, and the sanctification of men' (p. 202).

As we concentrate now on the theme of 'conquest', it may be helpful if we look first at the historic victory of Christ at the cross, and then at the victory of his people, which his victory has made possible.

The victory of Christ

What the New Testament affirms, in its own uninhibited way, is that at the cross Jesus disarmed and triumphed over the devil, and all the 'principalities and powers' at his command. First-century hearers of the gospel will have had no difficulty in accepting this, for 'it is perhaps hard for modern man to realize how hag-ridden was the world into which Christ came'.[4] Still today in many countries people live in dread of malevolent spirits. And in the supposedly sophisticated West a new and alarming fascination with the occult has developed, which has been ably documented by Michael Green in his *I Believe in Satan's Downfall*. And yet at the same time many ridicule continuing belief in a personal devil, with evil spirits under him, as a superstitious anachronism. Rudolf Bultmann's dogmatic statement is well known: 'it is impossible to use electric light and the wireless, and to avail ourselves of modern medical and surgical discoveries, and at the same time believe in the New Testament world of demons and spirits'.[5] Michael Green sums up this anomaly of the coexistence of curiosity and incredulity by suggesting that two opposite attitudes would be equally pleasing to the devil:

'The first is that of excessive preoccupation with the Prince of evil. The second is that of excessive scepticism about his very existence' (p. 16). Michael Green goes on to give seven reasons why he believes in the existence of that immensely powerful, evil and cunning being who is called Satan or the devil. They relate to philosophy, theology, the environment, experience, the occult, Scripture and above all Jesus. It is a cogent case; I have nothing to add to it.

But how did God through Christ win the victory over him? The conquest is depicted in Scripture as unfolding in six stages, although the decisive defeat of Satan took place at the cross. Stage one is *the conquest predicted*. The first prediction was given by God himself in the Garden of Eden as part of his judgment on the serpent: 'And I will put enmity between you and the woman, and between your offspring and hers; he will crush your head, and you will strike his heel' (Gn. 3:15). We identify the woman's seed as the Messiah, through whom God's rule of righteousness will be established and the rule of evil eradicated. This being so, every Old Testament text which declares either God's present rule (*e.g.* 'Yours, O LORD, is the greatness and the power … Yours, O LORD, is the kingdom …') or his future rule over the nations through the Messiah (*e.g.* 'Wonderful Counsellor, Mighty God, Everlasting Father, Prince of Peace') may be understood as a further prophecy of the ultimate crushing of Satan.[6]

The second stage was *the conquest begun* in the ministry of Jesus. Recognizing him as his future conqueror, Satan made many different attempts to get rid of him, for example, through Herod's murder of the Bethlehem children, through the wilderness temptations to avoid the way of the cross, through the crowd's resolve to force him into a politico-military kingship, through Peter's contradiction of the necessity of the cross ('Get behind me, Satan'), and through the betrayal of Judas whom Satan actually 'entered'.[7] But Jesus was determined to fulfil what had been written of him. He announced that through him God's kingdom had come upon that very generation, and that his mighty works were visible evidence of it. We see his kingdom advancing and Satan's retreating before it, as demons are dismissed, sicknesses are healed and disordered nature itself acknowledges its Lord.[8] Moreover, Jesus sent out his disciples to preach and to heal as his representatives, and when they returned, excited that the demons had submitted to them in his name, he responded that he had seen 'Satan fall like lightning from heaven'. Here, however, is his most striking statement on this topic: 'When a strong man, fully armed, guards his own house, his possessions are safe. But when someone stronger attacks and overpowers him (*nikaō*, to gain the victory over), he takes away the armour in which the man trusted and divides up the spoils.' It is not difficult to recognize the strong man as a picture of the devil, the 'someone stronger' as Jesus Christ, and the dividing of the spoils (or, in Mark, the robbing of his house) as the liberation of his slaves.[9]

The 'overpowering' and 'binding' of the strong man did not take place, however, until the third and decisive stage, *the conquest achieved*, at the cross. Three times, according to John, Jesus referred to him as 'the prince of this world', adding that he was about to 'come' (*i.e.* launch his last offensive), but would be 'driven out' and 'condemned'.[10] He was evidently anticipating that at the time of his death the final contest would take place, in which the powers of darkness would be routed. It was by his death that he would 'destroy him who holds the power of death – that is, the devil –' and so set his captives free (Heb. 2:14–15).

Perhaps the most important New Testament passage in which the victory of Christ is set forth is Colossians 2:13–15.

> He forgave us all our sins, having cancelled the written code, with its regulations, that was against us and that stood opposed to us; he took it away, nailing it to the cross. And having disarmed the powers and authorities, he made a public spectacle of them, triumphing over them by the cross.

Paul here brings together two different aspects of the saving work of Christ's cross, namely the forgiveness of our sins and the cosmic overthrow of the principalities and powers.[11] He illustrates the freeness and graciousness of God's forgiveness (*charizomai*) from the ancient custom of cancelling debts. 'The written code, with its regulations, that was against us' can hardly be a reference to the law in itself, since Paul regarded it as 'holy, righteous and good' (Rom. 7:12); it must rather refer to the broken law, which on that account was 'against us and stood opposed to us' with its judgment. The word Paul uses for this 'written code' is *cheirographon*, which was 'a hand-written document, specifically a certificate of indebtedness, a bond' (AG) or a 'signed confession of indebtedness, which stood as a perpetual witness against us'.[12] The apostle then employs three verbs to describe how God has dealt with our debts. He 'cancelled' the bond by 'wiping' it clean (as *exaleiphō* literally means) and then 'took it away, nailing it to the cross'. Jeremias thinks the allusion is to the *titulus*, the tablet fixed over a crucified person's head on which his crimes were written, and that on Jesus' titulus it was our sins, not his, which were inscribed.[13] In any case, God frees us from our bankruptcy only by paying our debts on Christ's cross. More than that. He has 'not only cancelled the debt, but also destroyed the document on which it was recorded'.[14]

Paul now moves from the forgiveness of our sins to the conquest of the evil powers, and uses three graphic verbs to portray their defeat. The first could mean that God in Christ 'stripped' them from himself like foul clothing, because they had closed in upon him and were clinging to him, and so 'discarded' them (NEB). Or better, it means that he 'stripped' them either of their weapons and so 'disarmed' them (NIV), or of 'their dignity and might'[15] and so degraded them. Secondly, 'he made a public spectacle of them', exhibiting them as the 'powerless powers'[16] they now are, and so, thirdly, 'triumphing over them by the cross', which is probably a reference to the procession of captives which celebrated a victory. Thus the cross, comments Handley Moule, was 'his scaffold from one viewpoint, his imperial chariot from another'.[17] Alexander Maclaren suggests a unified picture of Christ as 'the victor stripping his foes of arms and ornaments and dress, then parading them as his captives, and then dragging them at the wheels of his triumphal car'.[18]

All this is vivid imagery, but what does it actually mean? Are we to visualize a literal cosmic battle, in which the powers of darkness surrounded and attacked Christ on the cross, and in which he disarmed, discredited and defeated them? If it was unseen, as it would surely have to be, how did Christ make 'a public spectacle' of them? It seems that we are to think of his victory, though real and objective, in other terms.

First, it is surely significant that Paul brackets what Christ did to the *cheirographon* (cancelling and removing it) with what he did to the principalities and powers (disarming and conquering them). The bond he nailed to the cross; the powers he defeated by the cross. It does not seem necessary to insist on the latter being any more literal than the former. The important point is that both happened together. Is not his payment of our debts the way in which Christ has overthrown the powers? By liberating us from these, he has liberated us from them.

Secondly, he overcame the devil by totally resisting his temptations. Tempted to avoid the cross, Jesus persevered in the path of obedience, and 'became obedient to death – even death on a cross' (Phil. 2:8). His obedience was indispensable to his saving work. 'For just as through the disobedience of the one man the many were made sinners, so also through the obedience of the one man the many will be made righteous' (Rom. 5:19). If he had disobeyed, by deviating an inch from the path of God's will, the devil would have gained a toehold and frustrated the plan of salvation. But Jesus obeyed; and the devil was routed. Provoked by the insults and tortures to which he was subjected, Jesus absolutely refused to retaliate. By his self-giving love for others, he 'overcame evil with good' (Rom. 12:21). Again, when the combined forces of Rome and Jerusalem were arrayed against him, he could have met power with power. For Pilate had no ultimate authority over him; more than twelve legions of angels would have sped to his rescue if he had summoned them; and he could have stepped down from the cross, as in jest they challenged him to do.[19] But he declined any resort to worldly power. He was 'crucified in weakness', though the weakness of

God was stronger than human strength. Thus he refused either to disobey God, or to hate his enemies, or to imitate the world's use of power. By his obedience, his love and his meekness he won a great moral victory over the powers of evil. He remained free, uncontaminated, uncompromised. The devil could gain no hold on him, and had to concede defeat.[20] As F. F. Bruce has put it:

> As he was suspended there, bound hand and foot to the wood in apparent weakness, they imagined they had him at their mercy, and flung themselves upon him with hostile intent ... But he grappled with them and mastered them.[21]

So the victory of Christ, predicted immediately after the Fall and begun during his public ministry, was decisively won at the cross. Its remaining three stages were the outworkings of this.

Fourthly, the resurrection was *the conquest confirmed and announced*. We are not to regard the cross as defeat and the resurrection as victory. Rather, the cross was the victory won, and the resurrection the victory endorsed, proclaimed and demonstrated. 'It was impossible for death to keep its hold on him', because death had already been defeated. The evil principalities and powers, which had been deprived of their weapons and their dignity at the cross, were now in consequence put under his feet and made subject to him.[22]

Fifthly, *the conquest is extended* as the church goes out on its mission, in the power of the Spirit, to preach Christ crucified as Lord and to summon people to repent and believe in him. In every true conversion there is a turning not only from sin to Christ, but 'from darkness to light', 'from the power of Satan to God', and 'from idols to serve the living and true God'; there is also a rescue 'from the dominion of darkness ... into the kingdom of the Son God loves'.[23] So every Christian conversion involves a power encounter in which the devil is obliged to relax his hold on somebody's life and the superior power of Christ is demonstrated. This being so, it may well be right to interpret the 'binding' of the dragon for a thousand years as coinciding with the 'binding' of the strong man which took place at the cross. For the result of the binding of Satan is that he is kept from 'deceiving the nations any more', which seems to refer to the evangelization of the nations which began after the great victory of the cross and its immediate sequel of Easter Day and Pentecost.[24]

Sixthly, we are looking forward to *the conquest consummated* at the parousia. The interim between the two advents is to be filled with the church's mission. The Lord's Anointed is already reigning, but he is also waiting until his enemies become a footstool for his feet. On that day every knee will bow to him and every tongue confess him Lord. The devil will be thrown into the lake of fire, where death and Hades will join him. For the last enemy to be destroyed is death. Then, when all evil dominion, authority and power have been destroyed, the Son will hand over the kingdom to the Father, and he will be all in all.[25]

Is it correct, however, thus to attribute Christ's victory to his death? Was it not rather achieved by his resurrection? Was it not by rising again from death that he conquered death? In fact, does not this book's whole emphasis lie too heavily on the cross, and insufficiently on the resurrection? Do the two events not belong together, as Michael Green has argued powerfully in his recent book, *The Empty Cross of Jesus*? It is essential that we address ourselves to these questions.

To begin with, it is true beyond doubt that the death and resurrection of Jesus belong together in the New Testament, and that the one is seldom mentioned without the other. Jesus himself, in the three successive predictions of his passion which Mark records, each time added that after three days he would rise again.[26] According to John, he also said both that he would 'lay down' his life and that he would 'take it up again'.[27] Moreover, it happened as he said it would: 'I am the Living One; I was dead, and behold I am alive for ever and ever' (Rev. 1:18). Next, it is equally clear that the apostles spoke of the two together. The earliest apostolic *kerygma* according to Peter was that he 'was handed over ... by God's set purpose and foreknowledge and ... put to death ... But God raised him from the dead', while Paul states as the original and universal gospel that 'Christ died for our sins ... was buried ... was raised ... and ... appeared'.[28] And Paul's letters are full of phrases such as 'we believe that Jesus died and rose again' and 'those who live should ... live ... for him who died for them and was raised again'.[29] Moreover, the two gospel sacraments were acknowledged from the beginning to bear witness to both, since in baptism the candidate symbolically dies and rises with Christ, while at the Lord's Supper it is the risen Lord who makes himself known to us through the very emblems which speak of his death.[30] So this is not – or should not be – in dispute. It would be seriously unbalanced to proclaim either the cross without the resurrection (as I am afraid Anselm did) or the resurrection without the cross (as do those who present Jesus as a living Lord rather than as an atoning Saviour). It is therefore healthy to maintain an indissoluble link between them.

Nevertheless, we need to be clear about the nature of the relation between the death and resurrection of Jesus, and careful not to ascribe saving efficacy to both equally. Michael Green avoids this trap, for he strongly affirms that 'the cross of Jesus is the very core of the gospel'.[31] It is indeed. When we examined the four images of salvation in chapter 7, it became apparent that it is 'by the blood of Jesus' that God's wrath against sin was propitiated, and by the same blood of Jesus that we have been redeemed, justified and reconciled. For it was by his death, and not by his resurrection, that our sins were dealt with. Even in the earliest apostolic *kerygma*, already quoted, Paul writes that 'Christ died for our sins'. Nowhere in the New Testament is it written that 'Christ rose for our sins'. But was it not by his resurrection that Christ conquered death? No, it was by his death that he destroyed him who holds the power of death (Heb. 2:14).

Of course the resurrection was essential to confirm the efficacy of his death, as his incarnation had been to prepare for its possibility. But we must insist that Christ's work of sin-bearing was finished on the cross, that the victory over the devil, sin and death was won there, and that what the resurrection did was to vindicate the Jesus whom men had rejected, to declare with power that he is the Son of God, and publicly to confirm that his sin-bearing death had been effective for the forgiveness of sins. If he had not been raised, our faith and our preaching would be futile, since his person and work would not have received the divine endorsement.[32] This is the implication of Romans 4:25, which at first sight seems to teach that Christ's resurrection is the means of our justification: 'He was delivered over to death for our sins and was raised to life for our justification.' Charles Cranfield explains: 'What was necessitated by our sins was, in the first place, Christ's atoning death, and yet, had his death not been followed by his resurrection, it would not have been God's mighty deed for our justification.'[33] In addition, because of the resurrection it is a living Christ who bestows on us the salvation he has won for us on the cross, who enables us by his Spirit not only to share in the merit of his death but also to live in the power of his resurrection, and who promises us that on the last day we too will have resurrection bodies.

James Denney expresses the relation between Jesus' death and resurrection in this way:

> There can be no salvation from sin unless there is a living Saviour: this explains the emphasis laid by the apostle [*sc.* Paul] on the resurrection. But the living One can be a Saviour only because he has died: this explains the emphasis laid on the cross. The Christian believes in a living Lord, or he could not believe at all; but he believes in a living Lord who died an atoning death, for no other can hold the faith of a soul under the doom of sin.[34]

To sum up, the gospel includes both the death and resurrection of Jesus, since nothing would have been accomplished by his death if he had not been raised from it. Yet the gospel emphasizes the cross, since it was there that the victory was accomplished. The resurrection did not achieve our deliverance from sin and death, but has brought us an assurance of both. It is because of the resurrection that our 'faith and hope are in God' (1 Pet. 1:3, 21).

Entering into Christ's victory

For Christians as for Christ, life spells conflict. For Christians as for Christ, it should also spell victory. We are to be victorious like the victorious Christ. Did not John write to the 'young men' of the churches he supervised because they had 'overcome the evil one'? Did not Jesus deliberately draw a parallel between himself and us in this respect, promising to him who overcomes the right to share his throne, just as he had overcome and shared his Father's throne?[35]

Yet the parallel is only partial. It would be utterly impossible for us by ourselves to fight and defeat the devil: we lack both the skill and the strength to do so. It would also be unnecessary to make the attempt, because Christ has already done it. The victory of Christians, therefore, consists of entering into the victory of Christ and of enjoying its benefits. We can thank God that 'he gives us the victory through our Lord Jesus Christ'. We know that Jesus, having been raised from the dead, is now seated at the Father's right hand in the heavenly realms. But God has 'made us alive with Christ … and raised us up with Christ and seated us with him in the heavenly realms'. In other words, by God's gracious power we who have shared in Christ's resurrection share also in his throne. If God has placed all things under Christ's feet, they must be under ours too, if we are in him. To borrow Jesus' own metaphor, now that the strong man has been disarmed and bound, the time is ripe for us to raid his palace and plunder his goods.[36]

It is not quite so simple as that, however. For though the devil has been defeated, he has not yet conceded defeat. Although he has been overthrown, he has not yet been eliminated. In fact he continues to wield great power. This is the reason for the tension we feel in both our theology and our experience. On the one hand we are alive, seated and reigning with Christ, as we have just seen, with even the principalities and powers of evil placed by God under his (and therefore our) feet; on the other we are warned (also in Ephesians) that these same spiritual forces have set themselves in opposition to us, so that we have no hope of standing against them unless we are strong in the Lord's strength and clad in his armour.[37] Or here is the same paradox in different language. On the one hand, we are assured that, having been born of God, Christ keeps us safe 'and the evil one does not touch' us; on the other we are warned to watch out because the same evil one 'prowls around like a roaring lion looking for someone to devour'.[38]

Many Christians choose one or other of these positions, or oscillate unsteadily between them. Some are triumphalists, who see only the decisive victory of Jesus Christ and overlook the apostolic warnings against the powers of darkness. Others are defeatists, who see only the fearsome malice of the devil and overlook the victory over him which Christ has already won. The tension is part of the Christian dilemma between the 'already' and the 'not yet'. Already the kingdom of God has been inaugurated and is advancing; not yet has it been consummated. Already the new age (the age to come) has come, so that we have 'tasted ... the powers of the coming age'; not yet has the old age completely passed away. Already we are God's sons and daughters, and no longer slaves; not yet have we entered 'the glorious freedom of the children of God'.[39] An overemphasis on the 'already' leads to triumphalism, the claim to perfection – either moral (sinlessness) or physical (complete health) – which belongs only to the consummated kingdom, the 'not yet'. An overemphasis on the 'not yet' leads to defeatism, an acquiescence in continuing evil which is incompatible with the 'already' of Christ's victory.

Another way of approaching this tension is to consider the implications of the verb *katargeō*, which, though often translated in our English versions as 'destroy', really falls short of that. It means rather to 'make ineffective or inactive', and is used of unproductive land and unfruitful trees. They are still there. They have not been destroyed. But they are barren. When this verb is applied to the devil, to our fallen nature and to death,[40] therefore, we know that they have not been completely 'destroyed'. For the devil is still very active, our fallen nature continues to assert itself, and death will go on claiming us until Christ comes. It is not, then, that they have ceased to exist, but that their power has been broken. They have not been abolished, but they have been overthrown.

John makes the important assertion that 'the reason why the Son of God appeared was that he might "undo" or "do away with" the works of the devil' (1 Jn. 3:8, literally). He came to confront and defeat the devil, and so undo the damage he had done. What are these 'works of the devil', the effects of his nefarious activity? Luther loved, for example, in his classic commentary on *Galatians*, to give a string of them. In one place he wrote of 'law, sin, death, the devil and hell' as constituting 'all the evils and miseries of mankind' (p. 162), and in another of 'sin, death and the curse' as 'those invincible and mighty tyrants' from which only Christ can set us free (p. 275). Anders Nygren in his famous commentary on *Romans* suggests that chapters 5 to 8 describe the life of the person who has been justified by faith: 'Chapter 5 says it means to be free from *wrath*. Chapter 6 says it is to be free from *sin*. Chapter 7 says free from *the law*. And Chapter 8 says we are free from *death*' (p. 188). My concern is that these lists omit any reference to 'the flesh' (our fallen human nature) and to 'the world' (godless society), which are familiar at least to church people in the trio 'the world, the flesh and the devil'. So the four 'works of the devil' from which Christ frees us, on which the New Testament writers seem to me to concentrate, are the law, the flesh, the world and death.

First, through Christ we are no longer under *the tyranny of the law*. It comes to many people as a surprise that the law, God's good gift to his people, in itself 'holy, righteous and good', could ever have become a tyrant which enslaves us. But that is exactly Paul's teaching. 'Before this faith came, we were held prisoners by the law, locked up until faith should be revealed.' The reason is that the law condemns our disobedience and so brings us under its 'curse' or judgment. But Christ has redeemed us from the law's curse by becoming a curse for us. It is in this sense that 'Christ is the end of the law' and we are no longer 'under' it.[41] It emphatically does not mean that there are now no moral absolutes except love, as the advocates of 'the new morality' taught in the 1960s, or that we now have no obligation to obey God's law, as other antinomians teach. No, since the tyranny of the law is its curse, it is from this that we are liberated by Christ, so that we are not 'under' it any more. The law no longer enslaves us by its condemnation. The *cheirographon* we were thinking about earlier has been expunged. The first four verses of Romans 8 bring these strands together. They say that for those who are in Christ there is 'no condemnation' (v. 1), for God has already condemned our sins in Jesus Christ (v. 3), and he did it in order that 'the righteous requirements of the law might be fully met in us' (v. 4). So the same cross of Christ, which frees us from the law's condemnation, commits us to the law's obedience.

Secondly, through Christ we are no longer under *the tyranny of the flesh*. What Paul means by the 'flesh' (*sarx*) is our fallen nature or unredeemed humanity, everything that we are by birth, inheritance and upbringing before Christ renewed us. Because our 'flesh' is our 'self' in Adam, its characteristic is self-centredness. Paul supplies a catalogue of some of its worst and ugliest outworkings, including sexual immorality, idolatry and occult practices (misdirected worship), hatred, jealousy and anger, selfish ambition and dissensions, and drunkenness. Living this kind of life, we were 'enslaved by all kinds of passions and pleasures'. As Jesus himself said, 'everyone who sins is a slave to sin'. But he immediately added: 'if the Son sets you free, you will be free indeed'. And freedom from our fallen nature and its selfishness comes through the cross: 'For we know that our old self was crucified with him so that the body of sin might be rendered powerless, that we should no longer be slaves to sin.'[42] Christ by his cross has won the victory over the flesh as well as over the law.

Thirdly, through Christ we are no longer under *the tyranny of the world*. If the flesh is the foothold the devil has within us, the world is the means through which he exerts pressure upon us from without. For the 'world' in this context means godless human society, whose hostility to the church is expressed now by open ridicule and persecution, now by subtle subversion, the infiltration of its values and standards. John declares outspokenly that love for the world and love for the Father are mutually incompatible. For by worldliness he means 'the cravings of sinful man, the lust of his eyes and the boasting of what he has and does'. In the first expression 'sinful man' translates *sarx*. 'Flesh' and 'world' are inevitably linked, since 'world' is the community of unredeemed people, whose outlook is dictated by their un-redeemed nature. Putting the three expressions together, it seems that the characteristics of the world which John emphasizes are its selfish desires, its superficial judgments (the eyes seeing only the surface appearance of things) and its arrogant materialism. Jesus made the claim,however, 'I have over-come the world.' He totally rejected its distorted values and maintained his own godly perspective unsullied. John then adds that through Christ we can be overcomers too:

> for everyone born of God has overcome the world. This is the victory
> that has overcome the world, even our faith. Who is it that overcomes
> the world? Only he who believes that Jesus is the Son of God.[43]

It is when we believe in Jesus Christ that our values change. We no longer conform to the world's values, but find instead that we are being trans-formed by our renewed mind which grasps and approves the will of God. And nothing weans us from worldliness more than the cross of Christ. It is through the cross that the world has been crucified to us and we to the world,[44] so that we are freed from its tyranny.

Fourthly, through Christ we are no longer under *the tyranny of death*. It is sometimes said that, whereas our Victorian forebears had a morbid fas-cination with death, but never spoke of sex, the contemporary generation is obsessed with sex, while death is the great unmentionable. The fear of death is practically universal. The Duke of Wellington is reported as having said that 'that man must be a coward or a liar who could boast of never having felt a fear of death'. And Dr Samuel Johnson added that 'no rational man can die without uneasy apprehension'.[45] But Jesus Christ is able to set free even those who all their lives have been 'held in slavery by their fear of death'. This is because by his own death he has 'destroyed' (deprived of power) 'him who holds the power of death – that is, the devil' (Heb. 2:14).

Jesus Christ has not only dethroned the devil but dealt with sin. In fact, it is by dealing with sin that he has dealt with death. For sin is the 'sting' of death, the main reason why death is painful and poisonous. It is sin which causes death, and which after death will bring the judgment. Hence our fear of it. But Christ has died for our sins and taken them away. With great disdain, therefore, Paul likens death to a scorpion whose sting has been drawn, and to a military conqueror whose power has been broken. Now that we are forgiven, death can harm us no longer. So the apostle shouts defiantly: 'Where, O death, is your victory? Where, O death, is your sting?' There is of course no reply. So he shouts again, this time in triumph, not disdain: 'Thanks be to God! He gives us the victory through our Lord Jesus Christ' (1 Cor. 15:55–57).

What, then, should be the Christian's attitude to death? It is still an enemy, unnatural, unpleasant and undignified – in fact 'the last enemy to be destroyed'. Yet, it is a defeated enemy. Because Christ has taken away our sins, death has lost its power to harm and therefore to terrify. Jesus summed it up in one of his greatest affirmations: 'I am the resurrection and the life. He who believes in me will live, even though he dies; and whoever lives and believes in me will never die.'[46] That is, Jesus is the resurrection of believers who die, and the life of believers who live. His promise to the former is 'you will live', meaning not just that you will survive, but that you will be resurrected. His promise to the latter is 'you will never die', meaning not that you will escape death, but that death will prove to be a trivial episode, a transition to fullness of life.

The Christian conviction that Christ 'has destroyed death' (2 Tim. 1:10) has led some believers to deduce that he has also destroyed disease, and that from the cross we should claim healing as well as forgiveness. A popular exposition of this topic is *Bodily Healing and the Atonement* (1930) by the Canadian author T. J. McCrossan, which has recently been re-edited and re-published by Kenneth E. Hagin of the pentecostal Rhema Church. McCrossan states his case in these terms: 'All Christians should expect God to heal their bodies today, because Christ died to atone for our sicknesses as well as for our sins' (p. 10). He bases his argument on Isaiah 53:4, which he translates, 'Surely he hath borne our sicknesses and carried our pains.' He particularly emphasizes that the first Hebrew verb (*nasa'*) means to 'bear' in the sense of 'suffering the punishment for something'. Since it is also used in Isaiah 53:12 ('he bore the sin of many'), 'the clear teaching … is that Christ bore our sicknesses in the very same way that he bore our sins' (p. 120).

There are three difficulties in the way of accepting this interpretation, however. First, *nasa'* is used in a variety of Old Testament contexts, including the carrying of the ark and other tabernacle furniture, the carrying of armour, weapons and children. It occurs in Isaiah 52:11 with reference to those who 'carry the vessels of the LORD'. So the verb in itself does not mean to 'bear the punishment of'. We are obliged to translate it thus only when sin is its object. That Christ 'bore' our sicknesses may (in fact, does) mean something quite different.

Secondly, the concept McCrossan puts forward does not make sense. 'Bearing the penalty of sin' is readily intelligible, since sin's penalty is death and Christ died our death in our place. But what is the penalty of sickness? It has none. Sickness may itself *be* a penalty for sin, but it is not itself a mis-demeanour which attracts a penalty. So to speak of Christ 'atoning for' our sicknesses is to mix categories; it is not an intelligible notion.

Thirdly, Matthew (who is the evangelist most preoccupied with the fulfilment of Old Testament Scripture) applies Isaiah 53:4 not to the atoning death but to the healing ministry of Jesus. It was in order to fulfil what was spoken through Isaiah, he writes, that Jesus 'healed all the sick'. So we have no liberty to reapply the text to the cross. It is true that Peter quotes the following verse, 'by his wounds we are healed', but the contexts in both Isaiah and Peter make it clear that the 'healing' they have in mind is salvation from sin.[47]

We should not, therefore, affirm that Christ died for our sicknesses as well as for our sins, that 'there is healing in the atonement', or that health is just as readily available to everybody as forgiveness.

That does not mean, however, that our bodies are unaffected by the death and resurrection of Jesus. We should certainly take seriously these statements of Paul about the body:

> We always carry around in our body the death of Jesus, so that the life of Jesus may also be revealed in our body. For we who are alive are always being given over to death for Jesus' sake, so that his life may be revealed in our mortal body (2 Cor. 4:10–11).

The apostle is referring to the infirmity and mortality of our human bodies, specially (in his case) in relation to physical persecution. It is, he says, like experiencing in our bodies the dying (or putting to death) of Jesus, and the purpose of this is that the life of Jesus may be revealed in our bodies. He does not seem to be referring to the resurrection of his body, for he comes to that later. Nor are his words exhausted in his survival of physical assaults, in which he was 'struck down, but not destroyed' (v. 9). No, he seems to be saying that now in our mortal bodies (which are doomed to die) there is being 'revealed' (twice repeated) the very 'life' of Jesus (also twice repeated). Even when we are feeling tired, sick and battered, we experience a vigour and vitality which are the life of the risen Jesus within us. Paul expresses the same thought in verse 16: 'Though outwardly we are wasting away, yet inwardly we are being renewed day by day.'

That the life of Jesus should be constantly revealed in our bodies; that God has put into the human body marvellous therapeutic processes which fight disease and restore health; that all healing is divine healing; that God can and sometimes does heal miraculously (without means, instantaneously and permanently) – these things we should joyfully and confidently affirm. But to expect the sick to be healed and the dead to be raised as regularly as we expect sinners to be forgiven, is to stress the 'already' at the expense of the 'not yet', for it is to anticipate the resurrection. Not till then will our bodies be entirely rid of disease and death.

We must now return to the four tyrants over which Christ has won the victory and from which in consequence he sets us free. The four tyrannies characterize the old 'aeon' (age) which was inaugurated by Adam. In it the law enslaves, the flesh dominates, the world beguiles and death reigns. The new 'aeon', however, which was inaugurated by Christ, is characterized by grace not law, the Spirit not the flesh, the will of God not the fashions of the world, and abundant life not death. This is the victory of Christ into which he allows us to enter.

The book of Revelation

No book of the New Testament bears a clearer or stronger testimony to Christ's victory than the Christian apocalypse which we know as 'the book of Revelation' or 'the Revelation to John'. More than half the occurrences of the 'victory' word group (*nikaō*, to overcome, and *nikē*, victory) are to be found in this book. H. B. Swete wrote that from beginning to end it is a *Sursum corda*, because it summons its readers to lift up their drooping hearts, to take courage and to endure to the end. Michael Green has suggested that the liberation song 'We shall overcome' might have been written as 'the signature tune of the New Testament';[48] its triumphant strains are certainly heard throughout the book of Revelation.

In the ancient world it was assumed that every victory on the field of battle was won by gods rather than mere mortals: 'a god alone conquers, is unconquered and unconquerable'.[49] Hence the popularity of the goddess *Nikē*, who was often depicted on monuments, and in whose honour the graceful little temple near the entrance to the Parthenon was built. I have sometimes wondered if it was in conscious contrast to *Nikē* that in the Revelation Jesus is called *ho Nikōn*, 'the Overcomer', and that his title is passed on to Christian overcomers too.[50]

Written almost certainly during the reign of the Emperor Domitian (AD 81–96), its background is the growth both of the persecution of the church (now systematic rather than spasmodic) and of the practice of emperor worship, the refusal of which by Christians often sparked off fresh outbreaks of persecution. What the book of Revelation does, in keeping with its apocalyptic genre, is to lift the curtain which hides the unseen world of spiritual reality and to show us what is going on behind the scenes. The conflict between the church and the world is seen to be but an expression on the public stage of the invisible contest between Christ and Satan, the Lamb and the dragon. This age-long battle is set forth in a series of dramatic visions which have been variously interpreted as depicting the historical development at that time (the 'praeterist' school), through the succeeding centuries (the 'historicist') or as a prelude to the End (the 'futurist'). None of these is altogether satisfactory, however. The visions cannot portray successive events in a continuous sequence, since the final judgment and victory are dramatized several times. It seems more probable, therefore, that the scenes overlap; that the whole history of the world between Christ's first coming (the victory won) and second (the victory conceded) is several times recapitulated in vision; and that the emphasis is on the conflict between the Lamb and the dragon which has already had a number of historical manifestations, and will have more before the End.

The book opens with references to Jesus Christ as 'the firstborn from the dead', 'the ruler of the kings of the earth' (1:5), 'the First and the Last' and 'the Living One' (1:17–18), and with a magnificent vision of him to justify these titles as the risen, ascended, glorified and reigning Lord. Next come the letters to the seven churches of the Roman province of Asia, each of which concludes with an appropriate promise to 'him who overcomes'. From Christ patrolling his churches on earth the focus then changes to Christ sharing God's throne in heaven. For four chapters (4 – 7) the throne is central, and everything is described in relation to it. Jesus Christ is portrayed as both Lion and Lamb (a combination of images which may indicate that his power is due to his self-sacrifice). He is seen 'standing in the centre of the throne'. The reason why he alone is worthy to open the sealed scroll (the book of history and destiny) is that he 'has triumphed' (5:5). And the nature of his triumph is that he was slain and by his blood has purchased for God people from every nation (5:9). We are intended to understand that the grim events which follow the breaking of the seals and the blowing of the trumpets (war, famine, plague, martyrdom, earthquake and ecological disasters) are nevertheless under the control of the Lamb, who is already reigning and whose perfect kingdom will soon be consummated (11:15–18).

My concern, however, is to reach the vision of chapter 12, which in some ways seems to be the centre of the book. John saw a pregnant woman, who had the sun as her garment, the moon as her foot-stool and twelve stars as her crown, and who was about to give birth to a Son whose destiny was to 'rule all the nations' (v. 5). He is evidently the Messiah, and she the Old Testament church out of whom the Messiah came. An enormous and grotesque red dragon, identified in verse 9 as 'that ancient serpent called the devil or Satan', stood in front of the woman, ready to 'devour her child the moment it was born'. But the child was 'snatched up to God and to his throne', and the woman fled to a desert place prepared for her by God (vv. 5–6).

War in heaven followed, in which 'the dragon and his angels' were defeated. As the Christ had been snatched from earth to heaven, the dragon was now hurled from heaven to earth. The victory must surely refer to the cross, since it was 'by the blood of the Lamb' (v. 11) that Christ's people overcame the dragon. No other weapon could be adequate, for the dragon is 'filled with fury, because he knows that his time is short' (v. 12).

This, then, is the situation. The devil has been defeated and dethroned. Far from this bringing his activities to an end, however, the rage he feels in the knowledge of his approaching doom leads him to redouble them. Victory over him has been won, but painful conflict with him continues. And in this conflict he relies on three allies who now appear (in John's vision) in the guise of two ugly monsters and a lewd and gaudy prostitute. It becomes evident that all three are symbols of the Roman empire, although in three different aspects, namely Rome the persecutor, Rome the deceiver and Rome the seducer.

The first monster, which John sees arising out of the sea, has seven heads and ten horns just like the dragon, and the dragon delegates to him his power, throne and sovereignty, so that he has a world-wide following. There is no need to go into the detail of interpretation (*e.g.* which heads and horns represent which emperors). What is of first importance is that the monster utters proud blasphemies against God (13:5), is given 'power to make war against the saints' and even (temporarily) 'to conquer them' (v. 7), and is worshipped by all but the Lamb's followers (v. 8). This is the absolute power of the Roman state. But the prophecy's fulfilment was not completed in the Roman empire. In every violent state, which opposes Christ, oppresses the church and demands the unquestioning homage of citizens, the horrible 'beast from the sea' raises again its ugly heads and aggressive horns.

The second monster arises 'out of the earth' (v. 11). He is evidently the first monster's henchman, since he exercises his authority and promotes his worship, and performs miraculous signs in order to do so. If it is the characteristic of the first beast to persecute, it is the characteristic of the second to deceive (v. 14). People are forced to worship the image of the first beast (an obvious reference to emperor worship) and to wear the mark of the beast, without which they will be unable to take part in business. This second beast is later called 'the false prophet' (19:20). Although in that generation he symbolized the promoters of emperor worship, in our day he stands for all false religion and ideology, which deflects worship to any object other than 'the living and true God'.

The dragon's third ally is not introduced for another few chapters, during which the Lamb's final victory is several times confidently forecast and celebrated.[51] This ally is called 'the great prostitute' (17:1). Once again without doubt she represents Rome, for she is referred to as 'Babylon the Great' (14:8 and 17:5), 'the great city that rules over the kings of the earth' (17:18), and a city which is situated on 'seven hills' (v. 9). But this time what is symbolized is the moral corruption of Rome. She sits on a scarlet beast (one of the kings on whom her authority rests), is adorned with purple and scarlet, gold, jewels and pearls, and holds in her hand a golden cup 'filled with abominable things and the filth of her adulteries' (v. 4). Such is her seductive power that the inhabitants of the earth are said to be 'intoxicated with the wine of her adulteries' (v. 2). Whether these adulteries are sexual immorality or spiritual idolatry, they were not her only offence. We read later of her 'excessive luxuries' (18:3) which resulted from her international commerce including a trade in slaves (vv. 11–13), unspecified 'sins' and 'crimes' (v. 5), and her boastful arrogance (v. 7). Her kings will make war against the Lamb, 'but the Lamb will overcome them', because he is 'Lord of lords and King of kings' (17:14). And in chapters 18 and 19 the fall of 'Babylon the Great' is not only described in graphic detail, but also vindicated as inevitable and just. Jesus the Victor is glimpsed on a white horse, as 'with justice he judges and makes war' (19:11–16). Then in the last three chapters are described the final destruction of Satan and death, the new heaven and new earth, and the New Jerusalem, in which there will be no tears, death, pain or night, as God establishes his perfect rule.

The devil has not changed his strategy. Although the Roman empire has long since passed away, other persecuting, deceiving and corrupting structures have arisen in its place. In some Hindu and Muslim countries today, in defiance of the United Nations' Declaration of Human Rights, to propagate the gospel and to profess conversion are offences punishable by imprisonment and even death. In the Soviet Union the psychiatric hospital is still in use as an alternative to prison. In most Marxist countries severe restrictions are placed on the teaching of the young and on all religious activities outside specially registered buildings. Wherever a non-Christian culture predominates, opportunities for higher education and prospects for promotion tend to be limited, and the full rights of citizenship denied. As for the 'beast from the earth' or 'false prophet', he is active through other religions, new cults and secular ideologies. Michael Green supplies in two chapters of his *I Believe in Satan's Downfall* well-documented information about both 'the fascination of the occult' and 'counterfeit religion'. I agree with him that these are still two of 'the strongest weapons in Satan's armoury' (p. 194). As for the 'great prostitute', the assault on traditional (*i.e.* biblical) Christian morality has now penetrated the defences of the church itself. On the sanctity of human life (*e.g.* in relation to abortion and experimentation on embryos) the church tends to be equivocal. There is no united witness against the immorality of indiscriminate weapons. Divorce is increasingly tolerated, even among Christian leaders. Sexual lifestyles other than strict heterosexual monogamy are not always condemned. And we continue to enjoy in the West a level of affluence which is insensitive to the plight of the destitute millions.

The message of the book of Revelation is that Jesus Christ has defeated Satan and will one day destroy him altogether. It is in the light of these certainties that we are to confront his continuing malicious activity, whether physical (through persecution), intellectual (through deception) or moral (through corruption). How, then, can we enter into Christ's victory and prevail over the devil's power? How can we be numbered among the 'over-comers'? How can we hope to throw the enemy back, not only in our own lives but in the world he has usurped?

First, we are told to *resist the devil*. 'Resist him, standing firm in the faith.' Again, 'Resist the devil, and he will flee from you.'[52] We are not to be afraid of him. Much of his show of power is bluff, since he was overthrown at the cross, and we need the courage to call his bluff. Clad in the full armour of God, we can take our stand against him (Eph. 6:10–17). We are not to flee from him, but on the contrary to resist him so that he flees from us. Our own feeble voice, however, is not sufficiently authoritative to dismiss him. We cannot say in our own name, as Jesus could, 'Begone, Satan.' But we can do it in the name of Jesus. We have to claim the victory of the cross. 'In the name of Jesus Christ, of *Christus Victor*, who defeated you at the cross, begone, Satan.' It works. He knows his conqueror. He flees before him.

Secondly, we are told to *proclaim Jesus Christ*. The preaching of the cross is still the power of God. It is by proclaiming Christ crucified and risen that we shall turn people 'from darkness to light, and from the power of Satan to God' (Acts 26:18), and so the kingdom of Satan will retreat before the advancing kingdom of God. No other message has the same inherent force. No other name is defended and honoured by the Holy Spirit in the same way.

Both in our own lives, then, and in the church's mission it is only the cross of Christ, by which Satan has been defeated, which can prevail against him. It is still true today that 'they overcame him by the blood of the Lamb and by the word of their testimony; they did not love their lives so much as to shrink from death' (Rev. 12:11). Uncompromising witness to Christ is essential. So is the willingness, if necessary, to lay down our lives for his sake. But indispensable to both is the content of our faith and message, namely the objective, decisive victory of the Lamb over all the powers of darkness, which he won when he shed his blood on the cross.

Notes

[1] 1 Cor. 15:57; Rom. 8:37; 2 Cor. 2:14; Rev. 2 and 3.

[2] Rev. 3:21; 5:5; 12:11; Col. 2:15.

[3] Quoted from John Eadie's *Commentary on Colossians* (p. 174) by T. J. Crawford in *Doctrine of Holy Scripture*, p. 127.

[4] H. E. W. Turner, *Patristic Doctrine*, p. 47

[5] Rudolf Bultmann, *Kerygma and Myth*, pp. 4–5.

[6] 1 Ch. 29:11; Is. 9:6–7.

[7] Rev. 12:1ff.; Mt. 2:1–18; 4:1–11; Jn.6:15; Mt. 16:23, RSV; Jn. 13:27.

[8] *E.g.* Mk. 1:24 (demons); Mt. 4:23 (sicknesses) and Mk. 4:39 (nature).

[9] Lk. 10:18; 11:21–22; Mk. 3:27.

[10] Jn. 12:31; 14:30; 16:11.

[11] Since about the Second World War, and in particular the publication of Hendrik Berkhof's *Christ and the Powers* and G. B. Caird's *Principalities and Powers*, there has been lively debate about the identity of Paul's 'principalities and powers'. Previously everybody seems to have agreed that he meant personal spiritual agencies, both angelic and demonic. But, not least because *archai* (rulers) and *exousiai* (authorities) are used by him in relation to political powers, it has been suggested that Paul himself had begun to 'demythologize' the concept of angels and demons, and that he sees them rather as structures of earthly existence and power, especially the state, but also tradition, convention, law, economics and even religion. Although this attempted reconstruction is popular in some evangelical (as well as liberal) groups, it remains unconvincing. The addition of 'in the heavenly realms' in the Ephesians passages, and the antithesis to 'flesh and blood' in Eph. 6:10, not to mention the world-wide extent of the powers' influence, seem to me to fit the concept of supernatural beings much more readily, although of course such beings can and do use structures as well as individuals as media of their ministry. For further study see my discussion in *Ephesians*, pp. 267–275; E. M. B. Green in *Satan's Downfall*, pp. 84ff.; and especially the full discussion entitled 'Principalities and Powers', by P. T. O'Brien, pp. 110–150.

[12] F. F. Bruce, *Colossians*, p. 238.

[13] J. Jeremias, *Central Message*, p. 37.

[14] Peter O'Brien, *Colossians*, p. 133. *Cf.* p. 124.

[15] *Ibid.*, p. 127.

[16] *Ibid.*, p. 129.

[17] H. C. G. Moule, *Colossian Studies*, p. 159. It was 'as if the cross', wrote Calvin, 'which was full of shame, had been changed into a triumphal chariot!' (*Institutes*, II.xvi.6).

[18] Alexander Maclaren, *Colossians and Philemon*, p. 222.

[19] Jn. 19:11; Mt. 26:53; Mk. 15:30.

[20] 2 Cor. 13:4; 1 Cor. 1:25; Jn. 14:30.

[21] F. F. Bruce, *Colossians*, p. 239.

[22] Acts 2:24; Eph. 1:20–23; 1 Pet. 3:22.

[23] Acts 26:18; 1 Thes. 1:9; Col. 1:13. Among animists, now usually called 'traditional religionists', who live in fear of the spirits, the concept of a 'power encounter' with Jesus Christ is particularly important. 'The turning of a people to serve the true and living God is normally a response to some evident and convincing demonstration of the power of Christ over the spirit powers (experiential), rather than a mental assent to truths about Jesus Christ (cognitive)' (*Christian Witness to Traditional Religionists of Asia and Oceania*, Lausanne Occasional Paper No. 16, p. 10). See also the Lausanne Occasional Papers which relate to Christian witness among similar peoples in Latin America and the Caribbean (No. 17) and in Africa (No. 18).

[24] Rev. 20:1–3, Mt. 28:18–20.

[25] Ps. 110:l; Phil. 2:9–11; Rev. 20:10, 14; 1 Cor. 15:24–28.

[26] Mk. 8:31; 9:31; 10:34.

[27] Jn. 10:17–18; *cf.* 2:19.

[28] Acts 2:23–24; 1 Cor. 15:1–8.

[29] 1 Thes. 4:14; 2 Cor. 5:15.

[30] Rom. 6:1–4; Lk. 24:30–35.

[31] E. M. B. Green, *Empty Cross*, p. 11.

[32] *E.g.* Acts 2:24; 5:31; Rom. 1:4; 1 Cor. 15:12ff.

[33] C. E. B. Cranfield, *Romans*, Vol. I, p. 252.

[34] James Denney, *Death of Christ*, p. 73.

[35] 1 Jn. 2:13; Rev. 3:21.

[36] 1 Cor. 15:57; Eph. 1:20–23; 2:4–6; Mk. 3:27.

[37] Eph. 1:20–23; 6:10–17.

[38] 1 Jn. 5:18; 1 Pet. 5:8.

[39] Heb. 6:5; 1 Jn. 2:8; Rom. 8:21.

[40] Heb. 2:14 (the devil); Rom. 6:6 (the 'flesh' or fallen nature); 2 Tim. 1:10 (death).

[41] Gal. 3:23 and 13; Rom. 6:14; 10:4; Gal. 5:18.

[42] Gal. 5:19–21; Tit. 3:3; Jn. 8:34–36; Rom. 6:6.

[43] 1 Jn. 2:15–16; Jn. 16:33; 1 Jn. 5:4–5.

[44] Rom. 12:1–2; Gal. 6:14.

[45] Boswell's *Life of Johnson*, Vol. II, p. 212.

[46] 1 Cor. 15:26; Jn. 11:25–26.

[47] Mt. 8:16–17; Is. 53:5; 1 Pet. 2:24.

[48] E. M. B. Green, *Satan's Downfall*, p. 220.

[49] O. Bauernfeind's article on the *nikaō* word-group.

[50] For *ho nikōn* see Rev. 2:7, 11, 17, 26; 3:5, 12, 21 (twice); 6:2; 21:7.

[51] *E.g.* Rev. 14:1–5; 15:1–4; 16:4–7.

[52] 1 Pet. 5:8–9; Jas. 4:7.

PART FOUR

Living under the cross

Ten

The community of celebration

Perhaps the reader has so far found this presentation of Christ's cross too individualistic. If so, the balance should be redressed in this section. For the same New Testament which contains Paul's flash of individualism, 'I have been crucified with Christ ... I live by faith in the Son of God, who loved me and gave himself for me', also insists that Jesus Christ 'gave himself for us to redeem us from all wickedness and to purify for himself a people that are his very own, eager to do what is good'.[1] Thus the very purpose of his self-giving on the cross was not just to save isolated individuals, and so perpetuate their loneliness, but to create a new community whose members would belong to him, love one another and eagerly serve the world. This community of Christ would be nothing less than a renewed and reunited humanity, of which he as the second Adam would be head. It would incorporate Jews and Gentiles on equal terms. In fact, it would include representatives from every nation. Christ died in abject aloneness, rejected by his own nation and deserted by his own disciples, but lifted up on the cross he would draw all men to himself. And from the Day of Pentecost onwards it has been clear that conversion to Christ means also conversion to the community of Christ, as people turn from themselves to him, and from 'this corrupt generation' to the alternative society which he is gathering round himself. These two transfers – of personal allegiance and social membership – cannot be separated.[2]

Much space is devoted in the New Testament to the portraiture of this new, redeemed society – its beliefs and values, its standards, duties and destiny. The theme of this section is that the community of Christ is the community of the cross. Having been brought into being by the cross, it continues to live by and under the cross. Our perspective and our behaviour are now governed by the cross. All our relationships have been radically transformed by it. The cross is not just a badge to identify us, and the banner under which we march; it is also the compass which gives us our bearings in a disorientated world. In particular, the cross revolutionizes our attitudes to God, to ourselves, to other people both inside and outside the Christian fellowship, and to the grave problems of violence and suffering. We shall devote a chapter to each of these four relationships.

A new relationship to God

The four images of salvation, which we investigated in chapter 7, all bear witness to our new relationship to God. Now that he has acted in his love to turn aside his anger, we have been justified by him, redeemed for him and reconciled to him. And our reconciliation includes the concepts of 'access' and 'nearness', which are aspects of our dynamic knowledge of God or 'eternal life' (Jn. 17:3). This intimate relationship to God, which has replaced the old and painful estrangement, has several characteristics.

First, it is marked by *boldness*. The word the apostles loved to use for it is *parrēsia*, which means 'outspokenness, frankness, plainness of speech' (AG), both in our witness to the world and in our prayers to God. Through Christ we are now able to 'approach God with freedom (*parrēsia*) and confidence'. We have *parrēsia* because of Christ's high priesthood to come to God's 'throne of grace', and *parrēsia* by Christ's blood 'to enter the Most Holy Place' of God's very presence.[3] This freedom of access and this outspokenness of address to God in prayer are not incompatible with humility, for they are due entirely to Christ's merit, not ours. His blood has cleansed our consciences (in a way that was impossible in Old Testament days), and God has promised to remember our sins no more. So now we look to the future with assurance, not fear. We feel the power of Paul's logic that since, when we were God's enemies, we were both justified and reconciled through Christ's death, 'how much more', having been justified and reconciled, shall we be saved on the last day from God's wrath. Now that we are 'in Christ', we are confident that 'in all things' God is working for our good, and that nothing can separate us from his love.[4]

The second characteristic of our new relationship with God is *love*. Indeed, 'we love because he first loved us'. Previously we were afraid of him. But now love has driven out fear. Love begets love. God's love in Christ, which has in one sense liberated us, in another hems us in, because it leaves us no alternative but to live the rest of our lives for him, in adoring and grateful service.[5]

Joy is a third mark of those who have been redeemed by the cross. When the Babylonian exiles returned to Jerusalem, their 'mouths were filled with laughter' and their 'tongues with songs of joy'. The old alienation and humiliation were over; God had rescued and restored them. They likened their exhilaration to the revelries of harvest: 'Those who sow in tears will reap with songs of joy. He who goes out weeping, carrying seed to sow, will return with songs of joy, carrying sheaves with him.' How much more should we rejoice in the Lord, who have been redeemed from a much more oppressive slavery? The early Christians could hardly contain themselves: they shared their meals together 'with unaffected joy'.[6]

Boldness, love and joy are not to be thought of as purely private and interior experiences, however; they are to distinguish our public worship. The brief time we spend together on the Lord's Day, far from being divorced from the rest of our life, is intended to bring it into sharp focus. Humbly (as sinners), yet boldly (as forgiven sinners), we press into God's presence, responding to his loving initiative with an answering love of our own, and not only worshipping him with musical instruments but articulating our joy in songs of praise. W. M. Clow was right to draw our attention to singing as a unique feature of Christian worship, and to the reason for it:

> There is no forgiveness in this world, or in that which is to come, except through the cross of Christ. 'Through this man is preached unto you the forgiveness of sins.' The religions of paganism scarcely knew the word ... The great faiths of the Buddhist and the Mohammedan give no place either to the need or the grace of reconciliation. The clearest proof of this is the simplest. It lies in the hymns of Christian worship. A Buddhist temple never resounds with a cry of praise. Mohammedan worshippers never sing. Their prayers are, at the highest, prayers of submission and of request. They seldom reach the gladder note of thanksgiving. They are never jubilant with the songs of the forgiven.[7]

By contrast, whenever Christian people come together it is impossible to stop them singing. The Christian community is a community of celebration.

Paul expresses our common sense of joyful exhilaration by alluding to the best-known Jewish feast: 'Christ, our Passover lamb, has been sacrificed. Therefore let us keep the Festival ...' (1 Cor. 5:7). Strictly speaking, 'Passover' referred to the communal meal which was eaten during the evening of 15 Nisan, immediately after the killing of the paschal lambs that afternoon (14 Nisan), although it came to be applied also to the week-long Feast of Unleavened Bread which followed. The foundation of the people's rejoicing was their costly redemption from Egypt. Costlier still was the redeeming sacrifice of Jesus Christ on the cross. It is because he, our Paschal Lamb, has been slain, and because by the shedding of his precious life-blood we have been set free, that we are exhorted to keep the feast. In fact, the whole life of the Christian community should be conceived as a festival in which with love, joy and boldness we celebrate what God has done for us through Christ. In this celebration we find ourselves caught up in the worship of heaven, so that we join 'with angels and archangels, and with all the company of heaven' in giving God glory. And because the worship of God is in essence the acknowledgment of his worth, we unite with the heavenly chorus in singing of his worthiness as both Creator and Redeemer:

> 'You are worthy, our Lord and God,
>   to receive glory and honour and power,
>   for you created all things,
>   and by your will they were created
>   and have their being' (Rev. 4:11).

> 'Worthy is the Lamb, who was slain,
>   to receive power and wealth and wisdom and strength
>   and honour and glory and praise!' (Rev. 5:12).

It is surprising that Paul's references to the Passover Lamb and the Paschal Feast come in the middle of an extremely solemn chapter, in which it has been necessary for him to upbraid the Corinthians for their moral laxity. One of their members is involved in an incestuous relationship. Yet they show no signs of humble grief or penitence. He instructs them to excommunicate the offender, and warns them of the danger that sin will spread in the community if decisive steps are not taken to eradicate it. 'Don't you know that a little yeast works through the whole batch of dough?' he asks (1 Cor. 5:6). It is this allusion to yeast (leaven) which reminds him of the Passover and its Feast of Unleavened Bread. As Christians 'keep the Festival', they must do it 'not with the old yeast, the yeast of malice and wickedness, but with bread without yeast, the bread of sincerity and truth' (v. 8). For the Christian festival is radically different from pagan festivals, which were usually accompanied by frenzy and often degenerated into an orgy of drunkenness and immorality. Holiness is to mark the Christian celebration, for Christ's ultimate purpose through the cross is 'to present you holy in his sight, without blemish and free from accusation' (Col. 1:22).

Christ's sacrifice and ours

Although the Christian life is a continuous festival, the Lord's Supper is the particular Christian equivalent to the Passover. It is therefore central to the church's life of celebration. It was instituted by Jesus at Passover-time, indeed during the Passover meal itself, and he deliberately replaced the ceremonial recitation, 'This is the bread of affliction which our fathers ate', with 'This is my body given for you ... This is my blood shed for you ...' The bread and wine of the Christian festival oblige us to look back to the cross of Christ, and to recall with gratitude what he suffered and accomplished there.

Protestant churches have traditionally referred to baptism and the Lord's Supper as either 'sacraments of the gospel' (because they dramatize the central truths of the good news) or 'sacraments of grace' (because they set forth visibly God's gracious saving initiative). Both expressions are correct. The primary movement which the gospel sacraments embody is from God to man, not man to God. The application of water in baptism represents either cleansing from sin and the outpouring of the Spirit (if it is administered by affusion) or sharing Christ's death and resurrection (if by immersion) or both. We do not baptize ourselves. We submit to baptism, and the action done to us symbolizes the saving work of Christ. In the Lord's Supper, similarly, the essential drama consists of the taking, blessing, breaking and giving of bread, and the taking, blessing, pouring and giving of wine. We do not (or should not) administer the elements to ourselves. They are given to us; we receive them. And as we eat the bread and drink the wine physically, so spiritually by faith we feed on Christ crucified in our hearts. Thus, in both sacraments we are more or less passive, recipients not donors, beneficiaries not benefactors.

At the same time, baptism is recognized as an appropriate occasion for the confession of faith, and the Lord's Supper for the offering of thanksgiving. Hence the increasingly popular use of 'Eucharist' (*eucharistia*, 'thanksgiving') as a name for the Lord's Supper. And since 'sacrifice' is another word for 'offer', it is not surprising that the term 'eucharistic sacrifice' came to be invented. But is it legitimate? What does it imply?

To begin with, we should all be able to agree on five ways in which what we do at the Lord's Supper is related to the self-sacrifice of Christ on the cross. First, we *remember* his sacrifice: 'do this in remembrance of me', he said (1 Cor. 11:24–25). Indeed, the prescribed actions with the bread and wine make the remembrance vivid and dramatic. Secondly, we *partake* of its benefits. The purpose of the service goes beyond 'commemoration' to 'communion' (*koinōnia*): 'Is not the cup of thanksgiving for which we give thanks a participation in the blood of Christ? And is not the bread that we break a participation in the body of Christ?' (1 Cor. 10:16). For this reason the Eucharist is rightly called the 'Holy Communion' (since through it we may share in Christ) and the 'Lord's Supper' (since through it we may feed, even feast, on Christ). Thirdly, we *proclaim* his sacrifice: 'For whenever you eat this bread and drink this cup, you proclaim the Lord's death until he comes' (1 Cor. 11:26). Although his death took place centuries ago, the proclamation of it continues today. Yet the Supper is a temporary provision. It looks forward to the Lord's coming as well as back to the Lord's death. It is not only a feast upon Christ crucified but a foretaste of his heavenly banquet. It thus spans the whole period between his two comings. Fourthly, we *attribute our unity* to his sacrifice. For we never partake of the Lord's Supper alone, in the privacy of our own room. No, we 'come together' (1 Cor. 11:20) in order to celebrate. And we recognize that it is our common share in the benefits of Christ's sacrifice which has united us: 'Because there is one loaf, we, who are many, are one body, for we all partake of the one loaf' (1 Cor. 10:17). Fifthly, we *give thanks* for his sacrifice, and in token of our thanksgiving offer ourselves, our souls and bodies as 'living sacrifices' to his service (Rom. 12:1).

So then, whenever we share in the Lord's Supper, his sacrifice on the cross is remembered, partaken of, proclaimed, acknowledged as the ground of our unity, and responded to in grateful worship. The question which remains, however, is whether there is any closer relationship still between the sacrifice Christ offered on the cross and the sacrifice of thanksgiving we offer in the Eucharist, between his 'dying' sacrifice and our 'living' sacrifices. It is this which has divided Christendom since the sixteenth century, and is a topic of anxious ecumenical debate today. We cannot talk about the church as a 'community of celebration', without delving more deeply into the nature of the eucharistic celebration.

Already in the immediate post-apostolic period the early church Fathers began to use sacrificial language in relation to the Lord's Supper. They saw in it a fulfilment of Malachi 1:11. '"In every place incense and pure offerings will be brought to my name, because my name will be great among the nations," says the LORD Almighty.'[8] But the unconsecrated bread and wine as 'pure offerings' were symbols of the creation, for which the people gave thanks. The ancient authors also regarded the people's prayers and praises, and alms for the poor, as an offering to God. It was not until Cyprian, Bishop of Carthage in the middle of the third century, that the Lord's Supper itself was called a true sacrifice, in which the passion of the Lord was offered to God by priests, whose sacrificial role was said to parallel that of the Old Testament priests. From this beginning the eucharistic doctrine of medieval Catholicism eventually developed, namely that the Christian priest offered Christ, really present under the forms of bread and wine, as a propitiatory sacrifice to God for the sins of the living and the dead. And it was against this that the Reformers vigorously protested.

Although Luther and Calvin diverged from one another in their eucharistic teaching, all the Reformers were united in rejecting the sacrifice of the mass, and were concerned to make a clear distinction between the cross and the sacrament, between Christ's sacrifice offered for us and our sacrifices offered through him. Cranmer expressed the differences with lucidity:

> One kind of sacrifice there is, which is called a propitiatory or merciful sacrifice, that is to say, such a sacrifice as pacifieth God's wrath and indignation, and obtaineth mercy and forgiveness for all our sins ... And although in the Old Testament there were certain sacrifices called by that name, yet in very deed there is but one such sacrifice whereby our sins be pardoned, and God's mercy and favour obtained, which is the death of the Son of God, our Lord Jesu Christ; nor never was any other sacrifice propitiatory at any time, nor never shall be. This is the honour and glory of this our High Priest, wherein he admitteth neither partner nor successor ...
>
> Another kind of sacrifice there is, which doth not reconcile us to God, but is made of [*sc.* by] them that be reconciled by Christ, to testify our duties unto God, and to show ourselves thankful unto him. And therefore they be called sacrifices of laud, praise and thanksgiving.
>
> The first kind of sacrifice Christ offered to God for us; the second kind we ourselves offer to God by [*sc.* through] Christ.[9]

Once this vital distinction had been made, Cranmer was determined to be consistent in its application. The ordained minister could still be called a 'priest', because this English word is simply a contraction of the word 'presbyter' (elder), but every reference to an 'altar' was eliminated from the Book of Common Prayer and replaced by 'table', 'holy table', 'Lord's table' or 'Communion table'. For Cranmer saw clearly that the Communion service is a supper served by a minister from a table, not a sacrifice offered by a priest on an altar. The shape of his final Communion Service exhibits the same determination, for the thankful self-offering of the people was taken out of the Prayer of Consecration (where it was in his first Communion Service, replacing the offering of Christ himself in the medieval mass) and judiciously placed after the reception of the bread and wine as a 'Prayer of Oblation'. In this way, beyond any possibility of misunderstanding, the people's sacrifice was seen to be their offering of praise in responsive gratitude for Christ's sacrifice, whose benefits they had again received by faith.

Scripture undergirds Cranmer's doctrine, both in safeguarding the uniqueness of Christ's sacrifice and in defining our sacrifices as expressing our thanksgiving, not securing God's favour. The unique finality of Christ's sacrifice on the cross is indicated by the adverb *hapax* or *ephapax* (meaning 'once for all'), which is applied to it five times in the letter to the Hebrews. For example, 'Unlike the other high priests, he does not need to offer sacrifices day after day, first for his own sins, and then for the sins of the people. He sacrificed for their sins *once for all* when he offered himself.' Again, 'now he has appeared *once for all* at the end of the ages to do away with sin by the sacrifice of himself'.[10] That is why, unlike the Old Testament priests who stood to perform their temple duties, repeatedly offering the same sacrifices, Jesus Christ, having made 'one sacrifice for sins for ever', sat down at God's right hand, resting from his finished work (Heb. 10–12).

Although his work of atonement has been accomplished, he still has a continuing heavenly ministry, however. This is not to 'offer' his sacrifice to God, since the offering was made once for all on the cross; nor to 'present' it to the Father, pleading that it may be accepted, since its acceptance was publicly demonstrated by the resurrection; but rather to 'intercede' for sinners on the basis of it, as our advocate. It is in this that his 'permanent priesthood' consists, for intercession was as much a priestly ministry as sacrifice: 'he always lives to intercede' for us.[11]

The uniqueness of Christ's sacrifice does not mean, then, that we have no sacrifices to offer, but only that their nature and purpose are different. They are not material but spiritual, and their object is not propitiatory but eucharistic, the expression of a responsive gratitude. This is the second biblical undergirding of Cranmer's position. The New Testament describes the church as a priestly community, both a 'holy priesthood' and a 'royal priesthood', in which all God's people share equally as 'priests'.[12] This is the famous 'priesthood of all believers', on which the Reformers laid great stress. In consequence of this universal priesthood, the word 'priest' (*hiereus*) is never in the New Testament applied to the ordained minister, since he shares in offering what the people offer, but has no distinctive offering to make which differs from theirs.

What spiritual sacrifices, then, do the people of God as a 'holy priesthood' offer to him? Eight are mentioned in Scripture. First, we are to present our bodies to him for his service, as 'living sacrifices'. This sounds like a material offering, but it is termed our 'spiritual worship' (Rom. 12:1), presumably because it pleases God only if it expresses the worship of the heart. Secondly, we offer God our praise, worship and thanksgiving, 'the fruit of lips that confess his name'.[13] Our third sacrifice is prayer, which is said to ascend to God like fragrant incense, and our fourth 'a broken and contrite heart', which God accepts and never despises.[14] Fifthly, faith is called a 'sacrifice and service'. So too, sixthly, are our gifts and good deeds, for 'with such sacrifices God is pleased'.[15] The seventh sacrifice is our life poured out like a drink offering in God's service, even unto death, while the eighth is the special offering of the evangelist, whose preaching of the gospel is called a 'priestly duty' because he is able to present his converts as 'an offering acceptable to God'.[16]

These eight are all, in Daniel Waterland's words, 'true and evangelical sacrifices', because they belong to the gospel not the law, and are thankful responses to God's grace in Christ.[17] They are spiritual and 'intrinsic' too, being 'either good thoughts, good words or good ways, all of them issues of the heart'.[18] And, he continued, the Eucharist may be termed a 'sacrifice' only because it is an occasion both for remembering Christ's sacrifice and for making a responsive, comprehensive offering of ours.

The Catholic Counter-Reformation

The Protestant Reformation, including its careful distinctions between Christ's sacrifice and ours, was condemned by the Roman Catholic Church at the Council of Trent (1545–64). Its Session XXII (1562) focused on the sacrifice of the mass.

> Inasmuch as in this divine sacrifice which is celebrated in the mass is contained and immolated in an unbloody manner the same Christ who once offered himself in a bloody manner on the altar of the cross, the holy council teaches that this is truly propitiatory ... For, appeased by this sacrifice, the Lord grants the grace and gift of penitence, and pardons even the gravest crimes and sins. For the victim is one and the same, the same now offering by the ministry of priests who then offered himself on the cross, the manner alone of the offering being different.[19]

> If anyone says that in the mass a true and real sacrifice is not offered to God ... let him be anathema (Canon 1).

> If anyone says that by those words *Do this for a commemoration of me* Christ did not institute the Apostles priests, or did not ordain that they and other priests should offer his own body and blood, let him be anathema (Canon 2).

> If anyone says that the sacrifice of the mass is one only of praise and thanksgiving; or that it is a mere commemoration of the sacrifice consummated on the cross but not a propitiatory one, let him be anathema (Canon 3).

The Canons of the Council of Trent remain in force as part of the Roman Catholic Church's official teaching. Their substance has been confirmed within the last half-century, for example, in two papal encyclicals. Pius XI in *Ad Catholici Sacerdotii* (1935) described the mass as being in itself 'a real sacrifice ... which has a real efficacy'. Moreover, 'the ineffable greatness of the human priest stands forth in all its splendour', because he 'has power over the very body of Jesus Christ'. He first 'makes it present upon our altars' and next 'in the name of Christ himself he offers it a victim infinitely pleasing to the Divine Majesty' (pp. 8–9). In *Mediator Dei* (1947) Pius XII affirmed that the eucharistic sacrifice 'represents', 're-enacts', 'renews' and 'shows forth' the sacrifice of the cross. At the same time he described it as being itself 'truly and properly the offering of a sacrifice' (para. 72), and said that 'on our altars he [Christ] offers himself daily for our redemption' (para. 77). He added that the mass 'in no way derogates from the dignity of the sacrifice of the cross', since it is 'a reminder to us that there is no salvation but in the cross of our Lord Jesus Christ' (para. 83). But in spite of this claim, to call the Eucharist in the same paragraph 'the daily immolation' of Christ inevitably detracts from the historical finality and eternal sufficiency of the cross.

There are three particularly obnoxious elements in these statements of the Council of Trent and subsequent papal encyclicals, which need to be clarified. The implications are that the sacrifice of the mass, being a daily though unbloody immolation of Christ, (1) is distinct from his 'bloody' sacrifice on the cross, and supplementary to it, (2) is made by human priests and (3) is 'truly propitiatory'. By contrast the Reformers insisted, as we must, that the sacrifice of Christ (1) took place once for all on the cross (so that it cannot be re-enacted or supplemented in any way), (2) was made by himself (so that human beings cannot make it or share in making it), and (3) was a perfect satisfaction for sin (so that any mention of additional propitiatory sacrifices is gravely derogatory to it).

Theologians of the Catholic tradition in more recent times, however, together with some scholars of other traditions, have proposed a variety of more moderate positions. While wishing to retain a concept of eucharistic sacrifice which links our sacrifice to Christ's, they have at the same time denied that his unique sacrifice could in any way be repeated or supplemented, or that we can offer Christ, or that the Eucharist is propitiatory. Some make all three denials together.

Although slightly out of chronological sequence, it seems appropriate to begin with the Second Vatican Council (1962–65). On the one hand, the bishops quoted and endorsed the findings of the Council of Trent 400 years previously, for instance that Christ 'is present in the sacrifice of the mass ... "the same one now offering, through the ministry of priests, who formerly offered himself on the cross"'.[20] Crude statements also appear, as when priests are told to instruct the faithful 'to offer to God the Father the divine victim in the sacrifice of the mass'.[21] On the other hand, there are two new emphases, first that the Eucharist is not a repetition but a perpetuation of the cross, and secondly that the eucharistic offering is made not by priests but by Christ and his whole people together. For example, Christ is said to have 'instituted the Eucharistic Sacrifice ... in order to perpetuate the sacrifice of the Cross throughout the centuries until he should come again'.[22] Then the role of priests is stated thus that, 'acting in the person of Christ [they] join the offering of the faithful to the sacrifice of their Head. Until the coming of the Lord ... they re-present and apply in the sacrifice of the mass the one sacrifice of the New Testament, namely the sacrifice of Christ offering himself once and for all to his Father as a spotless victim'.[23]

One senses in these statements, both in what they say and in what they leave unsaid, the struggle to get away from the crudities of Trent. Yet the two new emphases are still unacceptable, for the offering of the cross cannot be 'perpetuated', nor can our offering be 'joined' to Christ's. The 'Agreed Statement on the Eucharist' produced by ARCIC (the Anglican Roman Catholic International Commission) seems to back away even further from Trent. The commissioners not only decline to call the Eucharist 'propitiatory', but insist strongly on the absolute finality of the cross: 'Christ's death on the cross ... was the one, perfect and sufficient sacrifice for the sins of the world. There can be no repetition of or addition to what was then accomplished once for all by Christ. Any attempt to express a nexus between the sacrifice of Christ and the Eucharist must not obscure this fundamental fact of the Christian faith.'[24]

The cross and the Eucharist

What nexus is there, then, between the cross and the Eucharist? Recent suggestions have emphasized two main ideas, namely the eternal, heavenly ministry of Jesus and the church's union with him as his body.

According to the former, Christ's sacrifice is thought of as 'prolonged' (or 'perpetuated', as at Vatican 11), so that he is conceived as continuously offering himself to the Father. Dom Gregory Dix, for example, developed this concept in *The Shape of the Liturgy*. He rejected the view that the death of Jesus was 'the moment of his sacrifice'. On the contrary, he argued, 'his sacrifice was something which began with his humanity and which has its eternal continuance in heaven' (pp. 242–243). R. J. Coates has explained the importance which this idea has for its advocates, namely that the church somehow shares in Christ's continuous self-offering, whereas of course 'the church cannot offer Christ at the earthly altar, if he is not offering himself at a heavenly altar'.[25] But the New Testament does not represent Christ as eternally offering himself to the Father. To be sure, Father, Son and Holy Spirit give themselves to each other in love eternally, but that is reciprocal, and in any case is quite different from Christ's specific historical sacrifice for sin. It is also true that the incarnation involved sacrifice, since by becoming flesh the Son both 'emptied himself' and 'humbled himself' (Phil. 2:7–8), and throughout his public ministry he demonstrated that he had come 'not to be served but to serve'. But, according to his teaching and that of his apostles, the climax of his incarnation and ministry was his self-giving on the cross as a ransom for many (Mk. 10:45). It is this historical act, involving his death for our sins, which Scripture calls his sin-bearing sacrifice and which was finished once for all. Not only can it not be repeated, but it cannot be extended or prolonged. 'It is finished,' he cried. That is why Christ does not have his altar in heaven, but only his throne. On it he sits, reigning, his atoning work done, and intercedes for us on the basis of what has been done and finished. Richard Coates was right to urge us to maintain 'the lonely eminence of the sacrifice of Calvary'.[26]

This is the theme of Alan Stibbs' neglected monograph *The Finished Work of Christ* (1954). He quotes Michael Ramsey's argument that since Christ is for ever priest and 'priesthood means offering', therefore in Christ 'there is for ever that spirit of self-offering which the sacrifice of Calvary uniquely disclosed in our world of sin and death' (p. 5). Similarly, Donald Baillie maintained that the divine sin-bearing was not confined to one moment of time, but that there is 'an eternal atonement in the very being and life of God', of which the cross was the incarnate part (p. 6). Over against such views Alan Stibbs shows that Christ's self-offering for our salvation 'is unmistakably represented in Scripture as exclusively earthly and historical, the purpose of the incarnation, wrought out in flesh and blood, in time and space, under Pontius Pilate', and that 'by this once-for-all finished happening the necessary and intended atoning work was completely accomplished' (p. 8). Could Christ not be continuously offering in heaven, however, the sacrifice which he made once for all on earth? Indeed is it not necessary to affirm this, since he is called in Hebrews 'a priest for ever'? No. Eternal priesthood does not necessitate eternal sacrifice. Stibbs goes on to draw a helpful analogy between priesthood and motherhood:

> Admittedly the act of offering was necessary to constitute Christ a priest ... just as the act of child-bearing is necessary to constitute a woman a mother. But that truth does not mean in the case of motherhood that henceforth, to those who resort to her as 'mother', such a woman is always giving them birth. Her act of child-bearing is for them not only an indispensable but also a finished work. What they now enjoy are other complementary ministries of motherhood, which lie beyond the child-bearing. Similarly with Christ's priesthood his propitiatory offering is not only an indispensable but also a finished work ... [Now, however,] as with motherhood, beyond such successful discharge of the fundamental function of priesthood there lie other complementary throne ministries of grace, which the priest fulfils for the benefit of his already reconciled people (in particular, his heavenly intercession) (pp. 30–31).

The second emphasis of what I have called more 'moderate' positions is related to the thoroughly scriptural teaching that the church is the body of Christ, living in union with its head. But this biblical doctrine has come to be developed in an unbiblical way, namely that the body of Christ offers itself to God in and with its head. This notion has been widely held. A popular exposition of it was given by Gabriel Hebert in 1951; it influenced the Anglican bishops who assembled at the 1958 Lambeth Conference:

> The eucharistic sacrifice, that storm-centre of controversy, is finding in our day a truly evangelical expression from the 'catholic' side, when it is insisted that the sacrificial action is not any sort of re-immolation of Christ, nor a sacrifice additional to his one sacrifice, but a participation in it. The true celebrant is Christ the High Priest, and the Christian people are assembled as members of his body to present before God his sacrifice, and to be themselves offered up in sacrifice through their union with him.[27]

In endorsing this, the Lambeth bishops added their own statement, that 'we ourselves, incorporate in the mystical body of Christ, are the sacrifice we offer. Christ with us offers us in himself to God.'[28] William Temple had earlier written something almost identical: 'Christ in us presents us with himself to the Father; we in him yield ourselves to be so presented.'[29]

What is important about these last statements is that there is no question either of Christ's sacrifice being repeated or of our offering him. Instead, it is Christ the head who offers his body with himself to the Father. The ARCIC Agreed Statement says something similar, namely that in the Eucharist 'we enter into the movement of Christ's self-offering' (pp. 14, 20), or are caught up into it by Christ himself. Professor Rowan Williams, a widely respected contemporary Anglo-Catholic theologian, has expressed his view that this, namely 'our being "offered" in and by Christ', is 'the basic fact of the Eucharist'.[30]

Other suggested reconstructions attempt to mingle not our sacrifice, but either our obedience or our intercession, with Christ's. Professor C. F. D. Moule, for example, stressing the *koinōnia* by which we are 'in Christ', united to him, has written that 'the two obediences – Christ's and ours, Christ's in ours and ours in Christ's – are offered to God together'.[31] *Baptism, Eucharist and Ministry*, on the other hand, the so-called 'Lima Text' (1982), which is the fruit of fifty years' ecumenical discussion and claims 'significant theological convergence', focuses on intercession rather than obedience. Declaring that the Christ events (*e.g.* his birth, death and resurrection) 'are unique and can neither be repeated nor prolonged', it nevertheless affirms that 'in thanksgiving and intercession the church is united with the Son, its great high priest and intercessor',[32] and that 'Christ unites the faithful with himself and includes their prayers within his own intercession, so that the faithful are transfigured and their prayers accepted' (II.4).

What can be objected to, it may be asked, in such statements as these? They deliberately avoid the three 'obnoxious elements' in traditional Roman Catholic documents which I mentioned earlier. Once it has been firmly established that Christ's self-sacrifice is unrepeatable, that the Eucharist is not propitiatory, and that our offerings are not meritorious, must Calvary and Eucharist still be kept apart? After all, the New Testament calls us priests and summons us to offer our eight 'spiritual sacrifices' to God. It also sets Christ's self-giving love and obedience before us as the model to which we should aspire. So what could be better or healthier than to allow our self-offering to be caught up in his? Would not the perfection of his compensate for the imperfection of ours? More than that, as Vatican II put it, would not 'the spiritual sacrifice of the faithful' then be 'made perfect in union with the sacrifice of Christ'?[33] Is this not appropriate and reasonable? Would it not be perversely obstinate to object?

I am afraid there are real and grave objections, however. The first is that, as a matter of fact, the New Testament authors never express the concept of our offering being united to Christ's. What they do is exhort us to give ourselves (as a sacrifice) in loving obedience to God in three ways. First, 'like' Christ: 'live a life of love, just as Christ loved us and gave himself up for us as a fragrant offering and sacrifice to God' (Eph. 5:2). His self-offering is to be the model of ours. Secondly, the spiritual sacrifices we offer to God are to be offered 'through' Christ (1 Pet. 2:5), our Saviour and Mediator. Since they are all tainted with self-centredness, it is only through him that they become acceptable. Thirdly, we are to give ourselves in sacrifice 'unto' or 'for' Christ, constrained by his love to live for him alone the new life-from-death which he has given us (2 Cor. 5:14–15). Thus, we are to offer ourselves 'like', 'through' and 'for' Christ. These are the prepositions which the New Testament uses; it never suggests that our offerings may be made 'in' or 'with' Christ. And if it were important to see our self-offering as identified with Christ's, it is strange that the New Testament never says so. To be sure, it is 'in Christ' that we are justified, forgiven, adopted and made a new creation, but it is never said that we worship God 'in' Christ, in union with him, joining our praises with his. Even when we shall join the heavenly host in worship, and our self-offering is at last purged of all imperfection – even then our praise is not said to be united with Christ's. No, he will remain the object of our worship; he will not become our fellow-worshipper, nor shall we become his (see Rev. 4 – 7).

That brings me to the second objection, which is surely the reason why the New Testament refrains from describing our worship as offered 'in and with' Christ. It is that the self-offerings of the Redeemer and of the redeemed are so qualitatively different from one another that it would be a glaring anomaly to attempt to mingle them. We need to go back to Cranmer's distinction between the two sorts of sacrifice, 'propitiatory' (atoning for sin) and – though he did not use this word – 'eucharistic' (expressing praise and homage). It is vital to remember that Christ's sacrifice was both, whereas ours are only 'eucharistic'. The death of Jesus was not only a perfect example of self-giving love, as Abelard stressed, in which he gave himself to the Father in obedience to his will; he also gave himself as a ransom for us, dying our death in our place. He therefore died both as our substitute, thus sparing us what otherwise we should have had to experience, and as our representative or example, thus showing us what we ourselves should also do. If the cross were only the latter, it might have been possible to associate our self-offering more closely with his, in spite of the difference, much as he called God 'Father' and permitted us to do the same. But the cross was first and foremost a propitiatory sacrifice, and in that sense absolutely unique. We need greater clarity in disentangling the two meanings of the cross, so that we see the uniqueness of what Daniel Waterland often called 'the grand sacrifice of the cross'[34] and 'the high tremendous sacrifice of Christ God-Man' (p. 37). Then we will conclude that it is not only anomalous, but actually impossible, to associate our sacrifices with his, or even to think of asking him to draw ours up into his. The only appropriate relationship between the two will be for ours to express our humble and adoring gratitude for his.

There is now an important criticism of this evangelical emphasis to consider. When we are thinking of our conversion, it is said, our sacrifices do indeed appear only as penitent and unworthy responses to the cross. But does not the situation change once we have come to Christ and been welcomed home? Do we not then have something to offer, which can be caught up into Christ's offering? This is a point Professor Rowan Williams has made. He wants to retrieve 'the idea that the effect of Christ's sacrifice is precisely to make us "liturgical" beings, capable of offering ourselves, our praises and our symbolic gifts to a God who we know will receive us in Christ'.[35] Again, 'the effect of Christ's offering is to make us capable of offering, to count us worthy to stand and serve as priests' (p. 30). Is it then necessary for the liturgy so to be constructed as to cast us in the role of unconverted unbelievers, and to recapitulate our salvation? Could it not rather regard us as being already in Christ, already God's children, and then unite our thanksgiving to our Father with Christ's self-offering on the cross (pp. 26–27)? These questions are not without appeal. They make a substantive point. Nevertheless, I think they must be answered in the negative. For our offerings are still tainted with sin and need to be offered 'through' Christ, rather than 'in and with' him. Besides, his sacrifice not only towers above ours in quality; it also differs from ours in character. It is not appropriate, therefore, to mix the two. Nor is it safe. The pride of our hearts is so deeply ingrained and so subtly insidious that it would be easy for us to nurse the idea that we have something of our own to offer God. Not that Rowan Williams thinks so. He is quite explicit that we have nothing to offer before we have received. This being so, and granted our hungry human vanity, should not this truth be explicitly set forth in the Lord's Supper? I agree with Roger Beckwith and Colin Buchanan, whom Rowan Williams quotes, that 'all progress in the Christian life depends upon a recapitulation of the original terms of one's acceptance with God' (p. 26). The liturgy must remind us of these, and not allow us to forget them. Michael Green got this right in preparation for the 1967 National Evangelical Anglican Congress at Keele:

> We never outgrow the fact that we are sinners still, totally dependent each day on the grace of God to the underserving. We do not come to offer; in the first place we come to receive. The very nature of a supper declares this. We are the hungry, coming to be fed. We are the un-deserving, welcomed freely at the Lord's Table.[36]

What can be said, in conclusion of this discussion of 'eucharistic sacrifice', about the relationship between Christ's sacrifice and ours? I think we have to insist that they differ from one another too widely for it ever to be seemly to associate them. Christ died for us while we were still sinners and enemies. His self-giving love evokes and inspires ours. So ours is always secondary and responsive to his. To try to unite them is to blur the primary and the secondary, the source and the stream, initiative and response, grace and faith. A proper jealousy for the uniqueness of Christ's sacrifice for sin will lead us to avoid any formulation which could conceivably detract from it.

I come back to where this chapter began. The Christian community is a community of the cross, for it has been brought into being by the cross, and the focus of its worship is the Lamb once slain, now glorified. So the community of the cross is a community of celebration, a eucharistic community, ceaselessly offering to God through Christ the sacrifice of our praise and thanksgiving. The Christian life is an unending festival. And the festival we keep, now that our Passover Lamb has been sacrificed for us, is a joyful celebration of his sacrifice, together with a spiritual feasting upon it. In this celebratory feast we are all participants. But what is it that we share in? Not in the offering of Christ's sacrifice, nor even in the movement of it, but only in the benefits he achieved by it. For this costly sacrifice, and for the precious blessings it has won for us, we shall never cease, even in eternity, to honour and adore the Lamb.

Notes

1 Gal. 2:20; Tit. 2:14; Acts 2:40–41.

2 Eph. 2:15; Rom. 5:12–19; Eph. 3:6; Rev. 7:9; Jn. 12:32 (*cf.* 11:52); Acts 2:40–47.

3 Eph. 3:12; Heb. 4:16; 10:19.

4 Heb. 9:14; 8:12 and 10:17 (*cf.* Je. 31:34); Rom. 5:9–10; 8:28, 38–39.

5 1 Jn. 4:18–19; 2 Cor. 5:14–15.

6 Ps. 126; Acts 2:46, NEB (*agalliasis* means 'exultation').

7 W. M. Clow, *Cross in Christian Experience*, p. 278. If it be objected that in the Koran Allah is regularly styled 'the Compassionate, the Merciful' and sometimes 'the Forgiving One' (*e.g.* *Sura* 40), we would respond that, nevertheless, his forgiveness has to be earned and is never bestowed as a free gift on the undeserving. Hence the absence from Muslim worship of the note of jubilant celebration.

8 Mal. 1:11 is quoted in the *Didache* xiv.l; it was also used by Irenaeus, Tertullian, Jerome and Eusebius. See the survey of patristic references to 'sacrifice' in Daniel Waterland's *Review of the Doctrine of the Eucharist*, pp. 347–388. See also Michael Green's essay 'Eucharistic Sacrifice', especially pp. 71–78.

9 *Cranmer On the Lord's Supper*, p. 235.

10 Heb. 7:27; 9:26. *Cf.* Heb. 9:12, 28; 10:10; and also Rom. 6:10 and 1 Pet. 3:18.

11 Heb. 7:23–25; 1 Jn. 2:1–2.

12 1 Pet. 2:5, 9; Rev. 1:6.

13 Heb. 13:15. *Cf.* Pss. 50:14, 23; 69:30–31; 116:17.

14 Rev. 5:8; 8:3–4; *cf.* Mal. 1:11; Ps. 51:17; *cf.* Ho. 14:1–2.

15 Phil. 2:17; 4:18; Heb. 13:16; *cf.* Acts 10:4.

16 Phil. 2:17; 2 Tim. 4:6; Rom. 15:16.

17 Daniel Waterland, *Review of the Doctrine of the Eucharist*, pp. 344–345.

18 *Ibid.*, p. 601.

19 H. J. Schroeder (ed.), *Canons and Decrees*, Session xxii, chapter 2.

20 *Constitution on the Sacred Liturgy*, I.1.7.

21 *Decree on the Ministry and Life of Priests*, II.5.

22 *Constitution on the Sacred Liturgy*, II.47.

23 *Dogmatic Constitution on the Church*, III.28.

24 *Final Report* of the Anglican Roman Catholic International Commission, p. 13. See also the evangelical assessment and critique entitled *Evangelical Anglicans and the ARCIC Final Report*, issued on behalf of the Church of England Evangelical Council.

25 R. J. Coates, 'Doctrine of Eucharistic Sacrifice', p. 135.

26 *Ibid.*, p. 143.

27 G. Hebert, in *Ways of Worship*, ed. P. Edwall, E. Hayman and W D. Maxwell. Quoted in the 1958 *Lambeth Conference Papers*, Part 2, pp. 84, 85.

28 Lambeth 1958, Part 2, p. 84.

29 William Temple, *Christus Veritas*, p. 242.

30 Rowan Williams, in *Essays on Eucharistic Sacrifice*, ed. Colin Buchanan, p. 34.

31 C. F. D. Moule, *Sacrifice of Christ*, p. 52.

32 *Baptism, Eucharist and Ministry*, II.8. See also *Evangelical Anglicans and the Lima Text*, an assessment and critique, drafted by Tony Price for the Church of England Evangelical Council.

33 *Decree on the Ministry and Life of Priests*, I.2.

34 Daniel Waterland, *Review of the Doctrine of the Eucharist*, p. 343.

[35] Rowan Williams, *Eucharistic Sacrifice*, p. 27.
[36] E. M. B. Green, from his chapter 'Christ's Sacrifice and Ours', relating Holy Communion to the cross, in *Guidelines*, p. 116.

ELEVEN

Self-understanding and self-giving

The cross revolutionizes our attitude to ourselves as well as to God. So the community of the cross, in addition to being a community of celebration, is also a community of self-understanding. This may sound like a reversion to individualism. But it should not be so, since self-understanding is with a view to self-giving. How can one give what one does not know one has? That is why the quest for one's own identity is essential.

Who are we, then? How should we think of ourselves? What attitude should we adopt towards ourselves? These are questions to which a satisfactory answer cannot be given without reference to the cross.

A low self-image is comparatively common today. Many people have crippling inferiority feelings. Sometimes their origin is in a deprived childhood, sometimes in a more recent tragedy of being unwanted and unloved. The pressures of a competitive society make matters worse. And other modern influences make them worse still. Wherever people are politically or economically oppressed, they feel demeaned. Racial and sexual prejudice, and the trauma of being declared 'redundant', can undermine anybody's self-confidence. Technology demotes persons, as Arnold Toynbee once put it, 'into serial numbers punched on a card, designed to travel through the entrails of a computer'. Meanwhile, ethologists such as Desmond Morris tell us that we are nothing but animals, and behaviourists such as B. F. Skinner that we are nothing but machines, programmed to make automatic responses to external stimuli. No wonder many people today feel worthless nonentities.

In over-reaction to this set of influences is the popular 'human potential' movement in the opposite direction. 'Be yourself, express yourself, fulfil yourself!' it cries. It emphasizes 'the power of positive thinking', together with the need for 'possibility thinking' and 'positive mental attitudes'. With the laudable desire to build self-esteem, it gives the impression that our potentiality for development is virtually limitless. A whole literature has grown up round this concept, which has been well described and documented by Dr Paul Vitz in his book *Psychology as Religion: The Cult of Self-worship*. 'Psychology has become a religion', he writes, 'in particular a form of secular humanism based on worship of the self' (p. 9). He begins by analysing 'the four most important self-theorists', namely Erich Fromm, Carl Rogers, Abraham Maslow and Rollo May, all of whom, with different twists and turns, teach the intrinsic goodness of human nature, and the consequent need for unconditional self-regard, self-awareness and self-actualization. These self-theories have been popularized by 'transactional analysis' ('I'm OK; you're OK') and EST (Erhard Seminar Training), which Dr Vitz rightly calls 'an amazingly literal self-deification' (pp. 31ff.). He also cites an advertisement in *Psychology Today* as an illustration of 'selfist jargon': 'I love me. I am not conceited. I'm just a good friend to myself. And I like to do whatever makes me feel good ...' (p. 62). This self-absorption has been well captured in a limerick:

> There once was a nymph named Narcissus,
> Who thought himself very delicious;
> So he stared like a fool
> At his face in a pool,
> And his folly today is still with us.[1]

Unfortunately, many Christians seem to have allowed themselves to be sucked into this movement, under the false impression that the Mosaic command, endorsed by Jesus, that we love our neighbour as ourselves is a command to love ourselves as well as our neighbour. But it really is not. Three arguments may be adduced.

First, and grammatically, Jesus did not say that 'the first commandment is to love the Lord your God, the second to love your neighbour, and the third to love yourself'. He spoke only of the first great commandment and of the second which was like it. The addition of 'as yourself' supplies a rough and ready, practical guide to neighbour-love, because 'no-one ever hated his own body' (Eph. 5:29). In this respect it is like the Golden Rule to 'do to others what you would have them do to you' (Mt. 7:12). Most of us do love ourselves. So we know how we would like to be treated, and this will tell us how to treat others. Self-love is a fact to be recognized and a rule to be used, not a virtue to be commended.

Secondly, and linguistically, the verb is *agapaō*, and *agapē* love means self-sacrifice in the service of others. It cannot therefore be self-directed. The concept of sacrificing ourselves in order to serve ourselves is a nonsense.

Thirdly, and theologically, self-love is the biblical understanding of sin. Sin is being curved in on oneself (as Luther put it). One of the marks of 'the last days' is that people will be 'lovers of self' instead of 'lovers of God' (2 Tim. 3:1–5). Their love will be misdirected from God and neighbour to self.

How then should we regard ourselves? How can we renounce the two extremes of self-hatred and self-love, and neither despise nor flatter ourselves? How can we avoid a self-evaluation which is either too low or too high, and instead obey Paul's admonition, 'think of yourself with sober judgment' (Rom. 12:3)? The cross of Christ supplies the answer, for it calls us both to self-denial and to self-affirmation. But before we are in a position to consider these complementary exhortations, it tells us that we are already new people because we have died and risen with Christ.

It is in this respect that the death of Jesus must rightly be called 'representative' as well as 'substitutionary'.

A 'substitute' is one who acts in place of another in such a way as to render the other's action unnecessary.

A 'representative' is one who acts on behalf of another, in such a way as to involve the other in his action.

Thus, a person who in former days served in the army (for pay) instead of a conscript was a 'substitute'. So is the footballer who plays instead of another who has sustained an injury. The conscript and the injured player are now inactive; they have been replaced.

An agent, however, who serves as the 'representative' of his firm, is deputed to act on its behalf. He does not speak instead of the firm, but for it. The firm is committed to what he says and does.

Just so, as our substitute Christ did for us what we could never do for ourselves: he bore our sin and judgment. But as our representative he did what we by being united to him have also done: we have died and risen with him.

Paul's most extensive exposition of this extraordinary yet wonderful theme comes at the beginning of Romans 6.[2] It was occasioned by the evil suggestion that since, when sin increased, grace increased all the more, we might just as well go on sinning, so that grace may increase still further (5:20 – 6:1). Paul indignantly repudiates the idea, for the simple reason that 'we died to sin' and therefore can live in it no longer (6:2). When did that death take place? At our baptism: 'don't you know that all of us who were baptized into Christ Jesus were baptized into his death? We were therefore buried with him through baptism into death in order that, just as Christ was raised from the dead through the glory of the Father, we too may live a new life' (6:3–4). So then baptism visibly dramatizes our participation in the death and resurrection of Jesus. That is why we may be said to have 'died to sin', so that we should live in it no longer.

The missing piece in the jigsaw puzzle is that Christ's death (in which we have shared by faith inwardly and by baptism outwardly) was a death to sin: 'the death he died, he died to sin once for all; but the life he lives, he lives to God' (v. 10). There is only one sense in which it may be said that Jesus 'died to sin', and that is that he bore its penalty, since 'the wages of sin is death' (v. 23). Having paid sin's wage (or borne its penalty) by dying, he has risen to a new life. So have we, by union with him. We too have died to sin, not in the sense that we have personally paid its penalty (Christ has done that in our place, instead of us), but in the sense that we have shared in the benefit of his death. Since the penalty of sin has been borne, and its debt paid, we are free from the awful burden of guilt and condemnation. And we have risen with Christ to a new life, with the sin question finished behind us. How then can we possibly go on living in the sin to which we have died? It is not impossible, for it is still necessary for us to take precautions against letting sin reign within us (vv. 12–14). But it is inconceivable, because it is incompatible with the fact of our death and resurrection with Jesus. It is death and resurrection which have cut us off from our old life; how can we ever think of returning to it? That is why we have to 'reckon' or 'count' ourselves 'dead to sin but alive to God in Christ Jesus' (v. 11). This does not mean that we are to pretend we have died to sin and risen to God, when we know very well that we have not. On the contrary, we know that, by union with Christ, we have shared in his death and resurrection, and so have ourselves died to sin and risen to God; we must therefore constantly remember this fact and live a life consistent with it. William Tyndale expressed it in characteristically vivid terms at the end of his prologue to his work on *Romans*:

Now go to, reader, and according to the order of Paul's writing, even so do thou ... Remember that Christ made not this atonement that thou shouldest anger God again; neither died he for thy sins, that thou shouldest live still in them; neither cleansed he thee, that thou shouldest return, as a swine, unto thine old puddle again; but that thou shouldest be a new creature, and live a new life after the will of God, and not of the flesh.[3]

Barth grasped the radical nature of this teaching and alluded to it in his section on Justification. 'The sentence which was executed as the divine judgment in the death of Jesus is that ... I am the man of sin, and that this man of sin and therefore I myself am nailed to the cross and crucified (in the power of the sacrifice and obedience of Jesus Christ in my place), that I am therefore destroyed and replaced ...' This is the negative side of justification. But 'in the same judgment in which God accuses and condemns us as sinners, and gives us up to death, he pardons us and places us in a new life before him and with him'. These two belong together, 'our real death and our real life beyond death', the destruction by death and the replacement by resurrection, the No and the Yes of God to the same person.[4]

Granted this fundamental fact about all who are in Christ, namely that we have died and risen with him, so that our old life of sin, guilt and shame has been terminated and an entirely new life of holiness, forgiveness and freedom has begun, what is to be our attitude to our new self? Because our new self, though redeemed, is still fallen, a double attitude will be necessary, namely self-denial and self-affirmation, both illumined by the cross.

Self-denial

First, the call to self-denial. The invitation of Jesus is plain: 'If anyone would come after me, he must deny himself and take up his cross and follow me' (Mk. 8:34). Jesus has just for the first time clearly predicted his sufferings and death. It 'must' happen to him, he says (v. 31). But now he expresses implicitly a 'must' for his followers as well. He must go to the cross; they must take up their cross and follow him. Indeed, they must do it 'daily'. And, as the negative counterpart, if anybody does not take his cross and follow him, he is not worthy of him and cannot be his disciple.[5] In this way, one might say, every Christian is both a Simon of Cyrene and a Barabbas. Like Barabbas we escape the cross, for Christ died in our place. Like Simon of Cyrene we carry the cross, for he calls us to take it up and follow him (Mk. 15:21).

The Romans had made crucifixion a common sight in all their colonized provinces, and Palestine was no exception. Every rebel condemned to crucifixion was compelled to carry his cross, or at least the *patibulum* (the cross beam), to the scene of his execution. Plutarch wrote that 'every criminal condemned to death bears his cross on his back'.[6] So John wrote of Jesus that 'carrying his own cross, he went out to The Place of the Skull' (19:17). To take up our cross, therefore, and follow Jesus, is 'to put oneself into the position of a condemned man on his way to execution'.[7] For if we are following Jesus with a cross on our shoulder, there is only one place to which we are going: the place of crucifixion. As Bonhoeffer put it, 'When Christ calls a man, he bids him come and die.'[8] Our 'cross', then, is not an irritable husband or a cantankerous wife. It is instead the symbol of death to the self.

Although Jesus may have had the possibility of martyrdom in his mind, the universal nature of his call ('if anyone ...') suggests a broader application. It is surely self-denial which, by this vivid imagery, Jesus is describing. To deny ourselves is to behave towards ourselves as Peter did towards Jesus when he denied him three times. The verb is the same (*aparneomai*). He disowned him, repudiated him, turned his back on him. Self-denial is not denying to ourselves luxuries such as chocolates, cakes, cigarettes and cocktails (though it may include this); it is actually denying or disowning ourselves, renouncing our supposed right to go our own way. 'To deny oneself is ... to turn away from the idolatry of self-centredness.'[9] Paul must have been referring to the same thing when he wrote that those who belong to Christ 'have crucified the sinful nature with its passions and desires' (Gal. 5:24). No picture could be more graphic than that: an actual taking of hammer and nails to fasten our slippery fallen nature to the cross and thus do it to death. The traditional word for this is 'mortification'; it is the sustained determination by the power of the Holy Spirit to 'put to death the misdeeds of the body', so that through this death we may live in fellowship with God.[10]

In fact, Paul writes in his letters of three different deaths and resurrections, which are part and parcel of our Christian experience. Much confusion arises when we fail to distinguish between them. The first (which we have already considered) is the death to sin and subsequent life to God, which happens to all Christians by virtue of our union with Christ in his death and resurrection. By it we share in the benefits both of Christ's death (its forgiveness) and of his resurrection (its power). This is inherent in our conversion/baptism.

The second is the death to self, called variously taking up the cross, or denying, crucifying or mortifying ourselves. As a result, we live a life of fellowship with God. This death is not something which has happened to us, and which we are now told to 'reckon' or remember, but something which we must deliberately do ourselves, though by the power of the Spirit, putting our old nature to death. Indeed all Christians have done it, in the sense that it is an essential aspect of our original and continuing repentance, and we cannot be Christ's disciples without it. But we have to maintain this attitude, that is, take up the cross daily.

The third kind of death and resurrection I mentioned in chapter 9. It is the carrying about in our bodies of the dying of Jesus, so that the life of Jesus may be revealed in our bodies (2 Cor. 4:9–10). Plainly the arena for this is our bodies. It refers to their infirmity, persecution and mortality. It is in this connection that Paul could say both, 'I die daily' (1 Cor. 15:30–31), and 'We face death all day long' (Rom. 8:36). For it is a continuous physical frailty. But then the 'resurrection', the inward vitality or renewal from the life of Jesus within us, is continuous too (2 Cor. 4:16).

To sum up, the first death is *legal*; it is a death to sin by union with Christ in his death to sin (bearing its penalty), and the resultant resurrection with him leads to the new life of freedom which justified sinners enjoy. The second death is *moral*; it is a death to self as we put to death the old nature and its evil desires, and the resurrection which follows leads to a new life of righteousness in fellowship with God. The third death is *physical*; it is a death to safety, a 'being given over to death for Jesus' sake', and the corresponding resurrection is Jesus' strength which he makes perfect in our weakness. The legal death was a 'death unto sin once and for all', but the moral and physical deaths are daily – even continuous – experiences for the Christian disciple.

I wonder how my readers have reacted thus far, especially to the emphasis on dying to self, or rather putting it to death by crucifying or mortifying it? I expect (and hope) that you have felt uneasy about it. I have expressed an attitude to the self so negative that I must almost seem to have aligned myself with the bureaucrats and technocrats, the ethologists and behaviourists, in demeaning human beings. It is not that what I have written is untrue (for it was Jesus who told us to take up our cross and follow him to death), but that it is only one side of the truth. It implies that our self is wholly bad, and that it must on that account be totally repudiated, indeed 'crucified'.

Self-affirmation

But we must not overlook another strand in Scripture. Alongside Jesus' explicit call to self-denial is his implicit call to self-affirmation (which is not at all the same thing as self-love). Nobody who reads the Gospels as a whole could possibly gain the impression that Jesus had a negative attitude to human beings himself, or encouraged one in others. The opposite is the case.

Consider, first, his *teaching* about people. It is true that he drew attention to the evil and ugly things which issue from the human heart (Mk. 7:21–23). He also spoke, however, of the 'value' of human beings in God's sight. They are 'much more valuable' than birds or beasts, he said.[11] What was the ground of this value judgment? It must have been the doctrine of creation, which Jesus took over from the Old Testament, namely that human beings are the crown of God's creative activity, and that he made man male and female in his own image. It is the divine image we bear which gives us our distinctive value. In his excellent little book *The Christian Looks at Himself* Dr Anthony Hoekema quotes a young American black who, rebelling against the inferiority feelings inculcated in him by whites, put up this banner in his room: 'I'm me and I'm good, 'cause God don't make junk' (p. 15). It may have been bad grammar, but it was good theology.

Secondly, there was Jesus' *attitude* to people. He despised nobody and disowned nobody. On the contrary, he went out of his way to honour those whom the world dishonoured, and to accept those whom the world rejected. He spoke courteously to women in public. He invited little children to come to him. He spoke words of hope to Samaritans and Gentiles. He allowed leprosy sufferers to approach him, and a prostitute to anoint and kiss his feet. He made friends with the outcasts of society, and ministered to the poor and hungry. In all this diversified ministry his compassionate respect for human beings shone forth. He acknowledged their value and loved them, and by loving them he further increased their value.

Thirdly, and in particular, we must remember Jesus' *mission and death* for human beings. He had come to serve, not to be served, he said, and to give his life as a ransom instead of the many. Nothing indicates more clearly the great value Jesus placed on people than his determination to suffer and die for them. He was the Good Shepherd who came into the desert, braving the hardship and risking the peril, in order to seek and to save only one lost sheep. Indeed, he laid down his life for the sheep. It is only when we look at the cross that we see the true worth of human beings. As William Temple expressed it, 'My worth is what I am worth to God; and that is a marvellous great deal, for Christ died for me.'[12]

We have seen so far that the cross of Christ is both a proof of the value of the human self and a picture of how to deny or crucify it. How can we resolve this biblical paradox? How is it possible to value ourselves and to deny ourselves simultaneously?

This question arises because we discuss and develop alternative attitudes to ourselves before we have defined the 'self' we are talking about. Our 'self' is not a simple entity that is either wholly good or wholly evil, and therefore to be either totally valued or totally denied. Instead, our 'self' is a complex entity of good and evil, glory and shame, which on that account requires that we develop more subtle attitudes to ourselves.

What we are (our self or personal identity) is partly the result of the creation (the image of God) and partly the result of the Fall (the image defaced). The self we are to deny, disown and crucify is our fallen self, everything within us that is incompatible with Jesus Christ (hence his commands, 'Let him deny *himself*' and then 'Let him follow *me*'). The self we are to affirm and value is our created self, everything within us that is compatible with Jesus Christ (hence his statement that if we lose ourselves by self-denial we shall find ourselves). True self-denial (the denial of our false, fallen self) is not the road to self-destruction but the road to self-discovery.

So then, whatever we are by creation we must affirm: our rationality, our sense of moral obligation, our sexuality (whether masculinity or femininity), our family life, our gifts of aesthetic appreciation and artistic creativity, our stewardship of the fruitful earth, our hunger for love and experience of community, our awareness of the transcendent majesty of God, and our inbuilt urge to fall down and worship him. All this (and more) is part of our created humanness. True, it has been tainted and twisted by sin. Yet Christ came to redeem it, not to destroy it. So we must gratefully and positively affirm it.

Whatever we are by the Fall, however, we must deny or repudiate: our irrationality, our moral perversity, our blurring of sexual distinctives and lack of sexual self-control, the selfishness which spoils our family life, our fascination with the ugly, our lazy refusal to develop God's gifts, our pollution and spoliation of the environment, the anti-social tendencies which inhibit true community, our proud autonomy, and our idolatrous refusal to worship the living and true God. All this (and more) is part of our fallen humanness. Christ came not to redeem this but to destroy it. So we must strenuously deny or repudiate it.

So far I have deliberately oversimplified the contrast between our createdness and our fallenness. The picture needs now to be modified, indeed enriched, in two ways. Both enrichments are due to the introduction into the human scene of the redemption of Christ. Christians can no longer think of themselves only as 'created and fallen', but rather as 'created, fallen and redeemed'. And the injection of this new element gives us both more to affirm and more to deny.

First, we have more to affirm. For we have not only been created in God's image, but re-created in it. God's gracious work in us, which is variously portrayed in the New Testament as 'regeneration', 'resurrection', 'redemption', *etc.*, is essentially a re-creation. Our new self has been 'created to be like God in true righteousness and holiness', and it 'is being renewed in knowledge in the image of its Creator'. Indeed, every person who is in Christ 'is a new creation'.[13] This means that our mind, our character and our relationships are all being renewed. We are God's children, Christ's disciples and the Holy Spirit's temple. We belong to the new community which is the family of God. The Holy Spirit enriches us with his fruit and gifts. And we are God's heirs, looking forward with confidence to the glory which will one day be revealed. Becoming a Christian is a transforming experience. By changing us, it also changes our self-image. We now have much more to affirm, not boastfully but gratefully. Dr Hoekema is right to make this his main emphasis in *The Christian Looks at Himself*. He mentions the hymn 'Beneath the Cross of Jesus', which in many ways is magnificent and moving. But not the end of one verse, which goes like this:

> And from my smitten heart, with tears,
>   Two wonders I confess,
> The wonder of his glorious love,
>   And my own worthlessness.

No, no, Dr Hoekema objects. We cannot sing that. 'And my unworthiness' would express the truth, but not 'my own worthlessness' (p. 16). How can we declare 'worthless' what Jesus Christ has declared of 'value'? Is it 'worthless' to be a child of God, a member of Christ and an heir of the kingdom of heaven? So then, a vital part of our self-affirmation, which in reality is an affirmation of the grace of God our Creator and Redeemer, is what we have become in Christ. 'The ultimate basis for our positive self-image must be God's acceptance of us in Christ' (p. 102).

Secondly, Christians have more to deny as well as more to affirm. So far I have included only our fallenness in what needs to be denied. Sometimes, however, God calls us to deny to ourselves things which, though not wrong in themselves or attributable to the Fall, yet stand in the way of our doing his particular will for us. This is why Jesus, whose humanity was perfect and not fallen, still had to deny himself. We are told that he 'did not consider equality with God something to be grasped', that is, to be selfishly enjoyed (Phil. 2:6). It was his already. He did not 'make himself equal with God' as his critics complained (Jn. 5:18); he was eternally equal with him, so that he and his Father were 'one' (Jn. 10:30). Yet he did not cling to the privileges of this status. Instead, he 'emptied himself' of his glory. Yet the reason he laid it aside is not that it was not his by right, but that he could not retain it and at the same time fulfil his destiny to be God's Messiah and Mediator. He went to the cross in self-denial, not of course because he had done anything to deserve death, but because this was his Father's will for him according to Scripture, and to that will he voluntarily surrendered himself. Throughout his life he resisted the temptation to avoid the cross. In Max Warren's succinct words, 'all Christ's living was a dying'.[14] He denied himself in order to give himself for us.

The very same principle is applicable to Christ's followers. 'Let this mind be in you', Paul wrote. For he knew the call to self-denial in his own apostolic experience. He had legitimate rights, for example to marriage and to financial support, which he deliberately denied himself because he believed this was God's will for him. He also wrote that mature Christians should be willing to renounce their rights and limit their liberties so as not to cause immature brothers and sisters to sin. Still today some Christian people are called to forgo married life, or a secure job, or professional promotion, or a comfortable home in a salubrious suburb, not because any of these things is wrong in itself, but because they are incompatible with a particular call of God to go overseas or live in the inner city or identify more closely with the world's poor and hungry people.

There is, therefore, a great need for discernment in our self-understanding. Who am I? What is my 'self'? The answer is that I am a Jekyll and Hyde, a mixed-up kid, having both dignity, because I was created and have been re-created in the image of God, and depravity, because I still have a fallen and rebellious nature. I am both noble and ignoble, beautiful and ugly, good and bad, upright and twisted, image and child of God, and yet sometimes yielding obsequious homage to the devil from whose clutches Christ has rescued me. My true self is what I am by creation, which Christ came to redeem, and by calling. My false self is what I am by the Fall, which Christ came to destroy.

Only when we have discerned which is which within us, shall we know what attitude to adopt towards each. We must be true to our true self and false to our false self. We must be fearless in affirming all that we are by creation, redemption and calling, and ruthless in disowning all that we are by the Fall.

Moreover, the cross of Christ teaches us both attitudes. On the one hand, the cross is the God-given measure of the value of our true self, since Christ loved us and died for us. On the other hand, it is the God-given model for the denial of our false self, since we are to nail it to the cross and so put it to death. Or, more simply, standing before the cross we see simultaneously our worth and our unworthiness, since we perceive both the greatness of his love in dying, and the greatness of our sin in causing him to die.

Self-sacrificial love

Neither self-denial (a repudiation of our sins) nor self-affirmation (an appreciation of God's gifts) is a dead end of self-absorption. On the contrary, both are means to self-sacrifice. Self-understanding should lead to self-giving. The community of the cross is essentially a community of self-giving love, expressed in the worship of God (which was our theme in the previous chapter) and in the service of others (which is our theme at the end of this chapter). It is to this that the cross consistently and insistently calls us.

The contrast between the standards of the cross and of the world is nowhere more dramatically set forth than in the request of James and John and in the response of Jesus to them.

> Then James and John, the sons of Zebedee, came to him. 'Teacher,' they said, 'We want you to do for us whatever we ask.'
> 'What do you want me to do for you?' he asked.
> They replied, 'Let one of us sit at your right and the other at your left in your glory.'
> 'You don't know what you are asking,' Jesus said. 'Can you drink the cup I drink or be baptized with the baptism I am baptized with?'
> 'We can,' they answered.
> Jesus said to them, 'You will drink the cup I drink and be baptized with the baptism I am baptized with, but to sit at my right or left is

not for me to grant. These places belong to those for whom they have been prepared.'

When the ten heard about this, they became indignant with James and John. Jesus called them together and said, 'You know that those who are regarded as rulers of the Gentiles lord it over them, and their high officials exercise authority over them. Not so with you. Instead, whoever wants to become great among you must be your servant, and whoever wants to be first must be slave of all. For even the Son of Man did not come to be served, but to serve, and to give his life as a ransom for many' (Mk. 10:35–45).

Verse 35 ('We want you to do for us whatever we ask') and verse 45 ('the Son of Man came to serve ... and to give'), the one introducing and the other concluding this story, portray the sons of Zebedee and the Son of Man in irreconcilable disagreement. They speak a different language, breathe a different spirit and express a different ambition. James and John want to sit on thrones in power and glory; Jesus knows that he must hang on a cross in weakness and shame. The antithesis is total.

There was, first, the choice *between selfish ambition and sacrifice*. The brothers' statement, 'We want you to do for us whatever we ask', surely qualifies as the worst, most blatantly self-centred prayer ever prayed. They seem to have anticipated that there would be an unholy scramble for the most honourable seats in the kingdom; so they judged it prudent to make an advance reservation. Their request to 'sit in state' (NEB) with Jesus was nothing but 'a bright mirror of human vanity'.[15] It was the exact opposite of true prayer, whose purpose is never to bend God's will to ours, but always to bend our will to his. Yet the world (and even the church) is full of Jameses and Johns, go-getters and status-seekers, hungry for honour and prestige, measuring life by achievement, and everlastingly dreaming of success. They are aggressively ambitious for themselves.

This whole mentality is incompatible with the way of the cross. 'The Son of Man did not come to be served, but to serve, and to give ...' He renounced the power and glory of heaven and humbled himself to be a slave. He gave himself without reserve and without fear, to the despised and neglected sections of the community. His obsession was the glory of God and the good of human beings who bear his image. To promote these, he was willing to endure even the shame of the cross. Now he calls us to follow him, not to seek great things for ourselves, but rather to seek first God's rule and God's righteousness.[16]

The second choice was *between power and service*. It seems clear that James and John wanted power as well as honour. Asking to 'sit' each side of Jesus in his glory, we may be quite sure they were not dreaming of seats on the floor, or on cushions, stools or chairs, but on thrones. They rather fancied themselves with a throne each. We know they came from a well-to-do family, because their father Zebedee had employees in his fishing business on the lake. Perhaps they missed having servants to wait on them, but were willing to forgo that luxury for a while, provided that they were compensated with thrones in the end. The world loves power. 'You know that those who are regarded as rulers of the Gentiles lord it over them,' said Jesus, 'and their high officials exercise authority over them' (v. 42). Was he thinking of Rome, whose emperors had coins struck featuring their head with the inscription 'He who deserves adoration'? Or was he thinking of the Herods, who, though only puppet kings, ruled like tyrants? The lust for power is endemic to our fallenness.

It is also totally incompatible with the way of the cross, which spells service. Jesus' affirmation that 'the Son of Man did not come to be served, but to serve' was startlingly original. For the Son of Man in David's vision was given power so that all nations would serve him (7:13–14). Jesus claimed the title, but changed the role. He had not come to be served, but rather to be the 'servant of the Lord' of the Servant Songs. He fused the two portraits. He was both the glorious Son of Man and the suffering servant; he would enter glory only by suffering. Again, he calls us to follow. In the secular world rulers continue to throw their weight about, manipulate, exploit and tyrannize others. 'Not so with you' (v. 43), said Jesus emphatically. His new community is to be organized on a different principle and according to a different model – humble service, not oppressive power. Leadership and lordship are two distinct concepts. The symbol of an authentically Christian leadership is not the purple robe of an emperor, but the coarse apron of a slave; not a throne of ivory and gold, but a basin of water for the washing of feet.

The third choice was, and still is, *between comfort and suffering*. By asking for thrones in glory, James and John were wanting comfortable security in addition to honour and power. Following Jesus, they had become vagrants, even vagabonds. Did they miss their pleasant home? When Jesus replied to their question with a counter-question as to whether they could share his cup and his baptism as well as his throne, their riposte was a glib 'We can' (vv. 38–39). But surely they did not understand. They were day-dreaming about the goblets of wine at the Messianic banquet, preceded by the luxurious pre-banquet baths which Herod was known to love. Jesus, however, was referring to his sufferings. They would indeed share his cup and baptism, he said, without enlightening them. For James was to lose his head at the hand of Herod Antipas, and John was to suffer a lonely exile.

The spirit of James and John lingers on, especially in us who have been cushioned by affluence. It is true that inflation and unemployment have brought to many a new experience of insecurity. Yet we still regard security as our birthright and 'Safety first' as a prudent motto. Where is the spirit of adventure, the sense of uncalculating solidarity with the underprivileged? Where are the Christians who are prepared to put service before security, compassion before comfort, hardship before ease? Thousands of pioneer Christian tasks are waiting to be done, which challenge our complacency, and which call for risk.

Insistence on security is incompatible with the way of the cross. What daring adventures the incarnation and the atonement were! What a breach of convention and decorum that Almighty God should renounce his privileges in order to take human flesh and bear human sin! Jesus had no security except in his Father. So to follow Jesus is always to accept at least a measure of uncertainty, danger and rejection for his sake.

Thus James and John coveted honour, power and comfortable security, while the whole career of Jesus was marked by sacrifice, service and suffering. Mark, who is increasingly acknowledged as a theologian-evangelist as well as a historian, sandwiches the request of James and John between two explicit references to the cross. It is the glory of Christ's cross which shows up their selfish ambition for the shabby, tatty, threadbare thing it was. It also highlights the choice, which faces the Christian community in every generation, between the way of the crowd and the way of the cross.

Spheres of service

Granted that the community of Christ is a community of the cross, and will therefore be marked by sacrifice, service and suffering, how will this work itself out in the three spheres of home, church and world?

Life in a Christian home, which should in any case be characterized by natural human love, should be further enriched by supernatural divine love, that is, the love of the cross. It should mark all Christian family relationships, between husband and wife, parents and children, brothers and sisters. For we are to 'submit to one another out of reverence for Christ' (Eph. 5:21), the Christ whose humble and submissive love led him even to the cross. Yet it is specially husbands who are singled out. 'Husbands, love your wives, just as Christ loved the church and gave himself up for her to make her holy ... and to present her to himself as a radiant church ...' (vv. 25–27). This Ephesians passage is commonly regarded as being very hard on wives, because they are to recognize the 'headship' God has given to their husbands and submit to them. But it is arguable that the quality of self-giving love required of husbands is even more demanding. For they are to love their wives with the love which Christ has for his bride the church. This is Calvary love. It is both self-sacrificial (he 'gave himself up for her', v. 25) and constructive ('to make her holy' and resplendent, growing into her full potential, vv. 26–27). It is also caring and protective: 'husbands ought to love their wives as their own bodies', for 'no-one ever hated his own body, but he feeds it and cares for it, just as Christ does the church' (vv. 28–29). Christian homes in general, and Christian marriages in particular, would be more stable and more satisfying if they were marked by the cross.

We turn now from the home to the church, and begin with pastors. We saw in an earlier chapter that there is a place for authority and discipline in the community of Jesus. Nevertheless, his emphasis was not on these things but on the new style of leadership which he introduced, distinguished by humility and service. Paul himself felt the tension. As an apostle he had received from Christ a special degree of authority. He could have come to the recalcitrant Corinthian church 'with a whip', and was 'ready to punish every act of disobedience', if he had to. But he did not want to be 'harsh' in the use of his authority, which the Lord Jesus had given him for building them up, not for tearing them down. He would much prefer to come as a father visiting his dear children. It was the tension between the death and resurrection of Jesus, between weakness and power. He could exercise power, since Christ 'lives by God's power'. But since 'he was crucified in weakness', it is 'the meekness and gentleness of Christ' which Paul wants most to exhibit.[17] If Christian pastors adhered more closely to the Christ who was crucified in weakness, and were prepared to accept the humiliations which weakness brings, rather than insisting on wielding power, there would be much less discord and much more harmony in the church.

The cross is to characterize all our relationships in Christ's community, however, and not just the relationship between pastors and people. We are to 'love one another', John insists in his first letter, both because God is love in his being and because he has showed his love by sending his Son to die for us. And this love always expresses itself in unselfishness. We are to 'do nothing out of selfish ambition or vain conceit, but in humility consider others better than' ourselves. Positively, we are each of us to look not only to our own interests, 'but also to the interests of others'. Why? Why this renunciation of selfish ambition and this cultivation of an unselfish interest in others? Because this was the attitude of Christ, who both renounced his own rights and humbled himself to serve others. In fact, the cross sweetens all our relationships in the church. We have only to remember that our fellow Christian is a 'brother [or sister] for whom Christ died', and we will never disregard, but always seek to serve, their truest and highest welfare. To sin against them would be to 'sin against Christ'.[18]

If the cross is to mark our Christian life in the home and the church, this should be even more so in the world. The church tends to become very pre-occupied with its own affairs, obsessed with petty, parochial trivia, while the needy world outside is waiting. So the Son sends us out into the world, as the Father had sent him into the world. Mission arises from the birth, death and resurrection of Jesus. His birth, by which he identified himself with our humanity, calls us to a similar costly identification with people. His death reminds us that suffering is the key to church growth, since it is the seed which dies which multiplies. And his resurrection gave him the universal lordship which enabled him both to claim that 'all authority' was now his and to send his church to disciple the nations.[19]

In theory we know very well the paradoxical principle that suffering is the path to glory, death the way to life, and weakness the secret of power. It was for Jesus, and it still is for his followers today. But we are reluctant to apply the principle to mission, as the Bible does. In the shadowy image of Isaiah's suffering servant, suffering was to be the condition of his success in bringing light and justice to the nations. As Douglas Webster has written, 'mission sooner or later leads into passion. In biblical categories ... the servant must suffer ... Every form of mission leads to some form of cross. The very shape of mission is cruciform. We can understand mission only in terms of the cross ...'[20]

This biblical vision of suffering service has been largely eclipsed in our day by the unbiblical 'prosperity gospel' (which guarantees personal success) and by triumphalist notions of mission (which employ military metaphors that do not comfortably fit the humble image of the suffering servant). By contrast, Paul dared to write to the Corinthians: 'so then, death is at work in us, but life is at work in you' (2 Cor. 4:12). The cross lies at the very heart of mission. For the cross-cultural missionary it may mean costly individual and family sacrifices, the renunciation of economic security and professional promotion, solidarity with the poor and needy, repenting of the pride and prejudice of supposed cultural superiority, and the modesty (and sometimes frustration) of serving under national leadership. Each of these can be a kind of death, but it is a death which brings life to others.

In all evangelism there is also a cultural gulf to bridge. This is obvious when Christian people move as messengers of the gospel from one country or continent to another. But even if we remain in our own country, Christians and non-Christians are often widely separated from one another by social sub-cultures and lifestyles as well as by different values, beliefs and moral standards. Only an incarnation can span these divides, for an incarnation means entering other people's worlds, their thought-world, and the worlds of their alienation, loneliness and pain. Moreover, the incarnation led to the cross. Jesus first took our flesh, then bore our sin. This was a depth of penetration into our world in order to reach us, in comparison with which our little attempts to reach people seem amateur and shallow. The cross calls us to a much more radical and costly kind of evangelism than most churches have begun to consider, let alone experience.

The cross calls us to social action too, because it summons us to the imitation of Christ:

This is how we know what love is: Jesus Christ laid down his life for us. And we ought to lay down our lives for our brothers. If anyone has material possessions and sees his brother in need but has no pity on him, how can the love of God be in him? Dear children, let us not love with words or tongue but with actions and in truth (1 Jn. 3:16–18).

According to John's teaching here, love is essentially self-giving. And since our most valuable possession is our life, the greatest love is seen in laying it down for others. Just as the essence of hate is murder (as with Cain), so the essence of love is self-sacrifice (as with Christ). Murder is taking another person's life; self-sacrifice is laying down one's own. God does more, however, than give us a paramount exhibition of love in the cross; he puts his love within us. With the love of God both revealed to us and indwelling us, we have a double, inescapable incentive to give ourselves in love to others. Moreover, John makes it clear that to lay down our life for others, though the supreme form of self-giving, is not its only expression. If one of us 'has' a possession, 'sees' someone else who needs it, and then fails to relate what he 'has' to what he 'sees' in terms of practical action, he cannot claim to have God's love in him. So love gives food to the hungry, shelter to the homeless, help to the destitute, friendship to the lonely, comfort to the sad, provided always that these gifts are tokens of the giving of the self. For it is possible to give food, money, time and energy, and yet somehow withhold oneself. But Christ gave himself. Though rich, he became poor, in order to make us rich. We know this grace of his, Paul writes, and we must emulate it. Generosity is indispensable to the followers of Christ. There was an almost reckless extravagance about Christ's love on the cross; it challenges the calculating coldness of our love.

Yet, as we have repeatedly noted throughout this book, the cross is a revelation of God's justice as well as of his love. That is why the community of the cross should concern itself with social justice as well as with loving philanthropy. It is never enough to have pity on the victims of injustice, if we do nothing to change the unjust situation itself. Good Samaritans will always be needed to succour those who are assaulted and robbed; yet it would be even better to rid the Jerusalem–Jericho road of brigands. Just so, Christian philanthropy in terms of relief and aid is necessary, but long-term development is better, and we cannot evade our political responsibility to share in changing the structures which inhibit development. Christians cannot regard with equanimity the injustices which spoil God's world and demean his creatures. Injustice must bring pain to the God whose justice flared brightly at the cross; it should bring pain to God's people too. Contemporary injustices take many forms. They are international (the invasion and annexation of foreign territory), political (the subjugation of minorities), legal (the punishment of untried and unsentenced citizens), racial (the humiliating discrimination against people on the ground of race or colour), economic (the toleration of gross North–South inequality and of the traumas of poverty and unemployment), sexual (the oppression of women), educational (the denial of equal opportunity for all) or religious (the failure to take the gospel to the nations). Love and justice combine to oppose all these situations. If we love people, we shall be concerned to secure their basic rights as human beings, which is also the concern of justice. The community of the cross, which has truly absorbed the message of the cross, will always be motivated to action by the demands of justice and love.

As an illustration of how a Christian community can be comprehensively stimulated by the cross, I would like to mention the Moravian Brethren, founded by Count Nikolaus von Zinzendorf (1700–60). In 1722 he welcomed some pietistic Christian refugees from Moravia and Bohemia to his estate in Saxony, where he helped them to form a Christian community under the name 'Herrnhut'. The Moravians' stress was on Christianity as a religion of the cross and of the heart. They defined a Christian as one who has 'an inseparable friendship with the Lamb, the slaughtered Lamb'.[21] Their seal bears the inscription in Latin, 'Our Lamb has conquered; let us follow him', and the ensign on their boats was of a lamb passant with a flag in a blood-coloured field (p. 97). They were deeply concerned for Christian unity and believed that the Lamb would be the ground of it, since all who 'adhere to Jesus as the Lamb of God' are one (p. 106). Indeed, Zinzendorf himself declared that 'the Lamb Slain' was from the beginning the foundation on which their church was built (p. 70).

They were certainly a community of celebration. They were great singers, and the focus of their worship at Herrnhut was Christ crucified.

> In Jesus' blood their element
> They swim and bathe with full content (p. 70).

No doubt they were too preoccupied with the wounds and the blood of Jesus. At the same time they never forgot the resurrection. They were sometimes called 'the Easter people' because it was the risen Lamb whom they adored (p. 74).

As for self-understanding, their particular brand of pietism seems to have enabled them to come to terms with themselves. Their emphasis on the cross brought them to genuine humility and penitence. But it also gave them a strong assurance of salvation and quiet confidence in God. 'We are the Saviour's happy people', Zinzendorf said (p. 73). It was in fact their joy and fearlessness, when face to face with death as their ship was sinking in an Atlantic storm, which brought John Wesley under conviction of sin and was an important link in the chain which led to his conversion.

But the Moravians are best known as a missionary movement. While still a schoolboy Zinzendorf founded 'the Order of the Grain of Mustard Seed', and he never lost his missionary zeal. Again, it was the cross which stimulated him and his followers to this expression of self-giving love. Between 1732 and 1736 Moravian missions were founded in the Caribbean, Greenland, Lapland, North and South America, and South Africa, while later they began missionary work in Labrador, among Australian aboriginals and on the Tibetan border. The heathen know there is a God, taught Zinzendorf, but they need to know of the Saviour who died for them. 'Tell them about the Lamb of God', he urged, 'till you can tell them no more' (p. 91).

This healthy emphasis on the cross arose largely from his own conversion experience. Sent as a young man of nineteen to visit the capital cities of Europe, in order to complete his education, he found himself one day in the art gallery of Dusseldorf. He stood before Domenico Feti's Ecce Homo, in which Christ is portrayed wearing the crown of thorns, and under which the inscription reads: 'All this I did for thee; what doest thou for me?' Zinzendorf was deeply convicted and challenged. 'There and then', A. J. Lewis writes, 'the young Count asked the crucified Christ to draw him into "the fellowship of his sufferings" and to open up a life of service to him' (p. 28). He never went back on this commitment. He and his community were passionately concerned for 'the enthronement of the Lamb of God'.

Notes

[1] Quoted by John Piper of Bethel College, Minneapolis, in a 1977 article in *Christianity Today*, entitled 'Is Self-love Biblical?'.

[2] Rom. 6:1–14; *cf.* Gal. 2:20; Col. 2:20 and 3:1–14; 2 Cor. 5:14–15.

[3] William Tyndale. *Doctrinal Treatises*, p. 510.

[4] K. Barth, *Church Dogmatics*, IV.1, pp. 515–516, 543.

[5] Lk. 9:23; Mt. 10:38; Lk. 14:27.

[6] Quoted by Martin Hengel in *Crucifixion*, p. 77.

[7] H. B. Swete, *St Mark*, p. 172.

[8] Dietrich Bonhoeffer, *Cost of Discipleship*, p. 79.

[9] C. E. B. Cranfield in his *Mark*, p. 281.

[10] Rom. 8:13. *Cf.* Col. 3:5; 1 Pet. 2:24.

[11] Mt. 6:26; 12:12.

[12] William Temple, *Citizen and Churchman*, p. 74.

[13] Eph. 4:24; Col. 3:10; 2 Cor. 5:17.

[14] M. A. C. Warren, *Interpreting the Cross*, p. 81.

[15] Calvin, *Commentary on a Harmony of the Evangelists*, Vol. II, p. 417.

[16] Je. 45:5; Mt. 6:33.

[17] 1 Cor. 4:21; 2 Cor. 10:6–18; 13:10; 1 Cor. 4:13–14; 2 Cor. 13:10 and 10:1.

[18] 1 Jn. 4:7–12; Phil. 2:3–4; 1 Cor. 8:11–13.
[19] Jn. 17:18; 20:21; 12:24; Mt. 28:18–20.
[20] Douglas Webster, *Yes to Mission*, pp. 101–102.
[21] A. J. Lewis, *Zinzendorf*, p. 107.

Twelve

Loving our enemies

'To live under the cross' means that every aspect of the Christian community's life is shaped and coloured by it. The cross not only elicits our worship (so that we enjoy a continuous, eucharistic celebration) and enables us to develop a balanced self-image (so that we learn both to understand ourselves and to give ourselves), but it also directs our conduct in relation to others, including our enemies. We are to 'be imitators of God ... as dearly loved children' and to 'live a life of love, just as Christ loved us and gave himself up for us ...' (Eph. 5:1–2). More than that, we are to exhibit in our relationships that combination of love and justice which characterized the wisdom of God in the cross.

Conciliation and discipline

But how in practice we are to combine love and justice, mercy and severity, and so walk the way of the cross, is often hard to decide and harder still to do. Take 'conciliation' or 'peace-making' as an example. Christian people are called to be 'peacemakers' (Mt. 5:9) and to 'seek peace and pursue it' (1 Pet. 3:11). At the same time, it is recognized that peace-making can never be a purely unilateral activity. The instruction to 'live at peace with everyone' is qualified by the two conditions, 'if it is possible' and 'as far as it depends on you' (Rom. 12:18). What are we to do, then, when it proves impossible to live at peace with somebody because he or she is unwilling to live at peace with us? The place to begin our answer is with the beatitude already quoted. For there, in pronouncing peacemakers 'blessed', Jesus added that 'they will be called sons (or daughters) of God'.[1] He must have meant that peace-making is such a characteristically divine activity, that those who engage in it thereby disclose their identity and demonstrate their authenticity as God's children.

If our peace-making is to be modelled on our heavenly Father's, however, we shall conclude at once that it is quite different from appeasement. For the peace which God secures is never cheap peace, but always costly. He is indeed the world's pre-eminent peacemaker, but when he determined on reconciliation with us, his 'enemies', who had rebelled against him, he 'made peace' through the blood of Christ's cross (Col. 1:20). To reconcile himself to us, and us to himself, and Jews, Gentiles and other hostile groups to each other, cost him nothing less than the painful shame of the cross. We have no right to expect, therefore, that we shall be able to engage in concil-iation work at no cost to ourselves, whether our involvement in the dispute is as the offending or offended party, or as a third party anxious to help enemies to become friends again.

What form might the cost take? Often it will begin with sustained, painstaking listening to both sides, the distress of witnessing the mutual bit-terness and recriminations, the struggle to sympathize with each position, and the effort to understand the misunderstandings which have caused the communication breakdown. Honest listening may uncover unsuspected faults, which will in their turn necessitate their acknowledgment, without resorting to face-saving subterfuges. If we are ourselves to blame, there will be the humiliation of apologizing, the deeper humiliation of making resti-tution where this is possible, and the deepest humiliation of all, which is to confess that the wounds we have caused will take time to heal and cannot light-heartedly be forgotten. If, on the other hand, the wrong has not been done by us, then we may have to bear the embarrassment of reproving or rebuking the other person, and thereby risk forfeiting his or her friendship. Although the followers of Jesus never have the right to refuse forgiveness, let alone to take revenge, we are not permitted to cheapen forgiveness by offering it prematurely when there has been no repentance. 'If your brother sins,' Jesus said, 'rebuke him', and only then 'if he repents, forgive him' (Lk. 17:3).

The incentive to peace-making is love, but it degenerates into appease-ment whenever justice is ignored. To forgive and to ask for forgiveness are both costly exercises. All authentic Christian peace-making exhibits the love and justice – and so the pain – of the cross.

Turning from social relationships in general to family life in particular, Christian parents will want their attitude to their children to be marked by the cross. Love is the indispensable atmosphere within which children grow into emotional maturity. Yet this is not the soft, unprincipled love which spoils the children, but the 'holy love' which seeks their highest welfare, whatever the cost. Indeed, since the very concept of human fatherhood is derived from the eternal fatherhood of God (Eph. 3:14–15), Christian parents will naturally model their love on his. Consequently, true parental love does not eliminate discipline, since 'the Lord disciplines those whom he loves'. Indeed, it is when God disciplines us that he is treating us as his sons and daughters. If he did not discipline us, it might show us to be his illegitimate, not his authentic, children (Heb. 12:5–8). Genuine love gets angry too, being hostile to everything in the children which is inimical to their highest good. Justice without mercy is too strict, and mercy without justice too lenient. Besides, children know this instinctively. They have an inborn sense of both. If they have done something which they know is wrong, they also know that they deserve punishment, and they both expect and want to receive it. They also know at once if the punishment is being administered either without love or contrary to justice. The two most poignant cries of a child are 'Nobody loves me' and 'It isn't fair'. Their sense of love and justice comes from God, who made them in his image, and who revealed himself as holy love at the cross.

The same principle applies to the church family as to the human family. Both kinds of family need discipline, and for the same reason. Yet nowadays church discipline is rare, and where it does take place, it is often administered clumsily. Churches tend to oscillate between the extreme severity which excommunicates members for the most trivial offences and the extreme laxity which never even remonstrates with offenders. Yet the New Testament gives clear instructions about discipline, on the one hand its necessity for the sake of the church's holiness, and on the other its constructive purpose, namely, if possible, to 'win over' and 'restore' the offending member. Jesus himself made it abundantly plain that the object of discipline was not to humiliate, let alone to alienate, the person concerned, but rather to reclaim him. He laid down a procedure which would develop by stages. Stage one is a private, one-to-one confrontation with the offender, 'just between the two of you', during which, if he listens, he will be won over. If he refuses, stage two is to take several others along in order to establish the rebuke. If he still refuses to listen, the church is to be told, so that he may have a third chance to repent. If he still obstinately refuses to listen, only then is he to be excommunicated (Mt. 18:15–17). Paul's teaching was similar. A church member 'caught in a sin' is to be 'restored' in a spirit of gentleness and humility; this would be an example of bearing each other's burdens and so fulfilling Christ's law of love (Gal. 6:1–2). Even a 'handing over to Satan', by which presumably Paul was referring to the excommunication of a flagrant offender, had a positive purpose, either that he might be 'taught not to blaspheme' (1 Tim. 1:20), or at least that 'his spirit [might be] saved on the day of the Lord' (1 Cor. 5:5). Thus all disciplinary action was to exhibit the love and justice of the cross.

More perplexing than these examples from the life of individuals, family and church is the administration of justice by the state. Can God's revelation in the cross be applied to this area too? More particularly, may the state use force, or would this be incompatible with the cross? Of course the cross was itself a conspicuous act of violence by the authorities, involving a gross violation of justice and a brutal execution. Yet it was an equally conspicuous act of non-violence by Jesus, who allowed himself to be unjustly condemned, tortured and executed without resistance, let alone retaliation. Moreover, his behaviour is set forth in the New Testament as the model of ours: 'if you suffer for doing good and you endure it, this is commendable before God. To this you were called, because Christ suffered for you, leaving you an example, that you should follow in his steps' (1 Pet. 2:20–21). Yet this text provokes many questions. Does the cross commit us to a nonviolent acceptance of all violence? Does it invalidate the process of criminal justice and the so-called 'just war'? Does it prohibit the use of every kind of force, so that it would be incompatible for a Christian to be a soldier, policeman, magistrate or prison officer?

Christian attitudes to evil

The best way to seek answers to these questions is to look carefully at the twelfth and thirteenth chapters of Paul's letter to the Romans. They are part of the apostle's plea to his Christian readers to respond adequately to 'the mercies of God'. For eleven chapters he has been unfolding God's mercy both in giving his Son to die for us and in bestowing on us the full salvation he thus obtained for us. How should we respond to the divine mercy? We are (1) to present our bodies to God as a living sacrifice, and with renewed minds to discern and to do his will (12:1–2); (2) to think of *ourselves* with sober judgment, neither flattering nor despising ourselves (v. 3); (3) to love *each other,* using our gifts to serve each other, and living together in harmony and humility (vv. 4–13, 15–16); and (4) we are to bless our persecutors and do good to our *enemies* (vv. 14, 17–21). In other words, when the mercies of God lay hold of us, all our relationships are radically transformed: we obey God, understand ourselves, love one another and serve our enemies.

It is the fourth of these relationships which particularly concerns us now. The opposition of unbelievers is assumed. The stumbling-block of the cross (which offers salvation as a free and unmerited gift), the love and purity of Jesus (which shame human selfishness), the priority commands to love God and neighbour (which leave no room for self-love) and the call to take up our cross (which is too threatening) – these things arouse opposition to us because they arouse opposition to our Lord and his gospel. This, then, is the background to our study of Romans 12. There are people who 'persecute' us (v. 14), who do 'evil' to us (v. 17), who may even be described as our 'enemies' (v. 20). How should we react to our persecutors and enemies? What do the mercies of God require of us? How should the cross, in which God's mercy shines at its brightest, affect our conduct? Specially instructive, in the following section of Romans 12 and 13, are Paul's four references to good and evil:

Love must be sincere. Hate what is evil; cling to what is good …

Bless those who persecute you; bless and do not curse. Rejoice with those who rejoice; mourn with those who mourn. Live in harmony with one another. Do not be proud, but be willing to associate with people of low position. Do not be conceited.

Do not repay anyone evil for evil. Be careful to do what is right in the eyes of everybody. If it is possible, as far as it depends on you, live at peace with everyone. Do not take revenge, my friends, but leave room for God's wrath, for it is written: 'It is mine to avenge; I will repay,' says the Lord. On the contrary:

'If your enemy is hungry, feed him;

if he is thirsty, give him something to drink.

In doing this, you will heap burning coals on his head.'

Do not be overcome by evil; but overcome evil with good.

Everyone must submit himself to the governing authorities, for there is no authority except that which God has established. The authorities that exist have been established by God. Consequently, he who rebels against the authority is rebelling against what God has instituted, and those who do so will bring judgment on themselves. For rulers hold no terror for those who do right, but for those who do wrong. Do you want to be free from fear of the one in authority? Then do what is right and he will commend you. For he is God's servant to do you good. But if you do wrong, be afraid, for he does not bear the sword for nothing. He is God's servant, an agent of wrath to bring punishment on the wrongdoer. Therefore, it is necessary to submit to the authorities, not only because of possible punishment but also because of conscience.

This is also why you pay taxes, for the authorities are God's servants, who give their full time to governing. Give everyone what you owe him: If you owe taxes, pay taxes; if revenue, then revenue; if respect, then respect; if honour, then honour (Rom. 12:9, 14 – 13:7).

This passage seems to be a self-conscious meditation on the theme of good and evil. Here are the apostle's four allusions to them:

Hate what is evil; cling to what is good (12:9).

Do not repay anyone evil for evil. Be careful to do what is right in the eyes of everybody (12:17).

Do not be overcome by evil; but overcome evil with good (12:21).

He is God's servant to do you good ... He is God's servant, an agent of wrath to bring punishment on the evildoer (13:4).

In particular, these verses define what our Christian attitude to evil should be.

First, *evil is to be hated.* 'Love must be sincere. Hate what is evil; cling to what is good' (12:9). This juxtaposition of love and hate sounds incongruous. Normally we regard them as mutually exclusive. Love expels hate, and hate love. But the truth is not so simple. Whenever love is 'sincere' (literally, 'without hypocrisy'), it is morally discerning. It never pretends that evil is anything else, or condones it. Compromise with evil is incompatible with love. Love seeks the highest good of others and therefore hates the evil which spoils it. God hates evil because his love is holy love; we must hate it too.

Secondly, *evil is not to be repaid.* 'Do not repay anyone evil for evil ... Do not take revenge, my friends' (12:17, 19). Revenge and retaliation are absolutely forbidden to the people of God. For to repay evil for evil is to add one evil to another. And if we hate evil, how can we add to it? The Sermon on the Mount is clearly being echoed here. 'Do not resist an evil person,' Jesus had said. That is, as the context clarifies, 'do not retaliate'. And at the cross Jesus perfectly exemplified his own teaching, for 'when they hurled their insults at him, he did not retaliate; when he suffered, he made no threats' (1 Pet. 2:23). Instead, we are to 'do what is right' (12:17) and to 'live at peace with everyone' (12:18). That is, good not evil, and peace not violence, are to characterize our lives.

Thirdly, *evil is to be overcome.* It is one thing to hate evil and another to refuse to repay it; better still is to conquer or overcome it. 'Do not be overcome by evil; but overcome evil with good' (12:21). How to do this Paul has indicated in the previous verses, echoing more words from the Sermon on the Mount. Jesus had said: 'Love your enemies, do good to those who hate you, bless those who curse you, pray for those who ill-treat you.'[2] Now Paul writes: 'Bless those who persecute you' (12:14), and 'if your enemy is hungry, feed him' (12:20). We are to wish good to people by blessing them, and to do good to people by serving them. In the new community of Jesus curses are to be replaced by blessings, malice by prayer, and revenge by service. In fact, prayer purges the heart of malice; the lips which bless cannot simultaneously curse; and the hand occupied with service is restrained from taking revenge. To 'heap burning coals' on an enemy's head sounds an unfriendly act, incompatible with loving him. But it is a figure of speech for causing an acute sense of shame – not in order to hurt or humiliate him, but in order to bring him to repentance, and so to 'overcome evil with good'. The tragedy of repaying evil for evil is that we thereby add evil to evil and so *increase* the world's tally of evil. It causes what Martin Luther King called 'the chain reaction of evil', as hate multiplies hate and violence multiplies violence in 'a descending spiral of destruction'.[3] The glory of loving and serving our enemies, however, is that we thereby *decrease* the amount of evil in the world. The supreme example is the cross. Christ's willingness to bear the scorn of men and the wrath of God has brought salvation to millions. The cross is the only alchemy which turns evil into good.

Fourthly, *evil is to be punished.* If we were to stop with the first three attitudes to evil, we would be guilty of grave biblical selectivity and therefore imbalance. For Paul goes on to write of the punishment of evil by the state. All careful readers of these chapters notice the contrast – even apparent contradiction – which they contain. We are told both that we are not to avenge ourselves and that God will avenge (12:19). Again, we are told both that we are not to repay anyone evil for evil and that God will repay (12:17, 19). Thus vengeance and retaliation are first forbidden us, and then attributed to God. Is that not intolerable? No. The reason these things are forbidden us is not because evil does not deserve to be punished (it does, and should be), but because it is *God's* prerogative to punish it, not ours.

So how does God punish evil? How is his wrath expressed against evildoers? The answer which immediately springs to mind is 'At the last judgment', and that is true. The unrepentant are 'storing up wrath' against themselves 'for the day of God's wrath, when his righteous judgment will be revealed' (Rom. 2:5). But must we wait till then? Is there no way in which God's wrath against evil is revealed now? There is, according to Paul. The first is in the progressive deterioration of a godless society, by which God 'gives over' to their uncontrolled depravity of mind and conduct those who deliberately smother their knowledge of God and of goodness (Rom. 1:18–32). That is an outworking of God's wrath. The second is through the judicial processes of the state, since the law-enforcement officer is 'God's servant, an agent of wrath to bring punishment on the wrongdoer' (13:4). In this sense, Dr Cranfield writes, the state is 'a partial, anticipatory, provisional manifestation of God's wrath against sin'.[4]

It is important to note that Paul uses the same vocabulary at the end of Romans 12 and at the beginning of Romans 13. The words 'wrath' (*orgē*) and 'revenge/punishment' (*ekdikēsis* and *ekdikos*) occur in both passages.

Forbidden to God's people in general, they are assigned to God's 'servants' in particular, namely officials of the state. Many Christians find great difficulty in what they perceive here to be an ethical 'dualism'.[5] I should like to try to clarify this issue.

First, Paul is not distinguishing between *two entities*, church and state, as in Luther's well-known doctrine of the two kingdoms, the kingdom of God's right hand (the church) having a spiritual responsibility exercised through the power of the gospel, and the kingdom of his left hand (the state) having a political or temporal responsibility exercised through the power of the sword. Jean Lasserre calls this 'the traditional doctrine' (for Calvin held it too, though he expressed it in different terms) and sums it up thus:

> God has charged the church with the duty of preaching the gospel, and the state with the duty of ensuring the political order; the Christian is both member of the church and citizen of the nation; as the former he must obey God by conforming to the gospel ethic ... as the latter he must obey God by conforming to the political ethic of which the state is the judge ...[6]

It is true that God gives church and state different responsibilities, even if it needs to be stressed that they overlap, are not directed by different ethics and are both under Christ's lordship. But this is not really the issue in Romans 12 and 13.

Secondly, Paul is not distinguishing between *two spheres* of Christian activity, private and public, so that (to put it crudely) we must love our enemies in private but may hate them in public. The concept of a double standard of morality, private and public, is to be firmly rejected; there is only one Christian morality.

Thirdly, what Paul is doing is to distinguish between *two roles*, personal and official. Christians are always Christians (in church and state, in public and private), under the same moral authority of Christ, but are given different roles (at home, at work and in the community) which make different actions appropriate. For example, a Christian in the role of a policeman may use force to arrest a criminal, which in the role of a private citizen he may not; he may as a judge condemn a prisoner who has been found guilty, whereas Jesus told his disciples 'do not judge, or you too will be judged'; and he may as an executioner (assuming that capital punishment may in some circumstances be justified) kill a condemned man, although he is forbidden to commit murder. (Capital punishment and the prohibition of murder go together in the Mosaic law.) This is not to say that arresting, judging and executing are in themselves wrong (which would establish different moralities for public and private life), but that they are right responses to criminal behaviour, which however God has entrusted to particular officials of the state.

This, then, is the distinction which Paul is making in Romans 12 and 13 between the non-repayment of evil and the punishment of evil. The prohibitions at the end of chapter 12 do not mean that evil should be left unrequited pending the day of judgment, but that the punishment should be administered by the state (as the agent of God's wrath) and that it is inappropriate for ordinary citizens to take the law into their own hands. It is this distinction which Christian pacifists find it hard to come to terms with. They tend to rest their case on Jesus' teaching and example of non-retaliation, assuming that retaliation is intrinsically wrong. But retaliation is not wrong, since evil deserves to be punished, should be punished, and in fact will be punished. Jesus himself said that 'the Son of Man … will reward each person according to what he has done' (Mt. 16:27, where the verb is similar to that in Rom. 12:19). This truth appears even in Peter's account of Jesus' own non-retaliation. When he was insulted, he did not answer back. When he suffered, he did not threaten. But we must not deduce from this that he was condoning evil. For what did he do in place of retaliation? 'He entrusted himself to him who judges justly' (1 Pet. 2:23). In Paul's language, he left it to the wrath of God. So even when Jesus was praying for the forgiveness of his executioners, and even when he was giving himself in holy love for our salvation, the necessity of divine judgment on evil was not absent from his mind. Indeed, he himself was overcoming evil at that very moment only by enduring its just punishment himself.

The authority of the state

This brings us to another perplexing question in seeking to relate the cross to the problem of evil, namely how Christians should regard the state and its authority. A careful study of Romans 13 should help us to avoid the extremes of divinizing it (pronouncing it always right) or demonizing it (pronouncing it always wrong). The Christian attitude to the state should rather be one of critical respect. Let me try to sum up Paul's teaching here about the state's authority under four heads relating to its origin, the *purpose* for which it has been given, the *means* by which it should be exercised and the *recognition* which it should be accorded. In each case a limitation is placed on the authority of the state.

First, the *origin* of its authority is God. 'Everyone must submit himself to the governing authorities, for there is no authority except that which God has established' (v. 1a). 'The authorities that exist have been established by God' (v. 1b). 'Consequently, he who rebels against the authority is rebelling against what God has instituted' (v. 2). This perspective was already clear in the Old Testament.[7] We are not to think of the functions of the state in terms of 'authority' only, however, but of 'ministry' too. For 'the one in authority' (which seems to be a generic reference which could include any state official from policeman to judge) 'is God's servant to do you good' (v. 4a). Again, 'he is God's servant, an agent of wrath to bring punishment on the wrongdoer' (v. 4b). Yet again, the reason why we are to pay taxes is that the authorities are 'God's servants, who give their full time to governing' (v. 6).

I confess that I find it extremely impressive that Paul writes of both the 'authority' and the 'ministry' of the state; that three times he affirms the state's authority to be God's authority; and that three times he describes the state and its ministers as God's ministers, using two words (*diakonos* and *leitourgos*) which elsewhere he applied to his own ministry as apostle and evangelist, and even to the ministry of Christ.[8] I do not think there is any way of wriggling out of this, for example by interpreting the paragraph as a grudging acquiescence in the realities of political power. No. In spite of the defects of Roman government, with which he was personally familiar, Paul emphatically declared its authority and ministry to be God's. It is the divine origin of the state's authority which makes Christian submission to it a matter of 'conscience' (v. 5).

Nevertheless, the fact that the state's authority has been delegated to it by God, and is therefore not intrinsic but derived, means that it must never be absolutized. Worship is due to God alone, and to his Christ, who is the lord of all rule and authority (Eph. 1:21–22) and 'the ruler of the kings of the earth' (Rev. 1:5; *cf.* 19:16). The state must be respected as a divine institution; but to give it our blind, unqualified allegiance would be idolatry. The early Christians refused to call Caesar 'lord'; that title belonged to Jesus alone.

Secondly, the *purpose* for which God has given authority to the state is in order both to reward (and so promote) good and to punish (and so restrain) evil. On the one hand, then, the state 'commends' (expresses its approbation of) those who do good (v. 3) – by the honours it bestows on its outstanding citizens – and exists to 'do you good' (v. 4). This phrase is not explained, but it surely covers all the social benefits of good government, preserving the peace, maintaining law and order, protecting human rights, promoting justice and caring for the needy. On the other hand, the state, as the minister of God and agent of his wrath, punishes wrongdoers (v. 4), bringing them to justice. Modern states tend to be better at the latter than the former. Their structures for law enforcement are more sophisticated than those for the positive encouragement of good citizenship by rewarding public service and philanthropy. Yet punishments and rewards go together. The apostle Peter also brackets them when, perhaps echoing Romans 13, and certainly writing after Christians had begun to suffer persecution in Rome, he affirms the same divine origin and constructive purpose of the state as 'sent by God to punish those who do wrong and to commend those who do right' (1 Pet. 2:14).

Nevertheless, the state's double function requires a high degree of discernment. Only the good is to be rewarded, only the evil punished. There is no warrant here for the arbitrary distribution of favours or penalties. This is specially so in relation to law enforcement. In peacetime the innocent must be protected, and in wartime non-combatants must be guaranteed immunity. Police action is discriminate action, and the Bible consistently expresses its horror at the shedding of innocent blood. The same principle of discrimination is an essential aspect of the 'just war' theory. It is why all use of indiscriminate weapons (atomic, biological and chemical) and all indiscriminate use of conventional weapons (*e.g.* the saturation bombing of civilian cities) are outlawed by this text and deeply offensive to the Christian conscience.

Thirdly, the *means* by which the state's authority is exercised must be as controlled as its purposes are discriminate. In order to protect the innocent and punish the guilty it is clearly necessary for coercion sometimes to be used. Authority implies power, although we have to distinguish between violence (the uncontrolled and unprincipled use of power) and force (its controlled and principled use to arrest evil-doers, hold them in custody, bring them to trial, and if convicted and sentenced oblige them to bear their punishment). The state's authority may even extend to the judicial taking of life. For most commentators interpret the 'sword' which the state bears (v. 4) as the symbol not just of its general authority to punish, but of its specific authority either to inflict capital punishment or to wage war or both.[9] Luther and Calvin argued that it was legitimate to extrapolate in this paragraph to include the 'just war', since the 'evil-doers' the state has authority to punish may be aggressors who threaten it from without, as well as criminals who threaten it from within.

Of course there are obvious differences between sentencing and punishing a criminal on the one hand, and declaring and waging war against an aggressor on the other. In particular, in warfare there is neither a judge nor a court. In declaring war a state is acting as judge in its own cause, since as yet no independent body exists to arbitrate in international disputes. And the set procedures and cool, dispassionate atmosphere of the lawcourt have no parallel on the battlefield. Nevertheless, as Professor Oliver O'Donovan has shown, the development of the 'just war' theory 'represented a systematic attempt to interpret acts of war by analogy with acts of civil government',[10] and so to see them as belonging to 'the context of the administration of justice' and as subject to 'the restraining standards of executive justice'.[11] In fact, the more a conflict can be represented in terms of the quest for justice, the stronger will be the case for its legitimacy.

The state's use of force, being strictly limited to the particular purpose for which it is given, must with equal strictness be limited to particular people, *i.e.* bringing criminals to justice. No possible excuse can be found in Romans 13 for the repressive measures of a police state. In all civilized nations both police and army have instructions to use 'minimum necessary force' – sufficient only to accomplish its task. In war force has to be controlled as well as discriminate. The Christian conscience protests against the appalling overkill capacity of current nuclear arsenals.

Fourthly, the due *recognition* of the state's authority is laid down. Citizens are to 'submit' to the governing authorities because God has established them (v. 1). In consequence, those who 'rebel' against them are rebelling against God, and bring his judgment upon them (v. 2). It is necessary to 'submit', however, not only to avoid punishment but also to maintain a good conscience (v. 5). What, then, is included in our 'submission'? Certainly we shall obey laws (1 Pet. 2:13) and pay taxes (v. 6). We shall also pray for rulers (1 Tim. 2:1–2). Example, taxes and prayer are three ways of encouraging the state to fulfil its God-given responsibilities. Whether we go further and suggest that due 'submission' will include co-operation, and even participation in the work of the state, is likely to depend on whether our ecclesiology is Lutheran, Reformed or Anabaptist. Speaking for myself, since the authority and ministry of the state are God's, I can see no reason for avoiding, and every reason for sharing in, its God-appointed service.

Nevertheless, there must be limits to our submission. Although (in theory, according to God's purpose) 'rulers hold no terror for those who do right, but for those who do wrong' (v. 3), Paul knew that a Roman procurator had condemned Jesus to death, and he had himself on occasion been the victim of Roman injustice. So what should Christians do if the state misuses its God-given authority, perverts its God-given ministry and begins to promote evil and punish good? What if it ceases to be God's minister and becomes the devil's, persecutes the church instead of protecting it, and exercises a malevolent authority derived not from God but from the dragon (Rev. 13)? What then? We reply that Christians should still respect an evil state, much as children should respect bad parents, but meek submission is not required of them. The apostle gives no encouragement to totalitarian rule. We have a duty to criticize and protest, agitate and demonstrate, and even (in extreme situations) resist to the point of law-breaking disobedience. Civil disobedience is, in fact, a biblical concept honoured particularly by Daniel and his friends in the Old Testament and by the apostles Peter and John in the New.[12] The principle is clear. Since the state's authority has been given it by God, we must submit right up to the point where to obey the state would be to disobey God. At that point, if the state commands what God forbids, or forbids what God commands, we disobey the state in order to obey God. As the apostles said to the Sanhedrin, 'We must obey God rather than men!'[13]

If in extreme circumstances disobedience is permissible, is rebellion permissible too? Certainly the Christian tradition of the 'just war' has sometimes been extended to include the 'just revolution'. But the same stringent conditions have been laid down for armed revolt as for war. These relate to justice (the need to overthrow a manifestly evil tyranny), restraint (last resort only, all other options having been exhausted), discrimination and control (in the use of force), proportion (the suffering caused must be less than that being endured), and confidence (a reasonable expectation of success). A conscientious application of these principles will make the drastic step of rebellion very rare.

Let me sum up the aspects and corresponding limitations of the state's authority. Because its authority has been delegated to it by God, we must respect but not worship it. Because the purpose of its authority is to punish evil and promote goodness, it has no excuse for arbitrary government. To fulfil this purpose it may use coercion, but only minimum necessary force, not indiscriminate violence. We are to respect the state and its officials, giving them a discerning submission, not an uncritical subservience.

Overcoming evil with good

Having moved, in our study of Romans 12 and 13, from the hatred of evil, through the non-repayment and the conquest of evil, to its punishment, we are left with a problem of harmonization. We have seen that evil is to be both not repaid and repaid, depending on who is the agent. But how can evil be at one and the same time 'overcome' (12:21) and 'punished' (13:4)? This is a more difficult question and goes to the heart of the debate between Christian pacifists and 'just war'
theorists. The Christian mind goes at once to the cross of Christ, because there they were reconciled. God overcame our evil by justifying us only because he first condemned it in Christ, and by redeeming us only because he first paid the ransom-price. He did not overcome evil by refusing to punish it, but by accepting the punishment himself. At the cross human evil was both punished and overcome, and God's mercy and justice were both satisfied.

How, then, can these two be reconciled in our attitudes to evil today? In the light of the cross, Christians cannot come to terms with any attitude to evil which either bypasses its punishment in an attempt to overcome it, or punishes it without seeking to overcome it. Certainly the state as the agent of God's wrath must witness to his justice, in punishing evil-doers. But Christian people also want to witness to his mercy. It is over-simple to say that individuals are directed by love, states by justice. For individual love should not be indifferent to justice, nor should the state's administration of justice overlook that love for neighbour which is the fulfilment of the law.

Moreover, the state is not under obligation in its pursuit of justice to demand the highest penalty the law permits. The God who laid down the 'life for life' principle himself protected the life of the first murderer (Gn. 4:15). Extenuating circumstances will help to temper justice with mercy. The retributive (punishing the evil-doer) and the reformative (reclaiming and rehabilitating him) go hand in hand, for then evil is simultaneously punished and overcome.

It is considerably more difficult to imagine such a reconciliation in war, when nations rather than individuals are involved. But at least Christians must struggle with the dilemma and try not to polarize over it. 'Just war' theorists tend to concentrate on the need to resist and punish evil, and to overlook the other biblical injunction to overcome it. Pacifists, on the other hand, tend to concentrate on the need to overcome evil with good, and to forget that according to Scripture evil deserves to be punished. Can these two biblical emphases be reconciled? Christians will at least stress the need to look beyond the defeat and surrender of the national enemy to its repentance and rehabilitation. The so-called 'politics of forgiveness', recently developed by Haddon Willmer,[14] is relevant here. David Atkinson sums up this emphasis well:

> Forgiveness is a dynamic concept of change. It refuses to be trapped into a fatalistic determinism. It acknowledges the reality of evil, wrong and injustice, but it seeks to respond to wrong in a way that is creative of new possibilities. Forgiveness signals an approach to wrong in terms, not of peace at any price, nor of a destructive intention to destroy the wrongdoer, but of a willingness to seek to reshape the future in the light of the wrong, in the most creative way possible.[15]

On the cross, by both demanding and bearing the penalty of sin, and so simultaneously punishing and overcoming evil, God displayed and demonstrated his holy love; the holy love of the cross should characterize our response to evil-doers today.

Notes

[1] Mt. 5:9; *cf.* 5:48 and Lk. 6:36.

[2] Lk. 6:27–28; *cf.* Mt. 5:44.

[3] Martin Luther King, *Strength to Love*, p. 51.

[4] C. E. B. Cranfield, *Commentary on Romans*, vol. II, p. 666.

[5] Discussion of this 'dualism' may be found, for example, in Jean Lasserre's *War and the Gospel*, pp. 23ff., 128ff. and 180ff.; in David Atkinson's *Peace in Our Time*, pp. 102–107 and 154–157; in the debate between Ronald Sider and Oliver O'Donovan, published as *Peace and War*, pp. 7–11 and 15; and to some extent in my own *Message of the Sermon on the Mount*, pp. 103–124.

[6] Jean Lasserre, *War and the Gospel*, p. 132.

[7] *E.g.* Je. 27:5–6; Dn. 2:21; 4:17, 25, 32; 5:21; 7:27.

[8] For *diakonos* applied to Christ see Rom. 15:8, and to Paul 2 Cor. 6:4. For *leitourgos* applied to Christ see Heb. 8:2, and to Paul Rom. 15:16.

[9] *Machaira*, the word Paul uses of the state's 'sword' here, may sometimes be translated 'dagger' or 'knife', but is used several times in the New Testament to symbolize death by execution or in war (*e.g.* Mt. 10:34; Lk. 21:24; Acts 12:2; Rom. 8:35; Heb. 11:37).

[10] Oliver O'Donovan, *Pursuit of a Christian View of War*, p. 13.

[11] *Ibid.*, p. 14.

[12] As examples of civil disobedience see Ex. 1:15–21; Dn. 3:1–18 and 6:1–14; Acts 4:13–20.

[13] Acts 5:29; *cf.* 4:19.

[14] Haddon Willmer, in *Third Way* (May, 1979).

[15] David Atkinson, *Peace in our Time?*, p. 167.

THIRTEEN

Suffering and glory

The fact of suffering undoubtedly constitutes the single greatest challenge to the Christian faith, and has been in every generation. Its distribution and degree appear to be entirely random and therefore unfair. Sensitive spirits ask if it can possibly be reconciled with God's justice and love.

On 1 November 1755 Lisbon was devastated by an earthquake. Being All Saints Day, the churches were full at the time, and thirty of them were destroyed. Within six minutes 15,000 people had died and 15,000 more were dying. One of many stunned by the news was the French philosopher and writer, Voltaire. For months he alluded to it in his letters in terms of passionate horror. How could anybody now believe in the benevolence and omnipotence of God? He ridiculed Alexander Pope's lines in his *Essay on Man,* which had been written in a secure and comfortable villa in Twickenham:

> And, spite of pride, in erring reason's spite,
> One truth is clear, Whatever is, is right.

Voltaire had always revolted against this philosophy of Optimism. Would Pope have repeated his glib lines if he had been in Lisbon? They seemed to Voltaire illogical (interpreting evil as good), irreverent (attributing evil to Providence) and injurious (inculcating resignation instead of constructive action). He first expressed his protest in his *Poem on the Disaster of Lisbon,* which asks why, if God is free, just and beneficent, we suffer under his rule. It is the old conundrum that God is either not good or not almighty. Either he wants to stop suffering but cannot, or he could but will not. Whichever it is, how can we worship him as God? Voltaire's second protest was to write his satirical novel *Candide,* the story of an ingenuous young man, whose teacher Dr Pangloss, a professsor of Optimism, keeps blandly assuring him that 'all is for the best in the best of all possible worlds', in defiance of their successive misfortunes. When they are shipwrecked near Lisbon, Candide is nearly killed in the earthquake, and Pangloss is hanged by the Inquisition. Voltaire writes: 'Candide, terrified, speechless, bleeding, palpitating, said to himself: "If this is the best of all possible worlds, what can the rest be?" '[1]

The problem of suffering is far from being of concern only to philosophers, however. It impinges upon nearly all of us personally; few people go through life entirely unscathed. It may be childhood deprivation resulting in lifelong emotional turmoil, or a congenital disability of mind or body. Or suddenly and without warning we are overtaken by a painful illness, redundancy at work, poverty or bereavement. Or again, perhaps we are afflicted by involuntary singleness, a broken love affair, an unhappy marriage, divorce, depression or loneliness. Suffering comes in many unwelcome forms, and sometimes we not only ask God our agonized questions 'Why?' and 'Why me?' but even like Job rage against him, accusing him of injustice and indifference. I know of no Christian leader who has been more forthright in confessing his anger than Joseph Parker, who was minister of the City Temple from 1874 until his death in 1902. He says in his autobiography that up to the age of sixty-eight he never had a religious doubt. Then his wife died, and his faith collapsed. 'In that dark hour', he wrote, 'I became almost an atheist. For God had set his foot upon my prayers and treated my petitions with contempt. If I had seen a dog in such agony as mine, I would have pitied and helped the dumb beast; yet God spat upon me and cast me out as an offence – out into the waste wilderness and the night black and starless.'[2]

It needs to be said at once that the Bible supplies no thorough solution to the problem of evil, whether 'natural' evil or 'moral', that is, whether in the form of suffering or of sin. Its purpose is more practical than philosophical. Consequently, although there are references to sin and suffering on virtually every page, its concern is not to explain their origin but to help us to overcome them.

My object in this chapter is to explore what relation there might be between the cross of Christ and our sufferings. So I shall not elaborate other standard arguments about suffering which the textbooks include, but only mention them as an introduction.

First, according to the Bible suffering is an alien intrusion into God's good world, and will have no part in his new universe. It is a Satanic and destructive onslaught against the Creator. The book of Job makes that clear. So do Jesus' description of an infirm woman as 'bound by Satan', his 'rebuking' of disease as he rebuked demons, Paul's reference to his 'thorn in the flesh' as 'a messenger of Satan' and Peter's portrayal of Jesus' ministry as 'healing all who were under the power of the devil'.[3] So whatever may be said later about the 'good' which God can bring out of suffering, we must not forget that it is good out of evil.

Secondly, suffering is often due to sin. Of course originally disease and death entered the world through sin. But I am now thinking of contemporary sin. Sometimes suffering is due to the sin of others, as when children suffer from unloving or irresponsible parents, the poor and hungry from economic injustice, refugees from the cruelties of war, and road casualties caused by drunken drivers. At other times suffering can be the consequence of our own sin (the reckless use of our freedom) and even its penalty. We must not overlook those biblical passages where sickness is attributed to the punishment of God.[4] At the same time we must firmly repudiate the dreadful Hindu doctrine of *karma* which attributes all suffering to wrong-doing in this or a previous existence, and the almost equally dreadful doctrine of Job's so-called comforters. They trotted out their conventional orthodoxy that all personal suffering is due to personal sin, and one of the major purposes of the book of Job is to contradict that popular but wrong-headed notion. Jesus categorically rejected it too.[5]

Thirdly, suffering is due to our human sensitivity to pain. Misfortune is made worse by the hurt (physical or emotional) which we feel. But the pain sensors of the central nervous system give valuable warning-signals, necessary for personal and social survival. Perhaps the best illustration of this is the discovery by Dr Paul Brand at Vellore Christian Hospital in South India that Hansen's disease ('leprosy') numbs the extremities of the body, so that the ulcers and infections which develop are secondary problems, due to loss of feeling. Nerve reactions have to hurt if we are to protect ourselves. 'Thank God for inventing pain!' wrote Philip Yancey; 'I don't think he could have done a better job. It's beautiful.'[6]

Fourthly, suffering is due to the kind of environment in which God has placed us. Although most human suffering is caused by human sin (C. S. Lewis reckoned four-fifths of it, and Hugh Silvester nineteen-twentieths, *i.e.* 95%),[7] natural disasters such as flood, hurricane, earthquake and drought are not. True, it can be argued that God did not intend the earth's 'inhospitable areas' to be inhabited, let alone increased by ecological irresponsibility.[8] Yet most people go on living where they were born and have no opportunity to move. What can one say, then, about the so-called 'laws' of nature which in storm and tempest relentlessly overwhelm innocent people? C. S. Lewis went so far as to say that 'not even Omnipotence could create a society of free souls without at the same time creating a relatively independent and "inexorable" Nature'.[9] 'What we need for human society', Lewis continued, 'is exactly what we have – a neutral something', stable and having 'a fixed nature of its own', as the arena in which we may act freely towards each other and him.[10] If we lived in a world in which God prevented every evil from happening, like Superman in Alexander Salkind's films, free and responsible activity would be impossible.

There have always been some who insist that suffering is meaningless, and that no purpose whatever can be detected in it. In the ancient world these included both the Stoics (who taught the need to submit with fortitude to nature's inexorable laws) and the Epicureans (who taught that the best escape from a random world was indulgence in pleasure). And in the modern world secular existentialists believe that everything, including life, suffering and death, is meaningless and therefore absurd. But Christians cannot follow them down that blind alley. For Jesus spoke of suffering as being both 'for God's glory', that God's Son might be glorified through it, and 'so that the work of God might be displayed'.[11] This seems to mean that in some way (still to be explored) God is at work revealing his glory in and through suffering, as he did (though differently) through Christ's. What then is the relationship between Christ's sufferings and ours? How does the cross speak to us in our pain? I want to suggest from Scripture six possible answers to these questions, which seem to rise gradually from the simplest to the most sublime.

Patient endurance

First, the cross of Christ is *a stimulus to patient endurance*. Even though suffering has to be recognized as evil and therefore resisted, there nevertheless comes a time when it has to be realistically accepted. It is then that the example of Jesus, which is set before us in the New Testament for our imitation, becomes an inspiration. Peter directed his readers' attention to it, especially if they were Christian slaves with harsh masters during the Neronian persecution. It would be no particular credit to them if they were beaten for some wrong-doing and took it patiently. But if they suffered for doing good and endured it, this would be pleasing to God. Why? Because undeserved suffering is part of their Christian calling, since Christ himself had suffered for them, leaving them an example, that they should follow in his steps. Though sinless, he was insulted, but he never retaliated (1 Pet. 2:18–23). Jesus set an example of perseverance as well as of non-retaliation, which should encourage us to persevere in the Christian race. We need to 'fix our eyes on Jesus', for he 'endured the cross, scorning its shame'. So then: 'Consider him who endured such opposition from sinful men, so that you will not grow weary and lose heart' (Heb. 12:1–3).

Although both these examples relate specifically to opposition or persecution, it seems legitimate to give them a wider application. Christians in every generation have gained from the sufferings of Jesus, which culminated in the cross, the inspiration to bear undeserved pain patiently, without either complaining or hitting back. True, there are many kinds of suffering he did not have to endure. Yet his sufferings were remarkably representative. Take Joni Eareckson as an example. In 1967, when she was a beautiful, athletic teenager, she had a terrible diving accident in Chesapeake Bay, which left her a quadriplegic. She has told her story with affecting honesty, including her times of bitterness, anger, rebellion and despair, and how gradually, through the love of her family and friends, she came to trust the sovereignty of God and to build a new life of mouth-painting and public speaking under the signal blessing of God. One night, about three years after her accident, Cindy, one of her closest friends, sitting by her bedside, spoke to her of Jesus, saying, 'Why, he was paralysed too.' It had not occurred to her before that on the cross Jesus was in similar pain to hers, unable to move, virtually paralysed. She found this thought deeply comforting.[12]

Mature holiness

Secondly, the cross of Christ is *the path to mature holiness*. Extraordinary as it may sound, we can add that 'it was for him, and it is for us'. We need to consider the implications of two rather neglected verses in the letter to the Hebrews:

> In bringing many sons to glory, it was fitting that God ... should make the Author of their salvation perfect through suffering (2:10).

> Although he was a son, he learned obedience from what he suffered and, once made perfect, he became the source of eternal salvation for all who obey him (5:8–9; *cf.* 7:28).

Both verses speak of a process in which Jesus was 'made perfect', and both ascribe the perfecting process to his 'suffering'. Not of course that he was ever imperfect in the sense that he had done wrong, for Hebrews underlines his sinlessness.[13] It was rather that he needed further experiences and opportunities in order to become *teleios*, 'mature'. In particular, 'he learned obedience from what he suffered'. He was never disobedient. But his sufferings were the testing-ground in which his obedience became full-grown.

If suffering was the means by which the sinless Christ became mature, so much the more do we need it in our sinfulness. Significantly, James uses the same language of 'perfection' or 'maturity' in relation to Christians. Just as suffering led to maturity through obedience for Christ, so it leads to maturity through perseverance for us.

> Consider it pure joy, my brothers, whenever you face trials of many kinds, because you know that the testing of your faith develops perseverance. Perseverance must finish its work so that you may be mature [*teleioi*] and complete, not lacking anything (Jas. 1:2–4; *cf.* Rom. 5:3–5).

Three graphic images are developed in Scripture to illustrate how God uses suffering in pursuance of his purpose to make us holy, in other words, Christlike. They are the father disciplining his children, the metalworker refining silver and gold, and the gardener pruning his vine. The father-children picture is already seen in Deuteronomy, where Moses says: 'Know then in your heart that as a man disciplines his son, so the LORD your God disciplines you.' The metaphor is taken up again in the book of Proverbs, where it is stressed that a father's discipline is an expression of his love for his children, and the Proverbs verses are quoted in the letter to the Hebrews and echoed in Jesus' message to the Laodicean church.[14] The Hebrews passage is the longest. It teaches that fatherly discipline marks out the true sons from the illegitimate; that God disciplines us only 'for our good', namely 'that we may share in his holiness'; that at the time discipline is painful not pleasant, but that later 'it produces a harvest of righteousness and peace', not indeed for everybody (for some rebel against the discipline), but for those who submit to it and so are 'trained by it'.

The second picture of God as the refiner of silver and gold occurs three times in the Old Testament, where it is made clear that the place of refinement for Israel was 'the furnace of affliction', and Peter applies it to the testing of our Christian faith in 'all kinds of trials'. The process will be distressing, but through it our faith ('of greater worth than gold') will both be proved genuine and result in glory to Jesus Christ.[15]

The third picture Jesus himself developed in his allegory of the vine, in which the fruitfulness of the branches (almost certainly a symbol of Christian character) will depend not only on their abiding in the vine, but also on their being pruned by the vine-dresser. Pruning is a drastic process, which often looks cruel, as the bush is cut right back and left jagged and almost naked. But when the spring and summer come round again, there is much fruit.[16]

All three metaphors describe a negative process, disciplining the child, refining the metal and pruning the vine. But all three also underline the positive result – the child's good, the metal's purity, the vine's fruitfulness. We should not hesitate to say, then, that God intends suffering to be a 'means of grace'. Many of his children can repeat the psalmist's statement:

'Before I was afflicted I went astray, but now I obey your word' (Ps. 119:67). For if God's love is holy love, as it is, then it is concerned not only to act in holiness (as in the cross of Christ), but also to promote holiness (in the people of God). As we have already seen, suffering fosters perseverance and purifies faith. It also develops humility, as when Paul's thorn in the flesh was to keep him 'from becoming conceited'. And it deepens insight, as through the pain of Hosea's unrequited love for Gomer there was revealed to him the faithfulness and patience of Yahweh's love for Israel.[17] Nor should we overlook the benefits which can come into other people's lives, such as the heroic unselfishness of those who care for the sick, the senile and the handicapped, and the spontaneous upsurge of generosity towards the hungry peoples of sub-Saharan Africa.

The Roman Catholic Church has traditionally spoken of 'redemptive suffering'. Its official teaching is that, even after the guilt of our misdeeds has been forgiven, their due of punishment still has to be completed either in this life or in purgatory (which is 'the church suffering'). Thus pardon does not remit penance, for punishment has to be added to forgiveness. The best penances, moreover, are not those appointed by the church but those sent from God himself – namely 'crosses, sicknesses, pains' – which atone for our sins. There are, in fact, 'two reasons for suffering for sin: first, atonement to God, and second the re-making of our souls'. For suffering subdues our bodily appetites, cleanses and restores us.[18]

This kind of teaching, which appears both to underplay the completeness with which God through Christ has redeemed and forgiven us, and to ascribe atoning efficacy to our sufferings, is very offensive to the Protestant mind and conscience. Some Roman Catholics use the term 'redemptive suffering', however, simply to indicate that affliction, although it embitters some, transforms others. Mary Craig writes of 'the redemptive power of suffering' in this sense. She describes how two of her four sons were born with severe abnormalities, her second son Paul with the disfiguring and incapacitating Höhler's syndrome, and her fourth Nicholas with Down's syndrome. She tells the story of her spiritual struggle without self-pity or melodrama. In the final chapter of her book, significantly entitled *Blessings*, she meditates on the meaning of suffering, and it is now that she introduces the word 'redemptive'. 'In the teeth of the evidence', she writes, 'I do not believe that any suffering is ultimately absurd or pointless', although 'it is often difficult to go on convincing oneself' of this. At first, we react with incredulity, anger and despair. Yet 'the value of suffering does not lie in the pain of it, ... but in what the sufferer makes of it ... It is in sorrow that we discover the things which really matter; in sorrow that we discover ourselves' (pp. 133–144).

Since Jesus Christ is the one and only Redeemer, and the New Testament never uses redemption language of anything we do, we will be wise not to talk of 'redemptive suffering'. 'Creative suffering', a term popularized by Dr Paul Tournier's last book, would be better, so long as it is not imagined that suffering actually creates anything. But it does stimulate 'creativity', which is his point. He begins by referring to an article written by Dr Pierre Rentchnick of Geneva in 1975 entitled 'Orphans Lead the World'. From the life-stories of history's most influential politicians he had made the astonishing discovery that nearly 300 of them were orphans, from Alexander the Great and Julius Caesar through Charles V and Louis XIV to George Washington, Napoleon and (less happily) Lenin, Hitler, Stalin and Castro. This naturally struck Dr Tournier, since he had long lectured on the importance for the child's development of a father and mother performing their roles harmoniously – which is exactly what the most influential politicians never had! Dr Rentchnick developed a theory that 'the insecurity consequent upon emotional deprivation must have aroused in these children an exceptional will to power'. The same was evidently true of religious leaders, since, for example, Moses, the Buddha, Confucius and Mohammed were also all orphans.[19] Professor André Haynal, a psychoanalyst, has worked further on the theory, and suggests that 'deprivation' of any kind (not just being orphaned) lies behind 'creativity' (which he prefers to 'will to power'). Finally, Dr Tournier confirms the theory from his own clinical experience. For fifty years his patients have confided in him their pains and conflicts. 'I have seen them change through suffering,' he says (p. 15). Not that suffering (which is an evil) is the cause of growth; but it is its occasion (p. 29). Why, then, do some grow through handicap, while others do not? Their reaction depends, he thinks, 'more on the help they receive from others than on their hereditary disposition' (p. 32), and in particular it depends on love. 'Deprivations without the aid of love spell catastrophe', while 'the decisive factor in making deprivation bear fruit is love' (p. 34). So it is not so much suffering which matures people, as the way they react to suffering (p. 37). 'While suffering may not be creative in itself, we are scarcely ever creative without suffering ... One could also say that it is not suffering which makes a person grow, but that one does not grow without suffering' (p. 110).

Biblical teaching and personal experience thus combine to teach that suffering is the path to holiness or maturity. There is always an indefinable something about people who have suffered. They have a fragrance which others lack. They exhibit the meekness and gentleness of Christ. One of the most remarkable statements Peter makes in his first letter is that 'he who has suffered in his body is done with sin' (4:1). Physical affliction, he seems to be saying, actually has the effect of making us stop sinning. This being so, I sometimes wonder if the real test of our hunger for holiness is our willingness to experience any degree of suffering if only thereby God will make us holy.

Suffering service

Thirdly, the cross of Christ is *the symbol of suffering service*. We are familiar with the four or five 'Servant Songs' of Isaiah which together make up the portrait of the 'suffering servant of the Lord',[20] and we began in the last chapter to consider the link between suffering and service. Meek in character and conduct (never shouting or raising his voice), and gentle in his dealings with others (never breaking bruised reeds or snuffing out smouldering wicks), he has nevertheless been called by Yahweh since before his birth, filled with his Spirit and receptive to his Word, with a view to bringing Israel back to him and being a light to the nations. In this task he perseveres, setting his face like a flint, although his back is beaten, his beard pulled out, his face spat upon, and he himself is led like a lamb to the slaughter and dies, bearing the sins of many. Nevertheless, as a result of his death, many will be justified and the nations sprinkled with blessing. What is particularly striking in this composite picture is that suffering and service, passion and mission belong together. We see this clearly in Jesus, who is the suffering servant *par excellence*, but we need to remember that the servant's mission to bring light to the nations is also to be fulfilled by the church (Acts 13:47). For the church, therefore, as for the Saviour, suffering and service go together.

More than this. It is not just that suffering belongs to service, but that suffering is indispensable to fruitful or effective service. This is the inescapable implication of the words of Jesus:

'The hour has come for the Son of Man to be glorified. I tell you the truth, unless an ear of wheat falls to the ground and dies, it remains only a single seed. But if it dies, it produces many seeds. The man who loves his life will lose it, while the man who hates his life in this world will keep it for eternal life. Whoever serves me must follow me; and where I am, my servant also will be. My Father will honour the one who serves me ...'

'But I, when I am lifted up from the earth, will draw all men to myself.' He said this to show the kind of death he was going to die (Jn. 12:23–26, 32–33).

It is hard to accept this lesson from the agricultural harvest. Death is more than the way to life; it is the secret of fruitfulness. Unless it falls into the ground and dies, the kernel of wheat remains a single seed. If it stays alive, it stays alone; but if it dies it multiplies. First and foremost Jesus was referring to himself. Did certain Greeks wish to see him? He was about to be 'glorified' in death. Soon he would be lifted up on his cross to draw people of all nations to himself. During his earthly ministry he restricted himself largely to 'the lost sheep of the house of Israel', but after his death and resurrection, he would have universal authority and a universal appeal.

But Jesus was not speaking only of himself. He was uttering a general principle, and went on to apply it to his disciples who must follow him and like him lose their lives (vv. 25–26) – not necessarily in martyrdom but at least in self-giving, suffering service. For us as for him, the seed must die to multiply.

Paul is the most notable example of this principle. Consider these texts taken from three different letters:

> For this reason I, Paul, the prisoner of Christ Jesus for the sake of you Gentiles – I ask you ... not to be discouraged because of my sufferings for you, which are your glory (Eph. 3:1, 13).

> Now I rejoice in what was suffered for you, and I fill up in my flesh what is still lacking in regard to Christ's afflictions, for the sake of his body, which is the church (Col. 1:24).

> This is my gospel, for which I am suffering ... Therefore I endure everything for the sake of the elect, that they too may obtain the salvation that is in Christ Jesus, with eternal glory (2 Tim. 2:8–10).

Paul states in all three texts that his sufferings are being endured 'for the sake of you Gentiles', 'for the sake of Christ's body' or 'for the sake of the elect'. Since he is doing it for them, he believes they will derive some benefit from his sufferings. What is this? In the Colossians verse he refers to his sufferings as filling up what was still lacking in Christ's afflictions. We can be certain that Paul is not attaching any atoning efficacy to his sufferings, partly because he knew Christ's atoning work was finished on the cross, and partly because he uses the special word 'afflictions' (*thlipseis*) which denotes his persecutions. It is these which were unfinished, for he continued to be persecuted in his church. What benefit, then, did Paul think would come to people through his sufferings? Two of the three texts link the words 'sufferings' and 'glory'. 'My sufferings ... are your glory', he tells the Ephesians. Again, 'salvation ... with eternal glory' will be obtained by the elect because of the sufferings Paul is enduring (2 Tim. 2:8–10). It sounds outrageous. Does Paul really imagine that his sufferings will obtain their salvation and glory? Yes, he does. Not directly, however, as if his sufferings had saving efficacy like Christ's, but indirectly because he was suffering for the gospel which they must hear and embrace in order to be saved. Once again, suffering and service were bracketed, and the apostle's sufferings were an indispensable link in the chain of their salvation.

The place of suffering in service and of passion in mission is hardly ever taught today. But the greatest single secret of evangelistic or missionary effectiveness is the willingness to suffer and die. It may be a death to popularity (by faithfully preaching the unpopular biblical gospel), or to pride (by the use of modest methods in reliance on the Holy Spirit), or to racial and national prejudice (by identification with another culture), or to material comfort (by adopting a simple lifestyle). But the servant must suffer if he is to bring light to the nations, and the seed must die if it is to multiply.

The hope of glory

Fourthly, the cross of Christ is *the hope of final glory*. Jesus clearly looked beyond his death to his resurrection, beyond his sufferings to his glory, and indeed was sustained in his trials by 'the joy set before him' (Heb. 12:2). It is equally clear that he expected his followers to share this perspective. The inevitability of suffering is a regular theme in his teaching and that of the apostles. If the world had hated and persecuted him, it would hate and persecute his disciples also. Suffering was, in fact, a 'gift' of God to all his people, and part of their calling. They should not therefore be surprised by it, as if something strange were happening to them. It was only to be expected. Nothing could be more forthright than Paul's assertion that 'everyone who wants to live a godly life in Christ Jesus will be persecuted'.[21] Further, in suffering *like* Christ they were suffering *with* Christ. They were more than spectators of his sufferings now, more than witnesses, more even than imitators; they were actually participants in his sufferings, sharing his 'cup' and his 'baptism'.[22] So, as they share in his sufferings, they would also share in his glory. The indispensability of suffering was to be seen not only as due to the antagonism of the world but as a necessary preparation. 'Through many tribulations we must enter the kingdom of God', the apostles warned the new converts in Galatia. It is understandable, therefore, that the countless multitude of the redeemed whom John saw before God's throne were described both as having 'come out of the great tribulation' (in the context surely a synonym for the Christian life) and as having 'washed their robes and made them white in the blood of the Lamb'.[23]

It is, then, the hope of glory which makes suffering bearable. The essential perspective to develop is that of the eternal purpose of God, which is to make us holy or Christlike. We ought frequently to meditate on the great New Testament texts which bring together the past and future eternities within a single horizon. For 'God chose us in Christ before the creation of the world to be holy and blameless in his sight'. His purpose is to present us 'before his glorious presence without fault and with great joy'. It is when these horizons are in our view that we 'consider ... our present sufferings are not worth comparing with the glory that will be revealed in us', because 'our light and momentary troubles are achieving for us an eternal glory that far outweighs them all'. And what is this 'glory', this ultimate destiny, towards which God is working everything together for good, including our sufferings? It is that we may 'be conformed to the likeness of his Son'. The future prospect which makes suffering endurable, then, is not a reward in the form of a 'prize', which might lead us to say 'no pain, no palm' or 'no cross, no crown', but the only reward of priceless value, namely the glory of Christ, his own image perfectly recreated within us. 'We shall be like him, for we shall see him as he is.'[24]

This is the dominant theme of the book *Destined For Glory* by Margaret Clarkson, the Canadian hymn-writer and authoress. Born into a 'loveless and unhappy' home, and afflicted from childhood with painful headaches and crippling arthritis, suffering has been her lifelong companion. In earlier days she experienced the full range of human responses to pain, including 'rage, frustration, despair' and even temptation to suicide (pp. viiff.). But gradually she came to believe in the sovereignty of God, namely that God 'displays his sovereignty over evil by using the very suffering that is inherent in evil to assist in the working out of his eternal purpose' (p. 37). In this process he has developed an alchemy greater than that sought by the early chemists who tried to turn base metals into gold. For 'the only true alchemist is God. He succeeds even in the 'transmutation of evil into good' (p. 13). We are 'destined for glory', the 'glory for which he created us – to make us like his Son' (p. 125). It is summed up in a verse of one of Margaret Clarkson's hymns (p. xii):

> O Father, you are sovereign,
>   The Lord of human pain,
> Transmuting earthly sorrows
>   To gold of heavenly gain.
> All evil overruling,
>   As none but Conqueror could,
> Your love pursues its purpose –
>   Our souls' eternal good.

We may well respond, of course, that we do not want God to change us, especially if the necessary means he uses is pain.. 'We may wish, indeed,' wrote C. S. Lewis, 'that we were of so little account to God that he left us alone to follow our natural impulses – that he would give over trying to train us into something so unlike our natural selves: but once again, we are asking not for more love, but for less ... To ask that God's love should be content with us as we are is to ask that God should cease to be God ...'[25]

This vision of suffering as the path to glory for the people of God is undoubtedly biblical. One cannot say the same, however, for attempts to universalize the principle and apply it to all suffering without exception.

Consider, for example, one of the official books published in preparation for the sixth assembly of the World Council of Churches in Vancouver (1983), whose advertised title was 'Jesus Christ, the Life of the World'. This book, although written by John Poulton, arose out of a meeting of twenty-five representative theologians, whose views he therefore incorporates. One of its main themes is that there is a parallel between the death and resurrection of Jesus on the one hand and the suffering and triumphs of the contemporary world on the other. In this way the whole of human life is represented as a eucharistic celebration. 'Might we not say', John Poulton asks, 'that wherever there is the conjunction of suffering and joy, of death and life, *there is eucharist?*'[26] The basis for this interpretation is the fact that 'the pattern of self-sacrifice and new beginnings is not one that only members of the Christian church experience and live by. Outside their circle, others too seem to reflect it, sometimes quite remarkably' (p. 66). Indeed, John Poulton continues, the criss-crossing of pain and joy, suffering and security, betrayal and love is discernible in everyday life everywhere. It reflects winter and spring, and Good Friday and Easter. Old-style evangelism is no longer needed, therefore. The new evangelism will be the Holy Spirit's work in 'bringing into focus in Jesus Christ a shape already glimpsed in human experience' (p. 66).

This is not the gospel of the New Testament, however. Scripture gives us no liberty to assert that all human suffering leads to glory. True, Jesus referred to wars, earthquakes and famines as 'the beginning of birth pains' heralding the emergence of the new world, and Paul similarly likened nature's frustration, bondage to decay and groans to 'the pains of childbirth'.[27] But these are references to the promise of cosmic renewal for both society and nature; they are not applied in the Bible to the salvation of individuals or peoples.

Another example is the moving attempt made by Dr Ulrich Simon, a German Jewish Christian who fled to England in 1933, and whose father, brother and other relatives perished in Nazi concentration camps, to apply the death-resurrection, sufferings-glory principle to the holocaust. In his *A Theology of Auschwitz* (1967) he tried to 'show the pattern of Christ's sacrifice, which summarizes all agonies, as the reality behind Auschwitz' (pp. 13–14). For the holocaust (which of course means 'burnt offering') 'is no less a sacrifice than that prefigured in the Scriptures', that is to say, in the suffering servant of the Lord (pp. 83–84). In this way, 'the mechanics of murder were turned into a Godward oblation', and those who gave their lives in the gas chambers became identified with 'the supreme sacrifice by way of a sharing analogy' (p. 84); they were even scapegoats, bearing the sins of the German people (p. 86). But now 'the dead of Auschwitz have risen from the dust' (p. 91), and their resurrection is seen in Israel's return to the land, in the conquest of anti-Semitism which 'both led to Auschwitz and was redeemed there' (p. 93), and in the contemporary Jewish witness to the world concerning the sacredness of human life and the loving brotherhood of all men (p. 95). The corn of wheat, having fallen into the ground, has borne this fruit. Thus the sufferings of Auschwitz, Ulrich Simon claims, are 'within the pattern of creation and redemption' (p. 102). In particular, by interpreting the holocaust 'in the light of the suffering Christ' and by seeing its aftermath as 'reflected in the triumph of the Crucified One', it has been possible to give 'spiritual meaning to the meaningless' (p. 104). 'We venture to attribute the glory of the ascended Christ to the gassed millions' (p. 105).

One cannot fail to be touched by this attempted reconstruction, and one fully appreciates Dr Simon's reasons for wanting to develop a 'timeless, universal and cosmic conception of Christ's work' (p. 110). But I fear this kind of 'theology of Auschwitz' is speculative rather than scriptural. I believe there is a better and more biblical way to relate the cross to Auschwitz, and I will come to it shortly. Meanwhile, within the community of those whom God in mercy has redeemed, it should be possible for us to echo Paul's affirmations that 'we also rejoice in our sufferings' because 'we rejoice in the hope of the glory of God' (Rom. 5:2–3).

So far, in seeking to discern the relationships between Christ's sufferings and ours, apart from the inspiration of his example, we have seen that suffering (for us as for Jesus) is God's appointed path to sanctification (mature holiness), multiplication (fruitful service) and glorification (our final destiny). I hope it does not sound glib. It is easy to theorize, I know. But things look different when the horizon closes in upon us, a horror of great darkness engulfs us, and no glimmer of light shines to assure us that suffering can yet be productive. At such times we can only cling to the cross, where Christ himself demonstrated that blessing comes through suffering.

Faith and the book of Job

Fifthly, the cross of Christ is *the ground of a reasonable faith*. All suffering, physical and emotional, sorely tries our faith. How can it be reasonable, when calamity overwhelms us, to continue to trust in God? The best answer to this question is provided by the book of Job. It will be worth our while to clarify its thesis.

Job is introduced as a 'blameless and upright' man, who 'feared God and shunned evil'. But then (after we as readers have been permitted a glimpse into the deliberations of the heavenly council chamber), Job is overtaken by a series of personal tragedies: he is deprived successively of his livestock, his servants, his sons and daughters, and his health. It would be hard to exaggerate the magnitude of the disasters which have overwhelmed him. In the rest of the book the full spectrum of possible responses to suffering is rehearsed in the dialogue which develops between Job, his three so-called 'comforters', the young man Elihu and finally God himself. Each of the four proposes a different attitude, and specially noteworthy in each is the place accorded to the self.

Job's own attitude is a mixture of *self-pity* and *self-assertion*. Refusing to follow his wife's advice that he should 'curse God and die', he nevertheless begins by cursing the day of his birth and then longs with anguish for the day of his death. He utterly rejects the accusations of his three friends. Instead, he frames his own accusations against God. God is being brutally cruel to him, even ruthless. Worse still, God has altogether denied him justice (27:2). The contest between them is grossly unfair, since the contestants are so unequal. If only there were a mediator to arbitrate between them! If only he himself could find God, in order personally to press charges against him! Meanwhile, he vehemently maintains his innocence and is confident that one day he will be vindicated.

By contrast, the attitude recommended by Job's friends may best be described as *self-accusation*. Job is suffering because he is sinful. His afflictions are the divine penalty for his misdeeds. That is the conventional orthodoxy about the wicked, which they repeat *ad nauseam*. 'All his days the wicked man suffers torment', says Eliphaz (15:20). 'The lamp of the wicked is snuffed out,' adds Bildad (18:5), while Zophar's contribution is that 'the mirth of the wicked is brief' (20:5). From this basic premise they draw the inevitable deduction that Job is suffering for his wickedness: 'Is not your wickedness great? Are not your sins endless?' (22:5). But Job will have none of it. His friends are 'worthless physicians' (13:4) and 'miserable comforters' (16:2), who talk nothing but 'nonsense' and even 'falsehood' (21:34). And God later confirms Job's verdict. He refers to their 'folly', and says that they 'have not spoken' of him 'what is right', as his servant Job has (42:7–8).

Elihu enters next. Although he is angry because Job has been 'justifying himself rather than God' (32:2), he is diffident on account of his youth to speak. When he does, it is not altogether easy to distinguish his position from that of Job's three comforters. For sometimes he too repeats the old orthodoxy. He also anticipates Yahweh's speech about creation. Yet it seems right to call the attitude he recommends *self-discipline*, for his distinctive emphasis is that God speaks in many ways (including suffering) in order 'to turn man from wrongdoing and keep him from pride' (33:14, 17). So God makes people 'listen to correction' and 'speaks to them in their affliction' (36:10, 15). Indeed, 'who is a teacher like him?' (v. 22). His teaching is even a kind of 'wooing' (v. 16), in which he pleads with people to repent and so seeks to deliver them from their distress.

At last, when Job, the comforters and Elihu have exhausted their arguments, Yahweh reveals himself and speaks. Judging from Job's response, the recommended attitude now may be called *self-surrender*. God is far from joining Job's three friends in their accusations, and he does not blame Job for maintaining his innocence (42:8). He takes his complaints seriously, and therefore replies to him. Yet Job has uttered 'words without knowledge', since it is never right to blame, accuse, let alone 'correct' God (40:2). 'Would you discredit my justice?' God asks (40:8). And Job replies: 'My ears had heard of you but now my eyes have seen you. Therefore I despise myself and repent in dust and ashes' (42:5–6). Previously he has defended, pitied and asserted himself, and accused God. Now he despises himself, and worships God. What has he 'seen' which has converted him from self-assertion to self-surrender?

Job has been invited to look afresh at the creation, and has glimpsed the glory of the Creator. God bombards him with questions. Where was he when the earth and the sea were made? Can he control the snow, the storm and the stars? Does he possess the expertise to supervise and sustain the animal world – lions and mountain goats, the wild donkey and the wild ox, the ostrich and the horse, hawks and eagles? Above all, can Job comprehend the mysteries and subdue the strength of *behemoth* the hippopotamus and *leviathan* the crocodile? What God gave Job was a comprehensive introduction to the wonders of nature, and thereby a revelation of his creative genius, which silenced Job's accusations and led him – even in the midst of his continued bereavement, suffering and pain – to humble himself, repent of his rebellion, and trust God again.

If it was reasonable for Job to trust the God whose wisdom and power have been revealed in creation, how much more reasonable is it for us to trust the God whose love and justice have been revealed in the cross? The reasonableness of trust lies in the known trustworthiness of its object. And no-one is more trustworthy than the God of the cross. The cross assures us that there is no possibility of a miscarriage of justice or of the defeat of love either now or on the last day. 'He who did not spare his own Son, but gave him up for us all – how will he not also, along with him, graciously give us all things?' (Rom. 8:32). It is the self-giving of God in the gift of his Son which convinces us that he will withhold nothing from us that we need, and allow nothing to separate us from his love (vv. 35–39). So between the cross, where God's love and justice began to be clearly revealed, and the day of judgment when they will be completely revealed, it is reasonable to trust in him.

We have to learn to climb the hill called Calvary, and from that vantage-ground survey all life's tragedies. The cross does not solve the problem of suffering, but it supplies the essential perspective from which to look at it. Since God has demonstrated his holy love and loving justice in a historical event (the cross), no other historical event (whether personal or global) can override or disprove it. This must surely be why the scroll (the book of history and destiny) is now in the hands of the slain Lamb, and why only he is worthy to break its seals, reveal its contents and control the flow of the future.

The pain of God

There is a sixth way in which Christ's sufferings are related to ours. It is the most important of the series. It is that the cross of Christ is *the proof of God's solidary love*, that is, of his personal, loving solidarity with us in our pain. For the real sting of suffering is not misfortune itself, nor even the pain of it or the injustice of it, but the apparent God-forsakenness of it. Pain is endurable, but the seeming indifference of God is not. Sometimes we picture him lounging, perhaps dozing, in some celestial deck-chair, while the hungry millions starve to death. We think of him as an armchair spectator, almost gloating over the world's suffering, and enjoying his own insulation from it. Philip Yancey has gone further and uttered the unutterable which we may have thought but to which we have never dared to give voice: 'If God is truly in charge, somehow connected to all the world's suffering, why is he so capricious, unfair? Is he the cosmic sadist who delights in watching us squirm?'[28] Job had said something similar: God 'mocks the despair of the innocent' (9:23).

It is this terrible caricature of God which the cross smashes to smithereens. We are not to envisage him on a deck-chair, but on a cross. The God who allows us to suffer, once suffered himself in Christ, and continues to suffer with us and for us today. Since the cross was a once-for-all historical event, in which God in Christ bore our sins and died our death because of his love and justice, we must not think of it as expressing an eternal sin-bearing in the heart of God. What Scripture does give us warrant to say, however, is that God's eternal holy love, which was uniquely exhibited in the sacrifice of the cross, continues to suffer with us in every situation in which it is called forth. But is it legitimate to speak of a suffering God? Are we not impeded from doing so by the traditional doctrine of the divine impassibility? The Latin adjective *impassibilis* means 'incapable of suffering' and therefore 'devoid of emotion'. Its Greek equivalent, *apathēs*, was applied by the philosophers to God, whom they declared to be above pleasure and pain, since these would interrupt his tranquillity.

The early Greek Fathers of the church took over this notion somewhat uncritically. In consequence, their teaching about God sometimes sounds more Greek than Hebrew. It was also ambivalent. True, they knew that Jesus Christ the Incarnate Son suffered, but not God himself. Ignatius wrote to Polycarp, for example, of the God 'who cannot suffer, who for our sakes accepted suffering', that is, in Christ.[29] Similarly, Irenaeus affirmed that by reason of the incarnation 'the invisible was made visible, the incomprehensible comprehensible, and the impassible passible'.[30] True again, they knew that the Old Testament authors wrote freely of the love, pity, anger, sorrow and jealousy of God. But they added that these were anthropomorphisms which are not to be taken literally, since the divine nature is unmoved by all emotions.[31] Gregory Thaumaturgus in the third century even wrote that 'in his suffering God shows his impassibility'.

These and other ancient church Fathers deserve our understanding. They were wanting above all to safeguard the truths that God is perfect (so that nothing can add to or subtract from him) and that God is changeless (so that nothing can disturb him).[32] We today should still wish to maintain these truths. God cannot be influenced against his will from either outside or inside. He is never the unwilling victim either of actions which affect him from without or of emotions which upset him from within. As William Temple put it, 'there is a highly technical sense in which God, as Christ revealed him, is "without passions"; for he is Creator and supreme, and is never "passive" in the sense of having things happen to him except with his consent; also he is constant, and free from gusts of feeling carrying him this way and that'. Nevertheless, Temple rightly went on to say that the term 'impassible' as used by most theologians really meant 'incapable of suffering', and that 'in this sense its predication of God is almost wholly false'.[33]

It is true that Old Testament language is an accommodation to our human understanding, and that God is represented as experiencing human emotions. Yet, to acknowledge that his feelings are not *human* is not to deny that they are *real*. If they are only metaphorical, 'then the only God left to us will be the infinite iceberg of metaphysics'.[34] In contrast to this, we may be thankful to the Jewish scholar Abraham Heschel, who in his book *The Prophets* refers to their 'pathetic theology', because they portray a God of feeling. The frequent Old Testament 'anthropopathisms' (which ascribe human suffering to God) are not to be rejected as crude or primitive, he writes, but rather to be welcomed as crucial to our understanding of him: 'the most exalted idea applied to God is not infinite wisdom, infinite power, but infinite concern' (p. 241). Thus, before the flood Yahweh was 'grieved' that he had made human beings, 'and his heart was filled with pain', and when his people were oppressed by foreigners during the time of the Judges, Yahweh 'could bear Israel's misery no longer'.[35] Most striking of all are the occasions when through the prophets God expresses his 'yearning' and 'compassion' for his people and addresses Israel direct: 'I have loved you with an everlasting love ... Can a mother forget the baby at her breast ...? Though she may forget, I will not forget you! ... How can I give you up, Ephraim? How can I hand you over, Israel? ... My heart is changed within me; all my compassion is aroused.'[36]

If God's full and final self-revelation was given in Jesus, moreover, then his feelings and sufferings are an authentic reflection of the feelings and sufferings of God himself. The Gospel writers attribute to him the whole range of human emotions, from love and compassion through anger and indignation to sorrow and joy. The stubbornness of human hearts caused him distress and anger. Outside Lazarus' tomb, in the face of death, he both 'wept' with grief and 'snorted' with indignation. He wept again over Jerusalem, and uttered a lament over her blindness and obstinacy. And still today he is able 'to sympathize with our weaknesses', feeling with us in them.[37]

The best way to confront the traditional view of the impassibility of God, however, is to ask 'what meaning there can be in a love which is not costly to the lover'.[38] If love is self-giving, then it is inevitably vulnerable to pain, since it exposes itself to the possibility of rejection and insult. It is 'the fundamental Christian assertion that God is love', writes Jürgen Moltmann, 'which in principle broke the spell of the Aristotelian doctrine of God' (*i.e.* as 'impassible'). 'Were God incapable of suffering ... then he would also be incapable of love', whereas 'the one who is capable of love is also capable of suffering, for he also opens himself to the suffering which is involved in love'.[39] That is surely why Bonhoeffer wrote from prison to his friend Eberhard Bethge, nine months before his execution: 'only the Suffering God can help'.[40]

Worthy of special mention, as a doughty opponent of false views of the divine impassibility, is the Japanese Lutheran scholar Kazoh Kitamori. He wrote his remarkable book *Theology of the Pain of God* in 1945, not long after the first atomic bombs had destroyed Hiroshima and Nagasaki. It was inspired, he tells us, by Jeremiah 31:20, where God describes his heart as 'yearning' or 'pained' for Ephraim, even as 'broken'. 'The heart of the gospel was revealed to me as the "pain of God",' he writes (p. 19). To begin with, God's anger against sin gives him pain. 'This wrath of God is absolute and firm. We may say that the recognition of God's wrath is the beginning of wisdom.' But God loves the very people with whom he is angry. So 'the "pain" of God reflects his will to love the object of his wrath'. It is his love and his wrath which together produce his pain. For here, in Luther's arresting phrase, is 'God striving with God'. 'The fact that this fighting God is not two different gods but the same God causes his pain' (p. 21). The pain of God is 'a synthesis of his wrath and love' (p. 26) and is 'his essence' (p. 47). It was supremely revealed in the cross. For 'the "pain of God" results from the love of the One who intercepts and blocks his wrath towards us, the One who himself is smitten by his wrath' (p. 123). This is strikingly bold phraseology. It helps us to understand how God's pain continues whenever his wrath and love, his justice and mercy, are in tension today.

Looking at the world during the second half of this century, there have probably been two outstandingly conspicuous examples of human suffering, the first being hunger and poverty on a global scale, and the second the Nazi holocaust of six million Jews. How does the cross speak to such evils as these?

It is reckoned that one thousand million people today, because they lack the basic necessities of life, may rightly be described as 'destitute'. Many of them eke out a pitiful existence in the slums and shanty towns of Africa and Asia, the *barriadas* of Spanish Latin America and the *favelas* of Brazil. The penury of the people, the overcrowding in their ramshackle shelters, the lack of elementary sanitation, the virtual nakedness of the children, the hunger, disease, unemployment and absence of education – all this adds up to a horrific tally of human need. It is not surprising that such slums are hotbeds of bitterness and resentment; the wonder is that the sheer inhumanity and injustice of it all does not breed an even more virulent anger. Rolf Italiaander imagines a poor man from one of the *favelas* of Rio de Janeiro, who climbs laboriously up to the colossal statue of Christ, 2,310 feet high, which towers above Rio, 'the Christ of Corcovado'. The poor man speaks to the statue:

> I have climbed up to you, Christ, from the filthy, confined quarters down there ... to put before you, most respectfully, these considerations: there are 900,000 of us down there in the slums of that splendid city ... And you, Christ ... do you remain here at Corcovado surrounded by divine glory? Go down there into the *favelas*. Come with me into the *favelas* and live with us down there. Don't stay away from us; live among us and give us new faith in you and in the Father. Amen.[41]

What would Christ say in response to such an entreaty? Would he not say, 'I did come down to live among you, and I live among you still'?

This is, in fact, how some Latin American theologians are presenting the cross today. In his *Christology at the Crossroads*, for example, Professor Jon Sobrino of El Salvador develops a protest both against a purely academic theology which fails to take appropriate action and against the traditional, mournful 'mystique' of the cross which is too passive and individualistic. Instead, he seeks to relate the cross to the modern world and its social injustice. Was God himself, he asks, 'untouched by the historical cross because he is essentially untouchable?' (p. 190). No, no. 'God himself, the Father, was on the cross of Jesus.' In addition, 'God is to be found on the crosses of the oppressed' (p. 201). Provided that Professor Sobrino is not denying the fundamental, atoning purpose of the cross, I do not think we should resist what he is affirming. Here is his summary: 'On the cross of Jesus God himself is crucified. The Father suffers the death of the Son and takes upon himself the pain and suffering of history.' And in this ultimate solidarity with human beings God 'reveals himself as the God of love' (pp. 224, 371).

What, then, about the holocaust? 'After Auschwitz', said Richard Rubinstein, 'it is impossible to believe in God.' One Sunday afternoon, in a sub-camp of Buchenwald, a group of learned Jews decided to put God on trial for neglecting his chosen people. Witnesses were produced for both prosecution and defence, but the case for the prosecution was overwhelming. The judges were Rabbis. They found the accused guilty and solemnly condemned him.[42] It is understandable. The sheer bestiality of the camps and the gas chambers, and the failure of God to intervene on behalf of his ancient people, in spite of their frequent and fervent prayers, have shaken many people's faith. I have already said that I do not think the way to interpret Auschwitz and its aftermath is in terms of death and resurrection. Is there, then, another way? I think Elie (Eliezer) Wiesel can help us. Born a Hungarian Jew, and now an internationally acclaimed author, he has given us in his book *Night* a deeply moving account of his boyhood experiences in the death camps of Auschwitz, Buna and Buchenwald. He was not quite fifteen when the Gestapo arrived to deport all Jews from Sighet in the spring of 1944. They travelled by train for three days, eighty in each cattle wagon. On arrival at Auschwitz, the men and women were segregated, and Elie never saw his mother or sister again. 'Never shall I forget that night, the first night in camp, which has turned my life into one long night, seven times cursed and seven times sealed. Never shall I forget that smoke [*sc.* of the crematorium] ... Never shall I forget those flames which consumed my faith for ever ... Never shall I forget those moments which murdered my God and my soul, and turned my dreams to dust ...' (p. 45). A bit later he wrote: 'Some talked of God, of his mysterious ways, of the sins of the Jewish people, and of their future deliverance. But I had ceased to pray. How I sympathised with Job! I did not deny God's existence, but I doubted his absolute justice' (p. 57).

Perhaps the most horrifying experience of all was when the guards first tortured and then hanged a young boy, 'a child with a refined and beautiful face', a 'sad-eyed angel'. Just before the hanging Elie heard someone behind him whisper, 'Where is God? Where is he?' Thousands of prisoners were forced to watch the hanging (it took the boy half an hour to die) and then to march past, looking him full in the face. Behind him Elie heard the same voice ask, 'Where is God now?' 'And I heard a voice within me answer him: "Where is he? Here he is – he is hanging here on this gallows ..."' (pp. 75–77). His words were truer than he knew, for he was not a Christian. Indeed, in every fibre of his being he rebelled against God for allowing people to be tortured, butchered, gassed and burned. 'I was alone – terribly alone in a world without God and without man. Without love or mercy' (p. 79). Could he have said that if in Jesus he had seen God on the gallows?

There is good biblical evidence that God not only suffered in Christ, but that God in Christ suffers with his people still. Is it not written of God, during the early days of Israel's bitter bondage in Egypt, not just that he saw their plight and 'heard their groaning', but that 'in all their distress he too was distressed'? Did Jesus not ask Saul of Tarsus why he was persecuting him, thus disclosing his solidarity with his church? It is wonderful that we may share in Christ's sufferings; it is more wonderful still that he shares in ours. Truly his name is 'Emmanuel', 'God with us'. But his 'sympathy' is not limited to his suffering with his covenant people. Did Jesus not say that in ministering to the hungry and thirsty, the stranger, the naked, the sick and the prisoner, we would be ministering to him, indicating that he identified himself with all needy and suffering people?[43]

I could never myself believe in God, if it were not for the cross. The only God I believe in is the One Nietzsche ridiculed as 'God on the cross'. In the real world of pain, how could one worship a God who was immune to it? I have entered many Buddhist temples in different Asian countries and stood respectfully before the statue of the Buddha, his legs crossed, arms folded, eyes closed, the ghost of a smile playing round his mouth, a remote look on his face, detached from the agonies of the world. But each time after a while I have had to turn away. And in imagination I have turned instead to that lonely, twisted, tortured figure on the cross, nails through hands and feet, back lacerated, limbs wrenched, brow bleeding from thorn-pricks, mouth dry and intolerably thirsty, plunged in God-forsaken darkness. That is the God for me! He laid aside his immunity to pain. He entered our world of flesh and blood, tears and death. He suffered for us. Our sufferings become more manageable in the light of his. There is still a question mark against human suffering, but over it we boldly stamp another mark, the cross which symbolizes divine suffering. 'The cross of Christ ... is God's only self-justification in such a world' as ours.[44]

The playlet entitled 'The Long Silence' says it all:

At the end of time, billions of people were scattered on a great plain before God's throne.

Most shrank back from the brilliant light before them. But some groups near the front talked heatedly – not with cringing shame, but with belligerence.

'Can God judge us? How can he know about suffering?' snapped a pert young brunette. She ripped open a sleeve to reveal a tattooed number from a Nazi concentration camp. 'We endured terror ... beatings ... torture ... death!'

In another group a Negro boy lowered his collar. 'What about this?' he demanded, showing an ugly rope burn. 'Lynched . ... for no crime but being black!'

In another crowd, a pregnant schoolgirl with sullen eyes. 'Why should I suffer?' she murmured, 'It wasn't my fault.'

Far out across the plain there were hundreds of such groups. Each had a complaint against God for the evil and suffering he permitted in his world. How lucky God was to live in heaven where all was sweetness and light, where there was no weeping or fear, no hunger or hatred. What did God know of all that man had been forced to endure in this world? For God leads a pretty sheltered life, they said.

So each of these groups sent forth their leader, chosen because he had suffered the most. A Jew, a Negro, a person from Hiroshima, a horribly deformed arthritic, a thalidomide child. In the centre of the plain they consulted with each other. At last they were ready to present their case. It was rather clever.

Before God could be qualified to be their judge, he must endure what they had endured. Their decision was that God should be sentenced to live on earth – as a man!

'Let him be born a Jew. Let the legitimacy of his birth be doubted. Give him a work so difficult that even his family will think him out of his mind when he tries to do it. Let him be betrayed by his closest friends. Let him face false charges, be tried by a prejudiced jury and convicted by a cowardly judge. Let him be tortured.

'At the last, let him see what it means to be terribly alone. Then let him die. Let him die so that there can be no doubt that he died. Let there be a great host of witnesses to verify it.'

As each leader announced his portion of the sentence, loud murmurs of approval went up from the throng of people assembled.

And when the last had finished pronouncing sentence, there was a long silence. No-one uttered another word. No-one moved. For suddenly all knew that God had already served his sentence.

Edward Shillito, shattered by the carnage of the First World War, found comfort in the fact that Jesus was able to show his disciples the scars of his crucifixion. It inspired him to write his poem 'Jesus of the Scars':

> If we have never sought, we seek thee now;
>   Thine eyes burn through the dark, our only stars;
> We must have sight of thorn-marks on thy brow,
>   We must have thee, O Jesus of the scars.
>
> The heavens frighten us; they are too calm;
>   In all the universe we have no place.
> Our wounds are hurting us; where is the balm?
>   Lord Jesus, by thy scars we know thy grace.
>
> If, when the doors are shut, thou drawest near,
>   Only reveal those hands, that side of thine;
> We know today what wounds are, have no fear;
>   Show us thy scars, we know the countersign.

> The other gods were strong; but thou wast weak;
> They rode, but thou didst stumble to a throne;
> But to our wounds only God's wounds can speak,
> And not a god has wounds, but thou alone.[45]

Notes

[1] See S. G. Tallentyre, *Life of Voltaire*, Vol. II, pp. 25–27 and *Voltaire* by Colonel Hamley, pp. 168–177.

[2] Quoted by Leslie J. Tizard in *Preaching*, p. 28.

[3] Lk. 13:16 and 4:35, 39; 2 Cor. 12:7; Acts 10:38.

[4] *E.g.* Dt. 28:15ff.; 2 Ki. 5:27; Pss. 32:3–5; 38:1–8; Lk. 1:20; Jn. 5:14; 1 Cor. 11:30.

[5] *E.g.* Lk. 13:1–5; Jn. 9:1–3.

[6] Philip Yancey, *Where is God When it Hurts?*, p. 23.

[7] C. S. Lewis, *Problem of Pain*, p. 77; Hugh Silvester, *Arguing with God*, p. 32.

[8] Hugh Silvester, *Arguing with God*, p. 80.

[9] C. S. Lewis, *Problem of Pain*, p. 17.

[10] *Ibid.*, p. 19.

[11] Jn. 11:4 and 9:3.

[12] Joni Eareckson with Joe Musser, *Joni*, p. 96. See also her second book *A Step Further*, in which she writes more about God's sovereignty and his eternal purpose.

[13] *E.g.* Heb. 4:15; 7:26.

[14] Dt. 8:5; Pr. 3:11–12; Heb. 12:5–11; Rev. 3:19.

[15] Ps. 66:10; Is. 48:10; Zc. 13:9; 1 Pet. 1:6–7.

[16] Jn. 15:1–8. *Cf.* Is. 5:1–7, especially v. 7, and Gal. 5:22–23, as evidence that the 'fruit' means righteous and Christlike character.

[17] 2 Cor. 12:7–10 and Ho. 1 – 3.

[18] George D. Smith (ed.), *Teaching of the Catholic Church*, pp. 1141–1146.

[19] Paul Tournier, *Creative Suffering*, pp. 1–5.

[20] Is. 42:1–4; perhaps 44:1–5; 49:1–6; 50:4–9; 52:13 – 53:12.

[21] *E.g.* Mt. 5:10–12; Jn. 15:18–21; Phil. 1:30; 1 Thes. 3:3; 1 Pet. 2:21; 4:12; 2 Tim. 3:12.

[22] *E.g.* Mk. 10:38; 2 Cor. 1:5; Phil. 3:10; 1 Pet. 4:13; 5:1.

[23] *E.g.* Acts 14:22, RSV; Rom. 8:17; 2 Tim. 2:11–12; 1 Pet. 4:13; 5:1, 9–10; Rev. 7:9, 14.

[24] Eph. 1:4; Jude 24; Rom. 8:18; 2 Cor. 4:17; Rom. 8:28–29; 1 Jn. 3:2.

[25] C. S. Lewis, *Problem of Pain*, pp. 32, 36.

[26] John Poulton, *Feast of Life*, p. 52.

[27] Mk. 13:8; Rom. 8:22.

[28] P. Yancey, *Where is God When it Hurts?*, p. 63.

[29] Ignatius, *Ad Polycarp* 3. *Cf.* his *Ad Eph.* vii. 2.

[30] Irenaeus, *Adversus Haereses* iii.16.6.

[31] See *e.g.* Clement of Alexandria's *Stromateis* v.11 and Origen's *Ezek. Hom.* vi.6. A useful survey of patristic quotations and references is given by J. K. Mozley in his *Impassibility of God*. See also *Suffering of the Impassible God* by B. R Brasnett.

[32] Statements that God does not change his mind, his justice or his compassion may be found in Nu. 23:19; 1 Sa. 15:29; Ezk. 18:25; and Mal. 3:6.

[33] William Temple, *Christus Veritas*, p. 269.

[34] Vincent Tymms, quoted by J. K. Mozley, *Impassibility of God*, p. 146.

[35] Gn. 6:6–7; Jdg. 10:16.

[36] Je. 31:20; 31:3; Is. 49:15; Ho. 11:8.

[37] Mk. 3:5; Jn. 11:35, 38; Lk. 13:34–35; 19:41–44; Heb. 4:15. See also B. B. Warfield's essay 'The Emotional Life of our Lord', reprinted from *Biblical and Theological Studies* (Scribners, 1912) in *The Person and Work of Christ*, ed. Samuel G. Craig, pp. 93–145.

[38] H. Wheeler Robinson, *Suffering Human and Divine*, p. 176.

[39] Jürgen Moltmann, *Crucified God*. See the whole section pp. 222–230.

[40] Dietrich Bonhoeffer, *Letters and Papers*, p. 361.

[41] Quoted from Walbert Bühlmann, *Coming of the Third Church*, p. 125.

[42] Rabbi Hugo Gryn first heard this story from an uncle of his who survied Buchenwald. It has been told by several Jewish authors, and also by Gerald Priestland in *Case Against God*, p. 13.

[43] Ex. 2:24; Is. 63:9; Acts 9:4; Mt. 1:23; 25:34–40.

[44] P. T. Forsyth, *Justification of God*, p. 32.

[45] Edward Shillito, *Jesus of the Scars*, published after World War I, and quoted by William Temple in his *Readings in St John's Gospel*, pp. 384–385.

The pervasive influence
of the cross

In the first chapter I sought to establish the centrality of the cross in the mind of Christ, in Scripture and in history; in the last we shall consider how from that centre the influence of the cross spreads outwards until it pervades the whole of Christian faith and life.

But before developing this theme, it may be helpful to survey the territory we have crossed.

In answer to the question 'Why did Christ die?' we reflected that, although Judas delivered him to the priests, the priests to Pilate, and Pilate to the soldiers, the New Testament indicates both that the Father 'gave him up' and that Jesus 'gave himself up' for us. That led us to look below the surface of what was happening, and to investigate the implications of Jesus' words in the upper room, the Garden of Gethsemane and the cry of dereliction.

It had already become evident that his death was related to our sins, and so in Part Two we came to the very heart of the cross. We began by broaching the problem of forgiveness as constituted by the conflict between the majesty of God and the gravity of sin. And although we rejected other 'satisfaction' theories, we concluded in chapter 5 that God must 'satisfy himself'. That is, he cannot contradict himself, but must act in a way that expresses his perfect character of holy love. But how could he do this? Our answer (chapter 6) was that in order to satisfy himself he substituted himself in Christ for us. We dared to affirm 'self-satisfaction by self-substitution' as the essence of the cross.

In Part Three we looked beyond the cross itself to its consequences, indeed its achievement in three spheres: the salvation of sinners, the revelation of God and the conquest of evil. As for salvation, we studied the four words 'propitiation', 'redemption', 'justification' and 'reconciliation'. These are New Testament 'images', metaphors of what God has done in and through Christ's death. 'Substitution', however, is not another image; it is the reality which lies behind them all. We then saw (chapter 5) that God has fully and finally revealed his love and justice by exercising them in the cross. When substitution is denied, God's self-disclosure is obscured, but when it is affirmed, his glory shines forth brightly. Having thus far concentrated on the cross as both objective achievement (salvation from sin) and subjective influence (through the revelation of holy love), we agreed that *Christus Victor* is a third biblical theme, which depicts Christ's victory over the devil, the law, the flesh, the world and death, and our victory through him (chapter 9).

Part Four I have entitled 'Living under the cross', because the Christian community is essentially a community of the cross. Indeed, the cross has radically altered all our relationships. We now worship God in continuous celebration (chapter 10), understand ourselves and give ourselves in the service of others (chapter 11), love our enemies, seeking to overcome evil with good (chapter 12), and face the perplexing problem of suffering in the light of the cross (chapter 13).

Seven affirmations in the letter to the Galatians

In order, in conclusion, to emphasize the pervasive influence of the cross, namely that we cannot eliminate it from any area of our thinking or living, we shall look through Paul's letter to the Galatians. There are two main reasons for this choice. First, it is arguably his first letter. This is not the place to assess the pros and cons of the 'South Galatian' and 'North Galatian' theories. The similarity of the contents with the letter to the Romans may suggest the later date, but the situation presupposed in Galatians fits the Acts chronology much better and strongly favours the earlier date. In this case the letter was written about AD 48, within fifteen years of the death and resurrection of Jesus. Secondly, the gospel according to Paul in Galatians (which he defends, along with his apostolic authority, as coming from God, not man) focuses on the cross. Indeed the letter contains seven striking affirmations about the death of Jesus, each of which illumines a different facet of it. When we put them together, we have an amazingly comprehensive grasp of the pervasive influence of the cross.

1. The cross and salvation (1:3–5)

> Grace and peace to you from God our Father and the Lord Jesus
> Christ, who gave himself for our sins to rescue us from the present evil
> age, according to the will of our God and Father, to whom be glory for
> ever and ever. Amen.

These words form part of Paul's introductory salutation. Usually such an
epistolary greeting would be casual or conventional. But Paul uses it to
make a carefully balanced theological statement about the cross, which indicates what his concern in the letter is going to be.

First, *the death of Jesus was both voluntary and determined.* On the one
hand, he 'gave himself for our sins', freely and voluntarily. On the other, his
self-giving was 'according to the will of our God and Father'. God the
Father purposed and willed the death of his Son and foretold it in the Old
Testament Scriptures. Yet Jesus embraced this purpose of his own accord.
He set his will to do his Father's will.

Secondly, *the death of Jesus was for our sins.* Sin and death are integrally
related throughout Scripture as cause and effect, as we have seen. Usually
the one who sins and the one who dies are the same person. Here, however,
although the sins are ours, the death is Christ's: *he* died for *our* sins, bearing
their penalty in our place.

Thirdly, *the purpose of Jesus' death was to rescue us.* Salvation is a rescue
operation, undertaken for people whose plight is so desperate that they
cannot save themselves. In particular, he died to rescue us 'out of the present
evil age'. Since Christ inaugurated the new age, the two ages at present
overlap. But he died to rescue us from the old age and secure our transfer
into the new, so that already we might live the life of the age to come.

Fourthly, *the present result of Jesus' death is grace and peace.* 'Grace' is his
free and unmerited favour, and 'peace' is the reconciliation with him and
with each other which grace has achieved. The life of the age to come is a
life of grace and peace. Paul continues to allude to it in the following verses,
in which he expresses his astonishment that the Galatians have so quickly
deserted the one who had called them 'by the grace of Christ' (v. 6). For the
call of God is a call of grace, and the gospel of God is the gospel of grace.

Fifthly, *the eternal result of Jesus' death is that God will be glorified for ever.*
The references in verses 3–5 to grace and glory, as part of the same sentence,
are striking. Grace comes from God; glory is due to God. The whole of
Christian theology is encapsulated in that epigram.

Here, then, in one pregnant sentence, is Paul's first statement in
Galatians about the cross. Although it was determined eternally by the
Father's will, Jesus gave himself voluntarily for us. The nature of his death
was the penalty for our sins, and its purpose was to rescue us from the old

age and transfer us to the new, in which we receive grace and peace now, and God receives glory for ever.

2. The cross and experience (2:19–21)

> For through the law I died to the law so that I might live for God. I have been crucified with Christ and I no longer live, but Christ lives in me. The life I live in the body, I live by faith in the Son of God, who loved me and gave himself for me. I do not set aside the grace of God, for if righteousness could be gained through the law, Christ died for nothing!

If we were not already familiar with verse 20, it would strike us as quite extraordinary. That Jesus Christ was crucified under Pontius Pilate is an established historical fact; but what could Paul possibly mean by writing that *he* had been crucified with Christ? As a physical fact it was manifestly not true, and as a spiritual fact it was hard to understand.

We need to examine the context. Verses 15–21 are in general about just-ification, how a righteous God can declare the unrighteous righteous. But in particular they assert that sinners are justified not by the law (referred to 7 times) but by God's grace through faith. Three times in verse 16 the apostle insists that nobody can be justified by the law. It would hardly have been possible to state more forcibly than this the impossibility of self justification, that is, of winning God's acceptance by obeying the law. Why is this? Because the law condemns sin and prescribes death as its penalty. Thus the function of the law is to condemn, not to justify.

Since the law clamours for my death as a law-breaker, how can I possibly be justified? Only by meeting the law's requirement and dying the death it demands. If I were to do this myself, however, that would be the finish of me. So God has provided another way. Christ has borne the penalty of my law-breaking, and the blessing of what he has done has become mine because I am united with him. Being one with Christ, I am able to say, 'I died to the law' (v. 19), meeting its demands, because 'I have been crucified with Christ' and now he lives in me (v. 20).

As in Romans 6, so in Galatians 2, the assertion of our death and resur-rection with Christ is Paul's answer to the charge of antinomianism. Granted, nobody can be justified by law-observance. But that does not mean that I am free to break the law. On the contrary, it is inconceivable that I should continue in sin. Why so? Because I have died; I have been cru-cified with Christ; my old sinful life has received the condemnation it deserved. In consequence I (the old, sinful, guilty I) live no longer. But Christ lives in me. Or, since plainly I am still alive, I can say that the life I now live is an entirely different life. It is the old 'I' (sinful, rebellious, guilty) which lives no longer. It is the new 'I' (justified and free from condemnation) who lives by faith in the Son of God who loved me and gave himself for me.

It is important to grasp that Paul is referring to the death and resurrection of Christ, and to our death and resurrection through union with him. He puts the same truth in two ways. Regarding the *death* of our old life, he can say both that 'he loved me and gave himself for me' and that 'I died ... I have been crucified with Christ'. Regarding the *resurrection* to new life, he can say both that 'Christ lives in me' and that 'I live for God' (v. 19) or 'I live by faith in the Son of God' (v. 20).

To sum up, Christ died for me, and I died with him, meeting the law's demands and paying sin's just penalty. Then Christ rose again and lives, and I live through him, sharing in his resurrection life. Justification by faith, then, does not set aside God's grace (v. 21). Nor (as in Rom. 6) does it presume on it, saying 'where sin abounds, grace abounds much more'. No, justification by faith magnifies the grace of God, declaring that it is by his grace alone. It is the notion of justification by law which sets aside the grace of God, for if a righteous status before God were attainable by law-obedience, then Christ's death was superfluous.

3. The cross and preaching (3:1–3)

> You foolish Galatians! Who has bewitched you? Before your very eyes Jesus Christ was clearly portrayed as crucified. I would like to learn just one thing from you: Did you receive the Spirit by observing the law, or by believing what you heard? Are you so foolish? After beginning with the Spirit, are you now trying to attain your goal by human effort?

Paul has just described (in 2:11–14) his public showdown with Peter in Antioch, because Peter had withdrawn from table fellowship with Gentile Christians and so in effect had contradicted God's free acceptance of them by his grace. He has gone on to rehearse the arguments he had used with Peter to prove the doctrine of justification by faith. Now he breaks out into an expression of astonished indignation. He accuses the Galatians of folly. Twice he uses the word 'senseless' (*anoētos*), which is to be lacking in *nous*, intelligence. Their folly is so uncharacteristic and so unacceptable that he asks who has 'bewitched' them. He implies that a spell must have been cast over them, perhaps by the Arch-deceiver, though doubtless through human false teachers. For their present distortion of the gospel is totally incompatible with what they have heard from Paul and Barnabas. He therefore reminds them of his preaching when he was with them. He 'publicly portrayed' (RSV) Jesus Christ before their eyes as having been crucified for them. How then could they imagine that, having begun their Christian life by faith in Christ crucified, they needed to continue it by their own achievement?

There is much to learn from this text about the preaching of the gospel.

First, *gospel-preaching is proclaiming the cross.* True, the resurrection must be added (1:1; 2:19–20). So must Jesus' birth of a woman, and under the law (4:4). But the gospel is in essence the good news of Christ crucified.

Secondly, *gospel-preaching is proclaiming the cross visually.* Paul uses a remarkable verb, *prographō.* Usually it means to 'write previously': for example, 'as I have already written' (Eph. 3:3). But *graphō* can sometimes mean to 'draw' or 'paint', rather than to 'write', and *pro* can mean 'before' in space (before our eyes) rather than in time (previously). So Paul here likens his gospel-preaching either to a huge canvas painting or to a placard publicly exhibiting a notice or advertisement. The subject of his painting or placard was Jesus Christ on the cross. Of course it was not literally a painting; the picture was created by words. Yet it was so visual, so vivid, in its appeal to their imagination, that the placard was presented 'before your very eyes'. One of the greatest arts or gifts in gospel-preaching is to turn people's ears into eyes, and to make them *see* what we are talking about.

Thirdly, *gospel-preaching proclaims the cross visually as a present reality.* Jesus Christ had been crucified at least fifteen years before Paul was writing, and in our case nearly two millennia ago. What Paul did by his preaching (and we must do by ours) was to bring that event out of the past into the present. The ministry of both word and sacrament can do this. It can overcome the time-barrier and make past events present realities in such a way that people have to respond to them. Almost certainly none of Paul's readers had been present at the crucifixion of Jesus; yet Paul's preaching brought it before their eyes so that they could see it, and into their existential experience so that they must either accept or reject it.

Fourthly, *gospel-preaching proclaims the cross as a visual, present and permanent reality.* For what we (like Paul) are to placard before people's eyes is not just *Christos staurōtheis* (aorist) but *Christos estaurōmenos* (perfect). The tense of the verb emphasizes not so much that the cross was a historical event of the past as that its validity, power and benefits are permanent. The cross will never cease to be God's power for salvation to believers.

Fifthly, *gospel-preaching proclaims the cross also as the object of personal faith.* Paul did not placard Christ crucified before their eyes so that they might simply gape and stare. His purpose was to persuade them to come and put their trust in him as their crucified Saviour. And this is what they had done. The reason for Paul's astonishment was that, having received justification and the Spirit by faith, they should imagine that they could continue in the Christian life by their own achievements. It was a contradiction of what Paul had presented before their eyes.

4. The cross and substitution (3:10–14)

All who rely on observing the law are under a curse, for it is written: 'Cursed is everyone who does not continue to do everything written in the Book of the Law.' Clearly no-one is justified before God by the law, because, 'The righteous will live by faith.' The law is not based on faith; on the contrary, 'The man who does these things will live by them.' Christ redeemed us from the curse of the law by becoming a curse for us, for it is written: 'Cursed is everyone who is hanged on a tree.' He redeemed us in order that the blessing given to Abraham might come to the Gentiles through Christ Jesus, so that by faith we might receive the promise of the Spirit.

These verses constitute one of the clearest expositions of the necessity, meaning and consequence of the cross. Paul expresses himself in such stark terms that some commentators have not been able to accept what he writes about the 'curse' which Christ 'became' for us. A. W. F. Blunt, for example, wrote in his commentary: 'The language here is startling, almost shocking. We should not have dared to use it.'[1] Jeremias also called it a 'shocking phrase' and spoke of its 'original offensiveness'.[2] Nevertheless, the apostle Paul did use this language, and Blunt was surely correct in adding that 'Paul means every word of it'. So we have to come to terms with it.

Several attempts have been made to soften it. First, it has been suggested that Paul deliberately de-personalized the 'curse' by calling it 'the curse of the law'. But the expression in Deuteronomy 21:23 is 'God's curse'; it cannot seriously be entertained that Paul is contradicting Scripture. Secondly, it has been proposed that his 'becoming' a curse expresses the sympathy of Christ for law-breakers, not an objective acceptance of their judgment. Here is Blunt's interpretation: 'It was not by a forensic fiction that Christ bore our sins, but by an act of genuine fellow feeling', like a mother who has a son who goes wrong and who 'feels his guilt to be hers as well'.[3] But this is an evasion; it does not do justice to Paul's words. As Jeremias put it, 'became' is 'a circumlocution for the action of God'.

Thirdly, it is said, Paul's statement that Christ became 'a curse' for us falls short of saying that he was actually 'cursed'. But according to Jeremias, 'curse' is 'a metonym for "the cursed one" ', and we should translate the phrase 'God made Christ a cursed one for our sake'. It is then parallel to 'God made him who had no sin to be sin for us' (2 Cor. 5:21). And we shall be able to accept the two phrases, and indeed worship God for their truth, because 'God was in Christ reconciling' (2 Cor. 5:19) even while he made Christ both sin and a curse.

Luther grasped very clearly what Paul meant, and expressed its implications with characteristic directness:

Our most merciful Father, seeing us to be oppressed and overwhelmed with the curse of the law, and so to be holden under the same that we could never be delivered from it by our own power, sent his only Son into the world and laid upon him all the sins of all men, saying: Be thou Peter that denier; Paul that persecutor, blasphemer and cruel oppressor; David that adulterer; that sinner which did eat the apple in Paradise; that thief which hanged upon the cross; and briefly, be thou the person which hath committed the sins of all men; see therefore that thou pay and satisfy for them.[4]

We need to feel the logic of Paul's teaching. First, *all who rely on the law are under a curse.* At the beginning of verse 10 Paul again uses the expression he used three times in 2:16, namely 'those who are of works of law' (literally), which NIV elaborates as 'all who rely on observing the law'. The reason Paul can declare such to be 'under a curse' is that Scripture says they are: 'Cursed is everyone who does not continue to do everything written in the Book of the Law' (*cf.* Dt. 27:26). No human being has ever 'continued' to do 'everything' the law requires. Such a continuous and comprehensive obedience has been given by no-one except Jesus. So 'clearly' (v. 11) nobody 'is justified before God by the law', because nobody has kept it. Besides, Scripture also says that 'the righteous will live by his faith' (Hab. 2:4), and living 'by faith' and living 'by law' are two completely different states (v. 12). The conclusion is unavoidable. Although theoretically those who obey the law will live, in practice none of us will, because none of us has obeyed. Therefore we cannot obtain salvation that way. On the contrary, far from being saved by the law, we are cursed by it. The curse or judgment of God, which his law pronounces on law-breakers, rests upon us. This is the appalling predicament of lost humankind.

Secondly, *Christ redeemed us from the curse of the law by becoming a curse for us.* This is probably the plainest statement in the New Testament of substitution. The curse of the broken law rested on us; Christ redeemed us from it by becoming a curse in our place. The curse that lay on us was transferred to him. He assumed it, that we might escape it. And the evidence that he bore our curse is that he hung on a tree, since Deuteronomy 21:23 declares such a person cursed (v. 13).

Thirdly, Christ did this *in order that in him the blessing of Abraham might come to the Gentiles ... by faith* (v. 14). The apostle moves deliberately from the language of cursing to that of blessing. Christ died for us not only to redeem us from the curse of God, but also to secure for us the blessing of God. He had promised centuries previously to bless Abraham and through his posterity the Gentile nations. And this promised blessing Paul here interprets as 'justification' (v. 8) and 'the Spirit' (v. 14); all who are in Christ are thus richly blessed.

To sum up, because of our disobedience we were under the curse of the law. Christ redeemed us from it by bearing it in our place. As a result, we receive by faith in Christ the promised blessing of salvation. The sequence is irresistible. It prompts our humble worship that God in Christ, in his holy love for us, was willing to go to such lengths, and that the blessings we enjoy today are due to the curse he bore for us on the cross.

5. The cross and persecution (5:11; 6:12)

> Brothers, if I am still preaching circumcision, why am I still being persecuted? In that case the offence of the cross has been abolished.

> Those who want to make a good impression outwardly are trying to compel you to be circumcised. The only reason they do this is to avoid being persecuted for the cross of Christ.

The cross of Christ is mentioned in both these verses, and in 5:11 it is called an 'offence' or 'stumbling-block' (*skandalon*). In both verses too there is a reference to persecution. According to 5:11 Paul is being persecuted because he preaches the cross; according to 6:12 the false teachers are avoiding persecution by preaching circumcision instead of the cross. So the alternative for Christian evangelists, pastors and teachers is to preach either circumcision or the cross.

To 'preach circumcision' is to preach salvation by the law, that is, by human achievement. Such a message removes the offence of the cross, which is that we cannot earn our salvation; it therefore exempts us from persecution.

To 'preach the cross' (as in 3:1) is to preach salvation by God's grace alone. Such a message is a stumbling-block (1 Cor. 1:23) because it is grievously offensive to human pride; it therefore exposes us to persecution.

There are, of course, no Judaizers in the world today, preaching the necessity of circumcision. But there are plenty of false teachers, inside as well as outside the church, who preach the false gospel (which is not a gospel, 1:7) of salvation by good works. To preach salvation by good works is to flatter people and so avoid opposition. To preach salvation by grace is to offend people and so invite opposition. This may seem to some to pose the alternative too starkly. But I do not think so. All Christian preachers have to face this issue. Either we preach that human beings are rebels against God, under his just judgment and (if left to themselves) lost, and that Christ crucified who bore their sin and curse is the only available Saviour. Or we emphasize human potential and human ability, with Christ brought in only to boost them, and with no necessity for the cross except to exhibit God's love and so inspire us to greater endeavour.

The former is the way to be faithful, the latter the way to be popular. It is not possible to be faithful and popular simultaneously. We need to hear again the warning of Jesus: 'Woe to you when all men speak well of you' (Lk. 6:26). By contrast, if we preach the cross, we may find that we are ourselves hounded to the cross. As Erasmus wrote in his treatise *On Preaching*: 'Let him [*sc.* the preacher] remember that the cross will never be lacking to those who sincerely preach the gospel. There are always Herods, Ananiases, Caiaphases, Scribes and Pharisees.'[5]

6. The cross and holiness (5:24)

> Those who belong to Christ Jesus have crucified the sinful nature with its passions and desires.

It is essential to see this text (as indeed every text) in its context. Paul in Galatians 5 is concerned with the meaning of moral freedom. He declares that it is not self-indulgence but self-control, not serving ourselves but serving each other in love (v. 13). Behind this alternative is the inner conflict of which all Christian people are conscious. The apostle calls the protagonists 'the flesh' (our fallen nature with which we are born) and 'the Spirit' (the Holy Spirit himself who indwells us when we are born again). In verses 16–18 he describes the contest between the two, because the desires of the flesh and of the Spirit are contrary to each other.

The acts of the flesh (vv. 19–21) include sexual immorality, religious apostasy (idolatry and witchcraft), social breakdown (hatred, discord, jealousy, temper, selfish ambition and factions) and uncontrolled physical appetites (drunkenness and orgies). The fruit of the Spirit (vv. 22–23), however, the graces which he causes to ripen in the people he fills, include love, joy and peace (specially in relation to God), patience, kindness and goodness (in relation to each other), and faithfulness, gentleness and self-control (in relation to ourselves).

How then can we ensure that the desires of the Spirit predominate over the desires of the flesh? Paul replies that it depends on the attitude which we adopt to each. According to verse 24 we are to 'crucify' the flesh, with its evil passions and desires. According to verse 25 we are to 'live by' and 'keep in step with' the Spirit.

My concern in this chapter is with verse 24, because of its assertion that those who belong to Christ have 'crucified' their flesh or sinful nature. It is an astonishing metaphor. For crucifixion was a horrible, brutal form of execution. Yet it illustrates graphically what our attitude to our fallen nature is to be. We are not to coddle or cuddle it, not to pamper or spoil it, not to give it any encouragement or even toleration. Instead, we are to be ruthlessly fierce in rejecting it, together with its desires. Paul is elaborating the teaching of Jesus about 'taking up the cross' and following him. He is telling us what happens when we reach the place of execution: the actual crucifixion takes place. Luther writes that Christ's people nail their flesh to the cross, 'so that although the flesh be yet alive, yet can it not perform that which it would do, forasmuch as it is bound both hand and foot, and fast nailed to the cross'.[6] And if we are not ready to crucify ourselves in this decisive manner, we shall soon find that instead we are 'crucifying the Son of God all over again'. The essence of apostasy is 'changing sides from that of the Crucified to that of the crucifiers'.[7]

The crucifixions of Galatians 2:20 and 5:24 refer to two quite different things, as mentioned in an earlier chapter. The first says that we have been crucified with Christ (it has happened to us as a result of our union with Christ), and the second that the people of Christ have themselves taken action to crucify their old nature. The first speaks of our freedom from the condemnation of the law by sharing in *Christ's* crucifixion, the second of our freedom from the power of the flesh by ensuring *its* crucifixion. These two, namely to have been crucified with Christ (passive) and to have crucified the flesh (active), must not be confused.

7. The cross and boasting (6:14)

> May I never boast except in the cross of our Lord Jesus Christ, through which the world has been crucified to me, and I to the world.

There is no exact equivalent in the English language to *kauchaomai*. It means to boast in, glory in, trust in, rejoice in, revel in, live for. The object of our boast or 'glory' fills our horizons, engrosses our attention, and absorbs our time and energy. In a word, our 'glory' is our obsession.

Some people are obsessed with themselves and their money, fame or power; the false teachers in Galatia were triumphalists, obsessed with the number of their converts (v. 13); but Paul's obsession was with Christ and his cross. That which the average Roman citizen regarded as an object of shame, disgrace and even disgust was for Paul his pride, boasting and glory. Moreover, we cannot dismiss this as Pauline idiosyncrasy. For, as we have seen, the cross was central to the mind of Christ, and has always been central to the faith of the church.

First, to glory or boast in the cross is to see it as *the way of acceptance with God*. The most important of all questions is how we, as lost and guilty sinners, may stand before a just and holy God. It was to answer this question loud and clear that Paul, in the passionate heat of his controversy with the Judaizers, dashed off his letter to the Galatians. Like them, some people today still trust in their own merits. But God forbid that we should boast except in the cross. The cross excludes all other kinds of boasting (Rom. 3:27).

Secondly, to glory or boast in the cross is to see it as *the pattern of our self-denial*. Although Paul writes of only one cross ('the cross of our Lord Jesus Christ'), he refers to two crucifixions, even three. On the same cross on which our Lord Jesus Christ was himself crucified, 'the world has been crucified to me, and I to the world'. The 'world' thus crucified (repudiated) does not of course mean the people of the world (for we are called to love and serve them), but the values of the world, its godless materialism, vanity and hypocrisy (for we are told not to love these, but to reject them). 'The flesh' has already been crucified (5:24); now 'the world' joins it on the cross. We ought to keep the two main crucifixions of 6:14 in close relation to each other – Christ's and ours. For they are not two, but one. It is only the sight of Christ's cross which will make us willing, and even anxious, to take up ours. It is only then that we shall be able with integrity to repeat Paul's words after him that we glory in nothing but the cross.

We have now considered Paul's seven great affirmations about the cross in the letter to the Galatians, and have looked at them in the order in which they occur. It may be helpful, in conclusion, to re-arrange and group them in theological rather than chronological order, in order to grasp yet more firmly the centrality and pervasiveness of the cross in every sphere of Christian living.

First, the cross is *the ground of our justification*. Christ has rescued us from the present evil age (1:4) and redeemed us from the curse of the law (3:13). And the reason why he has delivered us from this double bondage is that we may stand boldly before God as his sons and daughters, declared righteous and indwelt by his Spirit.

Secondly, the cross is *the means of our sanctification*. This is where the three other crucifixions come in. We have been crucified with Christ (2:20). We have crucified our fallen nature (5:24). And the world has been crucified to us, as we have been to the world (6:14). So the cross means more than the crucifixion of Jesus; it includes our crucifixion, the crucifixion of our flesh and of the world.

Thirdly, the cross is *the subject of our witness*. We are to placard Christ crucified publicly before people's eyes, so that they may see and believe (3:1). In doing so, we must not bowdlerize the gospel, extracting from it its offence to human pride. No, whatever the price may be, we preach the cross (the merit of Christ), not circumcision (the merit of man); it is the only way of salvation (5:11; 6:12).

Fourthly, the cross is *the object of our boasting*. God forbid that we should boast in anything else (6:14). Paul's whole world was in orbit round the cross. It filled his vision, illumined his life, warmed his spirit. He 'gloried' in it. It meant more to him than anything else. Our perspective should be the same.

If the cross is not central in these four spheres for us, then we deserve to have applied to us that most terrible of all descriptions, 'enemies of the cross of Christ' (Phil. 3:18). To be an enemy of the cross is to set ourselves against its purposes. Self-righteousness (instead of looking to the cross for justification), self-indulgence (instead of taking up the cross to follow Christ), self-advertisement (instead of preaching Christ crucified) and self-glorification (instead of glorying in the cross) – these are the distortions which make us 'enemies' of Christ's cross.

Paul, on the other hand, was a devoted friend of the cross. So closely had he identified himself with it, that he suffered physical persecution for it. 'I bear on my body the marks of Jesus' (Gal. 6:17), he wrote, the wounds and scars he had received in proclaiming Christ crucified, the *stigmata* which branded him as Christ's authentic slave.

The *stigmata* of Jesus, in the spirit if not in the body, remain a mark of authentication for every Christian disciple, and especially every Christian witness. Campbell Morgan expressed it well:

It is the crucified man that can preach the cross. Said Thomas, 'except I shall see in his hands the print of the nails … I will not believe'. Dr. Parker of London said that what Thomas said of Christ, the world is saying about the church. And the world is also saying to every preacher: Unless I see in your hands the print of the nails, I will not believe. It is true. It is the man … who has died with Christ, … that can preach the cross of Christ.[8]

Notes

1 A. W. F. Blunt, *Galatians*, p. 96.

2 Joachim Jeremias, *Central Message*, p. 35.

3 A. W. F. Blunt, *Galatians*, p. 97.

4 Martin Luther, *Epistle to the Galatians*, p. 272.

5 Quoted by Roland H. Bainton, in *Erasmus of Christendom*, p. 323.

6 Martin Luther, *Epistle to the Galatians*, p. 527.

7 Heb. 6:4–6; 10:26–27. *Cf.* C. F. D. Moule, *Sacrifice of Christ*, p. 30.

8 G. Campbell Morgan, *Evangelism*, pp. 59–60.

BIBLIOGRAPHY

Only works mentioned in the text are included in the Bibliography. With a few exceptions non-English works are given in an accessible English translation where a suitable one is widely available.

Abelard, P. See Fairweather, E. (ed.), *A Scholastic Miscellany*.

Anderson, J. N. D., *Morality, Law and Grace* (Tyndale Press, 1972).

Anglican Roman Catholic International Commission (ARCIC), *Final Report* (Catholic Truth Society and SPCK, 1982).

Anselm, *Cur Deus Homo?* (1098), tr. Edward S. Prout (Religious Tract Society, 1880).

Atkinson, David, *Peace in Our Time?* (IVP, 1985).

Atkinson, James, *Rome and Reformation Today*. Latimer Studies no. 12 (Latimer House, 1982).

Aulén, Gustav, *Christus Victor* (1930; SPCK, 1931).

Bailey, Kenneth, *The Cross and the Prodigal* (Concordia, 1973).

Bainton, Roland H., *Erasmus of Christendom* (1969; Collins, 1970).

Baptism, Eucharist and Ministry. Faith and Order Paper no. 111 (World Council of Churches, 1982).

Barclay, O. R., *Whatever Happened to the Jesus Lane Lot?* (IVP, 1977).

Barclay, William, *Crucified and Crowned* (SCM, 1961).

Barraclough, Geoffrey (ed.), *The Christian World: A Social and Cultural History of Christianity* (Thames & Hudson, 1981).

Barth, Karl, *Church Dogmatics*, ed. G. W. Bromiley and T. F. Torrance, tr. G. W. Bromiley (T. & T. Clark, 1956–57).

Bauernfeind, O., '*nikaō*', in *Theological Dictionary of the New Testament*, vol. IV (Eerdmans, 1967), pp. 942–945.

Baxter, Richard, *The Saints' Everlasting Rest* (1650), in *Practical Works*, vol. xxiii, ed. William Orme (James Duncan, 1830).

Beckwith, R. T., Duffield, G. E. and Packer, J. I., *Across the Divide* (Marcham Manor Press, 1977).

Beeson, Trevor, *Discretion and Valour: Religious Conditions in Russia and Eastern Europe* (Collins, 1974).

Behm, Johannes, '*haima*', in *Theological Dictionary of the New Testament*, vol. I (Eerdmans, 1964), pp. 172–177.

Berkhof, Hendrik, *Christ and the Powers*, tr. John Howard Yoder (Herald Press, 1962).

Berkouwer, G. C., *The Work of Christ* (Eerdmans, 1965).

Blunt, A. W. F., *The Epistle of Paul to the Galatians.* The Clarendon Bible (OUP, 1925).

Bonhoeffer, Dietrich, *The Cost of Discipleship*, tr. R. H. Fuller (1937; SCM, 1964).

— *Letters and Papers from Prison* (1953; SCM, 1971).

Boswell, James, *Life of Johnson.* 2 vols. (Dutton, 1927).

Brasnett, B. R., *The Suffering of the Impassible God* (SPCK, 1928).

Bruce, F. F., *Colossians. See under* Simpson, E. K. and Bruce, F. F.

Brunner, Emil, *Man in Revolt: A Christian Anthropology*, tr. Olive Wyon (1937; Lutterworth, 1939).

— *The Mediator*, tr. Olive Wyon (1927; Westminster Press, 1947).

Buchanan, Colin (ed.), *Essays on Eucharistic Sacrifice in the Early Church.* Grove Liturgical Study no. 40 (Grove Books, 1984).

Büchsel, F., '*allassō* and *katallassō*', in *Theological Dictionary of the New Testament*, vol. I (Eerdmans, 1964), pp. 251–259.

— and Hermann, J., '*hilaskomai*', in Theological Dictionary of the New Testament, vol. III (Eerdmans, 1965), pp. 300–323.

Bühlmann, Walbert, *The Coming of the Third Church* (1974; Orbis, 1978).

Bultmann, Rudolf, *Kerygma and Myth*, ed. Hans Werner Bartsch, tr. R. H. Fuller, 2 vols. (1948; SPCK, 1953).

Bushnell, Horace, *Forgiveness and Law, Grounded in Principles Interpreted by Human Analogies* (Scribner, Armstrong & Co, 1874).

— *The Vicarious Sacrifice, Grounded in Principles of Universal Obligation* (Alexander Strahan, 1866).

Buttrick, George A., *Jesus Came Preaching.* The 1931 Yale Lectures (Scribner, 1931).

Caird, G. B., *Principalities and Powers: A Study in Pauline Theology* (Clarendon Press, 1956).

Calvin, John, *Commentary on a Harmony of the Evangelists Matthew, Mark and Luke*, tr. W. Pringle. 3 vols. (Eerdmans, 1965).

— *Commentary on the Gospel According to St John*, tr. T. H. L. Parker. 2 vols. (Oliver & Boyd, 1961).

— *Institutes of the Christian Religion* (1559), in the Library of Christian Classics, vols. XX and XXI, ed. John T. McNeill, tr. Ford Lewis Battles (Westminster Press, 1960).

Campbell, John McLeod, *The Nature of the Atonement, and its Relation to Remission of Sins and Eternal Life* (1856; Macmillan, 4th ed. 1873).

Carey, George L., 'Justification by Faith in Recent Roman Catholic Theology', in *The Great Acquittal*, et. Gavin Reid (Collins, 1980).

— 'The Lamb of God and Atonement Theories', *Tyndale Bulletin* 32 (1983), pp. 97–122.

Christian Witness to Traditional Religionists of Asia and Oceania. Lausanne Occasional Paper no. 16 (Lausanne Committee for World Evangelization, 1980).

Church of England Evangelical Council, *Evangelical Anglicans and the ARCIC Final Report* (Grove Books, 1982).

Cicero, *Against Verres*, tr. L. H. G. Greenwood, *The Verrine Orations*. 2 vols. (Heinemann, 1928–35).

— *In Defense of Rabirius*, tr. H. G. Hodge, *The Speeches of Cicero* (Heinemann, 1927), pp. 452–491.

Clarkson, Margaret, *Destined for Glory: The Meaning of Suffering* (Eerdmans and Marshalls, 1983).

Clement of Alexandria, *Stromateis* (Miscellanies), in *The Ante-Nicene Fathers*, vol. II, ed. A. Roberts and J. Donaldson (1885; Eerdmans, 1975), pp. 299–567.

Clow, W. M., *The Cross in Christian Experience* (Hodder & Stoughton, 1910).

Coates, R. J., 'The Doctrine of Eucharistic Sacrifice in Modern Times', in *Eucharistic Sacrifice*, ed. J. I. Packer (Church Book Room Press, 1962), pp. 127–153.

Coggan, F. Donald (ed.), *Christ and the Colleges: A History of the Inter-Varsity Fellowship of Evangelical Unions* (IVFEU, 1934).

— *The Glory of God: Four Studies in a Ruling Biblical Concept* (CMS, 1950).

Council of Trent. *See* Schroeder, H. J., *Canons and Decrees.*

Cox, Harvey G., *On Not Leaving it to the Snake* (1964; SCM, 1968).

Craig, Mary, *Blessings: An Autobiographical Fragment* (Hodder & Stoughton, 1979).

Cranfield, C. E. B., *The Epistle to the Romans*. International Critical Commentary. 2 vols. (T. & T. Clark, 1975–79).

— *The Gospel According to St Mark*. Cambridge Greek New Testament Commentary (CUP, 1959).

Cranmer, Thomas, *On the Lord's Supper* (1550); reprinted from *The Remains of Thomas Cranmer*, ed. H. Jenkyns (1833; Thynne, 1907).

— *First Book of Homilies* (1547; SPCK, 1914).

Crawford, Thomas J., *The Doctrine of Holy Scripture Respecting the Atonement* (Wm Blackwood, 1871; 5th ed. 1888).

Cullmann, Oscar, *Baptism in the New Testament*, tr. J. K. L. Reid (1950; SCM, 1951).

— *The Christology of the New Testament*, tr. S. C. Guthrie and C. A. M. Hall (1957; SCM, 1959).

Cyprian, *Ad Thibaritanos* and *De Lapsis*, in *The Ante-Nicene Fathers*, vol. V, tr. Ernest Wallis (Eerdmans, 1981).

Dale, R. W., *The Atonement* (Congregational Union, 1894).

Denney, James, 'Anger', in *A Dictionary of Christ and the Gospels*, ed. James Hastings, vol. I (T. & T. Clark, 1906), pp. 60–62.

— *The Atonement and the Modern Mind* (Hodder & Stoughton, 1903).

— *The Death of Christ*, ed. R. V. G. Tasker (1902; Tyndale Press, 1951).

Didache, in *Early Christian Fathers*, vol. I, tr. and ed. Cyril C. Richardson (SCM, 1953), pp. 161–179.

Dimock, Nathaniel, *The Doctrine of the Death of Christ: In Relation to the Sin of Man, the Condemnation of the Law, and the Dominion of Satan* (Elliot Stock, 1890).

Dix, Gregory (ed.), *The Apostolic Tradition of St Hippolytus of Rome* (SPCK, 1937).

— *The Shape of the Liturgy* (Dacre Press, 1945).

Dodd, C. H., *The Bible and the Greeks* (Hodder & Stoughton, 1935).

— *The Epistle of Paul to the Romans*. The Moffatt New Testament Commentary (Hodder & Stoughton, 1932).

— '*hilaskesthai*, Its Cognates, Derivatives and Synonyms, in the Septuagint', *Journal of Theological Studies* 32 (1931), pp. 352–360.

— *The Johannine Epistles*. The Moffatt New Testament Commentary (Hodder & Stoughton, 1946).

Dunstone, A. S., *The Atonement in Gregory of Nyssa* (Tyndale Press, 1964).

Eareckson, Joni, *Joni* (Zondervan, 1976).

— *A Step Further* (Zondervan, 1978).

Edwall, P., Hayman, E. and Maxwell, W. D. (eds.), *Ways of Worship* (SCM, 1951).

England, R. G., *Justification Today: The Roman Catholic and Anglican Debate*. Latimer Studies no. 4 (Latimer House, 1979).

Epistle to Diognetus, in *The Ante-Nicene Fathers*, vol. I, ed. A. Roberts and J. Donaldson (1885; Eerdmans, 1981), pp. 23–30.

Fairweather, Eugene (ed.), *A Scholastic Miscellany: Anselm to Ockham*. Library of Christian Classics, vol. X (Macmillan, 1970).

Fichtner, Johannes, 'orgē', in *Theological Dictionary of the New Testament*, vol. V (Eerdmans, 1967), pp. 394–108.

Forsyth, P. T., *The Cruciality of the Cross* (Hodder & Stoughton, 1909).

— *The Justification of God* (Duckworth, 1916).

— *The Work of Christ* (Hodder & Stoughton, 1910).

Foxe, John, *Book of Martyrs* (1554; Religious Tract Society, 1926).

Franks, Robert S., *A History of the Doctrine of the Work of Christ, in its Ecclesiastical Development* (Hodder & Stoughton, 1918).

— *The Work of Christ: A Historical Study of Christian Doctrine* (1918; Thomas Nelson, 1962).

Gandhi, Mahatma, *An Autobiography* (1948; Jonathan Cape, 1966).

Glasser, William, *Reality Therapy: A New Approach to Psychiatry* (Harper & Row, 1965).

Glover, T. R., *The Jesus of History* (SCM, 1917; 2nd ed. 1920).

Gough, Michael, *The Origins of Christian Art* (Thames & Hudson, 1973).

Green, E. M. B., 'Christ's Sacrifice and Ours', in *Guidelines: Anglican Evangelicals Face the Future*, ed. J. I. Packer (Falcon, 1967), pp. 89–117.

— *The Empty Cross of Jesus* (Hodder & Stoughton, 1984).

— 'Eucharistic Sacrifice in the New Testament and the Early Fathers', in *Eucharistic Sacrifice*, ed. J. I. Packer (Church Book Room Press, 1962), pp. 58–83.

— *I Believe in Satan's Downfall* (1981; Hodder & Stoughton, 1984).

Green, Peter, *Watchers by the Cross: Thoughts on the Seven Last Words* (Longmans Green, 1934).

Gregory of Nazianzus, *Orations*, in *Nicene and Post-Nicene Fathers*, vol. III, ed. Philip Schaff and Henry Wace, tr. C. G. Browne and J. E. Swallow (1893; Eerdmans, 1981), pp. 203–434.

Gregory of Nyssa, *The Catechetical Oration*, in *Nicene and Post-Nicene Fathers*, vol. V, ed. Philip Schaff and Henry Wace, tr. W. Moore and H. A. Wilson (1892; Eerdmans, 1979), pp. 473–509.

Grotius, Hugo, *A Defence of the Catholic Faith concerning the Satisfaction of Christ against Faustus Socinus* (1617), tr. F. H. Foster (W. F. Draper, 1889).

Grubb, Norman P., *Once Caught, No Escape: My Life Story* (Lutterworth, 1969).

Guillebaud, H. E., *Why the Cross?* (IVF, 1937).

Hamley, Colonel (Edward Bruce), *Voltaire* (W. Blackwood & Sons, 1877).

Hanson, A. T., *The Wrath of the Lamb* (SPCK, 1959).

Hardy, Alister, *The Divine Flame* (Collins, 1966).

Hart, H. L. A., *Punishment and Responsibility* (OUP, 1968).

Hebert, G. *See under* Edwall, P. *et al.*, *Ways of Worship.*

Heiler, Friedrich, *The Gospel of Sadhu Sundar Singh* (1924; George Allen & Unwin, 1927).

Hengel, Martin, *The Atonement: The Origin of the Doctrine in the New Testament*, tr. John Bowden (1980; SCM, 1981).

— *Crucifixion*, tr. John Bowden (SCM, 1976; Fortress Press, 1977); originally *Mors turpissima crucis.*

Heschel, Abraham, *The Prophets* (Harper & Row, 1962).

Hoekema, Anthony A., *The Christian Looks at Himself* (Eerdmans, 1975).

Hooker, Richard, *Of the Laws of Ecclesiastical Polity* (1593-97), in *The Works of Richard Hooker*, ed. John Keble. 3 vols. (OUP, 3rd ed. 1845).

— 'Sermon on Habakkuk i. 4' (1585), in *The Works of Richard Hooker*, ed. John Keble, vol. III (OUP, 3rd ed. 1845), pp. 483-547.

Ignatius, *Ad Ephesios, in The Ante-Nicene Fathers*, vol. I, ed. A. Roberts and J. Donaldson (1885; Eerdmans, 1981), pp. 49–58.

— *Ad Polycarp*, in *The Ante-Nicene Fathers*, vol. I, ed. A. Roberts and J. Donaldson (1885; Eerdmans, 1981), 99–100.

Imbert, Jean, *Le Procès de Jésus* (Presses Universitaires de France, 1980).

Irenaeus, *Adversus Haereses*, in *The Ante-Nicene Fathers*, vol. I, ed. A. Roberts and J. Donaldson (1885; Eerdmans, 1981), pp. 315–567.

Jeeves, Malcolm A., Berry, R J. and Atkinson, David, *Free to Be Different* (Marshalls, 1984).

Jeremias, Joachim, *The Central Message of the New Testament* (1955; SCM, 1966).

— *The Eucharistic Words of Jesus*, tr. N. Perrin (OUP, 1955).

— and Zimmerli, W., '*pais Theou*', in *Theological Dictionary of the New Testament*, vol. V (Eerdmans, 1967), pp. 654–717.

— '*polloi*', in *Theological Dictionary of the New Testament*, vol. VI (Eerdmans, 1968).

— and Zimmerli, W., *The Servant of God* (1952; SCM, 1957).

Josephus, *Jewish Antiquities*, tr. H. St J. Thackeray, Ralph Marcus *et al.* 6 vols. (Heinemann, 1930–65).

— *Jewish War*, tr. H. St J. Thackeray. 2 vols. (Heinemann, 1927–28).

Justin Martyr, *Dialogue with Trypho a Jew*, in *The Ante-Nicene Fathers*, vol. I, ed. A. Roberts and J. Donaldson (1885; Eerdmans, 1981), pp. 194–270.

— *First Apology*, in *The Anti-Nicene Fathers*, vol. I, ed. A. Roberts and J. Donaldson (1885; Eerdmans, 1981), pp. 163–187.

Kidner, F. D., *Sacrifice in the Old Testament* (Tyndale Press, 1952).

King, Martin Luther, *Strength to Love* (1963; Hodder & Stoughton, 1964).

Kitamori, Kazoh, *Theology of the Pain of God* (1946; SCM, 1966).

Koran, The, tr. N. J. Dawood (Penguin, 3rd revised ed. 1958).

Küng, Hans, *Justification: The Doctrine of Karl Barth and a Catholic Reflection* (1957; Burns & Oates, 1964).

Lambeth Conference, *1958 Lambeth Conference Papers* (SPCK, 1958).

Lasserre, Jean, *War and the Gospel* (James Clarke, 1962).

Lewis, A. J., *Zinzendorf: The Eeumenical Pioneer. A Study in the Moravian Contribution to Christian Mission and Unity* (SCM, 1962).

Lewis, C. S., *The Four Loves* (Geoffrey Bles, 1960).

— 'The Humanitarian Theory of Punishment', in *Churchmen Speak*, ed. Philip E. Hughes (Marcham Manor Press, 1966), pp. 39–44.

— *The Problem of Pain* (1940; Collins Fontana, 1957).

— *Surprised by Joy* (Geoffrey Bles, 1955).

Lewis, W. H. (ed.), *Letters of C. S. Lewis* (Geoffrey Bles, 1966).

Loane, Marcus L., *Archbishop Mowll* (Hodder & Stoughton, 1960).

Lombard, Peter, *Book of Sentences (Sententiarum Libri Quatuor)*, in *Opera Omnia*, ed. J.-P. Migne, vol. 192 (Paris, 1880), pp. 521–1112.

Lucian, *The Passing of Peregrinus*, tr. A. M. Harman, in *The Works of Lucian*, vol. 5 (Heinemann, 1936), pp. 2–51.

Luther, Martin, *Commentary on the Epistle to the Galatians* (1535; James Clarke, 1953).

— *Letters of Spiritual Counsel*, in the Library of Christian Classics, vol. XVIII, ed. Theodore G. Tappert (SCM, 1955).

Mackintosh, Robert, *Historic Theories of the Atonement* (Hodder, 1920).

Maclaren, Alexander, *The Epistles of Paul to the Colossians and Philemon. The Expositor's Bible* (Hodder & Stoughton, 1896).

Marshall, 1. H., *The Work of Christ* (Paternoster Press, 1969).

McCrossan, T. J., *Bodily Healing and the Atonement*, ed. Roy Hicks and Kenneth E. Hagin (1930; Faith Library Publications, 1982).

McGrath, Alister, 'The Moral Theory of the Atonement: An Historical and Theological Critique', *Scottish Journal of Theology* 38 (1985), pp. 205–220.

Menninger, Karl, *Whatever Became of Sin?* (Hawthorn Books, 1973).

Miller, J. H., 'Cross' and 'Crucifix', in *The New Catholic Encyclopedia*, vol. 4 (McGraw Hill, 1980), pp. 473–479 and 485.

Moberly, R. C., *Atonement and Personality* (1901).

Moltmann, Jürgen, *The Crucified God: The Cross of Christ as the Foundation and Criticism of Christian Theology* (1973; SCM, 1974).

Morgan, G. Campbell, *Evangelism* (Henry E. Walter, 1964).

Morris, Leon, *The Apostolic Preaching of the Cross* (Tyndale Press, 1955).
— *The Atonement: Its Meaning and Significance* (IVP, 1983)
— *The Cross in the New Testament* (Paternoster Press, 1965).
— 'The use of *hilaskesthai* etc. in Biblical Greek', *The Expository Times* lxii.8 (1951), pp. 227–233.
Moule, C. F. D., *The Sacrifice of Christ* (Hodder & Stoughton, 1956).
Moule, Handley C. G., *Colossian Studies* (Hodder & Stoughton, 1898).
Mowrer, O. Hobart, *The Crisis in Psychiatry and Religion* (Van Nostrand, 1961).
Mozley, J. K., *The Doctrine of the Atonement* (Duckworth, 1915).
— *The Impassibility of God: A Survey of Christian Thought* (CUP, 1926).
Muggeridge, Malcolm, *Jesus Rediscovered* (Collins, 1969).
Murray, Iain H., *David Martyn Lloyd-Jones* (Banner of Truth, 1982).
Murray, John, *The Epistle to the Romans*. 2 vols. in 1 (Marshall, Morgan & Scott, 1960–65).
— *Redemption Accomplished and Applied* (Eerdmans, 1955; Banner of Truth, 1961).

Neil, William, *Apostle Extraordinary* (Religious Education Press, 1965).
Neill, S. C., *Christian Faith Today* (Penguin, 1955).
— *Crises of Belief* (Hodder & Stoughton, 1984).
— 'Jesus and History', in *Truth of God Incarnate*, ed. E. M. B. Green (Hodder & Stoughton, 1977).
Nicole, Roger R., 'C. H. Dodd and the Doctrine of Propitiation', *Westminster Theological Journal* xvii.2 (1955), pp. 117–157.
Nietzsche, Friedrich, *The Anti-Christ* (1895; Penguin, 1968).
Nygren, Anders, *Agape and Eros: A Study of the Christian Idea of Love*, tr. A. G. Hebert. 2 vols. (SPCK, 1932–39).
— *A Commentary on Romans* (1944; Fortress Press, 1949).

O'Brien, Peter, *Commentary on Colossians*. Word Biblical Commentary, vol. 44 (Word Books, 1982).
— 'Principalities and Powers, Opponents of the Church', in *Biblical Interpretation and the Church: Text and Context*, ed. D. A. Carson (Paternoster Press, 1984), pp. 110–150.
O'Donovan, Oliver, *In Pursuit of a Christian View of War*. Grove Booklets on Ethics no. 15 (Grove Books, 1977).
Origen, *Ezek. Hom.*, in *Opera Omnia*, ed. J.-P. Migne, vol. 13 (Paris, 1862), pp. 663–767.
Orr, James, *The Progress of Dogma* (Hodder & Stoughton, 1901).

Packer, J. I., 'Justification', in *New Bible Dictionary* (IVP, 2nd ed. 1982), pp. 646–619.

— 'What Did the Cross Achieve? The Logic of Penal Substitution', *Tyndale Bulletin* 25 (1974), pp. 3–45.

Paterson, W. P., 'Sacrifice', in *A Dictionary of the Bible*, ed. James Hastings (T. & T. Clark, 1902), pp. 329–349.

Philo, *Ad Gaium*, tr. C. D. Yonge, in *Works*, vol. 4 (Henty G. Bohn, 1855).

Piper, John, 'Is Self-love Biblical?', *Christianity Today*, 12 August 1977, p. 6.

Pius Xl, *Ad Catholici Sacerdotii* (Catholic Truth Society, 1935).

Pius Xll, *Mediator Dei* (Catholic Truth Society, 1947).

Plato, *Phaedo*, tr. H. N. Fowler (Heinemann, 1914), pp. 200–403.

Pocknee, Cyril E., *The Cross and Crucifix in Christian Worship and Devotion*. Alcuin Club Tracts xxxii (Mowbray, 1962).

Poulton, John, *The Feast of Life: A Theological Reflection on the Theme 'Jesus Christ – the Life of the World'* (World Council of Churches, 1982).

Price, Tony, *Evangelical Anglicans and the Lima Text*. Grove Worship series no. 92 (Grove Books, 1985).

Priestland, Gerald, *The Case Against God* (Collins, 1984).

— *Priestland's Progress: One Man's Search for Christianity Now* (BBC, 1981).

Ramsey, A. Michael, *The Glory of God and the Transfiguration of Christ* (Longmans Green, 1949).

Rashdall, Hastings, *The Idea of Atonement in Christian Theology* (Macmillan, 1919).

Robinson, H. Wheeler, *Suffering Human and Divine* (SCM, 1940).

Sanday, W. and Headlam, A. C., *The Epistle to the Romans*. International Critical Commentary (T. & T. Clark, 5th ed. 1902).

Schroeder, H. J., *The Canons and Decrees of the Council of Trent* (1941; Tan Books, 1978).

Shaw, George Bernard, *Major Barbara* (1905).

Sider, Ronald and O'Donovan, Oliver, *Peace and War: A Debate about Pacifism* (Grove Books, 1985).

Silvester, Hugh, *Arguing with God* (IVP, 1971).

Simon, Ulrich E., *A Theology of Auschwitz* (Gollancz, 1967).

Simpson, E. K. and Bruce, F. F., *Commentary on the Epistles to the Ephesians and the Colossians*. New London Commentary (Marshalls, 1957); New International Commentary on the New Testament (Eerdmans, 1957).

Simpson, P. Carnegie, *The Fact of Christ* (Hodder & Stoughton, 1900).

Skinner, B. F., *Beyond Freedom and Dignity* (1971; Pelican, 1973).

Smith, George D. (ed.), *The Teaching of the Catholic Church* (Burns & Oates, 2nd ed. 1952).

Sobrino, Jon, *Christology at the Crossroads* (1976; Orbis, SCM, 1978).

Socinus, Faustus, *De Jesu Christo Servatore* (1578), tr. Thomas Rees (London, 1818).

Stählin, Gustav, '*orgē*', in *Theological Dictonary of the New Testament*, vol. V (Eerdmans, 1967), pp. 419–447.

Stibbs, Alan M., *The Finished Work of Christ*. The 1952 Tyndale Biblical Theology Lecture (Tyndale Press, 1954).

— *The Meaning of the Word 'Blood' in Scripture* (Tyndale Press, 1948).

Stott, John R. W., *The Message of Ephesians: God's New Society*. The Bible Speaks Today series (IVP, 1979).

— *The Message of the Sermon on the Mount: Christian Counter-Culture*. The Bible Speaks Today series (IVP, 1978).

Swete, H. B., *The Gospel According to St Mark* (Macmillan, 1898).

Tallentyre, S. G., *The Life of Voltaire*. 2 vols. (London, 1903).

Tasker, R. V. G., *The Biblical Doctrine of the Wrath of God* (Tyndale Press, 1951).

Tatlow, Tissington, *The Story of the Student Christian Movement of Great Britain and Ireland* (SCM, 1933).

Taylor, Vincent, *The Atonenent in New Testament Teaching* (Epworth Press, 1940).

— *Forgiveness and Reconciliation: A Study in New Testament Theology* (Macmillan, 2nd. ed. 1946).

— *Jesus and His Sacrifice: A Study of the Passion-Sayings in the Gospels* (Macmillan, 1937).

Temple, William, *Christus Veritas* (Macmillan, 1924).

— *Citizen and Churchman* (Eyre & Spottiswoode, 1941).

— *Readings in St John's Gospel*. 2 vols. (Macmillan, 1939-40).

Tertullian, *Adversus Praxean*, in *The Ante-Nicene Fathers*, vol. III, ed. A. Roberts and J. Donaldson (Eerdmans, 1973), pp. 597–627.

— *De Carne Christi*, in *The Ante-Nicene Fathers* vol. III, ed. A. Roberts and J. Donaldson (Eerdmans, 1973), pp. 521–542.

— *De Corona*, in *The Ante-Nicene Fathers*, vol. III, ed. A. Roberts and J. Donaldson (Eerdmans, 1973), pp. 93–103.

Thompson, R. J. and Beckwith, R. T., 'Sacrifice and Offering', in *New Bible Dictionary* (IVP, 2nd ed. 1982), pp. 1045–1054.

Tizard, L. J., *Preaching: The Art of Communication* (OUP, 1959).

Tournier, Paul, *Creative Suffering* (1981; SCM, 1982).

Treuherz, J., *Pre-Raphaelite Paintings* (Lund Humphries, 1980).

Turner, H. E. W., *The Patristic Doctrine of Redemption* (Mowbray, 1952).

Tyndale, William, *Doctrinal Treatises*. Parker Society (CUP, 1848).

Vanstone, W. H., Love's *Endeavour, Love's Expense: The Response of Being to the Love of God* (Darton, Longman & Todd, 1977).

Vidler, Alec R., *Essays in Liberality* (SCM, 1957).

Vitz, Paul, *Psychology as Religion: The Cult of Self-Worship* (Eerdmans, 1977).

Vivekananda, Swami, *Speeches and Writings* (G. A. Natesan, Madras, 3rd ed.).

Wace, Henry, *The Sacrifice of Christ: Its Vital Reality and Efficacy* (1898; Church Book Room Press, 1945).

Wallace, Ronald S., *The Atoning Death of Christ* (Marshalls, 1981).

Warfield, B. B., *Biblical Doctrines* (OUP, 1929).

— *The Person and Work of Christ*, ed. Samuel G. Craig (Presbyterian & Reformed Publishing Company, 1950).

Warren, M. A. C., *Interpreting the Cross* (SCM, 1966).

Waterland, Daniel, *A Review of the Doctrine of the Eucharist* (1737; Clarendon Press, 1896).

Webster, Douglas, *In Debt to Christ* (Highway Press, 1957).

— *Yes to Mission* (SCM, 1966).

Wells, David F., *Revolution in Rome* (IVP, 1972).

— *The Search for Salvation* (IVP, 1978).

Wenham, G. J., *Numbers*. Tyndale Old Testament Commentaries (IVP, 1981).

Westcott, B. F., *Commentary on the Epistles of John* (Macmillan, 1883).

— *The Epistle to the Hebrews* (1889; Macmillan, 3rd ed. 1903).

— *The Historic Faith* (Macmillan, 6th ed. 1904).

Westminster Confession of Faith: *The Proposed Book of Confessions of the Presbyterian Church in the United States* (1976), pp. 77–101.

Whale, J. S., *Victor and Victim: The Christian Doctrine of Redemption* (CUP, 1960).

White, Douglas, 'The Nature of Punishment and Forgiveness', in *Papers in Modern Churchmanship*, no. II, ed. C. F. Russell (Longmans Green, 1924), pp. 6–9.

Wiesel, Elie, *Night* (1958; Penguin, 1981).

Williams, Rowan, *Eucharistic Sacrifice – The Roots of a Metaphor*. Grove Liturgical Study no. 31 (Grove Books, 1982).

Willmer, Haddon, in *Third Way*, May 1979.

Wright, Tom, 'Justification: The Biblical Basis and its Relevance for Contemporary Evangelicalism', in *The Great Acquittal*, ed. Gavin Reid (Collins, 1980).

Yancey, Philip, *Where is God When it Hurts?* (Zondervan, 1977).

Zwemer, Samuel M., *The Glory of the Cross* (Marshall, Morgan & Scott, 1928).

THE Contemporary Christian

ACKNOWLEDGMENTS

The lyric on p. 357 is from *Gethsemane* (*I Only Want to Say*) from the rock opera *Jesus Christ Superstar*. Lyrics by Tim Rice. Music by Andrew Lloyd Webber. © 1969 by MCA Music Ltd, a division of MCA Inc. Reproduced by kind permission of Tim Rice. International copyright secured. All rights reserved.

The lyric on p. 530 is *Love Changes Everything* from *Aspects of Love*. Music: Andrew Lloyd Webber. Lyrics: Don Black and Charles Hart. © 1988 The Really Useful Group Ltd. All rights for the US controlled by R. & H. Music Co. International copyright secured. All rights reserved.

Contents

Chief abbreviations

AV   The Authorized (King James) Version of the Bible (1611).
ET   English translation.
GNB   The Good News Bible (NT 1966, 4th edition 1976; OT 1976).
LXX   The Old Testament in Greek according to the Septuagint, third century BC.
NEB   The New English Bible (NT 1961, 2nd edition 1970; OT 1970).
NIV   The New International Version of the Bible (1973, 1978, 1984).
REB   The Revised English Bible (1989).
RSV   The Revised Standard Version of the Bible (NT 1946, 2nd edition 1971; OT 1952).
RV   The English Revised Version of the Bible (1881–85).
TDNT   *Theological Dictionary of the New Testament*, ed. G. Kittel and G. Friedrich, translated by G. W. Bromiley, 10 vols. (Eerdmans, 1964–76).

Preface

To be 'contemporary' is to live in the present, and to move with the times, without necessarily concerning ourselves with either the past or the future. To be a 'contemporary Christian', however, is to ensure that our present is enriched to the fullest possible extent both by our knowledge of the past and by our expectation of the future. Our Christian faith demands this. For the God we trust and worship is 'the Alpha and the Omega … who is, and who was, and who is to come, the Almighty',[1] while the Jesus Christ to whom we are committed is 'the same yesterday and today and for ever'.[2]

So this book is an essay in the Christian handling of time, in how we are meant to bring the past, the present and the future together in our thinking and living. Two main problems confront us. The first is the tension between the 'then' (past) and the 'now' (present), and the second the tension between the 'now' (present) and the 'not yet' (future).

The Introduction opens up the first problem: I ask whether it is possible for us truly to honour the past and live in the present simultaneously. Can we preserve Christianity's historic identity intact, without thereby cutting ourselves adrift from our contemporaries? And can we communicate the gospel in exciting, modern terms, without thereby distorting and even destroying it? Can we be authentic and fresh at the same time, or do we have to choose?

The Conclusion opens up the second problem, namely the tension

between the 'now' and the 'not yet'. I ask how far we can explore and experience now everything God has said and done through Christ, without
unwarrantably trespassing into the area of what has not yet been revealed or
given. Alternatively, how can we develop a proper humility before the un-
realized future, without becoming complacent about our present degree of
attainment?

In between these enquiries into the influence upon us of the past and the
future come twenty-one chapters about our present Christian responsibilities.

I think of *The Contemporary Christian* as a companion volume to *Issues
Facing Christians Today*, in that the latter explores questions of social ethics,
while this book relates to questions of doctrine and discipleship under the
five headings 'The Gospel', 'The Disciple', 'The Bible', 'The Church' and
'The World'. I make no attempt to be systematic, let alone exhaustive.
Instead, I have selected a number of issues which are either in the forefront
of current debate or of importance in my own thinking. And, although the
book is emphatically not a random collection of essays and sermons, much
of the material presented here has been used in lectures and addresses in different parts of the world.

In addition to the topic of time, and the relations between past, present
and future, there is a second theme which runs through this book. It concerns the need to talk less and listen more. Christians certainly have a reputation for being garrulous. Many of my readers will remember E. M.
Forster's description in *A Passage to India* of the elderly Mrs Moore's experience in one of the famous Marabar Caves, especially its monotonous but
terrifying echo 'boum'. While inside, she had almost fainted. Now outside
she was trying to write a letter. But a strange feeling of despair began to creep
over her, when 'suddenly, at the edge of her mind, Religion appeared, *poor
little talkative Christianity*, and she knew that all its divine words from "Let
there be light" to "It is finished" only amounted to "boum" '.[3]

Needless to say, the words of God are much more substantial than 'boum'
echoes in a cave, for they are words of truth and of life, which Mrs Moore
did not acknowledge. Nevertheless, the crucial thing is to listen to them
with reverent attention and not drown them by our own premature talk-
ativeness.

In particular, as indicated in this book's sub-title, I believe we are called
to the difficult and even painful task of 'double listening'. That is, we are to
listen carefully (although of course with differing degrees of respect) both to
the ancient Word and to the modern world, in order to relate the one to the
other with a combination of fidelity and sensitivity. Every chapter is, in fact,
an attempt at double listening, although I am sure that some are much less
successful than others. It is, however, my firm conviction that only if we can
develop our capacity for double listening will we avoid the opposite pitfalls

of unfaithfulness and irrelevance, and be able to speak God's Word to God's world with effectiveness today.

I express my special gratitude to Todd Shy, my current study assistant, who has worked laboriously through the whole book in draft and made some helpful suggestions; to Steve Andrews, one of my former study assistants, for his meticulous labours in compiling the indexes; to David Stone for his skill in composing the study guide; and to Frances Whitehead, my omnicompetent secretary, for producing yet one more immaculate typescript.

JOHN STOTT
Christmas, 1991

Notes

[1] Rev. 1:8.
[2] Heb. 13:8.
[3] E. M. Forster, *A Passage to India* (1924; Penguin, 1985), p. 144.

INTRODUCTION

The then and now

The very expressions 'the contemporary Christian' and 'contemporary Christianity' (as, for example, in 'the Institute for Contemporary Christianity') strike many people as a contradiction in terms. How can Christianity be called 'contemporary'? Is it not an ancient faith? Did not its Founder live and die nearly two millennia ago? Is not Christianity a period piece, a museum exhibit, an antique relic from the remote past, irrelevant to modern men and women? My purpose in this book is to try to answer these questions, and to demonstrate that there is such a thing as 'contemporary Christianity'. It is not a new version of Christianity which we are busy inventing, but original, historic, orthodox, biblical Christianity sensitively related to the modern world.

Christianity both historical and contemporary

The way to begin is to reaffirm without apology that Christianity is a historical religion. Of course every religion can claim to be to some degree 'historical', because each arose in a particular historical context and looks back to its founder (*e.g.* the Buddha, Confucius or Muhammad), and/or to a succession of formative teachers. Christianity, however, makes an even stronger claim to be historical because it does not rest only on a historical person, Jesus of Nazareth, but on certain historical events which involved him, especially his birth, death and resurrection. It is also events rather than persons which make Judaism historical. The Old Testament presents Yahweh not only as 'the God of Abraham, Isaac and Jacob' but as the God of the covenant which he made with Abraham, and renewed with Isaac and Jacob; not only as the God of Moses, but as the Redeemer responsible for the exodus, who went on to renew the covenant yet again at Mount Sinai. Christian people, then, are for ever tethered in heart and mind to these decisive, historical events of the past. We are constantly exhorted in Scripture to look back to them with thankfulness. Indeed God deliberately made provision for his people's regular recall of his saving actions. What the Passover was to the exodus, as an annual festival celebrating God's salvation, the Lord's Supper is to the atoning death of Christ, enabling us to call it regularly to mind and to feast on its great benefits. It is thus, through word and sacrament, that the past becomes present again.

The historical origins of Christianity are a great blessing. They give us a solid foundation. Our faith is not built on legends, fairy tales or even myths, but on actual events. These also constitute a problem, however, because they took place such a long time ago. The wide gap between then and now, the past and the present, the historical and the contemporary, is something of an embarrassment. The younger generation tell us they are not interested in history. It provokes from them only a long, rude, noisy yawn. They are concerned with the now, they say, not the then. They resemble Huckleberry Finn, when the widow Douglas first told him the story of Moses and the bulrushes:

> I was in a sweat to find out all about him; but by and by she let it out that Moses had been dead a considerable long time; so then I didn't care no more about him; because I don't take no stock in dead people.[1]

For more than twenty years I have been haunted by a conversation I had on this topic with two brothers, which I have related in full in *I Believe in Preaching*.[2] They were university students, who told me they had repudiated the faith of their parents, in which they had been brought up. One was now an agnostic, the other an atheist. I enquired why. Did they no longer believe in the truth of Christianity? No, that was not their problem, they replied. Their dilemma was not whether Christianity was true, but whether it was relevant. How could it be? Christianity, they went on, was a primitive, Palestinian religion. It had arisen in a primitive, Palestinian culture. So what on earth did it have to offer them, who lived in the exciting, modern world of space travel, transplant surgery and genetic engineering? It was irrelevant!

This feeling of the remoteness, obsolescence and irrelevance of Christianity is widespread. The world has changed dramatically since Jesus' day, and goes on changing with ever more bewildering speed. People reject the gospel, not necessarily because they think it false, but because it no longer resonates with them. Can the church survive the challenge of modernity? Or will it suffer the ignominious fate of the dinosaur, equally unable to adapt to a changing environment, and become extinct?

In response to this common feeling that Christianity is hopelessly out of date, we need to re-state our fundamental Christian conviction that God continues to speak through what he has spoken. His Word is not a prehistoric fossil, to be exhibited under glass, but a living message for the contemporary world. It belongs to the market place, not the museum. Through his ancient Word God addresses the modern world, for, as Dr J. I. Packer has said, 'the Bible is God preaching'. Even granted the historical particularities of the Bible, and the immense complexities of the modern world, there is still a fundamental correspondence between them, and God's Word remains a lamp to our feet and a light for our path.[3]

At the same time, our dilemma remains. Can the gospel really be 'modernized'? Is it feasible to expect the church to apply the historic faith to the contemporary scene, the Word to the world, without either betraying the former or alienating the latter? Can Christianity retain its authentic identity and demonstrate its relevance at the same time, or must one of these be sacrificed to the other? Are we obliged to choose between retreating into the past and making a fetish of the present, between reciting old truths which are stale and inventing new notions which are spurious? Perhaps the greater of these two dangers is that the church will attempt to recast the faith in such a way as to undermine its integrity and render it unrecognizable to its original heralds. I propose to focus on this problem now; the rest of the book is addressed in different ways to the complementary problem of relevance.

In 1937 the Harvard scholar Henry J. Cadbury's book *The Peril of Modernizing Jesus* was published. He conceded that the laudable purpose of the 'modernizers' of Jesus was to 'interpret him in terms that will seem real, that is, modern and congenial to the modern mind'.[4] But the result was often to falsify him, and in particular to lose sight of his first-century 'Jewishness'. Like the soldiers who mocked Jesus, 'stripped him and put on him a scarlet military cloak', and then after the mockery 'took the cloak off him and put on him his own raiment', so we put on Jesus our 'own kind of clothes', investing him with 'our own thoughts'.[5]

Yet the desire to present Jesus in a way that appeals to our own generation is obviously right. This was Bonhoeffer's preoccupation in prison: 'What is bothering me incessantly', he wrote to his friend Eberhard Bethge in 1944, 'is the question … who Christ really is for us today?'[6] It is without doubt a bothersome question. Yet in answering it, the church has tended in every generation to develop images of Christ which deviate from the portrait painted by the New Testament authors.

Helmut Thielicke was outspoken about this. 'Over and over the figure of Jesus has been horribly amputated', he wrote, to suit each age's taste.

> Throughout the whole history of the church Jesus Christ has suffered a process of repeated crucifixion. He has been scourged and bruised and locked in the prison of countless systems and philosophies. Treated as a body of thought, he has literally been lowered into conceptual graves and covered with stone slabs so that he might not arise and trouble us any more ... But this is the miracle, that from this succession of conceptual graves Jesus Christ has risen again and again![7]

Attempts to modernize Jesus

Here is a sample of the church's many attempts to present a contemporary picture of Christ. It will be seen that some have been more successful than others in remaining loyal to the original.

I think first of *Jesus the ascetic*, who inspired generations of monks and hermits. He was not markedly different from John the Baptist, for he too was clad in a camel's hair cloak, wore sandals or went barefoot, and munched locusts with evident relish, while otherwise renouncing the delights of the table and the joys of God's creation. It would be hard to reconcile this portrait with his contemporaries' criticism that he 'came eating and drinking'.[8]

Then there was *Jesus the pale Galilean*. It was the apostate emperor Julian, who tried to reinstate Rome's pagan gods after Constantine had replaced them with the worship of Christ, who is reported as having said on his deathbed in AD 363, 'You have conquered, O Galilean.' His words were popularized by the nineteenth-century poet Swinburne in his lines:

> Thou hast conquered, O pale Galilean;
> The world has grown grey from thy breath.

This image of Jesus was perpetuated in medieval art and stained glass, with a heavenly halo and a colourless complexion, his eyes lifted to the sky and his feet never quite touching the ground.

In contrast to the presentations of Jesus as weak, suffering and defeated, was *Jesus the cosmic Christ*, who was much loved by the Byzantine church leaders. Over against the advancing barbarians they depicted him as the King of kings and Lord of lords, the *pantokrator*, creator and ruler of the universe. Yet, exalted high above all things, glorified and reigning, he seemed aloof from the real world and even from his own humanity as revealed in the incarnation and the cross.

At the opposite end of the theological spectrum, the seventeenth- and eighteenth-century deists of the Enlightenment constructed in their own image *Jesus the teacher of common sense*,[9] all human and not divine. The most dramatic example is the work of that versatile genius Thomas Jefferson, President of the United States 1801–9. Rejecting the supernatural as incompatible with reason, he twice produced his own edition of the Gospels, calling the first *The Philosophy of Jesus of Nazareth* (1804) and the second *The Life and Morals of Jesus of Nazareth* (1820). From both books all miracles and mysteries were systematically eliminated. What is left is the plain man's guide to a merely human moral teacher.

Coming into the twentieth century, we are presented with a large variety of options. Two of the best known owe their popularity to musicals. There is *Jesus the clown* of *Godspell*, who spends his time singing and dancing, and thus captures something of the gaiety of Jesus, but hardly takes his mission seriously. Somewhat similar is *Jesus Christ Superstar*, the disillusioned celebrity, who once thought he knew who he was, but in Gethsemane was no longer sure:

> Then I was inspired;
> Now I'm sad and tired.

Next is that extraordinary invention, *Jesus the founder of modern business*. I am referring to a book entitled *The Man Nobody Knows* (1925), which for two years topped the best-seller list in the United States. Its author, Bruce Barton, was an American advertising man, who was rebelling against the anaemic, 'sissified' Jesus of his boyhood Sunday School. He depicted Jesus not only as a bronzed, muscular 'outdoor man', friendly, sociable and convivial, but as a leader of blazing conviction, whose whole life was a story of achievement, and who emphasized in his teaching the secrets of business success. Chapter 6 is headed 'The Founder of Modern Business'. Why, Bruce Barton writes, at the age of only twelve Jesus actually described himself as needing to be 'about his Father's *business*'!

Economics expertise as well as business success has been attributed to Jesus. Surprisingly enough, it is George Bernard Shaw who, doubtless with tongue in cheek, introduces us to *Jesus the economist*. 'Decidedly,' he wrote, 'whether you think Jesus was God or not, you must admit that he was a first-rate political economist', who among other things recommended equal distribution.[10] But writers have completely disagreed with one another about the nature of his economics. On the one hand there is the vision of *Jesus the capitalist*, the promoter of free enterprise, investment and conservation, so that T. N. Carver could claim in his *The Economic Factor in the*

Messiahship of Jesus (1922) that 'every essential feature of the modern economic system is explicitly set forth in the teachings of this young Jew'. [11]

On the other hand there is *Jesus the socialist*. I cite as my example Arthur Scargill, who was elected President of the National Union of Mineworkers in 1981. During a press interview at the time he said he was a Christian, and that he loved the old Moody and Sankey hymns, his favourite being 'What a friend we have in Jesus'. Pressed as to whether he believed the Creed, he first hedged and then declared: 'I do believe in Christianity in this sense: I believe that Jesus Christ was in fact a socialist.'[12]

Fidel Castro of Cuba has frequently referred to Jesus as 'a great revolutionary', and there have been many attempts to portray him as *Jesus the freedom fighter*, the urban guerrilla, the first-century Che Guevara, with black beard and flashing eyes, as in Pasolini's *Gospel according to Matthew*, whose most characteristic gesture was to overthrow the tables of the money changers and to drive them out of the temple with a whip.

Perhaps the most sustained effort to depict Jesus in revolutionary terms is Upton Sinclair's novel *They Call Me Carpenter*.[13] Over the altar in St Bartholomew's Church, New York, there was a stained-glass figure of Christ, who one day came alive, stepped down and began a public ministry in the city. 'Who are you?' people asked. 'They call me Carpenter,' he replied. So 'Mr Carpenter' he became, and later 'Prophet Carpenter', as his words and actions in New York paralleled those of Jesus in Palestine. He too was tempted (he was offered a $1,500-a-week contract as a movie star); he raised a dead child who had been knocked down by a car, and gathered other children round him; he healed the sick and handicapped; he rescued 'Mary Magna' from her life of prostitution; and he stood on the tail end of a truck in order to harangue the crowd about love and justice. But when he quoted Amos' denunciations of the idle rich, identified with strikers in a mass protest rally, inveighed against employers for alienating the workers from their product, and during a service in St Bartholomew's Church uttered a tirade against theologians and doctors of divinity ('Woe unto you Episcopalians, hypocrites!'), the local *Times* accused him of being a Bolshevik anarchist and of 'disguising the doctrine of Lenin and Trotsky in the robes of Christian revelation'.[14] He spent his last night in an upper room at the Socialist headquarters. And finally the mob, enraged by this 'Ranting Red Prophet', captured him, poured gallons of red paint over his head, stood him on top of a wagon, and hauled him through the streets shouting, 'Hi! Hi! the Bolsheviki Prophet!' Thrown out of a theatre window, he was unharmed, he returned running to St Bartholomew's Church, he leapt back into the window ... and behold, it had all been a dream.

Lest one should conclude that such reconstructions of Jesus have been attempted only by imaginative writers of fiction, I give as my final example a serious scholarly study entitled *Jesus the Magician*. I think it may justly be seen as another attempt to portray Jesus in ancient-modern dress, in that it is a convenient and contemporary way of getting rid of the miracles. It is surely significant that the book's most recent publisher is the Aquarian Press. Professor Morton Smith's thesis is that, although in the Gospels the followers of Jesus depict him as the mythical Son of God, yet his most ancient opponents saw him as a magician. Third-century documents, which Professor Smith claims were suppressed and destroyed by Christians, show (he declares) that Jesus went to Egypt as a young man, 'where he became expert in magic and was tattooed with magical symbols or spells'; that he returned to Galilee and 'made himself famous by his magical feats';[15] and that he finally united his followers to himself by the meal he instituted, 'an unmistakably magic rite'.[16] The evidence, Morton Smith concludes, gives 'a coherent picture of a magician's life and work'.[17]

This selection of thirteen different portraits of Jesus illustrates the perennial tendency to fashion a Christ with a modern appeal. It began already in the apostolic age, as Paul needed to warn people of false teachers who were preaching 'a Jesus other than the Jesus we [apostles] preached'.[18] And one is amazed by the ingenuity with which people have developed the representations of Jesus which we have considered. Yet all of them were anachronisms. Each generation read back into him its own ideas and aspirations, and created him in its own image. Their motive was right (to paint a contemporary portrait of Jesus), but the result was to some extent wrong (the portrait was unauthentic). The challenge before us is to present Jesus to our generation in a way that is both historical and contemporary, both authentic and appealing, new in the sense of 'fresh' (*neos*), not new in the sense of being a novelty (*kairos*).

The call for double listening

The main reason for every betrayal of the authentic Jesus is that we listen with exaggerated deference to contemporary fashion, instead of listening to God's Word. The demand for relevance becomes so imperious that we feel we have to capitulate to it, at whatever cost. We are familiar with this kind of pressure in the business world, in which it is the marketing people who determine the firm's product by discovering what will sell, what the public will buy. It sometimes seems as if market forces rule in the church as well. We become obsequious to the modern mood, slaves to the latest fad, even idolaters who are prepared to sacrifice truth on the altar of modernity. Then the quest for relevance has degenerated into a lust for popularity.

For the opposite extreme to irrelevance is accommodation which is a feeble-minded, unprincipled surrender to the *Zeitgeist*, the spirit of the time. Thielicke was haunted by this danger, because he could not forget how the so-called 'German Christians' during Hitler's Third Reich accepted and even defended the racial myths of the Nazis. He insisted, therefore, that true theology 'always involves a debate between the *kerygma* and the self-understanding of an age ... between eternity and time'. Moreover, in this debate 'faith believes *against* as well as *in*'; it is born in a conscious reaction to current ideas.[19] Thus Thielicke writes of theology's 'polar structure', one pole being 'a superior, eternal basis derived from revelation' and the other being 'specific constellations of the spirit of the age'.[20] 'Faith', he insists, 'will always be a venture ... it will involve not a Because but a Nevertheless in face of the reality of the human'.[21]

Peter Berger also, as a Christian sociologist, has some pertinent things to say about the need to tread delicately between irrelevance and accommodation:

> I would like to make it clear once more that I am *not* saying that Christians ought not to listen to others' ideas, or to take seriously what happens in their cultural milieu, or to participate in the political struggles of the times. What troubles me is not the stance of listening as such, but that of listening with uncritical adulation if not idolatrous intent – of listening, if you will, with wide-eyed and open-mouthed wonder.[22]

'It seems to me', Peter Berger goes on, 'that quite simply, it is time to say "Enough!" to the dance around the golden calves of modernity.'[23] More important than the question 'What does modern man have to say to the church?' is the question 'What does the church have to say to modern man?'[24]

The people of God live in a world which is often unfriendly and sometimes actively hostile. We are constantly exposed to the pressure to conform. Yet throughout Scripture the summons is given to a vigorous nonconformity, and warnings are sounded to those who give in to worldliness. In the Old Testament the Lord said to his people after the exodus: 'You must not do as they do in Egypt, where you used to live, and you must not do as they do in the land of Canaan, where I am bringing you. Do not follow their practices. You must obey my laws ...'[25] Yet the people said to Samuel: 'Now appoint a king to lead us, such as all the other nations have.'[26] And later Ezekiel had to rebuke them for their idolatry: 'You say, "We want to be like the nations, like the peoples of the world, who serve wood and stone."'[27] It was similar in New Testament days. In spite of the clear commands of Jesus, 'Do not be like them',[28] and of Paul, 'Do not conform ... to the pattern of this world',[29] the constant tendency of God's people was, and still is, to behave 'like the heathen',[30] until nothing much seems to distinguish the church from the world, the Christian from the non-Christian, in convictions, values or standards.[31]

Thank God, however, that there have always been some noble souls who have stood firm, sometimes alone, and refused to compromise. I think of Jeremiah in the sixth century BC, and Paul in his day ('everyone . . . has deserted me'),[32] Athanasius in the fourth century and Luther in the sixteenth. C. S. Lewis wrote his tribute to Athanasius, who maintained the deity of Jesus and the doctrine of the Trinity, when the whole church was determined to follow the heretic Arius: 'It is his glory that he did *not* move with the times; it is his reward that he now remains when those times, as all times do, have moved away.'[33]

So today, we are resolved to struggle to present the gospel in such a way as to speak to modern dilemmas, fears and frustrations, but we are equally determined not to compromise the biblical gospel in order to do so. Some stumbling-blocks are intrinsic to the original gospel and cannot be eliminated, or even soft-pedalled, in order to render it more palatable to contemporary taste. The gospel contains some features so alien to modern thought that it will always appear 'folly' to intellectuals, however hard we strive (and rightly) to show that it is 'true and reasonable'.[34] The cross will always constitute an assault on human self-righteousness and a challenge to human self-indulgence. Its 'scandal' (stumbling-block) simply cannot be removed. Indeed, the church speaks most authentically to the world not when it makes its shameful little prudential compromises, but when it refuses to do so; not when it has become indistinguishable from the world, but when its distinctive light shines most brightly.

Thus Christian people, who live under the authority of God's revelation, however anxious they are to communicate it to others, manifest a sturdy independence of mind and spirit. This is not obstinacy, for we are willing to listen to everybody. But we are determined to be faithful, and if necessary to suffer for it. God's word to Ezekiel is an encouragement to us: 'Do not be afraid of them . . . You must speak my words to them, whether they listen or fail to listen, for they are rebellious.'[35] So we have to apply the Word, but not manipulate it. We must do our utmost to ensure that it speaks to our time, but not bowdlerize it in order to secure a fake relevance. Our calling is to be faithful and relevant, not merely trendy.

How, then, can we be both conservative and radical simultaneously, conservative in guarding God's revelation and radical in our thoroughgoing application of it? How can we develop a Christian mind which is both shaped by the truths of historic, biblical Christianity, and acquainted with the realities of the contemporary world? How can we relate the Word to the world, understanding the world in the light of the Word, and even understanding the Word in the light of the world? We have to begin with a double refusal. We refuse to become either so absorbed in the Word, that we *escape* into it and fail to let it confront the world, or so absorbed in the world, that we *conform* to it and fail to subject it to the judgment of the Word. Escapism and conformity are opposite mistakes, but neither is a Christian option.

In place of this double refusal we are called to double listening, listening both to the Word and to the world. It is a truism to say that we have to listen to the Word of God, except perhaps that we need to listen to him more expectantly and humbly, ready for him to confront us with a disturbing, uninvited word. It is less welcome to be told that we must also listen to the world. For the voices of our contemporaries may take the form of shrill and strident protest. They are now querulous, now appealing, now aggressive in tone. There are also the anguished cries of those who are suffering, and the pain, doubt, anger, alienation and even despair of those who are estranged from God. I am not suggesting that we should listen to God and to our fellow human beings in the same way or with the same degree of deference. We listen to the Word with humble reverence, anxious to understand it, and resolved to believe and obey what we come to understand. We listen to the world with critical alertness, anxious to understand it too, and resolved not necessarily to believe and obey it, but to sympathize with it and to seek grace to discover how the gospel relates to it.

Everybody finds listening difficult. But are Christians for some reason (perhaps because we believe ourselves called to speak what God has spoken) worse listeners than others? Our symbol is rather the tongue than the ear. Yet we should have learned a lesson from Job's garrulous comforters. They began well. For when they heard about Job's troubles, they left their homes and visited him. And when they arrived, and could hardly recognize him because of his disfiguring sores, they wept, tore their robes, sprinkled dust on their heads, and then sat beside him on the ground for seven days. During that whole week they said nothing to him, because they saw how great his sufferings were. Indeed, nobody said anything, because there was simply nothing to say. One only wishes that they had continued as they began, and kept their mouths shut. Instead, they trotted out their conventional orthodoxy, that every sinner suffers for his own sins, in the most unfeeling, insensitive way. They did not really listen to what Job had to say. They merely repeated their own thoughtless and heartless claptrap, until in the end God rebuked them for not having spoken about him what was right.

We are familiar with the concept of 'double-think', an expression coined by George Orwell in his famous book *Nineteen Eighty-Four*. It denotes the ability to hold simultaneously in the mind two conflicting views or beliefs. Double-think is the speciality of unscrupulous propagandists. 'Double-speak' is even more disreputable. It is the ability to say one thing to one person and something entirely different to somebody else, and even to speak mutually contradictory things to the same person. Double-speak is the stock-in-trade of hypocrites, of consummate liars. 'Double listening', however, contains no element of self-contradiction. It is the faculty of listening to two voices at the same time, the voice of God through Scripture and the voices of men and women around us. These voices will often contradict one another, but our purpose in listening to them both is to discover how they relate to each other. Double listening is indispensable to Christian discipleship and Christian mission.

It is only through the discipline of double listening that it is possible to become a 'contemporary Christian'. For then we see that the adjectives 'historical' and 'contemporary' are not incompatible, we learn to apply the Word to the world, and we proclaim good news which is both true and new. In sum, we live in the 'now' in the light of the 'then'.

Notes

[1] Mark Twain, *The Adventures of Huckleberry Finn* (1884; Pan, 1968), p. 202.

[2] John Stott, *I Believe in Preaching* (Hodder and Stoughton, 1982), pp. 138–139.

[3] Ps. 119:105; *cf.* 2 Pet. 1:19.

[4] Henry J. Cadbury, *The Peril of Modernizing Jesus* (Macmillan, 1937; SPCK, 1962), p. 28.

[5] *Ibid.*, p. 42.

[6] Dietrich Bonhoeffer, *Letters and Papers from Prison* (SCM, enlarged edition, 1971), p. 279.

[7] Helmut Thielicke, *How Modern Should Theology Be?* (1967; ET Fortress, 1969, and Collins, 1970), pp. 18–19. See also his *Modern Faith and Thought* (1983; ET Eerdmans, 1990), p. 78.

[8] Mt. 11:19.

[9] See Jaroslav Pelikan, *Jesus Through the Centuries* (Yale University Press, 1985), pp. 182–193.

[10] Preface to *Androcles and the Lion* (1912; Constable, 1916), p. lxx.

[11] Quoted by H. J. Cadbury, *The Peril of Modernizing Jesus*, pp. 12–14.

[12] Interview with Terry Coleman, which appeared in the *Guardian Weekly* on 20 December 1981.

[13] Upton Sinclair, *They Call Me Carpenter* (Werner Laurie, 1922).

[14] *Ibid.*, pp. 127–128.

[15] Morton Smith, *Jesus the Magician* (1978; Aquarian Press, 1985), p. 67.

[16] *Ibid.*, p. 146.

[17] *Ibid.*, p. 152.

[18] 2 Cor. 11:4.

[19] H. Thielicke, *Modern Faith and Thought*, p. 5.

[20] *Ibid.*, p. 7.

[21] *Ibid.*, p. 563.

[22] Peter L. Berger, *Facing Up to Modernity* (1977; Penguin, 1979), p. 232.

[23] *Ibid*, p. 233.

[24] *Ibid.*, p. 233.

[25] Lv. 18:3–4a.

[26] 1 Sa. 8:5.

[27] Ezk. 20:32.

[28] Mt. 6:8.

[29] Rom. 12:2.

[30] 1 Thes. 4:5, *cf.* 1 Cor. 5:1; Eph. 4:17.

[31] For brave Christian challenges to the church to stand firm against the cultural and moral trends of today see, for example, *Christianity Confronts Modernity*, ed. Peter Williamson and Kevin Perrotta (Servant, 1981) and *The Gravedigger File: Papers on the Subversion of the Modern Church*, by Os Guinness (IVP USA, 1983).

[32] 2 Tim. 1:15; *cf.* 4:11, 16.

[33] From C. S. Lewis' Introduction to *St Athanasius on the Incarnation* (Mowbray, 1953), p. 9.

[34] Acts 26:25.

[35] Ezk. 2:6–7.

PART ONE

The Gospel

Christianity presents itself not as a religion, let alone as one religion among many, but as God's good news for the world. This implies that the gospel has both a divine origin (it comes from God) and a human relevance (it speaks to our condition). In consequence, before we are ready to ask the question 'What is the gospel?', we must obtain a satisfactory answer to the logically prior question, 'What is a human being?'

Chapter 1 ('The human paradox') is an attempt to do justice to what the Bible teaches and our own experience endorses, namely the glory and the shame of our humanness, both our dignity as creatures made in God's image and our depravity as sinners under his judgment. Chapter 2 then presents what is traditionally called 'salvation' in terms of 'Authentic freedom'.

Chapters 3 and 4 handle the central themes of the death and resurrection of Jesus, which secured our freedom. I try to face first the five main objections to the gospel of Christ crucified and then the current denials of his bodily resurrection. I argue that the New Testament significance of the resurrection of Jesus depends on the church's traditional belief that it was an event which involved the raising and transforming of his body.

In chapter 5 ('Jesus Christ is Lord') we review the far-reaching implications, for both faith and life, of this seemingly innocent affirmation. Radical indeed is the discipleship which takes Christ's lordship seriously.

ONE

The human paradox

Twice the question 'What is man?' (that is, 'What does it mean to be human?') is asked and answered in the Old Testament. And on both occasions the question expresses surprise, even incredulity, that God should pay so much attention to his human creation. For we are insignificant in comparison to the vastness of the universe, and impure in contrast to the brightness of the stars, even just 'a maggot' and 'a worm'.[1]

There are at least three major reasons for the importance of this question.

Personally speaking, to ask 'What is man?' is another way of asking 'Who am I?' Only so can we respond both to the ancient Greek adage *gnōthi seauton*, 'know yourself', and to the modern western preoccupation with the discovery of our true selves. There is no more important field for search or research than our own personal identity. For until we have found ourselves, we can neither fully discover anything else, nor grow into personal maturity. The universal cry is 'Who am I?' and 'Do I have any significance?'

The story is told that Arthur Schopenhauer, the philosopher of pessimism, was sitting one day in the Tiergarten at Frankfurt, looking somewhat shabby and dishevelled, when the park keeper mistook him for a tramp and asked him gruffly, 'Who are you?' To this enquiry the philosopher replied bitterly, 'I wish to God I knew.'

Professionally, whatever our work may be, we are inevitably involved in serving people. Doctors and nurses have patients, teachers pupils, lawyers and social workers clients, members of parliament constituents, and business people customers. How we treat people in our work depends almost entirely on how we view them.

Politically, it is arguable that the nature of human beings has been one of the chief points at issue between the rival visions of Jesus and Marx. Have human beings an absolute value because of which they must be respected, or is their value only relative to the state, because of which they may be exploited? More simply, are the people the servants of the institution, or is the institution the servant of the people? As John S. Whale has written, 'ideologies ... are really anthropologies'; they are different doctrines of man.[2]

The Christian critique of contemporary answers to the question 'What is man?' is that they tend to be either too naïve in their optimism or too negative in their pessimism about the human condition. Secular humanists are generally optimistic. Although they believe that *homo sapiens* is nothing but the product of a random evolutionary process, they nevertheless believe that human beings are continuing to evolve, have limitless potential, and will one day take control of their own development. But such optimists do not take seriously enough the human streak of moral perversity and self-centredness which has constantly retarded progress and so led to disillusion in social reformers.

Existentialists, on the other hand, tend to be extremely pessimistic. Because there is no God, they say, there are no values, ideals or standards any more, which is at least logical. And although we need somehow to find the courage to be, our existence has neither meaning nor purpose. Everything is ultimately absurd. But such pessimists overlook the love, joy, beauty, truth, hope, heroism and self-sacrifice which have enriched the human story.

What we need, therefore, to quote J. S. Whale again, is 'neither the easy optimism of the humanist, nor the dark pessimism of the cynic, but the radical realism of the Bible'.[3]

Our human dignity

The intrinsic value of human beings by creation is affirmed from the first chapter of the Bible onwards.

> Then God said, 'Let us make man in our image, in our likeness, and let them rule over the fish of the sea and the birds of the air, over the livestock, over all the earth, and over all the creatures that move along the ground.'

> So God created man
> in his own image.
> In the image of God

          he created him;
      male and female
          he created them.

God blessed them and said to them, 'Be fruitful and increase in number;
fill the earth and subdue it. Rule over the fish of the sea and the birds of
the air and over every living creature that moves on the ground.'[4]

There has been a long-standing debate about the meaning of the divine
'image' or 'likeness' in human beings, and where their superiority lies. Keith
Thomas collected a number of quaint suggestions in his book *Man and the
Natural World.*[5] He points out that a human being was described by
Aristotle as a political animal, by Thomas Willis as a laughing animal, by
Benjamin Franklin as a tool-making animal, by Edmund Burke as a religious animal, and by James Boswell the gourmet as a cooking animal.[6]
Other writers have focused on some physical feature of the human body.
Plato made much of our erect posture, so that animals look down, and only
human beings look up to heaven, while Aristotle added the peculiarity that
only human beings are unable to wiggle their ears.[7] A Stuart doctor was
greatly impressed by our intestines, by their 'anfractuous circumlocutions,
windings and turnings', whereas in the late eighteenth century Uvedale
Price drew attention to our nose: 'Man is, I believe, the only animal that has
a marked projection in the middle of the face.'[8]

Scholars who are familiar with ancient Egypt and Assyria, however,
emphasize that in those cultures the king or emperor was regarded as the
'image' of God, representing him on earth, and that kings had images of
themselves erected in their provinces to symbolize the extent of their
authority. Against that background God the Creator entrusted a kind of
royal (or at least vice-regal) responsibility to all human beings, appointing
them to 'rule' over the earth and its creatures, and 'crowning' them with
'glory and honour' to do so.[9]

In the unfolding narrative of Genesis 1 it is clear that the divine image or
likeness is what distinguishes humans (the climax of creation) from animals
(whose creation is recorded earlier). A continuity between humans and
animals is implied. For example, they share 'the breath of life'[10] and the
responsibility to reproduce.[11] But there was also a radical discontinuity
between them, in that only human beings are said to be 'like God'. This
emphasis on the unique distinction between humans and animals keeps
recurring throughout Scripture. The argument takes two forms. We should
be ashamed both when human beings behave like animals, descending to
their level, and when animals behave like human beings, doing better by
instinct than we do by choice. As an example of the former, men and
women are not to be 'senseless and ignorant' and behave like 'a brute beast',

or 'like the horse or the mule, which have no understanding'.[12] As an example of the latter, we are rebuked that oxen and donkeys are better at recognizing their master than we are,[13] that migratory birds are better at returning home after going away,[14] and that ants are more industrious and more provident.[15]

Returning to the early chapters of Genesis, all God's dealings with Adam and Eve presuppose their uniqueness among his creatures. He addresses them in such a way as to assume their understanding; he tells them which fruit they may eat and not eat, taking it for granted that they can discern between a permission and a prohibition, and choose between them. He planted the garden, and then put Adam in it 'to work it and take care of it',[16] thus initiating a conscious, responsible partnership between them in cultivating the soil. He created them male and female, pronounced solitude 'not good', instituted marriage for the fulfilment of their love, and blessed their union. He also 'walked in the garden in the cool of the day', desiring their companionship, and missed them when they hid from him. It is not surprising, therefore, that this cluster of five privileges (understanding, moral choice, creativity, love and fellowship with God) are all regularly mentioned in Scripture, and continue to be recognized in the contemporary world, as constituting the unique distinction of our 'humanness'.

To begin with, there is *our self-conscious rationality*. It is not only that we are able to think and to reason. For so, it may be said, can computers. They can perform the most fantastic calculations, and do so much faster than we can. They also have a form of memory (they can store information) and a form of speech (they can communicate their findings). But there is still one thing (thank God!) they cannot do. They cannot originate new thoughts; they can only 'think' what is fed into them. Human beings, however, are original thinkers. More than that. We can do what we (author and reader) are doing at this very moment: we can stand outside ourselves, look at ourselves, and evaluate ourselves, asking ourselves who and what we are. We are self-conscious and can be self-critical. We are also restlessly inquisitive about the universe. True, as one scientist said to another, 'astronomically speaking, man is infinitesimally small'. 'That is so,' responded his colleague, 'but then, astronomically speaking, man is the astronomer.'

Next, there is *our ability to make moral choices*. Human beings are moral beings. Although our conscience reflects our upbringing and culture, and is therefore fallible, nevertheless it remains on guard within us, like a sentinel, warning us that there is a difference between right and wrong. It is also more than an inner voice. It represents a moral order outside and above us, to which we sense an obligation, so that we have a strong urge to do what we perceive to be right, and feelings of guilt when we do what we believe to be wrong. Our whole moral vocabulary (commands and prohibitions, values and choices, obligation, conscience, freedom and will, right and wrong, guilt and shame) is meaningless to animals. True, we can train our dog to know what it is allowed and forbidden. And when it disobeys, and cringes from us by a reflex action, we can describe it as looking 'guilty'. But it has no sense of guilt; it knows only that it is going to be walloped.

Thirdly, there are *our powers of artistic creativity*. It is not only that God calls us into a responsible stewardship of the natural environment, and into partnership with himself in subduing and developing it for the common good, but that he has given us innovative skills through science and art to do so. We are 'creative creatures'. That is, as creatures we depend upon our Creator. But, having been created in our Creator's likeness, he has given us the desire and the ability to be creators too. So we draw and we paint, we build and we sculpt, we dream and we dance, we write poetry and we make music. We are able to appreciate what is beautiful to the eye, the ear and the touch.

In the next place, there is *our capacity for relationships of love*. God said, 'Let us make man in our image ... So God created man in his own image ... male and female he created them.'

Although we must be careful not to deduce from this text more than it actually says, it is surely legitimate to say that the plurality within the Creator ('Let us make man') was expressed in the plurality of his creatures ('male and female he created them'). It became even clearer when Jesus prayed for his own people 'that all of them may be one, Father, just as you are in me and I am in you'.[17] And this unity of love is unique to human beings. Of course all animals mate, many form strong pair bonds, most care for their young, and some are gregarious. But the love which binds human beings together is more than an instinct, more than a disturbance in the endocrine glands. It has inspired the greatest art, the noblest heroism, the finest devotion. God himself is love, and our experiences of loving are an essential reflection of our likeness to him.

Fifthly, there is *our insatiable thirst for God*. All human beings are aware of an ultimate personal reality, whom we seek, and in relation to whom alone we know we will find our human fulfilment. Even when we are running away from God, instinctively we know that we have no other resting-place, no other home. Without him we are lost, like waifs and strays. Our greatest claim to nobility is our created capacity to know God, to be in personal relationship with him, to love him and to worship him. Indeed, we are most truly human when we are on our knees before our Creator.

It is in these things, then, that our distinctive humanness lies, in our God-given capacities to think, to choose, to create, to love and to worship. 'In the animal,' by contrast, wrote Emil Brunner, 'we do not see even the smallest beginning of a tendency to seek truth for truth's sake, to shape beauty for the sake of beauty, to promote righteousness for the sake of righteousness, to reverence the Holy for the sake of its holiness ... The animal knows nothing "above" its immediate sphere of existence, nothing by which it measures or tests its existence ... The difference between man and beast amounts to a whole dimension of existence.'[18]

No wonder Shakespeare made Hamlet break out into his eulogy: 'What a piece of work is a man! how noble in reason! how infinite in faculty! ... in action how like an angel! in apprehension how like a god! the beauty of the world! the paragon of animals!'[19]

How I wish I could stop there and we could live the rest of our lives glowing with unadulterated self-esteem! But alas! There is another and darker side to our human being, of which we are only too well aware, and to which Jesus himself drew our attention.

Our human depravity

Here are some words of Jesus:

> Again Jesus called the crowd to him and said, 'Listen to me, everyone, and understand this. Nothing outside a man can make him "unclean" by going into him. Rather, it is what comes out of a man that makes him "unclean" ... For from within, out of men's hearts, come evil thoughts, sexual immorality, theft, murder, adultery, greed, malice, deceit, lewdness, envy, slander, arrogance and folly. All these evils come from inside and make a man "unclean".'[20]

Jesus did not teach the fundamental goodness of human nature. He undoubtedly believed the Old Testament truth that humankind, male and female, were made in the image of God, but he also believed that this image had been marred. He taught the worth of human beings, not least by devoting himself to their service, but he also taught our unworthiness. He did not deny that we can give 'good things' to others, but he added that even while doing good we do not escape the designation 'evil'.[21] And in the verses quoted above he made important assertions about the extent, nature, origin and effect of evil in human beings.

First, he taught *the universal extent of human evil.* He was not portraying the criminal segment of society or some particularly degraded individual or group. On the contrary, he was in conversation with refined, righteous and religious Pharisees, and generalized about 'a man' and 'men'. Indeed, it is often the most upright people who are the most keenly aware of their own degradation. As an example, take Dag Hammarskjöld, Secretary-General of the United Nations from 1953 to 1961. He was a deeply committed public servant, whom W. H. Auden described as 'a great, good and lovable man'. Yet his view of himself was very different. In his collection of autobiographical pieces entitled *Markings*, he wrote of 'that dark counter-centre of evil in our nature', so that we even make our service of others 'the foundation for our own life-preserving self-esteem'.[22]

Secondly, Jesus taught *the self-centred nature of human evil*. In Mark 7 he listed thirteen examples. What is common to them all is that each is an assertion of the self either against our neighbour (murder, adultery, theft, false witness and covetousness – breaches of the second half of the Ten Commandments – are all included) or against God ('pride and folly' being well defined in the Old Testament as denials of God's sovereignty and even of his existence). Jesus summarized the Ten Commandments in terms of love for God and neighbour, and every sin is a form of selfish revolt against God's authority or our neighbour's welfare.

Thirdly, Jesus taught *the inward origin of human evil*. Its source has to be traced neither to a bad environment nor to a faulty education (although both these can have a powerful conditioning influence on impressionable young people), but rather to our 'heart', our inherited and twisted nature. One might almost say that Jesus introduced us to Freudianism before Freud. At least what he called the 'heart' is roughly equivalent to what Freud called the 'unconscious'. It resembles a very deep well. The thick deposit of mud at the bottom is usually unseen, and even unsuspected. But when the waters of the well are stirred by the winds of violent emotion, the most evil-looking, evil-smelling filth bubbles up from the depths and breaks the surface – rage, hate, lust, cruelty, jealousy and revenge. In our most sensitive moments we are appalled by our potentiality for evil. Superficial remedies will not do.

Fourthly, Jesus spoke of *the defiling effect of human evil*. 'All these evils come from inside', he said, 'and make a human being "unclean".'[23] The Pharisees considered defilement to be largely external and ceremonial; they were preoccupied with clean foods, clean hands and clean vessels. But Jesus insisted that defilement is internal and moral. What renders us unclean in God's sight is not the food which goes into us (into our stomach) but the evil which comes out of us (out of our heart).

All those who have caught even a momentary glimpse of the holiness of God have been unable to bear the sight, so shocked have they been by their own contrasting uncleanness. Moses hid his face, afraid to look at God. Isaiah cried out in horror over his own pollution and lostness. Ezekiel was dazzled, almost blinded, by the sight of God's glory, and fell face down on the ground.[24] As for us, even if we have never like these men glimpsed the splendour of Almighty God, we know we are unfit to enter his presence in time or in eternity.

In saying this, we have not forgotten our human dignity with which this chapter began. Yet we must do justice to Jesus' own evaluation of evil in our human condition. It is universal (in every human being without exception), self-centred (a revolt against God and neighbour), inward (issuing from our heart, our fallen nature) and defiling (making us unclean and therefore unfit for God). We who were made by God like God are disqualified from living with God.

The resulting paradox

Here, then, is the paradox of our humanness: our dignity and our depravity. We are capable both of the loftiest nobility and of the basest cruelty. One moment we can behave like God, in whose image we were made, and the next like the beasts, from whom we were meant to be completely distinct. Human beings are the inventors of hospitals for the care of the sick, universities for the acquisition of wisdom, parliaments for the just rule of the people, and churches for the worship of God. But they are also the inventors of torture chambers, concentration camps and nuclear arsenals. Strange, bewildering paradox! – noble and ignoble, rational and irrational, moral and immoral, Godlike and bestial! As C. S. Lewis put it through Aslan, 'You come of the Lord Adam and the Lady Eve. And that is both honour enough to erect the head of the poorest beggar, and shame enough to bow the shoulders of the greatest emperor on earth.'[25]

I do not know any more eloquent description of the human paradox than one which was given by Richard Holloway, now Bishop of Edinburgh, at the Catholic Renewal Conference at Loughborough in April 1978:

> This is my dilemma ... [he said], I am dust and ashes, frail and wayward, a set of predetermined behavioural responses ... riddled with fears, beset with needs ... the quintessence of dust and unto dust I shall return ... But there is something else in me ... Dust I may be, but troubled dust, dust that dreams, dust that has strange premonitions of transfiguration, of a glory in store, a destiny prepared, an inheritance that will one day be my own ... So my life is stretched out in a painful dialectic between ashes and glory, between weakness and transfiguration. I am a riddle to myself, an exasperating enigma ... this strange duality of dust and glory.

Faced with the horror of their own dichotomy, some people are foolish enough to imagine that they can sort themselves out, banishing the evil and liberating the good within them. The classic expression both of our human ambivalence and of our hopes of self-salvation was given by Robert Louis Stevenson in his famous tale *The Strange Case of Dr Jekyll and Mr Hyde* (1886). Henry Jekyll was a wealthy and respectable doctor, inclined to religion and philanthropy. But he was conscious that his personality had another and darker side, so that he was 'committed to a profound duplicity of life'. He discovered that 'man is not truly one, but truly two'. He then began to dream that he could solve the problem of his duality if only both sides of him could be 'housed in separate identities', the unjust going one way, and the just the other. So he developed a drug by which he could assume the deformed body and evil personality of Mr Hyde, his *alter ego*, through whom he gave vent to his passions – hatred, violence, blasphemy and even murder.

At first Dr Jekyll was in control of his transformations, and boasted that the moment he chose he could be rid of Mr Hyde for ever. But gradually Hyde gained ascendancy over Jekyll, until he began to become Hyde involuntarily, and only by great effort could resume his existence as Jekyll. 'I was slowly losing hold of my original and better self, and becoming slowly incorporated with my second and worse.' Finally, a few moments before his exposure and arrest, he committed suicide.

The truth is that every Jekyll has his Hyde, whom he cannot control and who threatens to take him over. In fact, the continuing paradox of our humanness throws much light on both our private and our public lives. Let me give an example of each.

I begin with *personal redemption*. Because evil is so deeply entrenched within us, self-salvation is impossible. So our most urgent need is redemption, that is to say, a new beginning in life which offers us both a cleansing from the pollution of sin and a new heart, even a new creation, with new perspectives, new ambitions and new powers. And because we were made in God's image, such redemption is possible. No human being is irredeemable. For God came after us in Jesus Christ, and pursued us even to the desolate agony of the cross, where he took our place, bore our sin and died our death, in order that we might be forgiven. Then he rose, ascended and sent the Holy Spirit, who is able to enter our personality and change us from within. If there is any better news for the human race than this, I for one have never heard it.

My second example of our paradoxical human situation relates to *social progress*. The fact that men and women – even very degraded people – retain vestiges of the divine image in which they were created is evident. This is why, on the whole, all human beings prefer justice to injustice, freedom to oppression, love to hatred, and peace to violence. This fact of everyday observation raises our hopes for social change. Most people cherish visions of a better world. The complementary fact, however, is that human beings are 'twisted with self-centredness' (as Archbishop Michael Ramsey used to define original sin), and this places limits on our expectations. The followers of Jesus are realists, not Utopians. It is possible to improve society (and the historical record of Christian social influence has been notable), but the perfect society, which will be 'the home of righteousness' alone,[26] awaits the return of Jesus Christ.

Notes

[1] Jb. 7:17; 25:4–6; Ps. 8:3–4.

[2] J. S. Whale, *Christian Doctrine* (1941; Fontana, 1957), p. 33.

[3] *Ibid.*, p. 41.

[4] Gn. 1:26–28.

[5] Keith Thomas, *Man and the Natural World: Changing Attitudes in England 1500–1806* (1983; Penguin, 1984).

[6] *Ibid.*, p. 31.

[7] *Ibid.*, p. 31.

[8] *Ibid.*, p. 32. See also pp. 37–39, 43, 166 and 177.

[9] Gn. 1:26, 28; Ps. 8:5–8.

[10] Gn. 2:7; 7:22.

[11] Gn. 1:22, 28.

[12] Ps. 73:22; 32:9.

[13] Is. 1:3.

[14] Je. 8:7.

[15] Pr. 6:6–8.

[16] Gn. 2:8, 15.

[17] Jn. 17:21.

[18] Emil Brunner, *Man in Revolt* (1937; ET Lutterworth, 1939), pp. 419–420.

[19] Act II, Scene 2.

[20] Mk. 7:14–15, 21–23.

[21] Mt. 7:11.

[22] Dag Hammarskjöld, *Markings*, translated by Leif Sjöberg and W. H. Auden (Faber, 1964), pp. 128–129.

[23] Mk. 7:23.

[24] Ex. 3:1–6; Is. 6:1-5; Ezk. 1, especially verse 28.

[25] C. S. Lewis, *Prince Caspian* (Geoffrey Bles, 1951), p. 185.

[26] 2 Pet. 3:13.

TWO

Authentic freedom

One of the best ways of sharing the gospel with modern men and women is to present it in terms of freedom. At least three arguments may be used for this approach.

First, freedom is an extremely appealing topic. The worldwide revolt against authority, which began in the 1960s, is seen as synonymous with a worldwide quest for freedom. Many people are obsessed with it, and are spending their lives in pursuit of it. For some it is still *national* freedom, emancipation from a colonial or neo-colonial yoke. For others it is *civil* rights, as they protest against racial, religious or ethnic discrimination and demand the protection of minority opinions. Yet others are preoccupied with the search for *economic* freedom, freedom from hunger, poverty and unemployment. At the same time, all of us are concerned for our *personal* freedom. Even those who campaign most vigorously for the other freedoms I have mentioned (national, civil and economic) often know that they are not liberated people themselves. They cannot always put a name to the tyrannies which oppress them. Yet they feel frustrated, unfulfilled and unfree.

In an interview with the widely acclaimed novelist John Fowles, published under the title 'A Sort of Exile in Lyme Regis', Daniel Halpern asked him: 'Is there a particular picture of the world that you would like to develop in your writing? Something that has remained important to you?'

'Freedom, yes,' John Fowles replied, 'how you achieve freedom. That obsesses me. All my books are about that.'[1]

Secondly, freedom is a great Christian word. Jesus Christ is portrayed in the New Testament as the world's supreme liberator. 'The Spirit of the Lord is on me,' he claimed, applying an Old Testament prophecy to himself, 'because he has anointed me to preach good news to the poor. He has sent me to proclaim freedom for the prisoners and recovery of sight for the blind, to release the oppressed, to proclaim the year of the Lord's favour.'[2] Whether Jesus intended the poor, the prisoners, the blind and the oppressed to be understood as material or spiritual categories or both (the question continues to be hotly debated), the good news he proclaimed to them was certainly 'freedom' or 'release'. Later in his public ministry he added the promise: 'If the Son sets you free, you will be free indeed.'[3] Then the apostle Paul became the champion of Christian liberty and wrote: 'It is for freedom that Christ has set us free. Stand firm, then, and do not let yourselves be burdened again by a yoke of slavery.'[4] For those who find 'salvation' a bit of meaningless religious jargon, and even an embarrassment, 'freedom' is an excellent substitute. To be saved by Jesus Christ is to be set free.

Thirdly, freedom is much misunderstood. Even those who talk loudest and longest about freedom have not always paused first to define what they are talking about. A notable example is the Marxist orator who was waxing eloquent on the street corner about the freedom we would all enjoy after the revolution. 'When we get freedom', he cried, 'you'll all be able to smoke cigars like that,' pointing at an opulent gentleman walking by.

'I prefer my fag,' shouted a heckler.

'When we get freedom,' the Marxist continued, ignoring the interruption and warming to his theme, 'you'll all be able to drive in cars like that,' pointing to a sumptuous Mercedes which was driving by.

'I prefer my bike,' shouted the heckler.

And so the dialogue continued until the Marxist could bear his tormentor no longer. Turning on him, he said: 'When we get freedom, you'll do what you're told.'

The negative: freedom *from*

So what is freedom? A true definition is bound to begin negatively. We have to identify the forces which tyrannize us and so inhibit our freedom. Only then can we grasp how Christ is able to liberate us.

First, Jesus Christ offers us *freedom from guilt*. We should be thankful for the current reaction against Freud's insistence that guilt feelings are pathological, symptoms of mental sickness. Some doubtless are, especially in certain kinds of depressive illness, but not all guilt is false guilt. On the contrary, an increasing number of contemporary psychologists and psychotherapists, even if they make no Christian profession, are telling us that we must take our responsibilities seriously. The late Dr Hobart Mowrer of the University of Illinois, for example, understood human life in contractual terms and saw 'sin' as a breach of contract for which restitution must be made. Certainly the Bible has always emphasized both our obligations as human beings and our failure to meet them. In particular, we have asserted ourselves against the love and authority of God and against the welfare of our neighbours. To use straightforward Christian language, we are not only sinners but guilty sinners, and our conscience tells us so. According to one of Mark Twain's witticisms, 'Man is the only animal that blushes – or needs to.'[5]

Now no-one is free who is unforgiven. If I were not sure of God's mercy and forgiveness, I could not look you in the face, or (more important) God. I would want to run away and hide, as Adam and Eve did in the Garden of Eden. For it was in Eden, not at Watergate, that the device called 'cover-up' was first invented. I would certainly not be free. Not long before she died in 1988, in a moment of surprising candour on television, Marghanita Laski, one of our best-known secular humanists and novelists, said: 'What I envy most about you Christians is your forgiveness; I have nobody to forgive me.'

'But', as Christians want to shout from the housetops, echoing the penitential psalmist, 'there is forgiveness with God.'[6] For in his love for sinners like us, God entered our world in the person of his Son. Having lived a life of perfect righteousness, he identified himself in his death with our unrighteousness. He bore our sin, our guilt, our death in our place, in order that we might be forgiven.

So freedom begins with forgiveness. I remember a student at a university in the north of England, who had been brought up in spiritism but was taken by a fellow student to a Christian meeting, where he heard the gospel. The following weekend the battle for his soul began in earnest, until (as he wrote later) he cried in despair to Jesus Christ to save him. Then, he went on, 'he really came to me. I felt actual, real love, I can't describe it. It was just pure beauty and serenity. And despite the fact that I knew nothing about salvation and sin, and did not even know what they meant, I just *knew* I was forgiven ... I was unbelievably happy.'

Secondly, Jesus Christ offers us *freedom from self.* Talking once with some Jewish believers, he is recorded as having said to them: 'If you hold to my teaching, you are really my disciples. Then you will know the truth, and the truth will set you free.'

They were immediately indignant. How dared he say that they needed in some way to be liberated? 'We are Abraham's descendants', they expostulated, 'and have never been slaves of anyone. How can you say that we shall be set free?'

Jesus replied, 'I tell you the truth, everyone who sins is a slave to sin.'[7]

So if guilt is the first slavery from which we need to be freed, sin is the second. And what does that mean? Like 'salvation', 'sin' is a word which belongs to the traditional Christian vocabulary. 'I am not a sinner,' people often say, because they seem to be associating sin with specific and rather sensational misdeeds like murder, adultery and theft. But 'sin' has a much wider connotation than that. I can myself remember what a revelation it was to me to learn, especially through the teaching of Archbishop William Temple, that what the Bible means by 'sin' is primarily self-centredness. For God's two great commandments are first that we love him with all our being and secondly that we love our neighbour as we love ourselves. Sin, then, is the reversal of this order. It is to put ourselves first, virtually proclaiming our own autonomy, our neighbour next when it suits our convenience, and God somewhere in the background.

That self-centredness is a world-wide phenomenon of human experience is evident from the rich variety of words in our language which are compounded with 'self'. There are more than fifty which have a pejorative meaning – words like self-applause, self-absorption, self-assertion, self-advertisement, self-indulgence, self-gratification, self-glorification, self-pity, self-importance, self-interest and self-will.

Moreover, our self-centredness is a terrible tyranny. Malcolm Muggeridge used often to speak and write of 'the dark little dungeon of my own ego'. And what a dark dungeon it is! To be engrossed in our own selfish concerns and ambitions, without regard either for the glory of God or for the good of others, is to be confined in the most cramped and unhealthy of prisons.

Yet Jesus Christ, who rose from the dead and is alive, can liberate us. It is possible for us to know 'the power of his resurrection'.[8] Or, to put the same truth in different words, the living Jesus can enter our personality by his Spirit and turn us inside out. Not of course that we claim to be perfect, but that by the power of his indwelling Spirit we have at least begun to experience a transformation from self to unself. Our previously closed personality is starting to unfold to Christ, like a flower to the rising sun.

Thirdly, Jesus Christ offers us *freedom from fear*. The ancient world into which he came lived in apprehension of the powers which, it was believed, inhabited the stars. Still today the traditional religion of primitive tribespeople is haunted by malevolent spirits who need to be placated. The lives of modern men and women are also overshadowed by fear. There are the common fears which have always plagued human beings – the fear of sickness, bereavement, old age and death, together with the fear of the unknown, the occult and of nuclear extinction. Most of us have also sometimes suffered from irrational fears, and it is extraordinary how many educated people entertain superstitious fears. They touch wood, cross their fingers, carry charms and refuse to sit down thirteen to a meal because it is an unlucky number. For this reason many highrise hotels in the United States have no thirteenth floor. As you go up in the elevator and watch the illuminated panel, the numbers jump from 10, 11 and 12 to 14. For people are too superstitious to sleep on the thirteenth floor and do not seem to realize that it is still the thirteenth even if you call it the fourteenth! As for us in Britain, according to a recent opinion poll, although nine tenths of the population still believe in a God of some kind, twice as many adults read their horoscope each week as their Bible.

All fear brings a measure of paralysis. Nobody who is afraid is free. Moreover, fear is like fungus: it grows most rapidly in the dark. It is essential, therefore, to bring our fears out into the light and look at them, especially in the light of the victory and supremacy of Jesus Christ. For he who died and rose has also been exalted to his Father's right hand, and everything has been put 'under his feet'.[9] So where are the things of which we were previously afraid? They are under the feet of the triumphant Christ. It is when we see them there that their power to terrify is broken.

That fear and freedom are mutually incompatible was well illustrated for me once by a young African lecturer. We had been discussing the need for Christians to take a greater interest in natural history as God's creation. 'Before I became a Christian,' he responded, 'I was afraid of many things, especially snakes. But now I find it hard to kill one because I enjoy watching them. I thank God that now I am really free.'

The positive: freedom *for*

So far we have related the tyrannies which impede our freedom to the three major events in the experience of Jesus Christ, his death, resurrection and exaltation. There is freedom from guilt because he died for us, freedom from self because we may live in the power of his resurrection, and freedom from fear because he reigns, with all things under his feet.

It is a serious error, however, to define freedom in entirely negative terms, even if dictionaries make this mistake. According to one, freedom is 'the absence of hindrance, restraint, confinement, repression', while according to another to be free is to be 'not enslaved, not imprisoned, unrestricted, unrestrained, unhampered'. Every negative, however, has its positive counterpart. The true cry for freedom is not only for rescue from some tyranny, but also for liberty to live a full and meaningful life. Once a country has been delivered from a colonial regime, it is free to discover and develop its own national identity. Once the press is delivered from governmental control and censorship, it is free to publish the truth. Once a racial minority is delivered from discrimination, it is free to enjoy self-respect and dignity. For it is nationhood which is denied when a country is not free, truth when the press is not free, and self-respect when a minority is not free.

What, then, is the positive freedom of human beings? In 1970 Archbishop Michael Ramsey preached a series of four Cambridge University sermons, which were subsequently published under the title *Freedom, Faith and the Future.* In the first he posed the question: 'We know what we want to free men *from.* Do we know what we want to free men *for?'* He went on to answer his own question. Our striving for those freedoms 'which most palpably stir our feelings' (*e.g.* freedom from persecution, arbitrary imprisonment, crippling hunger and poverty) should always be 'in the context of the more radical and revolutionary issue of the freeing of man from self and for the glory of God'.[10]

It is this question of what we are set free for by Christ which we need to pursue. The principle is this: *True freedom is freedom to be our true selves, as God made us and meant us to be.* How can this principle be applied?

We must begin with God himself. Have you ever considered that God is the only being who enjoys perfect freedom? You could argue that he is not free. For his freedom is certainly not absolute in the sense that he can do absolutely anything whatsoever. Scripture itself tells us that he cannot lie, tempt or be tempted, or tolerate evil.[11] Nevertheless, God's freedom is perfect in the sense that he is free to do absolutely anything which he wills to do. God's freedom is freedom to be always entirely himself. There is nothing arbitrary, moody, capricious or unpredictable about him. He is constant, steadfast, unchanging. In fact the chief thing Scripture says he 'cannot' do (cannot because he will not) is to contradict himself. 'He cannot deny himself.'[12] To do this would not be freedom, but self-destruction. God finds his freedom in being himself, his true self.

What is true of God the Creator is also true of all created things and beings. Absolute freedom, freedom unlimited, is an illusion. If it is impossible for God (which it is), it is most certainly impossible for God's creation. God's freedom is freedom to be himself; our freedom is freedom to be ourselves. The freedom of every creature is limited by the nature which God has given it.

Take fish. God created fish to live and thrive in water. Their gills are adapted to absorb oxygen from water. Water is the only element in which a fish can find its fishiness, its identity as a fish, its fulfilment, its freedom. True, it is limited to water, but in that limitation is liberty. Supposing you keep a tropical fish at home. It lives not in a modern, rectangular, aerated tank, but in one of those old-fashioned, Victorian, spherical goldfish bowls. And supposing your fish swims round and round its blessed bowl until it finds its frustration unbearable, decides to make a bid for freedom and leaps out of its confinement. If somehow it manages to leap into a pond in your garden, it will increase its freedom. It is still in water, but there is more water to swim in. If instead it lands on the carpet, or on a concrete path, then of course its attempt to escape spells not freedom but death.

What, then, about human beings? If fish were made for water, what are human beings made for? I think we have to answer that, if water is the element in which fish find their fishiness, then the element in which humans find their humanness is love, the relationships of love. Morris West gives a striking example of this in his book *Children of the Sun*, which tells the story of the *scugnizzi*, the abandoned street children of Naples, and of Father Mario Borelli's love for them. 'There is one thing about us [that is Neapolitans]', Mario said to Morris, 'that never changes. *We have need of love as a fish has need of water*, as a bird has need of air.'[13] He went on to explain that every single one of the *scugnizzi* he knew 'had left home because there was no longer any love for him'.

But it is not the world's street children only who need to love and to be loved, and who discover that life spells love. It is all of us. It is in love that we find and fulfil ourselves. Moreover, the reason for this is not far to seek. It is that God is love in his essential being, so that when he made us in his own image, he gave us a capacity to love as he loves. It is not a random thing, therefore, that God's two great commandments are to love him and each other, for this is our destiny. A truly human existence is impossible without love. Living is loving, and without love we wither and die. As Robert Southwell, the sixteenth-century Roman Catholic poet, expressed it: 'Not when I breathe, but when I love, I live.' He was probably echoing Augustine's remark that the soul lives where it loves, not where it exists.

True love, however, places constraints on the lover, for love is essentially self-giving. And this brings us to a startling Christian paradox. True freedom is freedom to be my true self, as God made me and meant me to be. And God made me for loving. But loving is giving, self-giving. Therefore, in order to be myself, I have to deny myself and give myself. In order to be free, I have to serve. In order to live, I have to die to my own self-centredness. In order to find myself, I have to lose myself in loving.

True freedom is, then, the exact opposite of what many people think. It is not freedom from all responsibility to God and others, in order to live for myself. That is bondage to my own self-centredness. Instead, true freedom is freedom from my silly little self, in order to live responsibly in love for God and others.

Yet the secular mind cannot come to terms with this Christian paradox of freedom through love. For example, Françoise Sagan, the French novelist, was interviewed shortly before her fiftieth birthday in 1985. She said she was perfectly satisfied with her life and had no regrets.

'You have had the freedom you wanted?'

'Yes.' Then she qualified her statement. 'I was obviously less free when I was in love with someone … But one's not in love all the time. Apart from that … I'm free.'

The implication was clear: love inhibits liberty. The more you love, the less free you are, and *vice versa*. Presumably, therefore, the way to be completely free is to avoid all the entanglements of love, indeed to give up loving altogether.[14]

But Jesus taught the opposite in one of his favourite epigrams, which he seems to have quoted in different forms and contexts. In the formerly familiar language of the King James Version, he said: 'Whoever would save his life will lose it; and whoever loses his life for my sake and the gospel's will save it.'[15] I used to imagine that Jesus was referring to martyrs who lay down their life for him. And the principle he is enunciating certainly includes them. But the 'life' he is talking about, which can be either saved or lost, is not our physical existence (*zōē*) but our soul or self (*psychē*), which is not infrequently used in place of the reflexive 'himself' or 'herself'. One could, then, perhaps paraphrase Jesus' epigram in these terms: 'If you insist on holding on to yourself, and on living for yourself, and refuse to let yourself go, you will lose yourself. But if you are willing to give yourself away in love, then, at the moment of complete abandon, when you imagine that everything is lost, the miracle takes place and you find yourself and your freedom.' It is only sacrificial service, the giving of the self in love to God and others, which is perfect freedom.

Authentic freedom, then, combines the negative (freedom from) with the positive (freedom for). Or, to put it another way, it brings together freedom from tyranny and freedom under authority. Jesus illustrated this in one of his best-known invitations:

> Come to me, all you who are weary and burdened, and I will give you rest. Take my yoke upon you and learn from me, for I am gentle and humble in heart, and you will find rest for your souls. For my yoke is easy and my burden is light.[16]

Here are actually two invitations, to which is attached a single promise. The promise is 'rest', which seems to include the notion of freedom. 'I will give you rest,' Jesus says (verse 28). Again, 'you will find rest for your souls' (verse 29). But to whom does he promise rest? He gives it first to those who come to him 'weary and burdened', for he lifts their burdens and sets them free. He gives it secondly to those who take his yoke upon them and learn from him. Thus, true rest is found in Jesus Christ our Saviour, who frees us from the tyranny of guilt, self and fear, and in Jesus Christ our Lord, when we submit to his teaching authority. For his yoke is easy, his burden is light, and he himself is 'gentle and humble in heart'.

Notes

1 *London Magazine*, March 1971.

2 Lk. 4:18–19, quoting Is. 61:1–2.

3 Jn. 8:36.

4 Gal. 5:1.

5 *Following the Equator* (1897), Vol. 1, ch. 27.

6 *Cf.* Ps. 130:4.

7 Jn. 8:31–34.

8 Phil. 3:10.

9 Eph. 1:22.

10 Michael Ramsey, *Freedom, Faith and the Future* (SPCK, 1970), p. 12.

11 *E.g.* Heb. 6:18; Jas. 1:13; Hab. 1:13.

12 2 Tim. 2:13 (RSV).

13 Morris West, *Children of the Sun* (1957; Pan, 1958), pp. 94–95.

14 The interview appeared in *Le Monde,* and in an English translation in the *Guardian Weekly* on 23 June 1985.

15 Mk. 8:35.

16 Mt. 11:28–30.

THREE

Christ and his cross

The gospel is good news of freedom. That was my theme in the last chapter. Yet this on its own is a one-sided emphasis. For what the gospel announces, according to the New Testament, is not just what Christ offers people today, but what he once did to make this offer possible. The apostolic gospel brings together the past and the present, the once and the now, historical event and contemporary experience. It declares not only that Jesus saves, but that he died for our sins, and was raised from death, in order to be able to do so. The gospel is not preached if the saving power is proclaimed and the saving events omitted, especially the cross.

In this chapter we will reflect on one of Paul's greatest statements about the origin, content and power of the gospel, and in particular about the centrality of Christ's cross.

When I came to you, brothers, I did not come with eloquence or superior wisdom as I proclaimed to you the testimony about God. For I resolved to know nothing while I was with you except Jesus Christ and him crucified. I came to you in weakness and fear, and with much trembling. My message and my preaching were not with wise and persuasive words, but with a demonstration of the Spirit's power, so that your faith might not rest on men's wisdom, but on God's power.[1]

From this essentially trinitarian text three major lessons about evangelism stand out. They concern the Word of God, the cross of Christ and the power of the Spirit.

The Word of God

The gospel is truth from God. What Paul proclaimed to the Corinthians, he said, was not 'superior wisdom', that is, human wisdom or the wisdom of the world,[2] but the word of God or the wisdom of God, which he here calls either God's 'testimony' (*martyrion*) or God's 'mystery' (*mystērion*). The Greek words are similar and the manuscript evidence between them is fairly evenly balanced. Further, both occur within the first two chapters of this letter: *martyrion* may look back to 1:6, while *mystērion* may look forward to 2:7. Whichever is the correct reading, the sense is the same, namely that Paul's message came from God. If 'testimony' is right, then it is 'God's attested truth' (NEB). If 'mystery' is right, then it is God's secret truth (GNB). In either case the apostle's gospel is God's truth.

This is where all true evangelism must begin. We have not invented our message. We do not come to people with our own human speculations. We are rather bearers of God's word, trustees of God's gospel, stewards of God's revealed secrets.

Moreover, Paul's delivery was compatible with his message. He came to the Corinthians neither with 'eloquence' nor with 'superior wisdom' (verse 1). As to content, he renounced proud human wisdom, humbly submitting instead to the word of God about Christ (verse 2). As to delivery, he renounced proud human rhetoric, humbly relying instead on the Holy Spirit's power (verses 3–5). As C. H. Hodge put it in his commentary, he came 'neither as a rhetorician nor as a philosopher'.[3]

Please do not misinterpret this. There is no possible justification here either for a gospel without content or for a style without form. What Paul was renouncing was neither doctrinal substance, nor rational argument, but only the wisdom and the rhetoric of the world. We know this because Luke tells us in Acts 18 what Paul's evangelistic ministry in Corinth had been like. First, 'he reasoned in the synagogue' every sabbath, 'trying to persuade Jews and Greeks' (verse 4). Then he stayed on for eighteen months 'teaching them the word of God' (verse 11). In consequence, he could sum up his preaching in Corinth in terms of 'trying to persuade people'.[4] He both taught the truth and convinced people of the truth.

We have no liberty, then, to invite people to come to Christ by closing, stifling or suspending their minds. No. Since God has made them rational beings, he expects them to use their minds. To be sure, they will never believe apart from the illumination of the Spirit. Without this all our arguments will be fruitless. 'But', wrote Gresham Machen, 'because argument is insufficient, it does not follow that it is unnecessary. What the Holy Spirit does in the new birth is not to make a person a Christian regardless of the evidence, but on the contrary to clear away the mists from his eyes and enable him to attend to the evidence.'[5]

So then, the gospel is truth from God, which has been committed to our trust. Our responsibility is to present it as clearly, coherently and cogently as we can, and like the apostles to argue it as persuasively as we can. And all the time, as we do this, we will be trusting the Holy Spirit of truth to dispel people's ignorance, overcome their prejudices and convince them about Christ.

The cross of Christ

We come now to verse 2: 'I resolved to know nothing while I was with you except Jesus Christ and him crucified.' Some people misread this as if Paul had written 'except Jesus Christ crucified' and conclude that his sole topic was the cross. What Paul actually wrote, however (and what is consistent with Luke's description in the Acts of his evangelistic labours), was that he determined to know nothing 'except Jesus Christ' (his message focused on him) and (especially though not exclusively) 'him crucified'. What about Christ's resurrection, then? It certainly loomed large in the preaching of the apostles. Yet they understood and proclaimed it not as an isolated or in-dependent event, but in relation to the cross. For the resurrection was not only the sequel to the death of Jesus; it was the reversal of the human verdict passed on him and the public vindication of the divine purpose in his death.

We now note that, before Paul arrived in Corinth, he made a decision to concentrate in his preaching on Christ, and especially on the cross. 'I decided' (RSV), he wrote, 'I determined' (AV), 'I resolved' (NEB, NIV) to do so. It is this decision which we have to investigate; why did he need to make it?

The popular reconstruction of the situation is well known. Paul arrived in Corinth from Athens. His sermon to the Athenian philosophers (so the theory goes) had been a flop. Not only had it been too intellectual, but Paul had not preached the gospel. He had focused on the creation instead of the cross. As a result, there had been no conversions. So, on his way from Athens to Corinth, Paul repented of the distorted gospel he had preached in Athens and resolved in Corinth to limit his message to the cross.

I confess that when I first heard this theory propounded, many years ago now, I swallowed it hook, line and sinker. Since then, however, I have had to reject it, for it does not stand up to examination. First, Paul's Athens mission had not been a failure. On the contrary, 'some men joined him and believed, among them Dionysius the Areopagite and a woman named Damaris and others with them'.[6] Secondly, Luke in his Acts narrative gives no hint that he thinks Paul's Athenian sermon a mistake; on the contrary he records it as a model of the apostle's preaching to Gentile intellectuals. Thirdly, Paul almost certainly did preach the cross in Athens, since he proclaimed 'Jesus and the resurrection',[7] and you cannot preach the resurrection without the death which preceded it. To be sure, because of his Gentile audience Paul began situationally with idolatry and creation, rather than with Old Testament Scripture, but he did not stop there. The sermon Luke records would have taken only two minutes to preach; Paul must have elaborated this outline considerably. Fourthly, Paul did not in fact change his tactics in Corinth. As in Athens, so in Corinth, Luke portrays him continuing to argue, to teach and to persuade.[8]

What was Paul's decision, then? Behind every resolute decision there lies some previous indecision, a situation in which various options present themselves and we are obliged to choose, deciding for one of them over against the others. Evidently, then, behind Paul's decision to preach only Christ, and especially the cross, there lay an alternative, indeed a temptation, either to preach Christ without the cross, or not to preach Christ at all but rather the wisdom of the world. So why was this a temptation to Paul as he travelled from Athens to Corinth? It was not surely his imagined failure in Athens, but rather his fear of the reception awaiting him in Corinth. So who were these Corinthians that Paul should have been so intimidated by them and so apprehensive as he approached them ('in weakness and fear, and with much trembling', verse 3), and that he should have found it necessary to make a firm decision in relation to them?

As we ask and answer these questions, we shall also uncover the chief contemporary objections to the message of Christ and his cross. Indeed, we shall see why we ourselves need to make the same resolute decision today.

(a) *The intellectual objection*, or the foolishness of the cross. Paul had already encountered intellectual scorn in Athens. The philosophers had insulted him by calling him a *spermologos* or 'seed-picker'. The word was applied literally to scavenging birds, and so to vagrants who lived on scraps they could find in the gutter. Metaphorically it denoted teachers who trade only in second-hand ideas. The Athenians worshipped at the shrine of originality;[9] they despised the old-fashioned and the obsolete.

The philosophers scoffed when the resurrection was mentioned.[10] 'They made fun of him' (GNB). I think that means they burst out laughing. How they reacted when Paul preached the cross Luke does not say. But Paul knew that it was 'a stumbling block to Jews and foolishness to Gentiles'.[11] To the unbelieving Jew it was inconceivable that the Messiah should die 'on a tree', that is, under the curse of God.[12] To the unbelieving Gentile it was ludicrous to suppose that a god, one of the immortals, should die. Celsus, the second-century cynic, was scathing in criticizing Christians for this. He imagined, wrote Origen, that '"in worshipping him who", as *he* says, "was taken prisoner and put to death, we are acting like"' others who actually worshipped dead people.[13]

Corinth had not escaped the intellectual arrogance of Athens. These cities were only about fifty miles apart as the crow flies. Paul's first letter to the Corinthians provides plenty of evidence that pride of intellect was one of the chief sins of the Corinthian church. This was the background against which Paul made his decision to renounce the wisdom of the world in favour of 'the foolishness of the cross'. Sneers and jeers awaited him. But he knew that 'the foolishness of God is wiser than man's wisdom'.[14]

Still today the message of the cross is deeply despised. The biblical, evangelical doctrine of the atonement (that Christ died instead of us, as our substitute, the death we deserved to die) is opposed and even mocked. It is said to be 'primitive', 'forensic', 'unjust', 'immoral' and 'barbaric'. A. J. Ayer called the allied Christian doctrines of sin and atonement 'intellectually contemptible and morally outrageous'.[15] And a contemporary liberal theologian has described aspects of my own presentation in *The Cross of Christ* as 'untenable', 'unintelligible', 'not only inexplicable but also incomprehensible', and so 'incommunicable'. How are we to respond to this battery of negative epithets? We do not deny that some evangelical formulations have been unbalanced and unbiblical. Whenever we have cast Jesus Christ in the role of a third party, who intervened to rescue us from an angry God, we have been guilty of a travesty which stands condemned, since it is God who loved the world and God who took the initiative to send his Son to die for us. Yet the initiative he took led to Christ being 'made sin' and 'made a curse' for us,[16] and such language often arouses an extraordinarily emotional hostility. Hence the temptation to trim the gospel of Christ crucified, to eliminate its more objectionable features, and to try to make it more palatable to sensitive modern palates. No wonder the apostle sounds almost fierce in expressing his decision to know only Jesus Christ and especially his cross. It was a choice between faithfulness and popularity.

(b) *The religious objection*, or the exclusiveness of the gospel. If Paul found Athens 'full of idols',[17] he is not likely to have found Corinth less idolatrous. It is known to have had at least two dozen temples, each dedicated to a different deity. Even today, surviving from the ancient temple of Apollo, seven massive pillars are still standing among the ruins of Corinth. And behind the city the rocky Acrocorinth rises nearly 2,000 feet above it, on which the temple of Aphrodite once stood. So the Corinthians, like the Athenians, were 'very religious'.[18] They honoured many gods, who tolerated one another in amicable co-existence.

The Corinthians would not have raised any objection if the Christian evangelists were content to add Jesus to their already well-stocked pantheon. But the apostle Paul had a very different object in view when he visited the city. He wanted Corinth, with all its inhabitants and all its gods, to bow down and worship Jesus. He came to Corinth with the firm intention of knowing nothing 'except Jesus Christ and him crucified'. He knew very well, as he wrote to them later, that there were 'many "gods" and many "lords"' who were competing for their allegiance. But, as far as he was concerned, 'there is but one God, the Father, from whom all things came and for whom we live; and there is but one Lord, Jesus Christ, through whom all things came and through whom we live',[19] and he was not prepared to compromise. He thought of his visit as having effected their betrothal to Christ, and he felt a godly jealousy for them. 'I promised you to one husband, to Christ, so that I might present you as a pure virgin to him,' he wrote. 'But I am afraid that just as Eve was deceived by the serpent's cunning, your minds may somehow be led astray from your sincere and pure devotion to Christ.'[20] For Jesus Christ would not share his glory with Apollo or Aphrodite or anybody else.

The world's religious situation has not greatly changed. True, the old gods of Greece and Rome have long since been discredited and discarded. But new gods have arisen in their place, and other ancient faiths have experienced a resurgence. As a result of modern communication media and ease of travel, many countries are increasingly pluralistic. What people want is an easygoing syncretism, a truce in inter-religious competition, a mishmash of the best from all religions. But we Christians cannot surrender either the finality or the uniqueness of Jesus Christ. There is simply nobody else like him; his incarnation, atonement and resurrection have no parallels. In consequence, he is the one and only mediator between God and the human race.[21] This exclusive affirmation is strongly, even bitterly, resented. It is regarded by many as intolerably intolerant. Yet the claims of truth compel us to maintain it, however much offence it may cause. I elaborate this topic in chapter 18.

(c) *The personal objection*, or the humbling of human pride. Common to all religions except Christianity is the flattering notion (expressed in different ways) that we are capable, if not of achieving our salvation, at least of contributing substantially to it. This doctrine of self-salvation is exceedingly conducive to our self-esteem. It appeals to our proud ego; it saves us from the ultimate embarrassment of being humbled before the cross.

The Corinthians were no exception; they were a proud people. They were proud of their city, which had been beautifully rebuilt by Julius Caesar in 46 BC, following its destruction for rebellion a century previously; proud that Augustus had promoted Corinth over Athens to be the capital of the new province of Achaia; proud of their trade, their affluence, their culture, their Isthmian games, and their religious zeal.

Then along came this brash Christian missionary, this whippersnapper, this ugly little fellow with a bald pate, bandy legs and beetle brows, who appeared to have no respect for their distinguished city. He presumed to tell them that neither their wisdom, nor their wealth, nor their religion could save them; that they could not in fact save themselves from the judgment of God – or even help towards their salvation – by anything they could do; that this was why Jesus Christ had died for them; and that apart from him they would perish. Who did he think he was to insult them in this way? It was a stunning humiliation to a proud people. The message of the cross was a stumbling-block to proud Jews and proud Gentiles alike. No wonder the main response to the gospel in Corinth came from the lower echelons of society: 'Not many of you were wise by human standards; not many were influential; not many were of noble birth.' Instead, it was the foolish, the weak, the lowly, and the despised, who knew they had nothing to offer, whom God chose and called.[22]

Still today nothing keeps people out of the kingdom of God more than pride. As Emil Brunner put it, in all other religions 'man is spared the final humiliation of knowing that the Mediator [*sc.* Jesus Christ] must bear the punishment instead of him ... He is not stripped absolutely naked'.[23] But the gospel strips us naked (we have no clothing in which to appear before God), and declares us bankrupt (we have no currency with which to buy the favour of heaven).

(d) *The moral objection*, or the call to repentance and holiness. Corinth was a flourishing commercial centre, which commanded the trade routes both north–south by land and east–west by sea. So the city was full of merchants, travellers and sailors. Being strangers in a strange city, they exercised little moral restraint. Besides, Aphrodite, known to the Romans as Venus, the goddess of love, held court in her temple above the city, encouraged sexual promiscuity among her devotees, and provided a thousand prostitutes to roam the city's streets by night. Corinth was the Vanity Fair of the ancient world. The Greek verb *korinthiazomai* meant 'to practise immorality'.

A brazenly immoral city like Corinth could hardly be expected to welcome the gospel, with its summons to repentance, its warnings that the sexually dissolute will not inherit God's kingdom,[24] and its insistence that after justification comes sanctification (growth in holiness) and after sanctification glorification (when evil will be abolished).

The modern world is no more friendly to the gospel's call to self-control than was the ancient world. It likes to say that there are no such things as moral absolutes any longer, that sexual morality is only a matter of sexual mores, that restraint is bad and permissiveness good, and that Christianity with its prohibitions is the enemy of freedom.

(e) *The political objection*, or the lordship of Jesus Christ. There was a lot of political fervour – even fanaticism – in the Roman Empire. Loyal Roman procurators tended to encourage it, and acted ruthlessly to put down any attempt at rebellion. We need to remember that Jesus himself was condemned in a Roman court for the political offence of sedition, for claiming to be a king in rivalry to Caesar. Similarly, Paul and Silas were accused in Philippi of 'advocating customs unlawful for us Romans to accept or practise',[25] while in Thessalonica they were said to be 'defying Caesar's decrees, saying that there is another king, one called Jesus'.[26]

Were these charges true or untrue? They were both. Of course neither Jesus nor the apostles ever stirred up armed rebellion against Rome. They were not zealots. But they did proclaim that Jesus had ushered in God's kingdom, that his kingdom took precedence over all lesser loyalties, that it would spread throughout the world, and that the king was coming back to take his power and reign. It sounded positively seditious. Indeed, it *was* seditious if 'sedition' means denying undisputed authority to the state by according it to God's Christ.

Still today the one thing a totalitarian regime cannot endure is to be refused the total allegiance which it covets. Christians submit conscientiously to the state, in so far as its God-given authority is used to promote good and punish evil, but we will not worship it. It is Christ we worship, to whom all authority in heaven and on earth has been given. For he died and rose in order to be Lord of all.

Here then are five objections which are levelled against the gospel of Christ and his cross, and which Paul expected to encounter in Corinth. He knew that his message of Christ crucified would be regarded as intellectually foolish (incompatible with wisdom), religiously exclusive (incompatible with tolerance), personally humiliating (incompatible with self-esteem), morally demanding (incompatible with freedom) and politically subversive (incompatible with patriotism).

No wonder Paul felt 'weak ... nervous and shaking with fear',[27] and recognized that he had to make a decision. It was on the one hand a negative decision to renounce the wisdom of the world, namely every system which is offered as an alternative to the gospel, and on the other hand a positive decision to proclaim nothing but Jesus Christ, and especially his cross. The same alternative faces us today. It is the choice between the wisdom of the world, which is foolishness to God, and the foolishness of the cross, which is the wisdom of God.

The power of the Spirit

Some contemporary Christians, hearing Paul's confession of weakness, fear and trembling, would doubtless have rebuked him. 'Paul,' they might have said, 'you've no business to feel nervous or afraid. Pull yourself together! Don't you know what it is to be filled with the Spirit? You ought to be strong, confident and bold.'

But Paul was not afraid to admit that he was afraid. To be sure, he had a mighty intellect and a strong personality, and these powers he had dedicated to Christ. But he was also physically weak and emotionally vulnerable. According to tradition his appearance was unprepossessing. His critics said that 'in person he is unimpressive and his speaking amounts to nothing'.[28] So he was nothing much to look at or to listen to. In addition, disease of some kind (his so-called 'thorn in the flesh')[29] seems to have affected his eyesight and even disfigured him.[30] And he knew the unpopularity of his gospel, the opposition it would arouse in Corinth, and so the cost of being faithful to it.

In what, then, did he put his trust? He tells us in 1 Corinthians 2:4–5. His confidence was not in 'wise and persuasive words' (NIV) or 'plausible words of wisdom' (RSV). That is, he relied neither on the wisdom nor on the eloquence of the world. Instead of the world's wisdom he preached Christ and his cross (verses 1–2), and instead of the world's rhetoric he trusted in the powerful demonstration which the Holy Spirit gives to the word. For only the Holy Spirit can convince people of their sin and need, open their eyes to see the truth of Christ crucified, bend their proud wills to submit to him, set them free to believe in him, and bring them to new birth. This is the powerful 'demonstration' which the Holy Spirit gives to words spoken in human weakness.

This theme of 'power through weakness' is a vital element in Paul's Corinthian correspondence. In both extant letters the apostle emphasizes that it is through human weakness that divine power operates best. He hints that God deliberately makes and keeps his people weak in order to show that the power is his.[31] Paul even adds that the principle applies to God as well as to us, for it is through his own weakness in the cross that he puts forth his power to save.

In 1 Corinthians 1 and 2 the same theme of power through weakness is repeated in three variations. First, we have a weak and foolish message (Christ and the cross). Secondly, it is proclaimed by weak and foolish preachers. Thirdly, it is welcomed by weak and foolish people. Thus God chose a weak instrument (Paul) to bring a weak message (the cross) to weak people (the Corinthian working class). Why? It was 'so that no-one may boast before him' and so that he who does boast will 'boast in the Lord' alone.[32]

The first five verses of 1 Corinthians 2 are perhaps the noblest and richest statement on evangelism in the New Testament. They tell us that the gospel is truth from God about Christ and his cross in the power of the Spirit. Thus the gospel is not human speculation but divine revelation; not popular wisdom but Christ and his despised cross; not by the pressures of advertisement or personality, but by the Holy Spirit. The gospel comes from God, focuses on Christ and him crucified, and is authenticated by the Holy Spirit. This is the trinitarian evangelism of the New Testament.

Notes

[1] 1 Cor. 2:1–5.

[2] 1 Cor. 1:20–21.

[3] C. H. Hodge, *The First Epistle to the Corinthians* (1857; Banner of Truth, 1959), p. 29.

[4] 2 Cor. 5:11; *cf.* Acts 18:13.

[5] J. Gresham Machen, *The Christian Faith in the Modern World* (1936, Eerdmans, 1947), p. 63.

[6] Acts 17:34 (RSV).

[7] Acts 17:18.

[8] For a fuller refutation of the popular reconstruction, see my *The Message of Acts* in the Bible Speaks Today series (IVP, 1990), pp. 289–290.

[9] Acts 17:18, 21.

[10] Acts 17:32.

[11] 1 Cor. 1:23.

[12] Gal. 3:13.

[13] Origen, *Against Celsus*, III. 34.

[14] 1 Cor. 1 :25.

[15] The *Guardian Weekly*, 30 August 1979.

[16] 2 Cor. 5:21; Gal. 3:13.

[17] Acts 17:16.

[18] Acts 17:22.

[19] 1 Cor. 8:5–6.

[20] 2 Cor. 11:2–3.

[21] 1 Tim. 2:5.

[22] 1 Cor. 1:26–29.

[23] Emil Brunner, *The Mediator* (1927; Westminster, 1947), p. 474.

[24] 1 Cor. 6:9–10.

[25] Acts 16:21.

[26] Acts 17:7.

[27] 1 Cor. 2:3 (NEB).

[28] 2 Cor. 10:10.

[29] 2 Cor. 12:7.

[30] *E.g.* Gal. 4:13–14.

[31] See *hina* ('in order that') in 2 Cor. 4:7 and 12:9–10.

[32] 1 Cor. 1:29–31.

FOUR

The relevance of the resurrection

The most fantastic of all Christian claims is that Jesus Christ rose from the dead. It strains our credulity to the limit. Human beings have tried with all possible ingenuity both to defy and to deny death. But only Christ has claimed to conquer it, that is, to defeat it in his own experience, and to deprive it of its power over others. 'I am the resurrection and the life,' he declared. 'He who believes in me will live, even though he dies; and whoever lives and believes in me will never die.'[1] Again, 'I am the Living One; I was dead, and behold I am alive for ever and ever! And I hold the keys of [*i.e.* have authority over] death and Hades.'[2]

Moreover, the very first Christians already enjoyed this confidence. This is clear both from their brave and even joyful readiness to die for Christ, and from the earliest preaching of the apostles. Soon after Pentecost, Luke tells us, the Jewish authorities in Jerusalem 'were greatly disturbed because the apostles were ... proclaiming in Jesus the resurrection of the dead'.[3] The heart of their sermons follows the same pattern: 'you killed him, God raised him, and we are witnesses'.[4] And Paul did not deviate from this,[5] so that the Athenian philosophers, listening to him in the market-place, concluded that he was advocating two foreign deities, because they heard his repeated references to *Iēsous* and *Anastasis* (*resurrection*).[6] Then, when he came later to pass on to the Corinthians an outline of the original gospel he had himself received, he concentrated 'as of first importance' on the death, burial, resurrection and appearances of Jesus.[7] Those earliest followers of Jesus seem to have been both clear and confident about his resurrection.

Three major questions are raised by the claim that Jesus rose (or was raised) from the dead. First, what does it mean (a question of semantics)? Secondly, did it really happen (a question of history)? Thirdly, is it important (a question of relevance)?

What does the resurrection mean?

The semantic question was forced into the public mind in the 1980s by some provocative remarks of David Jenkins, Bishop of Durham. These were interpreted, at least by the popular press, as a rather shocking denial of the resurrection of Jesus Christ.

It is important to be fair to Dr Jenkins, however. He describes himself as a 'believing', not a 'doubting', bishop. He insists that he responded to the questions put to him when he was consecrated a bishop 'unhesitatingly', 'affirmatively' and 'in complete good faith'. Certainly in his earlier books he clearly affirmed the doctrines of the divine-human person of Jesus and of the Trinity. Thus, in his 1966 Bampton Lectures entitled *The Glory of Man* he wrote: 'God and man are distinct realities, who, in and as Jesus Christ, are in perfect union.'[8] And in his 1974 Edward Cadbury Lectures in Birmingham University, which were entitled *The Contradiction of Christianity* and explored what it means to be human, he spoke of the Trinity as 'the necessary legitimate interpretation of the experienced and perceived story of God, Jesus and the Spirit'.[9]

Dr Jenkins also declares that he believes in the resurrection of Jesus Christ. He made the following statement to his Diocesan Synod in early November 1984: 'I do believe in the resurrection of Jesus Christ from the dead ... Anyone who says that I do not believe in the resurrection ... is a liar. This I must say fiercely and categorically.' He will not convince people, however, merely by the use of strong and rather intemperate language. We still have to press the semantic question: what does he mean? In what sense does he believe in the resurrection?

During the service in York Minster in which he was made a bishop, he was asked: 'Do you accept the doctrine of the Christian faith as the Church of England has received it?' Those last eight words are an important qualification. They imply a distinction between two possible ways of 'accepting' Christian doctrine. One might be called 'traditional', namely the acceptance of doctrine in the same way as the Church of England has itself received and understood it from the Scriptures and the Creeds. The other might be called 'idiosyncratic', namely the acceptance of doctrine in the way in which the individual person questioned feels able to receive it, which may deviate widely from biblical teaching and traditional understanding.

Dr Jenkins must have answered 'yes' to the question in the latter sense, since he does not believe that the resurrection involved the transformation of the body of Jesus, which is what the Church of England has always believed and taught. Indeed, he caricatured this view in 1988 as 'a conjuring trick with bones', and at Easter 1989 declared that the risen Lord was 'neither a corpse nor a ghost', as if we were shut up to that alternative.

What light can be thrown on the semantic question? What is meant in the Creed by the resurrection of Jesus Christ? How should we think of the risen Lord? It may be helpful if we clarify what we do not believe, before coming on to affirm what we do.

First, the risen Lord is not just *a surviving influence*. On the one hand, we are not to think of him as having merely survived death, like a ghost. 'Look at my hands and my feet,' he said. 'It is I myself! Touch me and see; a ghost does not have flesh and bones, as you see I have.'[10] On the other hand, 'resurrection' does not mean the mere survival of an influence. Many leaders, who during their lifetime have held sway over their contemporaries' hearts and minds, live on after death in the sense that the memory of their example is a continuing inspiration.

This was certainly true of Che Guevara. He had an extraordinary following. Sartre once described him as 'the most complete man of his age'. In his thirty-nine years (before he was killed in the jungle) he had been a doctor, author, economist, banker, political theorist and guerrilla fighter. He became a legend during his lifetime, a folk hero. In every Cuban classroom the children would chant, 'We will be like Che.' And after his death his influence became greater still. He provided Marxists with the image of a secular saint and martyr. For years the walls of Latin American student buildings were chalked with the words 'Che lives!'[11]

It was similar when Archbishop Makarios of Cyprus died in August 1977. His followers paint-sprayed public buildings with the words 'Makarios lives!'

Is this all Christians mean when they say that 'Jesus lives'? Some seem to be saying little more than this, namely that he exerts his power and spreads his love in the world. Others are affirming some kind of continuing, personal existence for Jesus, so that 'he walks with me and talks with me along life's narrow way'. Yet the grand affirmation of the New Testament is not 'he lives', but 'he is risen'. The resurrection becomes an experience for us only because it was first an event which actually inaugurated a new order of reality.

Secondly, the risen Lord is not *a resuscitated corpse*. Resurrection is not a synonym for resuscitation in either of this word's two uses. To 'resuscitate' can mean either to revive a patient who has gone into a coma or to bring someone back to life who has been pronounced clinically dead. In this second sense Jesus is recorded as having performed three resuscitations during his public ministry. He 'raised from death' (*i.e.* restored to this life) the daughter of Jairus, the son of the widow of Nain, and Lazarus. Each of these three was dead, but was brought back to this life by Jesus. One understands the sympathy which C. S. Lewis expressed for Lazarus: 'To be brought back and have all one's dying to do again was rather hard.'[12]

But Jesus' own resurrection was not a resuscitation in either sense. On the one hand, he was not revived from a swoon or coma, for he had been dead for about thirty-six hours. On the other hand, he was not brought back to this life, with the need to die again. Yet it is popularly supposed that this is what Christians believe about 'resurrection', namely that the body is miraculously reconstituted out of the identical particles of which it is at present composed, and that it then resumes this vulnerable and mortal life. But on the contrary, Jesus was raised to a new plane of existence, in which he was now no longer mortal but 'alive for ever and ever'.[13]

In these first two negatives we agree with the Bishop of Durham. The resurrection was not 'a conjuring trick with bones', and the risen Lord is 'neither a corpse nor a ghost'. The tragedy is that, in using this rather sensational language, the bishop gave the impression that traditional Christian believers are committed to one or other of these options. But, whatever popular notions some people may have entertained, the faith of the church has never been to regard the risen Lord either as a rather ethereal ghostly influence or as a resuscitated corpse.

Thirdly, the risen Lord is not *a revived faith* in the experience of his disciples. This was Rudolf Bultmann's 'demythologized' reconstruction. He began by declaring that the resurrection of Jesus was 'obviously ... not an event of past history'. Why was this so obvious to him? Because 'an historical fact which involves a resurrection from the dead is utterly inconceivable'. But since the church in every age seems to have had very little difficulty in conceiving what Bultmann pronounced inconceivable, what was his problem? It lay in the 'incredibility of a mythical event like the resuscitation of a corpse – for that is what the resurrection means'. What is truly incredible, however, is not the resurrection of Jesus, but the misunderstanding of Bultmann who confused it with a resuscitation. How then did he interpret the 'myth' of Jesus' resurrection? In this way: 'if the event of Easter Day is in any sense an historical event additional to the event of the cross, it is nothing else than the rise of faith in the risen Lord ... All that historical criticism can establish is the fact that the first disciples came to believe in the resurrection.' In other words, Easter was not an event, but an experience; not the objective, historical resurrection of Jesus from the dead, but a subjective, personal recovery of faith in the hearts and minds of his followers.[14]

Fourthly, the risen Lord is not just *an expanded personality.* Yet this seems to express what David Jenkins believes. In 1969 he wrote: 'The resurrection means that God acted to establish Jesus in his person, in his achievements and in his continuing effect.'[15] In a later statement he declared his conviction that Jesus 'rose from the dead', and went on to explain this by affirming that 'the very life and power and purpose and personality which was in him was actually continuing … in the sphere of history, so that he was a risen and living presence and possibility'.[16] Elsewhere, he has spoken of the resurrection as an 'explosion' of the personality of Jesus. In fact, he constantly refers to Jesus' 'personality', and thinks of the resurrection as its 'establishment' or 'liberation' or 'explosion'. So the resurrection was a kind of event, even though it did not involve his body. Dr Jenkins believes in the 'risenness' and 'livingness' of Jesus, though his personality is not now embodied (except in the church).

Fifthly, the risen Lord is not merely *a living experience of the Spirit*. Probably the most comprehensive treatment of the resurrection theme in recent years is *The Structure of Resurrection Belief* by Dr Peter Carnley, Anglican Archbishop of Perth, Western Australia. Like Dr Jenkins he emphasizes that we should think of the resurrection as a present experience rather than a past event, especially as an experience of the Spirit. In his opening chapter he makes plain his sceptical stance. He asserts that Paul nowhere alludes to the empty tomb, even in 1 Corinthians 15:3–8, and that the so-called appearances were not objective. He argues that *ōphthē* ('he appeared') means not so much perception through sight (a visible appearance) as the reception of a new revelation (an intellectual apprehension), or at most a mixture of the two, with the emphasis on the second.[17]

Next come three long chapters in which Archbishop Carnley urges that there was, in fact, no post-mortem event; the real Easter event was the disciples' coming to faith.[18] Consequently, from chapter 5 onwards he refers no longer to 'the resurrection' (an event) but to 'the raised Christ' (an experience). For the Easter faith 'involves a post-mortem experience of encounter with the raised Christ', who is known as the Spirit.[19] And the way we come to recognize the true Spirit of Jesus is that he continues to manifest today in the Christian fellowship the same self-giving love which he displayed on the cross.[20] But, ingenious as this attempted reconstruction is, it cannot be said to do justice to the data of the New Testament, as I hope soon to show.

Sixthly, and in contrast to the previous five proposals, the risen Lord is *a transformed person*. The evidence adduced by the Gospels is that, before and after the resurrection, Jesus is the same person with the same identity ('It is I myself'),[21] but that the resurrection gave him a transformed, transfigured, glorified body. The resurrection was a dramatic act of God by which he arrested the natural process of decay and decomposition ('you will not … let your Holy One see decay'),[22] rescued Jesus out of the realm of death, and changed his body into a new vehicle for his personality, endowed with new powers and possessing immortality.

'I believe in the resurrection', Dr Jenkins has said, 'in exactly the same sense as St Paul believed in the resurrection.'[23] But how can he say this when he does not believe in a bodily resurrection? It is because of 1 Corinthians 15. This great chapter is in two parts, the first relating to the *fact* (verses 1–34), and the second to the *nature* (verses 35–58), of the resurrection. In the first part the resurrection appearances of Jesus appear to be physical; but in the second part the body is said to be 'sown a natural [RSV 'physical'] body ... raised a spiritual body' (verse 44). How, then, are we to harmonize the two halves of 1 Corinthians 15 with each other? Some scholars seize on the expression 'a spiritual body' and insist that the resurrection appearances of verses 5–8 must be understood in the light of it.

According to the New Testament as a whole, however, the assimilation process should be the other way round, and the nature of the 'spiritual body' must be interpreted in such a way as not to contradict the evidence that the resurrected Jesus had a physical body. This evidence is not to be found only in the Gospel narratives of the empty tomb (which liberal scholars tend to dismiss as being in their view too late to be trustworthy), but in the first sermons of Peter and in the early verses of 1 Corinthians 15. I will focus on the latter. In Paul's statement of the gospel, which he claims to be both the *original* gospel, which he had himself 'received' (verse 3), and the *universal* gospel, which they and he all believed (verse 11), he made four affirmations, namely that 'Christ died ... that he was buried, that he was raised on the third day ... and that he appeared ...' Two aspects of the resurrection of Jesus are clear from this.

First, it was *an objective, historical event*. Indeed, it was datable; it happened 'on the third day'. David Jenkins has called it 'not an event, but a series of experiences'. But no, it became a series of experiences only because it was first an event. And in God's providence the words 'on the third day' witness to the historicity of Jesus' resurrection, much as the words 'under Pontius Pilate' in the Apostles' Creed witness to the historicity of his sufferings and death.

Secondly, the resurrection was *a physical event*; it involved his body. The argument now is that the four verbs (died, was buried, was raised, appeared) all have the same subject, namely 'Christ' as a historical, physical person. This is beyond question in the case of the first two. It was his body which died and his body which was buried. The natural presumption, then, is that the very same historical, physical Christ is the subject of the third and fourth verbs, namely that he was raised and then appeared. It would take a high degree of mental gymnastics to claim that without warning the subject changes in the middle of the sentence, that although his body died and was buried, only his personality was raised and seen, and that in fact he was raised while still remaining buried. No, since it was his body which was buried, it must have been his body which was raised. This probably explains the mention of his burial in some of the early apostolic sermons.[24] It is entirely gratuitous, in the light of this, to maintain that the apostle Paul was ignorant of the empty tomb.

It is true that, when the dead and buried body of Jesus was 'raised', it was changed in the process. We are envisaging neither a resuscitation (in which he was raised bodily but not changed), nor a survival (in which he was changed into a ghost, but not raised bodily at all), but a resurrection (in which he was both raised and changed simultaneously).

Did the resurrection really happen?

Let us grant that the apostles, including Paul, did believe in a literal, datable, physical resurrection and transformation of Jesus; were they correct? Can we, who live in the sophisticated, contemporary world of astrophysics, microbiology and computer science, also believe in the resurrection? Yes, we can and we should. Many millions do.

Several books have been written to marshal the evidence for the resurrection.[25] This is an important part of Christian apologetics. All I can attempt here is a straightforward summary of the main lines of evidence.

First, there is *the disappearance of the body*. Everybody agrees that Joseph's tomb was empty, even those who deny the Gospel writers' stories; the rumours of resurrection could never have gained credence if people could have visited the tomb and found the body still in position. So the body had gone. The question has always been, 'What became of it?' No satisfactory explanation has been given of its disappearance, except for the resurrection.

We cannot accept that Jesus only fainted on the cross, then revived in the tomb, and subsequently came out of it by himself. For one thing, first the centurion and later Pilate assured themselves that Jesus was dead. For another, when he did emerge, he gave people the impression that he had conquered death, not that he had almost been conquered by it and was now a seriously sick man in need of hospital treatment.

So did the authorities (Roman or Jewish) deliberately remove the body, in order to prevent the disciples from spreading the rumour that he had risen? It is hard to believe this, since, when the apostles began to proclaim 'Jesus and the resurrection',[26] the authorities could have immediately scotched the new movement by producing the body, instead of which they resorted to violence.

In this case, did the disciples steal the body as part of a hoax, in order to deceive people into thinking that he had risen? That is an impossible theory, for they were prepared to suffer and die for the gospel, and people are not willing to become martyrs for a lie which they have themselves perpetrated.

No explanation of the empty tomb holds water except that God had raised him from the dead.

Secondly, there is *the reappearance of the Lord.* For if Jesus' body had disappeared from the tomb where it had been laid to rest, Jesus himself kept reappearing during a period of nearly six weeks. He is said to have showed himself to certain individuals (*e.g.* Mary Magdalene, Peter and James), to the Twelve, both with and without Thomas, and on one occasion 'to more than five hundred of the brothers at the same time', most of whom were still alive when Paul wrote this in about AD 54,[27] and could therefore have been cross-examined.

These resurrection appearances cannot be dismissed as inventions, since it is plain beyond doubt that the apostles really believed that Jesus had risen. The stories had not been made up. But nor were they hallucinations. Tough fishermen like Peter, James and John are not the kind of personalities who might be susceptible to such symptoms of mental disorder. Further, the great variety of time, place, mood and people in regard to the appearances, together with people's initial reaction of unbelief, make the theory of wishful thinking untenable. The only alternative to inventions and hallucinations is valid, objective appearances.

Thirdly, there is *the emergence of the church.* Something happened to change the apostles and to send them out on their mission to the world. When Jesus died, they were heartbroken, confused and frightened. But within less than two months they came out of hiding, full of joy, confidence and courage. What can account for this dramatic transformation? Only the resurrection, together with Pentecost which followed soon afterwards. From that bunch of disillusioned nobodies has grown a universal community numbering one third of the population of the world. It would take a lot of credulity, even of cynicism, to believe that the whole Christian edifice had been built on a lie, since Jesus Christ never rose from the dead.

The disappearance of the body, the reappearance of the Lord and the emergence of the church together constitute a solid foundation for believing in the resurrection.

Why is the resurrection important?

What we have to ask about the resurrection is not only whether it happened, but whether it really matters whether it happened. For if it happened, it happened nearly 2,000 years ago. How can an event of such remote antiquity have any great importance for us today? Why on earth do Christians make such a song and dance about it? Is it not irrelevant? No; my argument now is that the resurrection resonates with our human condition. It speaks to our needs as no other distant event does or could. It is the mainstay of our Christian assurance.

First, the resurrection of Jesus assures us of *God's forgiveness*. We have already noted that forgiveness is one of our most basic needs and one of God's best gifts. The head of a large English mental hospital has been quoted as saying, 'I could dismiss half my patients tomorrow if they could be assured of forgiveness.'[28] For we all have a skeleton or two in some dark cupboard, memories of things we have thought, said or done, of which in our better moments we are thoroughly ashamed. Our conscience nags, condemns, torments us.

Several times during his public ministry Jesus spoke words of forgiveness and of peace, and in the upper room he referred to the communion cup as his 'blood of the covenant ... poured out for many for the forgiveness of sins'.[29] Thus he linked our forgiveness with his death. And since throughout Scripture death is always welded to sin as its just desert ('the wages of sin is death'),[30] he can have meant only that he was going to die in our place the death which we deserved to die, in order that we might be spared and forgiven.

That is what he said. But how can we know that he was right, that he achieved by his death what he said he would achieve, and that God accepted his death in our place as 'a full, perfect, and sufficient sacrifice, oblation, and satisfaction, for the sins of the whole world'? The answer is that, if he had remained dead, if he had not been visibly and publicly raised from death, we would never have known. Rather, without the resurrection we would have to conclude that his death was a failure. The apostle Paul saw this logic clearly: 'If Christ has not been raised, our preaching is useless and so is your faith.' Again, 'if Christ has not been raised, your faith is futile; you are still in your sins. Then those also who have fallen asleep in Christ are lost.'[31] The terrible consequences of no resurrection would be that the apostles are false witnesses, believers are unforgiven, and the Christian dead have perished. But in fact, Paul continued, Christ was raised from the dead, and by raising him God has assured us that he approves of his sin-bearing death, that he had not died in vain, and that those who trust in him receive a full and free forgiveness. The resurrection validates the cross.

Secondly, the resurrection of Jesus assures us of *God's power*. For we need God's power in the present as well as his forgiveness of the past. Is God really able to change human nature, which appears to be so intractable, to make cruel people kind, selfish people unselfish, immoral people self-controlled, and sour people sweet? Is he able to take people who are dead to spiritual reality, and make them alive in Christ? Yes, he really is! He is able to give life to the spiritually dead, and to transform us into the likeness of Christ.

But these are great claims. Can they be substantiated? Only because of the resurrection. Paul prays that the eyes of our heart may be enlightened, so that we may know 'his incomparably great power for us who believe'.

And to help us grasp the measure of this power, not only does God give us an inward illumination by his Spirit, but he has given us an outward, public, objective demonstration of it in the resurrection. For the power available for us today is the very power 'which he exerted in Christ when he raised him from the dead ...'[32] The resurrection is thus portrayed as the supreme evidence in history of the creative power of God.

We are always in danger of trivializing the gospel, of minimizing what God is able to do for us and in us. We speak of becoming a Christian as if it were no more than turning over a new leaf, making a few superficial adjustments to our usual patterns of behaviour, and becoming a bit more religious. Then scratch the surface, crack the veneer, and behold! underneath we are still the same old pagan, unredeemed and unchanged. But no, becoming and being a Christian according to the New Testament is something much more radical than this. It is a decisive act of God. It is nothing less than a resurrection from the death of alienation and self-centredness, and the beginning of a new and liberated life. In a word, the same God of supernatural power, who raised Jesus from physical death, can raise us from spiritual death. And we know he can raise us because we know he raised *him*.

Thirdly, the resurrection of Jesus assures us of *God's ultimate triumph*. One of the major differences between the religions and ideologies of the world concerns their vision of the future. Some offer no hope, but sink into existential despair. Bertrand Russell, when still a young man of only thirty, expressed his conviction that

> no fire, no heroism, no intensity of thought and feeling, can preserve an individual life beyond the grave; that all the labours of the ages, all the devotion, all the inspiration, all the noonday brightness of human genius, are destined to extinction in the vast death of the solar system, and that the whole temple of man's achievement must inevitably be buried beneath the debris of a universe in ruins.[33]

Others think of history more in circular than in linear terms, as an endless cycle of reincarnations, with no release but the non-existence of *nirvana*. Marxists continue to promise Utopia on earth, but the vision has lost credibility. Secular humanists dream of taking control of their own evolution, but, in so far as this would involve genetic manipulation, the dream degenerates into a nightmare.

Christians, on the other hand, are confident about the future, and our Christian 'hope' (which is a sure expectation) is both individual and cosmic. Individually, apart from Christ, the fear of personal death and dissolution is almost universal. For us in the West, Woody Allen typifies this terror. It has become an obsession with him. True, he can still joke about it. 'It's not that I'm afraid to die,' he quips; 'I just don't want to be there when it happens.'[34] But mostly he is filled with dread. In a 1977 article in *Esquire* he said: 'The fundamental thing behind *all* motivation and *all* activity is the constant struggle against annihilation and against death. It's absolutely stupefying in its terror, and it renders anyone's accomplishments meaningless.'

Jesus Christ, however, rescues his disciples from this horror. We will not only survive death, but be raised from it. We are to be given new bodies like his resurrection body,[35] with new and undreamed-of powers.[36] For he is called both the 'firstfruits' of the harvest[37] and 'the firstborn from the dead'.[38] Both metaphors give the same assurance. He was the first to rise; all his people will follow. We will have a body like his. 'Just as we have borne the likeness of the earthly man [Adam] so shall we bear the likeness of the man from heaven [Christ].'[39]

Our hope for the future, however, is also cosmic. We believe that Jesus Christ is going to return in spectacular magnificence, in order to bring history to its fulfilment in eternity. He will not only raise the dead, but regenerate the universe;[40] he will make all things new.[41] We are persuaded that the whole creation is going to be set free from its present bondage to decay and death; that the groans of nature are the labour pains which promise the birth of a new world;[42] and that there is going to be a new heaven and a new earth, which will be the home of righteousness.[43]

So then, the living hope of the New Testament is an impressively 'material' expectation for both the individual and the cosmos. The individual believer is promised not survival merely, not even immortality, but a resurrected, transformed body. And the destiny of the cosmos is not an ethereal 'heaven', but a re-created universe.

Is there any evidence, however, for this amazing assertion that both we and our world are to be totally renewed? Yes, the resurrection of Jesus is the ground of both expectations. It provides solid, visible, tangible, public evidence of God's purpose to complete what he has begun, to redeem nature, to give us new bodies in a new world. As Peter expressed it, God 'has given us new birth into a living hope through the resurrection of Jesus Christ from the dead'.[44] For the resurrection of Jesus was the beginning of the new creation of God. It is not enough to believe that the personality, presence and power of Jesus live on. We need to know that his body was raised. For the resurrection body of Jesus was the first bit of the material order to be redeemed and transfigured. It is the divine pledge that the rest will be redeemed and transfigured one day.[45]

Thus the resurrection of Jesus assures us of God's forgiveness, power and ultimate triumph. It enables us to face our past (however much reason we have to be ashamed of it), confident of God's forgiveness through him who died for our sins and was raised; to face our present (however strong our temptations and heavy our responsibilities), confident of the sufficiency of God's power; and to face our future (however uncertain it may be), confident of God's final triumph, of which the resurrection is the pledge. The resurrection, precisely because it was a decisive, public, visible act of God, within the material order, brings us firm assurance in an otherwise insecure world.

Notes

[1] Jn. 11:25–26.

[2] Rev. 1:18.

[3] Acts 4:2.

[4] *E.g.* Acts 2:23–24, 32; 3:13–15; 5:30–32.

[5] *E.g.* Acts 13:28–31.

[6] Acts 17:18.

[7] 1 Cor. 15:3–8.

[8] (SCM, new edition, 1971), p. 99.

[9] (SCM, 1976), p. 154.

[10] Lk. 24:39.

[11] See Andrew Sinclair, *Guevara* (Fontana, 1970), especially pp. 70 and 88.

[12] *Letters of C. S. Lewis*, ed. W. H. Lewis (Geoffrey Bles, 1966), p. 307.

[13] Rev. 1:18.

[14] Rudolf Bultmann, *Kerygma and Myth* (1941; ET SPCK, 1953), pp. 38–42.

[15] David Jenkins, *Living with Questions* (SCM, 1969), pp. 138–139. See also the critique by J. Murray Harris entitled *Easter in Durham* (Paternoster, 1985).

[16] From the television programme *Credo* in April 1984.

[17] Peter Carnley, *The Structure of Resurrection Belief* (Clarendon Press, 1987), pp. 17ff.

[18] *Ibid.*, p. 164.

[19] *Ibid.*, pp. 200, 266.

[20] *Ibid., p.* 368.

[21] Lk. 24.39.

[22] Acts 2:27.

[23] Although I cannot trace this exact quotation, Bishop Jenkins has written similarly: 'I share the faith of the Apostles and I follow St Paul's account of the Resurrection' (*Free to Believe* by David Jenkins and his daughter Rebecca, BBC Enterprises, 1991, p. 44).

[24] *E.g.* Acts 2:23–32; 13:28–31, 37.

[25] See for example Frank Morison, *Who Moved the Stone?* (Faber, 1930); J. N. D. Anderson, *The Evidence for the Resurrection* (IVP, 1950); Stuart Jackman, *The Davidson File* (Lutterworth, 1982); E. M. B. Green, *The Day Death Died* (IVP, 1982); J. W. Wenham, *Easter Enigma* (Paternoster, 1984).

[26] Acts 4:2.

[27] 1 Cor. 15:6.

[28] Jack C. Winslow, *Confession and Absolution* (Hodder and Stoughton, 1960), p. 22.

[29] Mt. 26:28.

[30] Rom. 6:23.

[31] 1 Cor. 15:14, 17–18.

[32] Eph. 1:18–20.

[33] Bertrand Russell, *A Free Man's Worship* (1902; Unwin Paperbacks, 1976), pp. 10–17.

[34] Graham McCann, *Woody Allen, New Yorker* (Polity Press, 1990), pp. 43 and 83.

[35] *E.g.* Phil. 3:21.

[36] 1 Cor. 15:42–44.

[37] 1 Cor. 15:20, 23.

[38] Rom. 8:29; Col. 1:18; Rev. 1:5.

[39] 1 Cor. 15:49.

[40] Mt. 19:28.

[41] Rev. 21:5.

[42] Rom. 8:20–23.

[43] 2 Pet. 3:13; Rev. 21:1.

[44] 1 Pet. 1:3.

[45] Professor Oliver O'Donovan goes much further than this in his formative book *Resurrection and Moral Order: An Outline for Evangelical Ethics* (IVP and Eerdmans, 1986). He argues that the resurrection of Jesus is the foundation on which Christian ethics rests, because it proclaims that the created world order has been vindicated and reaffirmed by God; indeed, redeemed, renewed and transformed. 'From the resurrection we look not only back to the created order which is vindicated, but forwards to our eschatological participation in that order' (p. 22), not only 'back to what is reaffirmed there, the order of creation', but also 'forward to what is anticipated there, the kingdom of God' (p. 26).

FIVE

Jesus Christ is Lord

The apostolic gospel went beyond the fact and significance of the cross and resurrection to their purpose: 'For to this end Christ died and lived again, that he might be Lord both of the dead and of the living.'[1]

Indeed, it is well known that the earliest, shortest, simplest of all Christian creeds was the affirmation 'Jesus is Lord'. Those who acknowledged his lordship were baptized and received into the Christian community. For it was recognized, as Paul wrote, on the one hand that 'if you confess with your mouth, "Jesus is Lord," and believe in your heart that God raised him from the dead, you will be saved',[2] and on the other that 'no-one can say, "Jesus is Lord," except by the Holy Spirit'.[3]

It may at first sight seem extraordinary that two Greek words, *Kyrios Iēsous* or 'Lord Jesus' (for there is no connecting verb in either of the two verses quoted in the previous paragraph), could possibly be a satisfactory basis for identifying and welcoming somebody as a genuine Christian. Are they not hopelessly inadequate? Is this not theological reductionism at its worst?

The answer to these questions is 'No'. For the two words concerned, which sound like a minimal Christian confession, are pregnant with meaning. They have enormous implications for both Christian faith and Christian life. In particular, they express first a profound theological con-

viction about the historic Jesus and secondly a radical personal commitment to him in consequence. It is this conviction and this commitment
which I propose to explore in this chapter.

Theological conviction

Perhaps the best way to investigate the doctrinal overtones of calling Jesus
'Lord' is to take a fresh look at Philippians 2:9–11. These verses form the
climax of what is sometimes called *carmen Christi*, 'the song of Christ'. For
Paul is probably quoting an early Christian hymn about Christ. In doing
so, he gives it his apostolic imprimatur. He affirms that Christ, although he
shared God's nature and enjoyed equality with him, yet both emptied
himself of his glory and humbled himself to serve, becoming obedient even
to death on a cross (verses 6–8). He continues:

> Therefore God exalted him to the highest place
>   and gave him the name that is above every name,
> that at the name of Jesus every knee should bow,
>   in heaven and on earth and under the earth,
> and every tongue confess that Jesus Christ is Lord,
>   to the glory of God the Father (verses 9–11).

As a Christian hymn, used by the church and endorsed by the apostle, it
indicates how the early Christians thought of Jesus. Three points stand out.

First, *Paul gave Jesus a God-title.* That is, he referred to him as 'Lord'. It
is true, of course, that *kyrios* was used with different meanings in different
contexts. Sometimes it meant no more than 'sir', as when Mary Magdalene
thought the risen Jesus was the gardener[4] and when the priests asked Pilate
to have the tomb made secure.[5] But when used by Jesus' disciples in relation to him, *kyrios* was more than a polite form of address; it was a title, as
when they called him 'the Lord Jesus' or 'the Lord Jesus Christ'. This
becomes clear against the background of the Old Testament.

When the Old Testament came to be translated into Greek in Alexandria
about 200 BC, the devout Jewish scholars did not know how to handle the
sacred name Yahweh or Jehovah. They were too reticent to pronounce it;
they did not feel free to translate or even to transliterate it. So they put the
paraphrase *ho kyrios* ('the Lord') instead, which is why 'Yahweh' still appears
in most English versions as 'the LORD'. Lovers of biblical numerology may
like to know that it occurs 6,156 times in this Greek version, the
Septuagint. Or so I have read somewhere; I have not had the inclination or
the patience to check it.

What is truly amazing is that the followers of Jesus, knowing that at least
in Jewish circles *ho kyrios* was the traditional title for Yahweh, Creator of the

universe and covenant God of Israel, did not scruple to apply the same title to Jesus, or see any anomaly in doing so. It was tantamount to saying that 'Jesus is God'.

Secondly, *Paul transferred to Jesus a God-text.* In Isaiah 45:23 Yahweh had soliloquized:

> By myself I have sworn,
>> my mouth has uttered in all integrity
>> a word that will not be revoked:
> Before me every knee will bow;
>> by me every tongue will swear.

Now Paul, or the hymn-writer he is quoting, has the audacity to lift this text out of Isaiah and reapply it to Jesus. The implication is unavoidable. The homage which the prophet said was due to Yahweh, the apostle says is due to Christ; it was also to be universal, involving 'every knee' and 'every tongue'.

A similar example is the New Testament use of Joel 2:32. The prophet had written that 'everyone who calls on the name of the LORD [*sc.* God] will be saved'. On the Day of Pentecost, however, Peter reapplied this promise to Jesus, urging his hearers to believe in Jesus and be baptized in his name.[6] Similarly, Paul wrote later that the Lord Jesus 'is Lord of all and richly blesses all who call on him, for, "Everyone who calls on the name of the Lord will be saved."'[7] Thus the saving power of Yahweh to Israel has become the saving power of Jesus to Jewish and Gentile believers alike.

Thirdly, *Paul demanded for Jesus God-worship.* However we may interpret the confession of the tongue that he is Lord, the bowing of the knee to him is certainly worship. Indeed, prayer is regularly addressed to Jesus in the New Testament, especially when Paul links 'God our Father' and 'our Lord Jesus Christ' as being together the source of grace and the object of petition.[8] One is reminded too of Hebrews 1:6: 'Let all God's angels worship him.' It is assumed in the New Testament documents that grace flows from Christ, and that prayer and worship are due to him. Indeed, Christolatry (the worship of Christ) preceded Christology (the developed doctrine of Christ). But Christolatry is idolatry if Christ is not God, as Athanasius saw clearly in the fourth century when arguing against the Arian heresy that Christ was a created being.

Here, then, are three important data contained in the Christian hymn Paul was quoting. The early Christians gave Jesus a God-title ('Lord'), transferred to him God-texts (regarding the salvation he bestows and the homage he deserves) and offered him God-worship (the bowed knee). These facts are incontrovertible, and they are all the more impressive for being uncontrived and almost casual.

It is noteworthy, moreover, that the New Testament writers did not argue the rightness of making the daring identification that Jesus is God, for there was no need for them to do so. Paul defended the gospel of justification by grace through faith, and that fiercely, because it was being challenged. But he did not debate the divine lordship of Jesus (the truth that 'there is but one Lord, Jesus Christ'),[9] which must mean that it was not being disputed. So already within a few years of the death and resurrection of Jesus his deity was part of the universal faith of the church.

The confession that 'Jesus is Lord' has a second theological inference, namely that he is Saviour as well as God. The tradition in some evangelical circles is to distinguish sharply between Jesus the Saviour and Jesus the Lord, and even to suggest that conversion involves trusting him as Saviour, without necessarily surrendering to him as Lord. The motive behind this teaching is good, namely to safeguard the truth of justification by faith alone and not introduce works-righteousness (obeying Christ as Lord) by the back door. Nevertheless this position is biblically indefensible. Not only is Jesus 'our Lord and Saviour', one and indivisible, but his lordship implies his salvation and actually announces it. That is, his title 'Lord' is a symbol of his victory over all the forces of evil, which have been put under his feet. The very possibility of our salvation is due to this victory. It is precisely because he is Lord that he is able also to be Saviour.[10] There can be no salvation without lordship. The two affirmations 'Jesus is Lord' and 'Jesus saves' are virtually synonymous.

Radical commitment

The word *kyrios* could be used, as we have seen, as no more than a respectful designation. But it was most commonly employed of owners, whether of land, property or slaves. Possession carried with it full control and the right of disposal. It is with this understanding that Paul, Peter and James began their letters by designating themselves 'slave of Jesus Christ'. They knew that he had bought them at the cost of his lifeblood, and that in consequence they belonged to him and were entirely at his service.

This personal ownership by Christ, and commitment to Christ, is to penetrate every part of his disciples' lives. It has at least six dimensions.

First, it has *an intellectual dimension*. I begin with our mind because it is the central citadel of our personality and effectively rules our lives. Yet it is often the last stronghold to capitulate to the lordship of Jesus. The truth is that we rather like to think our own thoughts and ventilate our own opinions, and if they conflict with the teaching of Jesus, so much the worse for him!

But Jesus Christ claims authority over our minds. 'Take my yoke upon you and learn from me,' he said.[11] His Jewish hearers will immediately have understood him. For they commonly spoke of 'the yoke of Torah' (the law), to whose authority they submitted. Now Jesus spoke of *his* teaching as a yoke. His followers were to become his pupils, his disciples, to subject themselves to his instruction, and to learn from him. Nor need they be afraid of this. For on the one hand he was himself 'gentle and humble in heart', and on the other his yoke was 'easy' and under its light discipline they would find 'rest' for their souls. In other words, true 'rest' is found under Christ's yoke (not in resisting it), and true freedom under his authority (not in discarding it). The apostle Paul was later to write something similar, when he expressed his resolve to 'take captive every thought to make it obedient to Christ'.[12]

The contemporary Christian, who is anxious to respond sensitively to the challenges of the modern world, nevertheless may not jettison the authority of Jesus Christ in order to do so. Disciples have no liberty to disagree with their divine teacher. What we believe about God, about man, male and female, made in his image, about life and death, duty and destiny, Scripture and tradition, salvation and judgment, and much else besides, we have learned from him. There is an urgent need in our day, in which wild and weird speculations abound, to resume our rightful position at his feet. 'Only the person who follows the command of Jesus without reserve', wrote Dietrich Bonhoeffer, 'and submits unresistingly to his yoke, finds his burden easy, and under its gentle pressure receives the power to persevere in the right way. The command of Jesus is hard, unutterably hard, for those who try to resist it. But for those who willingly submit, the yoke is easy and the burden is light.'[13]

Secondly, radical commitment to Jesus Christ has *a moral dimension*. All round us today moral standards are slipping. People are confused whether there are any moral absolutes left. Relativism has permeated the world and is seeping into the church.

Even some evangelical believers misrepresent Scripture on the subject of the law. They quote the apostle Paul's well-known statements that 'Christ is the end of the law'[14] and 'you are not under law',[15] turn a blind eye to their context, and misinterpret them as meaning that the category of law has now been abolished, that we are no longer under obligation to obey it, but are free to disobey it. But Paul meant something quite different. He was referring to the way of salvation, not the way of holiness. He was insisting that for our acceptance with God we are 'not under law but under grace', since we are justified by faith alone, not by works of the law. But we are still under the moral law for our sanctification. As Luther kept saying, the law drives us to Christ to be justified, but Christ sends us back to the law to be sanctified.

The apostle is quite clear about the place of the law in the Christian life. He insists that both the atoning work of Christ and the indwelling presence of the Spirit are with a view to our obeying the law. Why did God send his Son to die for our sins? Answer: 'in order that the righteous requirements of the law might be fully met in us, who ... live ... according to the Spirit.'[16] And why has God put his Spirit in our hearts? Answer: in order to write his law there.[17] Consequently, God's Old Testament promise of the new covenant could be expressed equally as 'I will put my law in their minds and write it on their hearts'[18] and as 'I will put my Spirit in you and move you ... to keep my laws'.[19]

So Jesus Christ calls us to obedience. 'Whoever has my commands and obeys them, he is the one who loves me. He who loves me will be loved by my Father, and I too will love him and show myself to him.'[20] The way to prove our love for Christ is neither by loud protestations of loyalty like Peter, nor by singing sentimental ditties in church, but by obeying his commandments. The test of love is obedience, he said, and the reward of love is a self-revelation of Christ.

Thirdly, Christian commitment has *a vocational dimension*. That is to say, it includes our life work. To say 'Jesus is Lord' commits us to a lifetime of service. We should not hesitate to say that every single Christian is called to ministry, indeed to give his or her life in ministry. If this strikes you as an extraordinary statement, it is probably because you are thinking of 'ministry' as synonymous with the ordained pastoral ministry. But the pastoral ministry is only one of many ministries. My point is that we are all called to ministry or service (*diakonia*) of some kind. The reason it is possible to say this is that we are followers of one who assumed 'the very nature of a servant',[21] insisted that he had 'not come to be served but to serve'[22] and added 'I am among you as one who serves'.[23] If we claim to follow Jesus, therefore, it is inconceivable that we should spend our lives in any other way than in service. And this means that we must be able to see our job or profession in terms of service. Our daily work is meant to be a major sphere in which Jesus exercises his lordship over us. Beyond and behind our earthly employer we should be able to discern our heavenly Lord. Then we can be 'working for the Lord, not for men', since 'it is the Lord Christ [we] are serving'.[24]

In November 1940 the city of Coventry was devastated by aerial bombardment, including its fourteenth-century cathedral. After the war the ruins of the old cathedral were preserved, while a new cathedral was built beside it. From medieval times the old cathedral had, situated round its walls, a series of guild chapels (*e.g.* for the smiths, the drapers, the mercers and the dyers), symbolizing the close link between the church and the crafts. These chapels were destroyed, but in their place 'hallowing places' have been set round the ruined walls, expressing the implications of the prayer 'Hallowed be your name':

In industry, God be in my hands and in my making.
In the arts, God be in my senses and in my creating.
In the home, God be in my heart and in my loving.
In commerce, God be at my desk and in my trading.
In healing, God be in my skill and in my touching.
In government, God be in my plans and in my deciding.
In education, God be in my mind and in my growing.
In recreation, God be in my limbs and in my leisure.

Fourthly, the lordship of Christ has *a social dimension*. This means partly that the followers of Jesus have social as well as individual responsibilities, for example, to family, firm, neighbourhood, country and world. But it means more than this.

There is a sense in which to confess 'Jesus is Lord' is to acknowledge him as Lord of society, even of those societies or segments of society which do not explicitly acknowledge his lordship. Consider this dilemma which the New Testament sets before us. On the one hand, we are told that Jesus is Lord. He has dethroned and disarmed the principalities and powers, triumphing over them in the cross.[25] God has exalted him to his right hand and put everything under his feet.[26] In consequence, he can claim that all authority has been given to him.[27] On the other hand, we continue to struggle against the principalities and powers of darkness. They may have been defeated, even deprived of power; but they are still active, influential and unscrupulous.[28] The apostle John even goes so far as to declare that 'the whole world is under the control of the evil one'.[29] In fact, this dilemma is well summed up in Psalm 110:1, which was quoted by Jesus and several New Testament writers: 'The LORD says to my Lord: "Sit at my right hand until I make your enemies a footstool for your feet."' Within the compass of this one verse the Messiah is depicted both as *reigning* at God's right hand and as *waiting* for the overthrow of his enemies.

How can we reconcile these two perspectives? Is Jesus Lord, or is Satan? Is Christ reigning over his enemies, or waiting for them to surrender? The only possible answer to these questions is 'both'. We have to distinguish between what is *de jure* (by right) and what is *de facto* (in fact or reality). *De jure* Jesus is Lord, for God has exalted him to the highest place. *De facto*, however, Satan rules, for he has not yet conceded defeat or been destroyed.

How does this tension affect our discipleship? Because Jesus is Lord by right, that is, by divine appointment, we cannot acquiesce in any situation which denies it. We long that he who is Lord should be acknowledged as Lord; this is our evangelistic task. But even in a society which does not specifically acknowledge his lordship, we are still concerned that his values will prevail, that human rights and human dignity be accorded to people of all races and religions, that honour be given to women and children, that justice be secured for the oppressed, that society become more just, compassionate, peaceful and free. Why? Why do we care about these things? Because Jesus is Lord of society by right, and because he cares about them. This is not to resurrect the old 'social gospel' of theological liberalism, which made the mistake of identifying a caring society with the kingdom of God. It is rather to take seriously the truth that Jesus is Lord of society and therefore to seek to make it more pleasing to him.

It was during his inaugural address at the opening of the Free University of Amsterdam in 1880 that Abraham Kuyper, who was later to become Prime Minister of the Netherlands, said: 'There is not one inch in the entire area of human life about which Christ, who is Sovereign of all, does not cry out "Mine!"' Similarly, Dr David Gill of New College, Berkeley, has written: 'Jesus is Lord not just of the inner life, after life, family life and church life, but of intellectual life, political life – all domains."[29]

Fifthly, a radical commitment to Christ has *a political dimension.* We need to remember that Jesus was condemned for both a political and a religious offence. In the Jewish court he was found guilty of blasphemy, because he called himself the Son of God, while in the Roman court he was condemned for sedition because he called himself a king, and Rome recognized no king but Caesar. Thus the claims of Jesus had inescapable political implications. His statement that we are to 'give to Caesar what is Caesar's and to God what is God's'[30] may have been deliberately enigmatic. But it certainly implied that there are areas over which God is Lord, into which Caesar may not intrude.

The early Christians faced a continuing conflict between Christ and Caesar. During the first century the emperors manifested an ever-increasing megalomania. They had temples erected in their honour, and demanded divine homage from their subjects. These claims came into direct collision with the lordship of Christ, whom Christians honoured as king,[31] indeed as 'the ruler of the kings of the earth'.[32] Pliny, the early-second-century governor of Bithynia, described in a letter to the Emperor Trajan how he brought before him in court those Christians he suspected of disloyalty, and how he discharged only those who 'offered invocation with wine and frankincense to your [*sc.* the Emperor's] image'.[33] But how could believers say 'Caesar is Lord' when they had confessed that 'Jesus is Lord'? They went to prison and death rather than deny the lordship of Christ.

The deification of the state did not end with the Roman Empire. Still today there are totalitarian regimes which demand from their citizens an unconditional allegiance which Christians cannot possibly give. The disciples of Jesus are to respect the state, and within limits submit to it, but they will neither worship it, nor give it the uncritical support it covets. Consequently, discipleship sometimes calls for disobedience. Indeed, civil disobedience is a biblical doctrine, for there are four or five notable examples of it in Scripture.[34] It arises naturally from the affirmation that Jesus is Lord. The principle is clear, even though its application may involve believers in agonies of conscience. It is this. We are to submit to the state, because its authority is derived from God and its officials are God's ministers,[35] right up to the point where obedience to the state would involve us in disobedience to God. At that point our Christian duty is to disobey the state in order to obey God. For if the state misuses its God-given authority, and presumes either to command what God forbids or to forbid what God commands, we have to say 'no' to the state in order to say 'yes' to Christ. As Peter put it, 'we must obey God rather than men!'[36] Or in Calvin's words, 'obedience to man must not become disobedience to God'.[37]

Let me give a fairly recent example from South Africa. In 1957 Hendrik Verwoerd, then Minister of Native Affairs, announced the 'Native Laws Amendment Bill', whose 'church clause' would have prevented any racial association in 'church, school, hospital, club or any other institution or place of entertainment'. The Archbishop of Cape Town at the time was a gentle scholar called Geoffrey Clayton. He decided with his bishops, albeit with reluctance and apprehension, to disobey. He wrote to the Prime Minister to say that if the Bill were to become law, he would be 'unable to obey it or to counsel our clergy and people to do so'. The following morning he died, perhaps under the pain and strain of threatened civil disobedience. The Bill was amended, but in a mischievous way which would have penalized the black worshippers rather than the church leaders. After it became law, a letter was read out in all Anglican churches calling on the clergy and people to disobey it.

Sixthly, commitment to Christ has *a global dimension.* To affirm 'Jesus is Lord' is to acknowledge his universal lordship. For God has 'super-exalted' Jesus,[38] as we might render *hyperypsoō* – a word that occurs nowhere else in the New Testament, and may even have been coined by Paul. It means that God has raised him 'to the loftiest heights'.[39] And God's purpose in doing so was that every knee should bow to him and every tongue confess him Lord. We have no liberty to place any limitation on the repeated word 'every'. Therefore, if it is God's desire that everybody acknowledge Jesus, it must be our desire as well. Hindus speak of 'the Lord Krishna' and Buddhists of 'the Lord Buddha', but we cannot accept these claims. Only Jesus is Lord. He has no rivals.

There is no greater incentive to world mission than the lordship of Jesus Christ. Mission is neither an impertinent interference in other people's private lives, nor a dispensable option which may be rejected, but an unavoidable deduction from the universal lordship of Jesus Christ.

The two-word affirmation *Kyrios Iēsous* sounded pretty harmless at first hearing. But we have seen that it has far-reaching ramifications. Not only does it express our conviction that he is God and Saviour, but it also indicates our radical commitment to him. The dimensions of this commitment are intellectual (bringing our minds under Christ's yoke), moral (accepting his standards and obeying his commands), vocational (spending our lives in his liberating service), social (seeking to penetrate society with his values), political (refusing to idolize any human institution) and global (being jealous for the honour and glory of his name).

Notes

[1] Rom. 14:9 (RSV).
[2] Rom. 10:9.
[3] 1 Cor. 12:3.
[4] Jn. 20:15.
[5] Mt. 27:62–63.
[6] Acts 2:21, 38.
[7] Rom. 10:12–13.
[8] *E.g.* 1 Thes. 1:1; 3:11; 2 Thes. 1:2, 12; 2:16.
[9] 1 Cor. 8:6.
[10] *Cf.* Acts 2:33–39.
[11] Mt. 11:29.
[12] 2 Cor. 10:5.
[13] Dietrich Bonhoeffer, *The Cost of Discipleship* (1937; ET SCM, 1948), p. 31.
[14] Rom. 10:4.
[15] Rom. 6:14.
[16] Rom. 8:3–4.
[17] 2 Cor. 3:3, 6.
[18] Je. 31:33.
[19] Ezk. 36:27.
[20] Jn. 14:21.
[21] Phil. 2:7.
[22] Mk. 10:45.
[23] Lk. 22:27.
[24] Col. 3:23–24.
[25] Col. 2:15.
[26] Eph. 1:20–22.
[27] Mt. 28:18.
[28] Eph. 6:11–18.
[28] 1 Jn. 5:19.
[29] David W. Gill, *The Opening of the Christian Mind* (IVP USA, 1989), p. 131.
[30] Mk. 12:17.
[31] Acts 17:7.
[32] Rev. 1:5.
[33] *Epistles*, 10:96.
[34] *E.g.* Ex. 1:15–17; Dn. 3 and 6; Acts 4:19; 5:29.
[35] Rom. 13:1–7.
[36] Acts 5:29.

[37] *Institutes*, IV.xx.32.

[38] Phil. 2:9.

[39] Walter Bauer, *A Greek-English Lexicon of the New Testament and Other Early Christian Literature*, translated and adapted by W. F. Arndt and F. W. Gingrich (University of Chicago Press, second edition, 1979).

PART TWO

The disciple

We turn now from 'the gospel' to 'the disciple'. For if Christ crucified and risen is our Lord, we are his servants; if he is our teacher, we are his pupils.

Christian discipleship (that is, following Christ) is a many-faceted responsibility. My choice of four aspects of it could be described as random, except that all of them tend to be underrated and even overlooked.

I begin with 'The listening ear'. For, although all our bodily organs are to be consecrated and presented to God (including our eyes and lips, our hands and feet), a good case can be made for regarding our ears as the most important. Every true disciple is a listener.

Chapter 7 ('Mind and emotions') not only recalls that our Creator has made us both rational and emotional persons, but explores some of the more significant relations between these two components of the human personality.

In chapter 8, under the title 'Guidance, vocation and ministry', we reflect that discipleship implies service, and consider how we can discern the will of God and the call of God in our lives.

For the final chapter of Part Two I have reserved a discussion of the first fruit of the Spirit, which is love. Its primacy in Christian disciples is well expressed in *The Book of Common Prayer*, which describes it as 'that most excellent gift of charity, the very bond of peace and of all virtues, without which whosoever liveth is counted dead before God'.

Six

The listening ear

One of the most important – and much neglected – ingredients of Christian discipleship is the cultivation of a listening ear. Bad listeners do not make good disciples. The apostle James was clear about this. His strictures on the tongue as 'a restless evil, full of deadly poison'[1] are well known, but he has no comparable criticism of the ear. He urges us not to talk too much, but seems to suggest that we can never listen too much. Here is his exhortation:

> My dear brothers, take note of this: Everyone should be quick to listen, slow to speak and slow to become angry, for man's anger does not bring about the righteous life that God desires.[2]

What a remarkable organ God has created in the human ear! In comparison with it, the most sophisticated computer (it has been said) is 'as crude as a concrete mixer'. Of course what we usually call the ear is only the *outer ear*, that fleshy excrescence on the side of the head which comes in a variety of shapes and sizes. From it a one-inch canal leads to the ear drum, behind which is the *middle ear*, where the body's three tiniest bones (popularly known as the anvil, the hammer and the stirrup) amplify sound twenty-two times and pass it on to the *inner ear*, where the real hearing takes place. Its main component is the snail-shaped tube named the cochlea. It contains thousands of microscopic, hairlike cells, each of which is tuned to one particular vibration. The vibrations are now converted into electric impulses which convey sound to the brain for decoding along 30,000 circuits of the auditory nerve, enough for a sizeable city's telephone service. The human ear has rightly been celebrated as 'a triumph of miniaturization'.[3]

When you think how versatile and sensitive this organ is, which God has made, it is a thousand pities that we do not put it to better use and develop our capacity for listening. I am not thinking only of music, bird song and animal calls, but also of the value of conversation for our relationships. Involuntary deafness is a grievous handicap; deliberate deafness is both a sin and a folly.

This is one of the main themes of Alan Parker's film *Birdy*, which is based on William Wharton's novel. Its key statement seems to be the throwaway line near the end that 'nobody listens to anybody any longer'. The film depicts the friendship of two adolescent boys in Philadelphia, Al and Birdy, which blossoms in spite of Birdy's weird obsession with bird flight. Drafted to Vietnam, they are both blown up. Al has to have surgery on his disfigured face, while Birdy is damaged psychologically, retreats into impenetrable silence, and is committed to a mental hospital. He cowers in his cell like a caged bird, and constantly looks up at the barred window, dreaming of escape. The two men urgently need each other's support in the cruel aftermath of war, but they cannot communicate. At last, however, the breakthrough takes place, and their friendship is restored. But the background to it is a hostile world in which people are out of touch with each other – an unsympathetic mother, an uncomprehending girlfriend, a bloody and senseless war, and a psychotherapist who lacks both insight and compassion. Al and Birdy are now listening to each other again, but they seem to be the exceptions in a world in which 'nobody listens to anybody any longer'.

James's appeal to us to be 'quick to listen' is not one we find easy to heed. Many of us are compulsive talkers, especially preachers! We prefer to talk than to listen, to volunteer information than to confess our ignorance, to criticize than to receive criticism. But who am I to be saying these things? I have myself been as great an offender in this area as anybody. Let me share with you an experience of about twenty-five years ago, which proved to be formative. It was Monday morning in London, the All Souls church staff team had gathered for our weekly meeting, and I was in the chair. The others were carrying on about something which did not particularly interest me (I now forget what it was), and I am ashamed to say that I had switched off. Suddenly Ted Schroder, who might not unfairly be described at that time as 'a brash young colonial from New Zealand', and who is now a close and valued friend, blurted out: 'John, you're not listening!' I blushed. For he was quite right, and it is intolerably rude not to listen when somebody is speaking. Moreover, the tensions which were surfacing in our staff team relationships at that time were largely due to my failure to listen. So I repented, and have many times since prayed for grace to be a better listener.

To whom, then, shall we listen? First and foremost to God.

Listening to God

One of the distinctive truths about the God of the biblical revelation is that he is a speaking God. Unlike heathen idols which, being dead, are dumb, the living God has spoken and continues to speak. They have mouths but do not speak; he has no mouth (because he is spirit), yet speaks. And since God speaks, we must listen. This is a constant theme of the Old Testament in all three of its main sections. Take the Law: '… love the LORD your God, listen to his voice.'[4] And the wisdom literature in the Writings: 'To-day, Oh that ye would hear his voice!'[5] There are also many examples in the Prophets. For instance, Israel's 'stubbornness' of heart, of which God kept complaining to Jeremiah, was precisely that they 'refuse to listen to my words'.[6] The tragedy inherent in this situation is that what constituted Israel a special, a distinct, people was precisely that God had spoken to her and called her. Yet she neither listened nor responded. The result was judgment: 'When I called, they did not listen; so when they called, I would not listen.'[7] One might almost say that the epitaph engraved on the nation's tombstone was: 'The LORD God spoke to his people, but they refused to listen.' So then God sent his Son, saying, 'They will listen to my Son,' but they killed him instead.

Still today God speaks, although there is some disagreement in the church as to how he does so. I do not myself believe that he speaks to us nowadays directly and audibly, as he did for example to Abraham,[8] to the boy Samuel[9] or to Saul of Tarsus outside Damascus.[10] Nor should we claim that he addresses us 'face to face, as a man speaks with his friend',[11] since this intimate relationship which God had with Moses is specifically said to have been unique.[12] To be sure, Christ's sheep know the Good Shepherd's voice and follow him,[13] for this is essential to our discipleship, but we are not promised that his voice will be audible.

What, then, about indirect utterances of God through prophets? We should certainly reject any claim that there are prophets today comparable to the biblical prophets. For they were the 'mouth' of God, special organs of revelation, whose teaching belongs to the foundation on which the church is built.[14] There may well, however, be a prophetic gift of a secondary kind, as when God gives some people special insight into his Word and his will. But we should not ascribe infallibility to such communications. Instead, we should evaluate both the character and the message of those who claim to speak from God.[15]

The principal way in which God speaks to us today is through Scripture, as the church in every generation has recognized. The words which God spoke through the biblical authors, which he caused in his providence to be written and preserved, are not a dead letter. One of the special ministries of the Holy Spirit is to make God's written Word 'living and active' and 'sharper than any double-edged sword'.[16] So we must never separate the Word from the Spirit or the Spirit from the Word, for the simple reason that the Word of God is 'the sword of the Spirit',[17] the chief weapon he uses to accomplish his purpose in his people's lives. It is this confidence which enables us to think of Scripture equally as written text and as living message. Thus, Jesus could ask, 'What is written?'[18] and, 'Have you never read?',[19] while Paul could ask, 'What does the Scripture say?',[20] almost personifying it. In other words, Scripture (which means the written Word) can be either read or listened to, and what it says is what he (God) says through it. Through his ancient Word God addresses the modern world. He speaks through what he has spoken.

And God calls us to listen to what through Scripture 'the Spirit says to the churches'.[21] The tragedy is that still today, as in Old Testament days, people often do not, cannot or will not listen to God. The non-communication between God and us is not because God is either dead or silent, but because we are not listening. If we are cut off during a telephone conversation, we do not jump to the conclusion that the person at the other end has died. No, it is the line which has gone dead.

The same state of being cut off from God is often true of us Christians. Is this not the main cause of the spiritual stagnation we sometimes experience? We have stopped listening to God. Perhaps we no longer have a daily quiet time of Bible reading and prayer. Or if we continue to do so, perhaps it is more a routine than a reality, because we are no longer expecting God to speak. We need, then, to adopt the attitude of Samuel and say, 'Speak, LORD, for your servant is listening.'[22] Like the servant of the Lord we should be able to say: 'He wakens me morning by morning, wakens my ear to listen like one being taught.'[23] We should imitate Mary of Bethany who 'sat at the Lord's feet listening to what he said'.[24] Of course we have to be active as well as contemplative, to work as well as pray, to be Marthas as well as Marys. But have we allowed the Martha in us to crowd out the Mary? Have we neglected what Jesus called the 'better' option?[25]

Listening to one another

In this second sphere of listening, the principle is clear: community depends on communication. It is only when we speak and listen to one another that our relationships develop and mature, whereas when we stop listening to each other, they fall apart. There is a heavy emphasis in the book of Proverbs on the necessity and value of mutual listening. For example, 'the way of a fool seems right to him, but a wise man listens to advice'.[26] Similarly, 'he who listens to a life-giving rebuke will be at home among the wise'.[27] Again, 'the heart of the discerning acquires knowledge; the ears of the wise seek it out'.[28] Here, then, are exhortations to listen to advice, to rebuke and to instruction, together with the statement that those who do so are wise. Moreover, this need to listen applies in every sphere of life, including the home, the workplace, the state and the church.

First, it applies to *the home*. Although I almost feel the need to apologize for saying something so traditional, children and young people need to listen to their parents. 'Listen, my son, to your father's instruction, and do not forsake your mother's teaching.'[29] For the fact is that parents have more experience, and therefore usually more wisdom, than their offspring tend to give them credit for. Mark Twain had the candour to admit this. 'When I was a boy of fourteen,' he said, 'my father was so ignorant I could hardly stand to have the old man around. But when I got to be twenty-one, I was astonished at how much he had learned in seven years!'[30]

But if children need to listen to their parents, parents need to be humble enough to listen to their children, or they will never understand their problems. For the world in which their children are growing up is vastly different from the world of their own youth. Only patient, mutual listening can bridge the generation gap.

Next, husband and wife need to listen to one another. Marriage breakdown is nearly always preceded by communication breakdown. For whatever reason (neglect, fatigue, self-centredness or pressure of business), husband and wife are no longer taking time to listen to each other. So they drift apart, and misunderstandings, suspicions, grievances and resentments increase, until it is too late – although in fact it is never too late to start listening again.

Secondly, listening is essential in *the workplace*. This seems to be widely recognized, as the art of listening is now included in books and seminars on business management. For example, there is *The Language of Effective Listening* by Arthur Robertson, founder and president of Effective Communication and Development Inc.[31] It is an American self-help book, based on the conviction that 'effective listening is the number one communication skill requisite to success in your professional and personal life'.[32]

Listening is specially important in conflict situations. Whenever there is an industrial dispute, it is almost certain that both sides have a reasonable case. Neither side is totally selfish or totally crazy. The essence of conciliation, therefore, is to persuade each side to listen to the other. There have been several painful examples of this in Britain in recent years. Management and labour (sometimes with the Government involved as well) have been at loggerheads, with strikes and picketing on one side, sackings on the other, and bitter recriminations all round. It has been a case of almost total mutual deafness and non-comprehension. People prefer to shout at one another than to listen to one another. Yet only when both sides are willing to sit down together, put aside their prejudiced positions and listen, does any possibility of reconciliation emerge.

Thirdly, the same principle is applicable to *the state*. If democracy is government with the consent of the governed, then the governed have to be li tened to. Otherwise, they cannot be deemed to have given their consent. In 1864, shortly before the end of the American Civil War and before Congress's adoption of the Thirteenth Amendment abolishing slavery, Harriet Beecher Stowe interviewed Abraham Lincoln and wrote: 'Surrounded by all sorts of conflicting claims, by traitors, by half-hearted timid men, by Border States men and Free States men, by radical Abolitionists and Conservatives, Lincoln has listened to all, weighed the words of all ...'[33] I guess that the willingness to listen to all shades of opinion is a *sine qua non* of statesmanship.

Fourthly, it is true in *the church*. Church history has been a long and somewhat dismal record of controversy. Usually, important theological issues have been at stake. But, as often as not, they have been exacerbated by an unwillingness or inability to listen. I have myself tried to observe the rule never to engage in theological debate without first listening to the other person, or reading what he or she has written, or preferably both. Some evangelical friends joined me in meeting Bishop John Robinson after the publication of *Honest to God*, five contributors to *The Myth of God Incarnate* after its publication, and Bishop David Jenkins after his provocative remarks about the resurrection. I do not of course claim that disagreement is overcome by such dialogue, but at least our misunderstanding is diminished and our integrity preserved.

This is even more so in the case of domestic evangelical debate. When we stay apart, and our only contact is to lob hand grenades at one another across a demilitarized zone, a caricature of one's 'opponent' develops in one's mind, complete with horns, hooves and tail! But when we meet, and sit together, and begin to listen, not only does it become evident that our opponents are not after all demons, but actually normal human beings, and even sisters and brothers in Christ, the possibility of mutual understanding and respect grows. More than this: when we listen not only to what others are saying, but to what lies behind what they are saying, and in particular to what it is that they are so anxious to safeguard, we often find that we want to safeguard the same thing ourselves.[34]

I am not claiming that this discipline is easy. Far from it. Listening with patient integrity to both sides of an argument can cause acute mental pain. For it involves the interiorizing of the debate until one not only grasps but feels the strength of both positions. Yet this is another aspect of the 'double listening' for which I am pleading in this book.

It is perhaps specially to pastors that God has committed the ministry of listening. Bonhoeffer wrote of it with his customary insight:

> The first service that one owes to others in the fellowship consists in listening to them. Just as love to God begins with listening to his Word, so the beginning of love for the brethren is learning to listen to them. It is God's love for us that he not only gives us his Word but also lends us his ear. So it is his work that we do for our brother when we learn to listen to him. Christians, especially ministers, so often think they must always contribute something when they are in the company of others, that this is the one service they have to render. They forget that listening can be a greater service than speaking ...
>
> Brotherly pastoral care is essentially distinguished from preaching by the fact that, added to the task of speaking the Word, there is the obligation of listening. There is a kind of listening with half an ear that presumes already to know what the other person has to say. It is an impatient, inattentive listening, that despises the brother, and is only waiting for a chance to speak and thus get rid of the other person. This is no fulfilment of our obligation ...
>
> Christians have forgotten that the ministry of listening has been committed to them by him who is himself the great listener and whose work they should share. We should listen with the ears of God that we may speak the Word of God.[35]

Listening to the world

The contemporary world is positively reverberating with cries of anger, frustration and pain. Too often, however, we turn a deaf ear to these anguished voices.

First, there is the pain of those who have never heard the name of Jesus or, having heard of him, have not yet come to him, and in their alienation and lostness are hurting dreadfully. Our evangelical habit with such is to rush in with the gospel, to climb on to our soapbox, and to declaim our message with little regard for the cultural situation or felt needs of the people concerned. In consequence, more often than we care to admit, we put people off, and even increase their alienation, because the way we present Christ is insensitive, clumsy and even irrelevant. Truly, 'he who answers before listening – that is his folly and his shame'.[36]

The better way is to listen before we speak, to seek to enter into the other person's world of thought and feeling, to struggle to grasp what their objections to the gospel may be, and to share with them the good news of Jesus Christ in a way which speaks to their need. This humble, searching, challenging activity is rightly called 'contextualization'. But it is essential to add that to contextualize the gospel is not in any way to manipulate it. Authentic evangelism necessitates 'double listening'. For Christian witnesses stand between the Word and the world, with the consequent obligation to listen to both. We listen to the Word in order to discover ever more of the riches of Christ. And we listen to the world in order to discern which of Christ's riches are needed most and how to present them in their best light.

This shows the nature and purpose of inter-faith dialogue. Dialogue is neither a synonym nor a substitute for evangelism. Dialogue is a serious conversation in which we are prepared to listen and learn as well as to speak and teach. It is therefore an exercise in integrity. 'It is an activity in its own right,' Max Warren wrote. 'It is in its very essence an attempt at mutual "listening", listening in order to understand. Understanding is its reward.'[37] Besides, Max Warren knew what he was talking about, as he tells us in his autobiography:

> My earliest memory is of dancing firelight, and of my mother reading to me. I am looking into the flames and listening. I must have been three or four years old ... Long before I could read I was learning to listen, perhaps the most valuable lesson I ever learnt ... What is more, reading has always been for me a form of listening. Books have always been 'persons' to me, not just the person of the author so much as the book itself talking, while I listened.[38]

Secondly, there is the pain of the poor and the hungry, the dispossessed and the oppressed. Many of us are only now waking up to the obligation which Scripture has always laid on the people of God to care about social justice. We should be listening more attentively to the cries and sighs of those who are suffering. Let me share with you a Bible verse which we have neglected, and which on that account we should perhaps underline. It contains a solemn word from God to those of his people who lack a social conscience. It is Proverbs 21:13: 'If a man shuts his ears to the cry of the poor, he too will cry out and not be answered.'

To turn a deaf ear to somebody is a signal mark of disrespect. If we refuse to listen to someone, we are saying that we do not consider that person worth listening to. But there is only one person we should refuse to listen to, on the ground that he is not worth listening to, and that is the devil, together with his emissaries. It is the essence of wisdom to be a discerning, discriminating listener and to choose carefully whom to listen to. Failure to do this was the folly of our first parents in the Garden of Eden. Instead of listening to the truth of God, they gave credence to the lies of Satan. And we are often crazy enough to copy them!

But we should nor listen to the devil's talk, whether it be lies or propaganda, slander or gossip, filth or insults. 'A prudent man overlooks an insult.'[39] The same applies to anonymous letters. It is possible to be very upset by them, since they are usually rude. But why should we take seriously the criticisms of a correspondent who lacks the courage to disclose his or her identity? A good story illustrating this is told of Joseph Parker, who was minister of the City Temple in London at the end of the last century. As he climbed into his tall pulpit one Sunday morning, a lady in the gallery threw a piece of paper at him. Picking it up, he found that it contained the single word 'Fool!' Dr Parker commented: 'I have received many anonymous letters in my life. Previously they have been a text without a signature. Today for the first time I have received a signature without a text!'

If we steadfastly refuse to listen to anything that is untrue, unfair, unkind or impure, we should at the same time listen carefully to instruction and advice, criticism, reproof and correction, together with other people's views, concerns, problems and troubles. For, as has been well said, 'God has given us two ears, but only one mouth, so that he evidently intends us to listen twice as much as we talk.'

To take time to listen to God and to our fellow human beings begins as a mark of courtesy and respect, continues as the means to mutual understanding and deepening relationships, and above all is an authentic token of Christian humility and love. So, dear sisters and brothers, 'everyone should be quick to listen, slow to speak and slow to become angry'.

Notes

[1] Jas. 3:8.

[2] Jas. 1:19–20.

[3] See Alan E. Nourse, *The Body* (Time Life, 1968); also two books by Paul Brand and Philip Yancey entitled *In His Image* (Hodder and Stoughton, 1984) and *Fearfully and Wonderfully Made* (Hodder and Stoughton, 1981).

[4] Dt. 30:20.

[5] Ps. 95:7 (RV).

[6] Je. 13:10; *cf.* Is. 30 9.

[7] Zc. 7:13; *cf.* Je. 21:10–11.

[8] Gn. 22:1.

[9] 1 Sa. 3:4, 6, 8, 10.

[10] Acts 9:3–7.

[11] Ex. 33:11.

[12] Dt. 34:10.

[13] Jn. 10:3–5.

[14] Eph. 2:20.

[15] Mt. 7:16; 1 Thes. 5:20–22.

[16] Heb. 4:12.

[17] Eph. 6:17.

[18] *E.g.* Lk. 10:26.

[19] *E.g.* Mt. 19:4; 21:42.

[20] *E.g.* Rom. 4:3; Gal. 4:30.

[21] *E.g.* Rev. 2:7.

[22] 1 Sa. 3:9–10.

[23] Is. 50:4.

[24] Lk. 10:39.

[25] Lk. 10:42.

[26] Pr. 12:15; *cf.* 13:10; 15:12, 22; 20:18.

[27] Pr. 15:31; *cf.* 9:8; 17:10; 25:12; 27:5.

[28] Pr. 18:15.

[29] Pr. 1:8.

[30] *Reader's Digest*, September 1937.

[31] Arthur Robertson, *The Language of Effective Listening* (Scott Foresman Professional Books, 1991).

[32] *Ibid.*, p. xv.

[33] Stephen B. Oates, *Abraham Lincoln: The Man Behind the Myths* (New American Library, 1984), pp. 125–126.

[34] See, for example, *Evangelism and Social Responsibility: An Evangelical Commitment*, known as 'The Grand Rapids Report' (Paternoster, 1982), especially pp. 5–7.

[35] Dietrich Bonhoeffer, *Life Together* (Harper and Brothers, l954), pp. 97–99.

[36] Pr. 18:13.

[37] From a paper entitled *Presence and Proclamation* read at a European Consultation on Mission Studies in April, 1968.

[38] M. A. C. Warren, *Crowded Canvas* (Hodder and Stoughton, 1974), pp. 16, 18.

[39] Pr. 12:16.

SEVEN

Mind and emotions

Christian discipleship involves the whole of our human personality. We are to love the Lord our God with all our heart, soul, mind and strength.[1] Our mind is to be renewed,[2] our emotions purified,[3] our conscience kept clear[4] and our will surrendered to God's will.[5] Discipleship entails all that we know of ourselves being committed to all that we know of God. Yet, of the various constituent elements which go to make up our human being, it is our mind and our emotions which the biblical writers treat most fully. So we will consider each separately, and then the two in relation to each other.

The mind

The story is told of two women who were having a chat in their local supermarket. One said to the other: 'What's the matter with you? You look so worried.'

'I am,' responded her friend; 'I keep thinking about the world situation.'

'Well,' said the first lady, 'you want to take things more philosophically, and stop thinking!'

It is a rather delicious idea that the way to become more philosophical is to do less thinking. Yet those two ladies were reflecting the modern anti-intellectual mood, which has given birth to the ugly twins called mindlessness and meaninglessness.

Over against this trend we need to set the instruction of the apostle Paul: 'Brothers, stop thinking like children. In regard to evil be infants, but in your thinking be adults.'[6] It is noteworthy that he begins with the very words used by one of the ladies in the supermarket, 'Stop thinking'; but he continues, 'like children'. True, Jesus told us to become like children, but he did not mean that we are to copy children in everything. Similarly, Paul urges us to be children, indeed 'infants' or 'babies', in evil (the less sophisticated we are in relation to evil, the better); but in our thinking, he adds, we are to grow up, to become mature. The whole biblical revelation lies behind Paul's appeal.

First, a responsible use of our minds *glorifies our creator.* For he is (among other things) a rational God, who made us in his own image rational beings, has given us in nature and in Scripture a double, rational revelation, and expects us to use our minds to explore what he has revealed. All scientific research is based on the convictions that the universe is an intelligible, even meaningful, system; that there is a fundamental correspondence between the mind of the investigator and the data being investigated; and that this correspondence is rationality. In consequence, 'a scientist faced with an apparent irrationality does not accept it as final … He goes on struggling to find some rational way in which the facts can be related to each other … Without that passionate faith in the ultimate rationality of the world, science would falter, stagnate and die …'[7] It is therefore no accident that the pioneers of the scientific revolution were Christians. They believed that the rational God had stamped his rationality both upon the world and upon them. In this way all scientists, whether they know it or not, are 'thinking God's thoughts after him', as the seventeenth-century German astronomer Johannes Kepler put it.

Conscientious Bible students are also 'thinking God's thoughts after him'. For God has given us in Scripture an even clearer and fuller revelation of himself. He has 'spoken', communicating his thoughts in words. In particular, he has disclosed his love for sinners like us and his plan to save us through Jesus Christ.

Has God, then, made us rational persons, and shall we deny this essential feature of our creation? Has he taken the trouble to reveal himself, and shall we neglect his revelation? No, the proper use of our minds is neither to abdicate our responsibility and go to sleep, nor to proclaim the autonomy of human reason (as the leaders of the Enlightenment did) and so stand in judgment on the data of divine revelation, but to sit in humility under them, to study, interpret, synthesize and apply them. Only so can we glorify our Creator.

Secondly, a responsible use of our minds *enriches our Christian life.* I am not now thinking of education, culture and art, which enhance the quality of human life, but of our discipleship in particular, no part of which is possible if we stifle our minds. 'Looking back over my experience as a pastor for some thirty-four years,' wrote Martyn Lloyd-Jones, 'I can testify without the slightest hesitation that the people I have found most frequently in trouble in their spiritual experience have been those who have lacked understanding. You cannot divorce these things. You will go wrong in the realms of practical living and experience if you have not a true understanding.'[8]

Let me illustrate this in relation to faith. It is amazing how many people suppose that faith and reason are incompatible. But they are never set over against each other in Scripture. Faith and sight are contrasted,[9] but not faith and reason. For faith according to Scripture is neither credulity, nor superstition, nor 'an illogical belief in the occurrence of the improbable',[10] but a quiet, thoughtful trust in the God who is known to be trustworthy. Consider Isaiah 26:3–4:

> You will keep in perfect peace
>   him whose mind is steadfast,
>   because he trusts in you.
> Trust in the LORD for ever,
>   for the LORD, the LORD, is the Rock eternal.

In these verses to trust in God and to set the mind steadfastly upon him are synonyms, the reasonableness of trusting him is that he is an immovable rock, and the reward of faith is peace. It is only by reflecting on the changelessness of God that our faith grows. And the more we perceive his steadfastness, the more steadfast does our faith become.

Or take our need of divine guidance. Too many people regard it as an alternative to human thought, even a convenient device for saving them the bother of thinking. They expect God to flash on to their inner screen answers to their questions and solutions to their problems, in such a way as to bypass their minds. And of course God is free to do this; perhaps occasionally he does. But Scripture gives us the warrant to insist that God's normal way of guiding us is rational, not irrational, namely through the very thought processes which he has created in us.

Psalm 32 makes this clear. Verse 8 contains a marvellous threefold promise of divine guidance, in which God says, 'I will instruct you and teach you in the way you should go; I will counsel you and watch over you' (RSV 'counsel you with my eye upon you'). But *how* will God fulfil his promise? Verse 9 continues: 'Do not be like the horse or the mule, which have no understanding, but must be controlled by bit and bridle or they will not come to you.' If we put together the promise and the prohibition, what God is saying to us is this: 'I promise that I will guide you, and show you the way to go. But do not expect me to guide you as you guide horses and mules (namely by force, not intelligence), for the simple reason that you are neither a horse nor a mule. They lack "understanding", but you don't. Indeed, I myself have given you the precious gift of understanding. Use it! Then I will guide you *through* your minds.'

Thirdly, a responsible use of our minds *strengthens our evangelistic witness.* So much modern evangelism is an assault on the emotions and the will, without any comparable recognition of the mind. But our evangelistic appeal should never ask people to close or suspend their minds. The gospel requires us to humble our minds, indeed, but also to open them to God's truth.

That this is God's way is clear from the practice of the apostles. We saw in chapter 3 that Paul in Corinth renounced the wisdom of the world and the rhetoric of the Greeks,[11] but that he did not renounce either doctrinal content in his preaching or the deployment of arguments. In Corinth itself Luke describes him as 'reasoning' with people and trying to 'persuade' them,[12] while in Ephesus he lectured and debated daily in a secular lecture hall for two years.[13] To be sure, his confidence was in the Holy Spirit. But, being the Spirit of truth, the Holy Spirit brings people to faith in Christ because of the evidence, and not in spite of it. There is an urgent need in our day to include apologetics in our evangelism, that is, to defend the gospel as well as to proclaim it. In all our evangelism we need to be able to declare, as Paul did to Festus: 'What I am saying is true and reasonable.'[14] In addition, God is surely calling some men and women in our generation, as he has done in the past, to dedicate their God-given intellect to the task of 'defending and confirming the gospel'.[15]

So then, we need to repent of the cult of mindlessness, and of any residual anti-intellectualism or intellectual laziness of which we may be guilty. These things are negative, cramping and destructive. They insult God, impoverish us and weaken our testimony. A responsible use of our minds, on the other hand, glorifies God, enriches us and strengthens our witness in the world.

Two qualifications seem to be needed, however, since there are two 'isms' which, if we are not on our guard, might result from this emphasis on the mind, namely elitism and intellectualism. Elitism in this context would limit Christian thinking to a small minority of university-educated people. It would give the impression that only a select, even exclusive, bunch of eggheads are capable of using their minds. We must set ourselves fiercely against this bizarre notion, however. True, Christians have been the pioneers of education, and want everybody to have the best possible education to develop their maximum potential. But formal education is not indispensable to the development of Christian thinking. For *all* human beings are created rational in God's image and are able to learn how to think. A few years ago I was addressing a group of clergy in Liverpool and said something about the need to use our God-given minds. As soon as I had finished, somebody stood up and objected that I was limiting Christianity to intellectuals and excluding the working classes, among whom he worked. I did not need to reply. For immediately several inner-city workers were on their feet, flushed with anger. 'You're insulting the working classes,' they said to the first speaker. 'They may not have had as much formal education as you, but they're just as intelligent and just as able to think.' Our task, then, is to encourage all God's people to think, and not to develop an intellectual elite.

The second danger is intellectualism, the encouragement of a Christianity which is too cerebral, and not visceral enough. That is, it is all brain, with no gut. But in order to urge people to use their minds, it is not necessary to urge them to suppress their feelings. I often say to our students at the Institute for Contemporary Christianity in London that we are not in the business of 'breeding tadpoles'. A tadpole is a little creature with a huge head and nothing much else besides. Certainly there are some Christian tadpoles around. Their heads are bulging with sound theology, but that is all there is to them. No, we are concerned to help people to develop not only a Christian mind, but also a Christian heart, a Christian spirit, a Christian conscience and a Christian will, in fact to become whole Christian persons, thoroughly integrated under the lordship of Christ. This will include our emotions.

Chaim Potok's book *The Chosen*[16] and the film based on it illustrate this well. He tells the story of two Jewish youths who were brought up in Brooklyn, New York, during and after the Second World War. Danny Saunders' father was a strict Hasidic rabbi, while Ruevan Malter's father was a writer in the liberal Jewish tradition. In the boys' friendship these two traditions came into conflict. Throughout most of the book Rabbi Saunders astonishes us because, although he is a very human person, he never talks to Danny except when he is teaching him out of the Talmud. Instead, he maintains between them a 'weird silence'.[17] Not until near the end is the mystery explained. Rabbi Saunders says that God had blessed him with a brilliant son, 'a boy with a mind like a jewel'. When Danny was only four years old, his father saw him reading a book and was frightened because he 'swallowed' it. The book described the sufferings of a poor Jew, yet Danny had enjoyed it! 'There was no soul in my four-year-old Daniel, there was only his mind. He was a mind in a body without a soul.'[18] So the rabbi cried to God: 'What have you done to me? A mind like this I need for a son? A *heart* I need for a son, a *soul* I need for a son, compassion … righteousness, mercy, strength to suffer and carry pain.' *That* I want from my son, not a mind without a soul!'[19] So Rabbi Saunders followed an ancient Hasidic tradition and brought the boy up in silence, for then 'in the silence between us he began to hear the world crying'.[20] In the final scene of reconciliation between father and son, the rabbi says that Danny had to learn 'through the wisdom and the pain of silence that a mind without a heart is nothing'.

The emotions

My readers will probably not suspect me of being an emotional person. For I am one of those cold fish called an Englishman descended from hard Norsemen and blunt Anglo-Saxons, with no spark of Celtic or Latin fire in my blood. With that ancestry, I am supposed to be shy, reserved and even buttoned up. Moreover, I was brought up in an English public school on the philosophy of the 'stiff upper lip'. That is, since a trembling of the upper lip is the first visible sign of emotion, the tradition was to stiffen it. I was taught the manly virtues of courage, fortitude and self-discipline, and warned that, if I should ever feel any emotion, I was on no account to show it. Weeping was strictly for women and children only, not for men.

But then I was introduced to Jesus Christ. I learned to my astonishment that God, whose 'impassibility' I thought meant that he was incapable of emotion, speaks (though in human terms) of his burning anger and vulnerable love.[21] I discovered too that Jesus of Nazareth, the perfect human being, was no tight-lipped, unemotional ascetic. On the contrary, I read that he turned on hypocrites with anger, looked on a rich young ruler and loved him, could both rejoice in spirit and sweat drops of blood in spiritual agony, was constantly moved with compassion, and even burst into tears twice in public.

From all this evidence it is plain that our emotions are not to be suppressed, since they have an essential place in our humanness and therefore in our Christian discipleship.

First, there is a place for emotion in *spiritual experience.* The Holy Spirit is the Spirit of truth, as we have noted. But his ministry is not limited to illuminating our minds and teaching us about Christ. He also pours God's love into our hearts.[22] Similarly, he bears witness with our spirit that we are God's children, for he causes us to say '*Abba,* Father'[23] and to exclaim with gratitude 'how great is the love the Father has lavished on us, that we should be called children of God!'[24] In addition, although we have not yet seen Christ, nevertheless already we love him and trust him, and so 'are filled with an inexpressible and glorious joy'.[25]

There are, of course, many varieties of spiritual experience, and we must not try to stereotype them, insisting that everybody has exactly the same experience. Nevertheless, all Christian people, at least from time to time, have feelings both of profound sorrow and of profound joy. On the one hand, we 'groan inwardly', in solidarity with the fallen creation, burdened with our own fallenness and longing for our final redemption.[26] On the other, we rejoice in the Lord, overwhelmed with gratitude for the great love with which he has loved us.

Secondly, there is a place for emotion in *public worship.* We are told in Hebrews 12:22–24 that when we assemble for worship, we do not just 'come to church', that is, to a building. For already we 'have come to Mount Zion, to the heavenly Jerusalem, the city of the living God'. We 'have come to thousands upon thousands of angels in joyful assembly, to the church of the firstborn, whose names are written in heaven'. We 'have come to God, the judge of all men, to the spirits of righteous men made perfect, to Jesus the mediator of a new covenant, and to the sprinkled blood that speaks a better word than the blood of Abel'. The recognition of this cosmic dimension transforms worship. On some particular Sunday perhaps only a handful of God's people have gathered, and a heterogeneous handful at that. But then we remember, as the 1928 Prayer Book put it, that we have come together 'in the presence of Almighty God and of the whole company of heaven'. And in the communion service we expressly join 'with angels and archangels, and with all the company of heaven' in praising God's glorious name. That is, we are transported beyond ourselves into eternal, unseen reality. We are deeply moved by the glories of which we speak and sing, and we bow down before God in humble and joyful worship.

Thirdly, there is a place for emotion in *gospel preaching*. The apostle Paul used his mind, as we have seen. He believed in the truth of his message. He took time and trouble to defend, explain, argue and proclaim it in its fulness. But his unfolding of the whole plan of God was never cold or arid. On the contrary, he wrote that God 'has committed to us the message of reconciliation. We are therefore Christ's ambassadors, as though God were making his appeal through us. We implore you on Christ's behalf: Be reconciled to God.'[27] Paul was not satisfied with a statement of the gospel; he went on to beg people to respond to it. To his systematic exposition he added an urgent personal appeal. And often, he added, his proclamation was accompanied by tears.[28]

Some preachers are impeccable in both doctrine and diction, but would never lean over the pulpit with tears in their eyes, imploring people to be reconciled to God. Others whip themselves up into a frenzy of excitement, begging for a decision, but never make a careful, cogent statement of the gospel. Why must we polarize? It is the combination of truth and tears, of mind and emotion, of reason and passion, of exposition and appeal, which makes the authentic preacher. For 'What is preaching?' asked Dr Lloyd-Jones, and went on to answer his own question. 'Logic on fire! Eloquent reason! Are these contradictions? Of course they are not. Reason concerning this Truth ought to be mightily eloquent ... Preaching is theology coming through a man who is on fire.'[29]

Fourthly, there is a place for emotion in *social and pastoral ministry*. In this, as in all things, Jesus himself is our perfect model. Let us visualize him at the graveside of Lazarus, face to face with the reality of death. According to Scripture death is an alien intrusion into God's good world, and is no part of either his original or his ultimate purpose. The Bible calls death an 'enemy', in fact 'the last enemy to be destroyed'.[30] How, then, will Jesus react when confronted by this arch-enemy of God and of the human race? He reacted, surprisingly, with two violent emotions.

First, he was moved with anger, or indignation. In John 11:33 and 38 we are told that he 'groaned' (AV), 'sighed' (NEB), or 'was deeply moved' (RSV, NIV). The Greek verb *enebrimēsato* (verse 33) means that he 'snorted'; the word is used literally of horses and metaphorically of indignation.[31] C. K. Barrett in his commentary on John 11 writes: 'It is beyond question that *embrimasthai* implies anger.' B. B. Warfield went even further: 'What John tells us ... is that Jesus approached the grave of Lazarus in a state not of uncontrollable grief but of irrepressible anger.' Why? Because he saw 'the evil of death, its unnaturalness, its "violent tyranny" as Calvin phrases it.' He 'burns with rage against the oppressor of men ... Fury seizes upon him; his whole being is discomposed and perturbed ... It is death that is the object of his wrath, and behind death him who has the power of death, and whom he has come into the world to destroy.'[32]

Then we are told of a second emotional response of Jesus, namely sorrow and compassion. On seven separate occasions in the Gospels Jesus was 'moved with compassion', for example towards the hungry and leaderless crowds, the widow of Nain, leprosy sufferers and a blind beggar. And in John 11 we read that 'Jesus wept' (verse 35) – not now tears of anger in the face of death but tears of sympathy for the bereaved sisters. Is it not beautiful to see Jesus, when confronted by death and bereavement, so deeply moved? He felt indignation in the face of death, and compassion towards its victims. First, he 'snorted' (verse 33) and then he 'wept' (verse 35).

Speaking personally, I long to see more Christian anger towards evil in the world, and more Christian compassion for its victims. Think of social injustice and political tyranny, of the callous killing of human foetuses in the womb as if they were no more than pieces of tissue, or the cynical wickedness of drug-pushers and pornographers who make their fortunes out of other people's weaknesses and at the cost of their ruin. Since these and many other evils are hateful to God, should his people not react against them in anger? And what about the victims of evil – the poor, the hungry and the homeless, street kids abandoned by their parents, unborn children at risk in a selfish society, tortured prisoners of conscience, and the alienated and lost who have never heard the gospel? Where is our sense of outrage? Where is the compassion of Jesus, which will express itself in practical action for those who suffer?

I do not know how much Christian profession Bob Geldof makes, but his social conscience and drive put many of us Christians to shame. What happened, then, to transform the 'scruffy Irish pop singer' into 'St Bob', the cult hero who alerted the world to the famine holocaust in Africa? Watching the televised news report on famine in Ethiopia towards the end of 1984, he experienced what one might call a 'secular conversion'. The people he saw on his TV screen were 'so shrunken by starvation that they looked like beings from another planet'.[33] 'I felt disgusted, enraged and outraged', he has said, 'but more than all those, I felt deep shame.'[34] Out of this experience came Band Aid and Live Aid and other initiatives, which raised many millions of pounds. What drove him? It was a combination of 'pity and disgust'.[35]

Mind and emotions

So far we have looked at our intellect and our emotions separately, and we have seen that both have an indispensable place in our Christian discipleship. We are to be neither such emotional Christians that we never think, nor such intellectual Christians that we never feel. No, God has made us human beings, and human beings are by creation both rational and emotional.

But how are our mind and our emotions to be related to one another? There are two particular relationships on which Scripture lays emphasis, and in which the mind exercises the primary role. They are also complementary, in that the first is negative, and the second positive.

First and negatively, *the mind controls the emotions*, or should do so. There have always been some who campaign for the unfettered expression of human emotions. Bacchus, for example, whom the Greeks identified with Dionysus, was worshipped in orgies of wine, dance and sex. In our day popular Freudianism, which has not entirely grasped what Freud meant by 'repression', has taught the peril of suppressing our emotions. And some forms of existentialism have added impetus to these ideas by urging us to find our authenticity in being and expressing ourselves.

But Christians cannot possibly follow this teaching and give free rein to our emotions. For our whole human being has been tainted and twisted by inherited sin, and that includes our emotions. They are ambiguous because we are ambiguous. Some are good, but others evil, and we have to learn to discriminate between them.

Take anger. The instruction 'In your anger do not sin'[36] recognizes that there are two different kinds of anger. There is righteous anger, such as God himself feels towards evil, and there is unrighteous anger (contaminated by pride, envy, malice, spite and revenge) which is one of the 'acts of the sinful nature'.[37] Consequently, when feelings of anger arise within us, it would be very foolish to give vent to them uncritically. Instead, we should say to ourselves: 'Wait a minute! What is this anger which is beginning to burn inside me? Is it righteous anger or unrighteous? Is it anger against evil, or merely injured vanity?'

Or take love. What should we say to a married man who confesses that he has fallen in love with another woman, that he cannot help himself, that this is 'the real thing', and that he must divorce his wife? I think we would have to say: 'Wait a minute! You are not the helpless victim of your emotions. You have accepted a life-long commitment to your wife. You should (and can) put this other woman out of your mind.'

In these two examples, the one of anger and the other of love, there is a recognition that both emotions can be tainted with self-centredness, and that we should never give in to either without first asking ourselves some searching questions. In both cases, the mind is meant to stand censor over the emotions.

Secondly and positively, the *mind stimulates the emotions.* It is when we reflect on the truth that our heart catches fire. Think of the Emmaus disciples on the afternoon of Easter Day. The risen Lord joined them on their walk and explained to them out of the Scriptures how the Messiah had to suffer before entering his glory. Later, after he had left them, they said to each other: 'Were not our hearts burning within us while he talked with us on the road and opened the Scriptures to us?'[38] This inner burning of the heart is a profound emotional experience, but it was Jesus' biblical teaching which prompted it. Nothing sets the heart ablaze like fresh vistas of truth. As F. W. Faber put it, 'deep theology is the best fuel of devotion; it readily catches fire, and once kindled it burns long.'[39]

Or consider Paul's well-known statement that 'Christ's love compels us'.[40] Literally, it 'hems us in' or 'leaves us no choice' (NEB), so that we must live our lives for him. But how does the love of Christ constrain or move us? Is it that we are overwhelmed emotionally at the foot of the cross? Yes and no! Yes, in that we cannot contemplate the cross and not be moved by it. But no, if we suppose that our mind plays no part in the process. For what Paul writes is that 'Christ's love compels us, because we are convinced that ...' It is through certain convictions that Christ's love tightens its grip upon us. In brief, it is because we have received our life from Christ crucified and risen, that we realize we must live it for him. It is as we reflect upon this logic that the fires of love within us are fanned into flame.

One more example may be mentioned. In the area of social responsibility it is essential that we both think clearly and feel deeply. A cool analysis of injustice is necessary, so long as it leads to hot anger and action.

It is important, then, to keep our mind and our emotions together, allowing our mind both to control and to stimulate our emotions. I think it was Bishop Handley Moule at the end of the last century who gave this good advice: 'Beware equally of an undevotional theology [*i.e.* mind without heart] and of an untheological devotion [*i.e.* heart without mind].'

Notes

1 Mk. 12:30.
2 Rom. 12:2; Eph. 4:23.
3 *E.g.* Eph. 4:26; 1 Pet. 1:22.
4 Acts 24:16.
5 *E.g.* Mk. 14:36; Mt. 6:10; Col. 4:12.
6 1 Cor. 14:20.
7 Lesslie Newbigin, *Foolishness to the Greeks* (SPCK, 1986), p. 70.
8 D. Martyn Lloyd-Jones, *The Christian Warfare* (Banner of Truth, 1976), p. 114.
9 2 Cor. 5:7.
10 H. L. Mencken, who wrote for the *Baltimore Sun* and was sometimes called 'the sage of Baltimore'.
11 1 Cor. 2:1–5.
12 Acts 18:4.
13 Acts 19:9–10.
14 Acts 26:25.
15 Phil. 1:7.
16 Chaim Potok, *The Chosen* (1967; Penguin, 1970).
17 *Ibid.*, p. 200.
18 *Ibid.*, p. 273.
19 *Ibid.*, p. 274.
20 *Ibid.*, p. 277.
21 *E.g.* Ho. 11:8–9.
22 Rom. 5:5.
23 Rom. 8:15–16.
24 1 Jn. 3:1.
25 1 Pet. 1:8.
26 Rom. 8:22–25; 2 Cor. 5:2–4.
27 2 Cor. 5:19–20.
28 *E.g.* Acts 20:19, 31; Phil. 3:18.
29 D. Martyn Lloyd-Jones, *Preaching and Preachers* (Hodder and Stoughton, 1971), p. 97.
30 1 Cor. 15:26.
31 *Cf.* Mk. 14:5.
32 B. B. Warfield, *The Person and Work of Christ* (Presbyterian and Reformed, 1950), pp. 115–117.
33 Bob Geldof with Paul Vallely, *Is That It?* (Penguin, 1986), p. 269.
34 *Ibid.*, p. 271.
35 *Ibid.*, p. 386.
36 Eph. 4:26.
37 Gal. 5:19–21.
38 Lk. 24:32.
39 Quoted by Ralph G. Turnbull in *A Minister's Obstacles* (1946; Baker, 1972), p. 97.
40 2 Cor. 5:14.

EIGHT

Guidance, vocation and ministry

If God has a purpose for the lives of his people, and if his purpose is discoverable, then nothing could be more important for us than to discern and do it. The apostle Paul certainly indicated that this was his expectation. 'We are God's workmanship,' he affirmed, 'created in Christ Jesus to do good works, which God prepared in advance for us to do.'[1] If, therefore, there are good works which God has planned and designed for us, presumably from before we were born, we surely must find out what they are. No wonder Paul wrote later in the same letter: 'Do not be foolish, but understand what the Lord's will is.'[2]

In the companion letter to the Colossians Paul also prayed that God would 'fill [them] with the knowledge of his will through all spiritual wisdom and understanding',[3] and mentioned how Epaphras was 'always wrestling in prayer' for them, that they might 'stand firm in all the will of God, mature and fully assured'.[4]

Whenever we talk about discovering God's will for our lives, three words are almost bound to crop up in the conversation; they are 'guidance', 'vocation' and 'ministry'. Each has a distinctive meaning. 'Guidance' implies that God is willing to direct us, 'vocation' that he calls us, and 'ministry' that he wants us to give our lives in service. At the same time, what is common to the three concepts is that the initiative in each is God's, and that each has both a general aspect (which applies equally to all of us) and a particular (which is different for each of us). This will become clearer as we go on.

Guidance

We sometimes say with a sigh, 'If only I had ten lives ...' There is a myth that cats have nine, but we human beings have only one, and we cannot duplicate or replicate ourselves. Hence the urgency that we should discover God's will for the one and only life he has given us.

But before we are in a position to discover God's will, it is essential to draw a distinction between his 'general' will and his 'particular' will. God's general will is so called because it is his will for the generality of his people; it is the same for all of us in all places and at all times. God's particular will is so called, however, because it is his will for particular people at particular places and times. His general will is that we should 'be conformed to the likeness of his Son'.[5] Christlikeness is God's will for all of us; it does not vary from disciple to disciple. His particular will, on the other hand, concerns such questions as the choice of a life work and of a life partner, and how we should spend our energies, time, money and holidays. These will be different for each of us. Only when we have made this essential distinction between the 'general' and the 'particular' are we in a position to repeat our earlier question how we can discover God's will. His general will has been revealed in Scripture. Not that Scripture contains slick solutions to complex twentieth-century ethical problems, but that it contains principles which can be applied to them. Generally speaking, it is correct to say that the will of God for the people of God is in the Word of God.

The particular will of God will not be found in Scripture however. I cannot deny that occasionally God seems to have guided individuals through a specific verse wrenched out of its context. But I must add that he has done it only in condescension to our weakness. For Scripture is not an anthology of unrelated texts, but a cumulative, historical revelation. We have no liberty to ignore its original meaning in order to oblige it to speak to us. What the Bible does contain, however, is principles which are relevant to particular questions. Take marriage as an example. Scripture gives us general guidance and settles some issues in advance. It tells us that marriage is God's good purpose for human beings and that singleness is the exception, not the rule; that one of his primary purposes in instituting marriage is companionship, so that this is an important quality to look for in a spouse; that a Christian is at liberty to marry only a fellow-Christian; and that marriage (as a lifelong, loving, monogamous and heterosexual commitment) is the only God-ordained context for sexual intercourse. These general guidelines are clearly laid down in the Bible. But the Bible will not tell any individuals whether God is calling them to marriage or to remain single, or (if they should marry) who their spouse should be.

How, then, are we meant to discover God's particular will, if he does not disclose it through Scripture? Since God is sovereign and free, I do not think we have the liberty to stereotype our answer. But I have found that the following five monosyllables are safe guides. First, *yield.* The word is a familiar road sign in the United States, telling traffic to give way to other vehicles. Just so, we are to give in to, or give way to, God's purpose. An unsurrendered will is the most serious of all obstacles to the discovery of God's will. If God does not reveal his truth to those who are not willing to believe it, neither does he reveal his will to those unwilling to do it. No, 'he guides the humble in what is right and teaches them his way'.[6]

Secondly, *pray.* A vague surrender is not enough; sustained, expectant prayer is also necessary. 'Ask and it will be given to you,' Jesus taught, and 'You do not have, because you do not ask God,' James added.[7] Our heavenly Father does not spoil his children. He does not disclose his will to us unless we really want to know it and express our desire in our prayers.

Thirdly, *talk.* Although one of the strengths of Protestant Christianity is its insistence on 'the right of private judgment', we must not imagine that this means we should make all our decisions alone. On the contrary, God has given us to each other in his family. So we need to be humble enough to talk to others, including our parents, in order to seek their counsel, for 'wisdom is found in those who take advice'.[8] Let our decisions be group decisions, taken responsibly in the rich fellowship in which God has put us.

Fourthly, *think.* Although we must yield, pray and ask advice, ultimately we have to make up our own minds. As we saw in the last chapter, God balances his promises of guidance with his prohibition of behaviour like horses and mules which lack understanding.[9] We must not expect him to fulfil his promises to guide us either by using 'bit and bridle' (*i.e.* force) or by giving us irrational hunches, but rather through the minds he has given us, as in every situation we carefully weigh up the pros and cons.

Fifthly, *wait.* It is a mistake to be in a hurry or grow impatient with God. It took him about 2,000 years to fulfil his promise to Abraham in the birth of Christ. It took him eighty years to prepare Moses for his life work. It takes him about twenty-five years to make a mature human being. So then, if we *have* to make a decision by a certain deadline, we must make it. But if not, and the way forward is still uncertain, it is wiser to wait. I think God says to us what he said to Joseph and Mary when sending them into Egypt with the child Jesus: 'Stay there until I tell you.'[10] In my experience, more mistakes are made by precipitate action than by procrastination.

Vocation

'Vocation' is one of many biblical words which over the years has changed its meaning and become devalued. In popular usage it refers to our work or career. 'What's your vocation?' is a rather grandiose way of asking somebody what his job is, and 'vocational training' means training for a particular trade. In biblical usage, however, 'vocation' has a much broader and nobler connotation. Its emphasis is not on the human (what *we* do) but on the divine (what *God* has called us to do). For 'vocation' is a Latin word, whose Anglo-Saxon equivalent is 'calling'.

In the New Testament the Greek verb to 'call' occurs about 150 times, and in most cases of God calling human beings. In the Old Testament God called Moses, Samuel and the prophets; in the New Testament Jesus called the Twelve and later Saul of Tarsus. Today, although we are neither prophets nor apostles, he still calls us into his service. It is a wonderful fact that God cares about us enough to call us personally and individually. In consequence, God is 'he who called you';[11] and we are the 'called according to his purpose'.[12]

The question before us is this: what, according to Scripture, does God call us to? What is our divine vocation? In answer to this question about 'vocation', we have to make a similar distinction to the one we made with regard to 'guidance', namely between our 'general' calling and our particular 'callings'. Our general calling is that of all God's people, and is therefore the same. Our particular calling is that of each of us, and is therefore different. We all share in the same general call of God; we have each received a different particular call from God.

God's *general call* to us is not so much to do something (a job) as to be something (a person). Although he does call us to different tasks, as we shall shortly see, he first calls us to something even more significant, namely to be a disciple of Jesus Christ, to live a new life in his new society and in the world. So if somebody asks us, 'What is your calling?', our first and correct answer should be: 'I am called to belong to Jesus Christ.'[13] In fact, we are called to embrace and enjoy all the blessings which God has locked up in Jesus Christ: 'to this you were called so that you may inherit a blessing'.[14] What, then, is this blessing? It has many facets.

First, we are called to *fellowship with Jesus Christ*. This is basic. His invitation is still 'Come to me' and 'Follow me'. For 'God ... has called you into fellowship with his Son Jesus Christ our Lord'.[15] Just as Christ called the Twelve to be 'with him',[16] so he calls us to know him and to enjoy his fellowship. Eternal life is to know God and his Christ,[17] and nothing can take the place of this fundamental relationship with him.

Secondly, we are called to *freedom*. 'You, my brothers,' Paul wrote to the Galatians, 'were called to be free.'[18] The kind of freedom to which the apostle was alluding here is freedom from the condemnation of the law through God's forgiveness and acceptance of us in Christ. It is freedom from guilt and from a guilty conscience, the freedom of access to God as his adopted sons and daughters. It is not, however, freedom to sin or freedom from social responsibilities. On the contrary, Paul goes on: 'But do not use your freedom to indulge the sinful nature; rather serve one another [literally, 'be slaves to one another'] in love.' It is the paradox we have already noted that it is only through serving that we become free.

Thirdly, we are called to *peace*. 'Let the peace of Christ rule in your hearts, since as members of one body you were called to peace.'[19] The reference to the 'one body' gives us the clue to Paul's meaning. He is not here referring to peace of mind, heart or conscience, but to the peace (*shalom*) of reconciliation with each other in the kingdom community of Christ. Our calling is to belong not only to Christ, but also to the people of Christ.

Fourthly, we are called to *holiness*,[20] or 'called to be saints'.[21] Since God himself is holy, he calls us to be holy too.[22] Unfortunately, 'holiness' suggests to many people the false image of pious folk with an anaemic look and a vacant stare, who seem to have contracted out of life. But true holiness is a Christlikeness which is lived out in the real world.

Fifthly, we are called to *witness*. 'But you are ... a people belonging to God, that you may declare the praises of him who called you out of darkness into his wonderful light.'[23] Peter is contrasting what we once were with what we now are. We were in darkness, but now we are in light. We were not a people, but now we are God's people. We had not received mercy, but now we have. The logical deduction is that we cannot possibly keep these blessings to ourselves. Having been called into God's light, we are inevitably called to let our light shine.

Sixthly, we are called to *suffering*. 'If you suffer for doing good and you endure it, this is commendable before God. To this you were called.'[24] Peter was writing when Nero's hostility to Christians was growing and the storm clouds of persecution were gathering ominously on the horizon. At any moment the storm might break. How then should Christians react if they suffered unjustly? Peter's answer was straightforward. They were called to follow Christ's example of non-retaliation. It comes as a shock to many people that unjust suffering is an unavoidable part of the Christian calling. But Jesus himself warned us of it. 'If the world hates you, keep in mind that it hated me first ... If they persecuted me, they will persecute you also.'[25]

Seventhly, we are called to *glory*. The Christian calling is a 'heavenly calling'.[26] 'The God of all grace, who called you to his eternal glory in Christ, after you have suffered a little while, will himself ... make you strong, firm and steadfast.'[27] Suffering and glory are constantly bracketed in the New Testament. It was through suffering that Jesus entered his glory, and it will be the same for us. If we share in Christ's suffering, we will also share in his glory.[28] Thus, the call of God is not for this life only; it is also to spend eternity with him in the new universe.

Here, then, is God's sevenfold, general calling. He calls all of us to Christ, freedom, peace, holiness, witness, suffering and glory. More simply, it is a call to belong to Christ in time and eternity, to love one another in the peace of his new community, and to serve, witness and suffer in the world. This is the fundamental meaning of 'Christian vocation'. It is the same for all of us, and we are exhorted to live a life that is worthy of it.[29]

If our general call (which is the same for us all) is to be free and holy and Christlike, our *particular calling* (which is different for each of us) relates to the highly individual details of our lives. Consider the teaching of Paul: 'Each one should remain in the situation [literally, 'the calling'] which he was in when God called him.'[30] We note at once the two senses in which the apostle uses the notion of 'calling'. The words 'when God called him' refer to a person's conversion when God's general call is heard and obeyed. 'The situation' ('calling') which he was 'in', on the other hand, is a reference to his particular calling at the time of his conversion. This situation is regarded as something God has 'called' us to and something God has 'assigned' to us.[31] And the general principle the apostle lays down, repeating it three times,[32] is that we should 'remain' in it. He gives three examples – our domestic situation (married or single), cultural situation (Jewish or Gentile) and social situation (slaves or free). In order to understand Paul's teaching, we need to grasp the background and context. It appears that the Corinthian converts found life in Christ so new ('a new creation')[33] and exciting, and so radically different from their unregenerate state, that they imagined that nothing belonging to the old life could be retained; everything had to be repudiated.

Take the example of marriage. Now that they belonged to Christ, they seem to have been asking, how could a pre-conversion contractual obligation still be valid post-conversion? Would not such a relationship be 'unclean'?[34] Paul answers, 'No.' Why not? Because God's providence embraced both their pre- and their post-conversion lives. Their marriage, though entered into before they became Christians, was a part of the 'calling' they were in when God called them. They had no liberty therefore to repudiate it. Transform it by God's grace – yes; reject it – no.

We have to be very cautious in applying this teaching to ourselves. Paul is laying down a general rule, not absolute one. For example, he himself had not remained a Pharisee when called to be an apostle of Christ. Similarly, the Twelve had given up their fishing and their tax-collecting when called to become apostles. And Paul says here that if a slave can gain his freedom he should do so.[35] We too need to be open to the possibility that God is calling us to something different. What Paul was opposing was thoughtless and reckless actions, change for change's sake, and especially the notion that nothing before conversion and nothing outside religion has any value to God.

From Scripture we turn to history, and to the teaching of the Reformers and the Puritans in this area. The Reformers insisted that every Christian man and woman has a divine 'calling'. They were reacting against the teaching of medieval Catholicism that bishops, priests, monks and nuns had a superior, because a 'religious', calling. The Reformers rejected this as both 'clericalism', separating clergy from laity, and 'dualism', separating 'sacred' activities like prayer from 'secular' ones like running a home or earning a living. They affirmed that God is interested in the whole of life, and that to be a farmer, craftsman. magistrate or housewife was just as much a divine calling as to be a 'priest' or 'pastor'. Luther insisted much on this:

> Those who are now called 'spiritual', that is, priests, bishops or popes, are neither different from other Christians nor superior to them, except that they are charged with the administration of the word of God and the sacraments, which is their work and office.

But 'tailors, cobblers, stonemasons, carpenters, cooks, innkeepers, farmers and all the temporal craftsmen' have also been 'consecrated' like priests, each to 'the work and office of his trade'.

> Further, everyone must benefit and serve every other by means of his own work or office, so that in this way many kinds of work may be done for the bodily and spiritual welfare of the community, just as all the members of the body serve one another (1 Cor. 12:14–26).[36]

Again, 'serving God is not tied to one or two works, nor is it confined to one or two callings, but it is distributed over all works and all callings'.[37] 'But what I want to do is to keep a distinction between the callings and offices, so that everyone can see to what God has called him and fulfil the duties of his office faithfully and sincerely in the service of God.'[38]

Calvin's teaching was similar:

> The Lord bids each one of us in all life's actions to look to his calling ... Therefore, lest through our stupidity and rashness everything be turned topsy-turvy, he has appointed duties for every man in his particular way of life. And that no one may thoughtlessly transgress his limits, he has named these various kinds of living 'callings'. Therefore each individual has his own kind of living assigned to him by the Lord as a sort of sentry post so that he may not heedlessly wander about throughout life ... From this will arise also a singular consolation: that no task will be so sordid and base, provided you obey your calling

in it, that it will not shine and be reckoned very precious in God's sight.[39]

The Puritans developed this theme further. William Perkins, for example, who had a very influential ministry in Cambridge, wrote *A Treatise of the Vocations or Callings of Men* (published in 1603). Here is a sample of his thesis:

The action of a shepherd in keeping sheep … is as good a work before God as is the action of a judge in giving sentence, or of a magistrate in ruling, or a minister in preaching. Thus then we see there is good reason why we would search how every man is rightly to use his particular calling.[40]

A century later, and on the other side of the Atlantic, Cotton Mather, the Harvard Puritan, wrote *A Christian at his Calling* (1701). In it he taught that every Christian has two callings – 'a general calling' ('to serve the Lord Jesus Christ …') and 'a personal calling' ('a particular employment by which his usefulness in his neighbourhood is distinguished').[41]

Moreover, the two callings should be pursued in balance. For 'a Christian at his two callings is a man in a boat rowing for heaven … If he mind but one of his callings, be it which it will, he pulls the oar but on one side of the boat, and will make but a poor dispatch to the shore of eternal blessedness.'[42]

It would be easy to criticize this kind of teaching. The Reformers and the Puritans were people of their age and culture, as we are of ours. They held a static, medieval view of society. In their reaction against the revolutionary overtones of some Anabaptist teaching, they tended to be too resistant to change. Sometimes they got close to the embarrassing verse in the hymn 'All Things Bright and Beautiful':

The rich man in his castle,
The poor man at his gate,
God made them, high or lowly,
And ordered their estate.

We certainly should not use the biblical teaching about 'callings' to resist social change.

Paul in the first century, the Reformers in the sixteenth, and the Puritans in the seventeenth all seem rather remote from us. So what is the underlying principle, which Paul taught and the Reformers and Puritans recovered, which we need to hold on to today? I think it is this. The whole of our life belongs to God and is part of his calling, both before conversion and outside religion. We must not imagine that God first became interested in us when we were converted, or that now he is interested only in the religious bit of our lives.

Consider our life before conversion. What was our calling in which we were when God called us? If at the time of our conversion we were looking after elderly relatives, we should not abandon them now. If we were students, we have no liberty to give up our studies and drop out of college or university. If we had entered into a contract with somebody, we have no right to break it. If we were musical, artistic, athletic, or intelligent when God called us, we must not now disown these good things which a good Creator gave us. For these things were not accidental aspects of our life. They were part of God's providence to which he had called us and which he had assigned to us. God's sovereignty extends over both halves of our life. He did not begin to work in and for us at our conversion, but at our birth, even before our birth in our genetic inheritance, as later in our temperament, personality, education and skills. And what God made us and gave us before we became Christians, he redeems, sanctifies and transforms afterwards. There is a vital continuity between our pre- and post-conversion life. For although we are a new person in Christ, we are still the same person we were by creation, whom Christ has made new.

Now consider our life outside religion. The God many of us worship is altogether too religious. We seem to imagine that he is interested only in religious books and buildings and services. But no, he is interested in us, in our home, family and friends, in our work and hobbies, in our citizenship and community. So God's sovereignty extends over *both* halves and over *all* sections of our life. We must not marginalize God, or try to squeeze him out of the non-religious section of our life. We must remember that our vocation (*i.e.* God's calling) includes these things. It is in these that we are to serve and glorify God.

Ministry

If we are concerned to discover where God is leading us (guidance) and to what he is calling us (vocation), we may be sure that this will relate to how best we may serve him (ministry). Moreover, as with the words 'guidance' and 'vocation', so with the word 'ministry', we need to distinguish between a broader and a narrower meaning, between a general and a particular application.

Here are three affirmations about ministry.

First, *all Christians without exception are called to ministry*, indeed to spend their lives in ministry. Ministry is not the privilege of a small elite, but of all the disciples of Jesus. You will have noticed that I did not say that all Christians are called to *the* ministry, but to ministry, *diakonia*, service.

We do a great disservice to the Christian cause whenever we refer to the pastorate as 'the ministry'. For by our use of the definite article we give the impression that the pastorate is the only ministry there is, much as medieval churchmen regarded the priesthood as the only (or at least the most 'spiritual') vocation there is. I repented of this view, and therefore of this language, about twenty-five years ago, and now invite my readers, if necessary, to join me in penitence. Nowadays, whenever somebody says in my presence that 'So-and-so is going into the ministry', I always ask innocently, 'Oh really? Which ministry do you mean?' And when my interlocutor probably replies, 'The pastoral ministry', I come back with the gentle complaint, 'Then why didn't you say so?!' The fact is that the word 'ministry' is a generic term; it lacks specificity until we add an adjective.

I come back to my first proposition that all Christians without exception are called to ministry. How can I make such a dogmatic statement? Because of Jesus Christ. His lordship over us has a vocational dimension, as we saw in chapter 5. Since he is 'the servant' *par excellence*, who gave himself without reserve to the service of God and human beings, it would be impossible to be his disciple without seeking to follow his example of service. He preached the kingdom, healed the sick, fed the hungry, befriended the friendless, championed the oppressed, comforted the bereaved, sought the lost and washed his apostles' feet. No task was too demanding, and no ministry too mean, for him to undertake. He lived his life and died his death in utterly self-forgetful service. Shall we not imitate him? The world measures greatness by success; Jesus measures it by service.

Secondly, *there is a wide variety of Christian ministries*. This is because 'ministry' means 'service', and there are many different ways in which we can serve God and people. Acts 6:1–4 provides a firm biblical base for this conviction. An ethnic or cultural squabble was tearing the Jerusalem church apart. The 'Grecian Jews' were complaining against the 'Hebraic Jews' that their widows were being discriminated against in the daily distribution of food. Moreover, the apostles had become embroiled in this quarrel; it was occupying a great deal of their time, and threatening to distract them from the preaching and teaching role to which Jesus had commissioned them. So they wisely called a church meeting and said: 'It would not be right for us to neglect the ministry of the word of God in order to wait on [*diakonein*] tables.' The church was then asked to choose seven men for that responsibility, while, the apostles added, 'We ... will give our attention to prayer and the ministry [*diakonia*] of the word.'

It is essential to note that both distributing food and teaching the word were referred to as ministry (*diakonia*). Indeed, both were Christian ministry, could be full-time Christian ministry, and required Spirit-filled people to perform them. The only difference between them was that one was pastoral ministry, and the other social. It was not that one was 'ministry' and the other not; nor that one was spiritual and the other secular; nor that one was superior and the other inferior. It was simply that Christ had called the Twelve to the ministry of the word and the Seven to the ministry of tables.

I was myself brought up as a young Christian to think of different vocations or ministries as forming a hierarchy or pyramid. Perched precariously at the top of the pyramid was the cross-cultural missionary. He was our hero, she our heroine. I was taught that if I was really out and out for Christ I would undoubtedly join their ranks overseas. If I was not as keen as that, I would stay at home and be a pastor. If I did not aspire even to that, I would probably become a doctor or a teacher, whereas, if I were to go into business, politics or the media, I would not be far from backsliding! Please do not misunderstand me. It is a wonderful privilege to be a missionary or a pastor, *if God calls us to it*. But it is equally wonderful to be a Christian lawyer, industrialist, politician, manager, social worker, television scriptwriter, journalist, or home-maker, *if God calls us to it*. According to Romans 13:4 an official of the state (whether legislator, magistrate, policeman or policewoman) is just as much a 'minister of God' (*diakonos theou*) as a pastor. It is the hierarchy we have to reject, the pyramid we have to demolish.

There is still, of course, an urgent need for missionaries of the right kind, men and women who are characterized above all by humility – for example, the humility to repent of cultural imperialism and identify with another culture, the humility to work under national church leadership, the humility to serve people's felt needs (social as well as evangelistic), and the humility to rely on the Holy Spirit as the chief communicator.[43] World evangelization remains at the top of the church's agenda, and the fifth section of this book is devoted to it. Pastors also are greatly needed to teach the word of God. Chapters 13 and 17 take up this ministry.

At the same time, there is a crying need for Christian men and women who see their daily work as their primary Christian ministry and who determine to penetrate their secular environment for Christ.

Christian people in business and industry are needed to specify 'service to the public' as the first goal on their 'mission' statement, to make bold experiments in labour relations, worker participation and profit-sharing, and to accept their responsibility to produce an annual 'social audit' alongside their annual financial audit.

Christian politicians are needed to identify the major injustices in their society, refuse to come to terms with them, and determine to secure legislative change, however long it takes. And Christian economists are needed to find a way of controlling inflation and reducing unemployment simultaneously.

Christian film-makers are needed to produce not only overtly Christian or evangelistic films, but wholesome films which indirectly commend

Christian personal and family values, and so honour and glorify Christ.

More Christian doctors are needed who, in co-operation with moral theologians, face the contemporary challenges of medical ethics and develop ways of maintaining the uniquely Christian vision of the human person and the human family.

Dedicated Christian teachers are needed, in both Christian and secular schools, who count it a privilege to serve their students in such a way as to help them develop their full God-given potential.

And more Christian social workers are needed who, in their concern for the handicapped in mind or body, abused children, drug-abusers, Aids victims and others, combine the latest medical treatment and social care with Christian love, believing prayer and church support.

Thirdly, *the particular ministry to which Christ calls us is likely to be determined by our gifts.* That is, the major factor in deciding on our life work will probably be what kind of person we are by God's creation and redemption. God is not a random creator; he has not given us natural gifts in order that they may be wasted. Nor is he a random redeemer, who has given us spiritual gifts to be wasted. Instead, he wants his gifts to us to be discerned, cultivated and exercised. He surely does not want us to be frustrated (because our gifts are lying idle), but rather fulfilled (because our gifts are being used).

It seems to me fully compatible with our Christian doctrines of creation and redemption that we should talk to ourselves somewhat as follows: 'I am a unique person. [That is not conceit. It is a fact. If every snowflake and every blade of grass is unique, how much more is every human being?] My uniqueness is due to my genetic endowment, my inherited personality and temperament, my parentage, upbringing and education, my talents, inclinations and interests, my new birth and spiritual gifts. By the grace of God I am who I am. How then can I, as the unique person God has made me, be *stretched* in the service of Christ and of people, so that nothing he has given me is wasted, and everything he has given me is used?'

There may be exceptions to this principle, but it appears to me to be the right question to ask oneself. And in trying thus to evaluate ourselves honestly, with neither pride nor false modesty, our parents and friends who know us best are likely to help us most.

The three words we have been considering (guidance, vocation and ministry) all relate to God's will for our lives and how to discover it. As I conclude, let me anticipate two fears which my readers may be feeling, and try to relieve them.

First, there is no need to fear God's will on the assumption that it is bound to be difficult. Some Christians seem to imagine that the more disagreeable some prospect is, the more likely it is to be God's will! But God is not an ogre, bent on spoiling our lives; he is our Father, committed to our welfare and determined to give us only what is for our good. 'If you … though you are evil, know how to give good gifts to your children,' Jesus said, 'how much more will your Father in heaven give good gifts to those who ask him!'[44] We can be assured that God's will is 'good, pleasing and perfect'.[45]

Secondly, there is no need to fear that we shall never discover God's will. We have no cause to fret or worry, to work ourselves into a state of nervous tension, or spend sleepless nights of anxiety. Strangely enough, one of my earliest childhood memories, when I cannot have been more than six or seven, was of my mother coming into my bedroom daily to say goodnight. I plagued her with the constantly repeated, anguished question: 'Mummy, what am I going to be when I grow up?' She replied to the effect that I need not worry, since it would be shown me in due time. And now, more than sixty years later, with the benefit of hindsight, I know that she was right, and that all those childish apprehensions were unnecessary. We have every reason to be confident that our Father's will is discoverable as well as good. He has ways and means of showing us what he wants us to do. The main condition is that we ourselves really want to discern his will, in order to do it.

Notes

[1] Eph. 2:10.
[2] Eph. 5:17.
[3] Col. 1:9.
[4] Col. 4:12.
[5] Rom. 8:29.
[6] Ps. 25:9.
[7] Mt. 7:7; Jas. 4:2.
[8] Pr. 13:10.
[9] Ps. 32:8–9.
[10] Mt. 2:13.
[11] *E.g.* Gal. 5:8; 1 Pet. 1:15.
[12] *E.g.* Rom. 8:28; Heb. 9:15.
[13] Rom. 1:6.
[14] 1 Pet. 3:9.
[15] 1 Cor. 1:9.
[16] Mk. 3:14.
[17] Jn. 17:3.
[18] Gal. 5:13.
[19] Col. 3:15.
[20] 1 Cor. 1:2.
[21] Rom. 1:7.
[22] *E.g.* 1 Pet. 1:15; 1 Thes. 4:7; 2 Tim. 1:9.
[23] 1 Pet. 2:9.

[24] 1 Pet. 2:20–21.

[25] Jn. 15:18, 20.

[26] Heb. 3:1; *cf.* Phil. 3:14.

[27] 1 Pet. 5:10.

[28] Rom. 8:17.

[29] Eph. 4:1.

[30] 1 Cor. 7:20.

[31] 1 Cor. 7:20, 17.

[32] 1 Cor. 7:17, 20, 24.

[33] 2 Cor. 5:17.

[34] 1 Cor. 7:14.

[35] 1 Cor. 7:21.

[36] Luther *Weimarer Ausgabe* (1883–), vol. 44, pp. 130–131.

[37] *Ibid.*, vol. 52, p. 124.

[38] *Ibid.*, vol. 46, p. 166.

[39] Calvin, *Institutes*, III.x.6.

[40] William Perkins, *A Treatise of the Vocations or Callings of Men* in *The Work of William Perkins*, The Courtenay Library of Reformation Classics, ed. Ian Breward (Sutton Courtenay Press, 1970), p. 458.

[41] Cotton Mather, *A Christian at his Calling* (1701), p. 37.

[42] *Ibid.*, pp. 37–38.

[43] See *The Willowbank Report: Gospel and Culture*, especially chapter 6: 'Wanted: Humble Messengers of the Gospel' (Lausanne Committee for World Evangelization, 1978).

[44] Mt. 7:11.

[45] Rom. 12:2.

NINE

The first fruit of the Spirit

I invite you in this chapter to reflect on a biblical text which has come to mean much to me. Every day for perhaps twenty years I have quoted it to myself in my morning devotions, and prayed for its fulfilment in my life. When I am asked what my favourite text is, I usually give this one. It seems to me to contain truths which are of enormous importance to all the people of God. Here it is:

> But the fruit of the Spirit is love, joy, peace, patience, kindness, goodness, faithfulness, gentleness and self-control. Against such things there is no law.[1]

From these two verses I think we may legitimately derive five affirmations about love.

Love, joy and peace

The first truth is that *love is the pre-eminent Christian grace:* 'the fruit of the Spirit is love'. True, Paul lists a cluster of nine qualities, which together he calls the Spirit's 'fruit', but love has pride of place. We hear much about the Holy Spirit nowadays (he is no longer the 'neglected' person of the Trinity), and many people are claiming spectacular manifestations of his power, but the first fruit of his indwelling presence is not power, but love.

It is salutary to ask ourselves this question: What is the chief distinguishing mark of a Christian? What is the hallmark which authenticates people as the children of God? Different answers are given by different people.

Some reply that what distinguishes the genuine Christian is *truth,* orthodoxy, correct belief, loyalty to the doctrines of Scripture, the Catholic Creeds and the Reformation Confessions. Right! Truth is sacred. Sound doctrine is vital to the health of the church. We are summoned to 'fight the good fight of the faith',[2] to 'guard the deposit' of revealed religion,[3] to 'stand firm and hold to the teachings' of the apostles,[4] and to 'contend for the faith that was once for all entrusted to the saints'.[5] We must never forget these solemn exhortations. Nevertheless, 'if I ... can fathom all mysteries and all knowledge ... but have not love, I am nothing'.[6] Besides, 'knowledge puffs up, but love builds up'.[7] So love is greater than knowledge.

Others insist that the hallmark of genuine disciples is *faith.* 'For we maintain that a man is justified by faith apart from observing the law.'[8] As Luther wrote, justification by faith is 'the principal article of all Christian doctrine' which 'maketh true Christians indeed'.[9] And Cranmer added the negative counterpart: 'This [*sc.* doctrine] whosoever denieth is not to be counted for a true Christian man.'[10] Or to quote from a modern evangelical statement, justification by faith is 'the heart and hub, the paradigm and essence, of the whole economy of God's saving grace'.[11] I agree. *Sola fide,* 'by faith alone', which was the watchword of the Reformation, must be our watchword too. Nevertheless, 'if I have a faith that can move mountains, but have not love, I am nothing'.[12] The great apostle of faith is clear that love is greater than faith.

A third group emphasizes *religious experience* as the hallmark of the Christian, often of a particular and vivid kind, which they believe must be reproduced in everybody. And this group also is to some extent correct. A first-hand personal relationship with God through Christ is essential. The internal witness of the Spirit is real. There is such a thing as 'unutterable and exalted joy',[13] and 'compared to the surpassing greatness of knowing Christ Jesus my Lord' everything else is indeed a loss.[14] Nevertheless, 'if I speak in the tongues of men and of angels' and 'if I have the gift of prophecy' (claiming a direct communication from God), 'but have not love, I am nothing'.[15] So love is greater than experience.

A fourth and final category of people, being of a practical bent, emphasize *service* as the distinguishing mark of the people of God, especially the service of the poor. Right again! Without good works faith is dead. Since Jesus was himself a champion of the poor, his disciples must be also. If we see people in need, and have the wherewithal to meet it, but do not take pity on them, how can we claim to have God's love in us?[16] Thank God for the renewed emphasis on his 'preferential option' or priority concern for the poor. Nevertheless, 'if I give all I possess to the poor and surrender my body to the flames' (perhaps in a heroic gesture of sacrifice), 'but have not love, I gain nothing'.[17] So love is greater than service.

To sum up, knowledge is vital, faith indispensable, religious experience necessary, and service essential, but Paul gives precedence to love. Love is the greatest thing in the world. For 'God is love'[18] in his innermost being. Father, Son and Spirit are eternally united to each other in self-giving love. So he who is love, and has set his love upon us, calls us to love him and others in return. 'We love because he first loved us.'[19] Love is the principal, the paramount, the pre-eminent, the distinguishing characteristic of the people of God. Nothing can dislodge or replace it. Love is supreme.

Secondly, *love brings joy and peace*. For 'the fruit of the Spirit is love, joy, peace'. The sequence is surely significant.

Human beings have always pursued joy and peace, though they have usually employed the more secular word 'happiness'. Thomas Jefferson, before becoming the third President of the United States, was so convinced that 'the pursuit of happiness' was an inalienable human right that he wrote it into the Declaration of Independence and called it a 'self-evident truth'.

But Christians feel obliged to add that those who pursue happiness never find it. Joy and peace are extremely elusive blessings. Happiness is a will-o'-the-wisp, a phantom. Even as we reach out a hand to grasp it, it vanishes into thin air. For joy and peace are not suitable goals to pursue; they are by-products of love. God gives them to us, not when we pursue *them*, but when we pursue *him* and *others* in love.

It is urgent that we bear witness to this truth in the contemporary world, in which 'self-realization' is the rage and the 'human potential movement' continues to gather momentum. In his perceptive book *Psychology as Religion*,[20] sub-titled *The Cult of Self-Worship*, Dr Paul Vitz of New York University began by analysing the four principal 'self-theorists' of that decade – Erich Fromm (who argued that vice is indifference to one's self and virtue self-affirmation), Carl Rogers (whose 'client-centred' therapy aimed at helping the client become an integrated, autonomous person through 'unconditional self-regard'), Abraham Maslow (who emphasized creative 'self-actualization') and Rollo May (who, influenced by existentialism, stressed decision and commitment as the means to becoming oneself). These four writers, who reached their peak in the 1970s, were all self-confessed secular humanists. They believed in human beings, not in God. They have had many popularizers, and their basic emphasis on self-esteem and self-actualization seems to have seeped into almost every segment of society. Dr David Wells comments that 'in the mid-1980s a full 87.5% of what was published in the USA was catering to the interests and appetites of the self-movement'.[21]

To be sure, there is a right and healthy kind of self-affirmation, which balances the self-denial to which Jesus called his disciples. It is not, however, the humanist's uncritical, unqualified affirmation of the self, for it is heavily qualified by the acknowledgment of our own sinfulness. Christian believers are able to affirm only those aspects of the self which derive from our creation in God's image (*e.g.* our rationality, moral responsibility and capacity for love), while at the same time denying (that is, disowning and repudiating) all those aspects of the self which derive from the fall and from our own personal fallenness (*e.g.* our selfishness, covetousness, malice, hypocrisy and pride). These Christian forms of self-affirmation and self-denial are very far from being expressions of a preoccupation, let alone an infatuation, with ourselves. For, on the contrary, they are directed not towards self but towards God. They are part and parcel of our worship of God as our Creator and our Judge.

Yet some Christian writers have tried to argue that Christianity itself is about self-esteem, that we must give up concentrating on sin, guilt, judgment and atonement, that we must present salvation instead as the discovery of the self, and that this is what Jesus meant when he endorsed the second commandment, thereby implicitly telling us to love ourselves as well as our neighbour. But this is really not so. Self-love in Scripture is a synonym for sin, not the path to freedom. Besides, *agapē*-love means the sacrifice of oneself in the service of others. By its very nature it cannot be self-directed. How can we sacrifice ourselves to serve ourselves? It is impossible. The very idea is a nonsense. The way of Jesus is the opposite, as we saw in chapter 2 on 'Authentic freedom'. He taught the great paradox that only when we lose ourselves do we find ourselves, only when we die to ourselves do we learn to live, and only through serving others are we ourselves free. Or, to return to Paul in Galatians, only when we love, do joy and peace follow. The self-conscious pursuit of happiness will always end in failure. But when we forget ourselves in the self-giving service of love, then joy and peace come flooding into our lives as incidental, unlooked-for blessings.

Love in action

Thirdly, *love issues in action.* For if love is the first fruit of the Spirit, with joy and peace following in its wake, next come 'patience, kindness, goodness'. Love is not just romance, let alone eroticism. It is not even pure sentiment or emotion. It sounds abstract, but it leads to positive attitudes and concrete actions, namely 'patience', 'kindness' and 'goodness'. And, as I believe Dostoyevsky wrote, 'love in action is much more terrible than love in dreams'. For love is always seeking the true welfare of others, at whatever personal cost.

'Patience' (*makrothymia*) is a negative quality. It is often translated 'long-suffering', for it denotes patience with people rather than with circumstances. It includes forbearance towards those who are demanding or aggravating. It never forgets the 'unlimited patience' of Christ towards us.[22]

'Kindness' (*chrēstotēs*) and 'goodness' (*agathōsynē*) are both positive qualities. The former is benevolence, generosity of thought, *wishing* good to other people, while the latter is beneficence, generosity of deed, actually *doing* for them the good we wish them.

It seems right, then, to discern a progression in these three Christian graces. Patience endures the malice of others and refuses to retaliate. Kindness turns toleration into kindliness, not wishing people ill, but wishing them well. And goodness converts the wish into the deed, taking the initiative to serve people in action.

All three qualities are characteristics and outworkings of love. For, as the apostle writes elsewhere, 'love is patient [*makrothymei*], love is kind [*chrēsteuetai*]',[23] and we are to 'serve one another in love'.[24] It is of little value that we make noble protestations of love for the human race; we have to get involved with real people in real situations. It is then that love's 'patience, kindness, goodness' will be put to the test.

Fourthly, *love is balanced by self-control*. For 'the fruit of the Spirit is … faithfulness, gentleness and self-control'. These three qualities seem to be different nuances of the mastery of ourselves. 'Faithfulness' is reliability or trustworthiness in such areas as keeping our promises and fulfilling our undertakings. 'Gentleness' translates *prautēs*, which is often rendered 'meekness'. But it is not a compliant, spineless, unprincipled kind of meekness. It certainly means being gentle, humble and considerate towards other people, but to this end it will often necessitate the taming of our strengths and the harnessing of our energies. The third word 'self-control' is *egkrateia*, 'which expresses the power or lordship which one has either over oneself or over something'.[25] It includes disciplining our instincts, restraining our temper and our tongue, and curbing our passions.

But why have I written above that love is 'balanced' by self-control? Because love is self-giving, and self-giving and self-control complement one another. For how can we give ourselves until we have first learned to control ourselves? Our self has to be mastered before it can be offered in the service of others. It is surely significant, therefore, that the ninefold fruit of the Spirit begins with self-giving and ends with self-control.

Love is the fruit of the Spirit

The fifth truth which emerges from this great text is that the *love* we have been thinking about (pre-eminent, bringing joy and peace, issuing in action, and balanced by self-control) *is the fruit of the Spirit*, that is, the natural consequence of the supernatural work of the Holy Spirit within us.

In the context Paul is drawing a contrast between 'the flesh' and 'the Spirit', between 'the works of the flesh' and 'the fruit of the Spirit'. We need to pause for some definitions. By 'flesh' he means neither the soft tissue of skin and muscle which covers our bony skeleton, nor the human body (a mistake people make when they talk of greed and sexual immorality as 'the sins of the flesh'), but rather our inherited, fallen, twisted nature with its bias towards evil, its corrupt desires and its selfish demands. It has been well said that if we erase the last letter of the word 'flesh' and read it backwards, we discover exactly what it is.

By 'Spirit' Paul means neither the breath which animates our body, nor the spiritual side of human beings in contrast to the material, but the Holy Spirit himself, who enters our personality when we repent and trust in Jesus, and whose indwelling presence is the mark of Christian identity[26] and the secret of Christian holiness.

Here, then, are the two protagonists in the struggle which Paul describes. On the one hand, there is 'the flesh', our self-centred fallen nature, and on the other 'the Spirit', the personal indwelling Spirit of God. Paul tells us three truths about the conflict between these forces.

First, the desires of the flesh and of the Spirit are *active* desires. 'For the sinful nature (*i.e.* 'the flesh') desires what is contrary to the Spirit, and the Spirit what is contrary to the sinful nature. They are in conflict with each other.'[27] Thus both the flesh and the Spirit have desires, which are alive, active, energetic and strong. The reason for stressing this is that throughout church history perfectionist groups have taught that after the new birth our fallen nature is inert and inactive, even dead. But Scripture is not on their side. The command that we should 'not gratify the desires of the sinful nature'[28] and the statement that 'the sinful nature desires what is contrary to the Spirit'[29] would both be nonsensical if our fallen nature no longer had any desires. No, the Christian life is one of unremitting conflict with the world, the flesh and the devil.

Secondly, the desires of the flesh and of the Spirit are *opposite* desires. A fierce antagonism exists between them. 'The desires of the flesh are against the Spirit, and the desires of the Spirit are against the flesh; for these are opposed to each other.'[30] As Bishop J. B. Lightfoot put it in his commentary on Galatians, 'between the Spirit and the flesh there is not only no alliance; there is an interminable deadly feud'.[31]

Moreover, the opposite desires of the flesh and the Spirit are made plain in the contrast between 'the works of the flesh'[32] and 'the fruit of the Spirit'.[33] The former are very unpleasant. Paul lists fifteen of them. They seem to fall into four categories – sexual sins (immorality and licentiousness), religious sins (idolatry and sorcery, the latter being the secret attempt to steal divine or demonic power by magic), social sins (eight of them including malice, jealousy, temper, quarrelling and selfish ambition) and personal sins (drunkenness and orgies). It is an ugly catalogue of activities in which people assert themselves against God and others.

The ninefold fruit of the Spirit,[34] which we have already considered, presents a beautiful contrast. Indeed, it would be hard to imagine a greater contrast. For here is godliness instead of godlessness, authentic joy and peace in place of the pursuit of sinful pleasure, kindness and goodness over against malice and envy, and self-control rather than self-indulgence.

Thirdly, Paul insists that the desires of the flesh and of the Spirit are *controllable* desires. It is possible, he writes, for the Spirit to gain ascendancy over the flesh and subdue it, for love to triumph over selfishness, and for goodness to be victorious over evil. How? The secret lies in our adopting the right attitude to both the flesh and the Spirit.

Our attitude to our fallen nature should be one of ruthless repudiation. For 'those who belong to Christ Jesus have crucified the sinful nature with its passions and desires'.[35] That is, we have taken this evil, slimy, slippery thing called 'the flesh' and nailed it to the cross. This was our initial repentance. Crucifixion is dramatic imagery for our uncompromising rejection of all known evil. Crucifixion does not lead to a quick or easy death; it is an execution of lingering pain. Yet it is decisive; there is no possibility of escaping from it.

Our attitude to the Holy Spirit, on the other hand, is to be one of unconditional surrender. Paul uses several expressions for this. We are to 'live by the Spirit', to be 'led by the Spirit' and to 'keep in step with the Spirit'.[36] That is, we are to allow him his rightful sovereignty over us, and follow his righteous promptings.

Thus both our repudiation of the flesh and our surrender to the Spirit need to be repeated daily, however decisive our original repudiation and surrender may have been. In Jesus' words, we are to 'take up [our] cross daily' and follow him.[37] We are also to go on being filled with the Spirit,[38] as we open our personality to him daily. Both our repudiation and our surrender are also to be worked out in disciplined habits of life. It is those who 'sow to the Spirit'[39] who reap the fruit of the Spirit. And to 'sow to the Spirit' means to cultivate the things of the Spirit, for example, by our wise use of the Lord's Day, the discipline of our daily prayer and Bible reading, our regular worship and attendance at the Lord's Supper, our Christian friendships and our involvement in Christian service. An inflexible principle of all God's dealings, both in the material and in the moral realm, is that we reap what we sow. The rule is invariable. It cannot be changed, for 'God cannot be mocked'.[40] We must not therefore be surprised if we do not reap the fruit of the Spirit when all the time we are sowing to the flesh. Did we think we could cheat or fool God?

To change the metaphor, I remember reading years ago of a visitor to the mountains of southern California. He met an old mountaineer, whose two dogs were continuously fighting. The visitor asked him which dog usually won. The mountaineer chewed his tobacco for a while in silence, and then replied: 'The one I feeds the most.' Just so, our new nature will gain the victory over the old only in so far as we feed the new and starve the old.

There is only one person, in the long history of the world, in whom the fruit of the Spirit has ever ripened to perfection. That person is Jesus of Nazareth. Indeed, Paul's ninefold fruit may be seen as a portrait of Jesus Christ. For he loved as no-one else has ever loved, in laying down his life for his enemies. He spoke both of 'my joy' and of 'my peace'.[41] He was wonderfully patient with his dim-witted apostles. He was invariably kind and full of good works. He was also steadfastly reliable and always gentle, in fact 'gentle and humble in heart'.[42] And he had perfect self-control so that, 'when they hurled insults at him, he did not retaliate'.[43]

Dr Kenneth Moynagh, who worked for many years as a medical missionary at Matana in Burundi, once summarized the fruit of the Spirit, with its emphasis on love, in this way:

> Joy is love exulting, and peace is love at rest;
> Patience, love enduring in every trial and test.
> Gentleness, love yielding to all that is not sin,
> Goodness, love in actions that flow from Christ within.
> Faith is love's eyes opened the living Christ to see;
> Meekness, love not fighting, but bowed at Calvary.
> Temperance, love in harness and under Christ's control,
> For Christ is love in person, and love, Christ in the soul.

Moreover, if the fruit of the Spirit is Christlikeness, Christlikeness is God's personal purpose for all his people. It is his *eternal* purpose, 'for those whom God foreknew he also predestined to be conformed to the likeness of his Son'.[44] Next, it is his *historical* purpose, as 'we … are being transformed into his likeness with ever-increasing glory'.[45] And thirdly, it is his *eschatological* purpose. For, although 'what we will be has not yet been made known', nevertheless 'we know that when he appears, we shall be like him, for we shall see him as he is'.[46]

The only way to understand the disappointments and frustrations of life, the loneliness, the suffering and the pain, is to see them as part of our loving Father's discipline in his determination to make us like Christ.[47]

I am sometimes asked, perhaps in a newspaper, radio or television interview, whether at my age I have any ambitions left. I always now reply: 'Yes, my overriding ambition is (and, I trust, will be until I die) that I may become a little bit more like Christ.'

Notes

[1] Gal. 5:22–23.

[2] 1 Tim. 6:12.

[3] 1 Tim. 6:20, literally; *cf.* 2 Tim 1:14.

[4] 2 Thes. 2:15.

[5] Jude 3.

[6] 1 Cor. 13:2.

[7] 1 Cor. 8:1.

[8] Rom. 3:28.

[9] Luther's *Commentary on the Epistle to the Galatians* (1531; James Clarke, 1953), pp. 101, 143.

[10] From the 'Sermon on Salvation' in the *First Book of Homilies* (1547).

[11] R. T. Beckwith, G. E. Duffield and J. I. Packer, *Across the Divide* (Lyttleton Press, 1977), p. 58.

[12] 1 Cor. 13:2.

[13] 1 Pet. 1:8 (RSV).

[14] Phil. 3:8.

[15] 1 Cor. 13:1–2.

[16] 1 Jn. 3:17.

[17] 1 Cor. 13:3.

[18] 1 Jn. 4:8, 16.

[19] 1 Jn. 4:19.

[20] Eerdmans, 1977.

[21] David Wells, *No Place for Truth* (Eerdmans, 1993).

[22] 1 Tim. 1:16.

[23] 1 Cor. 13:4.

[24] Gal. 5:13.

[25] From the article on *egkrateia* by Walter Grundmann in *TDNT*.

[26] Rom. 8:9.

[27] Gal. 5:17.

[28] Gal. 5:16.

[29] Gal. 5:17.

[30] Gal. 5:17 (RSV).

[31] J. B. Lightfoot, *Galatians* (1865), p. 209.

[32] Gal. 5:19–21.

[33] Gal. 5:22–23.

[34] Gal. 5:22–23.

[35] Gal. 5:24.

[36] Gal. 5:16, 18, 25.

[37] Lk. 9:23.

[38] Eph. 5:18.

[39] Gal. 6:8 (RSV).

[40] Gal. 6:7.

[41] *E.g.* Jn. 15:11; 14:27.

[42] Mt. 11:29.

[43] 1 Pet. 2:23.

[44] Rom. 8:29.
[45] 2 Cor. 3:18.
[46] 1 Jn. 3:2.
[47] *E.g.* Heb. 12:4–11.

PART THREE

The Bible

'We present you with this Book, the most valuable thing that this world affords. Here is wisdom; this is the royal law; these are the lively oracles of God.' With these words in the coronation service the Moderator of the General Assembly of the Church of Scotland handed to the newly crowned Queen Elizabeth a copy of the Bible.

It might be tempting to dismiss such claims for the Bible as idle rhetoric, were it not that successive generations of Christian people have found them to be true. Scripture has brought us light in darkness, strength in weakness, comfort in sadness. It is not difficult for us to endorse the psalmist's experience that the words of God 'are more precious than gold, than much pure gold; they are sweeter than honey, than honey from the comb'.[1]

This being so, it has been distressing in recent decades in the West to watch the Bible being dislodged from its position of acknowledged authority, not only in the nation but also in the church. There is little hope for thoroughgoing national reform or church renewal unless the Word of God is once more widely respected and read, and its teaching heeded.

Part Three of this book is my small contribution to this goal, as I write about the urgent need to continue in, respond to, interpret and expound God's Word.

Note

[1] Ps. 19:10.

TEN

Continuing in the Word

It is a regular theme of the New Testament authors that the people of God must be steadfast. On the one hand, we must resist the intellectual and moral pressures of our contemporary world, and refuse to conform to the fashions of the day. We are not to allow ourselves to slip, slither and slide in the mud of relativity or be torn from our moorings and carried away by the flood. On the other hand, and positively, we are summoned to persevere in the truth we have received, to cling to it as a secure handhold in the storm, and to stand firm on this foundation.

Here are some examples of this kind of exhortation by three of the major contributors to the New Testament.

Paul: 'So then, brothers, stand firm and hold to the teachings we passed on to you.'[1]

Hebrews: 'We must pay more careful attention, therefore, to what we have heard, so that we do not drift away.'[2]

John: 'See that what you have heard from the beginning remains in you.'[3] 'Anyone who runs ahead and does not continue in the teaching of Christ does not have God; whoever continues in the teaching has both the Father and the Son.'[4]

Common to these quotations is the recognition that certain truths had been 'taught' or 'passed on' by the apostles, and had consequently been 'heard' or 'received' by the church. This body of doctrine was now a sacred deposit to be guarded.[5] It had a normative quality. The church must remain in it and hold to it, neither going back from it, nor going on beyond it in such a way as to contradict it.

Part of Paul's final charge to Timothy elaborates this theme. In order to grasp its implications, we need to have the text before us. It is 2 Timothy 3:1 – 4:8.

3 [1]But mark this: There will be terrible times in the last days. [2]People will be lovers of themselves, lovers of money, boastful, proud, abusive, disobedient to their parents, ungrateful, unholy, [3]without love, unforgiving, slanderous, without self-control, brutal, not lovers of the good, [4]treacherous, rash, conceited, lovers of pleasure rather than lovers of God – [5]having a form of godliness but denying its power. Have nothing to do with them.

[6]They are the kind who worm their way into homes and gain control over weak-willed women, who are loaded down with sins and are swayed by all kinds of evil desires, [7]always learning but never able to acknowledge the truth. [8]Just as Jannes and Jambres opposed Moses, so also these men oppose the truth – men of depraved minds, who, as far as the faith is concerned, are rejected. [9]But they will not get very far because, as in the case of those men, their folly will be clear to everyone.

[10]You, however, know all about my teaching, my way of life, my purpose, faith, patience, love, endurance, [11]persecutions, sufferings – what kinds of things happened to me in Antioch, Iconium and Lystra, the persecutions I endured. Yet the Lord rescued me from all of them. [12]In fact, everyone who wants to live a godly life in Christ Jesus will be persecuted, [13]while evil men and impostors will go from bad to worse, deceiving and being deceived. [14]But as for you, continue in what you have learned and have become convinced of, because you know those from whom you learned it, [15]and how from infancy you have known the holy Scriptures, which are able to make you wise for salvation through faith in Christ Jesus. [16]All Scripture is God-breathed and is useful for teaching, rebuking, correcting and training in righteousness, [17]so that the man of God may be thoroughly equipped for every good work.

4 [1]In the presence of God and of Christ Jesus, who will judge the living and the dead, and in view of his appearing and his kingdom, I give you this charge: [2]Preach the Word; be prepared in season and out of season; correct, rebuke and encourage – with great patience and careful instruction. [3]For the time will come when men will not put up with sound doctrine. Instead, to suit their own desires, they will gather around them a great number of teachers to say what their itching ears want to hear. [4]They will turn their ears away from the truth and turn aside to myths. [5]But you, keep your head in all situations, endure hardship, do the work of an evangelist, discharge all the duties of your ministry.

⁶For I am already being poured out like a drink offering, and the time has come for my departure. ⁷I have fought the good fight, I have finished the race, I have kept the faith. ⁸Now there is in store for me the crown of righteousness, which the Lord, the righteous Judge, will award to me on that day – and not only to me, but also to all who have longed for his appearing.

Standing in the Word

Paul's exhortation to Timothy was given against the background of the kind of society he was living in (3:1–13). It was not at all friendly to the gospel. Nor could the gospel possibly be reshaped in order to accommodate to its ideas and standards. On the contrary, Paul was aware of a radical incompatibility between the Word and the world. 'Mark this,' he wrote: 'There will be terrible times in the last days.'

It is important to realize that by 'the last days' the apostle was not alluding to a future epoch which would immediately precede the return of Christ. For in verse 5 he tells Timothy to 'have nothing to do' with the people he has been describing. How could Timothy avoid them if they had not even been born? No, 'the last days' from the perspective of the New Testament began with Jesus Christ. He ushered them in.⁶ The last days are therefore these days, the days in which Timothy lived and in which we also live, that is, the whole era which stretches between the first and second comings of Christ. What are the characteristics of the last days? Three seem to stand out from Paul's description.

The first is *misdirected love*. Of the nineteen distinguishing marks which the apostle lists (verses 2–4), it is striking that six have to do with love. 'People will be lovers of themselves, lovers of money … without love … not lovers of the good … lovers of pleasure rather than lovers of God.' The expression 'without love' must be understood as meaning 'without true love'. For the people in view are not altogether devoid of love; they love themselves, they love money and they love pleasure. But these are examples of misdirected love. Self, money and pleasure are inappropriate objects of human love. They even become idolatrous when they displace God from his rightful place as the One to be loved with all our being. Yet we see misdirected love everywhere today. Self-absorption, covetousness and hedonism are rife, while the first and second commandments, to love God and our neighbour, are neglected. Moreover, when people's love is directed to the wrong objects, all their relationships go wrong. They become 'boastful, proud, abusive, disobedient … ungrateful … unforgiving, slanderous' (verses 2–3).

The second characteristic of our age may be called *empty religion*. Our contemporaries are described as 'having a form of godliness but denying its power' (verse 5). It may seem extraordinary that people characterized by self-love could also be religious. But it is so. Indeed, it is possible for religion, which is intended to express the worship of God, to become perverted into a means of ego-inflation. The proper name for this sick distortion is hypocrisy, and Jesus inveighed against it.[7] Such religion is 'form' without 'power', outward show without inward reality. It is also an enemy of the gospel, because nominal Christianity hardens people against real Christianity.

Thirdly, the last days are distinguished by *the cult of an open mind*. Paul writes here of people who are 'always learning but never able to acknowledge the truth' (verse 7). They sit on the fence and refuse to come down on either side of it. Tolerance is their watchword. Determined to avoid the pain of reaching definite conclusions, they make a fetish of keeping their mind open. They cannot endure what C. S. Lewis called 'the tyrannous noon of revelation';[8] they greatly prefer the twilight of free thought. They have overlooked the distinction which Allan Bloom has recently pointed out between two kinds of 'openness' – 'the openness of indifference ... and the openness that invites us to the quest for knowledge and certitude'.[9] The latter is an aspect of the Christian virtue of humility, acknowledging that our understanding is provisional and incomplete, and always seeking to increase it. The former, on the other hand, is not only insulting to truth but personally perilous. It exposes us to the danger, as a bishop of the American Episcopal Church has put it, of having our minds so open that our brains fall out!

Here, then, are three characteristics of our time, which Scripture trenchantly criticizes and tells us to avoid. We are to love God and our neighbour, and not misdirect our love to self, money or pleasure. We are to value the reality and power of religion above its outward forms. And we are to submit humbly to God's revelation and not cultivate a wishy-washy, undemanding agnosticism.

Thus Paul calls Timothy to be different from the world around him. After his portrayal of these ungodly trends, Paul twice writes *su de*, meaning 'You, however', or 'But as for you' (verses 10 and 14). These words introduce the apostle's two exhortations to Timothy to resist the mood of the world, and to stand firm against it. The first exhortation focuses on what Timothy has already come to know about Paul (verses 10–13) – his 'teaching', his 'way of life', his 'purpose', together with his 'faith, patience, love, endurance, persecutions, sufferings'. Timothy had seen Paul's ministry with his own eyes, including the opposition and persecution which he had had to endure in Antioch, Iconium and Lystra (verse 11). For the fact is that 'everyone who wants to live a godly life in Christ Jesus will be persecuted' (verse 12), since 'evil men and impostors', who reject the gospel, 'will go from bad to worse' (verse 13).

Thus the apostle sets over against each other the low standards of the world and his own teaching and conduct. The two were in irreconcilable antagonism to one another. Hence the persecution Paul had had to bear. If Timothy were to stand firm, taking Paul's side against the world's, he would undoubtedly have to suffer too.

Continuing in the Word

Paul's mention of the 'evil men and impostors', deceived and deceiving, who would 'go from bad to worse' (verse 13), leads him to his second *su de*, 'But as for you'. This time, rather than just looking back to his past teaching, conduct and sufferings which Timothy had come to know, he also looks to the future: 'But as for you, continue in what you have learned and have become convinced of, because you know those from whom you learned it' (verse 14). These teachers from whom Timothy had learned are probably first his mother and grandmother who had taught him the Old Testament from his infancy (verse 15, *cf.* 1:5) and secondly the apostle, whose 'teaching' (verse 10) Timothy knew and which for us is preserved in the New Testament. Thus Paul contrasts two sets of teachers – on the one hand the impostors and deceivers of verse 13 and on the other Timothy's mother and his mentor (the apostle himself) who had taught him the Scriptures.

We who live at the end of the twentieth century need, ourselves, to heed the same summons. We are not to be like reeds blown by the wind. We are not to bow down before the prevailing trends of society, its covetousness and materialism, its relativism, and rejection of all absolute standards of truth and goodness. Instead, we are to continue faithfully in the Old and New Testament Scriptures. But why? What is Scripture that it should occupy such an important place in our lives? The apostle goes on to stress three fundamental aspects of it.

First, *Scripture is able to instruct us for salvation* (verse 15, RSV). Its primary purpose is practical. It is more a guidebook than a textbook, more a book of salvation than a book of science. This is not to say that the biblical and scientific accounts of the world are in conflict, but rather that they are complementary. Further, God's purpose in Scripture is not to reveal facts which can be discovered by the scientific method of observation and experiment, but rather to reveal truths which are beyond the scope of science, in particular God's way of salvation through Christ.

This is why Jesus Christ is himself the centre of the biblical revelation, since it bears witness to him.[10] As J.-J. von Allmen has expressed it, 'the heart of the Scripture (what sums it up and makes it live) or the head of the Scripture (... what explains it and justifies it) ... is Jesus Christ. To read the Bible without meeting him is to read it badly, and to preach the Bible without proclaiming him is to preach it falsely.'[11] It is because Scripture instructs us for salvation that it instructs us about Christ, by faith in whom salvation is received. Moreover, the reason we love the Bible is that it speaks to us of Christ. It is God's picture, God's portrait, of Christ.

Secondly, *Scripture is God-breathed.* The better-known AV phrase consists of five words, 'given by inspiration of God'. But the NIV is correct to use the one word 'God-breathed' as the precise equivalent of the Greek expression *theopneustos.* This indicates that Scripture is the Word of God, spoken by God, or breathed out of the mouth of God. The implied combination of mouth, breath and word shows that the model of inspiration which is intended is that of human speech. For speech is communication between minds. Often we keep what is 'on our mind' to ourselves. But when we speak, we clothe the thoughts of our minds in the words of our mouth.

We observe also that the text reads 'All Scripture is God-breathed' (verse 16). The NEB, on the other hand, translates the clause 'every inspired Scripture is useful ...' This is almost certainly incorrect. It implies that if every inspired Scripture is useful, there must be other Scriptures which are not inspired and therefore not useful. But, in the first place, the concept of 'uninspired Scripture' is a contradiction in terms; the word 'Scripture' simply means inspired writing. Secondly, the NEB omits, without sufficient warrant, the little word *kai*, meaning 'and' or 'also'. It shows that Paul is not making one statement ('every inspired Scripture is useful') but two ('every Scripture is inspired *and* useful'). Indeed, it is useful to us precisely because it is inspired by God.

Nevertheless, we must not mis-state the truth of inspiration. When God spoke, he did not speak into space. Nor did he write documents and leave them around to be discovered, as Joseph Smith (founder of the Mormon Church) claimed regarding his golden plates. Nor did God dictate Scripture to non-participating secretaries, as Muslims believe Allah dictated the Qur'an to Muhammad in Arabic. No, by the process of inspiration we mean that the human authors, even while God was speaking to and through them, were themselves actively engaged in historical research, theological reflection and literary composition. For much of Scripture is historical narrative, and each author has his own particular theological emphasis and literary style. Divine inspiration did not dispense with human co-operation, or iron out the peculiar contributions of the authors.

So 'God-breathed' is not the only account which Scripture gives of itself, since God's mouth was not the only mouth involved in its production. The same Scripture which says 'the mouth of the LORD has spoken'[12] also says that God spoke 'by the mouth of his holy prophets'.[13] Out of whose mouth did Scripture come, then? God's or man's? The only biblical answer is 'both'. Indeed, God spoke through the human authors in such a way that his words were simultaneously their words, and their words were simultaneously his. This is the double authorship of the Bible. Scripture is equally the Word of

God and the words of human beings. Better, it is the Word of God through the words of human beings.

It is essential to keep the two authorships together. Some theologians, ancient and modern, Catholic and Protestant, have appealed to the two natures of Christ as an analogy. Although the parallel is not exact, it is illuminating. Just as in the person of Christ (who is both God and human) we must neither affirm his deity in such a way as to deny his humanity, nor affirm his humanity in such a way as to deny his deity, but rather affirm both equally, refusing to allow either to contradict the other, so in our doctrine of Scripture we must neither affirm that it is the Word of God in such a way as to deny that it is the words of human beings (which is fundamentalism), nor affirm that it is the words of human beings in such a way as to deny that it is the Word of God (which is liberalism), but rather affirm both equally, refusing to allow either to contradict the other. Thus on the one hand God spoke,[14] determining what he wanted to say, yet without smothering the personality of the human authors. On the other hand, human beings spoke,[15] using their faculties freely, yet without distorting the truth which God was speaking through them.

We have no liberty to declare that such a combination is impossible. To say so, Dr J. I. Packer has written, would indicate

> a false doctrine of God, here particularly of his providence ... For it assumes that God and man stand in such a relationship to each other that they cannot both be free agents in the same action. If man acts freely (*i.e.* voluntarily and spontaneously), God does not, and *vice versa*. The two freedoms are mutually exclusive. But the affinities of this idea are with Deism, not Christian theism ... The cure for such fallacious reasoning is to grasp the biblical idea of God's *concursive operation* in, with and through the free working of man's own mind.[16]

The way we understand Scripture will affect the way we read it. In particular, its double authorship demands a double approach. Because Scripture is the Word of God, we should read it as we read no other book – on our knees, humbly, reverently, prayerfully, looking to the Holy Spirit for illumination. But because Scripture is also the words of human beings, we should read it as we read *every* other book, using our minds, thinking, pondering and reflecting, and paying close attention to its literary, historical, cultural and linguistic characteristics. This combination of humble reverence and critical reflection is not only not impossible; it is indispensable.[17]

Thirdly, *Scripture is useful* (verses 16–17). It is able to do more than instruct us for salvation (verse 15); it is also 'useful for teaching, rebuking, correcting and training in righteousness' (verse 16). In other words, it is profitable both for doctrine (teaching truth and correcting error) and for ethics (rebuking sin and training in right living), thus leading us on in Christian belief and behaviour until we become men and women of God, 'thoroughly equipped for every good work' (verse 17). In these ways the Bible has an essential part to play in our growth into maturity in Christ, as we will consider more fully in the next chapter. Over against the errors of the 'evil men and impostors', Timothy was to continue in the Word of God, both the Old Testament Scriptures and the apostle's teaching.

Thank God for the Bible! God has not left us to grope our way in the darkness; he has given us a light to show us the path. He has not abandoned us to flounder in heavy seas; Scripture is a rock on which we may stand. Our resolve should be to study it, believe it and obey it.

Preaching the Word

Neither Timothy nor anybody else has the liberty to monopolize Scripture. For Scripture is nobody's private possession; it is public property. Having been given by God, it belongs to all. His Word has been spoken, in order to be passed on. So the apostle, conscious of God's presence and of Christ's future appearing for judgment (4:1), gives Timothy this charge: 'Preach the Word' (verse 2). He must proclaim it like a herald or town crier in the market-place. He must do so boldly, urgently and relevantly, correcting, rebuking and encouraging according to people's state and need, and 'with great patience and careful instruction' (verse 2).

This was all the more necessary, Paul added, because the time was coming when people will 'not put up with sound doctrine'. Instead, suffering from a strange pathological condition called 'itching ears', they will listen to teachers who say what they want to hear, rather than to the truth which God wants to say to them (verses 3–4). Yet the unwillingness of some to listen to the Word of God is no reason why we should give up preaching it! On the contrary, Timothy was to persevere, to keep his head, to endure opposition and to fulfil his ministry faithfully, both as an evangelist and as a teacher (verse 5).

One of the greatest needs of the contemporary church is conscientious biblical exposition from the pulpit (see below, chapter 13). Ignorance of even the rudiments of the faith is widespread. Many Christian people are immature and unstable. And the major reason for this sorry state of affairs is the paucity of responsible, thorough, balanced biblical preachers. The pulpit is not the place to ventilate our own opinions, but to unfold God's Word.

The climax of the apostle's exhortation is reached in verses 6–8. In a previous letter, written about two years earlier, he has described himself as 'an old man'.[18] Now he writes that the time of his departure has come. Indeed, the pouring out of his life like a drink offering has already begun (verse 6). Looking back over his apostolic career, he is able to say that he has fought the good fight, finished the race and kept the faith (verse 7). He has no regrets. He is probably incarcerated in the underground Mamertine Prison in Rome, from which he is not expecting to be released. Already with his mind's eye he sees the flash of the executioner's sword, and beyond it 'the crown of righteousness' which on the last day Jesus, the righteous Judge, will give both him and 'all who have longed for his appearing' (verse 8). It is his sense that his ministry is nearing its end which prompts him to exhort Timothy to stand firm in the Word, continue in it and pass it on.

I hope I shall not be thought too personal if I say that I understand and feel the poignancy of Paul's words, although I do not of course presume to compare myself with him. But as I write these words, I have recently celebrated my seventieth birthday, my statutory 'three score years and ten'.[19] At this age I do not expect to live very much longer. Every new day is a bonus which I receive gratefully from God's hand.

So naturally I ask myself: where are the Timothys of the next generation? Where are the young evangelical men and women, who are determined by God's grace to stand firm in Scripture, refusing to be swept off their feet by the prevailing winds of fashion, who are resolved to continue in it and live by it, relating the Word to the world in order to obey it, and who are committed to passing it on, as they give themselves to the ministry of conscientious exposition?

Notes

[1] 2 Thes. 2:15.
[2] Heb. 2:1.
[3] 1 Jn. 2:24.
[4] 2 Jn. 9.
[5] *E.g.* 1 Tim. 6:20; 2 Tim. 1:14.
[6] *Cf.* Mk. 1:15; 1 Cor. 10:11.
[7] *E.g.* Mt. 6:1–18.
[8] C. S. Lewis, *Surprised by Joy* (Geoffrey Bles, 1955), p. 63.
[9] Allan Bloom, *The Closing of the American Mind* (Simon and Schuster, 1987), p. 41.
[10] *Cf.* Jn. 5:39; 20:31.
[11] J.-J. von Allmen, *Preaching and Congregation* (Lutterworth, 1962), p. 24.
[12] *E.g.* Is. 1 20.
[13] *E.g.* Acts 3:18, 21 (RSV).
[14] Heb. 1:1.
[15] 2 Pet. 1:21.
[16] J. I. Packer, *'Fundamentalism' and the Word of God* (IVP, 1958), pp. 81–82.
[17] *Cf.* 2 Tim. 2:7.
[18] Phm. 9.
[19] Ps. 90:10 (AV).

ELEVEN

Responding to the Word

The concept of divine revelation, and of our need to submit to it, is both eminently reasonable and practically wholesome. It is reasonable because it acknowledges that the infinite God is altogether beyond his finite creatures, and that we could never have known him if he had not taken the initiative to make himself known. It is also wholesome because submission to God's self-revelation in Christ and in the full biblical witness to Christ, far from inhibiting the health and growth of the church, is actually indispensable to them. My thesis in this chapter is that God's Word, received and responded to, has a central role in the faith and life of God's people. I give five examples.

Mature discipleship

First, submission to the authority of Scripture is *the way of mature discipleship*. I am not saying that it is impossible to be a disciple of Jesus without a high view of Scripture, for this is manifestly not the case. There are genuine followers of Jesus Christ who are not 'evangelical', whose confidence in Scripture is small, even minimal, and who put more faith in the past traditions and present teaching of the church, or in their own reason or experience. I have no desire to deny the authenticity of their Christian profession. Yet I venture to add that their discipleship is bound to be impoverished on account of their attitude to the Bible. A full, balanced and mature Christian discipleship is impossible whenever disciples do not submit to their Lord's teaching authority as it is mediated through Scripture.

For what is discipleship? It is a many-faceted lifestyle, an amalgam of several ingredients. In particular, it includes worship, faith, obedience and hope. Every Christian is called to worship God, to trust and obey him, and to look with confident hope towards the future. Yet each of these is a response to revelation, and is seriously impaired without a reliable, objective revelation of God.

1. *Worship.* Every Christian is a worshipper. In both public and private, we recognize our duty to worship Almighty God. But how can we worship God unless we know both who he is and what kind of worship pleases him? Without this knowledge, our attempts at worship are almost certain to degenerate into idolatry. At best we would copy that famous altar which Paul found in Athens and which was inscribed 'TO AN UNKNOWN GOD'.[1] But Christians are not agnostic Athenians; we are to love the Lord our God with all our mind[2] and to worship him 'in spirit and in truth'.[3]

What, then, does it mean to worship God? It is to 'glory in his holy name',[4] that is, to revel adoringly in who he is in his revealed character. But before we can glory in God's name, we must know it. Hence the propriety of the reading and preaching of the Word of God in public worship, and of biblical meditation in private devotion. These things are not an intrusion into worship; they form the necessary foundation of it. God must speak to us before we have any liberty to speak to him. He must disclose to us who he is before we can offer him what we are in acceptable worship. The worship of God is always a response to the Word of God. Scripture wonderfully directs and enriches our worship.

2. *Faith.* If every Christian is a worshipper, every Christian is a believer also. Indeed, the Christian life is a life of faith. 'Where is your faith?' Jesus asked the Twelve when they were afraid, and exhorted them, 'Have faith in God.'[5]

But what is faith? It too is a response to the revelation of God. We can no more trust a God we do not know than we can worship an unknown God. Consider Psalm 9:10: 'Those who know your name will trust in you, for you, LORD, have never forsaken those who seek you.' If worship is to 'glory' in God for who he is (his 'name'), then faith is to 'trust' him because of who he is. So faith is neither naivety nor gullibility. It is neither illogical nor irrational. On the contrary, faith is a reasoning trust. It rests on knowledge, the knowledge of God's name. Its reasonableness arises from the reliability of the God who is being trusted. It is never unreasonable to trust God, since no more trustworthy person exists.

Faith will grow, therefore, as we reflect on the character of God (who never lies) and on the covenant of God (who has pledged himself to his people). But how can we discover his character and covenant? Only from the Bible, in which these twin truths have been revealed. So the more we meditate on God's self-disclosure in Scripture, the riper our faith will become, whereas without Scripture our faith is bound to be weak and sickly.

3. *Obedience.* Jesus calls his disciples to a life of obedience, as well as of worship and faith.

But how can we obey him, unless we know his will and commandments? Without a knowledge of these, obedience would be impossible. 'If you love me, you will obey what I command,' he said.[6] And again, 'Whoever has my commands [that is, knows them, and treasures them up in his mind and memory] and obeys them, he is the one who loves me.'[7]

Once more, then, the Bible is seen to be indispensable to mature discipleship. For it is there that we learn the commands of Christ and so take the first necessary step towards understanding and doing his will.

4. *Hope.* The Christian hope is a confident expectation regarding the future. No Christian can be a cynic or a pessimist. To be sure, we do not believe that human beings will ever succeed in building Utopia on earth. But, although we have little confidence in human achievement, we have great confidence in the purposes and power of God. We are certain that error and evil are not going to be allowed the last word. On the contrary, truth and righteousness will triumph in the end. For Jesus Christ is going to return in strength and splendour, the dead will be raised, death will be abolished, and the universe will be liberated from decay and suffused with glory.

But how can we be so sure of these things? There are no obvious grounds for such confidence. Evil flourishes. The wicked get away with their wickedness. World problems appear intractable. And the mushroom cloud of a nuclear explosion still overshadows the horizon. Is there not more reason for despair than for hope? Yes, there would be – if it were not for the Bible! It is the Bible which arouses, directs and nurtures hope. For Christian hope is quite different from secular optimism. It is a confidence in God, kindled by the promises of God. 'Let us hold unswervingly to the hope we profess,' the author of Hebrews exhorts his readers. Why? 'For he who promised is faithful.'[8] Jesus himself said that he would come again. 'Men will see the Son of Man coming in clouds with great power and glory … And you will see the Son of Man … coming on the clouds of heaven.'[9] It is promises like these which stimulate our hope. It is 'in keeping with his promise' that we are looking for a new world, in which righteousness will reign.[10]

Here, then, are four basic ingredients of Christian discipleship – worship, faith, obedience and hope. All four would be irrational without an objective basis in God's revelation, to which they are a response. Worship is a response to the revelation of God's name, faith to the revelation of his character and covenant, obedience to the revelation of his will and commandments, and hope to the revelation of his purpose and promises. And God's name, covenant, commands and promises are all found in Scripture. That is why Scripture is fundamental to Christian growth, and why submission to its authority is the way of mature discipleship.

Intellectual integrity

Secondly, submission to biblical authority is *the way of intellectual integrity.*

Many people would immediately deny this statement and even affirm the contrary. They cannot understand how apparently intelligent Christians at the end of the twentieth century can possibly be so perverse as to believe in biblical inspiration and authority. They regard a commitment to the truth and trustworthiness of Scripture as untenable. They therefore charge those of us who hold it with a lack of intellectual integrity. They accuse us of obscurantism, mental schizophrenia, intellectual suicide and other equally horrid conditions. To these charges, however, we plead 'Not guilty'. We insist that our conviction about Scripture arises from the very integrity which our critics say we lack.

'Integrity' is the quality of an integrated person. In particular, integrated Christians are at peace, not at war, with themselves. Instead of being conscious of a dichotomy between our various beliefs, or between our beliefs and our behaviour, so that we are 'torn apart' inside, there is an inner harmony. We are 'all of a piece', or whole. What is the secret of this integration?

There is no more integrating Christian principle than the affirmation we considered in chapter 5, 'Jesus Christ is Lord'. It is of the essence of integrated discipleship that we both confess his lordship with our lips and enthrone him as Lord in our hearts. We assume the easy yoke of his teaching authority. We seek to 'take captive every thought to make it obedient to Christ'.[11] And when Jesus is Lord of our beliefs, opinions, ambitions, standards, values and lifestyle, then we are integrated Christians, since then 'integrity' marks our life. Only when *he* is Lord do *we* become whole.

But Jesus our Lord himself submitted to the Old Testament Scriptures. In his ethical conduct, in his understanding of his mission, and in his public debates with contemporary religious leaders, his primary concern was to be true to Scripture. 'What does the Scripture say?' he would ask. It was always his final court of appeal. Moreover, he indicated his expectation that his disciples would follow his example in this. He also made provision for the Scriptures of the New Testament to be written by choosing, calling, equipping and commissioning his apostles to be the teachers of the church, and he expected the church to submit to them. 'He who listens to you listens to me,' he said.[12] In consequence of this, submission to

Scripture by Christian disciples is part and parcel of our submission to Jesus as Lord. For the disciple is not above his teacher. We cannot therefore accommodate ourselves to selective submission. It would be inherently illogical, for example, to agree with Jesus' doctrine of God but disagree with his view of the Word of God. No, selective submission is not authentic submission.

This gives us the clue we need regarding how to deal with the problems in the Bible. For in affirming the inspiration and authority of Scripture, I am not denying that there are problems. There are textual, literary, historical, scientific, philosophical, cultural, theological and moral problems. The observable phenomena of Scripture (which we see inductively) sometimes seem to conflict with our doctrine of Scripture (which we hold deductively, inferring it from the attitude and teaching of Jesus). So what should we do with problems? How can we handle them with integrity?

We need to remember that every Christian doctrine raises problems, not excluding the central doctrines of God (his being, creation, sovereignty, providence and justice), of Jesus Christ (his one person in two natures, his work of atonement, his bodily resurrection, present reign and future return) and of the Holy Spirit (his activity in the church and the world). Or take the love of God. It is a fundamental Christian doctrine. Every Christian without exception believes that God is love (Roman Catholic, Orthodox, Reformed, Lutheran, Episcopal, Independent, Pentecostal); if they denied it, they would not be Christians. Yet the problems surrounding this belief are enormous: for example, the origin and spread of evil, the suffering of the innocent, the 'silences' of God and the 'acts' of God, the vastness of the universe, and the apparent insignificance of individual human beings.

Supposing somebody comes to us with a personal problem or dilemma (perhaps the birth of a handicapped child, a natural disaster, or a tragic bereavement) and challenges us: 'Why should this happen to me? How can God be love if he allows this?' How do we react? Do we say that, in order to preserve our intellectual integrity, we must suspend our belief in the love of God until we have solved the problem? I hope not. Nor do we sweep the problem under the carpet and try to forget it. No, instead, in addition to the question how we should respond pastorally to our questioner, we wrestle with the problem in our own mind and heart. We think about it conscientiously, read about it, talk about it and pray about it. And during this process some light is thrown upon the problem. Yet some of the perplexity remains. So what next? The way of intellectual integrity, I suggest, is to determine to retain our conviction about God's love, in spite of the residual difficulties, ultimately for one reason only, namely that Jesus our Lord himself taught it and exhibited it. It was because of Jesus that we came to believe in God's love in the first place; it is for the same reason that we should continue to do so.

It is the same with problems relating to the Bible. We need to learn to face them as we face problems surrounding other Christian doctrines. If somebody comes to us with a biblical problem (a discrepancy, for example, between theology and science, or between two Gospel accounts, or a moral dilemma), what should we do? We should not (from a mistaken integrity) suspend our belief in the truth of Scripture until we have solved the problem. Nor should we place the problem either on a shelf (indefinitely postponing its challenge) or under a carpet (permanently concealing it, even from ourselves). Instead, we should struggle conscientiously with the problem in thought, discussion and prayer. As we do so, some difficulties will be either wholly or partly cleared up. But then, in spite of those which remain, we should retain our belief about Scripture on the ground that Jesus himself taught and exhibited it.

If a critic says to me, 'You are an obscurantist to believe the Bible to be the Word of God in defiance of the problems', I nowadays return the compliment and say, 'OK, if you like, I am. But then you are an obscurantist to believe in the love of God in defiance of the problems.' Actually, however, to believe a Christian doctrine in spite of its problems, because of the acknowledged lordship of Jesus Christ, is not obscurantism (preferring darkness to light) but faith (trusting him who said he was the light of the world). It is more than faith; it is the sober, intellectual integrity of confessing Jesus as Lord.

Ecumenical progress

Thirdly, submission to the authority of Scripture is *the way of ecumenical progress*, that is to say, the means by which to secure an acceptable coming together of churches.

Now I realize that some of my readers may entertain no desire to make any ecumenical progress. You may be (I am guessing) suspicious of the whole ecumenical movement, and of the World Council of Churches to which it has given birth. You see (although it is always misleading to generalize) its tendency to doctrinal indifferentism, its attempted reinterpretation of the Christian mission in terms of socio-political action, and its leaning towards syncretism and universalism in the face of the challenges of other faiths. Indeed, I understand your qualms, for I share them. There is much in contemporary ecumenism to perplex and even distress us. We cannot accept uncritically everything which emanates from Geneva.

Nevertheless, I am also disturbed by the blanket condemnation of ecumenical activity which is expressed by a large section of the evangelical constituency. It is clear to me that we cannot simply dismiss the whole non-evangelical section of Christendom as if it did not exist, or, since it does exist, regard it as non-Christian and resolve to have nothing to do with it. Besides, Jesus our Lord prayed that his people might be one, in order that the world might believe,[13] and his apostle Paul urges us to 'make every effort to keep the unity of the Spirit through the bond of peace'.[14]

There is, of course, room for disagreement among us regarding what shape Christian unity should take. But it should be possible for us to agree that competition between different churches is unseemly, and that the visible unity of the church in some form is a desirable goal. In his reply to a letter from Thomas Cranmer, Archbishop of Canterbury, in 1552, Calvin wrote as follows:

> Doubtless it must be counted among the greatest misfortunes of our century that churches are thus separated from each other … and that the holy communion of the members of Christ, which many confess with their mouth, is only sincerely sought after by few … From this it follows that the members being so scattered, the body of the church lies bleeding. This affects me so deeply, that, if anybody could see that I might be of any use, I should not hesitate to cross ten seas for this business, if that were needful … Indeed, if learned men were to seek a solid and carefully devised agreement according to the rule of Scripture, an agreement by which the separated churches should unite with each other, I think that for my part I ought not to spare any trouble or dangers.[15]

Calvin's letter to Cranmer is significant, not only because of the end he had in view (the uniting of separated churches), but also because of the means he proposed (agreement according to the rule of Scripture). For the unity Christ himself desires for his church is certainly a unity in truth. His prayer recorded in John 17 clearly links the two, as we shall see in chapter 16. Besides, since the church is built on the foundation of the apostles and prophets, with Christ himself as the chief cornerstone,[16] it will certainly not grow in size or stability by neglecting, let alone undermining, its foundation. And in its official position the World Council of Churches agrees with this. Its accepted definition of 'the unity we seek' (1961) speaks of 'one fully committed fellowship, holding the one apostolic faith, preaching the one gospel, breaking the one bread' and enjoying a corporate life of prayer, witness and service.[17]

The 'one apostolic faith' has, of course, come down to us in the New Testament, and no union of churches could or should be contemplated which deviates from this rule. In particular, one of the greatest obstacles to unity has been the failure to distinguish between Scripture and tradition. Jesus himself drew a clear distinction between written Scripture and the oral tradition of the elders, subordinated the latter to the former, and even went so far as to reject tradition as 'the words of men' in order that Scripture as the Word of God might have the supremacy.[18] The very same distinction needs to be made today. Yet an example of why some church unity schemes have failed is the tendency of Anglican or Episcopal churches to insist on a particular view of the 'historic episcopate' as non-negotiable. One can understand the historical reasons for this, and I myself would want to defend an episcopal form of government as a pastoral ideal which is consonant with Scripture and conducive to the health of the church. But one cannot insist on it as indispensable, since it belongs to the tradition of the church, and is not required by Scripture.

If only we could agree that Scripture is 'God's Word written' (Anglican Article XX), that it is supreme in its authority over all human traditions however venerable, and that it must be allowed to reform and renew the church, we would take an immediate leap forward in ecumenical relationships. Reformation according to the Word of God is indispensable to reunion.

Effective evangelism

Fourthly, submission to the authority of Scripture is *the way of faithful and effective evangelism*. My argument so far has been domestic and ecclesiastical, as we have thought about personal discipleship and integrity, and about church relations. All the time the world outside is in great confusion and darkness. Has the church any light for this darkness, any word of hope for the bewildered modern world?

One of the tragedies of the contemporary church is that, just when the world seems to be ready to listen, the church often seems to have little or nothing to say. For the church itself is confused; it shares in the current bewilderment, instead of addressing it. The church is insecure; it is uncertain of its identity, mission and message. It stammers and stutters, when it should be proclaiming the gospel with boldness. Indeed, the major reason for its diminishing influence in the West is its diminishing faith.

A recovery of evangelism is impossible without a recovery of the evangel, the good news. For evangelism according to its simplest definition is 'sharing the evangel'. So biblical evangelism is impossible without the biblical evangel. Many churches throughout the world are regarding the 1990s as a 'decade of evangelism'. It sounds fine. But we shall never agree on what we mean by 'evangelism' if we decline to discuss the content of the 'evangel'. Evangelism really has to be defined in terms of the evangel.

We should be able to agree that Christian witness is essentially witness to Christ, and that the only authentic Christ there is is the Christ of the apostolic witness. For the apostles were the original witnesses, the eyewitnesses; our witness, vital though it is, always remains secondary to theirs. We have no authority to edit their gospel. Our calling is rather to preserve it like stewards, proclaim it like heralds, and argue it like advocates.

In his book on evangelism entitled *Go and Make Disciples,* David Read, who for many years was minister of Madison Avenue Presbyterian Church, New York, wrote: 'Those of us who enjoy visiting other countries are familiar with that solemn moment when at the frontier we encounter a customs official who ... fixes us with steely eyes and asks "Have you anything to declare?" I have not yet had the nerve to answer "Yes, as a minister of the gospel, it is my duty to declare that Jesus Christ is your Lord and Saviour".' So David Read calls his final chapter 'The crux: have you anything to declare?' It is lack of conviction about the gospel, he writes, which makes 'most of us ... reluctant evangelists'.[19]

I agree. I think there is no chance of the church taking its evangelistic task seriously unless it first recovers its confidence in the truth, relevance and power of the gospel, and begins to get excited about it again. For this, however, it will have to return to the Bible in which the gospel has been revealed.

Personal humility

Fifthly, submission to the authority of Scripture is *the way of personal Christian humility.* Nothing is more obnoxious in us who claim to follow Jesus Christ than arrogance, and nothing is more appropriate or attractive than humility. And an essential element in Christian humility is the willingness to hear and receive God's Word. Perhaps the greatest of all our needs is to take our place again humbly, quietly and expectantly at the feet of Jesus Christ, in order to listen attentively to his Word, and to believe and obey it. For we have no liberty to disbelieve or disobey him.

The ultimate issue before us and the whole church is whether Jesus Christ is Lord (as we say he is) or not. The question is whether Christ is Lord of the church (to teach and command it) or the church is lord of Christ (to edit and manipulate his teaching). In the contemporary crisis of authority in the world, and loss of authority in the church, my plea is that we return to a humble submission to Scripture as God's Word, and that we do so out of a humble submission to Jesus Christ as Lord, who himself humbly submitted to Scripture in his own faith, life, mission and teaching.

In so doing, we will find the way of mature discipleship and intellectual integrity, the way to unite churches and evangelize the world, and the way to express a proper humility before our Lord Jesus Christ. That is what I mean by the 'wholesomeness' of submitting to the authority of Scripture.

Notes

[1] Acts 17:23.
[2] Mk. 12:30.
[3] Jn. 4:24.
[4] Ps. 105:3.
[5] Lk. 8:25; Mk. 11:22.
[6] Jn. 14:15.
[7] Jn. 14:21.
[8] Heb. 10:23.
[9] Mk. 13:26; 14:62.
[10] 2 Pet. 3:13.
[11] 2 Cor. 10:5.
[12] Lk. 10:16.
[13] Jn. 17:20–23.
[14] Eph. 4:3.
[15] *Op. Calv.* XIV, pp. 312–314, quoted in Jean Cadier, *The Man God Mastered* (ET IVF, 1960), pp. 172–173.
[16] Eph. 2:20.
[17] *The New Delhi Report* (SCM, 1962), p. 116.
[18] *E.g.* Mk. 7:5–13.
[19] David H. C. Read, *Go and Make Disciples* (Abingdon, 1978), pp. 94–95.

TWELVE

Transposing the Word

Whenever we pick up the Bible and read it, even in a contemporary version like the Good News Bible, we are conscious of stepping back two millennia or (in the case of the Old Testament) even more. We travel backwards in time, behind the microchip revolution, the electronic revolution, the scientific revolution and the industrial revolution, until we find ourselves in an alien world which long ago ceased to exist. In consequence, the Bible feels odd, sounds archaic, looks obsolete and smells musty. We are tempted to ask impatiently, 'What on earth has that old book got to say to me?'

Our sense of incongruity when we read the Bible, and the consequent difficulty we often experience in receiving a meaningful communication from it, are due primarily neither to the passage of time in itself (from the first century to the twentieth) nor to the mere distance (from the Middle East to the West), but to the cultural differences which remoteness of time and place have caused.

In fact, two distinct but complementary problems confront us. The first is the problem of our own cultural imprisonment, and the second the problem of the cultural conditioning of the biblical authors. That is, both the writers and the readers of Scripture are culture-creatures, the products (and therefore to some degree the prisoners) of the particular cultures in which they were brought up. Consequently, in all our Bible reading there is a collision of cultures between the biblical world and the modern world.

Both God's speaking and our listening are culture-conditioned. This fact clearly affects our interpretation of Scripture; in the course of our discussion we will have to ask whether it also affects the authority of Scripture.

The hermeneutical problem

Biblical hermeneutics, that is, the art or science of interpreting Scripture, has become in recent decades a major preoccupation of scholars. Indeed, all Christian people who read the Bible come up against the question of how to understand it rightly.

The problem arises from the extreme cultural particularities of the ancient text and the modern interpreter. Each has a different 'horizon', a limited viewpoint or perspective, and what is needed is what Hans-Georg Gadamer called a 'fusion' of horizons. 'Understanding takes place', writes Dr Tony Thiselton in his classic and comprehensive study *The Two Horizons*,[1] 'when two sets of horizons are brought into relation to each other, namely those of the text and those of the interpreter.'[2]

In this process the interpreter's first task was called by Gadamer 'distancing'. That is, we have to acknowledge 'the pastness of the past', disengage ourselves from the text, and allow it its own historical integrity, without intruding ourselves into it or deciding prematurely how it applies to us. Careful exegesis of the text necessitates studying it in its own cultural and linguistic terms.

But this is only the beginning. If first we stand back from the text, next we seek to enter it. 'There must be present engagement with the text', writes Tony Thiselton, 'as well as critical distancing from it.'[3] Since the interpreter also belongs to a precise and particular context, though different from that of the text, this is not easy. It requires a high degree of imagination, of empathy, if we are to enter that alien world. 'Historical exegesis is essential, but it is not enough. We need *both* distancing *and* an openness to the text which will yield progress towards the fusion of horizons.'[4]

This leads to an active interaction or dialectic between text and interpreter. However hard we may work at distancing ourselves from the text, we can hardly help bringing to it our presuppositions and our own agenda of problems and questions. The Scripture may respond to these. But, because it has its own agenda, it may not. Instead, it may challenge us to go away and re-shape our questions, even replace them with better ones. We then return with our new agenda, and so the dialogue between us goes on. It is part of what is called 'the hermeneutical circle', although some European and Latin American scholars have preferred the expression 'hermeneutical spiral' because the movement is progressive and upward.[5]

During the sixties some German scholars, especially Ernst Fuchs and Gerhard Ebeling, former students of Bultmann, went further in developing a 'new hermeneutic'. Rejecting objectivity as impossible, on the ground that we cannot jump out of our own particularity into that of a biblical author, they stressed the need to let the text speak. According to their theory of language, its purpose is not so much to convey 'concepts' as to cause an 'event' (a 'language-event'), in which the roles of text and interpreter are reversed and the interpreter listens instead of talking. It seems clear that these post-Bultmannians went too far. Denying that the biblical text has an accessible, objective meaning, they lapsed into an uncontrolled subjectivity. What the text said to them might bear no relation to what it actually meant.

Nevertheless, there is abiding value in what these scholars are feeling for. They take seriously the cultural gulf between the past and the present. They recognize the independent historical particularity of both text and interpreter, and they seek to develop a dialectic between them. The old hermeneutic put into our hands a set of universal rules of interpretation, which we applied to the text; the new hermeneutic is concerned to allow the text to apply its message to us. The old hermeneutic concentrated on the text as *object*; we stood over it, studied it, scrutinized it, applied our rules to it, and almost took control of it. The new hermeneutic, however, concentrates on the text as *subject*; it stands over us, and we sit meekly 'under it', as the Reformers used to put it. It addresses, confronts, challenges and changes us.

Here, then, is the danger of a new polarization between the 'old' and the 'new'. Each is perilously lopsided without the other. For the text is both object and subject. We address it, and it addresses us. But as these two processes develop, we must insist that the object and the subject are the same text and have the same meaning.

We now return to the two cultural problems, and consider each separately.

Our own cultural imprisonment

Every human being who has ever lived has been a creature of culture. Culture is a convenient term with which to denote the complex of beliefs, values, customs and traditions which each generation receives from its predecessor and transmits to its successor, and which binds a society together. We have all drunk in our cultural inheritance with our mother's milk. The way we think, judge, act, talk, dress, eat, work and play are all to a large extent determined by our culture, and we usually do not realize how much our cultural upbringing has enslaved us.

Hence the great value of travel, for then we learn to listen to ourselves through the ears of another culture, and look at ourselves through another culture's eyes. I well remember my first visit to the United States about thirty-five years ago. After the first address I had given on American soil, a lady said to me, 'I do like your English accent.' Accent? Me? She of course had an American accent, but surely I spoke the Queen's English? My speech was the norm; hers was the deviation, the abnorm. Then, not so long afterwards, I was in Manila, and a little Filipino boy of only about eight years old came up to me, cocked his head, looked into my face and commented cheekily, 'You *do* talk funny!' He was right. I do. But then so do you, and so does everybody.

Our culture includes not only the general views and values, standards and customs, of our society, but also those which apply to our particular sex, age and class. They all affect the way we read the Bible. For example, how can I as a man read Scripture in the same way as a woman who has been hurt by male chauvinism? Or how can I as an old man hear from Scripture what young people hear when they read it? Or again, how can I as a member of an affluent society really listen to what Scripture says about the poor?

Men and women, old and young, black and white, African and Asian, capitalist and socialist, waged and unwaged, middle-class and working-class, all read Scripture differently. Our spectacles have cultural lenses. It is so difficult as to be almost impossible for us to read the Bible with genuine objectivity and openness, and for God to break through our cultural defences and to say to us what he wants to say. Instead, we come to our reading of the Bible with our own agenda, bias, questions, preoccupations, concerns and convictions, and, unless we are extremely careful, we impose these on the biblical text. We may sincerely pray before we read, 'Open my eyes that I may see wonderful things in your law,'[6] but still the same non-communication may persist. For even that introductory prayer, though to be sure it is taken from the Psalter, is suspect because it lays down the kind of message we want to hear.

'Please, Lord, I want to see some "wonderful thing" in your word.'

But he may reply, 'What makes you think I have only "wonderful things" to show you? As a matter of fact, I have some rather "disturbing things" to show you today. Are you prepared to receive them?'

'Oh no, Lord, please not', we stammer in reply. 'I come to Scripture only to be comforted; I really do not want to be challenged or disturbed.'

In other words, we come to the Bible with our agenda formulated uni-laterally, our expectations pre-set, our minds made up, laying down in advance what we want God to say to us. Then, instead of hearing the thunderclap of his voice, all we receive is the soothing echoes of our own cultural prejudice. And God says to us, as he did to his servant through Isaiah: 'Hear, you deaf; look, you blind, and see! Who is blind but my servant, and deaf like the messenger I send?'[7]

Hence the dismal record of the church's unfaithfulness. Seldom in its long history has it been sensitively in tune with God's Word. More often it has been exactly what it has been forbidden to be, namely conformist.[8] It has been influenced more by the world than by the Word. Instead of challenging the *status quo* with the values of the kingdom of God, it has acquiesced in it. Instead of resisting the encroachments of secularism, it has surrendered to them. Instead of rejecting the value system and lifestyle of the world, it has assimilated them. The church has accommodated itself to the prevailing culture, leaped on all the trendiest bandwagons, and hummed all the popular tunes of the day. Whenever the church does this, it reads Scripture through the world's eyes, and rationalizes its own unfaithfulness.

Is this unfair? I do not think so. Consider some examples from the past. For church history is full of the church's cultural blind spots.

How is it, I ask myself, that the Christian conscience not only approved but actually glamorized those terrible medieval Crusades as a Christ-glorifying form of mission, so that European Christian knights in shining armour rode forth to recover the holy places from Islam by force? It was an unholy blunder which Muslims have never forgotten, let alone forgiven, and which continues to obstruct the evangelization of the Muslim world, especially in the Middle East. Or how is it that torture could ever have been employed in the name of Jesus Christ to combat heresy and enforce orthodoxy, so that the thumbscrews were turned on some miserable dissident until he capitulated? One might almost characterize it 'evangelization by torture', and that in the name of the Prince of Peace! Or how is it that, although the Franciscans organized missions in the thirteenth century and the Jesuits in the sixteenth, Protestant churches were so inward looking that they had virtually no missions until the time of the Pietists two centuries after the Reformation? Even then, towards the end of the eighteenth century, when William Carey proposed a mission to India, he was greeted with the patronizing retort, 'Sit down, young man; when God wants to convert the heathen, he will do it without your help or mine.' Had his critic never read the Great Commission?

Again, how is it that the cruel degradations of slavery and of the slave trade were not abolished in the so-called Christian West until 1,800 years after Christ? Or how is it that racial prejudice and environmental pollution have become widely recognized as the evils they are only since the Second World War?

Such is a catalogue of some of the worst blind spots, which have marred the church's testimony down the ages. None of them can be defended from Scripture, although tortuous attempts have been made to do so. All are due rather to a misreading of Scripture or to an unwillingness to sit under its authority. God's people were blinded by tradition. They had other agendas; they were not in a mind or mood to listen to God.

What, then, about our own contemporary blindness? It is comparatively easy to criticize our forebears for theirs; it is much harder to be aware of ours. What will posterity see as the chief Christian blind spot at the end of the twentieth century? I cannot say with any degree of certainty, because of course I share in the same myopia myself. But I suspect that it will relate to two main areas. First, we Christians who live in the affluence of the North Atlantic still do not seem to have felt sufficiently the injustice of continuing North-South economic inequality, which was forcibly brought to the world's attention by the two Brandt Commission Reports, *North-South* (1980) and *Common Crisis* (1983). Apart from macro-economic questions of trade and development, we do not seem to have allowed the situation to affect our lifestyle. While a thousand million people are destitute, lacking the basic necessities for survival, and while about 10,000 people die of starvation daily, not counting mass starvation in famine conditions, should not the Christian voice of protest be louder and more strident? And should we not continue to simplify our own economic lifestyle, not because we imagine that this will solve the problem, but because it will enable us personally to share more and to express appropriately our sense of compassionate solidarity with the poor?

A second blind spot of at least evangelical Christians seems to me to be our comparative failure to condemn as immoral and indefensible all indiscriminate weaponry – both the use of atomic, biological and chemical weapons as being indiscriminate by nature, and the indiscriminate use of conventional weapons. We should surely be denouncing this as incompatible with the 'just war' theory, let alone with Christian pacifism. It was back in 1965 that the Roman Catholic Church condemned such weapons as 'a crime against God and man himself'. Ecumenical pronouncements followed, declaring indiscriminate warfare 'increasingly offensive to the Christian conscience'. But the evangelical voice, with notable exceptions, has been irresponsibly muted.

The first step towards the recovery of our Christian integrity will be the humble recognition that our culture blinds, deafens and dopes us. We neither see what we ought to see in Scripture, nor hear God's Word as we should, nor feel the anger of God against evil. We need to allow God's Word to confront us, disturbing our security, undermining our complacency, penetrating our protective patterns of thought and behaviour, and overthrowing our resistance.

It is not impossible for God to do this. Once we realize how strong a barrier to his communication with us our culture can be, we will be alert to the problem. Then we will begin to cry to him to open our eyes, unstop our ears, and stab our dull consciences awake, until we see, hear and feel what (through his Word) God has been saying to us all the time.

The Bible's cultural conditioning

It is not only Bible readers who are the products of a particular culture; so were the biblical authors. And God took this into account when he desired to communicate with his people. That is, when he spoke, he neither used his own language (if he has one), nor expressed himself in terms of his own heavenly culture, for such communication would have been unintelligible to human beings on earth. Nor did God shout culture-free maxims out of a clear, blue sky. On the contrary, he humbled himself to speak in the languages of his people (classical Hebrew, Aramaic and common Greek), and within the cultures of the ancient Near East (the Old Testament), Palestinian Judaism (the Gospels) and the hellenized Roman Empire (the rest of the New Testament). No word of God was spoken in a cultural vacuum; every word of God was spoken in a cultural context.

True, the cultural contexts in which the Bible was written are often alien to us. But we must not resent this on the ground that it causes us problems. We should rather rejoice in the divine condescension, that God should have stooped to our level in order to reveal himself in linguistically and culturally appropriate terms. This truth applies both to the incarnation of his Son, who took human flesh, and to the inspiration of his Word, which was spoken in human language.

Nevertheless, we are also faced with this question: How can a divine revelation given in transient cultural terms have permanent validity? How can a revelation addressed to a particular cultural situation have a universal application? Does not the cultural conditioning of Scripture limit its relevance to us, and even its authority over us? Must we not say with David Edwards, 'I admit that a lot in the Bible ... is culturally conditioned, and therefore out of date'?[9] Is his deduction logical?

My response to David Edwards is to agree that the Bible is a culturally conditioned book (as indeed are all books which have ever been written, including his and mine!), but to disagree that it is on that account necessarily out of date. How then shall we handle the cultural element in Scripture?

The principle, as I see it, can be set forth by an everyday illustration. We have little difficulty in distinguishing between a person and the particular clothing which he or she happens to be wearing. Most of us have several sets of clothes at home. Sometimes we dress up in maximum finery, for a wedding or party perhaps, or in our national costume. At other times we put on more sombre clothing, as when we attend a funeral. Occasionally we dress up in archaic garments, when playing charades or going to a fancy-dress party. We also have our work clothes, our sports clothes and our night clothes. In other words, there is variety in our wardrobe. But the person underneath the clothing remains the same. The clothing changes; the person does not.

Now just as we distinguish between persons and their clothing, so we need to distinguish between the essence of God's revelation (what he is teaching, promising or commanding) and the cultural clothing in which it was originally given. However dated the cultural setting may be, the essential message has permanent and universal validity. The cultural application may change; the revelation does not.

When we are faced with a biblical passage, therefore, whose teaching is obviously clothed in ancient cultural dress (because it relates to social customs which are either obsolete or at least alien to our own culture), how shall we react? We have three options.

The first possibility is *total rejection*. 'Because the culture is out of date,' we could say to ourselves, 'the teaching here is irrelevant. It has nothing to say to me. I may as well take a pair of scissors, cut this passage out of my Bible, and throw it away.' I am not recommending this response!

The second and opposite possibility is *wooden, unimaginative literalism*. The literalist says: 'Because this text is part of God's Word, it must be preserved and followed just as it stands, without modification. Both the substance and its cultural expression have equal authority. To discard either would be to tamper with the Word of God and be guilty of an incipient liberalism.' I do not recommend this response either.

There is a third and more judicious way, which is called *cultural transposition*. The procedure now is to identify the essential revelation in the text (what God is saying here), to separate this from the cultural form in which he chose to give it, and then to re-clothe it in appropriate modern cultural terms. 'Transposition' is a good word for this practice, since we are already familiar with it in musical contexts. To transpose a piece of music is to put it into a different key from that in which it was originally written. To transpose a biblical text is to put it into a different culture from that in which it was originally given. In musical transposition the tune and harmonization remain the same; only the key is different. In biblical transposition the truth of the revelation remains the same; only the cultural expression is different.

Cross-cultural missionaries illustrate the need for cultural transposition, although they have to wrestle with the dialectic between three cultures. Their task is to take the essence of the gospel, which was first revealed in the cultural settings of the Bible, and which they have received in their own cultures, and transpose it into the culture of the people to whom they go, without thereby either falsifying the message or rendering it unintelligible.[10] That, at least, is the theory. In practice, missionaries have often taken with them what Dr René Padilla at the Lausanne Congress in 1974 called a 'culture-Christianity'. In other words, they exported with the gospel their own cultural inheritance.

I remember the shock I felt on my first visit to West Africa and its churches. I saw Gothic spires rising incongruously above the coconut palms, and African bishops sweating profusely in the tropical heat, because they were wearing medieval European ecclesiastical robes. I heard western hymn tunes being sung to the accompaniment of western instruments, and African tongues attempting to get round Jacobean and even Elizabethan English! It is, of course, easy to criticize, and, if we had been in the position of the early missionaries, we would probably have made the same mistake. Nevertheless, this imposition of western cultural forms was a serious blunder. What is needed instead is what Stanley Jones in India called the 'naturalization' of the gospel,[11] which means its transposition into indigenous cultural forms.

Looking again at the three options before us, we might perhaps say that 'total rejection' is to throw out the baby with the bath water; that 'wooden literalism' is to keep both the baby and the bath water; while 'cultural transposition' is to keep the baby and change the bath water.

Examples of cultural transposition

The Bible is concerned about both doctrine and ethics, belief and behaviour, and in both areas cultural transposition is necessary.

Take first the doctrinal or theological teaching of the Bible. It seems obvious that we must learn to distinguish between the truth being affirmed, and the cultural terms in which it is presented; between meaning (the revelation) and medium (its communication). It is in this connection that we have to face the challenge posed by Bultmann's 'demythologization' programme. His argument may without too much distortion be reduced to three points, relating respectively to the biblical authors, their modern readers, and theological communicators. First, the intellectual framework of the biblical writers was pre-scientific and therefore 'mythical'. For example, they envisaged heaven above and hell below in a three-decker universe, so that they imagined Jesus literally 'descending to hell' and 'ascending to heaven'. Secondly, if modern scientific men and women are presented today with the gospel (*kerygma*) couched in terms of such an obsolete cosmology, they will reject it as frankly incredible. Thirdly, the task of theologians is therefore to strip away the mythical elements in the Bible, or 'demythologize the *kerygma*', because the purpose of myth is to speak not of historical events but of transcendent reality.

Let us agree at once with the spirit of the second point above. Our priority concern is how to communicate the *kerygma* to modern people in a way that is credible. In order to do so, we have to proclaim biblical *truth*, but not necessarily use biblical *terms*. We may (and must) transpose revealed truth into modern idiom.

With regard to Bultmann's first point, however, I am not myself at all convinced that the biblical authors were the literalists he imagines. To be sure, they used the imagery of the three-decker universe, for it was part of their intellectual framework. But were they actually affirming it? I think not. Take Psalm 75. God is said, when the earth quakes, to 'hold its pillars firm'.[12] So here is the earth (the middle deck) resting on pillars. But in the same psalm God both commands the wicked not to lift up their 'horns' or they will be cut off,[13] and warns that in his hand there is 'a cup full of foaming wine mixed with spices' which he will shortly pour out for the wicked to drink.[14] Now nobody (least of all the psalmist) believed literally that the wicked sprout horns or that God holds a cup of wine in his hand. If, therefore, these are examples of dramatic, poetic imagery, is it not gratuitous to insist that the earth's pillars are meant to be understood literally?

The Old Testament writers affirmed God's sovereign control of the world by saying that he held earth's pillars firm, without committing themselves to a three-decker cosmology. They affirmed God's power over evil by referring to his destruction of the primeval monster Leviathan,[15] without committing themselves to the Babylonian creation myth. They also affirmed his general revelation through nature by saying that the sun runs across the sky,[16] without committing themselves to a pre-Copernican universe. These forms of thought and speech, whether we call them 'imagery', 'poetry' or 'myth', were common currency in the ancient Near East. Old Testament writers used them to convey truths about God as Creator and Lord, without affirming the literal truth of the imagery or mythology they were using.

This brings us to Bultmann's third point. We should be able to agree with the need in some degree to 'demythologize', if what is meant is the need to transpose truth from one set of images to another, as we have just seen. But Bultmann goes much further than this, especially in relation to the New Testament. He attempts to reconstruct the *kerygma* (especially the death, resurrection and *parousia* of Jesus) by dissolving these historical events into a 'meaning' which is not historical. Thus, according to Bultmann, when the apostles said that 'Christ died for our sins', they were not referring to any literal sin-bearing sacrifice, but affirming God's love and our own existential experience of being crucified with Christ. When they said that 'he rose', they were not referring to an event but to an experience, namely that he rose in their own revived faith. And when they said that he is coming again to judge, they were not referring to a future event, but to a present challenge to make a responsible decision for Christ today.

The key question, however, is whether the affirmations that Christ died, rose and will return were deliberately mythical ways of referring to something other than historical events, or whether they were real happenings which were themselves part of the *kerygma* being proclaimed. The natural interpretation of the apostolic *kerygma is* that the apostles were intending to proclaim events in the career of Jesus which were both historically true and theologically significant.

It is, then, legitimate to distinguish between the meaning and the medium, between what is being affirmed and how the affirmation is made, between the revelation of truth and its communication. But it is also essential to ask whether the words and images used are literal or mythical. The defeat of Leviathan is a myth; the death, resurrection and coming of Jesus belong to history. The intention of the author will usually help us to know which is which.

We turn now to three examples of cultural transposition in the ethical field. I will begin with a fairly easy example, so that we may firmly grasp the principle and its application, namely the foot-washing. After Jesus had washed the feet of the Twelve in the upper room and resumed his place, he said: 'Now that I, your Lord and Teacher, have washed your feet, you also should wash one another's feet.'[17] In Jesus' day foot-washing was a common cultural practice. If we had been invited to a meal in a friend's house, we would have walked there barefoot or in sandals through dusty streets, and on arrival a slave would have washed our feet. Today, however, at least in the West, the whole culture has changed. We visit a friend by car or public transport. On arrival, there is certainly no slave to meet us and wash our feet. Instead, our host or hostess will probably ask us, 'Do you want to wash your hands?' How, then, shall we handle a text in which reciprocal foot-washing is commanded? Think of the three options. Shall we go the way of total rejection, on the ground that foot-washing has no place in our culture? No. Shall we obey Jesus' command literally, and go round asking people to take their shoes and socks or tights off, so that we may wash their feet? No. Although the Mennonites, and some African and Asian churches, have a ritual foot-washing as part of their communion service, it seems clear that Jesus' reference was to a social custom, not to a religious ceremony.

We are left then with the third option of cultural transposition. We ask what Jesus was getting at, what was the essence of his instruction. The answer is not far to seek. He was teaching that if we love one another, we must serve one another, and no service will be too dirty, menial or demeaning for us to perform. If, then, we cannot wash people's feet, we will gladly shine their shoes, or wash the dishes for them, or even clean out the toilets. Nothing will be beneath our dignity. Whatever in our culture is regarded as unpleasant work of low status, *that* will be our privilege out of love to undertake.

A second example of the need for cultural transposition relates to the eating of idol meats.[18] The question was whether it was permissible for the followers of Jesus to eat the meat of animals which, before being put on sale in a butcher's shop, had been offered in an idolatrous sacrifice. New converts, freshly rescued from heathen idolatry, had conscientious qualms about doing so. Would not the eating of idol meats contaminate and compromise them? Paul was clear that it would not. Idols were nothing, he said.

There was only one God, the Father, and only one Lord, Jesus Christ.[19] So he saw no reason why he should not eat idol meats. His conscience was 'strong', that is, well educated. But then there were the 'weak' believers to consider. Their 'weakness' was not in their will but in their conscience, which was under-educated and therefore over-scrupulous. If Paul were to eat idol meats in their presence, they might be encouraged to follow his example against their better judgment, in which case their conscience would be defiled. Consequently, out of deference to the weak Christians, Paul refrained.

Reading about this heated controversy in the New Testament sounds very alien to our context, at least in the West. There are no pagan temples in our culture, where animals are sacrificed to idols, nor are there any meat markets in which we could buy food which had been used in idolatrous worship. Yet at least two principles remain, which were laid down by Paul, and which are relevant to Christian people in every culture today. The first is that conscience is sacred. To be sure, it needs to be educated, but, even when it is weak, it must not be violated. 'Conscientious objection', not only to military service, but in other situations as well, is allowed in those countries which have had a Christian influence. Secondly, love limits liberty. Paul had liberty of conscience to eat, but he denied himself this freedom out of loving concern for those who would be offended if he did. These two principles can be applied in many different cultural contexts today.

My third example is the most controversial. It concerns the position and roles of women. Whole books have been written on this topic; I can hope here only to consider how far cultural transposition may be appropriate and helpful in this area. We are familiar both with Paul's prohibitions, that a woman may not 'teach or … have authority over a man',[20] and with his commands, that women are to wear veils and remain silent in public worship.[21] The question which these texts raise is this: Are all these instructions of permanent and universal validity? Or do they contain some cultural elements, which could allow us a little flexibility in interpretation and which may need transposition into our own culture? My response to these questions necessitates first the making of two affirmations, and then the asking of two more questions.

The first affirmation is that the sexes are equal. This is taught in Genesis 1:26–28. Men and women are equal bearers of the divine image, and equal sharers in the earthly dominion. Moreover, if they are equal by creation, they are even more equal (if that is possible) by redemption. For in Jesus Christ 'there is neither … male nor female'.[22] That is, we are absolutely equal in worth, dignity and relation to God. The second affirmation is that the sexes are complementary. This is taught in Genesis 2:18–24. Equality does not mean identity. Nor does it necessarily imply a complete interchangeability of roles. Moreover, within this complementary Paul affirmed the principle of masculine 'headship'. He derived it from the creation facts of Genesis 2, namely that woman was made after, out of and for man. And he evidently did not see any conflict between this and Galatians 3:28. I do not myself feel at liberty to disagree with the apostle Paul or to dismiss his teaching as rabbinic, cultural or mistaken. On the contrary, he roots it in creation, and what creation has established, no culture is able to destroy.

From the two affirmations I come to the two questions. First, what does 'headship' mean? I do not think we shall find our answer from the etymology of the Greek word *kephalē*, 'head', or from its use in secular Greek, where it may sometimes mean 'source'. The meaning of a word in Scripture is determined less by its origin or its use elsewhere than by its use in the biblical context. This being so, Ephesians 5:21–32 comes to our aid, since there Paul uses 'head' to convey responsibility rather than authority. He argues that the husband's headship (and therefore perhaps masculine headship in general) is to be modelled both on Christ's headship of the church (which led him to give himself up for her) and on our relation to our own body (which leads us to nourish it and care for it). In both cases 'headship' means sacrifice and service. It is the headship of care, not control. Its purpose is not to inhibit, let alone to crush, but to facilitate, to create conditions of love and security in which women are free to be and to develop themselves.

Secondly, how does 'headship' apply? Does it forbid ordination or other forms of ministry? In 1 Corinthians 11 Paul requires women to wear veils in public worship and refers to the veil as a symbol of authority, which in those days it was. It still is in some cultures, but not in the West. Wearing hats in church is a good example of bad transposition, for western ladies' hats tend to symbolize liberation rather than submission! What then about the requirement of silence?

My own belief is that commentators have not sufficiently noticed that Paul draws a double contrast when he writes: 'A woman should learn in quietness and full submission. I do not permit a woman to teach or to have authority over a man; she must be silent.'[23] The first contrast is between authority and submission; it seems to be permanent because creational. The second contrast is between teaching and silence. Is it possible that silence, like the veil, was a first-century cultural symbol of submission to masculine headship, which is not necessarily binding today? Certainly the situation has changed considerably. Women in many cultures today are just as educated as men. And the teaching office today, now that the New Testament canon has been finalized, is much less authoritative. So then, supposing (I ask myself) a woman were to teach men under the authority of Scripture (not claiming an authority of her own), in a meek and humble spirit (not throwing her weight about), and as a member of a pastoral team of which a man were head – might those three conditions enable her to teach men, without exercising an improper authority over them, and without infringing the principle of masculine headship? Would this be a legitimate example of cultural transposition?

My tentative answer to my own questions is, 'Yes, I think so.' I realize that this may seem to some nothing but an irrelevant theory, since in several denominations and in many parts of the world women's ordination is already a reality. But at least I hope it is clear what I have been trying to do. This is to identify and preserve the essence of God's revelation (in this case the creational relation of the sexes), while at the same time seeking to discern appropriate twentieth-century cultural symbols to express it.

I conclude this rather long chapter with two words of reassurance about the practice of cultural transposition.

First, cultural transposition is appropriate only where the biblical text contains two levels of discourse – first, doctrinal or ethical teaching, and, secondly, its cultural or social expression; first (for example) the command to love and serve one another, and secondly the foot-washing. Cultural transposition is impossible where there is only one level of discourse; it cannot be used to justify the rejection of what Scripture teaches, forbids or commands.

Take as an example the attempt to justify homosexual partnerships by declaring the biblical prohibitions to be culturally conditioned. The argument developed by some liberal thinkers runs like this: 'We grant that some forms of homosexual behaviour were forbidden by Moses in the Old Testament and by Paul in the New. But they were referring to particular cultural practices, in Leviticus to the ritual prostitution which was part of ancient Canaanite fertility religion, and in Paul's letters to promiscuous sexual behaviour, together with the corruption of the young. They were not referring to tender, loving, faithful relationships between two adult men or two adult women. Besides, Moses and Paul had a very limited understanding of human psycho-sexuality; we know much more than they did. So then, because the biblical prohibitions were of culturally specific taboos, they are irrelevant to us, and they cannot be taken to forbid a committed homosexual partnership which is equivalent to a heterosexual marriage.'

But this is a specious argument, which needs to be firmly rejected. The fact is that the reason for the biblical prohibitions of homosexual conduct was not cultural, but creational. They arose from the biblical definition of marriage, which was personally endorsed by Jesus Christ: 'For this reason a man will leave his father and mother and be united to his wife, and they will become one flesh.'[24] In other words, the only kind of marriage or sexual partnership envisaged in Scripture is heterosexual monogamy, which is also the only God-given context for the 'one flesh' experience. So what limits sexual intercourse to heterosexual marriage, and forbids it in all other relationships, is not culture but creation. No attempt at cultural transposition would be legitimate here.

Secondly, cultural transposition is not the thin end of the liberal wedge. It is not a conveniently respectable way to dodge awkward passages of Scripture by declaring them to be culturally relative. It is not a sophisticated way of rejecting biblical authority. No. If we go in for total rejection, we certainly cannot obey God's Word. If instead we embrace a position of wooden literalism, our obedience becomes artificial and mechanical. Only if we transpose the teaching of Scripture into modern cultural dress does our obedience become contemporary. Not disobedience, but meaningful obedience, is the purpose of cultural transposition.

Notes

[1] Anthony C. Thiselton, *The Two Horizons: New Testament Hermeneutics and Philosophical Description with Special Reference to Heidegger, Bultmann, Gadamer and Wittgenstein* (Paternoster, 1980). Two shorter essays have brought this debate within reach of ordinary mortals, namely Dr Thiselton's own 'Understanding God's Word Today' in *Obeying Christ in a Changing World*, vol. I, ed. John Stott (Collins 1977), pp. 90–122, and Dr J. I. Packer's 'Infallible Scripture and the Role of Hermeneutics' in *Scripture and Truth*, ed. D. A. Carson and John D. Woodbridge (Zondervan and IVP, 1983), pp. 323–356.

[2] A. C. Thiselton, *The Two Horizons*, p. 103.

[3] *Obeying Christ in a Changing World*, vol. 1, p. 118.

[4] A. C. Thiselton, *The Two Horizons*, p. 326.

[5] See *e.g. The Willowbank Report: Gospel and Culture* (Lausanne Committee for World Evangelization, 1978), pp. 10–11.

[6] Ps. 119:18.

[7] Is. 42:18–19.

[8] Rom. 12:2.

[9] From a book review in the *Church Times*.

[10] See *The Willowbank Report: Gospel and Culture*, especially chapter 5.

[11] See E. Stanley Jones, *The Christ of the Indian Road* (Hodder and Stoughton, 1926), *e.g.* p. 186.

[12] Verse 3.

[13] Verses 4, 5, 10.

[14] Verse 8.

[15] *E.g.* Ps. 74:14; Is. 27:1.

[16] Ps. 19:1–6.

[17] Jn. 13:14.

[18] Paul deals with this issue at some length in both Rom. 14 and 1 Cor. 8.

[19] 1 Cor. 8:4–6.

[20] 1 Tim. 2:12.

[21] 1 Cor. 11:4–10; 14:34–35; 1 Tim. 2:11–12.

[22] Gal. 3:28.

[23] 1 Tim. 2:11–12.

[24] Gn. 2:24, quoted by Jesus in Mk. 10:7–9, with the addition, 'Therefore what God has joined together, let man not separate.'

THIRTEEN

Expounding the Word

This chapter is about preaching, and as I begin it I am conscious of the need to make three preliminary points. The first is a personal one. There is something fundamentally anomalous about one preacher presuming to preach to other preachers about preaching. I wrote something similar ten years ago in my Introduction to *I Believe in Preaching*. I have not changed my mind in the meantime. For what do I know that you do not know? We have all preached, read and listened to sermons *ad nauseam*. I certainly claim no particular expertise. Often still in the pulpit I am seized with a communication frustration. Seldom if ever do I descend from the pulpit without feeling the need to confess my comparative failure and to pray for grace to do better next time. So I hope this puts us on the level. We are all struggling in this privileged but problematic ministry.

My second point is social. It concerns the widespread disillusion with preaching. Is it not an anachronism, an obsolete medium of communication, a dead art form, 'a sacred relic, a dubious thing of withered skin and dry bones enclosed in a reliquary of fond remembrance, still encrusted with the jewels of past glory'?[1] Who wants to listen to sermons nowadays? People are drugged by television, hostile to authority, weary and wary of words. When the sermon begins, they quickly grow impatient, fidgety and bored. We cannot assume that people want to listen to us; we have to fight for their attention.

Thirdly, and speaking pastorally, in spite of the acknowledged problems, we must persevere. For the health of the church depends on it. If it is true, as Jesus said, endorsing Deuteronomy, that human beings do 'not live on bread alone, but on every word that comes from the mouth of God',[2] it is equally true of churches. Churches live, grow and flourish by the Word of God; they wilt and wither without it. The pew cannot easily rise higher than the pulpit; the pew is usually a reflection of the pulpit. This is the lesson of history. 'Is it not clear', asked Dr Martyn Lloyd-Jones, 'that the decadent periods and eras in the history of the Church have always been those periods when preaching had declined?'[3] I am sure he was right. Indeed, we can see it illustrated in the world today. Although we rejoice in the statistics of church growth, we have to admit with shame that it is often growth without depth. There is much superficiality everywhere. And I am myself convinced from observation that the low level of Christian living is due more than anything else to the low level of Christian preaching. To be sure, it is the Holy Spirit who renews the church, but the Spirit's sword is the Word of God.[4] Nothing, it seems to me, is more important for the life and growth, health and depth of the contemporary church than a recovery of serious biblical preaching.

Let me seek to develop the case for biblical preaching. I begin with a straightforward definition in twenty-four words.

To preach is to open up the inspired text with such faithfulness and sensitivity that God's voice is heard and God's people obey him.

This definition of preaching contains six implications – two convictions about the biblical text, two obligations in expounding it, and two expectations as a result.

Two convictions

The first conviction about the biblical text is that it is an inspired text. 'To preach is to open up the inspired text.' A high view of the biblical text, as being unlike any other text, unique in its origin, nature and authority, is indispensable to authentic preaching. Nothing undermines preaching more than scepticism about Scripture. Without developing a sustained defence of this statement, I hope I shall carry you with me in reference to three words which belong together in our doctrine of Scripture, namely 'revelation', 'inspiration' and 'providence'.

'Revelation' describes the initiative God took to unveil or disclose himself. It is a humbling word. It presupposes that in his infinite perfections God is altogether beyond the reach of our finite minds. Our mind cannot penetrate his mind. We have no ability to read his thoughts. Indeed, his thoughts are as much higher than our thoughts as the heavens are higher than the earth.[5] Consequently, we would know nothing about God if he had not chosen to make himself known. Without revelation we would not be Christians at all but Athenians, and all the world's altars would be inscribed 'TO AN UNKNOWN GOD'.[6] But we believe God has revealed himself, not only in the glory and order of the created universe, but supremely in Jesus Christ his incarnate Word, and in the written Word which bears a comprehensive and variegated witness to him.

'Inspiration' describes the means God chose by which to reveal himself, namely by speaking to and through the biblical authors. As we have already noted, it was not a dictation process which would have demeaned them into machines, but a dynamic one which treated them as persons in active possession of their faculties. Many of the biblical authors were historians, and much of Scripture is history. For this they engaged in research, and made use of diaries, records and archives. They were also theologians, each with a distinct doctrinal emphasis, and writers, each with his own literary genre, style and vocabulary. These phenomena of historical research, theological concern and literary composition were neither incompatible with, nor smothered by, the process of inspiration. God spoke through them in such a way that the words spoken were simultaneously and equally his and theirs. This is the double authorship of Scripture, on which we reflected in chapter 10.

The third word is 'providence'. This is the loving foresight and provision of God by which he arranged for the words he had spoken first to be written, to form what we call 'Scripture', and then to be preserved across the centuries so as to be available to all people in all places at all times, for their salvation and enrichment.

Scripture then is 'God's word written',[7] his self-disclosure in speech and writing, the product of his revelation, inspiration and providence. This first conviction is indispensable to preachers. If God had not spoken, we would not dare to speak, for we would have nothing to say except our own threadbare speculations. But since God has spoken, we too must speak, communicating to others what he has communicated in Scripture. Indeed, we refuse to be silenced! As Amos put it, 'the Sovereign LORD has spoken – who can but prophesy?',[8] or pass on his Word. Similarly, Paul wrote, quoting Psalm 116, 'I believed; therefore I have spoken.'[9] That is, we speak because we believe what God has spoken.

I pity the preacher who enters the pulpit with no Bible in his hands, or with a Bible which is more rags and tatters than the Word of God. He cannot expound Scripture, because he has no Scripture to expound. He cannot speak, for he has nothing worth saying. But to enter the pulpit with the confidence that God has spoken, that he has caused what he has spoken to be written, and that we have this inspired text in our hands – ah! then our head begins to swim, our heart to beat, our blood to flow, and our eyes to sparkle, with the sheer glory of having God's Word in our hands and on our lips.

Our second conviction is that the inspired text is also a partially closed text. If to preach is 'to open up the inspired text', then it must be partially closed or it would not need to be opened up. And at once I think I see your Protestant hackles rising with indignation. 'What do you mean,' you ask me, 'that Scripture is partially closed? Do you not believe with the sixteenth-century Reformers in the "perspicuity" of Scripture (that it has a transparent or "see-through" quality)? Cannot even simple and uneducated people understand it by themselves? Is not the Holy Spirit our God-given teacher?' Yes, indeed; thank you for your questions. I can say a resounding 'Yes' to them. But what you are rightly saying also needs to be qualified.

The Reformers' insistence on the perspicuity of Scripture related to its central message, namely the gospel of salvation through faith in Christ crucified. That is as plain as day in the Bible. But they did not maintain that everything in Scripture is equally plain. How could they when Peter wrote that some things in Paul's letters 'are hard to understand'?[10] If one apostle did not always understand another apostle, it would hardly be modest for us to claim that we see no problems! Consequently, the church needs 'pastors and teachers' to expound or open up the Scriptures, and the ascended Christ still gives these gifts to his church.[11]

The story of the Ethiopian eunuch illustrates well this need for human teachers. While he was sitting in his chariot and reading Isaiah 53, Philip asked him: 'Do you understand what you are reading?' Did the Ethiopian reply, 'Why, of course I do. Don't you believe in the perspicuity of Scripture?'? No, he said: 'How can I [understand] unless someone explains it to me?'[12] Calvin rightly comments on the Ethiopian's humility, and contrasts it with those who, 'swollen-headed' with confidence in their own abilities, are too proud to submit themselves to teaching.

Here, then, is the biblical case for biblical exposition. It consists of two fundamental convictions, namely that God has given us in Scripture a text which is both inspired (having a divine origin and authority) and to some degree closed (difficult to understand). Therefore, in addition to the text, he gives the church teachers to open up the text, explaining it and applying it to people's lives.

Two obligations

My definition of preaching moves on from two convictions about the biblical text to two obligations in expounding it. 'To preach is to open up the inspired text with ... faithfulness and sensitivity ...' The main reason why the biblical text is partially closed and hard to understand is that a wide and deep cultural gulf yawns between the ancient world in which God spoke his Word and the modern world in which we listen to it. It is this cultural chasm, which occupied us in the last chapter, which also determines the task of the biblical expositor and lays down our two major obligations, namely faithfulness to the ancient Word and sensitivity to the modern world.

First comes the call to faithfulness. We have to accept the discipline of exegesis, that is, of thinking ourselves back into the situation of the biblical authors, into their history, geography, culture and language. This task has long been graced with the name 'grammatico-historical exegesis'. To neglect this discipline, or to do it in a half-hearted or slovenly way, is inexcusable; for it expresses contempt for the way God chose to speak. With what painstaking, conscientious and meticulous care should we study ourselves, and open to others, the very words of the living God!

Moreover, the worst blunder that we can commit is to read back our twentieth-century thoughts into the minds of the biblical authors (which is 'eisegesis'), to manipulate what they wrote in order to make it conform to what we want them to say, and then to claim their patronage for our opinions.

Calvin, centuries in advance of his time, understood this principle well. 'It is the first business of an interpreter', he wrote, 'to let his author say what he does say, instead of attributing to him what we think he ought to say.'[13] And some 300 years later, Charles Simeon of Cambridge enunciated the same principle in a letter to his publisher: 'My endeavour is to bring out of Scripture what is there, and not to thrust in what I think might be there.'[14] In our day we urgently need both the integrity and the courage to work by this basic rule, to give the biblical authors the freedom to say what they do say, however unfashionable and unpopular their teaching may be.

Secondly, biblical preaching demands sensitivity to the modern world. Although God spoke to the ancient world in its own languages and cultures, he intends his Word to be for everybody. This means that the expositor is more than an exegete. The exegete explains the original meaning of the text; the expositor goes further and applies it to the contemporary world. We have then to struggle to understand the rapidly changing world in which God has called us to live; to grasp the main movements of thought which have shaped it; to listen to its many discordant voices, its questions, its protests and its cries of pain; and to feel a measure of its disorientation and despair. For all this is part of our Christian sensitivity.

Here, then, are the two obligations which the calling to preach lays upon biblical expositors – faithfulness (to the Word) and sensitivity (to the world). We are neither to falsify the Word, in order to secure a phony relevance, nor to ignore the world in order to secure a phony faithfulness. We are not to fulfil either obligation at the expense of the other. It is the combination of faithfulness and sensitivity which makes the authentic preacher.

But, being difficult, it is also rare. The characteristic fault of conservative preachers is to be biblical, but not contemporary. The characteristic fault of liberal preachers is to be contemporary, but not biblical. Very few preachers manage to be both simultaneously.

In practice, as we study the text, we need to ask ourselves two distinct questions, and to ask them in the right order. The first is 'What did it mean?' and the second, 'What does it say?' In posing these two questions, our concern begins with the text's original meaning, when it was first spoken or written, and then moves on to its contemporary message, as it addresses people today. We must neither confuse these two questions, nor put them in the wrong order, nor ask either without also asking the other.

The first question, 'What did it mean?', could also be worded 'What *does* it mean?', since a text's actual meaning does not change. It still means today what it meant when it was first written. In his well-known book *Validity in Interpretation*, Dr E. D. Hirsch, formerly Kenan Professor of English at the University of Virginia, reaffirms the 'sensible belief that a text means what its author meant'.[15] He complains of the 'banishment of the author' from legal, biblical and literary texts. The result is pure subjectivism. In legal circles 'the meaning of a law is what present judges say the meaning is'; in Bultmannian biblical exegesis 'the meaning of the Bible is a new revelation to each succeeding generation', and in literary theory a text is 'what it means to us today'.[16] Indeed, in some university literature departments it is nowadays claimed that 'a text is infinitely interpretable', because it 'means' different things to different people. But this is a misleading use of the words 'mean' and 'meaning'. Professor Hirsch insists that it is only the author who determines the meaning of a text, and that to 'banish the original author as the determiner of meaning' is to 'reject the only compelling normative principle that could lend validity to an interpretation'.[17] So then a text's 'meaning' is what its author meant by it, and is therefore permanent, whereas its 'significance' is how it strikes different people and relates to different contexts, and is therefore variable.[18] There is all the difference in the world between Bultmann's 'a text means what it means to me' and E. D. Hirsch's 'a text means what its author meant'.

So the meaning of a text must be sought and found in the words themselves, the author's words, and not in the reader's thoughts and feelings. As Professor David Wells has put it, endorsing the emphasis of B. B. Warfield: 'Meaning is not to be found above the text, behind it, beyond it, or in the interpreter. Meaning is to be found *in the text*. It is the language of the text which determines what meaning God intends for us to have.' This is because 'words have meanings ... No language allows meaning to float free of the words used ... Unless words and their meaning are rejoined in hermeneutical practice, we can have no access to revelation in anything but a mystical sense'.[19]

The second question we have to ask of the text is, 'What does it say?' That is, having discerned its original meaning (which is fixed by its author), we need next to reflect on its contemporary message (how it applies to people today). This is where spiritual sensitivity comes in. We have to increase our familiarity with the modern world – its presuppositions and preoccupations, its mentality and mood, its volatile culture and falling standards, its values, goals, doubts, fears, pains and hopes, and not least its obsession with self, love and death. Only then shall we be able to discern how the unchanging Word speaks to the changing world. Nothing has helped me to do this more than the reading group of younger professionals who have been meeting with me in London about every six weeks for the last twenty years. We agree at the end of each session which book to read or film to see before our next meeting. We choose, in the main, books and films which express a non-Christian perspective. Then we ask ourselves, (1) What are the main issues which this raises for Christians? and (2) How does the gospel relate to people who think and live like this? In other words, we put our second question to the biblical text, 'What does it say?'

If we grasp the original meaning of a text, without going on to grapple with its contemporary message, we surrender to antiquarianism, unrelated to the present realities of the modern world. If, on the other hand, we begin with the text's contemporary message, without first having accepted the discipline of discovering its original meaning, we surrender to existentialism, unrelated to the past realities of revelation. Instead, we must ask both questions, first being faithful in working at the text's meaning and then being sensitive in discerning its message for today. Moreover, there are no short cuts to this. There is only the hard slog of study, seeking to become familiar both with the Scriptures in their fulness and with the modern world in all its variety.

It is, in fact, another case of the discipline of 'double listening', as we listen humbly to Scripture and critically to modernity, in order to relate the one to the other. Such listening is an indispensable preliminary to preaching. On 18 November 1991, the day on which Terry Waite was freed after nearly five years as a hostage in Lebanon, several other former hostages, whose liberation he himself had negotiated, were asked for a comment. One of them was Jean Waddell, who had served as a missionary in Iran. 'He's such a good communicator,' she said; 'he listens.'

Two expectations

After the two convictions about Scripture, and the two obligations in expounding it, come two expectations in consequence. If we do open up the inspired text with faithfulness and sensitivity, what can we expect to happen?

First, we expect God's voice to be heard. This expectation arises from our belief that the God who has spoken in the past also speaks in the present through what he has spoken.

Such an expectation, that through his ancient Word God addresses the modern world, is, however, at a low ebb today. As Dr Langmead Casserley, a scholar of the American Episcopal Church, has said, 'we have devised a way of reading the Word of God, from which no word from God ever comes'. When the time for the sermon arrives, the people clasp their hands and close their eyes with a fine show of piety, and sit back for their customary doze. Moreover, the preacher encourages it by his somnolent voice and manner.

How different it is when both preacher and people are expecting God to speak! The whole situation is transformed and becomes electric. The people bring their Bibles to church, and when they open them, they sit on the edge of their seats, hungrily waiting for what the Lord God may have to say to them. It is a re-enactment of the scene in the house of Cornelius the centurion when the apostle Peter arrived. Cornelius said to him: 'Now we are all here in the presence of God to listen to everything the Lord has commanded you to tell us.'[20] Why may a Christian congregation not experience the same degree of expectation today?

The preacher himself can encourage this attitude. He prepares carefully, in such a way that he is evidently expecting God to give him a message. He prays earnestly before he leaves home for church, and prays again in the pulpit before he preaches, that God will speak to his people. He reads and expounds his text with great seriousness of purpose, feeling deeply what he is talking about. Then, when he has finished, and he prays again, there is a stillness and a solemnity in the presence of the God who has spoken.

Our second expectation is that God's people will obey him. The Word of God always demands a response of obedience. We are not to be forgetful hearers, but obedient doers, of God's Word.[21] Throughout the Old Testament we hear the divine lament, 'Today, oh that you would listen to my voice!'[22] God kept sending his envoys to his people, 'but they mocked God's messengers, despised his words and scoffed at his prophets until the wrath of the LORD was aroused against his people and there was no remedy'.[23]

How then should people respond? What kind of obedience is required? Our answer is that the nature of the response expected is determined by the content of the word expounded. What we *do* in response to God's Word depends on what he *says* to us through it. Consider some examples. If, in and through the text expounded, God speaks about himself and his own glorious greatness, we respond by humbling ourselves before him in worship. If instead he speaks about us, our waywardness, fickleness, rebellion and guilt, then we respond in penitence and confession. If he speaks about Jesus Christ, who died to bear our sins and was raised from the dead to prove it, we respond in faith, laying hold of this heaven-sent Saviour. If he speaks about his promises, we determine to inherit them; if about his commands, we determine to keep them. If God speaks to us about the world, and its colossal spiritual and material need, then his compassion rises within us both to preach the gospel and to serve the needy. If, on the other hand, God speaks to us through his Word about the future, the coming of Christ and the glory to follow, then our hope is kindled, and we resolve to be holy and busy until he comes.

The preacher who has penetrated deeply into his text, has isolated and unfolded its dominant theme, and has himself been moved by its message, will hammer it home in his conclusion, and give people a chance to respond to it, often in silent prayer, as each person is brought by the Holy Spirit to an appropriate obedience.

This, then, is the definition of preaching which I venture to offer you. It contains two convictions (that the biblical text is an inspired text which yet needs to be opened up), two obligations (that we must open it up with faithfulness to the text itself and sensitivity to the modern context), and two expectations (that through the exposition and application of the written Word God himself will speak, and that his people will hear his voice and respond to him in obedience).

It is an enormous privilege to be a biblical expositor, that is, to stand in the pulpit with God's Word in our hands and minds, God's Spirit in our hearts, and God's people before our eyes, waiting expectantly for God's voice to be heard and obeyed.

Notes

[1] George Target, *Words That Have Moved the World* (Bishopsgate, 1987), p. 13.

[2] Mt. 4:4; Dt. 8:3.

[3] D. Martyn Lloyd-Jones, *Preaching and Preachers* (Hodder and Stoughton, 1971), p. 24.

[4] Eph. 6:17.

[5] Is. 55:9.

[6] Acts 17:23.

[7] Article XX of the Church of England's *Thirty-Nine Articles* (1563).

[8] Am. 3:8.

[9] 2 Cor. 4:13; Ps. 116:10.

[10] 2 Pet. 3:16.

[11] Eph. 4:11.

[12] Acts 8:26–39.

[13] Quoted by F. W. Farrer in his *History of Interpretation*, the 1885 Bampton Lectures (Macmillan, 1886), p. 347.

[14] Quoted by Hugh Evan Hopkins in *Charles Simeon of Cambridge* (Hodder and Stoughton, 1977), p. 57.

[15] E. D. Hirsch, *Validity in Interpretation* (Yale University Press, 1967), p. 1.

[16] *Ibid.*, p. viii.

[17] *Ibid.*, p. 5.

[18] *Ibid.*, pp. 8, 255. *Cf.* also E. D. Hirsch, *The Aims of Interpretation* (University of Chicago Press, 1976), pp. 2–3, 79.

[19] From Dr David Wells' essay 'Word and World' in *Evangelical Affirmations*, ed. Kenneth S. Kantzer and Carl F. H. Henry (Academie, Zondervan, 1990), pp. 161–162.

[20] Acts 10:33.

[21] Jas. 1:22–25.

[22] *E.g.* Ps. 95:7–10.

[23] 2 Ch. 36:16.

PART FOUR

The church

John Wesley was right when he described Christianity as essentially a 'social' religion, and added that to turn it into a 'solitary' religion would be to destroy it. This is not to deny that it offers individual salvation and calls to individual discipleship; it is rather to affirm that the church lies at the centre of God's purpose. Christ gave himself for us, we are told, not only 'to redeem us from all wickedness' but also 'to purify for himself a people that are his very own, eager to do what is good'.[1]

The problem we experience, whenever we think about the church, concerns the tension between the ideal and the reality. The ideal is beautiful. The church is the chosen and beloved people of God, his own special treasure, the covenant community to whom he has committed himself for ever, engaged in continuous worship of God and in compassionate outreach to the world, a haven of love and peace, and a pilgrim people headed for the eternal city. But in reality we who claim to be the church are often a motley rabble of rather scruffy individuals, half-educated and half-saved, uninspired in our worship, constantly bickering with each other, concerned more for our maintenance than our mission, struggling and stumbling along the road, needing constant rebuke and exhortation, which are readily available from both Old Testament prophets and New Testament apostles.

In consequence of this distinction between the ideal and the reality, people's opinions of the church vary enormously. On the one hand, P. T.

Forsyth could write that 'the church of Christ is the greatest and finest product of human history ... the greatest thing in the universe'.[2] On the other, Thomas Arnold wrote: 'The church as it now stands no human power can save ... When I think of the church, I could sit down and pine and die.'[3]

My purpose in Part Four of this book is to focus on the ideal, on what God intends his church to be, while all the time keeping in view the reality, so that we can more easily grasp the changes which need to be made. The first two chapters are complementary, since in chapter 14 we consider the world's challenge to the church and in chapter 15 the church's mission in the world. In chapter 16 the needed renewal of the church will be seen to include, as Jesus prayed, not one area only (*e.g.* its unity or its spirituality), but every area of its life. And to this end those of us who have been ordained to the pastoral ministry of the church need ourselves to be renewed according to God's purpose for us, which is the topic of chapter 17.

Notes

[1] Tit. 2:14.

[2] P. T. Forsyth, *The Work of Christ* (Hodder and Stoughton, 1910), p. 5.

[3] J. R. H. Moorman, *A History of the Church of England* (A. and C. Black, 1953), pp. 329, 331.

FOURTEEN

Secular challenges to the church

One of our greatest needs in today's church is a sensitive awareness of the world around us. If we are true servants of Jesus Christ, we will keep our eyes open (as he did) to human need, and our ears cocked to pick up cries of anguish. And we will respond compassionately and constructively (as again he did) to people's pain.

This does not mean that in every respect we 'let the world set the agenda for the church', as used to be said in the 1960s, or that we trot like a little dog at the world's heels. To behave like that would be to confuse service (which is our calling) with servility (which is not), and to interpret sensitivity (which is a virtue) in terms of conformity (which is a vice). No, first and foremost we have to declare and do what God has sent us to declare and do; we are not to pay obsequious homage to the world.

At the same time, unless we listen attentively to the voices of secular society, struggle to understand them, and feel with people in their frustration, anger, bewilderment and despair, weeping with those who weep, we will lack authenticity as the disciples of Jesus of Nazareth. Instead, we will run the risk (as has often been said) of answering questions nobody is asking, scratching where nobody is itching, supplying goods for which there is no demand – in other words, of being totally irrelevant, which in its long history the church has often been.

I would like to set before you in this chapter the threefold quest of modern, secularized men and women, which is, in fact, the universal, three-fold human aspiration, which Jesus Christ himself arouses within people, which he alone can satisfy, and which challenges the church to present him to the world in his fulness.

The quest for transcendence

Until quite recently 'transcendence' was regarded as a rather obscure word, whose use was limited to institutions of theological learning. There students were introduced to the distinction between 'transcendence' (meaning God above and outside the created world) and 'immanence' (meaning God present and active within it). Nowadays, however, nearly everybody has some notion of transcendence, because it has been popularized by the craze for 'transcendental meditation'. The quest for transcendence is, therefore, the search for ultimate reality beyond the material universe. It is a protest against secularization, that is, against the attempt to eliminate God from his own world. It is a recognition that human beings do not 'live on bread alone', for materialism cannot satisfy the human spirit. Consider some examples of the current disillusion with secularism and the persistent search for transcendence.

First, there is *the recent collapse of Euro-Marxism.* I am not now thinking about socialism as a politico-economic ideology, but about classical Marxism as a philosophy which denies the existence of God. Marxism was originally presented as a substitute for outmoded religious faith. But con-verts were few and far between. As Canon Trevor Beeson wrote about Eastern Europe in the 1970s, 'the basic doctrines of Communism have neither convinced the minds, nor satisfied the emotions, of the intelli-gentsia or of the proletariat. On the other hand, religious life has displayed remarkable resilience and, far from disappearing, has in many instances found new vitality and power'.[1] Solzhenitsyn said something similar in 1983, specifically about the Soviet Union. He drew attention to something which the Soviet leaders had not expected:

> that in a land where churches have been levelled, where a triumphant atheism has rampaged uncontrolled for two-thirds of a century, where clergy are utterly humiliated and deprived of all independence, where what remains of the church as an institution is tolerated only for the sake of propaganda directed at the west, where even today people are sent to the labour camps for their faith, and where, within the camps themselves, those who gather to pray at Easter are clapped in punishment cells – they [*sc.* the Soviet leaders] could not suppose that beneath this communist steam-roller the Christian tradition could survive in Russia! But there remain many

millions of believers; it is only external pressures that keep them from speaking out.[2]

The second sphere in which people are seen to be disillusioned with secularism is *the desert of western materialism*. Secularism is no more satisfying to the human spirit in its capitalistic, than in its communistic, guise. Theodore Roszak is an eloquent American exponent of its emptiness. The significant sub-title of his book *Where the Wasteland Ends* is *Politics and Transcendence in a Post-Industrial Society*.[3] He laments what he calls the 'coca-colonization of the world'.[4] We are suffering, he writes, from 'a psychic claustrophobia within the scientific worldview',[5] in which the human spirit cannot breathe. He castigates science (pseudo-science, I think he means) for its arrogant claim to be able to explain everything, its 'debunking spirit',[6] its 'undoing of the mysteries'. 'For what science can measure is only a portion of what man can know.'[7] This materialistic world of objective science, he goes on, is not nearly 'spacious enough' for us.[8] Without transcendence 'the person shrivels'.[9] His prescription (the recovery of Blake's 'visionary imagination') is woefully inadequate; but his diagnosis is surely right on target. Human beings know instinctively that Reality cannot be confined in a test tube, or smeared on a slide for microscopic examination, or apprehended by cool scientific detachment. For life has another and transcendent dimension, and Reality is 'awesomely vast'.[10]

Thirdly, the quest for transcendence is seen in *the epidemic of drug abuse*. There are, of course, a number of different interpretations of this almost world-wide phenomenon. It is neither a purely innocent experimentation, nor always a self-conscious protest against conventional mores, nor even an attempt to escape from the harsh realities of life. It is also a genuine search for a 'higher consciousness', and even for an objective transcendent reality. As evidence of this we could take Carlos Castaneda, whose books were extremely popular at the end of the 1960s and first half of the 1970s. He claimed that a Yaqui Indian from Mexico named Don Juan had initiated him. He taught him that there are two worlds of equal reality, the 'ordinary' world of living human beings and the 'non-ordinary' world of *diableros* or sorcerers. 'The particular thing to learn is how to get to the crack between the worlds and how to enter the other world ... There is a place where the two worlds overlap. The crack is there. It opens and closes like a door in the wind.'[11] The person who enters the other world of non-ordinary reality is 'the man of knowledge'; it is essential for him to have an 'ally', that is, 'a power capable of transporting him beyond the boundaries of himself'.[12] And the two main allies are *datura*, also called 'Jimson's weed' or 'devil's weed', which is feminine and gives power, and a mushroom called *humito* or 'little smoke', which is masculine and gives escstasy. The former was drunk or skin-absorbed, the latter smoked. The results were 'divination', bodily flight or bodilessness, adopting alternative bodies, and moving into and through objects.

The fourth example of the quest for transcendence is *the proliferation of religious cults*. Alongside the resurgence of ancient faiths, and the fascination of western youth with eastern mysticism, has gone the emergence of new religions. At least 800 have appeared in Britain since the Second World War,[13] and Alvin Toffler calculates that 1,000 new cults have won a following in the United States from about three million Americans.[14] One of the most alarming was the movement headed by Jim Jones of the People's Temple in San Francisco, nearly one thousand of whose followers died in 'Jonestown', their Guyana jungle colony, in 1978, mostly in a mass suicide by drinking poison. A leading article in *The Economist* warned that 'a groping has begun for new forms of spiritual experience', and added: 'In that search for God, it is all too easy to blunder into the arms of Satan instead.'[15] Peter Berger, the sociologist, has given a similar explanation: 'The current occult wave (including its devil component) is to be understood as resulting from the repression of transcendence in modern consciousness.'[16]

Most striking of all recent religious trends is the rise of the New Age movement. It is a bizarre assortment of diverse beliefs, religion and science, physics and metaphysics, ancient pantheism and evolutionary optimism, astrology, spiritism, reincarnation, ecology and alternative medicine. One of the movement's leaders, David Spangler, writes in his book *Emergence: The Rebirth of the Sacred* that 'from a very early age' he had himself been 'aware of an extra dimension' to the world around him, which as he grew older he came to identify as 'a sacred or transcendental dimension'. 'The rebirth of the sense of the sacred', he adds, 'is at the heart of the new age.'[17]

Here, then, are four contemporary pieces of evidence that materialism does not satisfy the human spirit, and that in consequence people are looking for another, a transcendent, reality. They seek it everywhere – through yoga, TM and the eastern religions, through sex (which Malcolm Muggeridge used to call 'the mysticism of the materialist'), through music and the other arts, through a drug-induced higher consciousness, through modern cults, New Age speculations, dangerous experiments with the occult and the fantasies of science fiction.

The immediate Christian reaction to this complex phenomenon should be one of sympathy. For we surely understand what is going on, and why. In the words of the apostle Paul before the Athenian philosophers, men and women are 'feeling after God', like blind people in the dark, groping after their Creator who leaves them restless until they find their rest in him.[18] They are expressing the human quest for transcendence. A contemporary example of it has been given by Richard North, environment correspondent of *The Independent*:

An awful lot of us just need to worship something. But in order to be able to worship, you have to be able to find something outside of yourself – and better than yourself. God is a construct for that. So is nature. We are all falling in love with the environment as an extension to and in lieu of having fallen out of love with God.[19]

This quest for transcendence is a challenge to the quality of the church's public worship. Does it offer what people are craving – the element of mystery, the 'sense of the numinous', in biblical language 'the fear of God', in modern language 'transcendence'? My answer to my own question is 'Not often'. The church is not always conspicuous for the profound reality of its worship. In particular, we who call ourselves 'evangelical' do not know much how to worship. Evangelism is our speciality, not worship. We seem to have little sense of the greatness and the glory of almighty God. We do not bow down before him in awe and wonder. Our tendency is to be cocky, flippant and proud. We take little trouble to prepare our worship services. Sometimes they are slovenly, mechanical, perfunctory and dull. At other times they are frivolous to the point of irreverence. No wonder those seeking Reality often pass us by!

We need to listen again to the biblical criticism of religion. No book, not even by Marx and his followers, is more scathing of empty religion than the Bible. The prophets of the eighth and seventh centuries BC were outspoken in their denunciation of the formalism and hypocrisy of Israelite worship. Jesus then applied their critique to the Pharisees of his day: 'These people … honour me with their lips, but their hearts are far from me.[20] And this indictment of religion by the Old Testament prophets and by Jesus is uncomfortably applicable to us and our churches today. Too much of our worship is ritual without reality, form without power, fun without fear, religion without God.

What is needed, then? Here are some suggestions. First, we need such a faithful reading and preaching of God's Word that through it his living voice is heard, addressing his people again. Secondly, we need such a reverent and expectant administration of the Lord's Supper that (I choose my words carefully) there is a Real Presence of Jesus Christ, not in the elements but among his people and at his table, Jesus Christ himself objectively and really present, coming to meet us, ready to make himself known to us through the breaking of bread, and anxious to give himself to us, that we may feed on him in our hearts by faith. Thirdly, we need such a sincere offering of praise and prayer, that God's people say with Jacob, 'Surely the LORD is in this place, and I was not aware of it,'[21] and unbelievers present will fall down and worship God, exclaiming, 'God is really among you!'[22]

In sum, it is a great tragedy that modern men and women, who are seeking transcendence, turn to drugs, sex, yoga, cults, mysticism, the New

Age and science fiction, instead of to the church, in whose worship services true transcendence should always be experienced, and a close encounter with the living God enjoyed.

The quest for significance

There is much in the modern world which not only smothers our sense of transcendence, but also diminishes (and even destroys) our sense of personal significance, our belief that life has any meaning. Three tendencies may be mentioned.

First, there is the effect of *technology.* Technology can be liberating, of course, in so far as it frees people from domestic or industrial drudgery. But it can also be dreadfully dehumanizing, as men and women feel themselves to be no longer persons but things, 'identified not by a "proper name" but by a serial number punched on a card that has been designed to travel through the entrails of a computer'.[23]

Secondly, there is *scientific reductionism.* Some scientists from different disciplines are arguing that a human being is nothing but an animal (Dr Desmond Morris's 'naked ape', to be more precise), or nothing but a machine, programmed to make automatic responses to external stimuli. It was statements like these which prompted the late Professor Donald MacKay to popularize the expression 'nothing buttery' as an explanation of what is meant by 'reductionism', and to protest against every tendency to reduce human beings to a level lower than the fully personal.

To be sure, our brain is a machine, a highly complex mechanism. And our anatomy and physiology are those of an animal. But that is not a complete account of our humanness. There is more to us than a body and a brain. It is when people affirm that we are 'nothing but' this or that, that they make a serious and dangerous mistake.

Thirdly, *existentialism* has the effect of diminishing people's sense of significance. Radical existentialists may be said to differ from humanists in general by their resolve to take their atheism seriously and face its terrible consequences. Because (in their view) God is dead, everything else has died with him. Because there is no God, there are now no values or ideals either, no moral laws or standards, no purposes or meanings. And although I exist, there is yet nothing that gives me or my existence any significance, except perhaps my decision to seek the courage to be. Meaning is found only in despising my own meaninglessness. There is no other way to authenticate myself.

Bleakly heroic as this philosophy may sound, there must be very few people able to perform the conjuring trick of pretending to have significance when they know they have none. For significance is basic to survival. This is what Viktor Frankl found when as a young man he spent three years in the Auschwitz concentration camp. He noticed that the inmates most likely to survive were those 'who knew that there was a task waiting for them to fulfil'.[24] Later he became Professor of Psychiatry and Neurology in the University of Vienna and founded the so-called 'Third Viennese School of Psychiatry'. He postulated that, in addition to Freud's 'will to pleasure' and Adler's 'will to power', human beings have a 'will to meaning'. Indeed, 'the striving to find a meaning in one's life is the primary motivational force in man'.[25] So he developed what he called 'logotherapy', using *logos* to mean neither 'word' nor 'reason' but 'meaning'. 'The mass neurosis of the present time', he wrote, is 'the existential vacuum',[26] that is, the loss of a sense that life is meaningful. He would sometimes ask his clients, 'Why don't you commit suicide?' (an extraordinary question for a doctor to put to a patient!). They would reply that there was something (perhaps their work or marriage or family) which made life worthwhile for them. Professor Frankl would then build on this.

Meaninglessness leads to boredom, alcoholism, juvenile delinquency and suicide. Commenting on Viktor Frankl's work, Arthur Koestler wrote:

> It is an inherent tendency in man to reach out for *meanings* to fulfil and for *values* to actualize ... Thousands and thousands of young students are exposed to an indoctrination ... which denies the existence of values. The result is a worldwide phenomenon – more and more patients are crowding our clinics with the complaint of an inner emptiness, the sense of a total and ultimate meaninglessness of life.[27]

According to Emile Durkheim, in his classic study of suicide, the greatest number of suicides are caused by *anomie*, which could be rendered 'normlessness' or 'meaninglessness'. And 'anomic' suicide takes place when somebody either has no goal in life or pursues an unattainable goal, whether power, success or prestige. 'No human being can be happy or even exist unless his needs are sufficiently proportioned to his means.'[28]

If the quest for transcendence was a challenge to the quality of the church's worship, the quest for significance is a challenge to the quality of the church's teaching. Millions of people do not know who they are, nor that they have any significance or worth. Hence the urgent challenge to us to tell them who they are, to enlighten them about their identity, that is, to teach without compromise the full biblical doctrine of our human being – its depravity, yes, but also (and in this context above all) its dignity. See chapter 1.

Christians believe in the intrinsic worth of human beings, because of our doctrines of creation and redemption. As we considered in chapter 1, God made man male and female in his own image and gave them a responsible stewardship of the earth and its creatures. He has endowed us with rational,

moral, social, creative and spiritual faculties which make us like him and
unlike the animals. Human beings are Godlike beings. As a result of the fall
our Godlikeness has indeed been distorted, but it has not been destroyed.
Further, 'God so loved the world' that he gave his only Son for our redemption. The cross is the chief public evidence of the value which God places
on us.

Christian teaching on the dignity and worth of human beings is of the
utmost importance today, not only for the sake of our own self-image and
self-respect, but even more for the welfare of society.

When human beings are devalued, everything in society turns sour.
Women are humiliated and children despised. The sick are regarded as a
nuisance, and the elderly as a burden. Ethnic minorities are discriminated
against. The poor are oppressed and denied social justice. Capitalism displays its ugliest face. Labour is exploited in the mines and factories.
Criminals are brutalized in prison. Opposition opinions are stifled. Belsen
is invented by the extreme Right, and Gulag by the extreme Left.
Unbelievers are left to live and die in their lostness. There is no freedom, no
dignity, no carefree joy. Human life seems not worth living, because it is
scarcely human any longer.

But when human beings are valued as persons, because of their intrinsic
worth, everything changes. Men, women and children are all honoured.
The sick are cared for, and the elderly enabled to live and die with dignity.
Dissidents are listened to, prisoners rehabilitated, minorities protected, and
the oppressed set free. Workers are given a fair wage, decent working conditions and a measure of participation in both the management and the
profit of the enterprise. And the gospel is taken to the ends of the
earth. Why? Because people matter. Because every man, woman and child
has worth and significance as a human being made in God's image and
likeness.

The quest for community

The modern technocratic society, which destroys transcendence and significance, is destructive of community also. We are living in an era of social
disintegration. People are finding it increasingly difficult to relate to one
another. So we go on seeking the very thing which eludes us – love in a loveless world. I summon as my witnesses three very different people.

The first is Mother Teresa. Born in Yugoslavia, she left for India when
she was only seventeen years old. Then, after about twenty years of teaching, she gave up this profession in order to serve the poorest of the poor in
Calcutta. The same year (1948) she became an Indian citizen, and two
years later founded her own order, the 'Missionaries of Charity'. So India
has been her home for over sixty years, and in consequence hers is an

authentic Third World vision and voice. This is what she has written about the West:

> People today are hungry for love, for understanding love, which is ... the only answer to loneliness and great poverty. That is why we [*sc.* the sisters and brothers of her order] are able to go to countries like England and America and Australia, where there is no hunger for bread. But there people are suffering from terrible loneliness, terrible despair, terrible hatred, feeling unwanted, feeling helpless, feeling hopeless. They have forgotten how to smile, they have forgotten the beauty of the human touch. They are forgetting what is human love. They need someone who will understand and respect them.[29]

I remember that, when I first read this assessment of the western world, I was a bit indignant and considered it exaggerated. But I have since changed my mind. I think it is accurate, at least as a generalization.

My second witness is Bertrand Russell, the brilliant mathematician and philosopher, and uncompromising atheist. He wrote with moving candour in the Prologue to his autobiography:

> Three passions, simple but overwhelmingly strong, have governed my life: the longing for love, the search for knowledge, and unbearable pity for the suffering of mankind. These passions, like great winds, have blown me hither and thither, in a wayward course, over a deep ocean of anguish, reaching to the very verge of despair. I have sought love, first, because it brings ecstasy ... I have sought it, next, because it relieves loneliness – that terrible loneliness in which one's shivering consciousness looks over the rim of the world into the cold unfathomable lifeless abyss ...[30]

Woody Allen is my third witness. Most people think of him as a comedian (he was selling jokes to the press while he was still at high school), but 'inside the clown there's a tragedian'.[31] For all his acclaimed brilliance as an author, director and actor, he never seems to have found either himself or anybody else. He describes love-making as 'two psychopaths under one quilt'. In his film *Manhattan* (1979) he quips that he thinks people ought to 'mate for life, like pigeons or Catholics', but he appears unable to follow his own precept. He confesses that all his films 'deal with that greatest of all difficulties – love relationships. Everybody encounters that. People are either in love, about to fall in love, on the way out of love, looking for love, or a way to avoid it.'[32] His biographer ends his portrait of him with these words: 'He is struggling, as *we* are surely struggling, to find the strength to found a life upon a love. As the character says in *Hannah and Her Sisters*,

"Maybe the poets are right. Maybe love is the only answer ..."[33]

Here are three people of very different backgrounds, beliefs, temperaments and experiences, who nevertheless agree with one another about the paramount importance of love. They speak for the human race. We all know instinctively that love is indispensable to our humanness. Love is what life is all about.

So people are seeking it everywhere. At least since the sixties, some have been breaking away from western individualism and experimenting with communal styles of living. Others are trying to replace the nuclear family (which is traditional in the West) with the extended family (which for centuries has been traditional in Africa and Asia). Yet others are repudiating the age-long institutions of marriage and the family in an attempt (vain and foolish, Christians believe) to find in this way the freedom and spontaneity of love. Everybody is searching for genuine community and the authentic relationships of love. The lyric from Andrew Lloyd Webber's musical *Aspects of Love* says it all:

> Love, love changes everything:
>   hands and faces, earth and sky.
> Love, love changes everything:
>   how you live and how you die.
> Love can make the summer fly
>   or a night seem like a life-time.
> Yes love, love changes everything;
>   now I tremble at your name.
> Nothing in the world will ever be the same.
>
> Love, love changes everything:
>   days are longer, words mean more.
> Love, love changes everything:
>   pain is deeper than before.
> Love will turn your world around
>   and that world will last for ever.
> Yes love, love changes everything,
>   brings you glory, brings you shame.
> Nothing in the world will ever be the same.

The world's third challenge, then, concerns the quality of the church's fellowship. We proclaim that God is love, and that Jesus Christ offers true community. We insist that the church is part of the gospel. God's purpose, we say, is not merely to save isolated individuals, and so perpetuate their loneliness, but to build a church, to create a new society, even a new humanity, in which racial, national, social and sexual barriers have been abolished. Moreover, this new community of Jesus dares to present itself as the true alternative society, which eclipses the values and standards of the world.

It is a high-sounding claim. But the tragedy is that the church has consistently failed to live up to its own ideals. Its theological understanding of its calling may be impeccable. But, comparatively speaking, there is little acceptance, little caring and little supportive love among us. People searching for community ought to be pouring into our churches, especially if they offer a small-group experience. Instead, the church is usually the one place they do not even bother to check out, so sure are they that they will not find love there.

Mel White, a Christian writer and film-maker, set out to investigate the causes of the tragic mass suicide at Jonestown in the Guyana jungle in 1978, and published his findings in a book and film entitled *Deceived*. 'How could it happen?' he asked, and 'What can we do to stop it happening again?' In talking to both defectors and survivors, he discovered to his surprise that 'Jones's victims were from our churches' (the title of the book's first chapter), but they did not find love there. Jean Mills, for example, a defector after seven years, said: 'I was so turned off in every church I went to, because nobody cared.'[34] And Grace Stoen, whose lawyer husband Tim became the second most powerful man in the People's Temple in San Francisco, said: 'I went to church until I was eighteen years old ... and nobody ever befriended me.' In the People's Temple, however, according to Jean Mills, 'everyone seemed so caring and loving. They hugged us and made us welcome ... and said they ... wanted us to come back.'[35] It was this discovery which led Mel White in his last chapter, entitled 'It must not happen again', to list eight resolutions. The first is this: 'I will do my best to help make my church a more loving community to our members, and the strangers in our midst.'[36]

It would be unjust, however, to be entirely negative in our evaluation of the contemporary church. For there are Christian communities all over the world where true, sacrificial, serving, supportive love is to be found. Where such Christian love flourishes, its magnetism is almost irresistible. Bishop Stephen Neill expressed it well:

Within the fellowship of those who are bound together by personal loyalty to Jesus Christ, the relationship of love reaches an intimacy and intensity unknown elsewhere. Friendship between the friends of Jesus of Nazareth is unlike any other friendship. This ought to be normal experience within the Christian community ... That in existing Christian congregations it is so rare is a measure of the failure of the church as a whole to live up to the purpose of its Founder for it. Where it is experienced, especially across the barriers of race, nationality and language, it is one of the most convincing evidences of the continuing activity of Jesus among men.[37]

Here, then, is a threefold quest on which human beings are engaged. Although they might well not articulate it thus, I think we may say that in looking for transcendence they are trying to find God, in looking for significance they are trying to find themselves, and in looking for community they are trying to find their neighbour. And this is humankind's universal search – for God, our neighbour and ourselves.

Moreover, it is the Christian claim (confident I know, humble I hope) that those who seek will find – in Christ and in his new society. The contemporary secular quest seems to me to constitute one of the greatest challenges – and opportunities – with which the church has ever been presented: people are openly looking for the very things that Jesus Christ is offering!

The only question is whether the church can be so radically renewed, by the Spirit and the Word of God, that it offers an experience of transcendence through its worship, of significance through its teaching, and of community through its fellowship. For if so, people will turn to it eagerly in their quest, and our proclamation of the good news will have a credibility which otherwise it lacks.

Notes

[1] Trevor Beeson, *Discretion and Valour* (Collins, 1974), p. 24.

[2] From an address by Solzhenitsyn, when accepting the Templeton Prize in London in May 1983.

[3] Theodore Roszak, *Where the Wasteland Ends* (1972; Anchor, 1973).

[4] *Ibid.*, p. 22.

[5] *Ibid.*, p. 66.

[6] *Ibid.*, pp. 227–228.

[7] *Ibid.*, p. 67.

[8] *Ibid.*, p. 70.

[9] *Ibid.*, p. xxi.

[10] Theodore Roszak, *The Making of a Counter Culture* (Anchor, 1969), p. 235.

[11] Carlos Castaneda, *The Teachings of Don Juan* (1968; Penguin, 1970), p. 182.

[12] *Ibid.*, pp. 54, 199.

[13] According to Dr Peter Clarke, a lecturer in the history and sociology of religion at King's College, London, as reported in *The Times* on 26 October 1990. He added that those so far documented were only the tip of the iceberg. 'Below the surface there would appear to be a large mass of new religion which has neither been located nor measured with any precision.'

[14] Alvin Toffler, *Third Wave* (Collins, 1980), p. 385.

[15] *The Economist*, 25 November 1978.

[16] Peter L. Berger, *Facing Up to Modernity* (1977; Penguin, 1979), p. 255.

[17] David Spangler, *Emergence: The Rebirth of the Sacred* (Dell Publishing 1984), pp. 12, 41.

[18] Augustine, *Confessions* (Bk. 1, ch. 1).

[19] Quoted by Jonathon Porritt and David Winner in *The Coming of the Greens* (Collins, 1988), pp. 251–252.

[20] Is. 29:13; Mk. 7:6.

[21] Gn. 28:16.

[22] 1 Cor. 14:24–25.

[23] Arnold Toynbee, quoted in *The Times* on 5 April 1969. See his *Experiences* (Oxford University Press, 1969).

[24] Viktor E. Frankl, *Man's Search for Meaning*, originally published with the title *From Death-Camp to Existentialism* (1959; Washington Square Press, 1963), p. 165.

[25] *Ibid.*, p. 154.

[26] *Ibid.*, pp. 167, 204.

[27] From the chapter 'Rebellion in a Vacuum', which was Arthur Koestler's contribution to the symposium *Protest and Discontent*, ed. Bernard Crick and William Robson (Penguin, 1970), p. 22.

[28] Emile Durkheim, *Suicide: A Study in Sociology* (1897; ET, 1952; Routledge and Kegan Paul, 1975), p. 246.

[29] Desmond Doig, *Mother Teresa, Her People and Her Work* (Collins, 1976), p. 159.

[30] *The Autobiography of Bertrand Russell* (George Allen and Unwin, 1967), p. 13.

[31] Jack Kroll in *Newsweek*, 24 April 1978.

[32] Graham McCann, *Woody Allen, New Yorker* (Polity Press, 1990), p. 222.

[33] *Ibid.*, p. 248.

[34] Mel White, *Deceived* (Spire Books, Revell, 1979), p. 19.

[35] *Ibid.*, p. 19.

[36] *Ibid.*, p. 184.

[37] Stephen C. Neill, *Christian Faith Today* (Pelican, 1955), p. 174.

Evangelism through the local church[1]

We should be very grateful to the African bishops for proposing, and to the other Anglican bishops for agreeing, that the last ten years of the twentieth century, indeed of the second millennium AD, should be declared 'A Decade of Evangelism'.

This decision of the 1988 Lambeth Conference has brought evangelism to the top of the Anglican Church's agenda and challenges us to ask ourselves what we know and believe about evangelism. For the whole Anglican Communion now finds itself obliged to face a responsibility which it has often shirked, namely the call to bear witness to Jesus Christ. Other denominations are also majoring on evangelism in the nineties and setting goals for AD 2000.

According to the definition which the Anglican primates have commended to us, to evangelize is 'to make known by word and deed the love of the crucified and risen Christ in the power of the Holy Spirit, so that people will repent, believe and receive Christ as their Saviour and obediently serve him as their Lord in the fellowship of his church'.

Not that evangelism is foreign to the ethos of Anglicanism. Far from it. The Second Book of Homilies, for example, written mostly by Bishop John Jewel of Salisbury, and published in 1571, contains the following admonition: 'If any man be a dumb Christian, not professing his faith openly, but cloaking and colouring himself for fear of danger in time to come, he giveth men occasion, justly and with good conscience, to doubt lest he have not the grace of the Holy Ghost within him, because he is tongue tied and doth not speak.'

Various forms of evangelism

Evangelism can of course take different forms. Ever since Jesus offered living water to the Samaritan woman at Jacob's well,[2] and Philip sat beside the Ethiopian in his chariot and told him the good news of Jesus,[3] *personal evangelism* has had impeccable biblical precedents. It is still our duty, when the opportunity is given and in a spirit of humility, to share Christ with those of our relatives, friends, neighbours and colleagues who do not yet know him.

Mass evangelism too (the preaching of an evangelist to crowds) has over the centuries been signally blessed by God. The recent disgracing of a few American televangelists does not contradict this fact. Besides, Jesus himself proclaimed the good news of the kingdom to the crowds in Galilee. So did the apostle Paul to the pagans of Lystra[4] and the philosophers of Athens,[5] and Wesley and Whitefield in eighteenth-century Britain and America. Gifted evangelists of many nationalities are still preaching effectively to large crowds today, although they know that their ministry depends on the active co-operation of churches and Christians. And all over the world there are clergy and lay people who take their preaching seriously, and who remember that in their congregation there will often be both non-Christians and nominal Christians who need to hear the gospel.

Nevertheless, *local church evangelism* can claim to be the most normal, natural and productive method of spreading the gospel today. There are two main reasons for commending it.

First, there is *the argument from Scripture*. According to the apostle Peter, the church is both 'a royal priesthood' to offer spiritual sacrifices to God (which is worship) and 'a holy nation' to spread abroad God's praises (which is witness).[6] Moreover, these responsibilities of the universal church devolve on each local church. Every Christian congregation is called by God to be a worshipping, witnessing community. Indeed, each of these two duties necessarily involves the other. If we truly worship God, acknowledging and adoring his infinite worth, we find ourselves impelled to make him known to others, in order that they may worship him too. Thus worship leads to witness, and witness in its turn to worship, in a perpetual circle.

The Thessalonians set a fine example of local church evangelism. Near the beginning of his first letter to them Paul points out this remarkable sequence: 'Our gospel came to you ... You welcomed the message ... The Lord's message rang out from you.'[7] In this way the local church becomes like a sounding-board which reflects and amplifies the vibrations it receives, or like a communications satellite which first accepts and then transmits a message. Every church which has heard the gospel must pass it on. This is still God's principal method of evangelism. If all churches had been faithful, the world would long ago have been evangelized.

Secondly, there is *the argument from strategy*. Each local church is situated in a particular neighbourhood. Its first mission responsibility must therefore be to the people who live there. The congregation is strategically placed to reach the locality. Any political party would be wildly jealous of the plant and personnel which are at our disposal. The churches in many countries have ample resources to disseminate the gospel throughout their land.

Thus biblical theology and practical strategy combine to make the local church the primary agent of evangelism.

But if the local church is to act out its God-appointed role, it must first fulfil four conditions. It must *understand* itself (the theology of the church), *organize* itself (the structures of the church), *express* itself (the message of the church), and *be* itself (the life of the church).

The church must understand itself

The theology of the church

I make no apology for beginning with theology. Many churches are sick because they have a false self-image. They have grasped neither who they are (their identity) nor what they are called to be (their vocation). We all know the importance for mental health of having an accurate self-image. What is true of persons is equally true of churches.

At least two false images of the church are prevalent today.

The first false image is *the religious club* (or *introverted Christianity*). According to this view, the local church somewhat resembles the local golf club, except that the common interest of its members happens to be God rather than golf. They see themselves as religious people who enjoy doing religious things together. They pay their subscription and reckon they are entitled to certain privileges. In fact, they concentrate on the status and advantages of being club members. They have evidently forgotten – or never known – the perceptive dictum attributed to Archbishop William Temple that 'the church is the only co-operative society in the world which exists for the benefit of its non-members'. Instead, they are completely introverted, like an ingrown toenail. To be sure, Temple was guilty of a slight exaggeration, for church members do have a responsibility to each other, as the many 'one another' verses of the New Testament indicate ('love one another', 'encourage one another', 'bear one another's burdens', *etc.*). Nevertheless, our primary responsibilities are our worship of God and our mission in the world.

At the opposite extreme to the religious club is *the secular mission* (or *religionless Christianity*). It was in the 1960s that some Christian thinkers became understandably exasperated by what they saw as the ecclesiastical self-centredness of the church. The church seemed to them so incorrigibly absorbed in its own petty domestic affairs, that they resolved to abandon it and drop out. For the arena of divine service they exchanged the church for the secular city. They were no longer interested in 'worship services', they said, but only in 'worship service'. So they tried to develop a 'religionless Christianity' in which they reinterpreted worship as mission, love for God as love for neighbour, and prayer to God as encounter with people.

How, some thirty years later, should we evaluate this movement? We must surely agree that their distaste for selfish religion was right. Since it is nauseating to God, it ought to sicken us also. But the concept of a 'religionless Christianity' was an unbalanced over-reaction. We have no liberty to confuse worship and mission, even though (as we have seen) each involves the other. There is always an element of mission in worship and of worship in mission, but they are not synonymous.

There is a third way to understand the church, which combines what is true in both false images, and which recognizes that we have a responsibility both to worship God and to serve the world. This is *the double identity of the church* (or *incarnational Christianity*). By its 'double identity' I mean that the church is a people who have been both called out of the world to worship God and sent back into the world to witness and serve. These are, in fact, two of the classical 'marks' of the church. According to the first, the church is 'holy', called out to belong to God and to worship him. According to the second, the church is 'apostolic', sent out into the world on its mission. Alternatively, we may say that the church is summoned by God to be simultaneously 'holy' (distinct from the world) and 'worldly' (not in the sense of assimilating the world's values and standards, but in the sense of renouncing other-worldliness and becoming instead immersed in the life of the world). It was Dr Alec Vidler who admirably captured the church's double identity by referring to its 'holy worldliness'.[8]

Nobody has ever exhibited the meaning of 'holy worldliness' better than our Lord Jesus Christ himself. His incarnation is the perfect embodiment of it. On the one hand, he came to us in our world, and assumed the full reality of our humanness. He made himself one with us in our frailty, and exposed himself to our temptations. He fraternized with the common people, and they flocked round him eagerly. He welcomed everybody and shunned nobody. He identified himself with our sorrows, our sins and our death. On the other hand, in mixing freely with people like us, he never sacrificed, or even for one moment compromised, his own unique identity. His was the perfection of 'holy worldliness'.

And now he sends us into the world as he was sent into the world.[9] We have to penetrate other people's worlds, as he penetrated ours – the world of their thinking (as we struggle to understand their misunderstandings of the gospel), the world of their feeling (as we try to empathize with their pain), and the world of their living (as we sense the humiliation of their social situation, whether poverty, homelessness, unemployment or discrimination). Archbishop Michael Ramsey put it well: 'We state and commend the faith only in so far as we go out and put ourselves with loving sympathy inside the doubts of the doubter, the questions of the questioner, and the loneliness of those who have lost the way.'[10] Yet this costly entry into other people's worlds is not to be undertaken at the expense of our own Christian integrity. We are called to maintain the standards of Jesus Christ untarnished.

Seldom in its long history has the church managed to preserve its God-given double identity of holy worldliness. Instead, it has tended to oscillate between the two extremes. Sometimes (in an over-emphasis on its holiness) the church has withdrawn from the world and so has neglected its mission. At other times (in an over-emphasis on its worldliness) it has conformed to the world, assimilating its views and values, and so has neglected its holiness. But in order to fulfil its mission, the church must faithfully respond to both its callings and preserve both parts of its identity.

'Mission' arises, then, from the biblical doctrine of the church in the world. If we are not 'the church', the holy and distinct people of God, we have nothing to say because we are compromised. If, on the other hand, we are not 'in the world', deeply involved in its life and suffering, we have no-one to serve because we are insulated. Our calling is to be 'holy' and 'worldly' at the same time. Without this balanced biblical ecclesiology we will never recover or fulfil our mission.

The church must organize itself

The structures of the church

The church must organize itself in such a way as to express its understanding of itself. Its structures must reflect its theology, especially its double identity.

The commonest fault is for the church to be structured for 'holiness' rather than 'worldliness', for worship and fellowship rather than mission. This was the emphasis of the report *The Church for Others* (1968), subtitled *A Quest for Structures for Missionary Congregations*. One does not have to agree with everything in the book in order to appreciate its thrust that

> the missionary church is not concerned with itself – it is a church for others ... Its centre lies outside itself; it must live 'excentredly' ... The

church has to turn itself outwards to the world ... We have to recognize that the churches have developed into 'waiting churches' into which people are expected to come. Its inherited structures stress and embody this static outlook. One may say that we are in danger of perpetuating 'come-structures' instead of replacing them by 'go-structures'. One may say that inertia has replaced the dynamism of the gospel and of participation in the mission of God.[11]

Further, our static, inflexible, self-centred structures are 'heretical structures' because they embody a heretical doctrine of the church.

Some zealous churches organize an overfull programme of church-based activities. Something is arranged for every night of the week. On Monday night the committees meet, and on Tuesday night the fellowship groups. On Wednesday night the Bible study takes place, and on Thursday night the prayer meeting. Even on Friday and Saturday evenings other good causes occupy people's time and energy. Such churches give the impression that their main goal is to keep their members out of mischief! Certainly they have neither time nor opportunity to get into mischief since they are busily engaged in the church every single night of the week!

But such a crowded, church-centred programme, admirable as it may look at first sight, has many drawbacks and dangers. To begin with, it is detrimental to Christian family life. Marriages break up and families disintegrate because father and/or mother are seldom at home. It also inhibits church members from getting involved in the local community because they are preoccupied with the local church. It thus contradicts an essential part of the church's identity, namely its 'worldliness'. As Bishop Richard Wilke of the United Methodist Church in the United States has put it, 'our structure has become an end in itself, not a means of saving the world'.[12] In that case it is a heretical structure.

I sometimes wonder (although I exaggerate in order to make my point) if it would not be very healthy for church members to meet only on Sundays (for worship, fellowship and teaching) and not at all midweek. Then we would gather on Sundays and scatter for the rest of the week. We would come to Christ for worship and go for Christ in mission. And in that rhythm of Sunday–weekday, gathering–scattering, coming–going and worship–mission the church would express its holy worldliness, and its structure would conform to its double identity.

How, then, should the local church organize itself? Ideally, it seems to me, every five or ten years each church should conduct a survey in order to evaluate itself and especially to discover how far its structures reflect its identity. In fact, it should conduct two surveys, one of the local community and the other of the local church, in order to learn how far the church is penetrating the community for Christ. This idea was recently taken up in

Britain by ACUPA (the Archbishop's Commission on Urban Priority Areas), whose influential report was entitled *Faith in the City*. It recommended what it called a 'local church audit', consisting of both 'the church profile' ('to build up an accurate picture of the local church') and 'the parish profile' ('to build up an accurate picture of the parish').[13] Perhaps I could take these in the opposite order:

A local community survey

Each church is set in a particular situation, and needs to become familiar with it in all its particularity. A questionnaire will need to be drawn up. Here are some of the questions which it will probably include:

1. What sort of people live in our parish or locality? What is their ethnic origin, nationality, religion, culture, media preference, and work? What proportions are there of normal families, single-parent families, single people, senior citizens, young people? What are the area's main social needs, relating to housing, employment, poverty, education?
2. Has the locality any centres of education, whether schools, colleges, adult education centres, or playgroups?
3. What places of business are found in it? Factories, farms, offices, shops, or studios? Is there significant unemployment?
4. Where do the people live? Do they occupy houses or flats, and do they own or rent them? Are there any hotels, hostels, student residences, apartment blocks, or homes for senior citizens?
5. Where do people congregate when they are at leisure? Café or restaurant, pub or disco, shopping mall, youth club or other clubs, bingo hall, concert hall, theatre or cinema, sports ground, park or street corner?
6. What public services are situated locally? Police, fire brigade, prison, hospital, public library, other social services?
7. Are there other religious buildings – church or chapel, synagogue, mosque, temple, or Christian Science reading room?
8. Has the community changed in the last ten years, and what changes can be forecast during the next ten?

A local church survey

In this second survey probing questions will need to be asked. Is the church in reality organized only for itself, for its own survival and convenience, and for the preservation of its privileges? Is it organized to serve itself, or to serve God and the community? What are its cherished traditions and conventions which unnecessarily separate it from the community? The questionnaire might include the following areas:

1. *The church building.* Church members tend to be most interested in its *interior* (its beauty, comfort and amenities). But we also need to walk round it and look at it through the eyes of an *outsider:* What image does it present? Is it a fortress (dark, forbidding and austere), or is it bright, inviting and welcoming?

   As an illustration, let me mention visiting the huge central square of the capital city of a Latin American republic. In the middle was the statue of the national hero, who had rescued the country at the beginning of the last century from the Spanish *conquistadores.* One side of the square was entirely occupied by the Roman Catholic cathedral. I tried to get in, but it was closed. On the steps leading up to its main door, however, were three human beings – a drunk who had vomited copiously, a blind beggar selling matches, and a prostitute who was offering herself to passers-by in broad daylight. A drunk, a beggar and a prostitute, three symbols of human tragedy, and behind them a locked cathedral, which seemed to be saying 'Keep out! We don't want you.' I realize that there may have been good reasons why the cathedral was closed. My concern is with the 'vibes' which were given off by that scene.

   A critical look at the inside of the church building will be necessary too, especially through the eyes of non-Christian visitors – its decoration and furniture, lighting and heating, its noticeboards, posters, bookstall and leaflets.

2. *The church services.* As with the first-century Jewish synagogue, so with the twentieth-century Christian church, there are 'Godfearers' on the edge of every congregation, who are attracted but not yet committed to Christ. Are our services exclusively for the committed, designed only for the initiated, and therefore mumbo jumbo to outsiders? Or do we remember the fringe members and non-members who may be present? What about the forms of service, the liturgy and language, the music (words, tunes and instruments), the seating, and the dress of both clergy and congregation? We need to ask ourselves what vibrations all these things give out.

3. *The church membership.* Is our membership mobilized for mission? Or is our church so clericalized (*i.e.* clergy-dominated) as to make this impossible? Has it grasped the New Testament teaching about the 'every-member ministry of the body of Christ'? Or is it less a body than a pyramid, with the clergy at the pinnacle and the lay people in their serried ranks of inferiority at the base? Are the members of the church also members of the community? Or are they either confined to church activities or practising a commuter-Christianity (travelling long distances to church), which makes local involvement difficult, even artificial?

4. *The church programme.* Do we imprison our members in the church? Or do we deliberately release at least some of them (including leaders) from church commitments in order to encourage them to be active for Christ in the community, and then support them with our interest and prayers as they do so? Do we ensure that the biblical truth of the double identity of the church is taught and embodied, and that training is available for those who want to commit themselves to Christian service and witness?

The two surveys (of community and church) will need to be studied by the church leadership (clergy and lay) both separately and in relation to each other. Out of this reflection will grow a strategy for mission. The leadership (preferably with others who may wish to be involved) will set both long-term and short-term goals, and establish a list of priorities. They may decide that the church is suffering from a false self-image and needs above all else some biblical teaching on its holy worldliness and on the implications of this for mission; or that a training programme must be arranged to equip members for evangelism; or that church-based activities should be reduced in order to increase members' involvement in the community. It might be decided to restructure radically the church building, decor, seating or services; or to organize a general visitation of the area, if possible in co-operation with other local churches; or to form specialist groups to penetrate particular, secular segments of the locality. For example, a group of committed young people could adopt a local disco, not in order to make occasional evangelistic raids into it, but between them (in pairs) to visit it regularly over a long period, in order to make friends with the other young people who congregate there. Again, the church may decide to arrange home meetings for neighbours, or a series of apologetic lectures in a local and neutral building, or regular guest services with an evangelistic thrust, to which members would be encouraged to bring their friends. Or the church may determine to take up some special social need in the area, which has surfaced during the surveys, and encourage a group to study it and then recommend action. All such decisions will be designed to help the church to identify with the community, and to develop structures which facilitate an authentically incarnational mission.

The church must express itself

The message of the church

It is not enough for the local church to understand itself and organize itself accordingly; it must also articulate its message. For evangelism, at its simplest and most basic, is sharing the evangel. So in order to define evangelism we must also define the good news.

There can be no doubt that the essence of the gospel is Jesus Christ himself. It would be impossible to preach the Christian good news without talking about Jesus. So we read that Philip, speaking to the Ethiopian, 'told him the good news about Jesus',[14] and that the apostle Paul described himself as 'set apart for the gospel of God ... regarding his Son ...'[15] Moreover, in bearing witness to Jesus we must speak above all of his death and resurrection. To quote Paul again in his famous summary of the apostolic gospel, 'What I received I passed on to you as of first importance: that Christ died for our sins according to the Scriptures, that he was buried, that he was raised on the third day according to the Scriptures, and that he appeared ...'[16] We simply do not share the gospel if we do not declare God's love in the gift of his Son to live our life, to die for our sins and to rise again, together with his offer through Jesus Christ, to all who repent and believe, of a new life of forgiveness and freedom, and of membership in his new society. The Anglican primates' recommended definition includes these essentials.

But how shall we formulate this good news in our world's increasingly pluralistic societies, in such a way that it resonates with them and makes sense? There are two opposite extremes to avoid.

The first extreme I will call *total fixity*. Some Christian people seem to be in bondage to words and formulae, and so become prisoners of a gospel stereotype. They wrap up their message in a nice, neat package; and they tape, label and price-tag it as if it were destined for the supermarket. Then, unless their favourite phraseology is used (whether the kingdom of God, or the blood of Jesus, or human liberation, or being born again, or justification by faith, or the cosmic lordship of Christ), they roundly declare that the gospel has not been preached. What these people seem not to have noticed is the rich diversity of gospel formulation which is found in the New Testament itself. The options I have listed are all biblical, but because all of them contain an element of imagery, and each image is different, it is impossible to fuse them into a single, simple concept. So it is perfectly legitimate to develop one or other of them, according to what seems most appropriate to the occasion.

The opposite extreme is *total fluidity*. Some years ago I heard a British bishop say: 'There's no such thing as the gospel in a vacuum. You don't even know what the gospel is until you enter each particular situation. You have to enter the situation first, and then you discover the gospel when you're there.' Now if he meant that he wanted a gospel in context, not in vacuum, and that we need to relate the gospel sensitively to each person and situation, I am in full agreement with him; but to say that 'there is no such thing as the gospel in a vacuum' and that 'you discover it' in each situation is surely a serious overstatement. For what the advocates of total fluidity seem not to have noticed is that, alongside the New Testament's rich diversity of gospel formulation, there is also an underlying unity (especially regarding the saving death and resurrection of Jesus) which binds the different formulations together. As Professor A. M. Hunter wrote, 'there is ... a deep unity in the New Testament, which dominates and transcends all the diversities'.[17]

Is there a middle way? Yes, there is. Both the extremes which I have described express important concerns which need to be preserved. The first ('total fixity') rightly emphasizes that the gospel has been revealed by God and received by us. It is both a *paradosis* (a tradition to be preserved) and a *parathēkē* (a deposit to be guarded). We did not invent it, and we have no liberty to edit it or tamper with it. The second ('total fluidity') rightly emphasizes that the gospel must be contextualized, that is to say, related appropriately to each particular person or situation. Otherwise it will be perceived as irrelevant.

Somehow, then, we have to learn to combine these two proper concerns. We have to wrestle with the dialectic between the ancient Word and the modern world, between what has been given and what has been left open, between content and context, Scripture and culture, revelation and contextualization. We need more fidelity to Scripture and more sensitivity to people. Not one without the other, but both.

The church must be itself

The life of the church

The church is supposed to be God's new society, the living embodiment of the gospel, a sign of the kingdom of God, a demonstration of what human community looks like when it comes under his gracious rule.

In other words, God's purpose is that the good news of Jesus Christ is set forth visually as well as verbally, or in the language of the primates' definition, that it be made known 'by word and deed'. Every educator knows how much easier it is for human beings to learn through what they see and experience than through what they hear. Or rather, word and deed, hearing and seeing, belong essentially together. This is certainly so in evangelism. People have to see with their own eyes that the gospel we preach has transformed us. As John Poulton put it, 'Christians ... need to look like what they are talking about. It is *people* who communicate primarily, not words or ideas ... What communicates now is basically personal authenticity.'[18] Conversely, if our life contradicts our message, our evangelism will lack all credibility. Indeed, the greatest hindrance to evangelism is lack of integrity in the evangelist.

No text has helped me to understand the implications of this for the life of the local church more than 1 John 4:12, 'No-one has ever seen God; but if we love one another, God lives in us and his love is made complete in us.' God is invisible. Nobody has ever seen him. All that human beings have ever seen of him is glimpses of his glory, of the outshining of his being.

Now the invisibility of God is a great problem for faith. It was so for the Jews in the Old Testament. Their heathen neighbours laughed at them for actually worshipping an invisible God. 'You say you believe in God?' they taunted them. 'Where is he? Come to our temples, and we will show you our gods. They have ears and eyes, hands and feet, and mouths and noses too. But where is your God? We can't see him. Ha, ha, ha!' The Jews found this ridicule hard to bear. Hence the complaint of psalmist and prophet: 'Why do the nations say, "Where is their God?"'[19] Of course Israel had its own apologetic. The idols of the heathen were nothing, only the work of human hands. True, they had mouths, but they could not speak, ears but could not hear, noses but could not smell, hands but could not feel, and feet but could not walk.[20] Yahweh, on the other hand, although (being spirit) he had no mouth, had spoken; although he had no ears, he listened to Israel's prayers; and although he had no hands, he had both created the universe and redeemed his people by his mighty power. At the same time, the people of God longed that he would make himself known to the nations, so that they might see him and believe in him.

The same problem of an unseen God challenges us today, especially young people who have been brought up on the scientific method. They are taught to examine everything by their five senses. Anything which is not amenable to empirical investigation they are told to suspect and even reject. So could it ever be reasonable to believe in an invisible God? 'Let us only see him,' they say, 'and we will believe.'

How, then, has God solved the problem of his own invisibility? First and foremost he has done so by sending his Son into the world. 'No-one has ever seen God; the only Son, who is in the bosom of the Father, he has made him known.'[21] Consequently Jesus could say, 'Anyone who has seen me has seen the Father,'[22] and Paul could describe him as 'the [visible] image of the invisible God'.[23]

To this people tend to reply: 'That is truly wonderful, but it happened nearly 2,000 years ago. Is there no way in which the invisible God makes himself visible *today*?' Yes, there is. 'No-one has ever seen God.'[24] John begins this verse in his first letter with the identical sentence which he has used in the prologue to his Gospel.[25] But now he concludes the sentence differently. In the Gospel he wrote that 'the only Son ... has made him known'. In the Epistle he writes that 'if we love one another, God lives in us and his love is made complete in us'. Because of John's deliberate repetition of the same statement, this can only mean one thing. The invisible

God, who once made himself visible in Christ, now makes himself visible in Christians, if *we love one another.*

God is love in his essential being, and has revealed his love in the gift of his Son to live and die for us. Now he calls us to be a community of love, loving each other in the intimacy of his family – especially across the barriers of age and sex, race and rank – and loving the world he loves in its alienation, hunger, poverty and pain. It is through the quality of our loving that God makes himself visible today.

We cannot proclaim the gospel of God's love with any degree of integrity if we do not exhibit it in our love for others. Perhaps nothing is so damaging to the cause of Christ as a church which is either torn apart by jealousy, rivalry, slander and malice, or preoccupied with its own selfish concerns. Such churches urgently need to be radically renewed in love. As one of the group reports of the 1978 Lambeth Conference put it, 'Mission without renewal is hypocrisy.' It is only if we love one another that the world will believe that Jesus is the Christ and that we are his disciples.[26]

Here, then, are the four main prerequisites for evangelism through the local church. First, the church must understand itself (theologically), grasping its double identity. Secondly, it must organize itself (structurally), developing a mission strategy which reflects its double identity. Thirdly, it must express itself (verbally), articulating its gospel in a way which is both faithful to Scripture and relevant to the contemporary world. And fourthly, it must be itself (morally and spiritually), becoming so completely transformed into a community of love that through it the invisible God again makes himself visible to the world.

Notes

[1] This chapter was written before Michael Green's mammoth book *Evangelism through the Local Church* (Hodder and Stoughton, 1990) was published and came into my hands. Michael Green is a rare combination of theologian and evangelist, and has had an unusually wide and varied experience of evangelism. With that rollicking infectious enthusiasm with which he always writes, he divides his theme into four parts: (1) 'Issues for the Church' (the nature, necessity, basis and sphere of evangelism in a multi-faith society), (2) 'The Secular Challenge' (four valuable chapters on apologetics), (3) 'Church-based Evangelism' (evangelistic preaching, personal evangelism, missions and other methods), and (4) 'Practical Appendices' (courses for enquirers, discovery groups for new Christians, the training of teams, the use of drama, leading worship *etc.*). Here are nearly 600 pages of guidance – theological, personal and practical – from one whose head, heart and hands are together committed to the evangelistic outreach of the local church.

[2] Jn. 4:4–15.

[3] Acts 8:26–35.

[4] Acts 14:14–18.

[5] Acts 17:22–23.

[6] 1 Pet. 2:5, 9.

[7] 1 Thes. 1:5, 6, 8.

[8] Alec Vidler, *Essays in Liberality* (SCM, 1957), ch. 5.

[9] Jn. 17:18; 20:21.

[10] Michael Ramsey, *Images Old and New* (SPCK, 1963), p. 14.

[11] *The Church for Others* (WCC, Geneva, 1967), pp. 7, 18–19.

[12] Richard Wilke, *And Are We Yet Alive?* (Abingdon, 1986).

[13] *Faith in the City* (Church House, 1985).

[14] Acts 8:35.

[15] Rom. 1:1, 3.

[16] 1 Cor. 15:3–5.

[17] A. M. Hunter, *The Unity of the New Testament* (SCM, 1943).

[18] John Poulton, *A Today Sort of Evangelism* (Lutterworth, 1972), pp. 60–61, 79.

[19] *E.g.* Ps. 115:2.

[20] *E.g.* Ps. 115:4–7.

[21] Jn. 1:18 (RSV).

[22] Jn. 14:9.

[23] Col. 1: 15.

[24] 1 Jn. 4:12.

[25] Jn. 1:18.

[26] Jn. 13:35; 17:21.

Dimensions of church renewal

The twentieth-century church has been characterized by a whole series of renewal movements, each focusing on a particular aspect of ecclesiastical life. At least six may be mentioned.

First, at the beginning of the century the missionary movement received fresh impetus at the World Missionary Conference in Edinburgh in 1910. The church growth movement founded by Dr Donald McGavran, and the Lausanne movement with its congresses on world evangelization (Lausanne 1974 and Manila 1989), have given it considerable further stimulus.

Secondly, there was the biblical theology movement, whose antecedent was the emphasis laid by Karl Barth and Emil Brunner between the wars on the 'otherness' of God and his Word. It flourished between 1945 and 1960 under biblical scholars like Gerhard von Rad (Old Testament) and Oscar Cullmann (New Testament), who stressed the inner unity of Scripture.

Next, the ecumenical movement, though stemming from the 1910 Edinburgh Conference, took shape in the formation of the World Council of Churches in Amsterdam in 1948 and has laid its stress on the need to unite the churches in their witness to the world.

Fourthly, the post-war liturgical movement, specially (though not exclusively) in the Roman Catholic Church, aimed to modernize the eucharistic worship of the congregation. The Second Vatican Council gave it a further boost.

Fifthly, the neo-pentecostal or charismatic movement has sought to incorporate the distinctive emphases of the pentecostal churches within the mainline denominations, and has been concerned for the restoration of spiritual power and spiritual gifts to the body of Christ.

Sixthly, the social justice movement, ranging from the cluster of liberation theologies to the recovery of the evangelical social conscience, has sought to balance the church's eternal and other-worldly preoccupations with its temporal, this-worldly responsibilities.

Thus mission, theology, unity, worship, power and justice are six legitimate Christian concerns, each of which has gathered round it a devoted clientele of protagonists. Yet the result has been an unhealthily fragmented agenda. What seems to be needed is a holistic or integrated vision of renewal in every dimension of the church's life.

The Roman Catholic word for this, at least since Vatican II (1963-65), has been *aggiornamento*, the process of bringing the church up to date in order to meet the challenges of the modern world. It implies that the world is changing rapidly and that, if the church is to survive, it must keep pace with this change, although without either compromising its own standards or conforming to the world's.

Protestants use a different vocabulary to describe the continuously needed restoring and refreshing of the church. Our two favourite words are 'reform', indicating the kind of reformation of faith and life according to Scripture which took place in the sixteenth century, and 'revival', denoting an altogether supernatural visitation of a church or community by God, bringing conviction, repentance, confession, the conversion of sinners and the recovery of backsliders. 'Reformation' usually stresses the power of the Word of God, and 'revival' the power of the Spirit of God, in his work of restoring the church. Perhaps we should keep the word 'renewal' to describe a movement which combines revival by God's Spirit with reformation by his Word. Since the Word is the Spirit's sword, there is bound to be something lopsided about contemplating either without the other.

For an integrated vision of continuous renewal, we cannot do better than reflect on Jesus' prayer for his people recorded in John 17. It is a mistake to regard this chapter as an exclusively ecumenical text, concentrating on Christian unity. Unity is indeed included, but the concern Jesus expressed in his prayer was considerably wider than this.

John 17, without doubt, is one of the profoundest chapters of the Bible. Whole books have been written to expound it. Thomas Manton, for example, the seventeenth-century British Puritan, who for a while was Oliver Cromwell's chaplain, preached a course of forty-five sermons on John 17.[1] Then the Irish clergyman Marcus Rainsford, who occupied the pulpit of St John's Church, Belgrave Square in London from 1866 to 1897, preached a course of forty-one sermons on the same chapter.[2] Both courses of sermons were published, and both books ran to more than 450 pages; so what can we hope to learn in one brief chapter? There are depths here we will never fathom; all we can do is paddle in the shallows. Here are heights we cannot scale; we can only climb the foothills.

Nevertheless, we must persevere. For if the upper-room discourse (John 13 – 17) is the temple of Scripture, John 17 is its inner sanctuary or holy of holies. Here we are introduced into the presence, mind and heart of God. We are permitted to eavesdrop, as the Son communes with the Father. We need to take off our shoes, since this is holy ground.

Jesus prays first for himself (verses 1–5), as he approaches the cross; secondly for his apostles (verses 6–19), to whom he has revealed the Father, and who are gathered round him as he prays; and thirdly for the whole church present and future (verses 20–26), consisting of all those who will believe in him through the apostles' teaching. We will concentrate on the second and third sections (verses 6–26).

As a matter of fact, Jesus does not begin his prayer for his people until the end of verse 11. Before this, for five and a half verses (verses 6–11a) he describes the people he is going to pray for. It is quite an elaborate description and, although it refers primarily to the apostles, it delineates them rather as ordinary disciples than in their distinctive apostolic ministry. The description has three parts.

First, *they belong to Christ.* Three times Jesus repeats the truth that the Father has 'given' them to him out of the world (verses 6 and 9), so that in consequence they belong to him.

Secondly, *they know the Father.* For if the Father has given them to the Son, the Son has given them a revelation of the Father. This too is repeated. 'I have revealed you [literally, 'your name'] to those whom you gave me out of the world' (verse 6). Also, 'I gave them the words you gave me and they accepted them' (verse 8). Of course this revelation of God's name, this gift of God's words, was made in the first instance to the apostles, but from them it has been passed on to all Christ's disciples.

Thirdly, *they live in the world.* 'I will remain in the world no longer,' Jesus says, 'but they are still in the world, and I am coming to you' (verse 11a). Although they have been given to Christ 'out of the world' (verse 6), they nevertheless remain 'in the world' (verse 11a) out of which they have been taken. They are to be spiritually distinct, but not socially segregated. Jesus leaves them behind as his representatives or ambassadors.

Here, then, is Jesus' threefold characterization of his people, beginning with his apostles, but including all later disciples, reaching even to us. First, the Father has given us to the Son. Secondly, the Son has revealed to us the Father. Thirdly, we live in the world. It is this threefold orientation (to the Father, to the Son and to the world) which makes us the 'holy' (that is, distinct) people we are. We live in the world as a people who know God and belong to Christ, and therefore (it is implied) have a unique mission to make him known.

What, then, does Christ pray for his people whom he has so carefully described? The burden of his intercession consists of only two words, which are repeated. 'Holy Father, *protect them* ... My prayer is ... that you *protect them* from the evil one' (verses 11b and 15). It is a prayer that the holy Father will keep us the holy people we are, that he will protect and preserve us from any and every evil influence which might spoil the unique position he has given us. It is a prayer that we may be kept true to who we are, to our essential Christian identity, as a people who know God, belong to Christ and live in the world.

More particularly, Jesus prays that his people may have four characteristics, namely truth, holiness, mission and unity.

Truth (verses 11–13)

A literal translation of verse 11b would be 'Keep them in your name', but commentators are not agreed how to translate the preposition 'in'. The NIV renders it 'Protect them by the power of your name'. Yet the context seems to require that God's name is not so much the power by which, as the sphere in which, the disciples are to be kept. I think, then, that the Jerusalem Bible is correct to translate: 'Keep those you have given me true to your name.' The revelation of God's name was 'the enclosing wall, as it were, within which they were to be kept'.[3] For God's name is God himself, who he is, his being and his character. This the Father has revealed to the Son, and the Son in his turn has revealed to the apostles (verse 6). During his earthly ministry Jesus has kept them in it (verse 12, literally). Now, however, he is about to leave the world. So he prays that the Father will keep them loyal to the name he has revealed to them, 'so that they may be one as we are one' (end of verse 11). That is, the major means to their unity will be their loyalty to God's truth revealed in and through Christ.

Truth, then, was the first concern for his church which Jesus expressed in his prayer. He spoke of revelation, of the disclosure by him of God's otherwise hidden name. He made plain his longing that his people would be loyal to this revelation, and that their unity would be based on their common faithfulness to it. Instead, today, I fear that some contemporary church leaders are guilty of serious unfaithfulness. A few are brash enough to deny the fundamentals both of the historic Christian faith and of traditional Christian morality, while others seem as blushingly unsure of themselves and of their beliefs as an adolescent teenager.

There is no possibility of the church being thoroughly renewed until and unless it is renewed in its faith, in its commitment to God's revealed truth in Jesus Christ and in the full biblical testimony to him. Nor is there any chance of the church recovering its unity until it recovers the only authentic basis for unity, which is truth. Jesus prayed first for the truth of the church; we should do the same. For God intends his church to be 'the pillar and foundation of the truth'.[4]

Holiness (verses 1–16)

Jesus prayed that the Father would keep his people not only true to his name, but also 'from the evil one' (verse 15). That is, he desired on the one hand that they would be preserved from error and in truth, and on the other hand from evil and in holiness. The church's final destiny, Paul was later to declare, is to be presented to Christ 'as a radiant church, without stain or wrinkle or any other blemish, but holy and blameless'.[5] But the church's holiness must begin now. So what is meant by 'holiness'?

All down history the church has tended to go to extremes, as we considered in the last chapter. Sometimes, in its proper determination to be holy, it has withdrawn from the world and lost contact with it. At other times, in its equally proper determination not to lose contact, it has conformed to the world and become virtually indistinguishable from it. But Christ's vision for the church's holiness is neither withdrawal nor conformity.

Withdrawal was the way of the Pharisees. Anxious to apply the law to the details of everyday life, they had a false understanding of holiness, imagining that mere contact with evil and evil people would bring contamination. And a form of Christian pharisaism or separatism has lingered in the church. It has often been due to a passionate longing for holiness and a zeal to preserve Christian culture from destruction by the wicked world. These motives persuaded the hermits to flee into the desert in the fourth century, and led to the development of medieval monasticism. But, noble as the motives of monks and hermits often were, the kind of monasticism which entailed withdrawal from the world must be pronounced a betrayal of Christ. So is the kind of modern piety which imprisons Christians in a ghetto-like fellowship and effectively cuts them off from non-Christians. For Jesus specifically prayed that, although he wanted his disciples to be protected from the evil one, he did not want them to be taken out of the world (verse 15).

If 'withdrawal' was the way of the Pharisees, and even more of the Essenes who took refuge in their desert communities to pray and wait for the kingdom of God to come, 'conformity' was the way of the Sadducees. Belonging to wealthy, aristocratic families, they collaborated with the Romans and sought to maintain the political status quo. This compromising tradition also persisted in the early church, and still survives today. The motive for it can again be good, namely the resolve to break down barriers between the church and the world, and to be the friends of publicans and sinners, as Jesus was.[6] But he was also 'set apart from sinners'[7] in his values and standards.

In place of these two extreme positions Jesus calls us to live 'in the world' (verse 11), while remaining like himself 'not of the world' (verse 14), that is, neither belonging to it, nor imitating its ways. This is the 'holy worldliness' of the church, about which I wrote in the last chapter, in connection with the church's double identity. We are neither to give in, nor to opt out. Instead, we are to stay in and stand firm, like a rock in a mountain stream, like a rose blooming in mid-winter, like a lily growing in a manure heap.

Mission (verses 17–19)

There are fifteen references to 'the world' in Jesus' prayer, which indicates that one of his main concerns was how his people would relate to the world, that is, to non-Christian society or godless secularism. He indicated that they have been given to him out of the world (verse 6), but were not to be taken out of it (verse 15); that they were still living in the world (verse 11), but were not to be of the world (verse 14b); that they would be hated by the world (verse 14a), but were nevertheless sent into the world (verse 18). This is the multi-faceted relationship of the church to the world: living in it, not belonging to it, hated by it and sent into it.

Perhaps the best way to grasp this is that, in place of 'withdrawal' and 'conformity', which are wrong attitudes to the world, the right one is 'mission'. Indeed, the church's mission in the world is possible only if it avoids the two false tracks. If we withdraw from the world, mission is obviously impossible, since we have lost contact. Equally, if we conform to the world, mission is impossible, since we have lost our cutting edge.

It is particularly striking that, although we live 'in' the world (verse 11), we nevertheless need to be sent 'into' it (verse 18). But that is the case. It is all too possible for Christian people to live in the world without having any share in Christ's mission.

Christ's prayer for his people here is that the Father will 'sanctify' us by his word of truth (verse 17), indeed that we may be 'truly sanctified' like Christ who sanctified himself for us (verse 19). What kind of sanctification is in mind, we are obliged to ask, if it is one in which Christ himself participated? How can the sinless Christ be said to have sanctified himself? The answer is surely that sanctification has two complementary aspects, negative and positive. To be sanctified is to be separated *from* evil in all its forms. This is what we usually think about when the word 'sanctification' is used. But to be sanctified is also to be set apart *for* the particular ministry to which God has called us. It is in this sense that Jesus set himself apart for us, namely to come into the world to seek and to save us. We too have been 'sanctified', or set apart for our mission in the world. In fact, we can be described as 'separated from the world to be of service to the world'.[8]

In verse 18 (as in John 20:21) Jesus draws a deliberate parallel between his mission and ours: 'As you sent me into the world, I have sent them into the world.' In what sense, then, did Jesus intend his mission to be the model of ours? There are substantial differences, of course. His being sent into the world entailed both the incarnation and the atonement, whereas we are not God that we could 'become flesh' or die for sinners. Nevertheless, the fact that we are sent into the world like him will shape our understanding of mission. It tells us that mission involves being under the authority of Christ (we are sent, we did not volunteer); renouncing privilege, safety, comfort and aloofness, as we actually enter other people's worlds, as he entered ours; humbling ourselves to become servants, as he did;[9] bearing the pain of being hated by the hostile world into which we are sent (verse 14); and sharing the good news with people where they are. I shall have more to say about Christ as the model of mission in chapter 21, 'The Christology of mission'.

Unity (verses 20–26)

Jesus' prophetic eyes now peered into the future, into the post-apostolic era. He saw the coming generations of his disciples who would not have seen or heard him in the flesh, as the apostles had done, but who would believe in him through their teaching: 'My prayer is not for them [the apostles] alone. I pray also for those who will believe in me through their message' (verse 20). This means every Christian of every age and place, including us. True, we may have come to believe in Jesus through the witness of our parents, or of a pastor, evangelist, teacher or friend. Yet their witness was a secondary witness, an endorsement from their own experience of the primary witness of the apostles. The apostles were the eyewitnesses, specially chosen by Jesus to be with him, so that they could bear witness to what they had seen and heard. There is only one authentic Christ, the Christ of the apostolic witness (now preserved in the New Testament), and all believers since the apostolic age have believed in Jesus 'through their message'.

What, then, does Jesus desire for all his believing people throughout the world and the centuries? There can be no doubt about this because he expresses it three times:

> verse 21a: 'that all of them may be one'
> verse 22b: 'that they may be one'
> verse 23b: 'that they may become perfectly one' (RSV)

These are well-known petitions. What is usually not so well known or understood is the nature of the unity for which Christ prayed. He stressed two aspects of it.

First, he prayed that his people would enjoy *unity with the apostles.* Consider carefully what is recorded in verse 20 and at the beginning of verse 21: 'My prayer is not for them alone. I pray also for those who will believe in me through their message, that all of them may be one.' We have already noted that Jesus distinguishes between two groups of people. They are conveniently designated in RSV and NEB 'these' (the little band of apostles gathered round him) and 'those' (the huge company of all subsequent believers), or the teachers and the taught. He then prays that 'all of them', which must mean 'these' and 'those' together, 'may be one'. In other words, Jesus' prayer was first and foremost that there might be a historical continuity between the apostles and the post-apostolic church, that the church's faith might not change with the changing years but remain recognizably the same, and that the church of every generation might merit the epithet 'apostolic' because of its loyalty to the message and mission of the apostles. Christian unity begins, then, as unity with the apostles (through the New Testament which makes their teaching available to us); without this, church unity would not be distinctively Christian.

Secondly, Jesus prayed that his people would enjoy *unity with the Father and the Son.* Although the punctuation of verse 21 is disputed, most English versions regard its second clause as beginning a new sentence. We might render it as follows: 'Father, just as you are in me and I am in you, [I pray that they] may also be in us, that the world may believe …' The implications of this petition are staggering. For Jesus prays that the union of his people with God may be comparable to the unity of the Father and the Son with each other in the Godhead. He goes on in verse 23, 'I in them and thou in me, that they may become perfectly one' (RSV).

So then, the Christian unity for which Christ prayed was not primarily unity with each other, but unity with the apostles (a common truth) and unity with the Father and the Son (a common life). The visible, structural unity of the church is a proper goal. Yet it will be pleasing to God only if it is the visible expression of something deeper, namely unity in truth and in life. In our ecumenical concern, therefore, nothing is more important than the quest for more apostolic truth and more divine life through the Holy Spirit. As William Temple put it, 'the way to the union of Christendom does not lie through committee-rooms, though there is a task of formulation to be done there. It lies through personal union with the Lord so deep and real as to be comparable with his union with the Father.'[10]

It is this kind of unity (a shared truth and life) which will bring the world to believe in Jesus (verses 21 and 23). Indeed, the main reason why Jesus prays for the unity of his people is 'in order that' the world may believe in Jesus' divine origin and mission. He prays that all who will in future 'believe' in him (verse 20) may enjoy such unity of truth and life that the world may 'believe' in him too. Thus faith begets faith, and believers multiply.

In the final verses of his prayer (24–26) Jesus looks beyond history to eternity, for it is only in heaven that the unity of his people will be brought to perfection. They will see his glory (verse 24), and the end-result of the Son's revelation of the Father will be that they experience in themselves both the very same love which the Father has for the Son and the indwelling of the Son himself (verse 26). This ultimate unity, comprehending the Father, the Son and the church in love, is certainly beyond our imagination, but is not beyond our humble and ardent desire.

Jesus' prayer, then, is much more comprehensive than is commonly realized. It is a prayer for the church's truth ('keep them in your name'), holiness ('keep them from the evil one'), mission ('sanctify them … I have sent them into the world') and unity ('that they may be one').

In a notable intervention at the Third Assembly of the World Council of Churches in New Delhi (1961), Archbishop Michael Ramsey said: 'The seventeenth chapter of St John describes Jesus praying not only that his disciples may be one, but also that they may become holy and that they may realize the truth. Unity, holiness, truth go together.'[11] Even then he omitted the fourth topic, mission!

One of the tragedies of the contemporary church is its tendency to atomize this holistic vision of Christ, and to select one or other of his concerns to the exclusion of the rest. But, as Michael Ramsey also said at the New Delhi assembly, 'a movement which concentrates on unity as an isolated concept, can mislead the world and mislead us, as indeed would a movement which had the exclusive label of holiness or the exclusive label of truth'.

The major preoccupation of the twentieth-century church has been the search for structural unity, but often without a comparable quest for the truth and the life which constitute authentic unity and are the means by which it grows.

Others have been preoccupied with truth (doctrinal orthodoxy), sometimes becoming dry, harsh and unloving in the process, forgetting that truth is to be adorned with the beauty of holiness.

Holiness seems of paramount importance to others, that is, the state of the church's interior life. But such people sometimes withdraw into a self-centred piety, forgetting that we have been called out of the world in order to be sent back into it, which is 'mission'.

So mission becomes the obsession of a fourth group, who, however, sometimes forget that the world will come to believe in Jesus only when his people are one in truth, holiness and love.

Truth, holiness, mission and unity belonged together in the prayer of Jesus, and they need to be kept together in our quest for the church's renewal today. I think we may detect them in the earliest Spirit-filled church

in Jerusalem, since we are told in Acts 2:42 and 47 that 'they devoted themselves to the apostles' teaching' (truth), 'to the fellowship' (unity), and 'to
the breaking of bread and to prayer' (worship expressing their holiness),
while 'the Lord added to their number daily those who were being saved'
(mission). It seems to me legitimate also to see the same characteristics in
the four traditional 'notes' or 'marks' of the church, according to the Nicene
Creed, namely that it is 'one, holy, catholic and apostolic'. For 'catholic'
includes the concept of embracing all truth, and apostolic' includes the
vision of being committed to the apostolic mission. It is important that we
do not separate what God has joined. Instead, we must seek the renewal of
the church in all four dimensions simultaneously, so that it faithfully guards
the revelation which has once for all been entrusted to it, becomes sanctified and unified by this truth which it preserves, and goes out boldly into
the world on its God-given mission of witness and service.

Notes

[1] Republished in 1958 by the Sovereign Grace Book club under the title *An Exposition of
John Seventeen.*

[2] Republished in 1950 by Moody Press under the title *Our Lord Prays for His Own.*

[3] Charles Ross, *The Inner Sanctuary, An Exposition of John 13–17* (1888; Banner of Truth,
1967), p. 216.

[4] 1 Tim. 3:15.

[5] Eph. 5:27.

[6] Mt. 11:19 = Lk. 7:34.

[7] Heb. 7:26.

[8] Leon Morris, *The Gospel According to John*, in the New London Commentary on the New
Testament (Marshall, Morgan and Scott, 1971), p. 730.

[9] Phil. 2:7–8.

[10] William Temple, *Readings in St John's Gospel* (first published in two volumes, 1939 and
1940; Macmillan, 1947), p. 327.

[11] Michael Ramsey made the same point during the epilogue to his address on 'The Church,
its Scandal and Glory' during his mission in Oxford University in February 1960. His
addresses were published as *Introducing the Christian Faith* (1961; SCM, revised edition,
1970), p. 76.

SEVENTEEN

The church's pastors

It would be difficult to think about the life, mission and renewal of the church without giving thought to its ordained ministers. For it is plain from the New Testament that God has always intended his church to have some form of *episkopē*, that is, pastoral oversight. Moreover the condition of the church in every place depends very largely on the quality of the ministry it receives. As Richard Baxter put it: 'If God would but reform the ministry, and set them on their duties zealously and faithfully, the people would certainly be reformed. All churches either rise or fall as the ministry doth rise or fall, not in riches or worldly grandeur, but in knowledge, zeal and ability for their work.'[1]

Yet there is a great deal of contemporary confusion about the nature and function of ordained clergy. Are they priests, prophets, pastors, preachers or psychotherapists? Are they administrators, facilitators or social workers? Perhaps no more embarrassing exposure of this uncertainty has been made than David Hare's play *Racing Demon*, which won three Olivier Awards in 1990. It portrays four Anglican clergy in a team ministry in South London, together with the diocesan bishop of Southwark (the Rt Rev. Charlie Allen) and his suffragan bishop of Kingston (the Rt Rev. Gilbert Heffernan). Each has a different notion of the purpose of the ordained ministry. To Lionel Espy, the gentle and largely ineffective team rector, 'our job is mainly to learn. From ordinary, working people. We should try to understand and serve them.'[2] 'Mostly, in fact, it's just listening to the anger,' and like a punch-bag absorbing it.[3] In complete contrast, the young charismatic curate, Tony Ferris, is frighteningly self-confident. 'I have this incredible power,' he claims, which enables him to 'spread confidence' around him, but he does it at the expense of other people.[4]

The other characters are more modest in their expectations. The diocesan bishop emphasizes the administration of holy communion. 'Finally, that's what you're there for. As a priest you have only one duty. That's to put on a show.'[5] His suffragan, the episcopal diplomat *par excellence*, sees the heart of his job as 'preventing problems growing into issues'.[6] To Donald Bacon ('Streaky'), who sings tenor, gets drunk and describes himself as 'a happy priest', there are no complications. 'The whole thing's so clear. He's there. In people's happiness.'[7] Harry Henderson, the homosexual clergyman, is a trifle more ambitious. 'There is people as they are. And there is people as they could be. The priest's job is to try and yank the two a little bit closer.'[8] Meanwhile, the sincere, agnostic girl Frances Parnell sees the ordained ministry as the 'waste of a human being ... always to be dreaming'.[9]

This perplexity about the role of clergy is by no means recent, however. More than a century ago Mark Twain expressed it through his attractive character, Huckleberry Finn. Huck told Joanna that in her uncle Harvey's church in Sheffield there were 'no less than seventeen' clergy, although (he added) 'they don't *all* of 'em preach the same day – only *one* of 'em'.

'Well then,' Joanna responds, 'what does the rest of 'em do?'

'Oh, nothing much,' Huck explains. 'Loll around, pass the plate – and one thing or another. But mainly they don't do nothing.'

'Well, then,' cries Joanna in wide-eyed astonishment, 'what are they *for*?'

'Why, they're for *style*,' Huck replies. 'Don't you know nothing?'[10]

Contrary opinions have, in fact, been held about the importance of the ordained ministry. Some people, seeing clergy marginalized by secular society and the welfare state, and rejoicing in the recovery of Paul's vision of an every-member ministry in the body of Christ, question whether ordained ministers are necessary any longer and suggest that the church would be in a healthier condition without them.

Others react in the opposite way. Whether on theological or pragmatic grounds, they put clergy on a pedestal, or at least acquiesce when they put themselves there. Then, when the reins of ministry are entirely in their hands, the almost inevitable consequences are either clerical breakdown or lay frustration or both.

All down its long history the church has oscillated between these extremes of clericalism (clerical domination of the laity) and anticlericalism (lay disdain for the clergy). Yet the New Testament warns us against both tendencies. To the Corinthians who developed a personality cult of different apostles Paul expostulated: 'What [he deliberately used the neuter] do you think we are, that you pay such exaggerated deference to us? We are only servants, through whom God worked to bring you to faith.'[11] To others, however, who regarded their leaders with contempt, Paul wrote that they must 'respect' them and 'hold them in the highest regard in love because of their work'.[12] Again, 'Here is a trustworthy saying: If anyone sets his heart on being an overseer, he desires a noble task.'[13] Or 'to aspire to leadership is an honourable ambition' (NEB).

We must now return to the basic question what the nature and function of ordained clergy are. In general, the churches have given only two answers, according to whether they have seen the ministry as being directed primarily towards God or towards the church. On the one hand, there is the priestly model, in which the ministry is exercised towards God on behalf of the people. On the other hand, there is the pastoral model, in which the ministry is exercised towards the people on behalf of God.

The priestly model

The Roman Catholic and Orthodox churches see their clergy as priests, especially in relation to their role at the eucharist. Lutheran and Anglican churches have also traditionally called their clergy 'priests', but for a different reason. The Council of Trent affirmed that in the mass a true and propitiatory sacrifice is offered to God, and that the human priest who offers it represents the Christ who offers himself.[14] Moreover, the essence of this teaching was endorsed at the Second Vatican Council. Thus, priests are 'given the power of sacred Order to offer sacrifice ...'[15] 'They sacramentally offer the Sacrifice of Christ in a special way when they celebrate mass.'[16] True, they are said to represent the people of God, as well as representing Christ, when they do this. But the heart of their priesthood is still conceived as offering the eucharistic sacrifice.

Protestant Christians, who insist on subordinating all ecclesiastical traditions to the teaching of Scripture, cannot accept this. For the hard fact remains that the New Testament never calls Christian leaders 'priests' and never refers to the eucharist as a sacrifice which they offer. The word *hiereus*, a sacrificing priest, occurs many times in the New Testament. There is one reference to a pagan priest,[17] and there are several to the Jewish priests in the Gospels, the Acts and Hebrews. The word is also applied to the Lord Jesus, our great high priest, who offered himself once for all as a sacrifice for sins.[18] And fourthly it denotes Christian believers who are 'priests of God'.[19] This is 'the priesthood of all believers' on which the Reformers laid much emphasis. Collectively we are a royal and holy 'priesthood', who offer 'spiritual sacrifices acceptable to God through Jesus Christ'.[20] If we enquire what these sacrifices are, they will all come under the general rubric of the church's worship. In particular, they include our bodies,[21] our prayer, praise and penitence,[22] our gifts and good deeds,[23] our life laid down in God's service,[24] and our evangelism by which we present our converts as 'an offering acceptable to God'.[25] These eight sacrifices are offered to God by the whole church in its capacity as a holy priesthood. But not once is priestly language or imagery used of a particular group of Christian leaders who might correspond to the priests of the old covenant.

When we remember that the levitical priesthood had for centuries been central to Israel's life and worship, and still was in the Palestinian Judaism of Jesus' day, the fact that Christian leaders are never called or likened to priests must have been deliberate. Charles Hodge, the nineteenth-century Princeton theologian, put the matter forcibly:

> Every title of honour is lavished upon them [*sc.* Christian ministers]. They are called the bishops of souls, pastors, teachers, rulers, governors, the servants or ministers of God; stewards of the divine mysteries; watchmen, heralds, but never priests. As the sacred writers were Jews, to whom nothing was more familiar than the word priest, whose ministers of religion were constantly so denominated, the fact that they never once used the word, or any of its cognates, in reference to the ministers of the gospel ... is little less than miraculous. It is one of those cases in which the silence of Scripture speaks volumes.[26]

This being the case, it may at once be asked why in the sixteenth century some Reformed churches retained the word 'priest' as a designation of their ministers, including the Church of England. The answer is primarily one of etymology. The English word 'priest' was known to be derived from, and a contraction of, 'presbyter'. It therefore translated *presbyteros* ('elder'), not *hiereus* ('priest'). So 'priest' was kept only because its meaning was theologically unexceptionable and because 'presbyter' was not yet a word of common English currency. At the same time, there is evidence that the Reformers would have preferred the unambiguous word 'presbyter', for 'even in matter of nomenclature', wrote Professor Norman Sykes, 'there was considerable agreement' among them.[27] For instance, Calvin complained in the *Institutes* that the Roman bishops by their ordination created 'not presbyters to lead and feed the people, but priests to perform sacrifices'.[28] In England Richard Hooker, answering the Puritans who criticized the retention of 'priest' in the Prayer Book, expressed a plain preference for 'presbyter', since 'in truth the word *presbyter* doth seem more fit, and in propriety of speech more agreeable than *priest* with the drift of the whole gospel of Jesus Christ'.[29] If this was so at the end of the sixteenth century, it is much more so at the end of the twentieth. For today few people know that 'priest' is a contraction of 'presbyter', and even fewer are able to perform the mental gymnastic of saying 'priest' and thinking 'presbyter'. It would therefore be conducive to both theological clarity and biblical faithfulness to drop the word 'priest' altogether from our vocabulary. We could then follow the wisdom of such united churches as those of South India, North India and Pakistan, and refer to the three orders of ordained ministry as 'bishops, presbyters and deacons'.

Not all Protestant leaders are willing to cut the Gordian knot in this manner, however. Some have made valiant attempts in recent years not only to reinstate the word 'priest', but to defend the priestly character of the ordained ministry. Even though they frankly concede that ministers are never called priests in the New Testament, and were not so called until Tertullian about AD 200, they are still not prepared to renounce either the word or the notion.

The most widely acclaimed attempt is found in *Baptism, Eucharist and Ministry*, often referred to as 'the Lima text', and constituting the fruit of fifty years of ecumenical discussion.[30] It sums up 'the chief responsibility of the ordained ministry' as follows: 'to assemble and build up the body of Christ by proclaiming and teaching the Word of God, by celebrating the sacraments, and by guiding the life of the community in its worship, its mission and its caring ministry'.[31] The commentary adds that these tasks are not performed by the ordained ministry 'in an exclusive way' (since all Christian people can share in them) but 'in a representative way'. Not only is there nothing distinctive about these ministries (which might separate clergy from laity) but, we may add, there is nothing necessarily 'priestly' about them either. Nevertheless, the Lima text later affirms that ordained ministers 'may appropriately be called priests because they fulfil a particular priestly service by strengthening and building up the royal and prophetic priesthood of the faithful through word and sacraments, through their prayers and intercession, and through their pastoral guidance of the community'.[32] The commentary adds that priestly terms 'underline the fact that the ordained ministry is related to the priestly reality of Jesus Christ and the whole community', although the ordained ministry's priesthood 'differs in appropriate ways' from Christ's and the community's.

I confess that these statements baffle me. Why should the strengthening of the community's priesthood be *ipso facto* a 'priestly service'? And in what ways does the claimed priesthood of the ordained ministry differ from Christ's and the community's? The text makes no attempt to answer these questions.

In 1986 the Church of England's 'Faith and Order Advisory Group' produced a document entitled *The Priesthood of the Ordained Ministry*. 'There is no dispute', its authors confess, that *hiereus* is used in the New Testament of the priesthood of Christ and the priesthood of the whole people of God and 'never ... of an appointed Christian minister'.[33] But they do not follow these admissions to their logical conclusion. Instead, they affirm that 'the common priesthood of the community and the special priesthood of the ordained ministry are both derived from the priesthood of Christ'. Nevertheless the latter differs from the former in that the priestly ministry of the ordained 'is an appointed means through which Christ makes his priesthood present and effective to his people'.[34]

This statement prompts me to ask the same kind of questions as before: why should a ministry which makes the priesthood (and sacrifice) of Christ effective to his people be *ipso facto* a priestly ministry? Again, why must a ministry which helps the people of God 'to realise their priestly character' itself be called priestly?[35]

All this muddle, it seems to me, is due to our failure first to define what (according to Scripture) the essence of 'priesthood' is, and secondly to remember that the Old Testament priests were pastors too. They exercised a dual role. On the one hand, as *priests*, they had a *Godward* ministry: 'Every high priest is selected from among men and is appointed to represent them in matters related to God ... '[36] In this capacity it was their privilege to approach, or draw near to, God,[37] to offer sacrifices,[38] and to make intercession.[39]

On the other hand, as *pastors*, they had a *people-ward* ministry. In this capacity they cared for the people's welfare; they taught them the law;[40] they blessed the people, that is, sought or pronounced God's blessing upon them;[41] and they acted as judges and made decisions.[42]

In New Testament days, since the cross, no more sacrifices for sin can be offered. And the remaining Godward privileges of the priesthood have through the work of Christ been inherited by the whole people of God. We may all draw near to God,[43] and 'have confidence to enter the Most Holy Place by the blood of Jesus'.[44] We are all invited to offer the 'spiritual sacrifices' of our worship.[45] And we are all to pray for one another. None of these ministries now belongs, as they did in Old Testament days, to a privileged caste, to clergy in distinction from laity. One could argue that intercession is a ministry which belongs peculiarly to clergy. Indeed, it seems to have been in this sense that Archbishop Michael Ramsey thought of the ordained ministry as 'priestly'. 'We are called', he said to a group of men on the eve of their ordination, 'near to Jesus and with Jesus and in Jesus, *to be with God with the people on our heart*. That is what you will be promising when I say to you "Will you be diligent in prayers?" You will be promising to be daily with God with the people on your heart.'[46] Although this ministry of intercession may thus be a special responsibility of clergy, however, it cannot be claimed as a distinctively 'priestly' work which is restricted to them.

Something needs also to be said about the prophets in Old Testament days. The priests and the prophets complemented one another in that both ministries were representative, although in opposite directions. The priests represented the people to God, especially in offering sacrifices; the prophets were spokesmen of God to the people, especially in uttering oracles. Is it not of the essence of the new covenant relationship between God and his people, however, that this double mediatorial ministry is now exercised by Jesus Christ alone? Through him we come to God. Through him God speaks to us. He is the only priest through whom we enjoy access to God, and the only prophet through whom we enjoy the knowledge of God. Human mediators are no longer needed.

It is rather the pastoral ministry of the Old Testament priests, their caring responsibility for the spiritual well-being of the people of God, and in particular their teaching role, which have devolved in New Testament days on clergy. In so far as priests were pastors in the Old Testament, I suppose one could call pastors priests in the New Testament. But pastoral duties do not have anything distinctively priestly about them (except perhaps intercession), and in fact, as we have seen, neither Jesus nor his apostles ever referred to pastoral leaders as priests.

They did indicate, however, that God wants his church to have pastors. True, the pastoral responsibilities of caring and teaching belong in some degree to all the people of God, since we are called to 'teach and admonish one another' and to 'carry one another's burdens'.[47] Nevertheless, the plain New Testament assumption is that each church will have a group of elders or leaders, whose main task will be to pastor God's flock, especially by feeding, *i.e.* teaching, them.[48]

The pastoral model

Since 'pastor' means 'shepherd', and the image comes from a rural context alien to today's burgeoning urban communities, it is sometimes suggested that we need to find a more appropriate term for the church's leaders. City flat-dwellers, perched on the ledges of their perpendicular cliffs of glass and concrete, know little about sheep and shepherds. Yet I doubt if we would be prepared to jettison the self-portrait of Jesus Christ as the 'good shepherd' who came to seek and save lost sheep, and laid down his life for us, or to stop singing the popular hymns which embody this imagery, such as 'The Lord's my shepherd, I'll not want' and 'The King of love my shepherd is'.

We are told that Jesus was moved with compassion when he saw the crowds, 'because they were harassed and helpless, like sheep without a shepherd'.[49] Shepherdless sheep must still arouse his distress and concern. Ultimately, he is himself their shepherd. But he delegates some of his responsibility to under-shepherds;[50] 'pastors and teachers' are still among the gifts with which he enriches his church.[51] In fact, all Christian ministry is derived from Christ. His ministry is the prototype. He is the true servant, who came 'not to be served but to serve'.[52] And now he calls us to follow him in the path of service, and to be the servants of others for his sake.[53]

Moreover, what is true of the servant, is true of the pastor as well. Jesus called himself 'the good shepherd'.[54] Elsewhere in the New Testament he is named 'the Chief Shepherd', 'that great Shepherd of the sheep' and 'the Shepherd and Overseer of your souls'.[55] If, then, pastors are under-shepherds, we will be wise to understudy the good, the great, the chief shepherd. For he both taught and exemplified all the main principles of pastoral ministry. It is right that the Gospel appointed for the Anglican ordination service is John 10:1–16, for here he describes what his ministry is, and what ours should be. The good pastor, who models his ministry on the good shepherd, has at least seven characteristics.

First, the good shepherd knows his sheep. He 'calls his own sheep by name ... I am the good shepherd; I know my sheep and my sheep know me – just as the Father knows me and I know the Father'.[56] Of course the ancient oriental shepherd was different in many ways from modern shepherds in other parts of the world. The main difference is due to whether the sheep are kept for wool or for mutton. Because in the West they are mostly reared for mutton, they live only a brief life and no personal relationship with the sheep farmer is possible. In Palestine, however, because the sheep were kept for their wool, and were sheared annually, the shepherd had them in his care for many years and a relationship of trust and intimacy developed between them. The shepherd would even know and call each of them by name.

This was certainly the relationship between Jesus and his disciples. He knew his sheep personally. As in the Old Testament Yahweh called Abraham, Moses, Samuel and others by name, so Jesus knew and called people personally. When he saw Nathanael approaching and said of him, 'Here is a true Israelite, in whom there is nothing false', Nathanael asked in astonishment, 'How do you know me?'[57] Jesus went on to call Zacchaeus by name to come down from the sycamore tree in which he was hiding, and after the ascension called Saul of Tarsus by name on the Damascus road.[58] And although at our own conversion we heard no audible voice, we too can say in truth that he called us personally.

Perhaps the first and most basic characteristic of Christ's undershepherds will be the personal relationship which develops between pastor and people. They are not our clients, constituents, patients or customers. Still less are they names on a register or, worse still, numbers on a computer card. Instead, they are individual persons, whom we know and who know us. Moreover, each of them has a 'proper' name, a symbol of his or her unique identity, and genuine pastors struggle to remember their names. Many years ago I had difficulty in recalling the names of two elderly ladies who came to church every Sunday together. Consequently, when greeting them after services, the best I could do was to hail them as 'you two'. It became a joke between us, not least because at that very time considerable publicity was being given to the shooting down by the Soviet Union of the American surveillance plane 'U2'. So when the ladies in question began to sign their letters 'U2', you can imagine my embarrassment. 'Greet the friends ... by name,' John wrote.[59]

What steps can be taken to overcome a bad memory? I have found two devices helpful. First, it is useless to ask people their name before we can recognize their face, for then we have numerous names floating round our mind with no faces to attach them to. In this situation we resemble the well-known Dr W. A. Spooner (of 'Spoonerism' fame), who is reputed to have accosted someone at a party with the words: 'I know your name so well; I just can't think of your face!' Instead, it is wiser to memorize the face first, and then we are ready to discover the correct name to attach to it.

The second way to remember people's names is to write them down and pray for them. When Paul told the Thessalonians, 'We always thank God for all of you, mentioning you in our prayers,'[60] it sounds as if he had some kind of list. It is, without doubt, the regular mentioning of people's names in prayer which – more surely and quickly than by any other means – fixes them in our mind and memory. To forget somebody's name is, as likely as not, a token of our pastoral prayerlessness.

Jesus also indicated that his relationship with his people would be both reciprocal ('I know my sheep and my sheep know me')[61] and intimate ('just as the Father knows me and I know the Father').[62] There was something transparently open and guileless about Jesus. He had nothing to hide. It was a mark of his true friendship, he said, that he made himself known to his disciples.[63] This does not of course mean that pastors have to disclose all their secrets to the congregation, but at least they should be willing for the costly and humbling step of forgoing some of their privacy and of being known to be frail and vulnerable human beings like everybody else.

At the same time it is possible in some cultures to be too forward, and even presumptuous, in exchanging names with people, because our name symbolizes our personal and private identity. Vincent Donovan discovered this when he was working among the Masai in Tanzania. At first, he has written, 'I quite naturally acted out of my American background, and saw nothing wrong in telling them my name and asking theirs.' He was advised, however, that the Masai regarded this as very rude. In public and with strangers they used titles or designations, not names. One day a Masai man said to him: 'Do not throw my name about. My name is important. My name is me. My name is for my friends.'[64] So, when Vincent Donovan moved to a new area, he adopted the custom of not knowing or disclosing each other's names. Then 'after working among them for a long period of time, and, perhaps as a parting gift to me, one of the elders told me his name, and I told him mine. I was flattered at the exchange. "My name is for my friends".'[65] It would be good in the West too, I think, to cultivate something of this respect for persons and their names. To divulge our name and discover another person's is not to be done lightly; for it is to claim an intimacy of relationship which, however, does belong properly to the family of God.

Secondly, the good shepherd *serves* his sheep. 'I am the good shepherd', Jesus said. 'The good shepherd lays down his life for the sheep.'[66] For he is devoted to their welfare, and his whole life is dominated by their needs. God's chief complaint against Israel's leaders was this: 'Woe to the shepherds of Israel who only take care of themselves! Should not shepherds take care of the flock?'[67] Now sheep are not particularly pleasant animals. We cherish a rather romantic picture of woolly, cuddly lambs. But in their natural state sheep have no concern for their cleanliness, and are afflicted by a variety of nasty pests. Hence the need to plunge them several times a year into powerful chemical solutions. They also have a reputation for being stupid. So there is a good deal of dirty and menial work in shepherding; it includes strengthening the weak ones, healing the sick, binding up the injured and bringing back the strays.[68]

Jesus himself laid down his life for his sheep. He was no hired hand or 'hireling', doing his work for money. He genuinely cared for them, even to the extent of dying for them. His great love was revealed in sacrifice and service, sacrificing himself to serve others. Pastors need this sacrificial, serving love in their ministry today. For like sheep human beings can often be 'perverse and foolish' in straying from the path. Some can also be demanding and unappreciative, and we will find it hard to love them. But then we will remember that they are God's flock, purchased with Christ's blood and entrusted by the Holy Spirit to our care.[69] And if the three persons of the Trinity are committed to their welfare, how can we not be also? We need to hear Christ's words to us as Richard Baxter imagined them: 'Did I die for them, and wilt not thou look after them? Were they worth my blood, and are they not worth thy labour? ... Have I done and suffered so much for their salvation, and was I willing to make thee a co-worker with me, and wilt thou refuse that little that lieth upon thy hands?'[70]

Thirdly, the good shepherd *leads* his sheep. Here is another difference between oriental and occidental shepherds. In the West shepherds seldom if ever lead their sheep; they drive them from behind with the use of trained sheepdogs. Because of the Palestinian shepherd's close relationship with his sheep, however, he is able to walk in front of them, call them, perhaps whistle or play a pipe, and they will follow him. Chua Wee Hian, former General Secretary of the International Fellowship of Evangelical Students, tells us in his book *Learning to Lead* of an Arab guide who was explaining this tradition to some tourists, who then 'spotted a man in the distance driving a small flock of sheep with a rather menacing stick'. Was the guide mistaken, then? 'He immediately stopped the bus and rushed off across the fields. A few minutes later he returned, his face beaming. He announced, "I have just spoken to the man. Ladies and gentlemen, he is not the shepherd. He is in fact the butcher!"'[71]

Israel's relationship to Yahweh, and especially their passage across the wilderness, are likened to the movement of sheep following their shepherd: 'Hear us, O Shepherd of Israel, you who lead Joseph like a flock.'[72] The godly individual Israelite thought of Yahweh in the same way: 'the LORD is my shepherd, I shall not be in want ... he leads me beside quiet waters ...'[73] So Jesus, the good shepherd, took over and developed the same picture: 'The sheep listen to his voice. He calls his own sheep by name and leads them out. When he has brought out all his own he goes on ahead of them, and his sheep follow him because they know his voice.'[74] The reciprocity is clear. If the good shepherd knows his sheep's names, they in their turn come to know his voice. Christian ears are attuned to the voice of Christ. We develop a certain sensitivity to his mind and will. Gradually we come to know instinctively what would please or displease him. And so we follow where he leads and where he calls.

Something similar is true of Christian pastors. It is our solemn responsibility to lead people in such a way that it is safe for them to follow us. That is, we have to set them a consistent and reliable example. We need to remember that Jesus introduced into the world a new style of leadership, namely leadership by service and example, not by force. The apostle Peter grasped this and echoed it in his teaching: 'Be shepherds of God's flock that is under your care ... not lording it over those entrusted to you, but being examples to the flock.'[75] As a matter of fact, for good or evil, whether we like it or not, people will follow us. It is frightening to think how undiscerning many sheep are. That is why it is essential to lead well, to set a good example, with no dichotomy between our preaching and our practice, so that we will not lead them astray.

Fourthly, the good shepherd *feeds* his sheep. 'I am the gate,' Jesus said. 'Whoever enters through me will be saved. He will come in and go out, and find pasture.'[76] The chief concern of shepherds is always that their sheep will have enough to eat. Whether they are being kept for wool or for mutton, their health depends on their having nutritious pasture. So Jesus himself as the good shepherd was pre-eminently a teacher. He fed his disciples with the good food of his instruction.

Pastors today have the same paramount responsibility. The ordained ministry is essentially a ministry of the Word, with the sacraments understood as 'visible words' (as Augustine called them), dramatizing the promises of the gospel. The pastor is primarily a teacher. This is the reason for two qualifications for the presbyterate which are singled out in the Pastoral Epistles. First, the candidate must be 'able to teach'.[77] Secondly, he must 'hold firmly to the trustworthy message as it has been taught, so that he can encourage others by sound doctrine and refute those who oppose it'.[78] These two qualifications go together. Pastors must both be loyal to the apostolic teaching (the *didachē*) and have a gift for teaching it (*didaktikos*). And whether they are teaching a crowd or congregation, a group or an individual (Jesus himself taught in all three contexts), what distinguishes their pastoral work is that it is always a ministry of the Word.

Nothing is more necessary today, either in the tired churches of the West or in the vibrant churches of many Third World countries, than a faithful and systematic exposition of Scripture from the pulpit. 'Do you love me?' Jesus asked Peter. Then 'Feed my sheep'.[79] Too many congregations are sick and even starving for lack of the 'solid food'[80] of the Word of God. Indeed, the ultimate goal of our pastoral ministry is both 'to present everyone perfect [better, 'mature'] in Christ'[81] and 'to prepare God's people for works of service [better, 'for their work of ministry']'.[82] It would be hard to imagine a nobler ambition than through our teaching ministry to lead God's people both into maturity and into ministry.

How, then, do shepherds feed their sheep? Strictly speaking, they do not feed them at all. To be sure, if a newborn lamb is sickly, the shepherd may take it into his arms and bottle-feed it. But normally the shepherd's way is to lead his sheep into 'good pasture' or 'good grazing land',[83] where they can browse and so feed themselves. It is not, I think, far-fetched to see in this a parable of sound pastoral education. Spoon-feeding and bottle-feeding are for babes in Christ. Only pasture-feeding will lead them into maturity in Christ. As the preacher opens up the Scriptures, he invites people into them, in order that they may feed themselves in this rich pasturage.

Fifthly, the good shepherd *rules* his sheep, accepting that he has a certain authority over them. I am tempted to omit this dimension, but to do so would lack integrity. Bishop Lesslie Newbigin is right in his book *The Good Shepherd* to complain that 'the figure of the good shepherd has been sentimentalized'.[84] In classical Greek the king was known as the 'shepherd' of his people, and the king-shepherd analogy occurs not infrequently in the Old Testament. For example, the people reminded David how God had said to him: 'You shall shepherd my people Israel, and you shall become their ruler.'[85] Further, the Greek verb *poimainō*, meaning 'to shepherd a flock', came to be used of a harsh rule: 'You will rule them [LXX *poimainō*] with an iron sceptre.'[86] And this verse is applied in the Revelation to Jesus' authority over the nations as their judge.[87] Clearly, we have no liberty either to deduce from this that pastors are to be autocratic or to justify the medieval concept of the prince-bishop. No, regal language ('palaces', 'thrones' and 'reigns') is entirely inappropriate in reference to the biblical presbyter-bishop. Nevertheless, alongside the New Testament's emphasis on the humble service of presbyters, there are also allusions to their leadership role, their being 'over' a local church 'in the Lord',[88] and the need to 'obey' them and 'submit to their authority',[89] although their authority is to be exercised through their ministry of the Word and their example.[90] And it is plain from several New Testament passages that, if discipline has to be exercised, it will be done through the local congregation collectively, and not through a single pastor.[91]

Sixthly, the good shepherd *guards* his sheep. The sheep's chief enemy in ancient Palestine was the wolf, fierce and predatory, whether hunting singly or in a pack. Sheep were defenceless against them. If the shepherd was merely a hired hand, he would see the wolf coming, and would abandon the sheep and run away, leaving the wolf to attack and scatter the flock.[92] Only a good shepherd would stay and risk his own life in defending and rescuing his sheep.

There is no difficulty in interpreting Jesus' allegory. 'Watch out for false prophets,' he had said in another place. 'They come to you in sheep's clothing, but inwardly they are ferocious wolves.'[93] If the sheep are God's people and the shepherds are their faithful pastors, then the wolves are false teachers and the hired hands unfaithful pastors who do nothing to protect God's people from error. Alas, there are still wolves in Christ's flock today, deceivers who deny some of the fundamentals of the historic Christian faith. True pastors will not behave like hirelings and run away. They will stand up to the wolves. It will be a costly task. For shepherds cannot shoo wolves away by shouting at them or waving their arms about. They have to get to grips with them, as young David did with both a lion and a bear.[94] Similarly, pastors need to accept the pain and the danger of close combat with false teachers. Vague denunciations will not be enough. Instead, we have to study their literature, listen to their teaching, and wrestle with the issues they are raising, in order to counter their arguments effectively in our teaching.

Yet, if this is a risky ministry, it is also a necessary and compassionate one. We should never relish controversy. It can never be more than a distasteful duty. The only reason we engage in it is out of compassion for the sheep. The hireling takes to his heels because he 'cares nothing for the sheep'.[95] It is only because a good shepherd does care, and care deeply, for the welfare of the people he serves, that he will seek grace and courage to stand up to error in the church. Shepherdless sheep are an easy prey to wolves. Must it be said of God's flock today that 'they were scattered because there was no shepherd, and … they became food for all the wild animals'?[96] On the contrary, if we care, we will be vigilant and 'keep watch over our flock', like those shepherds in the fields near Bethlehem. True, it is sometimes said that we must always be positive in our teaching, never negative. But this is not so. Jesus himself opposed false teachers. And the duties of the pastor are not only to teach 'sound doctrine' but also to 'refute those who oppose it'.[97] Feeding the sheep and routing the wolves cannot be separated.

In the seventh place, the good shepherd *seeks* his sheep. 'I have other sheep', Jesus said, 'that are not of this sheep pen. I must bring them also. They too will listen to my voice, and there shall be one flock and one shepherd.'[98] It is clear that by these 'other sheep' Jesus was referring to Gentile outsiders. Yet he could also say 'I have' them and 'I must bring them' in. We need the same kind of assurance in our evangelism. Wherever we live and work, we may be sure that some of Christ's 'other sheep' are there, that they already belong to him in the purpose of God, and that he is determined to, he 'must', bring them in.

This outreach to people who are alienated and lost is an essential part of the pastor's ministry, even if it belongs even more to lay church members who live and work among them. It is true that we customarily distinguish between 'evangelists' who seek lost sheep and 'pastors' who nurture those who have been found. Yet their ministries overlap. If Jesus, the good shepherd, not only feeds the sheep in his fold but also seeks those outside it,[99] his undershepherds who understudy him must do the same. In the Anglican ordination service the candidates are exhorted by the bishop 'to seek for Christ's sheep that are dispersed abroad ... that they may be saved by Christ for ever'. If we were to evade this responsibility, God would again complain: 'My sheep ... were scattered over the whole earth, and no-one searched or looked for them.'[100] And Jesus himself would say to us: 'Did I come down from heaven to earth, to seek and to save that which was lost, and wilt thou not go to the next door or street or village to seek them?'[101] On the other hand, if we do go out in order to bring people in, we shall share in the heavenly rejoicing 'over one sinner who repents'.[102]

Here, then, is the beautiful ideal of pastoral ministry which Jesus painted. Wherever there are sheep, whether lost or found, there is a need for pastors to seek and to shepherd them. Following the example of the good shepherd himself, human pastors will endeavour to know and serve, to lead, feed and rule the sheep of Christ's flock, to guard them from marauding wolves and to seek them when they have gone astray. And then, however little they may have been recognized, appreciated or honoured on earth, or have wished to be, they will receive from the Chief Shepherd, when he appears, 'the crown of glory that will never fade away'.[103]

The pastoral ideal exemplified in Jesus the good shepherd, which he wanted leaders to copy, needs to be complemented by two other models which he warned them to avoid. First, he said, there are the secular rulers who 'lord it over' and 'exercise authority over' people. 'Not so with you,' he added emphatically. Leadership in his new community was to be entirely different from leadership in the world. 'Instead, whoever wants to become great among you must be your servant.'[104] As T. W. Manson put it, 'in the kingdom of God service is not a stepping-stone to nobility; it *is* nobility, the only kind of nobility that is recognized'.[105] Secondly, Jesus urged his disciples not to imitate the Pharisees. They loved both places of honour (at banquets and in the synagogues) and titles of honour, for these were signs of the people's obsequious respect. 'Do not do what they do,' Jesus said. Christian leaders are not to be called 'Rabbi' (Teacher), 'Father' or 'Master'. That is, we are not to adopt towards any human being in the church, or allow anybody to adopt towards us, an attitude of helpless dependence, as of a child on his or her father, or of slavish obedience, as of a servant to his or her master, or of uncritical acquiescence, as of a pupil to his or her teacher. To do so, Jesus implied, would be both to usurp the prerogatives of the Holy Trinity (God our Father, Jesus our master, and the Holy Spirit our teacher) and to disrupt the brotherly-sisterly relationships of the Christian family.[106]

Here are two different contemporary models of leadership, one secular (rulers) and the other religious (Pharisees), which nevertheless shared the same basic characteristic: a hunger for power and prestige. Today the most likely model presented to us for imitation is that of business management. It too, despite some acceptable parallels, is often more worldly than Christian. We have to beware lest, as the status of pastors in society declines, we seek to compensate for it by demanding greater power and honour in the church. The essential mark of Christian leadership is humility, not authority; servitude, not lordship; and 'the meekness and gentleness of Christ'.[107]

I will give the last word to Chuck Colson, who before his conversion to Christ had himself tasted the intoxicating wine of power: 'The lure of power can separate the most resolute of Christians from the true nature of Christian leadership, which is service to others. It is difficult to stand on a pedestal and wash the feet of those below.'[108] Again, 'nothing distinguishes the kingdoms of man from the kingdom of God more than their diametrically opposed views of the exercise of power. One seeks to control people, the other to serve people; one promotes self, the other prostrates self; one seeks prestige and position, the other lifts up the lowly and despised.'[109]

Notes

[1] Richard Baxter, *The Reformed Pastor* (1656; Epworth, second edition, 1950), p. 24.

[2] David Hare, *Racing Demon* (Faber and Faber, 1990), p. 3.

[3] *Ibid.*, pp. 34–35.

[4] *Ibid.*, pp. 75, 97.

[5] *Ibid.*, pp. 3–4.

[6] *Ibid.*, p. 43.

[7] *Ibid.*, p. 63.

[8] *Ibid.*, p. 71.

[9] *Ibid.*, pp. 66, 69.

[10] Mark Twain, *The Adventures of Huckleberry Finn* (1884; Pan, 1968), p. 343.

[11] 1 Cor. 3:5, paraphrased and expanded.

[12] 1 Thes. 5:12–13.

[13] 1 Tim.3:1.

[14] Session 22, 1562.

[15] *Decree on the Priestly Ministry and Life*, 1965, I.2.

[16] *Ibid.*, I.5.

[17] Acts 14:13.

[18] *E.g.* Heb. 10:12.

[19] Rev. 1:6; 5:10; 20:6.

[20] 1 Pet. 2:5, 9.

[21] Rom. 12:1.

[22] Rev. 5:8; Heb. 13:15; Ps. 51:17.

[23] Phil. 4:18; Heb. 13:16.

[24] Phil. 2:17, 2 Tim. 4:6.

[25] Rom. 15:16.

[26] C. H. Hodge, *Systematic Theology* (Thomas Nelson and Sons/Charles Scribner and Co., 1875), vol. II, p. 467.

[27] Norman Sykes, *Old Priest, New Presbyter* (CUP, 1956), p. 43.

[28] Calvin, *Institutes*, IV.v.4.

[29] Richard Hooker, *Laws of Ecclesiastical Polity* (1593–97), V.lxxviii.3.

[30] *Baptism, Eucharist and Ministry*, Faith and Order Paper no. 111 (WCC, 1982).

[31] *Ibid.*, 'Ministry', II.A.13.

[32] *Ibid.*, 'Ministry', II.C.17.

[33] *The Priesthood of the Ordained Ministry*, para. 44.

[34] *Ibid.*, para. 142.

[35] *Ibid.*, para. 143. Other documents germane to this debate are: R. T. Beckwith, *Priesthood and Sacraments, A Study in the Anglican-Methodist Report* (Marsham Manor Press, 1964), ch. 2; George Carey, 'Reflections upon the Nature of Ministry and Priesthood in the Light of the Lima Report' (*Anvil*, vol. 3, no. 1, 1986), and a response to this by David Wright entitled 'Ministry and Priesthood: Further Reflections' (*Anvil*, vol. 3, no. 3, 1986). In dispute among these authors is the thesis developed by R. C. Moberly in his *Ministerial Priesthood* (John Murray, second edition, 1899). He emphasized that ordained ministers are authorized to represent the whole priestly community, and that they therefore exercise a priestly ministry on their behalf. In particular, Moberly argued that, in offering the eucharistic sacrifice, they are offering on earth the same sacrifice that Christ is offering in heaven. But, we respond, Christ's self-offering was finished on the cross. It is therefore not possible for the church to offer on earth what Christ is not offering in heaven.

[36] Heb. 5:1.

[37] *E.g.* Ex. 19:22; Lv. 10:3; 16:2.

[38] *E.g.* Ex. 30:20; Heb. 8:3–6.

[39] *E.g.* Ex. 28:9–14, 29–30; Joel 2:17.

[40] *E.g.* Lv. 10:11; Dt. 17:11; 2 Ch. 15:3; 17:8–9; 35:3; Je. 2:8, Mal. 2:1, 4–9.

[41] *E.g.* Lv. 9:22–23; Nu. 6:22–27; Dt. 21:5.

[42] *E.g.* Ex. 28:30; Dt. 21:5.

[43] Eph. 2:18; Jas. 4:8.

[44] Heb. 10:19.

[45] *E.g.* 1 Pet. 2:5; Rom. 12:1.

[46] A. M. Ramsey, *The Christian Priest Today* (SPCK, 1972), p. 14.

[47] *E.g.* Col. 3:16; Gal. 6:2.

[48] *E.g.* Acts 14:23; 20:17, 28; 1 Tim. 3:1–2; Tit. 1:5–9.

[49] Mt. 9:36.

[50] Acts 20:28.

[51] Eph. 4:11.

[52] Mk. 10:45.

[53] 2 Cor. 4:5.

[54] Jn. 10:11, 14.

[55] 1 Pet. 5:4; Heb. 13:20; 1 Pet. 2:25.

[56] Jn 10:3, 14–l5.

[57] Jn. 1:47–48.

[58] Lk. 19:5; Acts 9:4.

[59] 3 Jn. 14.

[60] 1 Thes. 1:2.

[61] Jn. 10:14.

[62] Jn. 10:15.

[63] *E.g.* Jn. 14:21; 15:15.

[64] Vincent J. Donovan, *Christianity Rediscovered: An Epistle from the Masai* (1978; SCM, 1982), p. 187.

[65] *Ibid.*, p. 188.

[66] Jn. 10:11.

[67] Ezk. 34:2. The New Testament equivalent is Jude 12, which speaks of 'shepherds who feed only themselves'. That is, they use their position to minister to their own ego rather than to the people committed to their care.

[68] See Ezk. 34:4.

[69] Acts 20:28.

[70] Richard Baxter, *The Reformed Pastor* (1656; Epworth, 1939), pp. 121–122.

[71] Chua Wee Hian, *Learning to Lead* (IVP, 1987), p. 35.

[72] Ps. 80:1.

[73] Ps. 23:1–2.

[74] Jn. 10:3–4.

[75] 1 Pet. 5:2–3.

[76] Jn. 10:9.

[77] 1 Tim. 3:2.

[78] Tit. 1:9.

[79] Jn. 21:17.

[80] 1 Cor. 3:2; Heb. 5: 12.

[81] Col. 1:28.

[82] Eph. 4:12.

[83] Ezk. 34:14.

[84] Lesslie Newbigin, *The Good Shepherd: Meditations on Christian Ministry in Today's World* (Faith Press, 1977), p. 14.

[85] 2 Sa. 5:2.

[86] Ps. 2:9.

[87] Rev. 2:27; 12:5; 19:15.

[88] 1 Thes. 5:12.

[89] Heb. 13:17.

[90] Heb. 13:7.

[91] *E.g.* Mt. 18:15–20; 1 Cor. 5:4–5, 13.

[92] Jn. 10:12–13.

[93] Mt. 7:15; *cf.* Acts 20:29–30.

[94] 1 Sa. 17:34–35.

[95] Jn. 10:13.

[96] Ezk. 34:5.

[97] Tit. 1:9.

[98] Jn. 10:16.

[99] Lk. 19:10; *cf.* 15:3–7.

[100] Ezk. 34:6.

[101] Richard Baxter, *The Reformed Pastor* (1656; Epworth, 1939), pp. 121–122.

[102] Lk. 15:7.

[103] 1 Pet. 5:4.

[104] Mk. 10:42–45.

[105] T. W. Manson, *The Church's Ministry* (Hodder and Stoughton, 1948), p. 27.

[106] Mt. 23:1–12.

[107] 2 Cor. 10:1; *cf.* 2 Tim. 2–24.

[108] Charles W. Colson, *Kingdoms in Conflict: An Insider's Challenging View of Politics, Power and the Pulpit* (Morrow-Zondervan, 1987), p. 272.

[109] *Ibid.*, p. 274.

PART FIVE

The world

In Part Four our concern was with the church; in Part Five it will be with the world. 'Church' and 'world' are often bracketed and, more often still, are set in antithesis to one another. In any case, it is hard to think of either without simultaneously remembering the other. For, at least in theory, the world is the old and fallen community, while the church is God's new and redeemed society.

How, then, are these two communities related to each other? Several options have been proposed. Some theologians, anxious to minimize the difference between them, go so far as to identify them by applying to all human beings indiscriminately the epithet 'the people of God'. Others reach almost the same goal by a different route. They allow the world to dictate to the church what its views and values should be, until the church conforms to the world, and the two become virtually indistinguishable. A third group is content for the church and the world to live together in amicable co-existence, with neither invading the other's territory or interfering in the other's affairs.

The fourth possible scenario, however, is what Jesus and his apostles envisaged. It is that the church has a God-given responsibility to infiltrate the world, listening indeed to the world's challenges, but also bringing its own challenge to the world by sharing the good news with it in word and deed. The correct term for this task is 'mission'. 'Mission' is precisely what

God sends the church into the world to do. We are going to consider four major aspects of it.

First (in chapter 18), we take up the topic of the uniqueness of Jesus Christ, which is arguably the most important and the most urgent issue before the world-wide church today. Can we still apply to Jesus, and to God's claimed revelation and redemption through him, traditional words like 'unique', 'absolute' and 'final' ? Or must we surrender to the pressures of 'pluralism' which insists that Jesus was only one of a number of religious leaders, and that every religion has its own independent validity? If Jesus was and is unique in his person and work, then we are under obligation to make him known. If he is not, then the chief foundation of the Christian mission has been undermined, and we will have to give up our ambition to win the world for Christ.

In the following chapter (chapter 19) we will endeavour to lay down the full biblical basis for the Christian mission. This goes beyond the uniqueness of Christ to the nature of God himself. For mission begins in the heart of God. The living God of the biblical revelation is a missionary God. A rapid survey of the whole of Scripture will demonstrate that each of its five sections has an unavoidably missionary emphasis.

In chapter 20, entitled 'Holistic Mission', we will see that the church's communication of the gospel cannot be in words only, but must also be in works. In the church's mission, as in Christ's, good news and good deeds go together.[1] A multiple argument will be developed that evangelism and social responsibility are in God's purpose married; they must not be divorced.

In the last chapter of Part Five (chapter 21) we will return to Christ, since nothing is more important in the Christian mission than a clear and fresh vision of him. Under the title 'The Christology of Mission', we will rehearse the five main events in the saving career of Jesus, in such a way as to note that each has a missionary dimension. From them we will learn the model, costliness, mandate, motivation and urgency of the mission to which we are called.

Note

[1] *Cf.* Mt 5:16.

The uniqueness of Jesus Christ

A social worker in Nigeria once visited a youth in one of the back streets of Lagos. On his bedside table he found the following books: the Bible, *The Book of Common Prayer*, the Qur'an, three copies of *Watchtower* (the magazine of the Jehovah's Witnesses), a biography of Karl Marx, a book of yoga exercises, and – what the poor fellow evidently needed most – a popular paperback entitled *How to Stop Worrying.*[1]

On Commonwealth Day (May 24) 1966, the first multi-faith service was held in the church of St Martin-in-the-Fields in London. In it Hindus, Buddhists, Muslims and Christians took part on equal terms, making four affirmations of a supposedly common faith, giving four readings from their respective sacred scriptures (the Buddhist *Tripitaka*, the *Bhagavad Gita*, the Qur'an and the Bible), and pronouncing four blessings, in only one of which the name of Jesus was mentioned for the first and last time. The secular press was enthusiastic, hailing it as 'a significant milestone in religious history'. But the Christian newspapers described it as 'a betrayal of the Christian faith'. It is doubtful if they would write anything similar today, for multi-faith services are regularly held.

These two incidents, the one in Lagos and the other in London, are examples of the spirit of syncretism. Dr W. A. Visser't Hooft, the first General Secretary of the World Council of Churches, has defined syncretism as the view 'that there is no unique revelation in history, that there are many different ways to reach the divine reality, that all formulations of religious truth or experience are by their very nature inadequate expressions of that truth, and that it is necessary to harmonize as much as possible all religious ideas and experiences so as to create one universal religion for mankind'.[2] Dr Visser't Hooft was outspoken in his rejection of this outlook. 'It is high time that Christians should rediscover', he went on, 'that the very heart of their faith is that Jesus Christ did not come to make a contribution to the religious storehouse of mankind, but that in him God reconciled the world unto himself ...'[3]

The debate has moved on since the 1960s, however. Today the main challenge to the traditional understanding of the uniqueness of Christ is not 'syncretism', but 'pluralism', not the attempt to fuse the world's religions into a single, universal faith, but the recognition of the integrity of each in all its diverse particularities.

The options before us are now usually summarized as 'exclusivism', 'inclusivism' and 'pluralism'.[4]

'Exclusivism' (an unfortunately negative term, which gives the impression of wanting to exclude people from the kingdom of God) is used to denote the historic Christian view that salvation cannot be found in other religions, but only in Jesus Christ.

'Inclusivism' allows that salvation is possible to adherents of other faiths, but attributes it to the secret and often unrecognized work of Christ. Vatican II embraced this view in its statement that Christ's saving work holds good 'not only for Christians, but for all men of good will in whose hearts grace works in an unseen way'.[5]

'Pluralism' goes further still, for its advocates reject exclusivism as 'presumptuous' and 'arrogant', and inclusivism as 'patronizing' or 'condescending'. Whereas 'plurality' expresses the simple fact that there are many religions, 'pluralism' affirms their independent validity. It renounces every claim that Christianity is 'absolute', 'unique', 'definitive', 'final', 'normative', and 'ultimate' or 'universal'. 'Unlimited growth is cancer, and so would be an ever growing single Christian religion all over the world.'[6] Instead, Christianity must be viewed as only one religion among many, and Jesus as only one saviour among others. This is the so-called 'deeper and larger ecumenism that embraces the whole of humanity', of which the rainbow remains 'a timeless symbol'.[7]

Arguments for pluralism

What is it about 'pluralism' that many find attractive? We shall not be in a position to respond to them until we have listened to them and struggled to understand and feel the appeal of their arguments.

First, there is *the new global consciousness*. Threats to the natural environment, fears of a nuclear conflict and the continuing situation of economic injustice between the North and the South are stimulating people to develop a planetary perspective. The very survival of the human race seems to depend on our learning to live together in harmony and to co-operate for the common good. Whatever divides us, therefore, including our religions, is understandably regarded with increasing disfavour.

In response, Christians should indeed be in the forefront of those who are seeking global harmony. By God's creation we are one people in the world. We should be committed to international peace-making, participatory democracy, human rights, community relations, environmental responsibility and the search for a new international economic order. Moreover, people of different races and religions can, should and do co-operate in these kinds of social witness and action. In order to do so, however, it is not necessary to renounce our belief in the uniqueness of Jesus Christ. It would be folly to seek unity at the expense of truth, or reconciliation without Christ the mediator. Besides, Christ unavoidably divides people as well as uniting them. He said he had come not 'to bring peace, but a sword'.[8] He envisaged that some conflict would continue, as people ranged themselves for or against him.

Secondly, there is *the new appreciation of other religions.* Modern communications (especially television and travel) have caused the world to shrink. People of strange beliefs and customs, who hitherto have been very remote from us, now live next door to us, and actually enter our homes – on the screen if not in person. This is 'a newly experienced reality for many today'.[9] The sacred books of other faiths, translated into our languages, are now readily available to us. And as we become better acquainted with the world's religions, what Professor John Hick has called their 'immense spiritual riches' have 'tended to erode the plausibility of the old Christian exclusivism'.[10] Further, some ancient faiths are showing signs of resurgence, just when it is being perceived that Christianity, declining in the West, 'has not succeeded in breaking the power of the great historical religions'.[11]

We should welcome today's more thorough knowledge of world faiths, not least through the comparative study of religions in schools. But if we discover 'riches' in other religions, we also discern more clearly the absolute uniqueness of Jesus Christ, as we will see later. 'To make exclusive claims for our particular tradition', writes Stanley Samartha, 'is not the best way to love our neighbours as ourselves.'[12] But on the contrary, it is the very best and highest way to express neighbour-love, if the gospel is true. If it is, we cannot claim to love our neighbours if we leave them in ignorance of Christ. As for the vitality of other religions, and the comparative failure of Christianity, these things should lead us not to the conclusion that the gospel is untrue, but rather to self-examination, repentance, amendment of life, and the adoption of better ways of sharing the good news with others.

Thirdly, there is *the new post-colonial modesty.* For four centuries the West dominated the world in political, military, economic and scientific terms, and took for granted its moral and spiritual superiority as well. Indeed, Christianity's 'attitude to other religions has been shaped by the colonial mentality'.[13] The end of the Second World War, however, heralded the end of the colonial era. As the West underwent a profound cultural shift 'from a position of clear superiority to one of rough parity', a parallel shift took place in theological consciousness. 'This dramatic situation has forced ... a new understanding of the interrelationships of religions, a new balance of spiritual power, so to speak, on all,' Professor Langdon Gilkey has written. It has pushed us all out of 'superiority' into 'parity'.[14] To continue, therefore, to claim Christian universality, it is said, is to lapse into the old imperialist mindset.

It is certainly embarrassing for us in the West to have to acknowledge that during those centuries of colonial expansion, territorial and spiritual conquest, politics and religion, gun and Bible, the flag and the cross, went hand in hand, and that representatives of the imperial power often developed attitudes of proud superiority towards those they ruled. But 'superiority' is a slippery word. It can describe an air of intolerable conceit, and we need to repent of every vestige of this. But the Christian missionary enterprise, in seeking to win to Christ adherents of other religions, is not in itself a mark of arrogance; it indicates rather a profound and humble conviction that the gospel *is* superior to other faiths because it is God's revealed truth.

The attraction of pluralism is more, however, than a concern for global harmony, an appreciation of other religions and a desire for post-colonial modesty. It has even deeper roots, which the twelve contributors to *The Myth of Christian Uniqueness* have examined. These scholars describe themselves as having 'crossed a theological Rubicon', not only from exclusivism to inclusivism, but from inclusivism to pluralism,[15] and they tell us about the three 'bridges' which have led them to make the crossing.

The first they call the *historico-cultural* bridge, or *relativity*. Since people began to apply Einstein's general theory of relativity beyond physics to other spheres (including religion), nothing absolute has seemed to remain. A historical and comparative study of religions, argues Professor Gordon Kaufman, suggests that they are simply 'creations of the human imagination',[16] each from its particular cultural perspective. This being so, Christian theology must give up any claim to absolute or final truth, and understand itself instead as 'a human imaginative response to the necessity to find orientation for life in a particular historical situation'.[17] Professor Tom Driver goes further, declaring that 'even Scripture ... is the creation of us human beings'.[18]

Now of course we also affirm that the Bible is a culturally conditioned book, in the sense that each of its authors belonged to, and spoke within, his own particular culture. But is this emphasis on the human, historical and cultural background of the Bible a complete account of its nature? No. As we considered in chapter 10, there are good reasons for believing in the dual authorship of Scripture, namely that behind the human authors stood the divine author, who spoke his Word through their words, and that his Word transcends both history and culture. It may be that other religions could be described (whatever their claims may be) as 'products of the human imagination'. But the historic Christian belief and claim are that the gospel is the product of divine revelation, although mediated through the minds and mouths of the human authors.

The second 'bridge' across the 'theological Rubicon' is designated *theo-logico-mystical,* or *mystery.* That is, there is in every religion some sense of the Transcendent or experience of God who, being himself infinite and ineffable, always remains beyond our apprehensions of him. Our theologies are only 'conceptual images of God', and 'like other images, each may be less or more worthy of its Subject', writes Professor Wilfred Cantwell Smith. There is, in principle, he goes on, 'no fundamental difference ... between a doctrine and a statue'. The former is an intellectual image of God, the latter a visual. 'It is wrong for our intellects to absolutize their own handiwork.' For 'both theology and art proffer relative apprehensions of the Absolute'; to absolutize our image of God is idolatry.[19] He goes further: 'For Christians to think that Christianity is true, or final, or salvific, is a form of idolatry. For Christians to imagine that God has constructed Christianity ... rather than that He/She/It has inspired us to construct it ... that is idolatry.'[20] Or, as Tom Driver sums it up, 'idolatry is the insistence that there is only one way, one norm, one truth'.[21]

In response, we certainly agree that God is the Transcendent Reality beyond all possible human imagination, apprehension or description. Words cannot capture, let alone contain, him. Because he is infinite, we shall never come to the end of him, but spend eternity exploring and worshipping his fathomless being. Nevertheless, to say that he remains a mystery is not incompatible with affirming that he has revealed himself. Moreover, his Word incarnate in Jesus and his Word written in Scripture have a normative position for all Christian believers. It is somewhat extraordinary that the *Myth* contributors regard all Christians of all churches for two millennia, who have believed in the uniqueness of Jesus, as idolaters! If they are referring to 'Christianity' as a human construct, then perhaps to absolutize it could become an idolatry. To acknowledge the finality and absoluteness of Christ himself, however, is not idolatry but authentic worship.

Thirdly, there is the *ethico-practical* bridge, or *justice.* The four contributors to Part III of *The Myth of Christian Uniqueness* are outraged by the sufferings of the oppressed and united in their commitment to social justice. Borrowing a number of concepts from liberation theology, Professor Paul

Knitter writes that 'a preferential option for the poor and the non-person constitutes the necessity and the primary purpose of inter-religious dialogue'. In other words, pluralism is not an end in itself, but a means to the end of liberating the oppressed. For this is too big a task for any one religion to accomplish, which is why 'a worldwide liberation movement needs a worldwide inter-religious dialogue'.[22] The *Myth* contributors also believe that the only possible criterion by which to judge or 'grade' religions must be neither doctrinal nor mystical, but ethical, namely their effectiveness in promoting human well-being.

We must agree that contemporary issues of social justice should be of enormous concern to all Christian people, since we acknowledge the dignity of human beings as persons made in God's image. We should therefore be ashamed that evangelical Christians during this century have tended to be in the rearguard, instead of in the vanguard, of social reformers. We have no quarrel with the proposal to assess religions, including Christianity, according to their social record, since we claim that the gospel is the power of God to transform both individuals and communities. It is because we have both experienced this power in our own lives and seen it at work constructively in human history that we cannot agree with Professor Hick's very negative assessment of the Christian social record as 'a complex mixture of valuable and harmful elements', neither better nor worse than that of other religions.[23]

In sum, our response to the six reasons why some find pluralism attractive is in each case fundamentally the same. They beg the question of truth; we want to press the question of truth. Has God fully and finally revealed himself in Christ, and in the total biblical testimony to Christ, or not?

(1) We agree with the search for global harmony, but not at the expense of truth.

(2) We agree that a greater knowledge of other religions is enriching, but in comparing them we cannot surrender Christ's claim to be the truth.

(3) We agree that colonial attitudes of superiority are arrogant, but still insist that truth is superior to falsehood.

(4) We agree that Scripture is culture-conditioned, but affirm that through it God has spoken his Word of truth.

(5) We agree that the ultimate mystery of God is beyond human apprehension, but affirm that God has truly revealed himself in Christ.

(6) We agree that it is an essential part of our Christian calling to serve the poor, but we are also called to bear witness to the truth.

According to Professor Rosemary Radford Ruether, 'the idea that Christianity, or even the biblical faiths, have a monopoly on religious truth is an outrageous and absurd religious chauvinism'.[24] If by 'monopoly' she means either that other religions possess no truth, or that Christians keep God's revelation to themselves and do not share it, we could perhaps agree with her strident words. But if by 'monopoly' she is referring to the belief that God has revealed himself fully and finally in Christ, then this is neither outrageous nor absurd, but on the contrary humble, wise, sober and considered Christian faith.

It would indeed be arrogant, even 'outrageous', if we were claiming uniqueness or finality for our own fallible opinions and limited experiences. But we are not. As Bishop Lesslie Newbigin put it in his sermon at the fiftieth anniversary of the Tambaram Missionary Conference in 1988:

> If, in fact, it is true that almighty God, creator and sustainer of all that exists in heaven and on earth, has – at a known time and place in human history – so humbled himself as to become part of our sinful humanity, and to suffer and die a shameful death to take away our sin, and to rise from the dead as the first-fruit of a new creation, if this is a fact, then to affirm it is not arrogance. To remain quiet about it is treason to our fellow human beings. If it is really true, as it is, that 'the Son of God loved me and gave himself up for me', how can I agree that this amazing act of matchless grace should merely become part of a syllabus for the 'comparative study of religions'?[25]

The uniqueness of Jesus Christ

It is essential at the outset to clarify that Christians claim uniqueness and finality only for Christ and not for Christianity in any of its many institutional or cultural forms. I call three witnesses to endorse this statement, who come respectively from Africa, Asia and Europe. First, Professor John Mbiti of Kenya has written: 'The uniqueness of Christianity is in Jesus Christ.'[26] My Asian witness is Sadhu Sundar Singh, the Indian Christian mystic and evangelist. Brought up in a Sikh home, he was converted to Christ as a teenager, and later became a *sadhu*, an itinerant holy man. Visiting a Hindu college one day, he was asked by an agnostic professor of comparative religion what he had found in Christianity which he had not found in his old religion. 'I have Christ,' he replied. 'Yes, I know,' said the professor a little impatiently. 'But what particular principle or doctrine have you found that you did not have before?' 'The particular thing I have found', he replied, 'is Christ.'[27]

The European witness I call is that widely travelled Anglican scholar, the late Bishop Stephen Neill. He strongly emphasized the centrality of Christ in the debate with pluralism. In his fine book *Christian Faith and Other Faiths*,[28] which was replaced by *Crises of Belief*, he wrote: 'The old saying "Christianity is Christ" is almost exactly true. The historical figure of Jesus of Nazareth is the criterion by which every Christian affirmation has to be judged, and in the light of which it stands or falls.'[29] Then, as he approached the end of his wide-ranging, sensitive response to Judaism,

Islam, Hinduism, Buddhism, primal religion and secularism, in which he faced the critics of Christianity honestly, he asked:

> Have our interlocutors ever really looked at Jesus Christ and tried to see him as he is? For, if we take the Gospels seriously ... Jesus is not in the least like anyone else who has ever lived. The things that he says about God are not the same as the sayings of any other religious teacher. The claims that he makes for himself are not the same as those that have been made on behalf of any other religious teacher. His criticisms of human life and society are far more devastating than those that any other man has ever made. The demands he made on his followers are more searching than those put forward by any other religious teacher.[30]

Our claim, then, is not just that Jesus was one of the great spiritual leaders of the world. It would be hopelessly incongruous to refer to him as 'Jesus the Great', comparable to Alexander the Great, Charles the Great or Napoleon the Great. Jesus is not 'the Great'; he is the only.[31] He has no peers, no rivals and no successors.

So how did the early Christians think of him? They gave him many names and titles. Often he is plain 'Jesus' or 'Christ', or, when his human name and messianic title are combined, 'Jesus (the) Christ'. Often again 'the Lord' is added, whether 'the Lord Jesus' or 'the Lord Christ' or 'the Lord Jesus Christ'. But when his title is spelled out in full, he is 'our Lord and Saviour Jesus Christ'. It comes, for example, at the conclusion of Peter's second Letter: 'But grow in the grace and knowledge of our Lord and Saviour Jesus Christ.'[32]

Within this complete designation three distinct affirmations are implied, namely that Jesus is Lord, Jesus is Saviour, and Jesus is ours. All three declare him to be unique.

Jesus is Lord

We have already considered in chapter 5 that *Kyrios Iēsous* ('Lord Jesus') was the earliest of all Christian creeds. It is assuredly a witness to the incarnation, since it is an affirmation of the identity of the human Jesus and the divine Lord. The word *kyrios* was used with a wide variety of meanings. On the one hand, it could be used simply as a courtesy title ('Sir') or to designate the owner of any kind of property. On the other hand, it was used throughout the classical Greek period in reference to the gods, who were thereby acknowledged as having authority over nature and history. It then came to be used of human rulers, especially the emperor (*Kyrios Kaisar*), and it was the regular paraphrase used for Yahweh by the scholars who put the Hebrew Bible into Greek. That it came to be used in the New Testament of the risen Christ,[33] with the implication that his followers were his slaves committed to worship and obey him, is a clear indication that they acknowledged his deity. It is all the more remarkable that his first Jewish disciples used this epithet, because they were as fiercely monotheistic as any Muslim is today. They recited the *Shema* daily, confessing that 'the LORD our God, the LORD is one'.[34] Yet in spite of this, they boldly called Jesus Lord, and worshipped him as God.

There is nothing like this in any other religion. The Jews still reject the deity of Jesus, of course. So do Muslims. Misunderstanding the incarnation in grossly physical terms, Muhammad wrote in the Qur'an: 'Allah forbid that he himself should beget a son.'[35]

Early or classical Buddhism had no god and no worship. Divine status and honour were not accorded to the Buddha until some 500 years after his death. We cannot therefore accept the parallel Professor Hick makes when he writes: 'Buddhology and Christology developed in comparable ways.'[36] That is, each 'came to be thought of' as an incarnation, as a result of the religious devotion of his followers. The comparison is inept, however, for Jesus' own contemporaries called him 'Lord', while half a millennium passed before the Buddha was worshipped as God.

Hinduism, it is true, claims a number of *avatars* or divine 'descents', in which the god Vishnu is said to have appeared in Rama, Krishna and others. In the *Bhagavad Gita* Krishna tells Arjuna that he frequently takes human form: 'I have been born many times, Arjuna ... Although I am unborn, everlasting, and I am the Lord of all, I come to my realm of nature and through my wondrous power I am born.'[37] Perhaps even more striking was the claim of Ramakrishna, the nineteenth-century Hindu reformer, who spoke of himself as 'the same soul that had been born before as Rama, as Krishna, as Jesus, or as Buddha, born again as Ramakrishna'.[38]

But 'incarnation' is not an apt or accurate rendering of the Sanskrit word *avatar*; it tends to conceal the two fundamental differences between the Hindu and the Christian claims. First, there is the question of *historicity.* Vishnu's *avatars* belong to Hindu mythology. Hinduism is a philosophical, mystical and ethical religion, and it is of no importance to Hindus whether the *avatars* actually happened or not. Christianity, however, is essentially a historical religion, based on the claim that the incarnation of God in Jesus Christ was an event of history which took place in Palestine when Augustus was emperor of Rome. If its historicity could be disproved, Christianity would be destroyed.

The second difference lies in the *plurality* of the *avatars*. Krishna spoke of his multiple, even 'frequent', rebirths. But 'incarnation' and 'reincarnation' are two fundamentally different concepts. The *avatars* were temporary manifestations or embodiments of Vishnu in human beings. But none involved the actual assumption of humanity by divinity or is in any way central to Hinduism. The Christian claim, by contrast, is that in Jesus of Nazareth God took human nature to himself once and for all and for ever; that his incarnation in Jesus was decisive, permanent and unrepeatable, the turning-point of human history and the beginning of the new age; and that reigning at God's right hand today is precisely 'the man Christ Jesus', still human as well as divine, although now his humanity has been glorified. Having assumed our nature, he has never discarded it, and he never will.

So the first aspect of the uniqueness of Jesus is that he is Lord. He is God's eternal, personal 'Word' or 'Son' who became a human being. Consequently, 'in Christ all the fulness of the Deity lives in bodily form'.[39] He is the sovereign ruler of the universe and of the church. It is true that he exercises his rule through humble love, for the Lord became the servant and washed his disciples' feet. Yet our place is on our faces at his feet.

Jesus is Saviour

The second affirmation contained within the full title of Jesus is that he is Saviour. Indeed, the divine Lord is the divine Saviour. And, although the vocabulary of salvation is distasteful to many people today, we cannot possibly give it up. For Christianity is in essence a rescue religion; it announces good news of salvation. As the churches have recited for centuries in the Nicene Creed, 'for us men (human beings) and for our salvation he came down from heaven ...'.

Now 'salvation' is a comprehensive word, embracing the totality of God's redeeming purpose for his alienated creatures. In a word, as we saw in chapter 2, salvation is freedom, with corresponding negative and positive aspects. It includes freedom from the just judgment of God on our sins, from our guilt and our guilty conscience, into a new relationship with him in which we become his reconciled, forgiven children and we know him as our Father. It is freedom from the bitter bondage of meaninglessness into a new sense of purpose in God's new society of love, in which the last are first, the poor rich and the meek heirs. It is freedom from the dark prison of our own self-centredness into a new life of self-fulfilment through self-forgetful service. And one day it will include freedom from the futility of pain, decay, death and dissolution into a new world of immortality, beauty and unimaginable joy. All this – and more! – is 'salvation'.

It was to secure these great blessings that Jesus Christ came into the world, died on the cross, and rose again. It is he not we who took the initiative: 'the Son of Man came to seek and to save what was lost.'[40] He likened himself to a shepherd who left the rest of his sheep on their own in order to go after the one which was lost. Far from abandoning it, in the hope that it might bleat and stumble its way home, he risked his own life to search it out.[41] In fact, 'the good shepherd' did lay down his life for his sheep.[42] Deliberately and voluntarily Jesus went to the cross, in order to identify himself with us. God in Christ took our place, bore our sins, assumed our guilt, paid our penalty, died our death, in order that we might be forgiven and recreated. And then he was raised from death in a super-natural event, in order to reverse the human verdict upon him and to vin-dicate his divine-human person and saving work.

This too is unique. It is not only in his incarnation, but also in his atoning death and historical resurrection, that his uniqueness is to be seen. The whole concept of a gracious God, who refused either to condone our sins or to visit them upon us, who instead took the initiative to rescue us, who gave himself to the shame and pain of death on the cross, and who broke the power of death in his resurrection, has no parallel in other faiths. 'If any other religion has anything in the least like the doctrines of incarna-tion and atonement ...' wrote Bishop Stephen Neill, 'I have yet to find it.'[43] But it cannot be found. Emil Brunner was right to refer to 'the self-confi-dent optimism of all non-Christian religion', teaching various forms of self-salvation, whereas in the gospel the whole emphasis is on the gracious 'self-movement' of God towards sinners and on self-despair as 'the ante-chamber of faith'.[44]

Buddhism sees the human predicament in suffering rather than sin, and in the 'desire' which it sees as the root of suffering. Deliverance comes only through the abolition of desire by self-effort. There is no God and no Saviour. 'Strive without ceasing' were the Buddha's last words to his dis-ciples before he died.

Philosophical Hinduism locates our problem in *maya*, usually under-stood as the 'illusion' of our space-time experience. Popular Hinduism, on the other hand, teaches the inflexible doctrine of *karma*, retribution through reincarnation. Each person must eat the fruit of his own wrong-doings, in future lives if not in this one. From this endless cycle (*samsara*) of rebirths or reincarnations there is no escape by forgiveness, but only by that final release called Nirvana, involving the extinction of individual being and absorption into impersonal divine reality (Brahman).

Judaism continues, of course, to teach the possibility of forgiveness to the penitent, which the Old Testament promised, but denies both that Jesus is the Messiah and that his sin-bearing death is the only ground on which God can forgive. That painstaking and honest Jewish scholar, C. G. Montefiore, saw the 'greatness and originality' of Jesus in his new attitude to sinners. Instead of avoiding them, he actively sought them out. The rabbis had said that God receives sinners who return to him; they had not spoken of a divine love which makes the first move to seek and to save them:

This direct search for, and appeal to, the sinner, are new and moving notes of high import and significance. The good shepherd who searches for the lost sheep, and reclaims it and rejoices over it, is a new figure ...[45]

Islam clearly proclaims the mercy of God. Each of the 114 *suras* (chapters) of the Qur'an is introduced by the words 'In the Name of Allah, the Compassionate, the Merciful'. But it discloses no costly historical display of his mercy. And when we probe into its exercise, we find that Allah is merciful to the meritorious, to those who pray, and give alms, and fast in Ramadan. There is no message for sinners who deserve judgment, except that they will receive the judgment they deserve.

> Moreover, that which we ask the Muslim to look for in Jesus is in itself a cause of grave offence to Muslim pride. We suggest – we cannot do otherwise – that he find a Saviour. The Muslim affirms that he has no need of any such thing.[46]

There can be no doubt that the chief difference between Christianity and the world's religions, and the chief stumbling block which they find in it, is the cross. It humbles all pride and dashes all hopes of self-salvation. It also speaks of the uncalculating generosity of the love of God in providing this way of salvation. It was here that Toyohiko Kagawa (died 1960), the Japanese Christian leader, found Christianity's uniqueness:

> I am grateful for Shinto, for Buddhism, and for Confucianism. I owe much to these faiths ... Yet these three faiths utterly failed to minister to my heart's deepest needs. I was a pilgrim journeying upon a long road that had no turning. I was weary. I was footsore. I wandered through a dark and dismal world where tragedies were thick ... Buddhism teaches great compassion ... but since the beginning of time, who has declared, 'this is my blood of the covenant which is poured out for many unto remission of sins'?[47]

Jesus is ours

Jesus Christ's full title is not 'the Lord and Saviour' but '*our* Lord and Saviour'. We must not miss this personal possessive adjective. It is a small word, but a highly significant one. It indicates that there is a third affirmation hidden in his title, namely *Jesus is ours*.

Already in the Old Testament the possessive adjective 'my' regularly expressed the personal relationship which God's covenant people enjoyed with him, especially when they addressed him in prayer, as in the Psalms. For example, 'O LORD, my Rock and my Redeemer,' 'The LORD is my shepherd,' 'The LORD is my light and my salvation ... the stronghold of my life,' 'He alone is my rock and my salvation; he is my fortress,' and 'O God, you are my God, earnestly I seek you.'[48]

In the New Testament what is claimed is a comparable personal relationship with Jesus Christ. Both Paul and Peter give us notable examples. Here is Paul: 'I consider everything a loss compared to the surpassing greatness of knowing Christ Jesus my Lord.'[49] As for Peter, he claims this intimate relationship not for himself alone, but for his readers too: 'Though you have not seen him [*sc.* Christ], you love him; and even though you do not see him now, you believe in him and are filled with an inexpressible and glorious joy.'[50]

Here are assertions that Christ is our contemporary. The Jesus who was born into our world, and who lived and died in first-century Palestine, also rose from the dead, is now alive for ever, and is available and accessible to his people. Jesus Christ is not to be relegated, like other religious leaders, to history and the history books. He is not dead and gone, finished or fossilized. He is alive and active. He calls us to follow him, and he offers himself to us as our indwelling and transforming Saviour.

Often this is explained in the New Testament as meaning that his availability to us is through the Holy Spirit, who is his Spirit.[51] Paul indicates this when he prays for the Ephesians, that 'he [*sc.* the Father] may strengthen you with power through his Spirit in your inner being, so that Christ may dwell in your hearts through faith'.[52] Indeed, the Christian faith is essentially trinitarian. We come to the Father through the Son and by the Spirit,[53] and the Father comes to us through the Son by the Spirit.[54]

Once again this is unique. There is nothing comparable to it in the other religions. The Buddhist does not claim to know the Buddha, nor the Confucianist Confucius, nor the Muslim Muhammad, nor the Marxist Karl Marx. Each reveres the founder of his religion or ideology as a teacher of the past. To Christians too Jesus is a teacher, but even more he is our living Lord and Saviour. Phrases claiming this 'recur on page after page of the New Testament, and make clear that it is this intimate and personal relationship of trust, devotion and communion, which is the very heart of the Christian faith'.[55]

Lord Coggan, when Archbishop of Canterbury, drew attention to this when referring to the 164 occurrences of Paul's favourite formula, 'in Christ':

> It is a strange phrase. We can scarcely find a parallel use to it in ordinary life. If, let us say, an intimate friend of Churchill who had spent many years with him and then had given a decade to the writing of his life were talking to us about that great man, he might sum up his relationship to him in a wide variety of ways. He might say that he feared him, or admired him, or revered him, or even loved him. But he never

would say, 'I am a man in Churchill'. It would never occur to him to use such a phrase. But Paul was, above everything else, 'a man in Christ'.[56]

Although it is right to emphasize in this way the believer's personal, individual relationship to Christ, indicated by the singular possessive 'my', yet his full title actually includes the *plural* possessive 'our'. For God is calling out a people for himself, and the focus of his people's unity is Jesus Christ. It is he who comes and stands among us when we meet to worship. 'I am with you,' he says, even when only two or three assemble in his name.[57] And he repeats his promise to us when we go out to make disciples of the nations: 'I am with you always, to the very end of the age.'[58]

Here, then, are three major aspects of the uniqueness of Jesus Christ. He is Lord. He is Saviour. He is ours. For he is 'our Lord and Saviour, Jesus Christ'. Historically speaking, these are allusions to his birth, death and resurrection. Theologically speaking, they refer to the incarnation, the atonement and the risen Lord's gift of the Spirit.

Indeed, because in no other person but the historic Jesus of Nazareth has God become human, lived on earth, died for our sins, conquered death, been exalted to heaven, and sent the Holy Spirit, therefore there is no other Saviour. For there is no other person who possesses these qualifications, on account of which he is competent to save.

Hendrik Kraemer, the Dutch theologian who dominated the Tambaram Missionary Conference in 1938, laid great stress on the uniqueness of the Christ events. Fifty years later Bishop Lesslie Newbigin said:

> Kraemer did not claim uniqueness for Christianity, which is a changing, variegated and ambiguous human phenomenon; he claimed uniqueness for the events that form the substance of the gospel. In Kraemer's favourite phrase, these events are *sui generis.* There may be ideas, stories, myths, legends that reflect the same motifs, but if we are talking about history ... there is nothing to be put alongside this story. The gospel is, strictly, *sui generis*, unique.[59]

It is not enough, therefore, to declare that Jesus is unique in the sense that every human being is unique, as indeed every snowflake is unique, and every blade of grass. Nor can we follow Professor Paul Knitter in his attempt to interpret the 'one and only' phraseology of the New Testament in relation to Christ. It is the language of testimony, not theology, he says; of love, not science; of enthusiastic faith, not analytical philosophy. It is, he goes on, 'much like the language a husband would use of his wife ... "you are the most beautiful woman in the world ... you are the only woman for me"'.[60]

It is poetry, hyperbole, not literal truth. Later, Professor Knitter argues that it is 'action language', whose *primary* purpose was neither to define doctrine nor to exclude others, but rather to urge action for Christ in 'total commitment to his vision and way'.[61]

But no. This appeal to different uses of language, although ingenious, is surely special pleading. A careful study of the 'one and only' texts, in their context, should convince us that they are not purely poetic expressions of faith and love, meant to be taken with a pinch of salt. On the contrary, they are solemn affirmations of truth, which have eternal consequences in relation to salvation. Moreover, all of them, implicitly if not explicitly, draw their negative conclusion ('no other') from their positive statement (he alone). Thus, it is because only he knows the Father that only he can make him known,[62] and it is because he is 'the way and the truth and the life' that nobody can come to the Father except through him.[63] Similarly, it is because the name of Jesus Christ, whom God has raised from the dead, is mighty to save, that there is no other saving name.[64] So too (even in the thoroughgoing syncretism of the Graeco-Roman world) 'there is but one God, the Father ... and there is but one Lord, Jesus Christ ...'[65] there is one high priest who offered one sacrifice (of himself) as a sin offering once for all;[66] and in consequence of his death as a ransom for all, 'there is one God and one mediator between God and men, the man Christ Jesus'.[67]

Only one way, only one name, only one God, only one Lord, only one Mediator. The claim is exclusive, and the implication inescapable. What is genuinely unique has universal significance and must be universally made known, whereas, to quote Visser't Hooft again, 'there is no universality if there is no unique event'.[68] Thus uniqueness and universality belong together. It is because God has super-exalted Jesus, and given him the unique name of 'Lord', towering above every other name, that every knee must bow to him. It is because Jesus Christ is the only Saviour, that we are under obligation to proclaim him everywhere. The 'inclusivism' of the mission is precisely due to the 'exclusivism' of the Mediator. In addition, universal authority over the nations has been given to him; that is why he commissions us to go and disciple the nations.[69]

In conclusion, I would like to try to answer two questions which may well be in the reader's mind, as they are certainly in mine. Both concern our relationships with adherents of other faiths.

Your first question might be this: 'Are you suggesting a total discontinuity between Christianity and other religions, so that all truth is contained in it and no truth in them?' No. Christians do certainly believe that God has revealed himself in Jesus Christ, as witnessed to in Scripture, in a unique and final way, so that, in this life, he has nothing more to reveal than he has revealed, although of course we have much more to learn. But we are not suggesting that outside the church we consider God inactive and truth absent. Not at all. God sustains all his creatures, and therefore 'is not far from any of them'. By creation they are his 'offspring', who 'live and move and have [their] being' in him.[70] Also Jesus Christ, as the *logos* of God and the light of men,[71] is himself ceaselessly active in the world. Because he is described as 'the true light that gives light to every man',[72] we dare to claim that all beauty, truth and goodness, wherever they are found among human beings, derive from him, whether people know it or not. This is an aspect of God's so-called 'common grace', his love shown to all humankind; it is not, however, his 'saving grace', which he extends to those who humbly cry to him for mercy.

Your second question may well follow on from the first: 'Is there no hope of salvation, then, for those who belong to other religions, and who may never even have heard of Jesus?' In seeking to respond to this extremely poignant question, I shall try to do so biblically. That is to say, we need to combine confidence and agnosticism, what we know (because Scripture plainly teaches it) and what we do not know (because Scripture is either unclear or even silent about it).

What we know from Scripture is that there is no possibility of self-salvation. For all human beings, on account of God's general revelation, have some knowledge of God and of goodness; all have failed to live up to their knowledge; and all are therefore guilty before God, and are in the state of 'perishing' (unless God intervenes). This is the argument of Romans 1 – 3. Nobody can achieve salvation by his or her religion, sincerity or philanthropy. Those who claim to be Christians cannot, and nor can anyone else. Moreover, Cornelius the centurion is not an exception to this rule, as has sometimes been suggested. His story teaches that salvation is available to Gentiles as well as to Jews, and on the same terms; it does not teach that he attained it by his own righteousness, piety or generosity. On the contrary, he needed to hear the gospel and respond to it in order to receive salvation, life, cleansing and the Holy Spirit.[73] So self-salvation is impossible. We also know that Jesus Christ is the only Saviour (because he alone has the necessary qualifications, as we have seen), and that salvation is by God's grace alone, on the ground of Christ's cross alone, by faith alone.

What we do not know, however, is exactly how much knowledge and understanding of the gospel people need before they can cry to God for mercy and be saved. In the Old Testament, people were certainly 'justified by grace through faith', even though they had little knowledge or expectation of Christ. Perhaps there are others today in a somewhat similar position. They know they are sinful and guilty before God, and that they cannot do anything to win his favour, so in self-despair they call upon the God they dimly perceive to save them. If God does save such, as many evangelical

Christians tentatively believe, their salvation is still only by grace, only through Christ, only by faith.

Something else we know is that the final number of God's redeemed people will be actually countless,[74] in final fulfilment of God's promise to Abraham that his posterity (spiritual as well as physical) will be 'as numerous as the stars in the sky and as the sand on the seashore'.[75] In the same vein we seem to be assured by Paul that many more people will be saved than lost, because Christ's work in causing salvation will be more successful than Adam's in causing ruin, and because God's grace in bringing life will overflow 'much more' than Adam's trespass in bringing death.[76]

Although we have solid biblical grounds for cherishing this expectation, we are not told how God will achieve it. But while we remain agnostic about this, we can have no uncertainty about our duty. We are commissioned, by him who has authority to do so, to preach the gospel and make disciples. It is hard for people to call on one they have not believed in, or to believe in one of whom they have not heard, or to hear if no-one preaches to them.[77] It is much easier for people to believe once they have heard the good news of Christ crucified. It is when they learn from the cross about God's mercy to sinners that they cry, 'God be merciful to me, a sinner!' As Paul put it, 'faith comes from hearing the message, and the message is heard through the word of Christ'.[78]

So then, to deny the uniqueness of Christ is to cut the nerve of mission and make it superfluous. To affirm his uniqueness, on the other hand, is to acknowledge the urgency of making him universally known.

Notes

[1] The story is told by Douglas Webster in *Not Ashamed* (Hodder and Stoughton, 1970), p. 66.

[2] W. A. Visser't Hooft, *No Other Name* (SCM, 1963), p. 11.

[3] *Ibid.*, p. 95.

[4] These categories were first employed by Alan Race in *Christians and Religious Pluralism* (Orbis, 1982), were popularized by the Church of England General Synod's Board for Mission and Unity in their report *Towards a Theology for Inter-Faith Dialogue* (Anglican Consultative Council, 1984, second edition, 1986), and were further developed by Paul F. Knitter in *No Other Name?* (SCM, 1985), while the implications of 'pluralism' were explored in *The Myth of Christian Uniqueness*, ed. John Hick and Paul F. Knitter (SCM, 1987). A judicious critique by Dr Christopher Wright of *Towards a Theology for Inter-Faith Dialogue* appeared in *Anvil* (vol. 1, no. 3, 1984), and this material has now been incorporated in his booklet *What's so Unique about Jesus?* (MARC, 1990). Then, in 1991 (too late to be considered in this book) there appeared a vigorous riposte to *The Myth of Christian Uniqueness* entitled *Christian Uniqueness Reconsidered: The Myth of a Pluralist Theology of Relgions*, ed. Gavin D'Costa (Fowler Wright). It is another symposium, and includes contributions by such leading contemporary theologians as Jürgen Moltmann, Lesslie Newbigin, Wolfhart Pannenberg, Rowan Williams and M. M. Thomas.

[5] *Gaudium et Spes*, para. 22.

[6] This is one possible position described by Raimundo Panikkar in his contribution to *The Myth of Christian Uniqueness*, p. 91.

[7] Stanley J. Samartha in *The Myth of Christian Uniqueness*, pp. 79–80.

[8] Mt. 10:34.

[9] Paul F. Knitter, *No Other Name?* (SCM, 1985), p. 2.

[10] *The Myth of Christian Uniqueness*, p. 17.

[11] Rosemary Radford Ruether in *The Myth of Christian Uniqueness*, p. 139.

[12] *Ibid.*, p. 76.

[13] Tom F. Driver in *The Myth of Christian Uniqueness*, p. 207.

[14] *The Myth of Christian Uniqueness*, pp. 39–40.

[15] *Ibid.*, p. viii.

[16] *Ibid.*, p. 8.

[17] *Ibid.*, pp. 12–13.

[18] *Ibid.*, p. 211.

[19] *Ibid.*, pp. 56–57.

[20] *Ibid.*, p. 59.

[21] *Ibid.*, p. 216.

[22] *Ibid.*, p. 180.

[23] *Ibid.*, pp. 23–30.

[24] *Ibid.*, p. 141.

[25] The full text of his sermon appears in the *International Review of Mission*, July 1988, pp. 325–331.

[26] John Mbiti, *African Religions and Philosophy* (Heinemann, 1969), p. 277.

[27] Stanley Jones, *The Christ of the Indian Road* (1925; Hodder and Stoughton, 1926), p. 64.

[28] (OUP, 1961).

[29] Stephen C. Neill, *Crises of Belief* (Hodder and Stoughton, 1984), published in the States as *Christian Faith and Other Faiths* (IVP USA, 1984), p. 23.

[30] *Ibid.*, p. 286.

[31] See P. Carnegie Simpson, *The Fact of Christ* (1930; James Clarke, 1952), pp. 19–22.

[32] 2 Pet. 3:18.

[33] *E.g.* Acts 2:36; Rom. 10:9; *cf.* Mt. 28:18.

[34] Dt. 6:4.

[35] Chapter on Mary, in *The Koran*, translated by N. J. Dawood (Penguin, 1968), p. 34.

[36] John Hick (ed.), *The Myth of God Incarnate* (SCM, 1977), p. 169.

[37] Translated by Juan Mascaro, *Bhagavad Gita* (Penguin, 1962), pp. 61–62.

[38] Quoted by W. A. Visser't Hooft, *No Other Name* (SCM, 1963), pp. 36–37.

[39] Col. 2:9.

[40] Lk. 19:10.

[41] Lk. 15:1–7.

[42] Jn. 10:11, 15.

[43] From an artide in the *Church of England Newspaper* on 28 May 1976.

[44] Emil Brunner, *The Mediator* (1927; ET Westminster, 1947), pp. 291–299.

[45] C. G. Montefiore, *The Synoptic Gospels* (Macmillan, second edition, 1927), vol. I, pp. cxviii, 55; vol. II, pp. 520–521.

[46] S. C. Neill, *Crises of Belief/Christian Faith and Other Faiths*, p. 87.

[47] T. Kagawa, *Christ and Japan* (SCM, 1934), pp. 108, 113.

[48] Pss. 19:14; 23:1; 27:1; 62:2; 63:1.

[49] Phil. 3:8.

[50] 1 Pet. 1:8.

[51] *E.g.* Jn. 14:16–18, 21; Rom.8:9–10.

[52] Eph. 3:16–17.

[53] Eph. 2:18.

[54] Jn. 14:16–23.

[55] Stephen C. Neill, *Christian Faith Today* (Penguin, 1955), pp. 17–18.

[56] Donald Coggan, *Paul – Portrait of a Revolutionary* (Hodder and Stoughton, 1984), p. 75.

[57] *Cf.* Mt. 18:20.

[58] Mt. 28:20.

[59] *International Review of Mission*, July, 1988, p. 327.

[60] P. F. Knitter, *No Other Name?*, p. 185.

[61] *The Myth of Christian Uniqueness*, p. 196.

[62] Mt. 11:25–27.

[63] Jn. 14:6.

[64] Acts 4:10–12.

[65] 1 Cor. 8:5–6.

[66] Heb. 10:12–14.

[67] 1 Tim. 2:5–6.

[68] W. A. Visser't Hooft, *No Other Name*, p. 102

[69] Mt. 28:18–29.

[70] Acts 17:27–28.

[71] Jn. 1:1–5.

[72] Jn. 1:9.

[73] Acts 11:14, 18; 15:9.

[74] Rev. 7:9.

[75] Gn. 22:17.

[76] Rom. 5:15–21.

[77] Rom. 10:14.

[78] Rom. 10:17.

Our God is a missionary God

The whole concept of 'mission' is out of favour in today's world, and hostility to it is growing. Evangelism, missionary zeal, attempts to convert other people, are all rejected as 'incompatible with the spirit of tolerance', 'a gross infringement of individual liberties', and 'a most distasteful form of arrogance'. Even in the church some members are completely indifferent to the church's mission, while others are actively resistant to it. 'How can one religion claim a monopoly of truth?' people ask. 'Are there not many different ways to God?' 'What right have we to interfere in other people's privacy, or attempt to impose our views on them? Let's rather mind our own business, and devoutly hope that other people will mind theirs.'

Half hidden in this negative rhetoric lie three main objections to the Christian mission, namely that it is guilty of intolerance, arrogance and violence. How should we respond to these criticisms?

Tolerance is perhaps the most prized virtue in western culture today. But people do not always define what they mean by it. It contributes to clarity if we distinguish between three different kinds of tolerance. The first may be called *legal* tolerance; it seeks to ensure that every minority's religious rights (usually summarized as the freedom to 'profess, practise and propagate' religion) are adequately protected in law. Christians should be in the forefront of those demanding this. Another kind is *social* tolerance, which encourages respect for all persons, whatever views they may hold, seeks to understand and appreciate their position, and promotes good neighbourliness. This too is a virtue which Christians wish to cultivate; it arises naturally from our recognition that all human beings are God's creation and bear his image, and that he wants us to live together in amity. But what about *intellectual* tolerance, which is the third kind? To cultivate a mind so broad that it can accommodate every opinion, however false or evil, without ever detecting anything to reject, is not a virtue; it is the vice of the feebleminded and amoral. It ends up in an unprincipled confusion of truth with error and goodness with evil. Christians who believe that truth and goodness have been revealed in Christ cannot possibly come to terms with it. We are resolved to bear witness to Christ, who is the embodiment of both. It was this conviction which led William Temple, when Archbishop of Canterbury, to decline invitations to become associated with the World Congress of Faiths and to write that 'Christianity is, I am persuaded, a profoundly intolerant religion'.[1]

If mission is not in the wrong sense intolerant, is it arrogant? I think we should begin by agreeing that some Christian attitudes and evangelistic methods could justly be described as 'proud' and 'patronizing'. We need to be sensitive to these Christian failings, which other people see in us, and repent. Evangelists should never be imperialists, ambitious for the growth of their personal empire or for the prestige of their church or organization, but only for the kingdom of God. The crusading spirit, the triumphalist mindset and the swashbuckling style are all inappropriate in Christ's ambassadors. Humility is the pre-eminent Christian virtue and should characterize all our thoughts, words and deeds.

The Willowbank Report, which summarized the findings of an international consultation on 'Gospel and Culture', held in January 1978, included a whole section entitled 'Wanted: Humble Messengers of the Gospel!' Half of it is 'an analysis of missionary humility'; it focuses on the need for cultural humility. Some western missionaries have made the mistake of confusing Christ with culture. They have then become 'guilty of a cultural imperialism which both undermines the local culture unnecessarily and seeks to impose an alien culture instead'.[2] The report continues:

> We know we should never condemn or despise another culture, but rather respect it. We advocate neither the arrogance which imposes our culture on others, nor the syncretism which mixes the gospel with cultural elements incompatible with it, but rather a humble sharing of the good news – made possible by the mutual respect of a genuine friendship.[3]

Granted the need to repent of both personal and cultural arrogance, is the very concept of mission inherently arrogant? Bishop Kenneth Cragg, the acknowledged Christian expert in Islam, argues that the opposite is the case:

> The description of mission as religious egoism may have some validity in relation to some of its disloyalties. But it is finally the abeyance of mission which would be the supremely damnable egoism, for it would argue a proprietary right in that which is too big to belong to a few and too inclusive to be arrogated to some alone ... To believe in Christ at all is to acknowledge him a universal Christ. Because he is requisite for all, he is perquisite to none. The Christian mission is simply an active recognition of the dimensions of the love of God.[4]

The third objection to the Christian mission is that it is a violent assault on people. Evangelism seems to them both aggressive and intrusive, involving an unwelcome invasion of private territory. Again we have to acknowledge that this is sometimes true. But the Great Commission gives us no warrant to encroach on other people's personal space or crash the barriers with which they seek to protect themselves. Personally speaking, I wish we could agree to purge our evangelistic vocabulary of all violent metaphors. 'Crusades' are too reminiscent of medieval military expeditions to the Holy Land, 'campaigns' of army operations, and even 'missions' of bombing-raids in wartime, while talk of 'targeting' communities is more suggestive of bombs and bullets than of the gospel of peace. How can we evangelize with integrity if we do not display the 'meekness and gentleness' of the Christ we proclaim?[5]

When people talk disparagingly of 'proselytism', they generally seem to have in mind some kind of conversion by force. This being so, it must be sharply distinguished from true evangelism. Indeed, there is a broad measure of agreement among churches that 'proselytism' is a synonym for 'unworthy witness'.[6] Moreover, the 'unworthiness' of a proselytizing witness may refer to our motives (concern for our own glory, instead of the glory of Christ), or to our methods (trust in psychological pressure techniques or in the offer of benefits on condition of conversion, instead of in the power of the Holy Spirit), or to our message (focusing on the alleged falsehood and failures of others, instead of on the truth and perfection of Jesus Christ). Besides, there is no need to resort to any kind of 'unworthy witness'. For truth is going to prevail in the end. As Paul put it, 'we cannot do anything against the truth, but only for the truth'.[7] Those who use improper pressures are thereby admitting the weakness of their own case.

Authentic Christian mission, then, is fully compatible with a true tolerance, a genuine humility and a Christlike gentleness. It is also integral to historic Christianity. Christianity without mission is Christianity no longer.

This is partly, as we saw in the last chapter, because Christianity affirms both the finality of Christ (he has no successors) and the uniqueness of Christ (he has no peers or rivals). His uniqueness gives him universal significance; he must be made known throughout the world.

More than that. Christian mission is rooted in the nature of God himself. The Bible reveals him as a missionary God (Father, Son and Holy Spirit), who creates a missionary people, and is working towards a missionary consummation. If this chapter were a sermon, I would have to announce my text as being the whole Bible! It would not be possible to select a shorter one, if we are to lay an adequate biblical foundation for the Christian mission. I propose, therefore, to make a rapid survey or overview of the Bible, dividing it into its five main sections. We shall look first at the Old Testament and at God the Father, the Creator of the world, the covenant God of Israel; secondly at the Gospels, and at our Lord Jesus Christ, the Saviour of sinners; thirdly at the Acts, and at the Holy Spirit at work in and through the apostles; fourthly at the Letters, and at the church they depict, living and witnessing responsibly in the world; and fifthly at the Revelation, and at the climax of history, when the redeemed people of God will be gathered from all nations. Each successive stage is a fresh missionary disclosure.

The God of the Old Testament is a missionary God

The idea that the Old Testament is a missionary book, and that its God is a missionary God, comes as a surprise to many people. For they have always thought of the God of the Old Testament as having been exclusively the God of Israel. They remember how he called Abraham and made a covenant with him and his descendants; how he renewed his covenant with Isaac and Jacob, and then with the twelve tribes whom he rescued from their Egyptian slavery and brought to Mount Sinai, where he promised to be their God and to make them his people; how he settled them in the promised land and blessed them with kings, priests and prophets, preparing them for the coming of the Messiah.

And all this is true. But it is only a part of the truth. For the Old Testament begins not with Abraham but with Adam, not with the covenant but with the creation, not with the chosen race but with the human race. It declares emphatically that Yahweh, the God of Israel, was no petty tribal godling like Chemosh, the god of the Moabites, or Milcom, the god of the Ammonites, but the Creator of heaven and earth, the Lord of the nations, and 'the God of the spirits of all flesh'.[8] That is its perspective throughout.

Further, the call of Abraham did not contradict this world view; it established it. Yahweh had told Abraham to leave his country, people and household for another land he would be shown. Now God said to him:

'I will make you into a great nation
 and I will bless you;
I will make your name great,
 and you will be a blessing.
I will bless those who bless you,
 and whoever curses you I will curse;
and all peoples on earth
 will be blessed through you.'[9]

Thus Abraham was to leave his own country and be shown another, to leave his own people and be made into another. God promised not only to bless him, but to make him a blessing; not only to give him a posterity, but through it to bless 'all peoples on earth'.

It is no exaggeration to say that Genesis 12:1–4 is the most unifying text of the whole Bible. For God's saving purpose is encapsulated in it, namely to bless the whole world through Christ, who was Abraham's seed. The rest of the Bible is an unfolding of it, and subsequent history has been a fulfilment of it. For God first prepared Israel for Christ's coming, and then through his coming has been blessing the world ever since. We ourselves would not be followers of Jesus today if it were not for this text: we are beneficiaries of the promise God made to Abraham about four thousand years ago. 'If you belong to Christ,' Paul wrote, 'then you are Abraham's seed, and heirs according to the promise.'[10] Again, if we share his faith, 'he is the father of us all'.[11] For God's promise was an advance announcement to Abraham of the gospel, namely that he was going to 'justify the Gentiles by faith'.[12]

The tragedy of the Old Testament is that Israel kept forgetting the universal scope of God's promise. They overlooked the fact that God had chosen one family in order to bless all families. They became preoccupied with themselves and with their own history. They even perverted the truth of divine election into the error of divine favouritism, which led them to boast of their privileged status and to assume that they were immune to the judgment of God.

So the prophets had to keep trying to broaden their outlook, and to remind them that God's purpose through Abraham's descendants was to bless the nations. For example, God would make the *nations* the Messiah's 'inheritance' and 'possession';[13] *all nations* would serve him;[14] he would be a light for the Gentile nations,[15] and in that day *all nations* would stream to the mountain of the Lord's temple.[16]

The Christ of the Gospels is a missionary Christ

In 1850 David Livingstone, the intrepid pioneer missionary in Africa, wrote to his sister Agnes:

Forbid it that we should ever consider the holding of a commission from the King of kings a sacrifice, so long as other men esteem the service of an earthly government an honour ... I am a missionary heart and soul. God had an only son, and he was a missionary and a physician. A poor, poor imitation of him I am ... In this service I hope to live; in it I wish to die.[17]

A few years later Robert Speer, travelling secretary of the Student Volunteer Movement in the United States, wrote in his journal: 'If you want to follow Jesus Christ, you must follow him to the ends of the earth, for that is where he is going ... We cannot think of God without thinking of him as a missionary God.'

It is true that twice Jesus is recorded by Matthew as having restricted his mission to 'the lost sheep of Israel'. He told the Twelve not to evangelize Gentile or Samaritan areas, but to 'go rather' to Israel's lost sheep;[18] and later he told a Canaanite woman, who had appealed to him on behalf of her demonized daughter, that he 'was sent only' to Israel's lost sheep.[19] This sounds disturbing, even shocking, until we remember that it was merely a temporary, historical limitation, relating only to Jesus' earthly ministry. He added that through his death, resurrection and gift of the Spirit, salvation would be offered to all the nations, to whom he therefore later instructed his followers to take the good news.

Even the Gospel of Matthew, which is the most Jewish of the four, and is the only Gospel to include the two references to Israel's lost sheep, makes this global horizon clear. It begins with the genealogy of Jesus, which is traced to Abraham, surely to indicate that the promise is at last to be fulfilled.[20] Next, after the birth of Jesus, it describes the visit of those mysterious Magi, who perhaps were Zoroastrian astrologers from Persia, who brought their treasures to 'the king of the Jews', and whom Matthew sees as forerunners of the Gentile multitudes who would later do homage to Jesus.[21] Matthew also records Jesus' remarkable prediction that 'many will come from the east and the west, and will take their places at the feast with Abraham, Isaac and Jacob in the kingdom of heaven'.[22] And Matthew's Gospel ends with the fullest version we are given of the so-called 'Great' or 'Universal' Commission. The mission of the Twelve during Jesus' public ministry may have been restricted to 'the lost sheep of Israel', but the mission of the church has no such limitation. The followers of Jesus are to 'go and make disciples of all nations', welcoming them by baptism into the Christian community, and teaching them to obey all their Master's instructions.[23] This commission to the nations has never been rescinded; it is still binding on the people of God. It was issued by the risen Christ who was able to claim that 'all authority in heaven and on earth' had been conferred on him. A link between the 'all authority' he claimed and the 'all nations' he commissioned his followers to disciple is clearly intended. The universal mission of the church springs from the universal authority of Jesus.

The Holy Spirit of the Acts is a missionary Spirit

Roland Allen, that remarkable High Church Anglican missionary in northern China from 1895 to 1903, burned with a passionate longing that the church would recover those three indigenous principles (self-governing, self-supporting, self-propagating) which characterized the missionary policy of the apostle Paul. His best-known books are *Missionary Methods, St Paul's or Ours?* (1912) and *The Spontaneous Expansion of the Church* (1927). Less well known is his little study of the Acts, *Pentecost and the World,* sub-titled *The Revelation of the Holy Spirit in the Acts of the Apostles.* In it he writes: 'The book of the "Acts" is strictly a missionary book ... The conclusion is irresistible that the Spirit given was ... in fact a missionary Spirit.'[24] This, he continues, is 'the great, fundamental, unmistakable teaching of the book ... It is in the revelation of the Holy Spirit as a missionary Spirit that the "Acts" stands alone in the New Testament'.[25]

Roland Allen was right. The Holy Spirit is the chief actor in the Acts. The book begins with the 120 disciples waiting. In the upper room during his last evening with the Twelve, Jesus had promised the coming of the Spirit and had described the Spirit's future ministry of convincing, teaching and witnessing. During the forty days which elapsed between the resurrection and the ascension, the repeated message was that the Spirit would give them 'power' for witness[26] and that they must wait for him to come.[27]

So Pentecost was a missionary event. It was the fulfilment of God's promise through the prophet Joel to pour out his Spirit 'on all people',[28] irrespective of their race, sex, age or social standing. And the foreign languages which the disciples spoke (which seems clearly to have been what the 'tongues' were, at least on the Day of Pentecost) were a dramatic sign of the international nature of the Messiah's kingdom which the Holy Spirit had come to establish.

The rest of the Acts is a logical unfolding of that beginning. We watch enthralled as the missionary Spirit creates a missionary people and thrusts them out on their missionary task. They began to witness to their fellow Jews in and around Jerusalem, the Jewish headquarters. Then Philip took the bold initiative to witness to Samaritans, who were a half-way house between the Jews and the Gentiles.[29] Next came the conversion of the centurion Cornelius, one of those Gentile 'Godfearers', who accepted the monotheism and ethical standards of the Jews, but remained a Gentile, on the fringe of the synagogue without accepting full conversion. The Holy Spirit gave the clearest possible evidence that Cornelius was now a fully accredited member of the church.[30] Soon afterwards, some unknown believers took the plunge and 'began to speak to Greeks also, telling them the good news about the Lord Jesus'.[31] The three missionary journeys of Paul the apostle to the Gentiles followed, in which he evangelized the provinces of Galatia, Asia, Macedonia and Achaia, the Holy Spirit both restraining and leading him.[32] The book ends with Paul in Rome, the capital of the world and the city of his dreams, not as a free man but as a prisoner, yet still an indefatigable evangelist, preaching Jesus and the kingdom to all who visited him, 'boldly and without hindrance'.[33]

Throughout the Acts Luke makes it plain that the impetus for mission came from the Holy Spirit. This is Harry R. Boer's theme in his book *Pentecost and Missions*. The Acts, he writes,

> is governed by one dominant, overriding and all-controlling motif. This motif is the expansion of the faith through missionary witness in the power of the Spirit ... Restlessly the Holy Spirit drives the church to witness, and continually churches rise out of the witness.[34]

Harry Boer makes the further important point that the momentum for this evangelism came from the Holy Spirit, not from the Great Commission, which, in fact, is not mentioned again after Acts 1. He writes:

> We must cease preaching the Great Commission as a command to be obeyed, but must present it *as a law that expresses the nature, and that governs the life, of the church* ... The outpouring of the Spirit is in and by reason of its [? his] very nature the effectuation of the Great Commission in the life of the church.[35]

The church of the Letters is a missionary church

The members of the local church (whether in imagination or in reality) are often seen sitting in a circle facing each other. This picture is not wrong, inasmuch as we belong to each other and need each other's support. Indeed, we are frequently urged in the New Testament to love one another, encourage, comfort and exhort one another, and bear one another's burdens. And this 'one anotherness' of the Christian fellowship can be enjoyed and developed only when we face one another. Although legitimate, however, 'meeting in a circle' is also dangerous. For whenever we turn inwards towards one another, we have turned our backs on the world. In order to enjoy mutual fellowship, we have also extricated ourselves from the world. It is permissible – but only if it is temporary. We come apart from the world for worship and fellowship, in order to return to it strengthened to live as Christ's witnesses and servants.

Now the twenty-one Letters of the New Testament, even those addressed to individuals, are all intended in their different ways to build up the church and to secure its growth in both maturity and extent. True, the Letters address the domestic affairs of the church, its doctrine, worship, ministry, unity and holiness. But they also assume throughout that the church lives in the world and is responsible to reach out in compassion towards it.

To begin with, Paul assumes that the churches will share in his own apostolic ministry by their support, their gifts and above all their prayers. He thanks God for the Philippians' 'partnership in the gospel'.[36] He asks the Thessalonians to pray that through him 'the message of the Lord may spread rapidly and be honoured';[37] the Colossians that God will 'open a door for our message';[38] and the Ephesians that he may be given utterance, clarity and boldness in his preaching.[39]

The apostles also assume that the church will itself be involved in spreading the faith. Paul calls it 'the pillar and foundation of the truth',[40] which suggests that it must hold the truth high (as pillars thrust a building aloft) and hold it firm (acting like a structure's foundation). Peter calls the church 'a chosen people, a royal priesthood, a holy nation, a people belonging to God', in order that its members may 'declare the praises' or 'proclaim the triumphs' (NEB) of the Saviour who has called them 'out of darkness into his wonderful light'.[41]

And each local church is to exhibit the missionary character of the whole church. The Philippians, who lived 'in a crooked and depraved generation', were told both to 'shine like stars in the universe' and to 'hold out the word of life', displaying it as a merchant does his goods, or as a waiter does the dishes at a feast.[42] The Thessalonians are described as having not only 'welcomed' the Lord's message but as having made it ring out in the neighbouring regions.[43]

Individual church members are also to be involved in Christian witness. The apostles urge them to be conscious of the 'outsiders' who are watching them. Here is an example: 'Be wise in the way you act towards outsiders; make the most of every opportunity. Let your conversation be always full of grace, seasoned with salt, so that you may know how to answer everyone.'[44] It is a very practical instruction. We are to be sensible in our relationships with outsiders, to seize every chance to witness, to combine grace with salt (perhaps wholesomeness or even with) in our conversation, and to be ready to answer whatever questions are put to us. This last point reminds us of Peter's similar direction: 'Always be prepared to give an answer to everyone who asks you to give the reason for the hope that you have.'[45]

So the church of the Letters is a missionary church, whether we are thinking of the universal church or the local church or individual church members. As we saw in chapter 15, mission is an essential part of the church's identity. In Bishop Lesslie Newbigin's forthright words, 'the commission to disciple all the nations stands at the centre of the church's mandate, and a church that forgets this, or marginalizes it, forfeits the right to the titles "catholic" and "apostolic".[46]

The climax of the Revelation is a missionary climax

When John was permitted a peep through the 'door standing open in heaven',[47] he saw a great crowd of people standing before God's throne. They were wearing white robes (the symbol of righteousness) and holding palm branches (the symbol of victory), and they were joining in a mighty chorus of worship, attributing their salvation to God and to the Lamb. John also describes this great multitude as coming 'from every nation, tribe, people and language'.[48] So the mission of the church will not be fruitless. On the contrary, it will result in a huge ingathering of people, a multi-racial and multi-national throng, whose different languages and cultures will not prevent, but rather enrich, their ceaseless celebration of the grace of God.

The redeemed multitude will also be countless. Only then will God's ancient promise to Abraham be completely fulfilled. In order to emphasize the limitless numbers of Abraham's posterity, both physical (the Jews) and spiritual (believers, whether Jews or Gentiles), God promised that they would be as numerous as the dust of the earth,[49] the stars in the sky,[50] and the sand on the seashore.[51] Each metaphor symbolizes numberlessness. 'I will make your offspring like the dust of earth, so that *if anyone could count the dust*, then your offspring could be counted.'[52] 'Look up at the heavens and count the stars – *if indeed you can count them*.'[53] With our twentieth-century understanding of the universe, it seems that the myriads on myriads of stars in the billions of galaxies do perhaps number as many as all the grains of sand and specks of dust throughout the world. Although we must be content to remain agnostic about how God will achieve this end, we can meanwhile rejoice that the missionary labours of the church will come to such a glorious and God-honouring climax.

From this rapid overview of Scripture we have seen that the God of the Old Testament is a missionary God (he called one family in order to bless all the earth's families); that the Christ of the Gospels is a missionary Christ (he commissioned the church to go and make disciples of the nations); that the Holy Spirit of the Acts is a missionary Spirit (he drove the church out to witness); that the church of the Letters is a missionary church (a world-wide community with a world-wide vocation); and that the climax of the Revelation will be a missionary climax (a countless, international crowd).

So the religion of the Bible is a missionary religion. The evidence is overwhelming, irrefutable. Mission cannot be regarded as a regrettable deviation from religious toleration, or as the hobby of a few eccentric enthusiasts. On the contrary, it arises from the heart of God himself, and is communicated from his heart to ours. Mission is the global outreach of the global people of a global God.

If, then, we have resisted the missionary dimension of the church's life, or dismissed it as if it were dispensable, or patronized it reluctantly with a few perfunctory prayers and grudging coins, or become preoccupied with our own narrow-minded, parochial concerns, we need to repent, that is, change our mind and attitude. Do we profess to believe in God? He's a missionary God. Do we say we are committed to Christ? He's a missionary Christ. Do we claim to be filled with the Spirit? He's a missionary Spirit. Do we delight in belonging to the church? It's a missionary society. Do we hope to go to heaven when we die? It's a heaven filled with the fruits of the missionary enterprise. It is not possible to avoid these things.

If some of us need to repent, all of us need to take action. The authentic Christianity of the Bible is not a safe, smug, cosy, selfish, escapist little religion. On the contrary, it is deeply disturbing to our sheltered security. It is an explosive, centrifugal force, which pulls us out from our narrow self centredness and flings us into God's world to witness and to serve. So we must find practical ways, individually and through our local church, of expressing this commitment.

In 1885 General William Booth, 'his eyes twinkling, challenged a mass rally of London Salvationists: "How wide is the girth of the world?" From the serried ranks came the full-throated response: "Twenty-five thousand miles". "Then", roared Booth, arms outspread, "we must grow till our arms get right round about it".'[54]

Notes

[1] From a letter to Lord Samuel, dated 26 November 1942, published in *Some Lambeth Letters*, ed. F. S. Temple (OUP, 1963), pp. 40–41.

[2] *The Willowbank Report: Gospel and Culture* (Lausanne Committee for World Evangelization, 1978), p. 14.

[3] *Ibid.*, p. 16.

[4] Kenneth Cragg, *The Call of the Minaret* (OUP, 1956), pp. 182–183.

[5] 2 Cor. 10:1.

[6] See, for example, the joint Roman Catholic and World Council study document entitled *Common Witness and Proselytism* (1970).

[7] 2 Cor. 13:8.

[8] Nu. 16:22; 27:16 (RSV).

[9] Gn. 12:1–4.

[10] Gal. 3:29.

[11] Rom. 4:16-17.

[12] Gal. 3:8.

[13] Ps. 2:8.

[14] Ps. 72: 11.

[15] Is. 49:6.

[16] Is. 2:2.
[17] W. G. Blaikie, *David Livingstone* (1908).
[18] Mt. 10:6.
[19] Mt. 15:24.
[20] Mt. 1:2.
[21] Mt. 2:1–12.
[22] Mt. 8:11.
[23] Mt. 28:19–20.
[24] Roland Allen, *Pentecost and the World* (OUP, 1917), p. 36.
[25] *Ibid.*, p. 40.
[26] *E.g.* Lk. 24:49; Acts 1:8.
[27] Acts 1:4.
[28] Joel 2:28; Acts 2:17.
[29] Acts 8:5–8.
[30] Acts 10 and 11.
[31] Acts 11:20.
[32] Acts 16:6–10.
[33] Acts 28:31.
[34] Harry R. Boer, *Pentecost and Missions* (Lutterworth, 1961), pp. 161–162.
[35] *Ibid.*, p. 217.
[36] Phil. 1:5.
[37] 2 Thes. 3:1.
[38] Col. 4:3.
[39] Eph. 6:19–20.
[40] 1 Tim. 3:15.
[41] 1 Pet. 2:9.
[42] Phil. 2:15–16.
[43] 1 Thes. 1:6, 8.
[44] Col. 4:5–6.
[45] 1 Pet. 3:15.
[46] From his address, 'The Enduring Validity of Cross-Cultural Mission', given at the opening of the Overseas Ministries Study Centre's new premises in New Haven Connecticut, on 5 October 1987, and published in the *International Bulletin of Missionary Research*, April 1988.
[47] Rev. 4:1.
[48] Rev. 7:9–10.
[49] Gn. 13:16.
[50] Gn. 15:5.
[51] Gn. 22:17.
[52] Gn. 13:16.
[53] Gn. 15:5.
[54] Richard Collier, *The General Next to God* (Collins, 1965), p. 146.

TWENTY

Holistic mission

'Holistic' (from 'holism', the philosophical notion that 'the whole is greater than the sum of its parts') is perhaps not a very satisfactory epithet to apply to the Christian mission. Yet it is intended to emphasize that authentic mission is a comprehensive activity which embraces evangelism and social action, and refuses to let them be divorced.

During at least the last thirty years, beginning in the ecumenical community, but more recently in the evangelical constituency as well, there has been considerable disagreement about these two responsibilities. It has been stated in different ways: as the tension 'between God's action in and through the church and everything God is doing in the world apparently independently of the Christian community';[1] 'between the vertical interpretation of the gospel as essentially concerned with God's saving action in the life of individuals, and the horizontal interpretation of it as mainly concerned with human relationships in the world';[2] between God seeking the justification of sinners and God seeking justice in and among nations; between redemption and providence, the salvation of the soul and the improvement of society.

At times the difference between these viewpoints has not been a tension only, but a sterile polarization, usually along the lines of the evangelical–liberal divide, each overreacting to the other's position. The former have tended to focus exclusively on evangelism to the neglect of social need, whether food for the hungry or freedom and justice for the oppressed. The latter have gone to the opposite extreme and have tended to neglect evangelism, or have tried to reinterpret it in terms of socio-political action such as the humanization of communities or the liberation of the downtrodden. Thus, the evangelical stereotype has been to spiritualize the gospel, and deny its social implications; while the ecumenical stereotype has been to politicize it, and deny its offer of salvation to sinners. This polarization has been a disaster.

Most (though not all) Christians are agreed that our responsibilities are both evangelistic and social. For example, in his opening remarks to the World Congress on Evangelism in Berlin in 1966, Dr Carl Henry stressed

> that evangelical Christians have a message doubly relevant to the present social crisis ... For they know *the God of justice and of justi-fication* ... Whenever Christianity has been strong in the life of a nation, it has had an interest in both law and gospel, in the state as well as the church, in jurisprudence and in evangelism.[3]

Or, using more striking imagery, Dr Raymond Bakke has written that 'we Christians are the only people on this earth who have the integrated world view of matter and spirit that enables us to tackle sewer system development and the salvation of souls with equal gusto'.[4] Although we may be agreed in such 'both–and' statements as these, however, we have problems first in defining the *relationship* between evangelism and social responsibility, and secondly in what *vocabulary* we should use to express this relationship.

The relationship between evangelism and social responsibility

A broad welcome was given to the Lausanne Covenant (1974) which contained outspoken statements on 'The Nature of Evangelism' and 'Christian Social Responsibility'.[5] The latter also included the affirmation 'that evangelism and socio-political activity are both part of our Christian duty'. Again, however, it is only a 'both–and' statement. The paragraphs on evangelism and social responsibility stand side by side without any attempt to relate them to one another. Or rather, more accurately, the only mention of a relation between them is the statement in paragraph 6 that 'in the church's mission of sacrificial service evangelism is primary'.

The Lausanne movement has remained true to this assertion of the primacy of evangelism, and its 'Consultation on the Relationship between Evangelism and Social Responsibility', held in Grand Rapids in 1982, endorsed and explained this primacy in two ways. First, evangelism has a certain logical priority: 'The very fact of Christian social responsibility pre-supposes socially responsible Christians, and it can only be by evangelism and discipling that they have become such.' Secondly,

> evangelism relates to people's eternal destiny, and in bringing them good news of salvation, Christians are doing what nobody else can do. Seldom if ever should we have to choose between … healing bodies and saving souls … Nevertheless, if we must choose, then we have to say that the supreme and ultimate need of all humankind is the saving grace of Jesus Christ, and that therefore a person's eternal, spiritual sal-vation is of greater importance than his or her temporal and material well-being.[6]

The Manila Manifesto (1989) made a similar statement: 'Evangelism is primary because our chief concern is with the gospel, that all people may have the opportunity to accept Jesus Christ as their Lord and Saviour.'[7]

To reaffirm the primacy of evangelism does not solve the problem, however. It leaves the relationships between evangelism and social respons-ibility still undefined.

It was to tease out these relationships that the Grand Rapids Consultation was called in 1982. Its members clarified three of them. First, 'social activity is a *consequence* of evangelism'. For evangelism brings people to faith, 'faith works through love', and love issues in service.[8] Indeed, 'social responsibility is more than a consequence of evangelism; it is also one of its principal aims', since we are saved 'unto good works'.[9] Secondly, 'social activity can be a *bridge* to evangelism'. In spite of the danger of making 'rice Christians', who profess conversion only because of the mat-erial benefits they are offered, it remains true that love in action 'can break down prejudice and suspicion, open closed doors, and gain a hearing for the gospel'. Thirdly, 'social activity not only follows evangelism as its conse-quence and aim, and precedes it as its bridge, but also accompanies it as its *partner*. They are like the two blades of a pair of scissors or the two wings of a bird', as they were in the public ministry of Jesus. 'The partnership is, in reality, a marriage.'[10]

This partnership applies both to the individual Christian and to the local church. Of course different Christians receive different specialist gifts and callings (see chapter 8), qualifying them to concentrate on specialist min-istries, just as the Twelve were called to a pastoral, and the Seven to a social, ministry.[11] Of course also, different Christians find themselves in different emergency situations, which demand specialized responses. We do not blame either the good Samaritan for tending the traveller's wounds and not enquiring into his spiritual state, or Philip for sharing the gospel with the Ethiopian and not enquiring into his social needs. Nevertheless, these are particular callings and situations. Generally speaking, all followers of Jesus Christ have the responsibility, according to the opportunities which are given them, both to witness and to serve.

It is similar with each local church. The needs of its local community will be many and varied. But everybody cannot do everything. Consequently, in a church of any size, its members should be encouraged to form themselves into 'study and action groups', according to their gifts, callings and interests, each taking up a particular evangelistic, pastoral or social need in the neighbourhood. In this way it will be possible to respond to a number of different challenges. Nevertheless, it will be important for the local church to recognize its specialist groups, to support them with encouragement, advice, prayer and finance, as necessary, and to give them the opportunity from time to time to report on their progress. Thus 'owning' the groups, the church will be able through them to reach out in compassion to the community and serve a number of its diverse needs.

So far we have been thinking about the *relationships* between evangelism and social responsibility. The second problem we have concerns the *vocabulary* we should use to express the partnership between them. According to the report of the first National Evangelical Anglican Congress, held at Keele University in 1967, 'evangelism and compassionate service belong together in the mission of God'.[12] I myself tried to elaborate this later by writing: '"Mission" describes … everything the church is sent into the world to do', namely 'Christian service in the world comprising both evangelism and social action'.[13]

Some evangelical leaders have criticized this definition of 'mission'. They believe it is potentially damaging to the Christian mission, because it will deflect missionaries from their priority tasks of evangelizing, discipling and church planting. They therefore urge that we retain the traditional understanding of 'mission' and 'missionary' to refer only to these evangelistic activities, although they concede that all Christians have social and political responsibilities as well. Certainly, the last thing of which I would desire to be guilty is hindering the mission of the church! It is also true that 'mission' itself is not a biblical word, any more than 'Trinity' and 'sacrament' are. Yet it is a useful piece of shorthand for a biblical concept, namely what Christ sends his people into the world to do. I still insist that this cannot be limited to proclamation evangelism, even though I have already said that this has primacy in the church. The issue is not merely one of semantics (What does the word 'mission' mean?), but of substance (Why are we sent into the world?). Even if I were to concede that the word 'mission' cannot bear the weight I have put upon it, it would make no difference to the argument that we are sent into the world both to witness and to serve. Nor do I feel able to withdraw the conviction that our mission is to be modelled on Christ's. Just as his love for us is like the Father's love for him,[14] so his sending us into the world is like his Father's sending him into the world.[15] If words and works went together in his ministry, they should also in ours.

The main fear of my critics seems to be that missionaries will be side-tracked. The best way to avoid this, in my view, is not to deny that 'mission' is broader than evangelism, but rather to insist that each 'missionary' must be true to his or her particular calling. I have already suggested that in the local church, although some members are called to this ministry and some to that, yet the church itself will be lopsided if it does not include a variety of ministries. Similarly, although some missionaries are called to primary evangelism, discipling, church-planting, and Bible-translating, and others to specialist medical, educational, or developmental ministries, yet the national church (and the mission agencies co-operating with it) would be lopsided if together they did not include such a wide variety of ministries. Indeed, there is much to be said for multi-national, multi-functional mission teams, composed of nationals and expatriates, men and women, evangelists and social workers, specialists in church-planting and experts in development, pastors and teachers.

The biblical basis for this partnership

Evangelical Christians are nothing if not biblical Christians. At least our overriding desire (whether we are successful in doing it or not) is to live 'under' or 'according to' Scripture. Is there, then, good biblical warrant for holding evangelism and social action together? There is. It has been variously stated, but I will content myself with three fundamental arguments.

First, there is *the character of God*. The God of the biblical revelation, being both Creator and Redeemer, is a God who cares about the total well-being (spiritual and material) of all the human beings he has made. Having created them in his own image, he longs that they will discover their true humanness in their relationships to him and to each other. On the one hand, God yearns after his creatures in their lostness. He takes no pleasure in the death of the wicked, and is not willing that any should perish. So he begs them to listen to his word, to return to him in penitence, and to receive his forgiveness. On the other hand, God cares for the poor and the hungry, the alien, the widow and the orphan. He denounces oppression and tyranny, and calls for justice. He tells his people to be the voice of the voiceless and the defender of the powerless, and so to express their love for them. It is neither an accident nor a surprise, therefore, that God's two great commandments are that we love him with all our being and our neighbour as ourselves.

The outworking of these commandments is made clear in the law. For example, God's people were to 'fear', 'love' and 'serve' him. How? Partly by 'walking in his ways' and 'obeying his commands', because he is 'God of gods and Lord of lords', who is on that account to be worshipped; and partly by following his example who 'defends the cause of the fatherless and the widow, and loves the alien, giving him food and clothing'.[16] Thus worship and obedience on the one hand, philanthropy and justice on the other, belong together as the double duty of the people of God.

Then came the prophets, who kept reminding the people of the law and urging each of them to obey it. 'He has showed you, O man, what is good. And what does the LORD require of you? To act justly and to love mercy and to walk humbly with your God.'[17] Again, justice and mercy to the neighbour and humility before God are united.

Alongside this prophetic witness to God's law went bold denunciations of those who flouted it. Elijah was an outstanding example. Living in a time of national apostasy, his ministry was encapsulated in his two major confrontations, first at Mount Carmel when he challenged the people to choose between Yahweh and Baal,[18] and then at Jezreel when he accused King Ahab of murdering Naboth and confiscating his property, and warned him of God's judgment.[19] It is striking to find the same prophet acting as the champion of both religious loyalty and social justice.

Then 150 years later we find the two great exilic prophets, Jeremiah and Ezekiel, continuing the same tradition of protest. Why was disaster to fall upon Jerusalem? According to Jeremiah, because the people had 'forsaken' Yahweh in favour of 'foreign gods' and had filled Jerusalem with 'the blood of the innocent'.[20] According to Ezekiel, the city would bring down judgment upon itself 'by shedding blood in her midst and ... by making idols'.[21] In both cases the acme of Israel's sin was the combination of 'idols' and 'blood' – idolatry being the worst sin against God and murder the worst against the neighbour.

The law and the prophets thus reflect the character of God. What he is, his people must be also, sharing and reflecting his concerns. In particular, there is no dualism in the thinking of God.

> We tend to set over against one another in an unhealthy way soul and body, the individual and society, redemption and creation, grace and nature, heaven and earth, justification and justice, faith and works. The Bible certainly distinguishes between these, but it also relates them to each other, and it instructs us to hold each pair in a dynamic and creative tension.[22]

The second ground for keeping evangelism and social concern together is *the ministry and teaching of Jesus*. There can be no question that words and works went together in his public ministry. True, he was a preacher. He announced the coming of the kingdom of God. But he also demonstrated its arrival by his works of compassion and power. Thus we read both that 'he went about among the villages teaching ...[23] and that 'he went about doing good and healing'.[24] The similarity between these statements is the fact that 'he went about'; he had an itinerant ministry, and criss-crossed the Palestinian countryside. The dissimilarity concerns what he 'went about' for. According to Mark it was 'teaching', according to Luke 'doing good and healing'. There was in his ministry an indissoluble bond between evangelism and compassionate service. He exhibited in action the love of God he was proclaiming. 'He was concerned', Chuck Colson has written, 'not only with saving man from hell in the next world, but with delivering him from the hellishness of this one.'[25]

So then his words explained his works, and his works dramatized his words. Hearing and seeing, voice and vision, were joined. Each supported the other. For words remain abstract until they are made concrete in deeds of love, while works remain ambiguous until they are interpreted by the proclamation of the gospel. Words without works lack credibility; works without words lack clarity. So Jesus' works made his words visible; his words made his works intelligible.

What Jesus exhibited in his life and ministry he also included in his teaching. Let me share with you a reflection on two of his best-known, best-loved parables, namely those of the prodigal son[26] (which highlights conversion) and the good Samaritan[27] (which highlights social action). There are obvious similarities between them. Both, for example, are recorded by Dr Luke alone, who was concerned to portray Jesus (and so God) as the lover of the outsider and the underdog, in the one case the self-willed boy and in the other the victim of thugs. Again, both depict tragic situations which, it is implied, are displeasing to God. God does not want human beings made in his image either to become demoralized and lost in a far country or to be assaulted and abandoned half-dead in the gutter. His desire is that both the lost and the battered be brought home.

More important for my purpose now, however, are the dissimilarities between the two parables. If we hold them together, they enforce the necessary nexus between evangelism and social action. First, in both there is a victim, a man who finds himself in a desperate plight. In the parable of the prodigal son he is the victim of his own sin; in the parable of the good Samaritan he is the victim of other people's sins, that is, he is 'the sinned against' (to borrow an expression popularized by Raymond Fung at the 1980 Melbourne Consultation). Moreover, in the first parable it is personal sin which is described, in the second social sin, namely the evil of public disorder. Both should arouse our compassion. We are concerned both for the sinning and for the sinned against.

Secondly, in both parables there is a rescue – from alienation in a distant land and from violent assault on the road. In the first parable the sinner repents, comes back and is forgiven (it is salvation by faith); in the second the victim can do nothing; he owes his rescue to the charity of the Samaritan (it is a rescue by good works). Thirdly, in both there is a display of love. In the parable of the prodigal son we see the love of God, as the father welcomes the boy home; in the parable of the good Samaritan we see the love of neighbour for neighbour, as the Samaritan binds up the victim's wounds. Moreover, in both cases love triumphs over prejudice. The prodigal is forgiven *although* he deserves no such treatment; the Samaritan takes pity on the robbers' victim, *although* he is an unknown Jew who has no claim on him.

Fourthly, in both parables there is a sub-plot, which dramatizes the alternative to what is being commended. In the parable of the lost son, his elder brother refuses to rejoice in his repentance and return. In the parable of the Samaritan, the priest and Levite refuse to get involved in the battered man's plight. We might even say that those who resist the call to evangelism, and leave people alone in their sins, resemble the elder brother, while those who resist the call to social action, and leave people alone in their sufferings, resemble the priest and Levite who 'passed by on the other side'.

Thus each parable emphasizes a vital aspect of Christian discipleship – its beginning when like the prodigal son we come home for salvation, and its continuing when like the good Samaritan we go out in mission. Each of us resembles the prodigal; each of us *should* resemble the Samaritan. First we face our own sins, and then we face the world's sufferings. First we come in and receive mercy, and then we go out and show mercy. Mercy cannot be shown until it has been received; but once it has been received it must be shown to others. Let us not divorce what Christ has married. We have all been prodigals; God wants us all to be Samaritans too.

In addition to the example and teaching of Jesus Christ, I would like to mention his emotions. In chapter 7 we considered how, face to face with the 'last enemy', death, which he had come to destroy, Jesus both 'snorted' with anger against this evil and then 'wept' with compassion for its victims. I went on to suggest that the same two emotions should motivate us, whenever we find ourselves confronting evil – whether the evil of human lostness or the social evils of our day.

I have only recently read General William Booth's book *In Darkest England and the Way Out*. Published in 1890, its title was deliberately parallel to H. M. Stanley's *In Darkest Africa*, which had appeared earlier the same year. Part I is called 'The Darkness' and Part II 'Deliverance'. Booth wrote with deep feeling about the miseries caused by poverty, unemployment, homelessness, hunger, exploited labour, drunkenness, disease, slums, white slavery and prostitution. 'The blood boils with impotent rage at the sight of these enormities,' he confessed, 'callously afflicted, and silently borne by these miserable victims.'[28] Of course he longed for their conversion, and maintained that he always put salvation first. But 'what is the use of preaching the gospel', he asked, 'to people whose whole attention is concentrated upon a mad, desperate struggle to keep themselves alive?'[29] 'In providing for the relief of temporary misery,' he added, 'I reckon that I am only making it easy where it is now difficult, and possible where it is now all but impossible, for men and women to find their way to the cross of our Lord Jesus Christ.'[30] In pursuit of this policy, the second part of his book contains an amazing array of proposals – for a farm colony, an overseas colony, a travelling hospital, 'the prison gate brigade', rescue homes for prostitutes and 'preventive homes for unfallen girls in danger', an 'enquiry office for lost people', 'refuges for the children of the streets', 'industrial schools', 'model suburban villages', 'the poor man's bank', a legal aid scheme for the poor, *etc.* And as this remarkable combination of social and spiritual concerns became known, 'inevitably public fancy endowed the Army with a slogan which has stuck ever since: "soup, soap and salvation"!'[31]

The third biblical argument for the partnership of evangelism and social action concerns *the communication of the gospel.* How is it to be made known? To begin with, it must be verbalized. Since God himself chose to speak, that is, to communicate with human beings in words, Christians should not despise them nor share in the current disenchantment with speech as a medium of communication. There is a precision in verbal communication, whether the words are spoken or written, which is absent from all other media. At the same time, the personal Word of God 'became flesh', in consequence of which people 'have seen his glory'.[32] If God's Word became visible, our words must too. We cannot announce God's love with credibility unless we also exhibit it in action. So we cannot stand aloof from those to whom we speak the gospel, or ignore their situation, their context. We have to enter into their social reality and share in their sufferings and their struggles. At that point, says J. H. Bavinck, our actions 'become preaching'.[33]

This brings us back to the ministry of Jesus.

> We are called today (says the Manila Manifesto) to a similar integration of words and deeds. In a spirit of humility we are to preach and teach, minister to the sick, feed the hungry, care for prisoners, help the disadvantaged and handicapped, and deliver the oppressed. While we acknowledge the diversity of spiritual gifts, callings and contexts, we also affirm that good news and good works are inseparable.[34]

Five objections considered

Although the biblical basis for the partnership between evangelism and social responsibility appears to be well laid, a number of objections to it are raised.

First, *shouldn't Christians steer clear of politics?* This objection often continues with the comment that, although all Christians agree with social service (*i.e.* philanthropy), we are not so sure about social action (*i.e.* political involvement).

Our answer to this first objection will largely depend on the connotation we give to the word 'politics'. If we take the narrow definition (referring to policies and programmes for legislative change, developed by political parties), then Christians should not get involved unless they are prepared to do their homework. Politics is for the politicians, who have gained the necessary expertise. There is little more embarrassing than the sight of Christians pontificating on political issues from positions of ignorance.

The broader definition of 'politics', however, refers to the life of the *polis*, the city, and to the art of living together in community. In this sense all of us are involved in politics, since Jesus calls us to live in the secular world.

We must also agree that social service is not enough. Working – even agitating – for legislative change is an essential expression of neighbour-love. For example, we have to go beyond healing individuals to building hospitals where different medical specialities are concentrated; beyond feeding the hungry to the establishment of a new international economic order in which hunger is abolished; beyond binding up people's wounds like the good Samaritan to the task of ridding the Jericho road of brigands; and beyond the fair treatment of slaves to the abolition of the institution of slavery itself. There may be no explicit biblical warrant for these things, and certainly Jesus never called for the emancipation of slaves. But are we not profoundly thankful that his followers did centuries later? Political action (which could be defined as love seeking justice for the oppressed) is a legitimate extrapolation from the biblical emphasis on the practical priorities of love.

Secondly, *isn't this going back to the old 'social gospel'?* No, it is not. We must distinguish between the social gospel of theological liberalism, developed by Walter Rauschenbusch and his friends at the beginning of this century, and the social implications of the biblical gospel.

The 'social gospel' attempted to identify the kingdom of God with socialized society, and then spoke of socio-political action in terms of 'building the kingdom of God on earth'. The vision was proud, self-confident and Utopian. The social implications of the biblical gospel are different, however. Once we have become new people in Christ, and are members of his new society, we must accept the responsibility he gives us to permeate the old society as its salt and light.

Thirdly, *isn't this social concern the same as 'liberation theology'?* No, again it is not. Our main evangelical critique of liberation theology is that it attempts to equate the social, political and economic liberation of human beings with the 'salvation' which Christ came, died and rose to win. It has also tended to endorse Marxist theories (especially its social analysis) and to espouse violence. Having said that, the total liberation of human beings from everything which oppresses, demeans or dehumanizes them is surely pleasing to God their Creator. I wish evangelical Christians had got in first with a truly *biblical* theology of liberation. But to equate material 'liberation' with 'salvation' is to misunderstand and misrepresent Scripture.

Fourthly, *isn't it impossible to expect social change unless people are converted*? Once more, no it isn't. Of course we long for people to be converted. But Jesus Christ through his people has had an enormous influence for good on society as a whole. Think, for example, of the rising standards of health and hygiene, the wider availability of education, the growing respect for women and children, the concern for human rights and civil liberties, better conditions in factory, mine and prison, and the abolition of slavery and the slave trade.

Legislation can secure social improvement, even though it does not convert people or make them good. Even fallen human beings retain sufficient vestiges of the divine image to prefer justice to injustice, freedom to oppression, and peace to violence. Martin Luther King was right when he said:

> Morality cannot be legislated, but behaviour can be regulated. Judicial decrees may not change the heart, but they can restrict the heartless ... The law cannot make an employer love me, but it can keep him from refusing to hire me because of the colour of my skin.'[35]

Fifthly, *won't commitment to social action distract us from evangelism?* Yes, it might, but no, it need not. Certainly we should take warning of this possibility. We should be grateful for evangelical watchdogs who bark loud and long if they see any signs in us of a diminished commitment to evangelism. But if we live in the light of Jesus' death, resurrection and ascension, our incentives to evangelism will be continuously renewed at that perennial spring. In particular, his exaltation to the supreme place of honour will inspire us to desire that he be given the glory due to his name. Then social action, far from diverting us from evangelism, will make it more effective by rendering the gospel more visible and more credible.

Some examples of the partnership

'Social action in mission', wrote the American missiologist Dr R. Pierce Beaver, 'can be traced from the time of the apostles.' Moreover, 'concern was never limited to relief'; it included what today we call 'development', enabling communities to become self-reliant, whether by introducing improved plants and livestock, eliminating diseases, digging deeper wells for pure and constant water, or establishing industrial schools. In addition, the missionaries stood for social justice. They were

> constantly the protectors of native peoples against exploitation and injustice by government and commercial companies ... They played a very important part in the abolishing of forced labour in the Congo. They resisted black-birding in the South Pacific. They fought fiercely for human rights in combating opium, foot-binding, and exposure of girl babies in China. They waged war against widow-burning, infanticide and temple prostitution in India, and above all broke the social and economic slavery of the caste system for the low and outcaste peoples ...[36]

The main difference between those days and today is that the responsibility for social witness has now in many places passed from the missionaries to the national church. Expatriates should engage in it only if invited by church leaders to do so.

There was, in fact, a certain inevitability about these concerns. It was literally impossible for the early missionaries to proclaim the message of God's love in Christ for the salvation of sinners and at the same time ignore the people's social conditions. The gospel itself, whose messengers they were, obliged them to oppose whatever was incompatible with it, whether slavery in Africa, untouchability and other evils in India, or the exploitation of tribespeople and the degrading poverty of the masses in Latin America. Similarly, it is impossible to evangelize in the West and simply turn a blind eye to the plight of the unemployed and the homeless, or of alienated youth and single-parent families in decayed and deprived inner-city areas. Has the gospel nothing to say about these things? Is our God interested only in bringing people to heaven, and not in ameliorating their circumstances on earth? No, to ignore the dehumanizing evils of society, while preaching the humanizing influence of salvation, is to be guilty of an inner contradiction which misrepresents God and distorts the gospel. Compassionate involvement in other people's felt needs is part and parcel of incarnational mission, and is demanded by the gospel of Christ.

Dr David Howard, General Secretary of the World Evangelical Fellowship from 1982 to 1992, has written about the ministry of his friend Gregorio Landero. Describing him as 'one of the most gifted evangelists I have ever known', he goes on:

> As he travelled around in evangelistic outreach to many parts of northern Colombia, he became heavily burdened because the people to whom he was ministering concerning their souls were suffering for lack of nutrition. He agonized about how he could preach a gospel of

salvation when they were starving and suffering diseases which could be avoided with more adequate help. He began to study the possibilities of a more full-orbed outreach of the gospel. The result, over several years of hard work, was the development of United Action, a programme of total outreach for the needs of people. Gregorio is the leader of United Action and has given the vision and impetus to the entire development of the programme. Today, along with his evangelistic preaching, he and his colleagues are helping people to improve agricultural methods, developing family poultry projects that will put more protein into their diet, teaching home hygiene, carrying on dental work, literacy work and other things which will develop the family and community life of the people. There have also been efforts to help conserve the natural resources which are a part of the total creation.[37]

Festo Kivengere from Uganda had a similar holistic vision and commitment. He was first and foremost an evangelist. And when he became bishop of the diocese of Kigezi, he continued his extraordinarily effective worldwide evangelistic ministry, in which many were won to Christ. But he also concerned himself with development in his diocese, and especially with improved education, health and agriculture. His message centred on love and reconciliation through Christ, but he also pleaded for justice. Although not a political bishop, in the sense that he took no part in the work of the legislative, judicial or executive functions of the state, he nevertheless played a major role in the overthrow of Idi Amin. Several times he risked his life by confronting Amin in private and protesting against his reign of terror. 'Festo was so courageous,' his colleagues recalled. 'As the arrests continued, he kept going back to Amin to face him with the enormity of what he was doing.'[38]

Bishop Festo saw no inconsistency between these different aspects of his ministry. In a seminar he led at a 1987 convention in Amsterdam, he spoke of 'the tragic divide between what, according to the Old Testament and the New Testament, are the two sides of the same coin – *the salvation of the lost souls of men* ... and *the concern for their social needs*'.[39] And Bishop Shannon Mallory from California, who chaired the 'Partners in Mission' Consultation in Uganda in 1985, said of him:

Our dear Festo was a fiery prophet in the midst of that debate [*sc.* about human rights violations being perpetrated at the time], calling passionately on the one hand for the spiritual renewal and reconciliation of the Church of Uganda, and at the same time boldly standing up (almost alone, it seemed) to speak out and condemn the political and military tyranny that was still going on in the country.[40]

Thus evangelistic witness and political protest, far from being incompatible, were and are natural twins. Although few Christian people may be called to engage in them simultaneously, since different people are called to different ministries, nevertheless the church as a whole must engage in both, since both belong to its God-given mission in the world.

Notes

[1] See R. K. Orchard (ed.), *Witness in Six Continents* (Edinburgh House Press, 1964), p. 157.

[2] W. A. Visser't Hooft in Norman Goodall (ed.), *The Uppsala 1968 Report* (WCC, 1968).

[3] Carl F. H. Henry, *Evangelicals at the Brink of Crisis* (Word Books, 1967), pp. 71–72.

[4] Raymond Bakke, *Urban Mission*, September 1986, p. 7.

[5] The Lausanne Covenant, paras. 4 and 5.

[6] *Evangelism and Social Responsibility: An Evangelical Commitment*, The Grand Rapids Report (Paternoster, 1982), pp. 24–25.

[7] *The Manila Manifesto: An Elaboration of the Lausanne Covenant 15 Years Later* (Lausanne Committee for World Evangelization, 1989), para. 4, p. 15.

[8] *Cf.* Gal. 5:6, 13.

[9] *Cf.* Eph. 2:10; Tit. 2:14.

[10] *Evangelism and Social Responsibility*, pp. 21–24.

[11] Acts 6:1–7.

[12] *Keele '67*, the National Evangelical Anglican Congress Statement, ed. Philip Crowe (Falcon, 1967), para. 2.20, p. 23.

[13] John Stott, *Christian Mission in the Modern World* (Falcon, 1975; Kingsway, 1986), pp. 30, 34.

[14] Jn. 15:9.

[15] Jn. 17:18; 20:21.

[16] Dt. 10:12–20.

[17] Mi. 6:8.

[18] 1 Ki. 18.

[19] 1 Ki. 21.

[20] Je. 19:4.

[21] Ezk. 22:3–4; *cf.* 36:18–19.

[22] *Evangelism and Social Responsibility*, p. 20.

[23] Mk. 6:6 (RSV).

[24] Acts 10:38 (RSV).

[25] Charles Colson, *Loving God* (Zondervan, 1983), p. 145.

[26] Lk. 15:11–32.

[27] Lk. 10:30–37.

[28] William Booth, *In Darkest England and the Way Out* (Salvation Army, 1890), p. 14.

[29] *Ibid.*, p. 45.

[30] *Ibid.*, Preface, p. 4. *Cf.* p. 257.

[31] Richard Collier, *The General Next to God* (Collins, 1965), p. 199.

[32] Jn. 1:14.

[33] J. Herman Bavinck, An *Introduction to the Science of Missions* (1954, ET Presbyterian and Reformed, 1960), p. 113.

[34] *The Manila Manifesto,* para. 4: 'The Gospel and Social Responsibility, p. 15.

[35] Martin Luther King, in *Strength to Love* (Collins, 1963), p. 34, and in *Stride Toward Freedom: The Montgomery Story* (Harper and Row, 1958), p. 198.

[36] From his introduction to *Christian Mission and Social Justice* by Samuel Escobar and John Driver (Herald, 1978), pp. 7–9.

[37] David Howard, *The Great Commission for Today* (IVP USA, 1976), pp. 84–85.

[38] Anne Coomes, *Festo Kivengere: The Authorized Biography* (Monarch, 1990), p. 318.

[39] *Ibid.*, p. 455.

[40] *Ibid.*, p. 434.

TWENTY-ONE

The Christology of mission

'Missiology' is a recognized discipline with increasingly broad parameters. It includes the history of Christian missions; the comparative study of religions, the theology of religions and the uniqueness of Christ; the biblical basis for mission; mission strategies and church growth; missionary motives and methods; questions of culture, contextualization and church formation; the relations between evangelism and social responsibility; and the renewal of the church. Yet some times missing from this list is what might be called the 'Christology' of mission, which acknowledges Christ as the source and way, the heart and soul, the ground and goal, of all mission. Nothing is more important for the recovery of the church's mission (where it has been lost), or its development (where it is weak), than a fresh, clear and comprehensive vision of Jesus Christ. When he is demeaned, and specially when he is denied, in the fulness of his unique person and work, the church lacks motivation and direction, our morale crumbles and our mission disintegrates. But when we see Jesus, it is enough. We have all the inspiration, incentive, authority and power we need.

I propose in this chapter, then, that we take a fresh look at our Lord and Saviour, that we rehearse the six major events in his saving career (his incarnation, cross, resurrection, exaltation, Spirit-gift and parousia), and that we note the inescapable (though often neglected) missionary dimension of each.

The incarnation of Christ

The model for mission

According to the Willowbank Report on *Gospel and Culture* (1978), already mentioned several times, the incarnation was 'the most spectacular instance of cultural identification in the history of mankind'.[1] For the Son of God did not stay in the safe immunity of his heaven, remote from human sin and tragedy. He actually entered our world. He emptied himself of his glory and humbled himself to serve. He took our nature, lived our life, endured our temptations, experienced our sorrows, felt our hurts, bore our sins and died our death. He penetrated deeply into our humanness. He never stayed aloof from the people he might have been expected to avoid. He made friends with the dropouts of society. He even touched untouchables. He could not have become more one with us than he did. It was the total identification of love.

Reflecting on the meaning of mission, I have sometimes compared and contrasted in my mind Christ's mission to the earth with the Apollo mission to the moon. The analogy is shallow, no doubt, but it is also instructive, for there are both similarities and dissimilarities between them. They are similar, one might say, in that each is described as a 'mission', and consisted of a sensational, cross-cultural journey, in the case of Christ from heaven to earth, and of the astronauts from earth to moon. They are different, however, in the degree and depth of the identification involved. The Apollo astronauts never identified with the moon; if they had attempted to do so, they would have been dead in a moment. Instead, they took with them the accoutrements of the earth – earth's oxygen, equipment, clothing and food. But when Jesus came from heaven to earth, he left heaven behind him and brought nothing but himself. His was no superficial touchdown. He became a human being like us and so made himself vulnerable like us.

Yet, as we noted in chapter 15, when Christ identified with us, he did not surrender or in any way alter his own identity. For in becoming one of us, he yet remained himself. He became human, but without ceasing to be God.

Now he sends us into the world, as the Father sent him into the world.[2] In other words, our mission is to be modelled on his. Indeed, all authentic mission is incarnational mission. It demands identification without loss of identity. It means entering other people's worlds, as he entered ours, though without compromising our Christian convictions, values or standards.

I take the apostle Paul as an example. You could argue, and some people have argued, that Paul did *not* enter personally into the lives of the people he sought to evangelize; that he was essentially a preacher to anonymous faces, in the synagogue or in the open air; and that he kept his distance from the people he addressed. But no, that is not how he himself saw his ministry. On the contrary, although he was free, he made himself everybody's slave. 'To the Jews I became like a Jew, to win the Jews ... To those not having the law I became like one not having the law ... so as to win those not having the law. To the weak I became weak, to win the weak. I have become all things to all men so that by all possible means I might save some.'[3] That is the principle of the incarnation. It is identification with people where they are.

In the history of missions there have been many dramatic examples of Christians trying to apply this principle. I mention three, taken from the last three centuries. In 1732 Count Zinzendorf, the Moravian leader, sent two of his missionaries to the West Indian sugar plantations. They found that the only way to reach the African slaves was to join their chain gangs and share their huts. In 1882 Major Frederick Tucker launched the Salvation Army in India. General Booth's last words to him were, 'Get into their skins, Tucker.' He did. Deeply concerned for the outcastes, he decided that he and his soldiers must live their life. So they donned saffron robes, adopted Indian names, walked barefoot, cleaned their teeth with charcoal, and ate their curry and water sitting cross-legged on the floor.[4]

Then in 1950 a young Italian Roman Catholic priest, Mario Borelli, horrified by the loveless, homeless plight of the *scugnizzi*, Naples' street children, decided that the only way to reach them was to become one of them. He took on 'their dress, their speech, their habits'. He may well have gone too far.[5] And missionaries are not always wise to 'go native', 'principally because a foreigner's attempt to do this may not be seen as authentic but as play-acting'.[6] Nevertheless, one cannot but admire these daring attempts to follow the example of Christ's incarnation.

For most of us, however, the incarnational model will involve a more mundane struggle. First, there is the need to enter into other people's *thought* world. In this connection I have always liked the title of Jim Sire's book *The Universe Next Door*.[7] He sub-titles it *A Basic World View Catalogue* and sketches the meaning of deism, naturalism, nihilism, existentialism, eastern pantheistic monism, *etc.* His point is that such people live in another universe of thought; it will therefore take a kind of incarnation to reach them.

Similarly, at the ecumenical missionary conference in Melbourne in May 1980, John V. Taylor, then Bishop of Winchester, emphasized that we will never be able to commend the gospel to modem sceptics 'so long as we remain inside our own cultural stockades. Genuine outsiders', he continues, 'can only be reached outside ... If we do not naturally belong to the world of the particular "outsiders" we want to reach, some of us must take the trouble to cross over and learn to be at home in that alien territory ...'[8]

We should, I believe, be praying and working for a whole new generation of Christian thinkers and apologists who will dedicate their God-given minds to Christ, enter sympathetically into their contemporaries' dilemmas, unmask false ideologies, and present the gospel of Jesus Christ in such a way that he is seen to offer what other religious systems cannot, because he and he alone can fulfil our deepest human aspirations. At least in the West, where the Enlightenment has run out of steam, the time is now ripe, urges Bishop Lesslie Newbigin, for 'a genuinely missionary encounter with post-Enlightenment culture'.[9]

Secondly, we need to enter other people's *heart* world, the world of their *Angst* and their alienation, and to weep with those who weep.[10] In every non-Christian (and many Christians too), even in the jolliest extraverts, there are hidden depths of pain. We can reach them only if we are willing to enter into their suffering. It will also include entering into people's social reality, as we saw in the last chapter, for it is impossible to share the gospel with people in a social vacuum, isolating them from their actual context and ignoring their suffering.

The cross of Christ

The cost of mission

One of the most neglected aspects of biblical mission today is the indispensable place in it of suffering, even of death. Yet it is plain in Scripture. Let me give you three examples.

First, we see it clearly in *Isaiah's suffering servant.* Before the servant can be a light to the nations and bring salvation to the ends of the earth,[11] he offers his back to those who beat him, his cheeks to those who pull out his beard, and his face to mockery and spitting.[12] Before he can 'sprinkle many nations',[13] he is 'despised and rejected by men, a man of sorrows, and familiar with suffering'.[14] More than that, he bears our sins and dies for us as a guilt offering.[15] Douglas Webster laid a proper emphasis on this. He wrote:

> Mission sooner or later leads into passion. In biblical categories ... the servant must suffer ... it is that which makes mission effective ... Every form of mission leads to some form of cross. The very shape of mission is cruciform. We can understand mission only in terms of the Cross ...'.[16]

Secondly, *the Lord Jesus himself* taught and exhibited this principle, and extended it to his followers. When those Greeks wanted to see him, he said: 'The hour has come for the Son of Man to be glorified [*sc.* on the cross]. I tell you the truth, unless a grain of wheat falls to the ground and dies, it remains only a single seed. But if it dies, it produces many seeds.'[17] In other words, only through his death would the gospel be extended to the Gentile world. So death is more than the way to life; it is the condition of fruitfulness. Unless it dies, the seed remains alone. But if it dies, it multiplies. It was so for the Messiah; it is the same for the messianic community. For 'whoever serves me must follow me', Jesus said.[18]

Thirdly, *the apostle Paul* applied the same principle to himself. Consider these extraordinary texts:

> I ask you, therefore, not to be discouraged because of my sufferings for you, which are your glory.[19]

> Therefore I endure everything for the sake of the elect, that they too may obtain the salvation that is in Christ Jesus, with eternal glory.[20]

> So then, death is at work in us, but life is at work in you.[21]

These three verses contain some truly startling statements. Paul dares to claim that through his sufferings others will enter into glory, that through his endurance others will be saved, and that through his death others will live. Is the apostle out of his mind? No! Does he really mean it? Yes! It is not, of course, that he attributes any atoning efficacy to his own sufferings and death, as he does to the sufferings and death of Jesus Christ. It is rather this. People can receive salvation, life and glory only when the gospel is preached to them, and those who preach the gospel with faithfulness invariably suffer for it. Paul knew what he was talking about. The reason why he became a prisoner, and was chained, is that he had been faithful to the 'heavenly vision' that Gentiles would be received into the Christian community on precisely the same terms as Jews. It was this aspect of the gospel which aroused almost fanatical opposition to him. And the Gentiles owed their salvation to his willingness to suffer for his proclamation of this good news.

There have been many examples since Paul of suffering for the gospel. It is not an accident that the Greek word for 'witness' is *martys*. The pages of church history are replete with stories of persecution. Sometimes it has been *physical*. In 1880 soon after the Salvation Army had been founded in Britain,

> 'publicans and brothel-keepers were launching a savage all-out counter-attack ... The Army learned the bleak truth of the Spanish proverb: "He who would be a Christian must expect crucifixion" ... In one year – 1882 – 669 Salvation Army officers were knocked down or brutally assaulted.' When Salvationists dedicated their children in the

1880s, they confessed their willingness that their children should be 'despised, hated, cursed, beaten, kicked, imprisoned or killed for Christ's sake'.[22]

At other times the suffering was more *mental* than physical. The Maréchale, for example, as the eldest daughter of General Booth was always known, wrote an article in 1883 for the *War Cry* from her prison cell in Neuchâtel, Switzerland, in which she reflected on inward crucifixion.

> Jesus was crucified ... Ever since that day, men have tried to find an easier way, but the easier ways fail. If you would win thousands who are without God, you must be ready to be crucified: your plans, your ideas, your likes and your inclinations. Things have changed, you say, there is liberty now. Is there? Go and live Christ's life, speak as he spoke, teach what he taught, denounce sin wherever you find it, and see if the enemy will not turn on you with all the fury of hell ... Christ wasn't crucified in the drawing-room. His was no easy-chair business ... Do you shrink from being bated, misrepresented and spoken evil of? It is time you were crucified ...[23]

Yet a third kind of suffering is *social*. Vincent Donovan, an American Roman Catholic priest who laboured for seventeen years among the Masai in Tanzania, once asked himself what the distinguishing mark of a missionary was. This is the answer he gave himself:

> A missionary is essentially a *social martyr*, cut off from his roots, his stock, his blood, his land, his background, his culture ... He must be stripped as naked as a human being can be, down to the very texture of his being ... [he must] divest himself of his very culture, so that he can be a naked instrument of the gospel to the cultures of the world.[24]

This call to suffering and death, as the condition for mission fruitfulness, sounds very alien, however, in our contemporary western ears. The respectable middle-class captivity of the church is not exactly an arena for persecution. Where is the willingness to suffer for Christ today? In the evangelical tendency to triumphalism there seems little place for tribulation. And the false 'prosperity gospel', promising unlimited health and wealth, blinds people to the biblical warnings of adversity. Yet the fact remains that if we compromised less we would assuredly suffer more.

There are three main reasons for opposition; they belong to the spheres of doctrine, ethics and discipline. As for doctrine, the gospel of Christ crucified remains folly to the intellectually proud and a stumbling-block to the self-righteous; both groups find it humiliating. As for ethics, Christ's call is to self-denial and self-control; the self-indulgent find its challenge unacceptable. As for discipline, both baptism and the Lord's Supper presuppose repentance and faith in those who wish to receive them; to deny these gospel sacraments to anybody, even to those who openly admit that they neither repent nor believe, nevertheless provokes them to outrage. Thus those who seek to be faithful in doctrine, ethics and discipline are sure to arouse persecution, in the church as well as in the world.

Are we ready, then, to bear the pain of being ridiculed, the loneliness of being ostracized, the hurt of being spoken against and slandered? Indeed, are we willing if necessary to die with Christ to popularity and promotion, to comfort and success, to our ingrained sense of personal and cultural superiority, to our selfish ambition to be rich, famous or powerful?

It is the seed that dies, which multiplies.

A brother from Orissa, India, once told me that, when he was eight years old, his evangelist father had been martyred, killed by hired assassins. At the time of his father's death, he added, there were only twelve churches in the region; when he spoke to me, there were one hundred and fifty.

The resurrection of Christ

The mandate for mission

It is of the greatest importance to remember that the resurrection preceded the Great Commission. It was the risen Lord who issued his commission to his followers to go and make disciples of all nations. He could not have issued it earlier, before he had been raised from death and invested with authority. 'All authority in heaven and on earth has been given to me,' he could now say. 'Therefore go and make disciples ...'[25]

This is a major theme of a book by Johannes Blauw, a former secretary of the Netherlands Missionary Council. It was called *The Missionary Nature of the Church*, and sub-titled *A Survey of the Biblical Theology of Mission*. His thesis is that the Old Testament perspective was one of 'universalism' (God promising that all the nations he had made would come and worship him),[26] but not of 'mission' (Israel going out to win the nations). The prophetic vision of the last days was of a 'pilgrimage of the nations' to Jerusalem. Mount Zion would be exalted as chief among the mountains, and 'all nations will stream to it'.[27] In the New Testament, however, this 'centripetal missionary consciousness' is replaced by a 'centrifugal missionary activity'.[28] That is, instead of the nations streaming to the church, the church now goes out to the nations. And what was the moment of change? 'The Great Turning-Point',[29] argues Johannes Blauw, was the resurrection. It preceded the Great Commission to go, all authority having now been given to Christ in fulfilment of Daniel 7:13–14. 'With Easter a new age has begun, the enthronement of a new ruler of the world, and the proclamation of this new ruler among the nations. *Mission is the summons of the Lordship of Christ.*[30]

'If the mission of the New Testament', Johannes Blauw elaborates later, 'seems at first glance centrifugal, it is to enable it to be centripetal. We go out into the world to gather it together; we cast the net to draw it in; we sow to reap.'[31] Moreover, 'in Paul's own person the centripetal and centrifugal aspects of the preaching are brought together'.[32] That is, while going out to preach the gospel, he is gathering both Gentiles and Israel, and bringing them home.

The resurrection, however, is the key to both movements. It is the risen Lord who sends us out into the world, and it is the same risen Lord who gathers people in to his church. The universal mission of the church derives its legitimacy from the universal lordship of Christ. In this way the resurrection supplies the mandate for mission.

The exaltation of Christ

The incentive for mission

Motivation is a very important aspect of every human enterprise. We need to know not only *what* we should be doing, but *why* we should be doing it. When our motives are sound and strong, we can persist in any task almost indefinitely. But when our motivation is faulty, we immediately begin to flag. This is undoubtedly true of the Christian mission. To seek to win people for Christ is hard work, widely unappreciated and unpopular, and, as we have just seen, it often provokes active opposition. The church will need powerful incentives, therefore, if it is to persevere. My argument in this section is that the exaltation of Jesus Christ to the Father's right hand, that is, to the position of supreme honour, provides the strongest of all missionary incentives.

It is better in this context to refer to Christ's 'exaltation' than to his 'ascension', for, although it is true that 'he ascended into heaven', yet to say that 'he was exalted' indicates that it was God the Father who thus vindicated, promoted, enthroned and invested his Son. Moreover, the apostolic statements of Jesus' exaltation are at pains to emphasize that he was elevated above all possible rivals, indeed *far above* all rule and authority, power and dominion, and every title that can be given, not only in the present age but also in the one to come'.[33] This is 'the highest place' to which God has exalted Jesus[34] and the 'supremacy' which he wants him to enjoy.[35]

This throws light on the use of the word 'superiority', which is viewed with distaste by those who are forsaking the old exclusivism and inclusivism in favour of the new pluralism (see chapter 18). Certainly, to adopt an 'air of superiority' towards the adherents of other faiths is a horrid form of discourtesy and arrogance. Certainly too, as Professor Hick points out, 'in the eighteenth and nineteenth centuries the conviction of the decisive superiority of Christianity' gave a powerful impetus to the imperial expansion of the West.[36] But it is not 'Christianity' as an empirical institution or system for which Christians should claim superiority. It is Christ, and only Christ. We should affirm without any sense of embarrassment or shame that he is 'superior' to all other religious leaders, precisely because he alone humbled himself in love even to the cross and therefore God has raised him 'above' every other person, rank or title.

Consequent upon his elevation or exaltation to the highest place, God desires 'every knee' to bow to him and 'every tongue' to confess his lordship.[37] The repeated 'every' is absolute; it admits of no exceptions. If God has given this supreme honour to Jesus, and desires everybody else to honour him, then the people of God should share his desire. This is sometimes spoken of in Scripture in terms of 'zeal', and even 'jealousy'. The prophet Elijah, for example, deeply distressed by the apostasy of Israel, in particular their worship of the Canaanite Baals, said: 'I have been very zealous for the LORD, the God of hosts.'[38] The apostle Paul spoke of himself as 'jealous ... with a godly jealousy' for the Corinthians, because he had betrothed them to Christ as their one husband, but was afraid that they might now be led astray from their 'sincere and pure devotion to Christ'.[39] Similarly, Henry Martyn, that brilliant and faithful Christian missionary in Muslim Iran towards the beginning of the nineteenth century, once said: 'I could not endure existence if Jesus were not glorified; it would be hell to me if he were to be always thus dishonoured.'[40]

This same sense of pain whenever Jesus Christ is dishonoured, and this same sense of jealousy that he should be given the honour due to him, should stir within us at the end of the twentieth century, in whatever particular culture we live. The primary motive for mission is neither obedience to the Great Commission, nor even love for those who are oppressed, lonely, lost and perishing, important as both those incentives are, but rather zeal or 'jealousy' for the glory of Christ. It was 'for his name's sake',[41] in order that it might receive the honour which it deserved, that the first missionaries went out. The same passionate longing should motivate us.

This, surely, is our answer to those who tell us that we should no longer evangelize or seek conversions. Professor Gregory Baum of the University of Toronto, for example, has said that 'after Auschwitz the Christian churches no longer wish to convert the Jews', for 'the churches have come to recognize Judaism as an authentic religion before God, with independent value and meaning, not as a stage on the way to Christianity'.[42] Similarly a Greek Catholic bishop, on his resignation, wrote to his friends: 'As a bishop, a preacher of the gospel, I never tried to convert a Jew or Arab Moslem to

Christianity; rather to convert them to be a better Jew, a better Moslem.'[43] Have these men, then, no jealousy for the honour of Jesus Christ? Do they not care when he is despised and rejected? Do they not long, as God does, that all human beings, whatever their culture or religion, will bow their knee to Jesus, and submit to him as their Lord?

It is this zeal for Christ which integrates the worship and witness of the church. How can we worship Christ and not mind that others do not? It is our worship of Christ which impels us to witness to Christ, in order that others may come and worship him too.

The Spirit-gift of Christ

The power for mission

The World Missionary Conference held in Edinburgh in 1910 was described by John R. Mott, its leading figure, as 'the most significant gathering ever held in the interest of the world's evangelization'.[44] After surveying the opportunities, the problems and the encouragements, in relation to world evangelization, John Mott listed four 'requirements of the present situation'. He began with (1) an adequate plan, (2) an adequate home base, and (3) an efficient church on the mission field. Then the fourth requirement he called 'the super-human factor'. He went on to say that, although missionaries, nationals and mission leaders differ substantially regarding plans, means and methods, they

> are absolutely united in the conviction that the world's evangelization is a divine enterprise, that the Spirit of God is the great Missioner, and that only as he dominates the work and workers can we hope for success in the undertaking to carry the knowledge of Christ to all people. They believe that he gave the missionary impulse to the early church, and that today all true mission work must be inaugurated, directed and sustained by him.[45]

Already during his public ministry Jesus had drawn attention to the missionary nature and purpose of the Holy Spirit. He had likened him to 'streams of living water' irrigating the desert, and had promised that they would flow out from within every believer.[46] 'No one can ... be indwelt by the Spirit of God', comments William Temple, 'and keep that Spirit to himself. Where the Spirit is, he flows forth; if there is no flowing forth, he is not there.'[47] And so it proved to be in the early church from the Day of Pentecost onwards, as we saw in chapter 19.

There are, of course, differences between and within the churches regarding the charismatic or neo-pentecostal movement, the so-called 'baptism of the Spirit', the diversity of spiritual gifts, and the place of 'signs and wonders' in evangelism and church growth. But all of us should be able to affirm together that evangelism is impossible without the Holy Spirit, without God the Evangelist, as Professor David Wells calls him in a book of that title.[48] To summarize the Spirit's indispensable ministry, I do not think I could do better than quote from the Manila Manifesto (1989):

> The Scriptures declare that God himself is the chief evangelist. For the Spirit of God is the Spirit of truth, love, holiness and power, and evangelism is impossible without him. It is he who anoints the messenger, confirms the word, prepares the hearer, convicts the sinful, enlightens the blind, gives life to the dead, enables us to repent and believe, unites us to the Body of Christ, assures us that we are God's children, leads us into Christlike character and service, and sends us out in our turn to be Christ's witnesses. In all this the Holy Spirit's main preoccupation is to glorify Jesus Christ by showing him to us and forming him in us.
>
> All evangelism involves spiritual warfare with the principalities and powers of evil, in which only spiritual weapons can prevail, especially the Word and the Spirit, with prayer. We therefore call on all Christian people to be diligent in their prayers both for the renewal of the church and for the evangelization of the world.
>
> Every true conversion involves a power encounter, in which the superior authority of Jesus Christ is demonstrated. There is no greater miracle than this, in which the believer is set free from the bondage of Satan and sin, fear and futility, darkness and death.
>
> Although the miracles of Jesus were special, being signs of his Messiahship and anticipations of his perfect kingdom when all nature will be subject to him, we have no liberty to place limits on the power of the living Creator today. We reject both the scepticism which denies miracles and the presumption which demands them, both the timidity which shrinks from the fulness of the Spirit and the triumphalism which shrinks from the weakness in which Christ's power is made perfect.
>
> We repent of all self-confident attempts either to evangelize in our own strength or to dictate to the Holy Spirit. We determine in future not to 'grieve' or 'quench' the Spirit, but rather to seek to spread the good news 'with power, with the Holy Spirit and with deep conviction'.[49]

There is an urgent need for us to humble ourselves before the sovereign Holy Spirit today. Sociological knowledge and communications expertise are important. Indeed, they are gifts of God to be used in evangelism. But we have to beware lest they diminish our reliance on the power of the Holy Spirit. Only the Holy Spirit of God can take words spoken in human weakness and carry them home with power to the mind, conscience and will of the hearers.[50] Only he can open the eyes of the blind to see the truth as it is in Jesus, unstop the ears of the deaf to hear his voice, and loosen the tongues of the dumb to confess that he is Lord. The Holy Spirit is the chief witness; 'without *his* witness, *ours is* futile'.[51]

The parousia of Christ

The urgency of mission

There was something fundamentally anomalous about the attitude of the Twelve immediately after the ascension. They had been commissioned to go 'to the ends of *the earth*', but they were standing on the Mount of Olives 'looking into *the sky*'![52] They were then promised that the Jesus who had just disappeared would in due time reappear. For this event they must wait; no amount of sky-watching would hasten it. Meanwhile, once they had been clothed with the Spirit's power, they must get on with their task. Earth, not sky, was to be their preoccupation. Thus the four stages of the divine programme were plain. First, Jesus returned to the Father (ascension). Secondly, the Spirit came (Pentecost). Thirdly, the church goes out to make disciples (mission). Fourthly, Jesus will return (parousia). Between the first and the fourth events, the ascension and the parousia, the disappearance and the reappearance of Jesus, there was to be an unspecified 'inter-adventual' period. During it no further saving event would take place. The gap was to be filled with the world-wide witness of the church. So the implied message of the angels after the ascension was this: 'You have seen him go. You will see him come. But between that going and coming there must be another. The Spirit must come, and you must go – into the world for Christ.'[53]

It is in this way that the parousia of Jesus is linked with the mission of the church. The parousia will terminate the mission-period which began with Pentecost. We have only a limited time in which to complete our God-given responsibility. We need, then, to recover the eager eschatological expectation of the first Christians, together with the sense of urgency which it gave them. Jesus had promised that the end would not come until the gospel of the kingdom had been preached throughout the world to all nations.[54] But we have no liberty to presume that we have plenty of time, and so drag our feet or slacken our pace in mission. On the contrary, the church is 'on the move – hastening to the ends of the earth to beseech all men to be reconciled to God, and hastening to the end of time to meet its Lord who will gather all into one'.[55] The two ends will coincide.

Another important link between the church's mission and the Lord's return has to do with judgment. 'We must all appear before the judgment seat of Christ,' Paul wrote, 'that each one may receive what is due to him ...'[56] This is evidently not the universal judgment relating to our eternal destinies, but a particular judgment of God's people relating to our Christian life and ministry. It concerns the promise of recognition and recompense of some kind, or their opposite. The next verse reads: 'Since, then, we know what it is to fear the Lord, we try to persuade men.'[57] That is, the reason why we seek to persuade people of the truth of the gospel is that we stand in awe of the Lord Jesus and his tribunal, before which we will one day have to give an account. I am reminded of those solemn passages in the prophecy of Ezekiel,[58] in which God appoints him 'a watchman for the house of Israel' and makes him responsible to warn them of the coming judgment. If he fails to give a wicked person adequate warning, and does not speak out to dissuade him from his evil ways, God says, 'I will hold you accountable for his blood.'[59]

In a similar way the apostle grounded his charge to Timothy to 'preach the Word' with urgency not only on 'the presence of God and of Christ Jesus', but also 'in view of his appearing and his kingdom', who 'will judge the living and the dead'.[60] To live, work and witness in conscious anticipation of Christ's parousia and judgment is a wholesome stimulus to faithfulness. Scripture bids us remember that, from God's perspective, the time is short, the need is great, and the task is urgent.

Let me recapitulate what Christ's saving career says to us about mission. The *model* for mission is his incarnation (identification without loss of identity), its *cost* is his cross (the seed which dies multiplies), its *mandate* is his resurrection (all authority is now his), its *motivation* is his exaltation (the honour of his name), its *power* is his gift of the Spirit (who is the paramount witness), and its *urgency* is his parousia (we will have to give him an account when he comes).

It seems to me that the church needs to keep returning, for its inspiration and direction, to this christological basis of mission. The challenge before us is to see Jesus Christ as adequate for our task. We have to repent of our pessimism (especially in the West), our low expectations, our cynical unbelief that, although the church may grow elsewhere, it cannot grow among us. Fiddlesticks! If only we could gain a fresh and compelling vision of Jesus Christ, incarnate and crucified, risen and reigning, bestowing the Spirit and coming again! Then we would have the clarity of purpose and strength of motive, the courage, the authority, the power and the passion for world evangelization in our time.

In an early anniversary sermon of the Church Missionary Society (I believe in 1805), John Venn, the Rector of Clapham, described a missionary in the following terms. His eloquent portrait is equally applicable to every kind of Christian witness:

> With the world under his feet, with heaven in his eye, with the gospel in his hand and Christ in his heart, he pleads as an ambassador for God, knowing nothing but Jesus Christ, enjoying nothing but the conversion of sinners, hoping for nothing but the promotion of the kingdom of Christ, and glorying in nothing but in the cross of Christ Jesus, by which he is crucified to the world, and the world to him.[61]

Notes

[1] Page 28.

[2] Jn. 17:18; 20:21.

[3] 1 Cor. 9:19–22.

[4] Richard Collier, *The General Next to God* (Collins 1965), pp. 91–98.

[5] Morris West, *Children of the Sun* (1957; Pan, 1958), especially pp. 82–104.

[6] *The Willowbank Report: Gospel and Culture* (Lausanne Committee for World Evangelization, 1978), para. 6(b), p. 18.

[7] James Sire, *The Universe Next Door* (IVP, 1976; second edition, 1990).

[8] *Your Kingdom Come* (WCC, 1980), p. 143.

[9] Lesslie Newbigin, *The Other Side of 1984* (WCC, 1983), especially pp. 22 and 31. See also his *Foolishness to the Greeks* (SPCK, 1986), in which he appeals to us to challenge both 'the scientific worldview' and 'atheistic materialism'.

[10] Rom. 12:15 (RSV).

[11] Is. 49:6; cf. 42:1-4.

[12] Is. 50:6–7.

[13] Is. 52:15.

[14] Is. 53:3.

[15] Is. 53:4–12.

[16] Douglas Webster, *Yes to Mission* (SCM, 1966), pp. 101–102.

[17] Jn. 12:23–24.

[18] Jn. 12:26.

[19] Eph. 3:13.

[20] 2 Tim. 2:10.

[21] 2 Cor. 4:12.

[22] Richard Collier, *The General Next to God* (Collins, 1965), pp. 104–109.

[23] Carolyn Scott, *The Heavenly Witch: The Story of the Maréchale* (Hamish Hamilton, 1981), p. 113.

[24] Vincent Donovan, *Christianity Rediscovered: An Epistle from the Masai* (1978; SCM, 1982), pp. 193–194.

[25] Mt. 28:18–19.

[26] E.g. Ps. 86:9.

[27] E.g. Is. 2:1–3.

[28] Johannes Blauw, *The Missionary Nature of the Church* (1962; Eerdmans, 1974), pp. 34, 54, 66. See also Joachim Jeremias, *Jesus' Promise to the Nations* (1956; ET SCM, 1958), especially pp. 58–67 which emphasize the centripetal pilgrimage.

[29] *Ibid.*, p. 83.

[30] *Ibid.*, p. 84

[31] *Ibid.*, p. 166.

[32] *Ibid.*, p. 101.

[33] Eph. 1:21.

[34] Phil. 2:9.

[35] Col. 1:18.

[36] John Hick and Paul F. Knitter (eds.), *The Myth of Christian Uniqueness* (SCM, 1987), p. 20.

[37] Phil.2:9–11.

[38] 1 Ki. 19:10 (RV).

[39] 2 Cor. 11:2–3.

[40] Constance E. Padwick, *Henry Martyn: Confessor of the Faith* (1922; IVP, 1953), p. 146.

[41] Rom. 1:5; *cf.* 3 Jn. 7

[42] Quoted in Gerald H. Anderson and Thomas F. Stransky (ed.), *Christ's Lordship and Religious Pluralism* (Orbis, 1981), pp. 115–117. See also A *Theological Understanding of the Relationship between Christians and Jews*, a paper commended for study by the General Assembly of the Presbyterian Church, USA, in 1987.

[43] Quoted by Cormac Murphy-O'Connor, Bishop of Arundel and Brighton, in *The Family of the Church* (DLT, 1984), p. 41.

[44] From his Preface to *The Decisive Hour of Christian Missions* (Church Missionary Society, 1910).

[45] *Ibid.*, p. 193.

[46] Jn. 7:37–39.

[47] William Temple, *Readings in St John's Gospel* (1945; Macmillan, 1955), p. 130.

[48] David Wells, *God the Evangelist* (Eerdmans and Paternoster, 1987).

[49] *The Manila Manifesto: An Elaboration of the Lausanne Covenant 15 Years Later* (Lausanne Committee for World Evangelization, 1989), para. B.5.

[50] See 1 Cor. 2:1–5; 1 Thes. 1:5.

[51] The Lausanne Covenant, para. 14.

[52] Acts 1:8, 11.

[53] See John Stott, *The Message of Acts* (IVP, 1990), p. 51.

[54] Mt. 24:14; *cf.* Mk. 13:10.

[55] Lesslie Newbigin, *The Household of God* (SCM, 1953), p. 25.

[56] 2 Cor. 5:10.

[57] 2 Cor. 5:11.

[58] Ezk. 3 and 33.

[59] Ezk. 33:8.

[60] 2 Tim. 4:1–2.

[61] Michael Hennell, *John Venn and the Clapham Sect* (Lutterworth, 1958), p. 245.

CONCLUSION

The now and the not yet

I began in the Introduction with the tension between the 'then' (past) and the 'now' (present); I end with another tension, between the 'now' (present) and the 'not yet' (future). The first concerns the connection between the historical and the contemporary; the second between the contemporary and the eschatological. Yet the two tensions belong together. For in and through Jesus Christ, the then, the now and the not yet, the past, the present and the future are brought into a creative relationship. Christians live in the present, but do so in thankfulness for the past and in anticipation of the future.

This final chapter is an essay in what I like to call 'BBC'. In this context these letters stand neither for the British Broadcasting Corporation, nor for Beautiful British Columbia, nor for the Bangkok Bible College, but for Balanced Biblical Christianity. Balance is a rare commodity these days in almost every sphere, not least among us who profess to follow Christ.

I do not claim any close personal acquaintance with the devil: it is even possible that some of my readers know him better than I! But what I do know is that he is a fanatic, and the enemy of all common sense, moderation and balance. One of his favourite pastimes is to upset our equilibrium, and tip Christians (especially evangelical Christians) off balance. If he cannot induce us to deny Christ, he will get us to distort Christ instead. In consequence lopsided Christianity is widespread, in which we overemphasize one aspect of a truth, while under-emphasizing another. Thank God, however, that he has given us two ears, so that we may engage in double listening, and may pay careful attention to both sides of every question; two eyes, so that we may see straight and not squint; two hands, so that we may grasp both extremes of every biblical antinomy; and two feet, so that we may walk steadily and not limp our way through life.

A balanced grasp of the now–not yet tension would be very conducive to Christian unity, and especially to a greater harmony among evangelical believers. I confess to being deeply disturbed by the barriers which separate us who share the same fundamental biblical faith. I am not now thinking either of the divide between Rome and the churches of the Reformation, or of the gulf between conservative and liberal Christians, that is to say, between those who believe in the givenness of revealed truth and those whose chief authority is what they call 'the climate of modern opinion'. I am referring rather to disunity within the evangelical movement itself. It goes without saying that we believe the Apostles' and the Nicene Creeds, and the substance of the major Reformation confessions as well. More than that, we have recently found a useful theological rallying-point in the Lausanne Covenant (1974) and its elaboration in the Manila Manifesto (1989). So we are agreed on the doctrinal and ethical fundamentals of the faith. Yet we seem to be constitutionally prone to quarrelling and dividing, or simply to going our own way and building our own empire. We appear to suffer from a pathological inability to get on with each other or to co-operate in the cause of the kingdom of God. We ought not to make light of this grievous situation.

Do you know Saki's marvellous short story *The Secret Sin of Septimus Brope*?[1] In it Mrs Troyle expresses dismay at the thought of losing her maid, Florinda. 'I am sure I don't know what I should do without Florinda ... She understands my hair. I've long ago given up trying to do anything with it myself. I regard one's hair as I regard husbands; as long as one is seen together in public, one's private divergences don't matter!' But we have no liberty to regard each other as Mrs Troyle regarded her hair and her husband. Both our public and our private divergences do matter. For they are undoubtedly displeasing to God and damaging to our mission in the world.

One example concerns the extraordinary world-wide development of the Pentecostal churches and the charismatic movement. They are growing faster than any other Christian group. Yet some Christians take up towards them such a completely negative stance that they seem to be in danger of quenching the Spirit, while some charismatics are so triumphalistic that they find it hard to listen to those who have serious theological questions about their distinctive Pentecostal beliefs and practices. Is it possible, then, for charismatic and non-charismatic evangelicals to respect and accept each other sufficiently to permit genuine fellowship and active collaboration? I think it is possible, even if problematic, and that an insight into the tension between the 'already' and the 'not yet' should contribute considerably to mutual understanding.

Kingdom come and coming

Fundamental to New Testament Christianity is the perspective that we are living 'in between times' – between the past and the future, between the first and the second comings of Christ, between what has been done and what remains to be done, between present reality and future destiny, between kingdom come and kingdom coming, between the 'now already' in relation to the inauguration of the kingdom and the 'not yet' in relation to its consummation. Physically speaking, it is of course impossible to face in opposite directions simultaneously; but spiritually speaking, it is essential to do so, looking back to the incarnation and all that it involved, and looking forward to the parousia and all that it will bring. A sample text, if I may elaborate it a little, would be this: 'Dear friends, now already we are God's children, but not yet has it been revealed what we will be.'[2]

The theological basis for this tension is to be found in Jesus' own teaching about the kingdom of God. It is universally agreed both that the kingdom featured prominently in his teaching and that he announced its coming. Where scholars have disagreed, however, is over the time of its arrival. Has the kingdom already come, because Jesus brought it with him? Or is its coming still future, so that we await it expectantly? Or does the truth lie between these positions, and combine them?

Albert Schweitzer, the amazingly versatile German musician, doctor, theologian and missionary (who died in 1965), argued in his famous book *The Quest of the Historical Jesus* (1906) that, according to Jesus, the kingdom lay entirely in the future. He was an apocalyptic prophet, who taught (mistakenly) that at any moment God was about to intervene supernaturally and establish his kingdom. The radical demands Jesus made on his disciples (*e.g.* to sell their goods, to turn the other cheek, and not to resist evil) were an 'interim ethic' in the light of the imminent arrival of the kingdom. Schweitzer's position has been called either 'thoroughgoing' or 'consistent' eschatology, because he developed his single thesis with thoroughness and consistency.

At the opposite extreme was C. H. Dodd (who died in 1973). In his book *The Parables of the Kingdom* (1934) he elaborated his 'realized eschatology', namely that the coming of the kingdom is wholly past. Although God's rule is eternal, yet it irrupted into space and time in the person of Jesus. Dodd laid a heavy emphasis on two verses whose verbs are in the perfect tense, namely 'The kingdom of God has arrived'[3] and 'The kingdom of God has come upon you'.[4] Further, according to Dodd, there is no future coming of the kingdom. Verses which speak of one must be understood as concessions to a popular, primitive Christian eschatology; they were not part of Jesus' own teaching.

In place of these extreme polarities (Schweitzer declaring the kingdom's coming to be wholly future, and Dodd wholly past), most scholars have taken a median position, that Jesus spoke of the kingdom as both a present reality and a future expectation. On the one hand he had himself inaugurated it, and on the other he would at his parousia consummate it. Joachim Jeremias, for example, wrote in his book *The Parables of Jesus* (1947) of 'eschatology in process of realization'. A. M. Hunter, in his *Interpreting the Parables* (1960) preferred the term 'inaugurated eschatology'. A similar stance was adopted by the Dutch theologian Herman Ridderbos in *The Coming of the Kingdom* (1950) and by the American George Eldon Ladd both in his *The Gospel of the Kingdom* (1959) and in his mature treatment of the subject, *The Presence of the Future* (1974). Ladd's central thesis was that the kingdom of God, meaning God's redemptive and dynamic rule,

> which will appear as an apocalyptic act at the end of the age, has already come into human history in the person and mission of Jesus to overcome evil, to deliver men from its power, and to bring them into the blessings of God's reign.[5]

So the kingdom did come with Jesus. 'But it did not come without remainder: the consummation still lay in the indeterminate future.'[6]

That Jesus regarded and described the kingdom as a present phenomenon is indubitable. He taught that the time of fulfilment had arrived;[7] that 'the strong man' was now bound and disarmed, facilitating the plundering of his goods, as was evident from his exorcisms;[8] that the kingdom was already either 'within' or 'among' people;[9] that it could now be 'entered' or 'received';[10] and that, since the time of John the Baptist his forerunner, who had announced its imminent arrival, 'forceful men' had in fact been 'laying hold' of it or 'forcing their way' into it.[11]

Yet in Jesus' perspective the kingdom was a future expectation as well. It would not be perfected until the last day. So he looked forward to the end, and taught his disciples to do so also. They were to pray 'Your kingdom come'[12] and to 'seek' it first,[13] giving priority to its expansion. At times he also referred to the final state of his followers in terms of 'entering' the kingdom[14] or 'receiving' it.[15]

In particular, his agricultural parables (*e.g.* those of the seed growing secretly, the mustard seed, and the wheat and the tares)[16] bring together the processes of planting, growth and harvest. Like seed the kingdom had already been planted in the world; now it would grow by invisible divine activity until the end. This seems to be what Jesus meant by 'the mystery (or secret) of the kingdom'.[17] Its presence was unobtrusive, yet also revolutionary, as the power of God would cause it to grow until finally it would become manifest to all.

Another way in which Scripture expresses the tension between the 'now' and the 'not yet', the present and the future, is by the terminology of the two 'ages'. From the perspective of the Old Testament, history is divided into 'this age' and 'that age',[18] between 'this present age' (which is evil) and 'the age to come' or 'the last days', namely the kingdom of righteousness to be introduced by the Messiah.[19] Sometimes this age is likened to a long, dark night, to be followed by the dawn of a new day. This simple structure of two consecutive ages was decisively changed, however, by the coming of Jesus. For he brought in the new age, and died for us in order to deliver us 'from the present evil age'.[20] In consequence, through Jesus the Father has already 'rescued us from the dominion of darkness and brought us into the kingdom of the Son he loves'.[21] We have even been raised from death and seated with Christ in the heavenly realm.[22]

At the same time, the old age persists. So the two ages overlap. 'The darkness is passing and the true light is already shining.'[23] 'Side by side ... with the continuation of this older scheme [*sc.* the new age succeeding the old], the emergence of a new one, involving a co-existence of the two worlds or states, can be observed.'[24] One day the old age will be terminated (which will be 'the end of the age'),[25] and the new age, which was inaugurated by Christ's first coming, will be consummated at his second. Meanwhile, while the two ages continue, and we feel ourselves caught in the tension between them, we are summoned not to 'conform any longer to the pattern of this world', but rather to 'be transformed' according to God's will, in fact to live consistently as children of the light.[26]

Nevertheless, the tension remains. Indeed, it finds expression in almost every metaphor which the New Testament uses for the blessing of belonging to Christ. Thus, already we have been saved, yet also we shall be saved one day.[27] Already we 'have redemption', yet the day of redemption is still future.[28] Already we are God's adopted children, yet we also are waiting for our adoption.[29] Already we have 'crossed over from death to life', yet eternal life is also a future gift.[30] Already we are a new creation, although not yet has God made everything new.[31] We are already 'filled', but not yet up to the fulness of God.[32] Already Christ is reigning, although his enemies have not yet become his footstool.[33]

Caught between the present and the future, the characteristic stance of Christians is variously described as hoping,[34] waiting,[35] longing,[36] and groaning.[37] For we are still suffering grievous trials and tribulations.[38] Indeed, 'we must see the reality of this suffering as a concrete manifestation of the "not yet".[39] Meanwhile we must wait both 'eagerly'[40] and also 'patiently'.[41] As John Murray has written:

> Attempts to claim for the present life elements which belong to con-summated perfection ... are but symptoms of that impatience which would disrupt divine order. Expectancy and hope must not cross the bounds of history; they must wait for *the end*, 'the liberty of the glory of the children of God'.[42]

The essence of the interim period between the 'now' and the 'not yet', between kingdom come and kingdom coming, is the presence of the Holy Spirit in the people of God. On the one hand, the gift of the Spirit is the distinctive blessing of the kingdom of God, and so the principal sign that the new age has dawned.[43] On the other, because his indwelling is only the beginning of our kingdom inheritance, it is also the guarantee that the rest will one day be ours. The New Testament uses three metaphors to illustrate this. The Holy Spirit is the 'firstfruits', pledging that the full harvest will follow,[44] the 'deposit' or first instalment, pledging that the full payment will be made,[45] and the foretaste, pledging that the full feast will one day be enjoyed.[46] In this way the Holy Spirit is 'both a fulfilment of the promise and the promise of fulfilment: he is the guarantee that the new world of God has already begun, as well as a sign that this new world is still to come'.[47]

It is time now to develop some examples of the tension between the 'now' and the 'not yet'.

Revelation, holiness and healing

The first example is in *the intellectual sphere*, or the question of *revelation*.

Already, we affirm with joyful confidence, God has revealed himself to human beings, not only in the created universe, in our reason and our con-science, but supremely in his Son Jesus Christ, and in the total biblical witness to him. 'In the past God spoke to our forefathers through the prophets at many times and in various ways, but in these last days he has spoken to us by his Son.'[48] Already, therefore, we dare to say that we know God, because he has made himself known to us. He has himself taken the initiative to draw aside the curtain which would otherwise hide him from us. We rejoice greatly in the glories of God's self-disclosure. Truly, his Word throws light on our path.[49]

Not yet, however, do we know God as he knows us. Our knowledge is partial because his revelation has been partial. This must be what is meant by the proverb that 'it is the glory of God to conceal a matter ...'[50] He has revealed everything which he wills to reveal, and which he considers to be for our good, but not everything which there is to reveal. There are many mysteries left, into which we should not try to penetrate because God has kept them from us. 'We live by faith, not by sight.'[51]

In particular, to borrow the striking imagery Luther used when addressing his fellow Augustinian monks at Heidelberg in 1518, all we can see so far is 'the visible back of God as disclosed in suffering and the cross', not his face. As Dr Alister McGrath has put it, 'the God who addresses us in the cross is to use Luther's breathtakingly daring phrase – "the crucified and hidden God"'.[52]

We should take warning from Eunomius, who was bishop of Cyzicus in Mysia in the fourth century. He was one of the leaders of a heretical group called the 'Anomoeans', extreme Arians who taught that the Son was 'unlike' (*anomoios*) the Father, and indeed had been created by the Father. Eunomius was once brash enough to claim, 'I know God as well as he knows himself.' A modern (but more humorous) equivalent might be the old-fashioned revival preacher from the American Deep South who once said: 'Today I'm going to explain to you the unexplainable. I'm going to define the indefinable. I'm going to ponder the imponderable. I'm going to unscrew the inscrutable.'[53]

We would be much wiser to take our stand alongside those biblical authors who, although they knew themselves to be vehicles of divine revelation, nevertheless confessed humbly that their knowledge remained limited. Moses, 'whom the LORD knew face to face', acknowledged: 'O Sovereign LORD, you have only [RSV] begun to show to your servant your greatness and your strong hand.'[54] Then the apostle Paul, to whom the church is permanently indebted for his profound teaching, yet called his knowledge partial and imperfect, and likened it both to the immature thoughts of a child and to the distorted reflections of a mirror.[55] And the apostle John, who had penetrated deeply into the mind of Christ, admitted that 'what we will be has not yet been made known'.[56]

So then, although it is right to glory in the givenness and finality of God's revelation, it is also right to confess our ignorance of many things. We know and we don't know. 'The secret things belong to the LORD our God, but the things revealed belong to us and to our children for ever, that we may follow all the words of this law.'[57] It is very important to maintain this distinction between the revealed things and the secret things, for then we shall be confident, even dogmatic, about the former, which belong to us, while remaining agnostic about the latter, which belong to God. Then too we will be free to explore the revealed things, and firm in not trespassing into God's secrets. Conversely, while holding ourselves in check before the secret things, we must not be diffident in believing, expounding and defending what God has disclosed. I would like to see among us more boldness in proclaiming what has been revealed, and more reticence before what has been kept secret. Agreement in plainly revealed truth will be necessary for unity, even while we give each other liberty in the area of the *adiaphora*, the 'matters indifferent'. The criterion for discerning these will be when Christians who are equally anxious to be submissive to Scripture nevertheless reach different conclusions about them. I am thinking, for example, about controversies over baptism, church government, liturgy and ceremonial, charismatic claims and the fulfilment of prophecy.

The second tension is in *the moral sphere*, or the question of *holiness*.

Already God has put his Holy Spirit within us, in order to make us holy.[58] Already the Spirit is actively at work within us, subduing our fallen, selfish human nature and causing his ninefold fruit to ripen in our character.[59] Already, we can affirm, he is transforming us by degrees into the image of Christ.[60]

Not yet, however, has our fallen nature been eradicated, for still 'the sinful nature desires what is contrary to the Spirit',[61] so that 'if we claim to be without sin, we deceive ourselves'.[62] Not yet have we become completely conformed to God's perfect will, for not yet do we love God with all our being, or our neighbour as ourselves. These things await the coming of Christ. As Paul put it, we have 'not ... already been made perfect', but we 'press on towards the goal', confident that 'he who began a good work in [us] will carry it on to completion until the day of Christ Jesus'.[63]

So then, we are caught in a painful dialectic between the 'now' and the 'not yet', between defeat and victory, between dismay over our continuing failures and the promise of ultimate freedom, between the cry of longing, 'Who will rescue me from this body of death?' and the cry of assurance, 'Thanks be to God – through Jesus Christ our Lord!'[64] On the one hand, we must take with the utmost seriousness God's command, 'Be holy because I ... am holy',[65] Jesus' instruction, 'Go, and do not sin again',[66] and John's statements that he is writing so that his readers 'will not sin', and that 'no-one who is born of God will continue to sin'.[67] On the other hand, we have to acknowledge the reality of indwelling sin alongside the reality of the indwelling Spirit.[68] The sinless perfection we long for continues to elude us, although, in rejecting perfectionism, we refuse to embrace reductionism, that is, to acquiesce in low standards of attainment.

Bishop Handley Moule summed up this tension in the first chapter of his book *Thoughts on Christian Sanctity* (1888), entitled 'Aims, Limits, Possibilities'. Under 'Aims' he wrote: 'We aim at nothing less than to walk with God all day long; to abide every hour in Christ ... to love God with all the heart and our neighbour as ourselves ... to "yield ourselves to God" ... to break with all evil, and follow all good.'[69] He continued: 'We are absolutely bound to put quite aside all secret purposes of moral compromise, all tolerance of besetting sin ... We cannot possibly rest short of a daily, hourly, continuous walk with God, in Christ, by the grace of the Holy

Ghost.'[70] But then under 'Limits' (not in our aims but in our attainment) he added: 'I hold with absolute conviction, alike from the experience of the Church and from the infallible Word, that, in the mystery of things, there will be limits to the last, and very humbling limits, very real fallings short. To the last it will be a *sinner* that walks with God.'[71] Similarly, according to Bishop J. C. Ryle, 'Old John Newton, the converted slave-trader, said: "I am not what I ought to be, I am not what I want to be, I am not what I hope to be in another world, but still I am not what I once used to be, and by the grace of God I am what I am."'[72]

The third tension between the 'already' and the 'not yet' is to be found in *the physical sphere* or the question of *healing*.

Already, we affirm, the long promised kingdom of God has been inaugurated, since it broke into history with Jesus Christ. Moreover, Jesus was not content merely to proclaim the kingdom; he went on to demonstrate its arrival by his mighty works in the physical realm. He walked on water, and he changed water into wine. He rebuked the wind, stilled a storm and multiplied loaves and fishes. Nature was subservient to him. His power was specially evident in the human body as he healed the sick, expelled demons and raised the dead.

He also gave authority to both the Twelve and the Seventy to extend his messianic mission in Israel, and to perform miracles. How much wider he intended his authority to go is a matter of dispute. Generally speaking, miracles were 'the signs of a true apostle'.[73] Nevertheless, it would be ludicrous to attempt to limit or domesticate almighty God. The God who created the universe, and who through Jesus brought in the kingdom, cannot possibly be put in a strait-jacket by us. We must allow him his freedom and his sovereignty, and be entirely open to the possibility of physical miracles today.

Not yet, however, has God's kingdom come in its fulness. For 'the kingdom of the world' has not yet 'become the kingdom of our Lord and of his Christ' when 'he will reign for ever and ever'.[74] He is still waiting for that day. In particular, our bodies have not yet been redeemed. Nor has nature yet been entirely subjugated to Christ's rule. Instead, 'the whole creation has been groaning as in the pains of childbirth right up to the present time', waiting for the new world to be born. 'Not only so, but we ourselves … groan inwardly as we wait eagerly for our adoption as sons, the redemption of our bodies.'[75]

So then, we have to recognize the 'already'–'not yet' tension in this sphere too. To be sure, we have 'tasted … the powers of the coming age',[76] but so far it has been only a taste. Again, it is part of our Christian experience that the resurrection life of Jesus is 'revealed in our mortal body',[77] his life in the midst of our death, his strength in our weakness, giving us a certain physical vigour and vitality which we would not otherwise know. At the same time, our bodies remain frail and mortal, and to claim perfect health now is to anticipate our resurrection. The bodily resurrection of Jesus was the pledge, and indeed the beginning, of God's new creation. Not yet, however, has God risen from his throne to utter the decisive word, 'I am making everything new!'[78] To sum up, those dismissive of the very possibility of miracles today forget the 'already' of the kingdom, while those who expect them as what has been called 'the normal Christian life' forget the kingdom's 'not yet'.

Church and society

Fourthly, the same tension is experienced in *the ecclesiastical sphere*, or the question of *church discipline*.

Already, we rightly affirm, Jesus the Messiah is gathering round him a people of his own. And already the messianic community is characterized by the truth, love and holiness to which he has called it. The church is 'the pillar and foundation of the truth',[79] that is, its foundation to hold it firm and its pillar to thrust it high. As for love, Christ has by his cross 'destroyed … the dividing wall of hostility' between people of different races, nations, tribes and classes, in order 'to create in himself one new man'.[80] As for holiness, his new society is variously called a holy nation, a holy priesthood and a holy people.[81] So truth, love and holiness are already essential marks of the new society of Jesus Christ.

Not yet, however, has Christ presented his bride to himself 'as a radiant church, without stain or wrinkle or any other blemish, but holy and blameless'.[82] On the contrary, her present life and witness are marred by many blemishes, by error, discord and sin. Church history is the story of God's incredible patience with his wayward people.

So then, whenever we think about the church, we have to hold together the ideal and the reality. The church is both committed to truth and prone to error, both united and divided, both pure and impure. Not that we are to acquiesce in its failures. 'The undeniable "not yet" can never serve as an alibi for our defeats.'[83] We are to cherish the vision of both the purity and the unity of the church, namely its doctrinal and ethical purity and its visible unity. Since these things are God's will, they must be our goal. In consequence, we are called to 'fight the good fight of the faith'.[84] We are also to 'make every effort to keep the unity of the Spirit through the bond of peace'.[85] And in pursuit of these things there is a place for discipline in cases of serious heresy or sin.

And yet error and evil are not going to be completely eradicated from the church in this world. They will continue to coexist with truth and goodness. 'Let both grow together until the harvest,' Jesus said in the parable of the wheat and the tares.[86] Some people argue that, because in this parable 'the field is the world',[87] the coexistence Jesus is referring to is in the world, not the church. But the enemy sows weeds 'among the wheat',[88] and it is 'out of his kingdom'[89] that the Son of Man will ultimately root out evil. Neither Scripture nor church history justifies the use of severe disciplinary measures in an attempt to secure a perfectly pure church in this world.

The fifth area of tension between the 'now' and the 'then', the 'already' and the 'not yet', is *the social sphere*, or the question of *progress*.

Already, we affirm, God is at work in human society. This is partly in his 'common grace', as he gives the world the blessings of family and government, by which evil is restrained and relationships are controlled. But it is also through the members of his redeemed community, who maintain without compromise the values of his kingdom. They must penetrate society, Jesus taught, like salt and light. It is legitimate to deduce from these models that Jesus intended his followers to influence the world for good. For both are effective commodities. They make a difference in the environment in which they are placed, salt hindering decay and light dispelling darkness. In consequence there has been over the centuries, alongside social decay, measurable social progress – the greater availability of health care, the spread of literacy and education, the defence of human rights, improved working conditions, the abolition of slavery and the slave trade, and the protection of the weak and the vulnerable.

Not yet, however, has God created the promised 'new heaven and ... new earth, the home of righteousness'.[90] Not yet has the justice of the kingdom ousted all oppression, and the peace of the kingdom all violence. There are still 'wars and rumours of wars'.[91] Not yet have swords been beaten into ploughshares and spears into pruning hooks.[92] The nations have not yet renounced war as a method of settling their disputes. Selfishness, cruelty and fear continue.

So then, although it is right to campaign for social justice and to expect to improve society further, in order to make it more pleasing to God, we know that we shall never perfect it. Christians are not utopians. Although we know the transforming power of the gospel and the wholesome effects of Christian salt and light, we also know that evil is ingrained in human nature and human society. We harbour no illusions. Only Christ at his second coming will eradicate evil and enthrone righteousness for ever. For that day we wait with eagerness.

Here, then, are five areas (intellectual, moral, physical, ecclesiastical and social) in which it is vital to preserve the tension between the 'already' and the 'not yet'. One might even say that there are three distinct types of Christian according to the degree to which they manage to maintain this biblical balance.

First, there are *the 'already' Christians*. These are the sunny optimists.

They rightly emphasize what God has already done for us through Christ and bestowed on us in Christ. But they give the impression that, in consequence, there are now no mysteries left, no sins which cannot be overcome, no diseases which cannot be healed, and no evils which cannot be eradicated from the church, or even from the world. In short, they seem to believe that perfection is attainable now. They remind me of those Corinthian believers to whom Paul wrote: 'Already you have all you want! Already you have become rich! You have become kings – and that without us!'[93]

The motive of the 'already' Christians is blameless. They want to glorify Christ. So they refuse to set limits to what he is able to do. They consider it derogatory to him not to claim the possibility of perfection now. But their optimism can easily degenerate into presumption and end up in disillusion. They forget the 'not yet' of the New Testament, and that perfection awaits the parousia.

Secondly, there are *the 'not yet' Christians*. These one might not unfairly style the gloomy pessimists. They rightly emphasize the incompleteness for the time being of the work of Christ, and they rightly look forward to the parousia when Christ will complete what he has begun. But they give the impression of being extremely negative in their attitudes. They seem to be preoccupied with our human ignorance and failure, the pervasive reign of disease and death, and the impossibility of securing either a pure church or a perfect society. They pour cold water on every claim that Christ may be victoriously active in any of these areas.

Their motive is excellent too. If the 'already' Christians want to glorify Christ, the 'not yet' Christians want to humble sinners. They are determined to be true to Scripture in their emphasis on our human depravity. But their pessimism can easily degenerate into complacency; it can also lead to an acquiescence in the status quo and to apathy in the face of evil. They forget the 'already' of what Christ has done by his death, resurrection and Spirit-gift, and of what he can do in our lives, and in church and society, as a result.

Thirdly, there are *the 'already–not yet' Christians*. These are the biblical realists. For they want to give equal weight to the two comings of Jesus, to what he has done and what he is going to do. They rejoice in the former and wait eagerly for the latter. They want simultaneously to glorify Christ and to humble sinners. On the one hand, they have great confidence in the 'already', in what God has said and done through Christ, and great determination to explore and experience to the fullest possible extent the riches of Christ's person and work. On the other hand, they exhibit a genuine humility before the 'not yet', humility to confess that much ignorance and sinfulness, much physical frailty, ecclesiastical unfaithfulness and social decay remain – and will remain as symptoms of a fallen, half-saved world until Christ perfects at his second coming what he began at his first.

It is this combination of the 'already' and the 'not yet', of kingdom inaugurated and kingdom consummated, of Christian confidence and Christian humility, which characterizes authentic biblical evangelicalism, and which exemplifies that 'BBC' which is so urgently needed today.

The three great acclamations about Christ sum up our position as 'contemporary Christians':

> Christ has died!
> Christ is risen!
> Christ will come again!

His death and resurrection belong to the 'already' of the past, his glorious parousia to the 'not yet' of the future. His ultimate triumph is nonetheless certain. Indeed, 'the hope of the final victory', wrote Professor Oscar Cullmann, 'is so much the more vivid because of the unshakeably firm conviction that the battle that decides the victory has already taken place'.[94]

Notes

[1] Saki (H. H. Munro), *The Chronicles of Clovis* (1911).
[2] 1 Jn. 3:2, my paraphrase.
[3] Mk.1:15, as he translated *ēngiken*.
[4] Mt. 12:28, *ephthasen*.
[5] G. E. Ladd, *The Presence of the Future* (1974; SPCK,1980), p. 218.
[6] *Ibid.*, p. 323.
[7] *E.g.* Mk. 1:14; Mt. 13:16–17.
[8] Mt. 12:28–29; *cf.* Lk. 10:17–18.
[9] Lk. 17:20–21.
[10] *E.g.* Mk. 10:15.
[11] Mt. 11:12; Lk. 16:16.
[12] Mt. 6:10.
[13] Mt. 6:33.
[14] Mk. 9:47; *cf.* Mt. 8:11.
[15] Mt. 25:34.
[16] Mk. 4:26–29; Mt. 13:31–32, 24–29, 36–42.
[17] Mk. 4:11.
[18] Lk. 20:34–35.
[19] *E.g.* Is. 2:2; Mt. 12:32; Mk. 10:30.
[20] Gal. 1 :4.
[21] Col. 1:13; *cf.* Acts 26:18; 1 Pet. 2:9.
[22] Eph. 2:6, Col. 3:1.
[23] 1 Jn. 2:8.
[24] Geerhardus Vos, *The Pauline Eschatology* (1930; Baker, 1979), p. 37; *cf.* Oscar Cullmann, *Christ and Time* (1946; ET SCM, 1951) and Stephen H. Travis, *I Believe in the Second Coming of Jesus* (Hodder, 1982).
[25] *E.g.* Mt. 13:39; 28:20.

[26] Rom. 12:2; 13:11–14; 1 Thes. 5:4–8.

[27] Rom. 8:24, 5:9–10; 13:11.

[28] Col. 1:14; Eph. 4:30.

[29] Rom. 8:15, 23.

[30] Jn. 5:24; 11:25–26; Rom. 8:10–11.

[31] 2 Cor. 5:17; Rev. 21:5.

[32] Col. 2:10; Eph. 5:18; 3:19.

[33] Ps. 110:1; Eph. 1:22; Heb.2:8.

[34] Rom. 8:24.

[35] Phil. 3:20–21; 1 Thes.1.9–10.

[36] Rom. 8:19.

[37] Rom. 8:22–23, 26; 2 Cor. 5:2; 4.

[38] Mk. 10:30; Acts 14:22; Rom. 8:17; 1 Pet. 4:12.

[39] G. C. Berkouwer, *The Return of Christ* (1961 and 1963; Eerdmans,1972), p. 116.

[40] Rom. 8:23; 1 Cor. 1:7.

[41] Rom. 8:25.

[42] John M. Murray, *The Epistle to the Romans*, New International Commentary on the New Testament (Eerdmans, 1959 and 1965), vol. I, p. 310.

[43] *E.g.* Is. 32:15; 44:3; Ezk. 39:29; Joel 2:28; Mk.1:8; Heb. 6:4–5.

[44] Rom. 8:23.

[45] 2 Cor. 5:5; Eph.1:14.

[46] Heb. 6:4–5.

[47] Johannes Blauw, *The Missionary Nature of the Church* (1962; Eerdmans, 1974), p. 89.

[48] Heb. 1:1–2.

[49] Ps. 119:105.

[50] Pr. 25:2.

[51] 2 Cor. 5:7.

[52] Alister McGrath, *The Enigma of the Cross* (Hodder and Stoughton, 1987) pp. 103–105.

[53] Quoted by Bruce Larson in *Wind and Fire: Living Out the Book of Acts* (Word, 1984), p. 11.

[54] Dt. 34:10; *cf.* Nu. 12:8; Dt. 3:24.

[55] 1 Cor. 13:9–12.

[56] 1 Jn. 3:2.

[57] Dt. 29:29.

[58] 1 Thes. 4:7–8.

[59] Gal. 5:16–26.

[60] 2 Cor. 3:18.

[61] Gal. 5:17.

[62] 1 Jn. 1:8.

[63] Phil. 3:12–14; 1:6.

[64] Rom. 7:24–25.

[65] *E.g.* Lv. 19:2.

[66] Jn. 8:11 (RSV).

[67] 1 Jn. 2:1; 3:9.

[68] *E.g.* Rom. 7:17, 20, 8:9, 11.

[69] H. C. G. Moule, *Thoughts on Christian Sanctity* (Seeley, 1888), p. 13.

[70] *Ibid.*, p. 15.

[71] *Ibid.*, p. 16.

[72] J. C. Ryle, *Home Truths* (Charles Thynne, ninth edition, undated), pp. 94–95.

[73] 2 Cor. 12:12 (RSV).

[74] Rev. 11:15.

[75] Rom. 8:22–23.

[76] Heb. 6:5.

[77] 2 Cor. 4:10–11.

[78] Rev. 21:5.

[79] 1 Tim. 3:15.

[80] Eph. 2:14–15

[81] *E.g.* 1 Pet. 2:5, 9.

[82] Eph. 5:27; *cf.* Rev. 21:2.

[83] G. C. Berkouwer, *op cit.*, p. 138.

[84] 1 Tim. 6:12.

[85] Eph. 4:3.

[86] Mt. 13:30.

[87] Mt. 13:38.

[88] Mt. 13:25.

[89] Mt. 13:41.

[90] 2 Pet. 3:13; Rev. 21:1.

[91] Mk. 13:7.

[92] Is. 2:4.

[93] 1 Cor. 4:8.

[94] Oscar Cullmann, *Christ and Time* (1946; ET SCM, 1951), p. 87.

John Stott: The making of a leader

TIMOTHY DUDLEY-SMITH

In this authorized biography, Timothy Dudley-Smith
tells the story of the first forty years in the life of
one of the great Christian leaders of this century.
He places his subject in the context of his times.
John Stott has been a key player in a remarkable
resurgence among evangelicals, yet when he was
ordained in 1945 it seemed that evangelicals would
be little more than a marginalized remnant.

Tracing the formative processes shaping his life and
character, Timothy Dudley-Smith draws on John
Stott's unpublished letters, diaries and other papers.
In the light of them it becomes clear why this multi-
gifted man preferred the simple vocation of a local
Christian minister to high rank in the church.

This engaging and intelligent biography uncovers
the secret of John Stott's worldwide impact upon
contemporary Christianity – the impact of a
preacher passionately discovering the validity of a
biblical and reasoned faith in a troubled and
tormented century.

*'John Stott is the most respected evangelical clergyman in
the world today.'*
Ruth and Billy Graham

*'This long-awaited biography will no doubt be rather
uncomfortable to this humble servant of God but a
blessing to the rest of us.'*
George and Eileen Carey

*'Worldwide, our debt to this glorious and good man is
immeasurable.'*
Dick Lucas

*'I commend this compelling account of the real man, his
life and influences to you. It makes fascinating reading.'*
Steve Chalke

512 pages   *Hardback*

Inter-Varsity Press